Stan Greenberg's
OLYMPIC
ALMANACK

Stan Greenberg's

OLYMPIC ALMANACK

The Encyclopedia of the Olympic Games

SPORTS
BOOKS

Published by SportsBooks Ltd

Copyright: Stan Greenberg ©
September 2007

SportsBooks Limited
PO Box 422
Cheltenham
GL50 2YN
United Kingdom
Tel: 01242 256755
Fax: 01242 254694
e-mail   randall@sportsbooks.ltd.uk
Website www.sportsbooks.ltd.uk

Cover photograph by Mark Shearman

Typeset in Garamond Premier Pro and Helvetica Nue

A CIP catalogue record for this book is available from the British Library.

ISBN 9781899807 53 6

Printed by Cromwell Press

ACKNOWLEDGEMENTS

I am greatly indebted to the original research by Olympic historians Erich Kamper (AUT), Volker Kluge (GER), Wolf Lyberg (SWE), Bill Mallon (USA) and Ian Buchanan (GBR). After extensive research, particularly by Bill Mallon and Wolf Lyberg, new participation figures have been agreed by the International Society of Olympic Historians. My main sources have been, in alphabetical order:

The Associated Press and Grolier – *Pursuit of Excellence, The Olympic Story* (1979)

Sandor Barcs (HUN) – *The Modern Olympics Story* (1964)

Pat Besford (GBR) – *Encyclopaedia of Swimming* (1976)

Ian Buchanan (GBR) – *British Olympians* (1991)

John Durant (USA) – *Highlights of the Olympics* (1961)

Erich Kamper (AUT) – *Enzyclopadie der Olympischen Spiele* (1972); *Lexicon der Olympischen Winter Spiele* (1964) ; and *Lexicon der 14,000 Olympioniken* (1983)

Erich Kamper (AUT) and Bill Mallon (USA) – *The Golden Book of the Olympic Games* (1992)

Lord Killanin (IRE) and John Rodda (GBR) – *The Olympic Games* (1976)

Volker Kluge (GER) – *Die Olympischen Spiele von 1896 bis 1980* (1981)
  – *Winter Olympia Kompakt* (1992)
  = *Olympia Guide, Salt Lake City* (2001)
  – *Olympische Sommerspiele I 1896-1936* (1997); *II 1948-1964* (1998); *III 1968-1984* (2000); *1988-1996* (2001)

Bill Mallon (USA) and Ian Buchanan (GBR) – *Quest for Gold* (1984)

Bill Mallon (USA) – *The Olympic Record Book* (1988)

Peter Matthews (GBR) – *Track and Field Athletics, The Records* (1986)

Norris and Ross McWhirter (GBR) – *The Guinness Book of Olympic Records* (1980)

Strömberg Media Group – *Olympiaboken* (1988-2006)

David Wallechinsky (USA) – *The Complete Book of the Olympics* (1984 1988, 1992)
  – *The Complete Book of the Summer Olympics* (1996, 2000)
  – *The Complete Book of the Winter Olympics* (1998, 2002)

Melvyn Watman (GBR) – *The Encyclopaedia of Track and Field Athletics* (1981)

Other experts and organizations whose publications and personal help have been invaluable include:
Richard Ayling, Howard Bass, Anthony Bijkerk (NED), Mark Butler, Harry Carpenter, Jim Coote, Peter Diamond (USA), Doug Gillon, Maurice Golesworthy, John Goodbody, Mark Heller, Richard Hymans, Peter Johnson, Ove Karlsson (SWE), Ekkehard zur Megede (GER), Ferenc Mezo (HUN), Rebecca Middleton, Jan Patterson, Philip Pope, Ron Pickering, Jack Rollin, Bob Sparks, Stuart Storey, Dave Terry, John Tidy, Lance Tingay, Martin Tyler, David Vine, Alan Weeks, Ture Widlund (SWE), Dorian Williams, Don Wood, the Association of Track and Field Statisticians (ATFS), British Olympic Association, the International Society of Olympic Historians (ISOH), the International Association of Athletics Federations (IAAF), International Olympic Committee (IOC), International Weightlifting Federation, National Ski Federation of Great Britain, National Union of Track Statisticians (NUTS), *New York Times, Sports Illustrated, The Times, Track and Field News, L'Equipe, USA Today*, and many other national and international bodies and individuals.

Key to notes in text
G = gold or gold medallist
S = silver
B = bronze
M = medallist
km/h = kilometres per hour
mph = miles per hour
yd = yards
m = metres

FOREWORD

MOST BOOKS ABOUT the Olympic Games tend to deal with them in Games order, i.e. starting with Athens in 1896 and following through until the latest celebration. Invariably, they deal with the various sports, breaking them up into those in the Summer Games, and then those in the Winter Games. Having been involved in reference work for most of my life, putting things into lists, files and classification systems, it seemed obvious to me that what was required was an Olympic compendium in an alphabetical order – similar to an encyclopedia.

You will find the different celebrations of the Games, whether Summer or Winter, in chronological order, i.e. by year, in a separate section. However, all the various sports, Summer, Winter and Discontinued, plus subsidiary subjects, such as Most Medals, Smallest, Tallest etc., are shown in alphabetical order. It is my opinion that this method of presentation, a unique one I believe, will enable the reader to find the information they require easier and faster than previously possible.

I would like to express my thanks to Keith Greenberg and Paul Sparks for their technical help, and Carole Greenberg for her good humour and understanding. Where contradictions have been found in different sources I have invariably arrived at my own, hopefully correct, conclusion. The political upheavals of the former eastern European bloc have caused Olympic chroniclers some problems. I have taken my own attitude to such matters and made my own, unusual, medal compilations. However, I have given all necessary data so that readers with different views can reconstruct tables to their own liking if they wish.

Stan Greenberg, London 2007

CONTENTS

ANCIENT GAMES

THE OLYMPIC GAMES originally evolved from legendary conflicts among the Greek Gods and the religious ceremonies held in their honour. Historical evidence dates the Games from about 900 BC, but there is good reason to believe that a similar festival existed four centuries previously. Indeed the modern word 'athlete' is said to derive from Aethlius, King of Elis. The area in which Olympia lies is in the plain of Elis, on the banks of the River Alpheios. It was a successor, Iphitus, who was instrumental in reviving the then faltering concept in the late ninth century BC. He also arranged for the truce (called ekecheiria) between the continually warring states of the region which recognized the neutrality and sanctity of Olympia, and which lasted for the period of the Games. The first firm record dates from 776 BC, and the Games were numbered at four-yearly intervals from then. At that time there was only one event, the stade race, and the winner, the first recorded Olympic champion, was Coroibis of Elis. The stade was 192.27m 210.26yd long, reputably 60 times the length of the god Heracles' (Hercules) stride. After thirteen Olympiads, in 724 BC, a race of two stade, the diaulus, was also contested, and in the following celebration the 24-stadia dolichus, about 4.5km 2.8 miles in length, was instituted. In 708 BC came the pentathlon, mythically invented by Jason (of Argonaut fame). This consisted of a run, standing long jump (with the aid of halteres, hand-held weights), throwing the discus and javelin, and wrestling. Eventually chariot racing, running in armour, and boxing were included, and in 648 BC the pankration, a brutal mix of boxing and wrestling. Numerous variants of these sports appeared over the years, as did also activities of a less sporting nature, such as contests for trumpeters.

Initially contestants wore simple shorts-like garments, but from about 720 BC they competed in the nude, and until 692 BC the Games lasted only for a single day. This was later increased to two days, and in 632 BC to a total of five days, of which the middle three were for actual competitions. For the next six centuries, the fame of Olympia spread throughout the known world, and many famous people visited the Games. Victors, in those early days, won only a crown of wild olive leaves, but were often richly rewarded by their home cities or states, and sometimes became very wealthy. Crowd figures were not published but archaeologists have estimated that the Stadium at Olympia could hold over 20,000 spectators.

For reasons not fully understood today women, and slaves, were strictly forbidden, under pain of death, to even attend the Games. An exception does appear to have been made for high ranking priestesses of the most important gods. However, it was possible for a woman to gain an Olympic prize. This was because in the chariot race the chaplet of olive leaves was awarded to the owner of the horses and not the drivers. One of the first women to win an Olympic title in this way was Belistike of Macedonia in 268 BC as owner of the champion 2-horse chariot, and an inscription at Olympia refers to Kyniska of Sparta as one of the first such female chariot owners. It is recorded that some women did defy the rules and disguised themselves, but, on discovery, were thrown over a cliff to their deaths. There is a story, perhaps apocryphal, that Pherenice of Rhodes acted as a second to watch her son, Pisidores, win his event. In her excitement she gave herself away, but when it was realised that not only her son, but also her father and brothers had all been Olympic champions, she was pardoned.

Possibly the most famous champion of early times was Leonidas of Rhodes who won the three 'track' events on four consecutive occasions 164-152 BC, making a total of 12 victories which has not been surpassed since. The first recorded triple gold medallist at one Games was Phanas of Pellene in 512 BC, while the Spartan runner Chionis won the stade in three successive Games 664-656 BC. Other excellent champions included Theagenes of Thassos who won eight titles at boxing, wrestling and pankration from 468-456 BC, and Milon of Croton who won six wrestling titles 536-516 BC. Eventually, the very success of the Games gave rise to its downfall. The importance of winning at Olympia, and the reflected glory it bestowed on the winner's birthplace, led cities to hire professionals and bribe judges. With the dawn of the Christian era the religious and physical backgrounds of the Games were attacked. An irreversible decline set in under Roman influence, so much so that in AD 67 a drunken Emperor Nero was crowned victor of the chariot race despite the fact that there were no other entrants (who could blame them) and he did not even finish the course. According to accepted belief, in AD 393 the Roman Emperor Theodosius I issued a decree in Milan which prohibited the Games. Some archaeological evidence seems to suggest that the Games may have continued, in some form, for another 100-120 years – recent scholarship putting a final date of 426AD. Then the ravages of foreign invaders, earthquakes and flooding virtually obliterated the site of Olympia, and the world forgot the glory that once had been.

There was a resurgence of interest in Ancient Greece in the 17th & 18th centuries and references to the Olympic Games in the poems of Pindar and other Greek poets were noted. In Britain, the Cotswold Olympic Games were inaugurated in the early 17th century, and in 1850 the Much Wenlock Olympic Society was founded by Dr William Penny Brookes. At the end of the 18th century, in Germany, the famed founder of modern gymnastics, Johann Guts Muths, had suggested the revival of the Olympic ideal. Some 50 years later a fellow-countryman, Ernst Curtius, who had done archaeological work at Olympia (started by the French in 1829) reiterated the idea in a lecture he gave in Berlin in 1852. In Greece itself Major Evangelis Zappas organized a Pan-Hellenic sports festival in 1859 which attracted a great deal of public support, and which was revived at intervals over the next 30 years.

However, the true founder of the modern Olympic Games is commonly acknowledged to be Pierre de Fredi, Baron de Coubertin, of France. In 1889 he met Brookes of Much Wenlock, and formed his own concept of a revived Games, which he first propounded publicly at a lecture in the Sorbonne, Paris, on 25 November 1892. In the following year, he met with representatives of the top American universities. In June 1894 he convened an international conference, also in the Sorbonne, the outcome of which was a resolution on 23 June, calling for competitions along the lines of the Ancient Games to be held every fourth year. The International Olympic Committee (IOC) was inaugurated under the presidency of Demetrius Vikelas of Greece with de Coubertin as secretary-general. The Frenchman had hoped to herald the new century with the first Games in Paris in 1900, but the delegates were impatient. There was strong sentiment in favour of London or Budapest, but, at the instigation of Vikelas, Athens was finally selected and the date set as 1896.

ATHENS 1896

1st Olympic Games. 6 – 15 April 1896
(25 March – 3 April by the Julian Calendar)
Attended by representatives of 14 countries, comprising 246 competitors (no women).

ALTHOUGH THE GREEK government was apparently not consulted, and were beset with internal financial and political problems, the Greek public were very enthusiastic. However, it was not until Crown Prince Constantine set up a committee and began organizing and collecting funds that the project became feasible, and the prospect of Budapest getting the honour by default faded. The turning point came with the generosity of a Greek businessman,

Georges Averoff (formerly Avykeris) who actually lived in Alexandria, Egypt. He offered to pay for the reconstruction of the Panathenean Stadium in Athens at a cost of 920,000 drachma (£36,500 at the 1896 exchange rate). The stadium had first been built in 330 BC by the orator Luycurgus, disciple of Plato. It was rebuilt 500 years later by Herodes Atticus, but had gradually disintegrated and was covered up until 1870 when King George of Greece had arranged for its excavation by a German, Ernst Ziller. The new track, which was laid by Britain's Charles Perry, measured 333.33m, had very sharp turns, and the competitors ran in a clockwise direction. There were supposed to be a total of 50 events in the Games, but the seven rowing competitions were cancelled due to inclement weather in Phaleron Bay.

The opening of the Games coincided with the 75th anniversary of the declaration of Greek independence from Turkish rule. Over 40,000 spectators in the stadium, plus thousands more on the surrounding hills, saw King George I formally open the proceedings. The great bulk of the competitors were from Greece itself. Many athletes entered privately, including holidaymakers, and the British contingent included two employees of the Embassy in Athens. Another member of the British team was an Irishman, John Boland, who was on holiday in Greece at the time and entered the tennis events. He won the singles and, partnering a German, also won gold in the pairs. A further nice touch of the period was provided by a French sprinter who insisted on wearing his gloves as he was running before royalty.

Not for the last time a gymnast, Hermann Weingärtner (GER), was the most successful competitor, with three first places, two seconds and a third; a Frenchman, Paul Masson, won three cycling events; but perhaps the most outstanding achievement was that of Carl Schuhmann of Germany who not only won three gymnastic events but also won the wrestling title. Another competitor to gain medals in two sports was gymnast Fritz Hofmann (GER) whose total of five placings included a silver medal in the 100 metres. In shooting, John and Sumner Paine (USA) became the first brothers to win Olympic gold medals, in military pistol and free pistol respectively. Their father had successfully defended yachting's America's Cup some years before, and John's great granddaughter later sculled in the 1996 Games.

The first competition of the modern Olympic Games was heat one of the 100m. It was won, in 12.5sec, by the American Francis Lane of Princeton University, thus carving a niche in history for himself. The first gold medallist of modern times was James Brendan Connolly (USA) who won the hop, step and jump (now known as the triple jump).

In fact the American team, composed exclusively of college students, dominated events in the stadium, despite arriving only the day before the start of the competitions, having travelled by ship to France and then by train to Greece. Victors actually received a silver medal and a crown of olive leaves; runners-up were given bronze medals and a crown of laurel; no awards were made for third place.

Two new sporting events were introduced at these Games; the discus throw and the marathon. Both were based on Greek antiquity and the hosts were eager to win them. However, the former was taken by Robert Garrett (USA) who had inadvertently practised with an implement much larger and heavier than the one actually used at Athens. The marathon had been proposed by Frenchman Michel Breal, to commemorate the legendary run of a Greek courier, possibly Pheidippides, with the news of a Greek victory over the Persians in 490 BC. He is supposed to have run from the site of the battle, and, after crying out 'Rejoice! We conquer', collapsed and died. To the great delight of the spectators the race was won by a Greek shepherd, Spiridon 'Spyros' Louis, who was escorted into the stadium by Crown Prince Constantine and Prince George.

The oldest gold medallist was Georgios Orphanidis (GRE) in the free rifle contest, aged 36yr 102days, while the youngest was swimmer Alfréd Hajós (HUN) aged 18yr 70days when he won the 100m and 1200m freestyle events. A member of the Greek bronze medal team in gymnastics has been reported to have been under 11 years of age, but some doubt exists about the veracity of this claim. In view of the modern saturation coverage of the Olympics by the media, it is noteworthy to record that the British press gave little space to reports from Athens, despite an earlier complaint in *The Times* about the lack of knowledge of the occasion in the country, and Britain's inadequate representation. Nevertheless, the Games were a tremendous success and Greece looked forward to the next celebration, which they also expected to host.

Athens 1896 Medals

	G	S	B
United States	11	7	1
Greece	10	19	18
Germany	7	5	2
France	5	4	2
Great Britain	3	3	1
Hungary	2	1	3
Austria	2	-	3
Australia	2	-	-
Denmark	1	2	4
Switzerland	1	2	-

PARIS 1900

IInd Olympic Games. 20 May – 28 October
Attended by representatives of 24 countries, comprising 1613 competitors, of which 22 were women.

DESPITE STRONG GREEK pressure for the exclusive rights to organize future Games, Baron de Coubertin won agreement to hold the 1900 Games in Paris, but made a serious mistake in making it part of the Fifth Universal Exposition also being held there. In the event the Games became merely a sideshow to the fair. Numerous internal rivalries within French sport left many of the sports without experienced officials or adequate venues. The track and field events were held on uneven turf at Croix-Catelan, in the Bois de Boulogne, where it is reported that the jumpers had to dig their own pits.

Many of the competitors, especially the Americans, had never run on a grass track before. Generally there were few spectators, and even these were nearly reduced in number when the 1896 discus champion threw the implement into the crowd on all three throws. Cricket, croquet and golf made their appearance, and amid the general confusion many competitors, even medal winners, were not aware until much later that they had been competing at the Olympic Games.

France, the host country, had a record-sized team numbering 884, the largest ever entered for the Games. Russia competed for the first time. The Americans were still represented by colleges and clubs, and the decision to have competition on Sunday upset many of those whose colleges were church controlled. Thus the long jump world record holder Myer Prinstein, a Russian-born Jew but under the aegis of the University of Syracuse, a strong Methodist institution, gained a silver medal with his Saturday qualifying round jump (such performances then counted for medals), but had to withdraw from the Sunday final. The eventual winner, Alvin Kraenzlein (USA) set a record of four individual gold medals, a feat never surpassed in track and field at one Games. Also much in evidence was America's Ray Ewry, the standing jump expert, at the start of his fabulous Olympic career, with three gold medals here. Behind him in those standing jumps was countryman Irving Baxter. He had already won the regular high jump and the pole vault, and reputedly became the first athlete of native American ancestry to win at the Olympic Games. Athlete Norman Pritchard, usually, and, though born there, mistakenly shown as representing India, but entered by Great Britain, won two silvers in the 200m flat and hurdles races, and later became an actor in Hollywood silent films.

Women were allowed to compete for the first

time, but not in the major sports, and the first female Olympic competitor (only recently researched) was Helen, Countess de Pourtalès (SUI), in the 1-2 tonnes sailing event in May. The first individual champion was Charlotte Cooper (GBR), who won the tennis singles on 7 July. A unique event occurred in the coxed pairs rowing final, in which a small French boy was drafted in at the last moment to cox the winning Dutch crew. His name was never recorded and he disappeared without trace afterwards, but there is an popular story that he was no more than ten years old, and possibly as young as seven, thus the youngest ever Olympic gold medallist. In 2006, a name, Marcel Depaillé, surfaced, but no one seems to know where it came from. The oldest gold medallist in 1900 was French-born Count Hermann de Pourtalès (SUI) in the 1-2 tonne class sailing aged 53yr 55days. The youngest female champion was Margaret Abbott (USA) in golf aged 20yr 110days, while the oldest was the above mentioned 31-year-old Helen, Countess de Pourtalès, a crew member for her father.

Press coverage was barely apparent, with many of the events not mentioned at all, and for years afterwards there was much confusion as to the names and nationalities of even the medallists. Thus it was that the first Olympic medals won by Canada, a gold and bronze gained by George Orton, were not 'discovered' for some years, as Orton had been entered by his American university and was billed as an American. Constantin Henriquez de Zubiera (FRA) gained a silver in the tug-of-war, and then a gold medal in Rugby in 1900 – he was Haitian-born and thus the first black athlete to (a) compete in the Games, (b) win a medal, and (c) gain a gold medal. Even more recently it has been found that the winner of the marathon, Michel Théato (FRA), was actually a Luxembourgeois – in this case the medal tables have not been altered.

Paris 1900 Medals

	G	S	B
France	27	39	34
United States	19	15	15
Great Britain	17	9	12
Switzerland	6	3	1
Belgium	5	5	3
Germany	3	2	2
Australia	3	-	4
Denmark	2	3	2
Italy	2	2	-
Netherlands	1	1	4
Hungary	1	2	2
Cuba	1	1	-
Canada	1	-	1
Sweden	1	-	1
Austria	-	3	3
Norway	-	2	3
Czechoslovakia	-	1	2

ST LOUIS 1904

IIIrd Olympic Games. 1 July – 23 November
Attended by representatives of 13 countries, comprising 649 competitors, of which 6 were women.

FOR A TIME the third celebration seemed likely to go to Britain, and then to Philadelphia, whilst de Coubertin had favoured New York. The IOC finally designated Chicago for these Games, but at the request of President Theodore Roosevelt, also president of the US Olympic Committee, the venue was changed to St Louis to coincide with the World's Fair, held to celebrate the centenary of the Louisiana Purchase. Thus again they became merely a sideshow. Held in the centre of the North American continent, the problems of distance and travel meant that there were very few overseas entrants. Indeed, even de Coubertin did not attend. Thus 85 per cent of the competitors were from the host country, and, not surprisingly, they won 84 per cent of the medals. In fact the Games were a virtual college and club tournament with the New York AC beating the Chicago Athletic Association for the track and field team title (a points table was actually published). It went so far that a German team applied to enter the gymnastics competition but was refused because all its members did not belong to one club. In swimming much was made of the fact that New York beat Germany and Hungary overall.

In such circumstances the Games degenerated into something of a farce, so that the cycling events, which had no foreign entrants at all, and included a number professional riders, were initially refused official Olympic status. However, recent scholarship suggests that they should be included in medal tables and results. So the unique achievement of Marcus Hurley in winning four cycling events should now be given due credit. Gymnast Anton Heida (USA) won five golds and one silver to be the most successful at these Games.

Under the rather loose controls imposed on most sports some strange things happened. In the 400m track race no heats were held, and all 13 entrants ran in the final. Rowing events were held over a 1½ mile *2.4km* course which entailed making a turn. The swimming events were held over Imperial distances, while the athletics track (in the grounds of Washington University, St Louis) measured one-third of a mile in circumference *536m* and had a 220 yard straightaway, which was quite an innovation for the visiting Europeans. In the track and field programme only two events went to non-Americans. The French-Canadian policeman Etienne Desmarteau won the 56lb *25.4kg* weight throw. He unfortunately died the following year of typhoid and a park was named after him in his home city of Montreal. The 10-event All-round competition, a forerunner of the decathlon, was won by Thomas Kiely, who incidentally like the silver medallist in the 2500m steeplechase, John Daly, was an Irishman. However, as Ireland at the time was part of the United Kingdom, they have to be taken as representing Great Britain, despite attempts by 'historical revisionists' to make it otherwise. The unfortunate Myer Prinstein redressed his grievance of four years previously by taking the long jump title, as well as winning the hop, step and jump. He also placed fifth in both the 60m and 400m finals. The ever liberal Prinstein here was representing the Greater New York Irish A.A.

The 200m final, uniquely held on a straightaway (i.e. no turns), was won by Archie Hahn, with all three of his opponents given a one-yard 0.99m handicap under the rules then governing false starts. Joseph Stadler won a silver medal in the standing high jump, while George Poage won bronzes in the 200m and 400m hurdle races. The significance of their performances was that they were thought to be the first black men to win medals in the Olympics. Recent research suggests that the French-Haitian in 1900 pre-dates them. Despite the lack of foreign opposition, the standard in many sports was very high, and the triple victories of Archie Hahn, Harry Hillman, James Lightbody, Ray Ewry and swimmer Charles Daniels were outstanding. Daniels, in winning three golds, a silver and a bronze, was the prototype of the American swimmers who were to dominate Olympic freestyle swimming for many years.

There was a scandal in the marathon when the first man out of the stadium, Fred Lorz (USA), was also the first man back, looking remarkably fresh. It later transpired that he had received a lift in a car after suffering cramp, and when the car itself broke down near the stadium he resumed running – as a joke he claimed. He was banned for life (but was competing again after only a year) and the title was awarded to British-born American Thomas Hicks who had finished in a daze due to being administered strychnine by his handlers as a stimulant – a practice then common and allowable. In ninth place was Len Tau (SAF), in St Louis as part of a World's Fair exhibit, the first black African distance runner to compete in the Olympics.

The youngest gold medallist was golfer Robert Hunter (USA) aged 17yr 301days, while the oldest was the Reverend Galen Spencer (USA), an archer, aged 64yr 2days. Another American archer, Samuel Duvall, won a silver medal aged 68yr 194days – the oldest American medallist ever. The oldest female champion was Lida Howell (USA) in archery aged 45yr 25days. The youngest medallist was another archer, Henry Richardson (USA), aged 15yr 124days. Another American, Frank Kungler, won a silver in wrestling, a bronze in tug-of-war, and two bronzes in weightlifting, to become the only Olympian to win medals at three different sports at a single Games.

A final insult to the Games were the Anthropology Days, during which competitions were held, parodying the regular Olympic events, for aboriginal peoples, such as American Indians, African pygmies, Patagonians, Ainus from Japan, and the like. Finally, in November, with the Association Football competition won by a Canadian college over two American teams, the IIIrd Olympic Games came to an end – and many in Europe wondered if the fledgling movement would recover.

St Louis 1904 Medals

	G	S	B
United States	80	84	84
Germany	4	4	5
Canada	4	1	1
Cuba	4	-	-
Austria	2	1	1
Hungary	2	1	1
Great Britain	1	1	-
Greece	1	-	1
Switzerland	1	-	1
France	-	1	-

ATHENS 1906

The Interim or Intercalated Games.
22 April – 2 May
Attended by representatives of 20 countries, comprising 841 competitors, of which 6 were women.

AFTER TWO DEBACLES, in Paris and St Louis, something was needed to revive the flagging Olympic movement and de Coubertin, with some misgivings, agreed a series of four-yearly meetings, interspersed with the main Games, to be held in Athens. Although these had the blessing of the IOC, it was decided that the Interim Games would not be numbered in sequence. This has caused an ambivalence in Olympic historians, when writing about the Games, leading to the ludicrous situation where some of them refuse to include these Games in their narratives, but do include the medals won in their overall totals. This author considers that as these Games were sanctioned by the IOC, numbered or no, they were genuine Olympic Games, and should be treated as such. In the event only this meeting of the projected series was ever held. Competitors were housed in the Zappeion, thus predating the first Olympic ' village' by 18 years. Again the Greeks showed their enthusiasm, and large crowds, missing for the past ten years, were in evidence. The marble stadium in Athens was full to capacity, and enthusiasm often helped to overcome organizational mishaps.

The 20 countries included the first 'official' American team, selected and sent by the US Olympic Committee, so ending the practice of colleges, clubs and private individuals entering. Also present was the first ever team from Finland, with the doyen of the famous Järvinen family, Werner, gaining his country's first ever Olympic gold medal. The programme of track and field events was altered by a reduction in the number of sprint and hurdles races, and the addition of a pentathlon and the javelin throw.

There were some excellent performances, especially by some of the 1904 champions such as the perennial Ray Ewry and the New York policeman Martin Sheridan. Another American, with the apt name of Paul Pilgrim, had only been added to the team at the last moment after he had privately raised the money for his fare. He had won a gold medal in 1904 as a member of the New York AC relay team, but in Athens surprisingly won both the 400m and 800m titles, a feat not equalled until 1976.

The new pentathlon event, consisting of a 192m run, standing long jump, discus and javelin throws, and Greco-Roman wrestling, was won by Hjalmar Mellander of Sweden. In third place was his countryman Erik Lemming who also gained bronze medals in the shot and tug-of-war as well as winning the first of three Olympic javelin titles. There was a real surprise in the 1500m walk, which was also the scene of a number of purely chauvinistic decisions by the various national judges. The American distance runner George Bonhag had disappointed in the 1500m and 5 mile runs, and had entered the walk, an entirely new event to him, in a last effort to win a medal. Owing mainly to the disqualifications of the favourites he won the gold. With all three previous Olympic marathons having been won by the host country, the Greeks were hopeful of continuing the tradition, but despite half of the entrants coming from Greece it was won by William Sherring of Canada, incidentally wearing a trilby hat, by a massive margin of nearly seven minutes. In addition to his medal he was given a goat. The most successful competitor at these Games was shooter Louis Richardet (SUI) who won three gold and three silver medals.

The oldest gold medallist was Maurice Lecoq (FRA) aged 52yr 31days when he won the rapid fire pistol event. Youngest was the coxswain of the Italian fours crew, Giorgio Cesana aged 14yr 12days. The youngest female champion was Marie Decugis (FRA) in tennis aged 21yr 261days. She and her husband, Max, became the first married couple to win Olympic gold medals. The oldest medallist was fencer Charles Newton-Robinson (GBR) at 52yr 195days.

Despite the soft cinder track in the stadium, poor facilities for the swimmers at Phaleron Bay, complaints about food and judging decisions, these, since much maligned, Interim Games put the whole Olympic concept back on the path towards de Coubertin's ideal.

Athens 1906 Medals

	G	S	B
France	15	9	16
United States	12	6	6
Greece	8	11	13
Great Britain	8	11	5
Italy	7	6	3
Switzerland	5	6	4
Germany	4	6	5
Norway	4	2	-
Austria	3	3	2
Denmark	3	2	1
Sweden	2	5	7
Hungary	2	5	3
Belgium	2	2	3
Finland	2	1	1
Canada	1	1	-
Netherlands	-	1	2
Australia	-	-	3
Czechoslovakia	-	-	2
South Africa	-	-	1

LONDON 1908

IVth Olympic Games. 27 April – 31 October
Attended by representatives of 22 countries, comprising 2002 competitors, of which 37 were women.

ORIGINALLY AWARDED TO Rome, the IVth Games were re-allocated to London when the Italian authorities informed the IOC during the 1906 Interim Games that they would have to withdraw due to financial problems caused by an eruption of Mt Vesuvius. London formally accepted on 19 November 1906. Nevertheless, they were the most successful held till then and set the pattern for future Games. Drawing on the expertise of many British sporting governing bodies – such as the Amateur Swimming Association, founded in 1869, and the Amateur Athletic Association, founded in 1880 – the organizing committee under Lord Desborough went to work. A 68,000 capacity stadium was built in West London for a reported cost of £40,000. (That stated 'capacity' was apparently well exceeded on a number of occasions). It contained an athletics track of three laps to the mile, inside a 660yd banked concrete cycle track. On the grass infield stood a giant (330ftx50ft, *100m x 15.24m*) pool for the swimming events. Rowing was on the Thames at Henley, tennis was held at the All-England Club, Wimbledon, and the new sport of motor boating was on Southampton Water. The sailing competitions took place at Ryde, Isle of Wight, with some on the River Clyde, at Glasgow – the only time that any Olympic events have been held in Scotland. The main competitions took place in July, although the overall programme lasted from April to October. There were 21 sports in all, including four ice skating events. There was also a demonstration sport, bicycle polo, in which Ireland beat Germany 3-1.

Entries were only by nations, as opposed to individuals. This tended to emphasis the nationalism that undoubtedly caused some of the disputes which marred this first truly international sporting occasion. These problems started during the formal opening, by King Edward VII, at what later became known as the White City stadium, on 13 July. Sweden and the United States were upset that their flags had been inadvertently missed from those flying around the stadium. Then Ralph Rose, the American flag bearer, and eventual winner of the shot, refused to dip the Stars and Stripes to King Edward in the march past. The Finnish team would not march behind the flag of Czarist Russia and came in without any banner. Later things got worse as complaints came from all sides, but especially from US officials. They complained about 'fixed' heats, illegal coaching, rule breaking and British chauvinism. The weather was also rather foul, even by British standards, and badly affected cycling and tennis in particular.

All the rancour came to a head in the 400m event final, in which three of the four finalists were Americans. Prior to the race officials had been tipped off to an American 'plot', after someone overheard them planning how to impede and beat the British favourite, Lieut Wyndham Halswelle. In the event, the race was declared void, and a re-run, with strings delineating the lanes, as ordered for the next day, and the winner of the disputed race, Carpenter, was disqualified. The other Americans refused to appear and Halswelle gained the gold medal in the only walk-over in Games history. One of the runners involved was John Taylor who, as a member of the winning medley relay team, has always been noted as the first black man to win an Olympic gold medal. However, recent research has indicated that the Haitian in the French team of 1900 has that distinction. A more imaginative resolution to a problem, apparently,

came in the 110m hurdles. The favourite, Forrest Smithson, an American student of theology, protested against the official decision to run the final on a Sunday, and then proceeded to break the world record with 15.0sec, supposedly carrying a bible in his left hand. While uplifting, the only 'evidence' of this story is a photograph that was obviously staged after the event.

Finally the bitterness reached such a level that it was thought necessary to produce a booklet entitled 'Replies to Criticism of the Olympic Games', which, owing to its rather pompous tone, did little to alleviate the situation. One result of all this was the decision that future control of competitions should be in the hands of the various international governing bodies of the sports and not left solely to the host country.

The previous year the IOC had decided that medals should be awarded for the first three places in all events. There were many excellent performances throughout the Games, despite all the problems. The ubiquitous Ray Ewry, now 33 years old, won his record-breaking ninth and tenth gold medals in the standing jumps, while John Flanagan (one of the so-called Irish-American 'Whales') won his third hammer title. Middle distance runner Mel Sheppard (USA) was a triple gold medallist, as was British swimmer Henry Taylor. Charles Daniels (USA) won the 100m freestyle to add to his three titles from the last two Games, and set a record of four individual event swimming gold medals that has been equalled, but not beaten since. The Hungarian swimmer Zoltán von Halmay increased his total medal haul to nine since 1900, a total unsurpassed in the sport until 1972.

The introduction of ice skating events gave the opportunity to Russia to win its first Olympic title, courtesy of Nikolai Panin (actually Kolomenkin) who four years later was a member of the fourth-placed revolver shooting team. Another Olympic first came in the London shooting programme when Oscar and Alfred Swahn of Sweden became the first father and son to win gold medals, with Oscar being the oldest gold medallist at these Games aged 60yr 265days. The youngest champion was Daniel Carroll (AUS) in rugby aged 16yr 245days, while the youngest female gold medallist was Gladys Eastlake-Smith (GBR) in tennis aged 24yr 273days. The oldest female champion was archer Queenie Newall (GBR) aged 53yr 275days.

Undoubtedly the most famous event in the IVth Games was the marathon. Originally the distance was to be about 25 miles *40km*, but the start was moved to Windsor Castle, an exact 26 miles *41.8km*. Then at the request of Princess Mary it was moved again to start beneath the windows of the royal nursery in the Castle grounds, making a final distance of 26 miles 385yd *42.195km*. This arbitrarily arrived-at distance was later (1924) accepted worldwide as the standard marathon length. The race itself was run in intensely hot and humid conditions, quite the opposite of most of the preceding weather, and was watched by an estimated 250,000 people. The little Italian Dorando Pietri reached the stadium first in a state of near collapse – it has been suggested that his gargling with wine during the race did not react well with the heat. He fell five times on the last part-lap of the track. Over-zealous officials, reputedly, but erroneously, including the famous author Sir Arthur Conan Doyle, helped him over the finish line, thus leading to his disqualification. Doyle was in the stadium, but sitting in the stand reporting the events for a newspaper. On behalf of the second finisher, Irish-born Johnny Hayes, the Americans lodged a protest which was upheld, and the Italian was disqualified. The wave of public sympathy found expression in the gift of Queen Alexandra to Pietri of a special gold cup.

Great Britain won the greatest number of medals overall, but the United States, as always, was well in front in the centrepiece of the Games, the track and field events. Two sportsmen, Ivan Osiier (DEN) a fencer, and Magnus Konow (NOR) a yachtsman, though unplaced in their events, began Olympic careers which continued until the next Games in London in 1948, setting a record breaking span for Olympic competition of 40 years. Colonel Joshua Millner, winner of the 1000y Free Rifle, aged at least 58yr 237days, was Britain's oldest ever Olympic gold medallist. The youngest British winner in 1908 was William Foster (GBR), in the 4x200m swimming relay six days past his 18th birthday.

London 1908 Medals

	G	S	B
Great Britain	56	50	39
United States	23	12	12
Sweden	8	6	11
France	5	5	9
Germany	3	5	5
Hungary	3	4	2
Canada	3	3	9
Norway	2	3	3
Italy	2	2	-
Belgium	1	5	2
Australia[1]	1	2	1
Russia	1	2	-
Finland	1	1	3
South Africa	1	1	-
Greece	-	3	1
Denmark	-	2	3
Czechoslovakia	-	-	2
Netherlands	-	-	2
Austria	-	-	1
New Zealand*	-	-	1

[1] *Australia and New Zealand combined as Australasia*

STOCKHOLM 1912

Vth Olympic Games. 5 May – 22 July
Attended by representatives of 28 countries, comprising 2381 competitors, of which 53 were women.

STOCKHOLM FINALLY ATTAINED the honour that Sweden had wanted from the very beginning, and Torben Grut designed and built a 31,000 capacity stadium, with a 383m *407yd* track laid out under the direction of Charles Perry, the Englishman responsible for the 1896 and 1908 tracks. Baron de Coubertin had insisted that the number of sports be cut, and now, with only 14, there were high standards of performance and sportsmanship, with few arguments or protests. Boxing was not held, the last time that it has been left out of the Olympic programme. The Games were opened officially by King Gustaf V. One of the rare complaints at these Games was from the Finns, again about competing under the Russian flag. Indeed the triple gold medallist Kolehmainen stated that he almost wished he had not won rather than see the hated flag raised for his victories.

Various innovations included the first use of electrical timing equipment for the running events. Baron de Coubertin had asked for a new event to be introduced, the modern pentathlon, which consisted of five disciplines of different sports. It was dominated by the Swedes but in fifth place was one Lieut George S Patton (USA), later to become a controversial World War II general. As previously, the American team lived on the liner that had brought them across the Atlantic, ironically named Finland – for this was the Games in which the first of the 'Flying Finns', Hannes Kolehmainen, made his appearance, winning the 5000m, 10,000m and 12,000m cross country. He also set a world record in a heat of the 3000m team race, in which the Finnish team surprisingly did not qualify for the final. Nevertheless, this was the beginning of a domination which lasted into the 1940s. Kolehmainen's race with Jean Bouin of France in the 5000m was one of the most enthralling races ever seen to that time with the Finn winning by a stride in 14min 36.6sec, improving the world record by a margin of 24.6sec. Other track stars were Ted Meredith (USA), gold medallist in the 800m in a new world mark, and Ralph Craig (USA) who took both sprints. Under current rules he would not have won as he was responsible for three of the seven false starts to the race. He reappeared at the Games, as a reserve yachtsman, 36 years later, in London, when he was given the honour of carrying the US team flag.

In the swimming pool, the first of the great Hawaiian competitors, Duke Paoa Kahanamoku, won the 100m freestyle. The son of Hawaiian royalty, he received his first name as a mark of respect for the then Duke of Edinburgh, Queen Victoria's second son, who was visiting the islands at the time of his birth. He competed in two more Games before becoming a movie star. There was only one cycling event, but it was unique in that it was the longest road race ever held in the Games. It was won by Rudolph Lewis (SAF), who took the 320km *198.8 miles* event in just short of 10¾ hours. A great impetus was given to the game of soccer at these Olympics, with 25,000 spectators present to see Great Britain beat Denmark 4-2 in the final. Gymnastics, which like wrestling, was held outdoors, also gained new status.

In wrestling, problems were caused by the extreme length of some of the bouts. In the light-heavyweight final the judges called a halt after the bout had gone on for nine hours and gave both wrestlers a silver medal, with no gold awarded. Even this was surpassed in the middleweight category where the tussle for the silver medal between Asikainen (FIN) and Klein, an Estonian representing Russia, went on for 11hr 40min, a record for the sport. Klein finally triumphed. The first known twins to win Olympic gold medals were the Carlberg brothers, Vilhelm (three) and Eric (two), in shooting, while an even rarer sibling combination came in the 6m class yachting when the French winner *Mac Miche* was crewed by the three Thubé brothers.

However, the star of the Games was undoubtedly Jim Thorpe. Of Irish, French, but mainly American Indian ancestry, Thorpe won both the newly constituted athletic pentathlon as well as the decathlon, with consummate ease. Additionally he was fourth in the individual high jump and seventh in the long jump. Thus, it can be said that he actually competed in a total of 17 events. Presenting him with his medals King Gustav V called him 'the greatest athlete in the world'. Thorpe reportedly replied 'Thanks King'. Six months later, a sportswriter for the *Worcester Telegram* in Massachusetts, Roy Johnson, reported that Thorpe had played minor baseball for money. Owing to the violent amateur/professional dichotomy of the time, perhaps reinforced by American anti-Indian prejudice, Thorpe's medals were taken back and his performances removed from Olympic annals. It seems almost certain that he was ignorant of the amateur laws of the time, and the amount involved was very small. Twenty years after his death in 1953 the American Athletic Union reinstated him as an amateur, but the IOC stubbornly refused all entreaties on his behalf. It has been suggested that his cause was not helped by the fact that the President of the IOC from 1952-72 was Avery Brundage, a teammate of Thorpe's in 1912 who had placed fifth (or sixth depending on your view) in the pentathlon. To their credit the runners-up to Thorpe, Hugo Wieslander (SWE) and Ferdinand Bie (NOR) initially refused to accept the gold medals when they were sent them, although their names were inscribed in Olympic annals as winners of the events. Finally, in October 1982, Thorpe, the man who had been voted in 1950 as the greatest athlete of the first half-century, was pardoned by the IOC and the medals presented to his family. However, they were in addition to the medals already presented, i.e. the amended result still stands, and two people are reckoned as winners.

The oldest gold medallist at these Games was the ubiquitous Oscar Swahn (SWE) now aged 64yr 258days, while teammate diver Greta Johansson was the youngest aged 17yr 186days. Only 40 days older was Isabella Moore (GBR) in the winning freestyle swimming relay team, who became Britain's youngest ever female gold medallist. The youngest male champion was fencer Nedo Nadi (ITA) aged 18yr 30days. British tennis player Edith Hannam was the oldest female gold medallist aged 33yr 171days. The youngest medallist was swimmer Grete Rosenberg (GER) in the relay at 15yr 280days.

At the Stockholm Games the Olympic movement finally 'came of age' and the marvellous efforts of the organizing committee under Viktor Balck, later, deservedly, President of the IOC, must take much of the credit. The only unfortunate incident at the Games was the collapse and death of Francisco Lazzaro (POR) during the marathon – ironically it was the first Games that his country had attended. Another new country was Japan, and the Games were beginning to achieve the wide-world support originally envisaged for them.

Stockholm 1912 Medals

	G	S	B
United States[1]	25	18	19
Sweden	24	24	16
Great Britain	10	15	16
Finland	9	8	9
France	7	4	3
Germany	5	13	7
South Africa	4	2	-
Norway	4	1	5
Hungary	3	2	3
Canada	3	2	2
Italy	3	1	2
Australia[2]	2	2	2
Belgium	2	1	3

Denmark	1	6	5
Greece	1	-	1
New Zealand[2]	1	-	1
Switzerland	1	-	-
Russia	-	2	3
Austria	-	2	2
Netherlands	-	-	3

[1]Adjusted by the reinstatement of Jim Thorpe in 1982; [2]Australia and New Zealand combined as Australasia

ANTWERP 1920

VIIth Olympic Games. 20 April – 12 September
Attended by representatives of 29 countries, comprising 2582 competitors, of which 65 were women.

WHEN THE VENUE of the VIth Games, due in 1916, came to be discussed in Stockholm, three cities were put forward as candidates – Budapest, Alexandria and Berlin. It is said that the latter was chosen in an attempt to avert the war that was then threatening Europe. With the outbreak of hostilities in 1914 hopes of holding the Games virtually disappeared, although the Germans still made preparations for them believing that the war would not last very long. In 1920, although Antwerp was sorely affected by the human tragedy and economic ruin of the conflict, the organizing committee under Count Henri de Baillet-Latour, later IOC President, overcame all difficulties to hold the Games. The recent enemies, Germany, Austria, Hungary and Turkey were not invited, but still a record number of countries and competitors attended. These included New Zealand as a separate entity (previously it had been part of an Australasian team), Argentina and Brazil. The Games were opened by King Albert, and the concept of the Olympic oath was introduced. This was taken by Victor Boin, who had competed in two previous Games, winning medals at water polo, and in Antwerp he gained another at fencing. Another newcomer at these Games was the newly devised Olympic flag, which consisted of five interlaced rings coloured blue, yellow, black, green, and red, from left to right. The rings were meant to symbolize the friendship of mankind, with the colours, including the white background of the flag itself, representing all nations, as every national flag contains at least one of these colours.

Unfortunately the 390m running track at the new 30,000-seat stadium was very poor (Charles Perry, the famous British groundsman, had not been able to do much with it) and was badly affected by the persistent rain. Due to the weather and the economic aftermath of the recent conflict, generally crowds were small. The competitors were housed in school buildings, which caused something of a revolt among the US team – though they were much more incensed by the intolerable conditions experienced aboard the old freighter that had brought them to Belgium.

For the first time Finland competed under its own flag, having gained independence in 1917, and they celebrated the occasion by halting the American track and field juggernaut by winning as many athletic gold medals as the United States team. The track star of 1912, Hannes Kolehmainen, made a surprise return to win the marathon. However his mantle had been taken over by another outstanding Finnish runner, Paavo Nurmi, who, although he lost his very first Olympic final, over 5000m to the gassed French war veteran Joseph Guillemot, was at the start of a brilliant career in which he won a record 12 Olympic medals, nine of them gold, and set 29 world records of one type or another. Britain's Albert Hill who had fought throughout the war, here won the 800m/1500m double, a feat not repeated for 44 years. In addition he also gained a silver medal in the 3000m team race. In second place in the 1500m was Philip Baker (GBR), who later in life, as Philip Noel-Baker MP, was the recipient of the 1959 Nobel Peace Prize – a unique achievement for an Olympian. Charley Paddock retained the 100m sprint title for the United States, delighting the spectators with his spectacular jump finish. Later, after appearing in some movies, he was killed in World War II as a Marine Corps captain, and posthumously had a ship named after him. The most successful competitors at these Games were Willis Lee (USA), who won five golds, one silver and one bronze, and his teammate Lloyd Spooner, who won four golds, one silver and two bronzes, both as shooting competitors. This sport also produced the first gold medal won by a South American country, when Guilherme Paraense (BRA) took the rapid-fire pistol title. Yet another shooter, the phenomenal Oscar Swahn (SWE), became the oldest ever Olympic medallist with a silver aged 72yr 280days. Also outstanding was fencer Nedo Nadi (ITA) who won two individual and three team golds. His younger brother, Aldo, added another three to the family total.

Returning to Olympic competition for the first time since 1906, when he had won two golds and a silver, archer Hubert van Innis (BEL) won four golds and two silvers, and was the oldest champion at these Games aged 54yr 187days. The youngest gold medallist was tiny (1.43m *4ft 8in*) diver Aileen Riggin (USA) at 14yr 119days. Indeed she was the youngest Olympic champion ever at the time, but almost lost the honour to Sweden's Nils Skoglund, who finished a very close second in high-diving when three months younger. Riggin won a diving silver four years later and, more unusually, a bronze in the 100m backstroke. The youngest male gold medallist was the

Dutchman Franciscus Hin in the yachting aged 14yr 163days. The oldest female champion was Winifred McNair (GBR) in tennis aged 43yr 15days.

Swimming was dominated by two Americans, who each captured three gold medals. Ethelda Bleibtrey, who had suffered from polio as a child, won all events open to her, in world record times. The year before she had been arrested in America and charged, under local decency laws, with swimming 'nude' at a public beach, when all she had done was to remove her stockings! Norman Ross won the 400m, 1500m and was part of the winning relay team, and also figured in an unusual incident when he was disqualified in the 100m final for impeding an Australian swimmer. The race had been won by Duke Kahanamoku in world record time. The re-swim was also won by the Hawaiian but in slower time. Another incident, of a more serious nature, occurred in the football final when the Czechoslovakian team were disqualified for leaving the field after 40 minutes play in protest at decisions by the British referee. Belgium were leading 2-0 at that point.

Daniel Carroll completed an unique double in the rugby final when he won a second gold medal as part of the US team. He had played in the victorious Australian team of 1908, but had since emigrated. The tennis events were the stage for one of the greatest players in the game, Suzanne Lenglen (FRA), eventually six times winner of the Wimbledon title. The winner of the single sculls, and, teamed with his cousin, the double sculls, was John Kelly. Earlier in the year the American had been refused entry to the Henley Regatta in England. One report said that it was on the grounds that as 'a bricklayer' he had an unfair advantage over 'gentlemen'. Another, probably more correct, is that his Philadelphia club, Vesper RC, had been banned. Ironically, after he had become a millionaire, his son John Jr won at Henley, in 1947, and his daughter, Grace, the film actress, became Princess of Monaco. Coincidentally, these were the first Games at which Monaco participated.

Two winter sports were also held, ice hockey and figure skating, attracting 74 men and 12 women from ten countries. The latter witnessed the first Winter-event gold medals won by a married couple, the pairs champions, German-born Ludowika, and Walter Jakobsson of Finland. On this topic it may be that the first Olympic marriage was that of American diver Alice Lord and high jump champion Dick Landon soon after they returned home. One final note on the subject of matrimonial bliss: it was revealed after the competitions that the ladies skating champion, Magda Mauroy-Julin (SWE), was three months pregnant.

Antwerp 1920 Medals

	G	S	B
United States	41	27	26
Sweden	19	20	25
Finland	15	10	9
Great Britain	14	15	13
Belgium	13	11	11
Norway	13	9	9
Italy	13	5	5
France	9	19	13
Netherlands	4	2	5
Denmark	3	9	1
South Africa	3	4	3
Canada	3	3	3
Switzerland	2	2	7
Estonia	1	2	-
Brazil	1	1	1
Australia	-	2	1
Japan	-	2	-
Spain	-	2	-
Greece	-	1	-
Luxembourg	-	1	-
Czechoslovakia	-	-	2
New Zealand	-	-	1

CHAMONIX/ MONT BLANC 1924

1st Winter Games. 25 January – 4 February
Attended by representatives of 16 countries, comprising 291 competitors, of which 13 were women.

AFTER SKATING (1908,1920) and ice hockey (1920) events were held previously as part of the Summer Games, it was finally decided to hold a separate Winter festival. Although initially opposed by the Scandinavian countries, who felt that a Winter Olympics would detract from their own Nordic Games, an 'International Winter Sports Week' was held at Chamonix, France. In 1926 it was accorded the title of Winter Games retrospectively. The French Under Secretary for Physical Education, Gaston Vidal, formally opened the proceedings, and the oath was taken by all the flag bearers, that of France being by a member of the Military Patrol team Camille Mandrillon. Seventeen countries marched in the opening ceremony, but Estonia did not have any competitors in the actual competitions. The first ever official Olympic Winter gold medallist was Charles Jewtraw (USA) who won the 500m speed skating on 26 January, which also made it the earliest gold medal ever won in an Olympic year. It was the only speed skating medal won by a competitor from other than Finland or Norway. Clas Thunberg (FIN) won three golds, one silver and a bronze (tied) to dominate the sport. In skiing only the Nordic variety was held as Alpine skiing was still in its infancy. Norway's Thorleif Haug won three gold medals. He was also, originally, awarded the bronze in the special jumping event, but 50 years later a Norwegian sports historian, Jakob Vaage, discovered that the points had been added incorrectly, and that the fourth placed jumper, Anders Haugen, a Norwegian-born American, had beaten Haug. In place of her deceased father, Haug's daughter presented the bronze medal to the 86-year-old Haugen in 1974. Canada retained its title from 1920 in ice hockey, scoring 110 goals to 3 against in five matches. At figure skating Gillis Grafström (SWE) gained the second of his three gold medals. He was later to gain even more fame as coach of Sonja Henie (NOR) who, as an 11-year-old competitor in Chamonix, placed eighth and last in the women's skating. Aside from her Olympic successes, she was to earn an estimated $47.5 million from her film and ice show activities, making her the richest ever female Olympian. The inaugural 4-man bobsleigh contest was won by the Swiss, the first of a record five titles they have won in this discipline. The curling and military patrol competitions, previously thought to be categorised as demonstration events, were historically 'reinstated' as medal events in 2006, and as such have been incorporated into the results and tables in this book.

The oldest champion was speed skater Julius Skutnabb (FIN) aged 34yr 229days, and the youngest was Heinrich Schläppi, in Switzerland's 4-man bob, aged 18yr 279days. The oldest medallist was pairs skater Walter Jakobsson (FIN) aged 41yr 357days, although it is possible that the Belgian bobsledder, René Mortiaux, was over 42yr. It is of note that Jakobsson and his partner/wife, Ludowika (herself well over 39yr) are the oldest married couple ever to win Winter Olympic medals. Two days before the closing ceremony a meeting established the International Ski Federation (FIS).

Chamonix/Mont Blanc 1924 Medals

	G	S	B
Norway	4	7	6
Finland	4	4	3
Austria	2	1	-
United States	1	2	1
Switzerland	2	-	1
Canada	1	-	-
Sweden	1	1	-
Great Britain	1	1	2
Belgium	-	-	1
France	-	-	3

Including curling and military patrol

PARIS 1924

VIIIth Olympic Games. 4 May – 27 July
Attended by representatives of 44 countries, comprising 3067 competitors, of which 135 were women.

ORIGINALLY SCHEDULED FOR Amsterdam, de Coubertin requested that the Games be transferred to Paris in the hope that the bad image acquired in 1900 could be eradicated. The IOC had taken steps to impose its authority on the staging of the Olympics so that never again could a host country add events as it wished. The Colombes stadium, with a 500m track built in 1909, was enlarged to hold 60,000 spectators. An Olympic village had been proposed but the idea was not carried through, although competitors were housed in huts scattered around the main site. Four of the five 'enemy' countries in the war were included in the record number of nations accepting invitations, but Germany was still not present due to the particularly frosty relations between them and France. Among the newcomers were Ireland, competing separately from Britain for the first time, Romania and Poland. Polish sportsmen had competed previously, but always in the teams of other countries. The Games were formally opened by the President of France, Gaston Doumergue, and were attended by well over 600,000 spectators in total. However, the chauvinism of the French supporters was outrageous at times. The weather was good, in fact sometimes too good – for the 10,000m cross-country event it was reported to be over 40°C and over half of the starters did not finish.

Despite, for the first time, all sports being organized by their international governing bodies and the instigation of Juries of Appeal, there were still many complaints of unfair decisions, notably in boxing. The newly instituted Olympic motto, *Citius, Altius, Fortius*, (faster, higher, stronger) originally composed by Father Henri Didon in 1895, was taken to heart. Numerous records were set, sometimes unexpectedly. The long jump was won by William DeHart Hubbard (USA), with 7.44m. Another American, Robert LeGendre, had been left out of that event but entered in the athletic pentathlon, during which he broke the world long jump record with 7.76m on the way to winning a bronze medal. Incidentally, Hubbard was the first black athlete to win a gold medal in an individual, as opposed to a team, event.

The track events were dominated by the resurgent Finns with their outstanding stars Paavo Nurmi and Ville Ritola. Nurmi won a then record five gold medals, and American-based Ritola four golds and two silvers. The remarkable Nurmi won the 1500m and 5000m title within 90 minutes on the same day – a unique performance. His other victories came in the 3000m team race and the 10,000m cross-country individual and team events. In this latter event, run in a record high temperature, only 15 of the 38 starters finished, as Nurmi beat Ritola by well over a minute. The statue of him which stands outside Helsinki stadium was sculpted in 1925 to commemorate his Paris triumphs. It is interesting to note that the only viable opposition to the 'Flying Finns' came from Edvin Wide of Sweden – but actually he was born in Finland. Two Britons scored upset wins when Harold Abrahams became the first European to win an Olympic sprint title, and Eric Liddell set a world record in taking the 400m crown. Abrahams, coached by Sam Mussabini who had also trained Reggie Walker to victory in 1908, later recollected that there were no victory ceremonies and that he received his gold medal in the post some time later. Third in that 100m final was New Zealand's Arthur Porritt, who later became Governor-General of his country. An Oscar-winning film *Chariots of Fire* was made in 1981 with a not too accurate account of the period leading up to the achievements of Abrahams and Liddell.

A unique double was achieved by Harold Osborn (USA), who won the decathlon title and the high jump. In that latter event, Osborn's habit of pressing the bar back against the uprights with his hand as he jumped using the Western Roll technique led to a change in the event's rules. The rules in another event resulted in a strange set of circumstances when the third finisher in the 400m hurdles was credited with a new Olympic record (also bettering the world mark). This happened because the winner, Frank Morgan Taylor (USA), had knocked down a hurdle, while the second finisher, Charles Brookins (USA), was disqualified for leaving his lane. Thus the eventual silver medallist, third finisher Erik Vilén (FIN) claimed the record. In fourth place was Georges André (FRA), who had taken the oath at the opening ceremony, and who had won a silver medal in the 1908 high jump.

In the pool, Johnny Weissmuller (USA) won three golds in freestyle swimming and a bronze at water polo. After more medals four years later, he turned to films, and in the 1930s he became the most famous screen 'Tarzan' of them all. His teammate in Paris, Gertrude Ederle, who had become the youngest person ever to set a world record in 1919 at the age of 12yr 298days, here won a gold in the relay, and two years later became the first woman to swim the English Channel. Incidentally, this Games was the first to introduce lane dividers in the pool. In rowing, another American to gain fame elsewhere was Benjamin Spock, number seven in the winning eight. He later gained renown as a best-selling writer and paediatrician. France came into her own in the fencing and cycling events. In the former Roger Ducret won three golds and one silver, while in the latter Armand Blanchonnet won the 188km 117 miles road race by a near-record margin of over nine minutes. A pointer to the future came in the soccer final which was won by Uruguay, the first South American country to enter the Olympic football competition.

Now aged 45, Alfred Swahn (SWE) won his ninth shooting medal in four Games. His father, the incredible Oscar, had been picked for the team, but at 76 was too ill. However, he and Alfred won a family total of six golds, four silvers and five bronzes. The American shooter Carl Osburn gained another silver to raise his individual total since 1912 to 11, comprising five gold, four silver and two bronze. Tennis made its last appearance for 64 years, but had an all-star entry with all titles won by Wimbledon champions. One of them, Norris Williams, who partnered Hazel Wightman in the mixed doubles, had been a survivor of the *Titanic* disaster in 1912. Rugby also disappeared from the Games, leaving the United States as reigning Olympic champions.

The oldest gold medallist at Paris was Allen Whitty (GBR) in the running deer shooting aged 57yr 59days. (There has been some confusion about his age as he falsified his date of birth in order to join the army). The youngest winner at Paris was featherweight boxer Jackie Fields (USA) at 16yr 162days. The youngest female winner was 400m freestyle champion Martha Norelius (USA) at 14yr 177days (Recent research has confirmed her as two years younger than originally thought). The oldest female gold medallist was Hazel Wightman (USA) in tennis aged 37yr 213days. The United States won the major share of the medals at Paris, but a record number of 30 countries shared in the total.

Paris 1924 Medals

(Summer)

	G	S	B
United States	45	27	27
Finland	14	13	10
France	13	15	10
Great Britain	9	13	12
Italy	8	3	5
Switzerland	7	8	10
Norway	5	2	3
Sweden	4	13	12
Netherlands	4	1	5
Belgium	3	7	3
Australia	3	1	2
Denmark	2	5	3
Hungary	2	3	4
Yugoslavia	2	-	-
Czechoslovakia	1	4	5
Argentina	1	3	2
Estonia	1	1	4
South Africa	1	1	1
Uruguay	1	-	-
Austria	-	3	1
Canada	-	3	1

Poland	-	1	1
Haiti	-	-	1
Japan	-	-	1
New Zealand	-	-	1
Portugal	-	-	1
Romania	-	-	1

ST MORITZ 1928

IInd Winter Games. 11 – 19 February
Attended by representatives of 25 countries, comprising 464 competitors, of which 28 were women.

THE DECISION THAT the same country should host both Summer and Winter editions of the Games had to be abandoned in 1928, although the principle was still thought to be a sound one. The Games were officially declared open by the President of Switzerland, Edmund Schulthess, and the oath was taken by Hans Eidenbenz, a skier. Japan, Holland, Romania and Mexico were making their debuts at the Winter Games. Unseasonal weather threatened the programme – on one day the temperature varied by over 20 C from morning to afternoon. One of the speed skating events had to be cancelled, and in the bobsleigh there were only two runs instead of four.

The cancellation of the 10,000m skating event by the Norwegian referee, caused particularly bad feeling among the American team, as at that point Irving Jaffee (USA) was surprisingly in front and seemed likely to retain that lead. Despite vigorous protests by all nationalities no medals were awarded. Perhaps the unfortunate circumstances at Lake Placid four years later provided Jaffee with a measure of rough justice. In the other events, Clas Thunberg (FIN) added two more golds to his 1924 haul to amass a total of five gold, one silver and one bronze, a record for the sport. There was a unique occurrence in the 500m in which two men tied for first place and three men for third, with no silver medals awarded. Another uncommon happening was in the skeleton toboggan race, conducted on the famous Cresta Run, where brothers Jennison and John Heaton (USA) gained the gold and silver respectively.

The bobsleigh, for the first and only time composed of 5-man teams, also went to the United States. The driver, William Fiske, was aged only 16yr 260days, and was then the youngest ever male Winter gold medallist. Also in the team was the oldest gold medallist at these Games, Nion Tucker, aged 42yr 182days. The youngest was Sonja Henie (NOR) taking the first of her three titles aged 15yr 316days. She was the 'star' of the Games with her interpretation of The Dying Swan, which began a whole new era for figure skating. The youngest medallist at these Games was Thomas Doe (USA) in the bob aged 15yr 129days, while the oldest was his teammate Jay O'Brien at 44yr 361days.

Pair skating witnessed the last appearance of the 1920 champions, Ludowika and Walter Jakobsson (FIN), who were placed fifth, their ages totalling 89 years. The men's skating event gave Gillis Grafström (SWE) his third consecutive gold medal.

In ski-jumping the defending champion Jacob Tullin-Thams (NOR) was nearly killed, crashing at the end of a 73m jump on a hill designed for jumps of considerably less. A true Olympian, he reappeared in 1936 to gain a silver medal in sailing. Johan Grøttumsbråten (NOR) won the 18km race and the Nordic Combination title to match Thunberg's two wins. As was becoming a habit, the Canadians easily won the ice hockey tournament scoring a total of 38 goals for and none against. The only demonstration event was a military patrol contest.

St Moritz 1928 Medals

	G	S	B
Norway	6	4	5
United States	2	2	2
Sweden	2	2	1
Finland	2	1	1
Canada	1	-	-
France	1	-	-
Austria	-	3	1
Belgium	-	-	1
Czechoslovakia	-	-	1
Germany	-	-	1
Great Britain	-	-	1
Switzerland	-	-	1

AMSTERDAM 1928

IXth Olympic Games. 17 May – 12 August
Attended by representatives of 46 countries, comprising 2869 competitors, of which 274 were women.

AFTER UNSUCCESSFULLY APPLYING for the Games of 1916, 1920 and 1924, the Dutch were finally rewarded, and built a new 33,000 capacity stadium on reclaimed land in Amsterdam. The size of the running track, 400m, encircled by a cycling track, was then standardized for future Games. The design of the stadium won the architect, Jan Wils, an Olympic prize in the architecture competition. One innovation was the erection of a large results board; others included the release of pigeons at the opening ceremony – to symbolize peace – and the burning of an Olympic flame throughout the period of competitions. The formal opening was by HRH Prince Hendrik, the consort of Queen Wilhelmina who was on a state visit to Norway, although the Queen herself did hand out medals at the end of the Games. The record number of countries included Rhodesia and Panama for the first time, and Germany made its return to the Olympics in great strength.

After much argument in world sporting circles, and despite the opposition of Baron de Coubertin, women were allowed to compete in track and field, albeit in only five events. World records were set in all five, although there were, reportedly, such harrowing scenes of distress at the end of the 800m that it was then omitted from the programme until 1960. In winning that 800m, Lina Radke won the first ever Olympic track and field gold medal for Germany. Her teammate, Anni Holdmann, became the first woman to win an Olympic track race by finishing first in heat one of the 100m on 30 July. Other firsts in the sport were a gold medal for Japan by Mikio Oda in the triple jump, and the appearance of the first Asian female competitor, his teammate Kinuye Hitomi. Reigning world record holder in the long jump, which was not included in these Games, Hitomi remarkably took a silver medal in that 800m. Incidentally, it should be noted that an entirely opposite view of women's athletics was created by the very attractive Canadian winner of the high jump, Ethel Catherwood.

The Finns again dominated the athletics, although the fabulous Paavo Nurmi won only one gold and two silvers. Looking far older than his 31 years, due to increasing baldness, the dour Finn offered some light relief when he competed in the steeplechase: unused to the event, he had problems with most of the barriers, and in his heat ignominiously fell into the water jump. Another competitor, a Frenchman, Lucien Duquesne, stopped and courteously helped him to his feet. Obviously grateful, Nurmi uncharacteristically acknowledged and thanked him, and then proceeded to 'shepherd ' the French runner for the rest of the race, even inviting him to break the tape first. This Duquesne, to his eternal credit, declined to do. Despite running his fifth distance race in seven days, Nurmi won the silver medal (behind a teammate) in the final. It was later reported that the great Finn had damaged his famous stopwatch in the fall.

The unheralded Canadian youngster Percy Williams took both sprints, and, with hurdler Lord Burghley becoming the first member of the British House of Lords to win an Olympic athletic title, and Douglas Lowe (GBR) successfully defending his 800m title, the Americans had a lean time. A pointer for the future was the victory in the marathon of Boughèra El Ouafi, representing France, but an Algerian and the pathfinder for future great African distance runners. The US team was under the control of the President of the US Olympic Committee, Major-General Douglas MacArthur, later in command of the victorious Americans in the Pacific theatre of the Second World War.

In the swimming pool another threat to United States dominance came from the Japanese. In Amsterdam they won their first ever swimming medals, giving an indication of things to come. American honour was saved by Johnny Weissmuller in the 100m and relay. Dorothy Poynton (USA) won a silver medal in springboard diving when only 24 days past her 13th birthday, one of the youngest medallists ever. She won gold medals at the next two Games. There was an unfortunate mix-up in the result of the men's high diving when Farid Simaika of Egypt was initially awarded the gold on the basis of his greater points score. The result was later reversed and the title given to Ulise 'Pete' Desjardins (USA) as the judges had made more first place decisions in his favour. Canadian-born Desjardins had been the first Olympic diver to be awarded a score of 10, in the 1924 springboard event.

Another Egyptian, Ibrahim Moustafa, won the light-heavyweight wrestling title to become the first non-European to take a Greco-Roman event. Not for the first time, nor the last, boxing was beset with protests about the standard of officiating. In sailing, Crown Prince Olav, later King Olav V of Norway, gained the first Olympic victory by a member of a Royal house when he was a crew member of the 6m yacht Norna. (His son, Crown Prince Harald, also competed in Olympic sailing 1964-1972, but not with his father's success). In the soccer tournament Uruguay retained its title, beating another South American country, Argentina, in the final. In front of 50,000 people India won the first of their six consecutive hockey gold medals, retaining the title until 1960. Their goalkeeper, Richard Allen, did not concede a single goal in the tournament.

A teammate of the Crown Prince in Norna, Johan Anker, a champion from 1912, was the oldest gold medallist in Amsterdam aged 57yr 44days, while the youngest gold medallist, and male medallist, also water-borne, was the Swiss pairs cox Hans Bourquin aged 14yr 222days. The youngest female champion was Elizabeth Robinson (USA) who won the 100m sprint aged 16yr 343days, while the oldest woman to win a gold medal was Virginie Hériot (FRA) in the 8m sailing aged 38yr 15days. The youngest medallist was Luigina Giavotti (ITA), silver in gymnastics aged 11yr 302days – she remains the youngest ever female medallist in Olympic history.

Amsterdam 1928 Medals

	G	S	B
United States	22	18	16
Germany	10	7	14
Finland	8	8	9
Sweden	7	6	12
Italy	7	5	7
Switzerland	7	4	4

France	6	10	5
Netherlands	6	9	4
Hungary	4	5	-
Canada	4	4	7
Great Britain	3	10	7
Argentina	3	3	1
Denmark	3	1	2
Czechoslovakia	2	5	2
Japan	2	2	1
Estonia	2	1	2
Egypt	2	1	1
Austria	2	-	1
Australia	1	2	1
Norway	1	2	1
Poland	1	1	3
Yugoslavia	1	1	3
South Africa	1	-	2
India	1	-	-
Ireland	1	-	-
New Zealand	1	-	-
Spain	1	-	-
Uruguay	1	-	-
Belgium	-	1	2
Chile	-	1	-
Haiti	-	1	-
Philippines	-	-	1
Portugal	-	-	1

LAKE PLACID 1932

IIIrd Winter Games. 4 – 15 February
Attended by representatives of 17 countries, comprising 252 competitors, of which 21 were women.

SNOW HAD TO be brought over to the United States from Canada by lorries for some of the venues at Lake Placid, and a thaw caused the 4-man bob event to be held after the official closing ceremony on 13 February. The Games were opened by the Governor of New York State, Franklin D Roosevelt, who became President of the United States the following year. Incidentally, Eleanor, his redoubtable wife, took a ride down the bob course. The oath was taken by Jack Shea, who won the 500m speed skating gold later in the day. An Olympic first was achieved in the opening ceremony by the British contingent when their flag was carried by a woman, skater Mollie Phillips. Innovatively, figure skating was held indoors, and drew large crowds, and three speed skating events for women were given demonstration status – 28 years later such events were on the programme proper. Demonstrations were also given of curling and dog sled racing, the latter won by Emile St Goddard of Canada.

Not surprisingly the Scandinavians swept the Nordic skiing, but an upset occurred in the speed skating where the Americans and Canadians dominated. It is arguable whether this was more to do with the abilities

of the North Americans than with the change of rules the organizing committee had invoked. Instead of the more usual European system of competition in pairs, with the fastest times deciding the medal places, American rules were in force. Under these, mass start races were held, similar to track running, with heats and finals. Lack of familiarity with the tactics employed, often quite physical, put the Europeans at a distinct disadvantage. Indeed, Finland's four time gold medallist Clas Thunberg did not even bother to appear at Lake Placid. The Canadians won the ice hockey title for the fourth consecutive time, but only on goal average after three periods of overtime against the United States in the final game.

In figure skating, the peerless Sonja Henie (NOR) easily retained her title, but triple champion Gillis Grafström (SWE), now 38, was the victim of an unfortunate accident. During the compulsory figures he collided with a badly positioned movie camera and fell, suffering a mild concussion. This may well have cost him an unprecedented fourth title. The oldest competitor was Joseph Savage (USA) aged 52yr 144days in the pairs skating. The winners of that title, Pierre and Andrée Brunet (FRA), became the first pair to win both as an unmarried and married couple. In so doing, Andrée was the oldest female gold medal winner in Lake Placid aged 30yr 149days. They later coached American gold medallists Carol Heiss (1960), Hayes (1956) and David (1960) Jenkins. In the ladies individual event, Cecilia Colledge was Britain's youngest ever Olympic competitor, at any sport, 11yr 73days. She was also the youngest ever competitor in the Olympic Winter Games.

History of a different kind was made by Eddie Eagan (USA) in the 4-man bob as a late and virtually untried draftee. As part of the winning team he became the only man to win gold medals in both Summer and Winter celebrations – he was a 1920 boxing champion. The 2-man bob was won by brothers Curtis and Hubert Stevens (USA), and a third brother, Paul, won a silver medal in the 4-man event. The oldest gold medallist at Lake Placid was Eagan's bob teammate Jay O'Brien aged 48yr 359days, while Sonja Henie was again the youngest, now aged 19yr 308days. The youngest male champion was ice hockey player Albert Duncanson (CAN) aged 20yr 134days. O'Brien is still the oldest person to win a winter Olympics gold medal.

Lake Placid 1932 Medals

	G	S	B
United States	6	4	2
Norway	3	4	3
Sweden	1	2	-
Canada	1	1	5

Finland	1	1	1
Austria	1	1	-
France	1	-	-
Switzerland	-	1	-
Germany	-	-	2
Hungary	-	-	1

LOS ANGELES 1932

Xth Olympic Games. 30 July – 14 August
Attended by representatives of 37 countries, comprising 1326 competitors, of which 126 were women.

AS EARLY AS 1920, the US delegation to the IOC led by William May Garland had applied for either the 1924 or 1928 Games to be held in Los Angeles. Despite trepidations felt over the memory of the 1904 'farce' at St Louis, in 1923 Los Angeles was awarded the 1932 Games. Against further worries of distance and cost of travel were set the advantages of favourable weather and competitive conditions. The announcement by the organizing committee that they would subsidize transportation, housing and feeding costs helped greatly at a time of the Depression, and did much to offset the critics. One source of income was from a new 3 cent postage stamp, which depicted a runner, for which the model was the anchor man of the 1924 gold medal relay team, Alfred Leconey. The concept of an Olympic 'village' came to fruition with the construction of 550 specially designed small houses for male competitors in the Baldwin Hills area. It was strictly guarded by cowboys who 'rode the fences' around the perimeter, and the strict rule preventing women in the village barred the Finnish team's lady cook. Female competitors were put up separately in the Chapman Park Hotel on Wilshire Boulevard. Despite Prohibition, the French team were allowed to bring in wine for their own consumption. After journeys often lasting two weeks the foreigners found excellent weather and facilities awaiting them.

The main stadium was the Los Angeles Coliseum which had begun construction in 1921 and opened two years later. In 1930 it had been enlarged to hold 101,000 seated spectators, and the track had a new crushed peat running surface. Also there was the 10,000 seat swimming stadium, the State Armory where fencing took place, the Olympic Auditorium, seating 10,000 to watch boxing, wrestling and weightlifting events, and a specially built wooden track was erected in the world famous Pasadena Rose Bowl for the cycling. Long Beach harbour was the venue for sailing, and the Long Beach Marine Stadium hosted the rowing. The LA Museum of History, Science and Art was the home for the fine art competitions. The Games were formally opened by the Vice President of the United States, Charles Curtis, on behalf of President Hoover

who was in the middle of an electioneering tour. (Interestingly, he lost the Presidency the following year, to Franklin D Roosevelt, who had officially opened the Winter Games at Lake Placid earlier in the year). The oath was taken by American fencer, Lieut George Calnan of the US Navy, who died the following April when the dirigible *Akron* crashed into the Pacific Ocean. Although the number of teams, and the total number of competitors, were lower than at Amsterdam, there were two countries making their Olympic debuts, Colombia and China, both with sole representatives, neither of whom achieved any success. However, another small team, Ireland with only eight men, finished well up the medal table with two gold medals.

At these Games new ideas included the use of photo-finish equipment – the Kirby Two-Eyed Camera – for track races. Although it could accurately provide times to one-hundredth of a second it was only used to decide close finishes, and only a few of the timings have ever come to light. Another innovation was the three-tiered victory stand, with medal awarding ceremonies involving the raising of national flags taking place at the end of each day's events. In boxing the system of having the referee in the ring with the boxers was introduced into the Games for the first time, although it did not settle all arguments in that sport.

As with all such international gatherings there were some unfortunate incidents, but in the main they were of minor importance. Prior to the arrival of teams there was a major 'scandal' with the banning by the IAAF of the great Finnish runner, Paavo Nurmi, under charges of professionalism – he was accused of accepting unduly large expenses on a German tour. Despite rigorous protests on his behalf, the Finnish Federation finally accepted the ruling although he had already be selected for the marathon and, indeed, arrived with the team in Los Angeles. It seems not unreasonable to suggest that he would have finished a remarkable career with another gold medal. Once the Games were underway, the Finns were also involved in another incident when the runners in the 3000m steeplechase ran an extra lap due to a miscalculation by the lap counter. Happily the error did not appear to have altered the final medal placings. Another minor irritant was the American habit of announcing all the field event results only in Imperial units of measurement, much to the annoyance, and bafflement, of the foreign competitors and spectators. But there were two more serious occurrences, one on the track and one in the swimming pool. The first was when the eventual winner, Lauri Lehtinen (FIN) deliberately blocked the American, Ralph Hill, twice in the final stages of the race, a not uncommon practice in Europe, but one which drew loud booing from the basically partisan crowd. They were quickly quietened by the announcer, Bill Henry, whose words 'Remember please, these people are our guests' have entered Olympic lore.

The second incident was of a much more serious nature when the Brazilian water polo team, after losing 7-3 to Germany, lost their tempers and insulted the referee. They were disqualified from the tournament. On the brighter side was the performance of the outstanding individual of the Games, Mildred 'Babe' Didrikson.(Since her death her family has insisted that the surname should be spelt with an 'e' not an 'o'). Much to her annoyance she was only allowed to enter three events. She set Olympic records in each of them, winning the javelin and 80m hurdles, and gaining a silver in the high jump. Thus she is the only athlete to win medals in individual running, jumping and throwing events. In the high jump there was a strange judgement made, for although Didrikson cleared the same height as her teammate, Jean Shiley, and then tied in a jump-off, the judges decided that her 'Western Roll' style of jump had been performed illegally, with her head preceding her body over the bar, and illogically they placed her second. She later became the world's greatest female golfer of her day under her married name of Zaharias.

Another unusual thing occurred in the 400m hurdles when Irishman Bob Tisdall, who reportedly spent most of the preceding days in bed recuperating from a long and tiring journey, won the gold medal in a time superior to the world record. However, because he knocked down the last hurdle, the world record was given to the runner-up Glenn Hardin (USA). Remarkably, the first four finishers were all gold medallists in the event – Tisdall (1932), Hardin (1936), Taylor (1924) and Burghley (1928).

In the 200m final Ralph Metcalfe was inadvertently made to start about 1.5m *5ft* before the correct place, thus almost certainly costing him a silver medal. As Americans had placed 1-2-3, Metcalfe, later a US Congressman, declined the offered re-run. The Indian hockey team, while not quite so invincible as previously, set a record score by defeating the United States by 24-1, with Roop Singh scoring 12 goals. Similarly, in the water polo competition, Hungary beat Japan with a record score of 18-0. Nevertheless, the Japanese were particularly noteworthy in swimming, highlighted by their superb 4x200m team breaking the world record by a remarkable 37.8 sec.

The oldest gold medallist at Los Angeles was yachtsman Pierpoint Davis (USA) aged 47yr 224days, while the youngest was 1500m freestyle champion Kusuo Kitamura (JPN) aged 14yr 309days. The youngest female champion was Claire

Dennis (AUS) who won the 200m breaststroke aged 16yr 117days. The oldest female winner was Lillian Copeland (USA) in the discus aged 27yr 251days. The youngest medallist was diver Katharine Rawls (USA) 58 days past her 14th birthday. The oldest medallist was Hiram Tuttle (USA) in the dressage aged 49yr 231days. As demonstration sports the hosts provided American football and lacrosse. During the closing ceremony the President of the IOC, Count Henri de Baillet-Latour, presented Olympic Merit Awards for Alpinism to Franz and Toni Schmid (GER) for the first climb of the north face of the Matterhorn. Despite all the economic and organizational misgivings, the Xth Games were a great success, attended by a total of 1.25 million spectators, and realized a profit of about $1 million.

One last innovation at these Games was the use of two sentences, attributed to Baron de Coubertin, but actually based on words used by the Bishop of Central Pennsylvania, Ethelbert Talbot, in a sermon at St Paul's Cathedral, London on 19 July 1908. Displayed on the scoreboard at every opening ceremony since 1932, the words are: 'The most important thing in the Olympic Games is not to win but to take part, just as the most important thing in life is not the triumph but the struggle. The essential thing is not to have conquered but to have fought well.'

Los Angeles 1932 Medals

	G	S	B
United States	41	32	30
Italy	12	12	12
France	10	5	4
Sweden	9	5	9
Japan	7	7	4
Hungary	6	4	5
Finland	5	8	12
Germany	3	12	5
Great Britain	4	7	5
Australia	3	1	1
Argentina	3	1	-
Canada	2	5	8
Netherlands	2	5	-
Poland	2	1	4
South Africa	2	-	3
Ireland	2	-	-
Czechoslovakia	1	2	1
Austria	1	1	3
India	1	-	-
Denmark	-	3	3
Mexico	-	2	-
Latvia	-	1	-
New Zealand	-	1	-
Switzerland	-	1	-
Philippines	-	-	3
Spain	-	-	1
Uruguay	-	-	1

GARMISCH-PARTENKIRCHEN 1936

IVth Winter Games. 6 – 16 February
Attended by representatives of 28 countries, comprising 668 competitors, of which 80 were women.

IT IS NOT always remembered that when the Winter and Summer Games of 1936 were awarded to Germany five years previously, Adolf Hitler was virtually unknown. However, by the year of the Games they were seen by many as a test case of how the German Olympic Committee would react to the demands of the National Socialist government of Germany. There had been much heated discussion around the world as to the advisability of attending these, or the later Summer, Games, due to the racialist policies of that government. In spite of this a record entry included teams from Bulgaria, Turkey, Australia, Spain and Liechtenstein for the first time. The Games were declared open by Chancellor Adolf Hitler, and Wilhelm Bogner, a cross-country skier, took the oath on behalf of competitors. By the end of the competitions, there were a record 17 events, more than 500,000 paying spectators had watched the six different sports. These now included Alpine skiing, although the only event was a combination one, for both men and women.

Birger Ruud (NOR) successfully defended his ski jump title, and then caused a major surprise by winning the downhill segment of the men's Alpine combination. By dint of a 5.9sec margin of victory in the slalom segment the title went to Franz Pfnür (GER) and Ruud fell back to fourth place. In the women's event there was a similar situation when the downhill race was won by 16-year-old Laila Schou Nilsen (NOR), who, a year later, broke five world speed skating records. She had entered the skiing in the absence of such events for women. In the slalom, Christl Cranz (GER), who was eventually to win 12 world skiing championships, won by the quite astounding margin of 11.3sec and took the overall gold medal. Despite falling in the downhill, Nilsen gained the bronze.

The top medal winner was speed skater Ivar Ballangrud (NOR) with three golds and a silver. Contrary to the Lake Placid conditions of four years earlier the racers competed under European-style rules with pairs of skaters racing against the clock. Instead of the four gold medals the Americans had won in 1932, here they only gained a solitary bronze. Sonja Henie (NOR) won her third consecutive figure skating title, to add to her ten world championships, and then went off to Hollywood, followed sometime later by the sixteenth-placed British girl, Gladys Jepson-Turner,

the youngest competitor at Garmisch aged 12yr 124days, who gained cinematic fame as Belita, and 17th placed Vera Hruba (TCH). The British caused a major upset by winning the ice hockey, with a team containing mainly British-born Canadians. Also in this competition was Rudi Ball, one of only two athletes of Jewish origin selected by Germany in 1936. A bronze medallist in 1932, he was especially requested to return from his exile in France – the hosts hoping to offset criticism of their attitude to Jewish competitors by this act.

A most unusual double nearly came the way of Ernst Baier (GER) who won the pairs skating, but came only second in the men's singles. It was still the best such double placing ever. His pairs partner, Maxi Herber was the youngest gold medallist aged 15yr 128days, and sister and brother Ilse and Erik Pausin (AUT), the pairs silver medallists, were the youngest ever couple to gain a medal in the event, their ages totalling a mere 32yr 307days. The oldest gold medallist was Carl Erhardt (GBR) one day past his 39th birthday in the ice hockey final. The demonstration events were German curling and the military patrol.

Garmisch-Partenkirchen 1936 Medals

	G	S	B
Norway	7	5	3
Germany	3	3	-
Sweden	2	2	3
Finland	1	2	3
Austria	1	1	2
Switzerland	1	2	-
Great Britain	1	1	1
United States	1	-	3
Canada	-	1	-
France	-	-	1
Hungary	-	-	1

BERLIN 1936

XIth Olympic Games. 1 – 16 August
Attended by representatives of 49 countries, comprising 3954 competitors, of which 329 were women.

THESE GAMES WERE awarded to Berlin just prior to the rise to power of Adolf Hitler and the National Socialist (Nazi) Party. Abhorrence of Germany's policies under this government led many countries, not least the United States, to propose a boycott, but the President of the US Olympic Committee, Avery Brundage, was strongly in favour of participation, and won the day. In Germany itself, the notorious Heinrich Himmler was opposed to the Games being held, but Josef Goebbels convinced Hitler that they would present tremendous propaganda opportunities. Political overtones over-shadowed the

Games until the last moment when Spain withdrew owing to the outbreak of the civil war there.

The original intention had been to enlarge the stadium that had been built for the aborted 1916 Games, but Hitler decreed that a brand new 100,000 capacity stadium be built. The architects were Werner and Walter March, whose father had designed the 1916 stadium. However, recent research has indicated that, according to Albert Speer, Hitler had expressed his displeasure with the finished stadium, and that Speer instigated some finishing touches, to placate him. It seems that the Fuhrer envisaged that after his final victory, all future Games would be held in this stadium. Other fine stadia and halls were erected, plus a magnificent 'village' of 150 buildings for the competitors. Sailing events were held at Kiel on the north-west coast. At the instigation of Carl Diem, the main organizer, a torch relay was inaugurated to bring the sacred Olympic flame from the Temple of Zeus at Olympia – where it was lit by 'priestesses' Koula Pratsika and Aleka Katseli, who handed it to a Greek runner, Kyril Kondylis, the first of 3,331 runners. The flame crossed seven countries (3187km *1980 miles*) in ten days. The last runner into the stadium to light the cauldron was athlete Fritz Schilgen. The Games were formally opened by Chancellor Hitler, as a specially commissioned 16½ ton bell was rung and thousands of pigeons set free. As the massive German contingent, 348 strong, entered, the giant airship *Hindenburg* flew over.

The German team, with full government backing, was probably the best prepared team ever in the Games. As a sop to foreign criticism it contained one athlete of Jewish origin, Helene Mayer, persuaded to return from America with the promise of full 'Aryan' classification. Ironically she placed second in the foil to the Hungarian Jewess, Ilona Elek, with another Jewish fencer in third. Perhaps even more ironic, at the Opening ceremony the 1896 marathon victor, Spiridon Louis, attired in national dress, presented Hitler with an olive branch – signifying peace – from Olympia. In the march-past of teams a number of them gave the Nazi salute, but the United States and Great Britain, to their credit and to the annoyance of the crowd, merely made the traditional 'eyes right'. The music for the ceremony was conducted by the famous composer Richard Strauss. An indication of the future came with the first ever use of television at the Games, with a closed circuit system to special halls in the city.

There were a record 144 events held, and attendances totalled over one million for the first time. Very high sporting standards were reached at these Games, and at the forefront of the record breaking were the ten black members of the US track and field team. Anathema to the German propaganda machine, which dubbed them 'Black Auxiliaries', they won seven gold, three silver and three bronze medals – more than any other national team, including their own white teammates. Outstanding among them was Jesse Owens with four gold medals, in the 100m, 200m, long jump, and as a member of the 4x100m relay team. In second place in the 200m was Mack Robinson, whose brother Jackie was the first black major league baseball player. It should be noted that the attitude of the German government to Owens was not shared by the majority of the fans – and he was in tremendous demand by autograph hunters.

Much has been written about Hitler refusing to meet and congratulate Owens and the other black gold medallists. In fairness it should be realized that after he had made a point of personally greeting the German victors on the first day, he was rebuked for the practice by the President of the IOC, Henri de Baillet-Latour, who informed him that only IOC designated people performed such duties in an Olympic stadium. After that he refrained from further congratulatory meetings, although it is reported that he met all German medallists in private. Thus, if he did snub anybody, it would have been the only black winner on the first day, high jumper Cornelius Johnson.

Other track highlights included the superb sprinting of Helen Stephens (USA), the decathlon victory of teammate Glenn Morris, later to be a screen Tarzan, and the 1500m world record by Jack Lovelock (NZL). This last event was considered by many to have been the highlight of the Games. The Finns took all three places in the 10,000m as well as the first two places in the 5000m and steeplechase, Volmari Iso-Hollo successfully defending his title in the latter. Outstanding in the pool were the Dutch women led by Hendrika Mastenbroek, who personally won three golds and a silver. The winner of the women's springboard diving, Marjorie Gestring (USA), became the youngest ever female gold medallist, and the youngest ever individual event champion, aged 13yr 268days. The oldest gold medallist at Berlin was Friedrich Gerhard (GER) in the dressage team aged 52yr 20days. The youngest male champion was fencer Edoardo Mangiarotti (ITA) aged 17yr 124days, while the oldest female champion was gymnast Friedl Iby (GER) at 31yr 128days. In taking the bronze medal in the 200m breaststroke, Inge Sørensen (DEN) became one of the youngest ever Olympic medallists aged 12yr 24days.

Robert Charpentier (FRA) won three gold medals in cycling, in which Toni Merkens (GER) won the 1000m sprint despite being fined, but not disqualified, for obstruction in the first race. In wrestling, Kristjan Palusalu of Estonia matched the achievement of Ivar Johansson (SWE) in 1932 by winning titles in both freestyle and Greco-Roman styles. Interestingly, the list of gold medallists at Berlin includes the name *Nurmi*, but in this case it was the name of the horse ridden by Ludwig Stubbendorff (GER) to his easy victory in the tough three-day event. Of the fourteen teams which started, only four finished with sufficient scorers. These included Britain, whose final placer, Capt Richard Fanshawe, gained his team the bronze medal despite numerous penalty points incurred resulting from having to chase his horse for 4km *2.5 miles* before remounting.

In the single-handed Olympia class sailing the bronze medal went to Peter Markham Scott, son of the tragic Antarctic explorer, and later himself a world-famous naturalist. Canoeing and basketball made their official debuts, with the inventor of the latter, Dr James Naismith, on hand to see the US team begin its remarkable sequence of victories. At the end of the Games a magnificent film *Olympische Spiele* was produced by Leni Riefenstahl, which although criticized as propaganda, is still the best documentary record of an Olympic Games. In addition to their traditional awards, gold medallists were given oak tree seedlings. Forty years later research by the US Olympic Committee indicated that at least 16 of the trees were still alive and well.

Berlin 1936 Medals

	G	S	B
Germany	33	26	30
United States	24	20	12
Hungary	10	1	5
Italy	8	9	5
Finland	7	6	6
France	7	6	6
Sweden	6	5	9
Japan	6	4	8
Netherlands	6	4	7
Great Britain	4	7	3
Austria	4	6	3
Czechoslovakia	3	5	-
Argentina	2	2	3
Estonia	2	2	3
Egypt	2	1	2
Switzerland	1	9	5
Canada	1	3	5
Norway	1	3	2
Turkey	1	-	1
India	1	-	-
New Zealand	1	-	-
Poland	-	3	3
Denmark	-	2	3
Latvia	-	1	1
Romania	-	1	-
South Africa	-	1	-
Yugoslavia	-	1	-
Mexico	-	-	3
Belgium	-	-	2
Australia	-	-	1
Philippines	-	-	1
Portugal	-	-	1

ST MORITZ 1948

Vth Winter Games. 30 January – 8 February
Attended by representatives of 28 countries, comprising 668 competitors, of which 77 were women.

IN 1936, THE Winter Games of 1940 were initially awarded to Sapporo, Japan, but as a consequence of the Sino-Japanese conflict they were reallocated to St Moritz. Due to some disagreements the IOC transferred them again in June 1939 to Garmisch-Partenkirchen, Germany, at the same time deciding that the 1944 meeting should be held at Cortina d'Ampezzo, Italy. The Second World War then upset these plans, and in 1946 a postal vote of IOC members relocated the 1948 Games in St Moritz, as neutral Switzerland had been virtually untouched by the war. Chile, Denmark, Iceland, Korea and Lebanon competed for the first time in the Winter Games, but Germany and Japan were not invited, although Italy was. The oath was taken by ice hockey player Richard Torriani on behalf of the competitors, and Swiss President Enrico Celio formally declared the Games open. There were now six Alpine events which attracted larger fields than the Nordic disciplines. Poor weather affected some of the competitions, and there were a number of disputes.

The most medals were won by Henri Oreiller (FRA) with gold in the downhill (by a record margin of 4.1sec), and combination, and a bronze in the slalom. Alpine skier Gretchen Fraser (USA) gained the first skiing title ever won by a non-European. In Nordic skiing the Swedes broke the Norwegian monopoly. They had the three medals and fifth place in the 18km, first two and fifth in the 50km, and won the 4x10km relay by a margin of nearly nine minutes. They also won their first ever speed skating title when Ake Seyffarth took the 10km event. The athletic American figure skaters brought a new concept to figure skating as Dick Button gained an easy victory. He became the first to successfully complete a double Axel in the Games.

The ice hockey competition was the cause of a major row. Two American teams appeared in St Moritz. One represented the Amateur Hockey Association of the United States (AHA) and the other was picked by the US Olympic Committee. The AHA, while not affiliated to the USOC, was a member of the International Hockey Federation (IHF). This last was the governing body of most of the other teams at the Games, and threatened to withdraw all the other teams if the AHA team were not allowed to play. The USOC in turn threatened to withdraw its whole Olympic team if it did. Initially the IOC decided to bar both teams, but then agreed with the Swiss organizers and the IHF to allow the AHA team to compete. Strangely, however, the USOC team members marched in the opening ceremony. The AHA team eventually finished fourth, but a year later the AHA was disqualified for non-affiliation to the Olympic movement. The Canadians won the title once again, but only just. The title was decided on goal average, with the Czechs taking the silver. The Swiss in third place contained the man who had taken the oath, Richard 'Bibi' Torriani, thus adding another bronze to that he had won 20 years earlier when he was just past his sixteenth birthday.

The US bobsleds were sabotaged prior to the competitions, but it did not prevent them from winning a gold and two bronzes. They have never won an Olympic bob event since. In the skeleton toboggan, which was held only in those days when the Games are at St Moritz on the Cresta Run, John Heaton (USA) won his second silver medal, 20 years after his first. The gold medal went to Nino Bibbia of Italy, a country perhaps surprisingly not refused an invitation like its wartime ally, Germany. Bibbia was a master of the Cresta Run and won many titles and championships over the next quarter of a century.

The great Norwegian ski jumper Birger Ruud, nearly 37 years old and a survivor of a wartime concentration camp, ended his Olympic career with a silver medal to add to his golds from 1932 and 1936. He and his brother Sigmund had made the event a family preserve since 1928. A third brother, Asbjørn, was also in the 1948 team.

A record thirteen countries shared out the medals, and Italy and Belgium won their first ever Winter Games titles. There were two demonstration events: a military ski patrol, and a winter pentathlon. This latter consisted of 10km cross-country skiing, pistol shooting, downhill skiing, fencing, and horse riding. No medals were awarded, but in second place was Capt Willie Grut (SWE), of whom much more was to be heard six months later, in London.

The oldest gold medallist was Francis Tyler, in the US 4-man bob aged 43yr 58days, while the youngest was skater Dick Button aged 18yr 202days. The youngest female champion was skater Barbara-Ann Scott (CAN) aged 19yr 273days, while the oldest female winner was Gretchen Fraser (USA) in the slalom aged 28yr 360days. The youngest medallist was skater Suzanne Morrow (CAN) with a pairs bronze aged 17yr 55days, while the oldest was bobsledder Max Houben (BEL) at 49yr 278days.

St Moritz 1948 Medals

	G	S	B
Norway	4	3	3
Sweden	4	3	3
Switzerland	3	4	3
United States	3	4	2
France	2	1	2
Canada	2	-	1
Austria	1	3	4
Finland	1	3	2
Belgium	1	1	-
Italy	1	-	-
Czechoslovakia	-	1	-
Hungary	-	1	-
Great Britain	-	-	2

LONDON 1948

XIVth Olympic Games. 29 July – 14 August
Attended by representatives of 59 countries, comprising 4071 competitors, of which 393 were women.

IN 1936 THE XIIth Games were awarded to Tokyo, to take place from 24 August–8 September 1940. When the Sino-Japanese war began in 1938, the Games were transferred to Helsinki, but the Soviet invasion of Finland cancelled these plans. In June 1939, a very optimistic IOC awarded the XIIIth Games, for 1944, to London, over competing claims from Detroit, Lausanne and Rome. A postal vote of IOC members called by the President, Sigfrid Edström of Sweden, in 1946, awarded the XIVth Games to London. In the meantime, Baron de Coubertin had died, in 1937, and his heart was buried at Olympia in Greece.

Organized by the British Olympic Association, under the Presidency of Lord Burghley, the 1948 Olympics were an austerity Games – after six years of war Britain still had rationing of food and clothing. Housing was in short supply due to wartime destruction, and competitors were housed at RAF and Army camps (for men) and colleges (for women). A temporary running track was laid at the 83,000 capacity Wembley Stadium, the home of British football. Other existing buildings were adapted. Rowing was held at Henley, on the River Thames, and the sailing was at Torbay, Devon. The total expenditure amounted to no more than £600,000, and final accounts suggested that a profit of over £10,000 was made. The Games were opened by King George VI. Not surprisingly Germany and Japan were not invited, but a record 59 countries attended. These included the first entries by countries under Communist governments. Some of the hottest weather for years occurred on the opening days, but later it rained. Photo-finish equipment, as used on race courses, was used for the track events, but only to decide places, and starting blocks were allowed for he first time in the Games. The first proper television coverage of the Games occurred with pictures beamed into an estimated 80,000 black and white receivers within range of the transmission from Wembley.

The undoubted star of the Games was Francina 'Fanny' Blankers-Koen (NED) who won four gold medals, a record for a woman. At the time 30 years of age, and a mother of two children, she had finished in sixth place in the 1936 high jump. In 1948 she held seven world records including those in the high and long jumps, neither of which she contested in London. The gap between her and the second girl in the 200m, 0.7sec, remains the largest margin of victory ever achieved in an Olympic sprint, by men or women. In the high jump Dorothy Tyler (née Odam) (GBR) placed second again, 12 years after her other silver medal – both times she had cleared the same height as the winner. Bob Mathias (USA) became the youngest ever male Olympic individual athletics champion when we won the decathlon aged 17yr 263days. He retained the title in 1952, became a movie actor, and later was elected a US Congressman. Another athlete to catch the eye was Emil Zátopek (TCH), not so much by his easy win in the 10,000m, but by his remarkable last 300m sprint to narrowly lose the 5000m. An American, Harrison Dillard, acknowledged as the world's best high hurdler, had fallen in the US trials and failed to make their team in his best event. In London he won his 'second-string' event, the 100m, and won another gold in the relay. Two of the debuting countries made their marks early in the Games. Duncan White of Ceylon (now Sri Lanka) gained the only medal his country has ever won with a silver in the 400m hurdles. Jamaica made an even bigger impact by collecting a gold, two silvers and two other finalists in the 200, 400, and 800m. The marathon provided its usual drama when Etienne Gailly, a Belgian paratrooper, entered the stadium first, but was so exhausted that he was passed by two runners prior to the tape. Incidentally, the female high jump champion, Alice Coachman, was the first black woman to win an Olympic gold medal, in any sport.

An outstanding competitor in the modern pentathlon was Willie Grut of Sweden who won three disciplines of the five-sport event, and placed fifth and eighth in the others, to win by a large margin. He was the son of the designer of the 1912 Olympic stadium. Another exceptional champion was South African boxer George Hunter, who not only won the light-heavyweight title, but also the Val Barker Trophy as the best stylist in the whole competition. However, lack of experienced referees and judges resulted in much criticism of the boxing tournament. There were problems too at Herne Hill stadium where some of the cycling events finished in very poor light due to the lack of floodlighting. There was an unfortunate turn of events in the equestrian competitions where the team dressage contest was won by the Swedes. However, the following year they were disqualified, and their medals taken away, when it was learned that one of their number, Gehnäll Persson, was not a commissioned officer, as the rules then required.

In fencing, Ilona Elek (HUN) retained her 1936 title even though she was now over 41 years of age. Her sister Margit placed sixth. The 1932 champion, Ellen Müller-Preis (AUT) gained the bronze medal. An even more outstanding veteran was 40-year-old Heikki Savolainen, the famous Finnish gymnast who, in his fourth Olympics, won his first gold medal, on the pommel horse.

The soccer gold medallists, Sweden, were involved in one of the strangest goals in the history of the sport, in their semi-final against Denmark. The Swedish centre-forward Gunnar Nordahl, one of three brothers in the team, quickwittedly leapt into the Danish goalnet to avoid being offside during a Swedish attack. At the end of the move his inside-left headed the ball into the goal, where in the absence of the Danish 'keeper it was caught by Nordahl. Sweden went on to win the gold medal. Sailing witnessed the end of a long Olympic career when Ralph Craig, the 1912 double sprint champion, reappeared in the American team. Although he carried the US flag in the opening ceremony he did not actually compete. Torbay was also the start of another exceptional career with the appearance of Durward Knowles competing for Britain. He competed in sailing events for the Bahamas in the next six Games, and made it an eighth time in 1988. A rare happening at the sailing was the victory of father/son combination Paul and Hilary Smart (USA) in the Star class. At the Empire Pool, site of the swimming competitions, US competitors won 12 of the 15 events there, excluding water polo. One of the few non-American champions was Greta Andersen (DEN) in the 100m freestyle, who, 16 years later, set a female record for swimming the English Channel. In diving, Vicki Draves (USA) won both titles, then a unique achievement.

The oldest gold medallist in London was Paul Smart (see above) in yachting aged 56yr 212days, and the youngest was Thelma Kalama (USA) in the swimming sprint relay for women aged 17yr 135days. Bob Mathias, the decathlon champion, was the youngest male champion (see above), while the oldest female winner was fencer Ilona Elek (HUN) aged 41yr 77days.

London 1948 Medals

	G	S	B
United States	38	27	19
Sweden	16	11	17
France	10	6	13
Hungary	10	5	12
Italy	8	11	8
Finland	8	7	5
Turkey	6	4	2
Czechoslovakia	6	2	3
Switzerland	5	10	5
Denmark	5	7	8
Netherlands	5	2	9
Great Britain	3	14	6
Argentina	3	3	1
Australia	2	6	5
Belgium	2	2	3
Egypt	2	2	1
Mexico	2	1	2
South Africa	2	1	1
Norway	1	3	3
Jamaica	1	2	-
Austria	1	-	3
India	1	-	-
Peru	1	-	-
Yugoslavia	-	2	-
Canada	-	1	2
Portugal	-	1	1
Uruguay	-	1	1
Ceylon (now Sri Lanka)	-	1	-
Cuba	-	1	-
Spain	-	1	-
Trinidad	-	1	-
Korea	-	-	2
Panama	-	-	2
Brazil	-	-	1
Iran	-	-	1
Poland	-	-	1
Puerto Rico	-	-	1

OSLO 1952

VIth Winter Games. 14 – 25 February
Attended by representatives of 30 countries, comprising 693 competitors, of which 109 were women.

A FEATURE OF these Games was the enormous crowds at all venues, including a record for any Olympic event, at the ski jumping at Holmenkollen, estimated at 150,000. An innovation was the Olympic flame coming, not from Olympia, but from Morgedal in southern Norway, the home of Sondre Nordheim, the father of modern skiing. The last relay 'runner' who brought the flame into the Bislett Stadium was Eigil Nansen, the grandson of the renowned Polar explorer Fridtjof Nansen. The oath was taken by ski jumper Torbjørn Falkanger. All entrants from Commonwealth countries wore black armbands as the opening day coincided with the funeral of Britain's King George VI. As King Haakon and the Crown Prince were in London for this, the Games were opened by HRH Princess Ragnhild. Back in the Olympic fold were Germany and Japan, and for the first time in the Winter Games entries included Portugal and New Zealand.

Bad weather conditions necessitated the start of some of the competitions, the women's giant slalom and the 2-man bob, the day before the opening ceremony. Of the three Alpine events, the giant slalom and downhill races were held some 120km from Oslo, at Norefjell. In the men's giant slalom Stein Eriksen (NOR) became the first ever winner of an Alpine skiing event from a Nordic country. This did not happen again until 1980. The star of the Games was Hjalmar Andersen of the host country who won three speed skating gold medals. In winning the women's figure skating title, Jeanette Altwegg won Britain's first skating gold medal since Madge Syers in 1908. Instead of turning professional, as did most of her predecessors and successors, she went to work at the famed village for orphan children, Pestalozzi in Switzerland. The men's title went to defending champion Dick Button (USA) with some of the most remarkable jumps ever seen in competition, including a triple loop. Finishing sixth, was Carlo Fassi (ITA), later to coach Olympic champions Peggy Fleming (USA), Dorothy Hamill (USA), John Curry (GBR) and Robin Cousins (GBR).

The basic running abilities required by cross-country skiers were highlighted in the Nordic skiing when the 18km gold medal was won by Hallgeir Brenden (NOR), who during following years won two national steeplechase titles. Also in the silver Norwegian relay team with him was Martin Stokken, who had placed fourth in the 1948 Olympic 10,000m run in London. By competing again at Helsinki, he became one of the few men to compete in a Winter and Summer Games in the same year. For the first time there was a Nordic ski race for women, dominated by Finland with four of the first five places. Bandy, a distant relative of ice hockey, was played as a demonstration sport and won by Sweden.

The oldest gold medallist at Oslo was Franz Kemser in the German 4-man bob aged 41yr 103days, and the youngest was slalom winner Andrea Mead-Lawrence (USA) aged 19yr 301days. The youngest male winner was Robert Dickson (CAN) in ice hockey aged 20yr 308days, while the oldest female champion was Lydia Wideman (FIN) in the 10km cross-country aged 31yr 282days. The youngest medallist was skater Tenley Albright (USA) with a silver aged 16yr 217days. Albert Madorin (SUI) won a bronze in the 4-man bob aged 46yr 342days.

Oslo 1952 Medals

	G	S	B
Norway	7	3	6
United States	4	6	1
Finland	3	4	2
Germany	3	2	2
Austria	2	4	2
Canada	1	-	1
Italy	1	-	1
Great Britain	1	-	-
Netherlands	-	3	-
Sweden	-	-	4
Switzerland	-	-	2
France	-	-	1
Hungary	-	-	1

HELSINKI 1952

XVth Olympic Games. 19 July – 3 August
Attended by representatives of 69 countries, comprising 4919 competitors, of which 521 were women.

ONE OF THE greatest Olympian countries, Finland, finally hosted the Games. President Juho Paasikivi formally opened them in the smallest city ever to be host, as his capital Helsinki had a population of only 367,000. There were two dramatic moments during the ceremony. Firstly, when a so-called 'Angel of Peace', an apparently mentally unstable German girl in a flowing white robe, ran around part of the track. More appropriate to the occasion was the moment when the last torch relay runner was due, and the scoreboard indicated the first letter of his name. The stadium erupted to cheers as 55-year-old Paavo Nurmi, arguably the greatest distance runner the world has seen, ran a lap and lit the flame in the stadium. The torch was then passed to 62-year-old Hannes Kolehmainen, the original 'Flying Finn', who was at the top of the stadium tower, and he lit another flame there.

After 40 years Russia returned to the Olympics, now in the guise of the Soviet Union. Fears of confrontation between them and the United States team proved unfounded, as the competitors seemed to treat each other quite cordially, if somewhat coolly. Attending the Games for the first time were teams from the Bahamas, Gold Coast (now Ghana), Guatemala, Dutch Antilles, Hong Kong, Indonesia, Israel, Nigeria, Thailand, Vietnam, and, for the only time ever, the Saar. Because mainland China had been invited, the Nationalist Chinese (Taiwan) had withdrawn. Although they all marched together there were two Olympic villages; surprisingly the IOC had allowed the Soviet bloc to set up their own at Otaniemi, while everybody else was at Kapyla.

The athlete of these Games was the Czech runner Emil Zátopek who won an unprecedented triple of the 5000m, 10,000m and marathon. To crown his achievements, his wife Dana, born on the same day as Emil, also won a gold medal, in the javelin, within an hour of his 5000m victory. The outstanding female track athlete was Australia's Marjorie Jackson who set world records winning the 100m and 200m, but dropped the baton when certain to win a third gold in the sprint relay. Incidentally, she retrieved the baton and finished in fifth place. In the winning American team was Barbara Pearl Jones who became the youngest ever track and field gold medallist aged 15yr 123days. However, the youngest gold medallist at Helsinki was French cox Bernard Malivoire at 14yr 94days in the rowing pairs event. Once again small nations did well, with Jamaican runners invincible over 400m, and Josy Barthel causing the band some problems as they tried to find the anthem of his native Luxembourg when he scored an upset win in the 1500m.

The 1948 100m sprint champion, Harrison Dillard (USA), was here back to his first love, winning the 110m hurdles and taking his fourth gold medal in the sprint relay. His teammate, Horace Ashenfelter gained America's first win in a distance run since 1908 when he set an inaugural official world record for the 3000m steeplechase. The Press had great fun with the fact that Ashenfelter, an FBI agent, was here followed home by a Russian. The Soviet Union's first ever Olympic gold medal was won by Nina Romashkova in the women's discus. Highly questionable disqualifications by blatantly biased judges marred the 10,000m track walk, but did not stop the Swiss and Russian second and third place medallists literally running the last 30m to the line, outsprinting the judge who vainly tried to reach them to rule them out. Incidentally, the judge was Giorgio Oberweger (ITA), who had won a bronze medal in the 1936 discus before becoming a walking official. The event was dropped from future Games. The winner of the high jump, Walt Davis (USA), was, at 2.04m 6ft 8in, probably the tallest competitor ever to win an individual event, in any sport, at the Games. In the swimming pool the Hungarians won four of the five events for women. Almost matching the Zátopeks were Éva Székely, who won the 200m breaststroke, and her husband Dezsö Gyarmati, a member of the victorious Hungarian water polo team four days later. Much media attention was gained by the 400m freestyle for men, when the father of the winner, Jean Boiteux (FRA), jumped into the pool fully clothed to congratulate his son. In diving, Dr Sammy Lee, an American of Korean origin, became the first man to successfully defend a title, in this case the platform. He later coached the next man to achieve the feat, Bob Webster in 1960 and 1964.

The gymnastics competitions were dominated by

the Soviet teams, led by Viktor Chukarin, four golds and two silvers, and his female counterpart Maria Gorokhovskaya with two golds and five silvers. The latter's total of seven is the most medals ever won by a woman at one Games in any sport. The Finnish veteran, Dr Heikki Savolainen, who had taken the oath at the opening ceremony, and gained a team bronze, the fifth consecutive Games at which he had won a medal, was just two months short of his 45th birthday. Other veterans did well in 1952. Ilona Elek (HUN) added a silver to her two fencing golds at the age of 45yr 71days. In the dressage André Jousseaume (FRA) won an individual bronze medal two days after his 58th birthday, and 20 years after his gold medal at Los Angeles. In all he placed in the first five positions in five Games. Another great sportsman, Károly Takács (HUN), won the rapid-fire pistol for the second time. Before the War he had won the European title as a right-handed shooter, but in 1938 he had lost his right hand when a grenade exploded while he was holding it. He painstakingly taught himself to shoot with his left hand and won two Olympic titles. On a less uplifting note there was the disqualification of Ingemar Johansson (SWE) in the heavyweight boxing final for 'not trying'. His silver medal was withheld for 14 years. In 1959 he won the world professional title from the 1952 Olympic middleweight champion Floyd Patterson (USA).

The oldest gold medallist at these Games was Everard Endt (USA) in the 6m yachting aged 59yr 112days. Another yachtsman, Ernst Westerlund (FIN), was the oldest medallist, 19 days older than Endt. The youngest male and female champions were Bernard Malivoire and Barbara Pearl Jones (see above). The oldest female winner was Sylvi Saimo (FIN) in the 500m kayak event aged 37yr 260days. At the end of the Games a then record 43 countries had won medals in Helsinki, and it was announced that Avery Brundage (USA) had taken over the Presidency of the IOC from the retiring Sigfrid Edström.

1952 Medals

	G	S	B
United States	40	19	17
Soviet Union	22	30	19
Hungary	16	10	16
Sweden	12	13	10
Italy	8	9	4
Czechoslovakia	7	3	3
France	6	6	6
Finland	6	3	13
Australia	6	2	3
Norway	3	2	-
Switzerland	2	6	6
South Africa	2	4	4
Jamaica	2	3	-
Belgium	2	2	-
Denmark	2	1	3
Turkey	2	-	1
Japan	1	6	2
Great Britain	1	2	8
Argentina	1	2	2
Poland	1	2	1
Canada	1	2	-
Yugoslavia	1	2	-
Romania	1	1	2
Brazil	1	-	2
New Zealand	1	-	2
India	1	-	1
Luxembourg	1	-	-
Germany	-	7	17
Netherlands	-	5	-
Iran	-	3	4
Chile	-	2	-
Austria	-	1	1
Lebanon	-	1	1
Ireland	-	1	-
Mexico	-	1	-
Spain	-	1	-
Korea	-	-	2
Trinidad	-	-	2
Uruguay	-	-	2
Bulgaria	-	-	1
Egypt	-	-	1
Portugal	-	-	1
Venezuela	-	-	1

CORTINA d'AMPEZZO 1956

VIIth Winter Games. 26 January – 5 February
Attended by representatives of 32 countries, comprising 821 competitors, of which 132 were women.

MOST OF THE money spent on these Games came from the Italian Football Pools, but despite excellent facilities there were still problems with the weather. Once again snow needed to be 'imported' for some venues. The President of Italy, Giovanni Granchi, formally opened the Games. Giuliana Chenal-Minuzzo, who won the 1952 bronze medal in downhill skiing, became the first woman in Olympic history to pronounce the oath on behalf of all competitors. The last runner in the torch relay, speed skater Guido Caroli, fell as he completed a circuit of the arena but happily the flame did not go out. The entry of the Soviet Union provided the first Soviet competitors in Olympic 'Winter' events since 1908. These were the first Winter Games to be televised, which undoubtedly resulted in smaller numbers of spectators than previously.

Most attention was gained by the Austrian plumber Toni Sailer who gained a grand slam of all three Alpine titles, downhill, slalom and giant slalom, winning in treacherous conditions by outstanding margins of 3.5sec, 4.0sec and 6.2sec respectively.

Second in the slalom was Asia's first Winter medallist, Chiharu Igaya (JPN), an American college student, who had to wait anxiously while the jury investigated an unsubstantiated claim, by Sweden and the United States, that he had missed a gate. Madeleine Berthod (SUI) won the women's downhill by a still record margin of 4.7sec.

The most medals won at Cortina was by Sixten Jernberg (SWE) with one gold, two silvers and a bronze in Nordic skiing. Hallgeir Brenden (NOR) successfully defended his 1952 title, the distance now reduced from 18km to 15km. Using a new style, the Finns dominated the ski jumping and the Norwegians, who had won 15 of the 18 medals available in the sport since 1924, failed to place in the first six. Though Germany competed as a single team, the jumping bronze, won by Harry Glass, was claimed by the GDR as its first Olympic medal. The speed skating surface on Lake Misurina, at an altitude of 1755m 5756ft, was considered to be the fastest ever, and witnessed a wholesale attack on the record book. The winner of the 500m title, Yevgeni Grishin (URS) had been a member of the Soviet cycling team in Helsinki. In figure skating Hayes (gold) and David (bronze) Jenkins were the first brothers to win medals in the same skating event. Their teammate, women's champion Tenley Albright, had been a victim of polio as a child.

A member of the winning Swiss 4-man bob, Franz Kapus, at 46yr 298days, was the oldest gold medallist at Cortina. The youngest champion was Elisabeth Schwarz (AUT) in pairs skating aged 19yr 260days. The youngest male winner was Toni Sailer (AUT) in the giant slalom aged 20yr 73days, and the oldest female champion was Siiri Rantanen (FIN) in the cross-country relay aged 31yr 49days. The youngest medallist was skater Ingrid Wendl (AUT) with a bronze aged 15yr 260days, and the youngest male medallist was speed skater Alv Gjestvang (NOR) at 18yr 137days. The Soviet competitors won a total of 16 medals to head the unofficial medal table – a position they were rarely to lose in future Winter Games.

Cortina d'Ampezzo Medals

	G	S	B
Soviet Union	7	3	6
Austria	4	3	4
Finland	3	3	1
Switzerland	3	2	1
Sweden	2	4	4
United States	2	3	2
Norway	2	1	1
Italy	1	2	-
Germany	1	-	1
Canada	-	1	2
Japan	-	1	-
Hungary	-	-	1
Poland	-	-	1

MELBOURNE 1956

XVIth Olympic Games. 22 November – 8 December (also at Stockholm. 10 – 17 June)
Attended by representatives of 67 countries, comprising 3182 competitors, of which 370 were women. (At Stockholm there were representatives of 29 countries, comprising 158 competitors, of which 13 were women).

IN 1949 THE IOC had decided on Melbourne by only one vote, and they were disquieted, to say the least, by first the apparent tardiness in finishing facilities, and second the inability of the Australians to hold the equestrian events. This was due to their stringent animal quarantine laws. Thus for the first and only time, contrary to the Olympic Charter, a sport was detached from the main Games and held elsewhere, in Stockholm. Except for the cross-country section of the three-day event the venue was the 1912 Olympic Stadium. The host country won three of the six titles, but there was strong criticism and accusations of chauvinism by the judges in the dressage competition. Also the above mentioned cross-country was thought to be too dangerous in the existing wet conditions.

The Games proper, the only celebration to that date in the Southern Hemisphere, opened in Melbourne under a cloud of international ill-will, occasioned by the Soviet invasion of Hungary, and the French and British intervention in the Suez Canal dispute between Israel and Egypt. The Netherlands, Spain and Switzerland withdrew because of the former, and Egypt and Lebanon because of the latter. This time mainland China withdrew because of the presence of Taiwan. Perhaps surprisingly, the Hungarians did compete, and with good effect. West and East Germany entered a combined team, and continued to do so until after 1964. In addition to Taiwan, Olympic debuts were made by teams from Ethiopia, Fiji, Kenya, Liberia, Uganda, Malaya and North Borneo (the two latter now combined as Malaysia). Cambodia's appearance in the Stockholm events was its Olympic debut. HRH The Duke of Edinburgh opened the Games at the Melbourne Cricket Ground, the main venue. The final torch bearer was a 19-year-old Australian miler, Ron Clarke, destined to be one of the world's greatest runners.

The distance runs in Melbourne were dominated by the Soviet sailor Vladimir Kuts, with record breaking victories at 5000m and 10,000m. Ireland won its first gold medal since 1932, when Ronnie Delany took the 1500m with an exceptionally fast last 300m. In the sprints both Bobby-Joe Morrow (USA) and Betty

Cuthbert (AUS) gained three gold medals, including the relays. Teamed with Cuthbert in the 4x100m was Shirley de la Hunty (née Strickland), who ended her three Games career with an unbeaten total of seven medals (three gold, one silver, three bronze). A photo-finish picture, which was not unearthed for many years after the event, indicates that she was also third, not fourth, in the 200m in 1948. She made no official claim and the result remains as it was. After placing second to Emil Zátopek in three Olympic races since 1948, Frenchman Alain Mimoun finally beat him, into sixth place, by taking the marathon – the oldest man to do so at only a month short of his 36th birthday. The 50km walk was won by Norman Read, representing his adopted country, New Zealand. As a former English junior mile walk champion Read had watched the 1952 Games as a spectator (sitting next to the author).

Another English-born competitor, Murray Rose (AUS), was the first male swimmer to win two individual freestyle events since 1924. He also won a third gold medal in the relay. Pat McCormick (USA) achieved a then unique double 'double' retaining both her diving titles from Helsinki. Boxing too had its record-breaker when László Papp did his bit to raise Hungarian spirits by gaining an unprecedented third gold medal at boxing. Not surprisingly, bad feelings erupted in the water polo semi-final between Hungary and the Soviet Union. By a nice touch of irony the referee was from the perennially neutral Sweden. With Hungary leading 4-0 he ended the game, as it had degenerated into a 'boxing match under water'. However, by beating Yugoslavia in the soccer final on the last day, December 8th, the Soviet Union went into history as the winners of the latest gold medal ever won in an Olympic year.

John Kelly Jr, the son of the 1920 gold medallist, won a bronze in the single sculls as Vyacheslav Ivanov (URS) gained the first of his record three consecutive titles. At the shooting range Gerald Ouellette (CAN) won the prone small bore rifle competition with a world record 'maximum' of 600, only to have the record, but not the gold medal, disallowed because the range was found to be 1.5m short of the international distance of 50m.

The oldest gold medallist in the 1956 Games, albeit in his case at Stockholm, was Henri St. Cyr (SWE) in dressage aged 54yr 93days, while the youngest was Sandra Morgan (AUS) in the 4x100m freestyle relay aged 14yr 183days. The youngest male winner was Murray Rose (AUS) aged 17yr 332days, while the oldest female champion was Hungarian gymnast Agnes Keleti at 35yr 331days. Although not even a medallist, Gunhild Larking, a beautiful Swedish high jumper, undoubtedly had more photographs taken of her than any of the more successful competitors. Actually a member of the combined Germany team, Wolfgang Behrendt, winner of the boxing bantamweight title, was the GDR's first Summer Games gold medallist.

At the closing ceremony for the first time the athletes entered en masse, signifying the friendship of the Games. The idea for this had come from an Australian-born Chinese boy, John Wing, in a letter to the chairman of the organizing committee, the Hon Wilfrid S Kent-Hughes. A happy postscript to these Games occurred in Prague in March 1957 when the American hammer winner, Harold Connolly, married Olga Fikotová, the Czech Olympic discus champion. The best man at this 'Olympic' wedding was, most appropriately, Emil Zátopek.

Melbourne 1956 Medals

	G	S	B
Soviet Union	37	29	32
United States	32	25	17
Australia	13	8	14
Hungary	9	10	7
Italy	8	8	9
Sweden	8	5	6
Germany	6	13	7
Great Britain	6	7	11
Romania	5	3	5
Japan	4	10	5
France	4	4	6
Turkey	3	2	2
Finland	3	1	11
Iran	2	2	1
Canada	2	1	3
New Zealand	2	-	-
Poland	1	4	4
Czechoslovakia	1	4	1
Bulgaria	1	3	1
Denmark	1	2	1
Ireland	1	1	3
Norway	1	-	2
Mexico	1	-	1
Brazil	1	-	-
India	1	-	-
Yugoslavia	-	3	-
Chile	-	2	2
Belgium	-	2	-
Argentina	-	1	1
Korea	-	1	1
Iceland	-	1	-
Pakistan	-	1	-
South Africa	-	-	4
Austria	-	-	2
Bahamas	-	-	1
Greece	-	-	1
Switzerland	-	-	1
Uruguay	-	-	1

SQUAW VALLEY 1960

VIIIth Winter Games. 18 – 28 February
Attended by representatives of 30 countries, comprising 664 competitors, of which 144 were women.

WHEN THE IOC voted narrowly, 32-30, to give the Games to Squaw Valley, USA, instead of Innsbruck, virtually nothing existed at the site. Due to the efforts of Alexander Cushing, who owned most of the area, it became the first purpose-built Winter Games venue. Despite initial delays everything was ready for the official opening, under the direction of Walt Disney. The formal opening was by Richard Nixon, then Vice-President of the United States. The last relay runner was Ken Henry, the 500m speed skating champion of 1952, and the oath was taken by figure skater Carol Heiss, who went on to win the women's title.

There were a number of protests and problems. Bobsledding was dropped as the organizers would not accept the cost of building a run for what they considered would be a small entry. Artificial obstacles were built into the downhill runs to make them more difficult, and concern was expressed over the altitude (over 1900m *6230ft*) at which the Nordic skiing events were held. East and West Germany competed as one entity with agreement reached on the popular theme from Beethoven's *Ninth Symphony* played for any victory ceremonies instead of their respective national anthems. A team from South Africa appeared, for the first time in the Winter Games – they were banned thereafter until 1992. The biathlon and speed skating for women made Olympics debuts. The biathlon was the successor to the military patrol event which had been a demonstration event on four previous occasions.

The speed skating times in general were excellent, with Knut Johannesen (NOR) beating the 10,000m world record by 46.0sec, the greatest margin achieved in the 20th century. Yevgeni Grishin (URS) equalled his own world mark to become the first man to successfully defend the 500m title. Helga Haase (GER) was the first ever women's Olympic champion in speed skating when she won the 500m. In figure skating David Jenkins kept the men's title in the family – his brother Hayes had won in 1956, and made the family even more Olympian by marrying Squaw Valley's lady champion Carol Heiss two months later.

There was a first in Nordic skiing when Georg Thoma, a German postman from the Black Forest, who was often forced to deliver mail on skis in bad weather, achieved the first victory by a non-Scandinavian in the sport. The winner of the inaugural biathlon, Klas Lestander (SWE) was only 15th in the cross-country segment of the contest, but scored a maximum possible 20 in the shooting. The Soviet Union's women dominated their 10,000m race, taking the first four places, but they lost the relay, a virtual certainty, when their first girl fell and broke a ski. A protest was made against the first Swedish woman who was accused of deliberate fouling, but it was not upheld.

In Alpine skiing, metallic skis were used in the Games for the first time. The medals were more widespread than usual, with no skier winning more than one event, and only Penny Pitou (USA) won more than one medal, with two silvers. The outstanding competitor was Anne Heggtveit (CAN) who won the women's slalom by a margin of 3.3sec, only ever bettered by the 1936 combination winner, Christl Cranz (GER).

The oldest gold medallist was Veikko Hakulinen (FIN) in the Nordic relay aged 35yr 52days, and the youngest Heidi Biebl (GER), the downhill champion three days past her 19th birthday. The youngest male champion was American ice hockey player Thomas Williams aged 19yr 317days. The oldest female gold medallist was Sonja Ruthström (SWE) in the Nordic relay aged 29yr 94days. The youngest medallist was skier Traudl Hecher (AUT) with a downhill bronze aged 16yr 145days.

Squaw Valley 1960 Medals

	G	S	B
Soviet Union	7	5	9
Germany	4	3	1
United States	3	4	3
Norway	3	3	-
Sweden	3	2	2
Finland	2	3	3
Canada	2	1	1
Switzerland	2	-	-
Austria	1	2	3
France	1	-	2
Netherlands	-	1	1
Poland	-	1	1
Czechoslovakia	-	1	-
Italy	-	-	1

ROME 1960

XVIIth Olympic Games. 25 August – 11 September
Attended by representatives of 83 countries, comprising 5338 competitors, of which 612 were women.

AFTER JUST MISSING out in 1908 the Games finally went to Rome, the home city of the Emperor Theodosius, who reputedly had ended the Ancient Games 1567 years before. A number of old Roman sites were utilized as well as a brand-new 90,000 capacity stadium. The Baths of Caracalla housed the gymnastics and the Basilica di Massenzio had the wrestling competitions. The marathon began at the Capitol Hill and finished on the Appian Way, near the Arch of Constantine. It was the first time that an Olympic marathon had not started or finished in the main Olympic stadium. Sailing was held in the bay of Naples under the shadow of Mt Vesuvius. The Games were opened by the President of Italy, Giovanni Gronchi, before 90,000 spectators. The oath was taken by the 1948 discus champion Adolfo Consolini. Barbados (as part of the Antilles team), Morocco, Sudan, San Marino and Tunisia made their debuts. Nationalist China protested, but competed, when they were told by the IOC to appear under the name of Taiwan and not China. These Games were the first to have worldwide television coverage.

The extreme heat undoubtedly caused upsets, but did nothing to hinder the successes of the Australasians in the middle distance running events. Peter Snell (NZL) won the 800m, Herb Elliott (AUS) won the 1500m by a record margin of 2.8sec in world record time, and Murray Halberg (NZL), handicapped by a withered arm, won the 5000m. An unknown runner, Abebe Bikila, won the marathon barefoot, and signalled the entry of Ethiopia on to the world distance running scene. The team from Taiwan was cheered up somewhat when their decathlete Chuan-Kwang Yang had a tremendous battle with Rafer Johnson (USA), a university teammate at UCLA, and lost the gold medal narrowly. The stadium was captivated by sprinter Wilma Rudolph (USA) who won three gold medals – she was one of 19 children and had suffered from polio as a child. Sisters Irina and Tamara Press (URS) won the 80m hurdles and shot respectively, while their countrywoman, Ludmila Shevtsova, won the first 800m event for women since 1928.

In the swimming pool the only one of the fifteen events not won by either Australia or the United States went to Anita Lonsbrough (GBR). The outstanding swimmer was America's Christine von Saltza, a descendant of Prussian/Swedish nobility, with three golds and a silver. The standard was very high with Olympic records broken in every event. An unfortunate incident occurred in the men's 100m freestyle when Lance Larson (USA) was timed at 0.01sec faster than John Devitt (AUS) but was placed second to him despite slow-motion film indicating that the American was first. In future Games full electronic timing was used. Only the second Royal gold medal in Olympic history was won by Crown Prince Constantine (later King Constantine II of Greece) in the Dragon

class yachting. It is reported that he received the traditional winner's ducking, being pushed into the water by his mother, Queen Frederika. In the Flying Dutchman class Peder Lunde Jr (NOR) became the third generation of his family to win a medal, equalling his grandfather's gold of 1924, but going one better than his mother and father in 1952. Paul Elvstrøm (DEN) won his fourth consecutive individual gold medal in dinghy sailing, the first sportsman from any sport to achieve this distinction. The canoeing, on Lake Albano, had a particularly distinguished spectator, as the Pope apparently watched some of the competitions from his summer palace. In boxing the light-welter silver medallist, Clement 'Ike' Quartey (GHA) became the first black African to win an Olympic medal, just five days before Bikila won his gold.

The most medals won in Rome were the seven (four gold, two silver, one bronze) gained by gymnast Boris Shakhlin (URS). Aladár Gerevich (HUN), at 50yr 178days the oldest champion in Rome, won his sixth team sabre gold medal in as many Games – a feat unsurpassed by any other Olympic competitor. In the foil and épée events Edoardo Mangiarotti (ITA) brought his total of fencing medals to a record 13 (six gold, five silver, two bronze) in five Games 1936-1960. The light-heavyweight boxing title went to Cassius Clay (USA), who, as Muhammad Ali, amassed the greatest amount ever earned by a sportsman, $68 million, when he became a professional after the Games. In soccer, Yugoslavia won the gold medal after three consecutive runner-up placings. The first loss to India in Olympic hockey since they entered the competition in 1928 occurred when Pakistan beat them 1-0 in the final.

The youngest champion was swimmer Carolyn Wood (USA) in the freestyle relay aged 14yr 260days, and the youngest male gold medallist was Klaus Zerta, cox of the German rowing pairs, aged 14yr 283days. The oldest female winner was discus champion Nina Ponomaryeva (URS) at 31yr 131days.(She had achieved notoriety in 1956, when it was alleged that she stole hats from an Oxford Street store, while on a trip to London for an international match, which was thereby cancelled). The oldest medallist was yachtsman Manfred Metzger (SUI) at 55yr 104days, while the oldest female medallist was Italian fencer Welleda Cesari at 40yr 201days.

A tragic note was struck by the collapse and death of cyclist Knut Jensen (DEN), originally diagnosed as due to the excessive heat, but later revealed as due to a drug overdose. At the end of the Games a then record 44 countries had shared in the medals.

Rome 1960 Medals

	G	S	B
Soviet Union	43	29	31
United States	34	21	16
Italy	13	10	13
Germany	12	19	11
Australia	8	8	6
Turkey	7	2	-
Hungary	6	8	7
Japan	4	7	7
Poland	4	6	11
Czechoslovakia	3	2	3
Romania	3	1	6
Great Britain	2	6	12
Denmark	2	3	1
New Zealand	2	-	1
Bulgaria	1	3	3
Sweden	1	2	3
Finland	1	1	3
Austria	1	1	-
Yugoslavia	1	1	-
Pakistan	1	-	1
Ethiopia	1	-	-
Greece	1	-	-
Norway	1		
Switzerland	-	3	3
France	-	2	3
Belgium	-	2	2
Iran	-	1	3
Netherlands	-	1	2
South Africa	-	1	2
Argentina	-	1	1
Egypt (UAR)	-	1	1
Canada	-	1	-
Ghana	-	1	-
India	-	1	-
Morocco	-	1	-
Portugal	-	1	-
Singapore	-	1	-
Chinese Taipei	-	1	-
Brazil	-	-	2
Jamaica*	-	-	2
Barbados*	-	-	1
Iraq	-	-	1
Mexico	-	-	1
Spain	-	-	1
Venezuela	-	-	1

* Double counted as part of the Antilles team

INNSBRUCK 1964

IXth Winter Games. 29 January – 9 February
Attended by representatives of 36 countries, comprising 1093 competitors, of which 199 were women.

AWARDED TO INNSBRUCK in 1959, these Games were the most successful yet with over one million spectators attending a now record 34 events. Among them were lugeing and a second ski jump. However, again weather was a problem, and snow had to be manhandled to some venues by the Austrian Army. During practice before the Games began there were two tragic deaths, of a British tobogganist and an Australian skier. The official opening by the Austrian President, Dr Adolf Schärf, took place at the Bergisel ski jump in front of 60,000 people. The last relay runner who lit the flame was a skier Joseph Rieder, and the oath was taken by bobsledder, Paul Aste. Mongolia and India competed for the first time, while Korea was split into North and South teams. South Africa was now banned from the Olympics. An innovation was the use, officially, of computers to aid judging, as well as provide electronic timing.

The Games were dominated by the Soviet Union and, for the first time, Switzerland failed to gain a single medal. Lydia Skoblikova (URS), a teacher from Siberia, won all four women's speed skating events, to total six gold medals in two Games, a record for the sport. The Soviet husband and wife skating pair, Ludmila Belousova and Oleg Protopopov, brought a new concept, classical ballet, to the sport. The silver medal went for the second consecutive occasion to Marika Kilius and Hansjürgen Bäumler (GER) – two years later they were disqualified owing to professional activities which had then come to light, but were reinstated in 1987 by the IOC. The women's individual skating title went to Sjoukje Dijkstra, Holland's first ever Winter Games gold medal.

The first sisters to win gold medals at the same Games were Marielle and Christine Goitschel (FRA) who swapped first and second places in the Alpine slalom events. The re-introduced bobsleigh events were won, for the first time, by countries which did not possess bob runs of their own. Also the victory by Tony Nash and Robin Dixon (GBR) in the 2-man bob was the first by a 'lowland' country, and owed much to a replacement bolt supplied by an Italian adversary Eugenio Monti. He was later awarded the Pierre de Coubertin Fair Play Trophy for this action. Klaudia Boyarskikh (URS) won three gold medals in Nordic skiing, while Sixten Jernberg (SWE) brought his total to a record nine medals in three Games. A demonstration of German curling was held.

The oldest gold medallist was Sixten Jernberg, winning his fourth gold medal two days after his 35th birthday. The youngest was Manfred Stengl (AUT) aged 17yr 310days in the 2-man luge, with Marielle Goitschel (FRA) the youngest female winner in the giant slalom aged 18yr 128days. The oldest female champion was Alevtina Koltschina (URS) in the Nordic relay at 33yr 88days. Scott Allen (USA) was the youngest medallist with his bronze in the men's figure skating just two days short of his 15th birthday, while the oldest was Eugenio Monti (ITA) aged 36yr 15days.

Innsbruck 1964 Medals

	G	S	B
Soviet Union	11	8	6
Austria	4	5	3
Norway	3	6	6
Finland	3	4	3
France	3	4	-
Sweden	3	3	1
Germany	3	3	3
United States	1	2	3
Canada	1	-	2
Netherlands	1	1	-
Great Britain	1	-	-
Italy	-	1	3
North Korea (PRK)	-	1	-
Czechoslovakia	-	-	1

TOKYO 1964

XVIIIth Olympic Games. 10 – 24 October
Attended by representatives of 93 countries, comprising 5134 competitors, of which 680 were women.

ASIA'S FIRST GAMES witnessed large crowds and a tremendous assault on the record books. Vast sums, estimated to be as much as $3 billion, were been spent not only on stadia but also on transport facilities. Teams from 14 countries made their first appearance at the Games, but South Africa no longer received an invitation. Also missing were Indonesia and North Korea, whose athletes, having competed in the previous year's unsanctioned GANEFO Games (Games of the New Emergent Forces), were banned. Emperor Hirohito performed the formal opening, and the flame was brought into the stadium by a young runner who had been born near Hiroshima on the day that the atom bomb had been dropped there in 1945. The Olympic flag was raised to the top of a flagpole which measured 15.21m *50ft 6¾in*, the distance reached in the triple jump by Mikio Oda in 1928 when he won Japan's first Olympic gold medal.

The growth of the Games can be highlighted by distance runner Ron Clarke's remark after failing to gain the gold medal over 10,000m. Having dropped all the known opposition, he looked over his shoulder and saw 'an Ethiopian, a North African Arab and an American Indian'. This latter, Billy Mills, a part-Sioux Marine officer, was America's first ever winner at the distance. In the marathon Abebe Bikila (ETH), only six weeks after having his appendix removed – and this time wearing shoes – became the first man to retain the title, and Peter Snell (NZL) won the rare 800/1500m double. The winner of the 100m, Bob Hayes, ran a phenomenal last leg in the 4x100m relay, to regain the title that the USA had lost in Rome for the first time in 40 years. There is a story told that one of the beaten teams decried the US team to the effect that all they had was Hayes. This was met by the now

famous rejoinder, 'Man, that's all we needed'. Britain won its first ever gold in women's athletics when Mary Rand took the long jump – her room-mate Ann Packer added the 800m gold for good measure.

At the much admired pool, Australia and the United States won all the titles bar one. That was the women's 200m breaststroke, the event which had also prevented a clean sweep by the two swimming superpowers in Rome. Here it was won by Galina Prozumenshchikova (later Stepanova), the Soviet Union's first ever swimming gold medallist – she won a further two silver and two bronze at the next two Games. Don Schollander (USA) became the first swimmer to win four golds in a single Games. Close behind him came Sharon Stouder (USA) with three gold and a silver in the women's events. Australia's Dawn Fraser, just past her 27th birthday, won her third consecutive 100m title, then a unique achievement in swimming, and added a relay silver to take her total haul to eight medals, a record for a female swimmer. Another competitor to complete a unique triple was Soviet rower Vyacheslav Ivanov by winning the single sculls once again. An unusual thing occurred in the eights where the cox of the winning American crew, Róbert Zimonyi, aged 46, had been cox of the third placed Hungarian pairs in 1948. In water polo the Hungarian veteran Desző Gyarmati won his third gold medal, his fifth medal in as many Games.

The most medals were won by a gymnast Larissa Latynina (URS) with two golds, two silvers and two bronzes. Her teammate Boris Shakhlin brought his total of golds since 1956 to seven, of which a record six were in individual events. In weightlifting Norbert Schemansky (USA) won a bronze to add to his previous gold, silver and bronze since 1948, giving him a record for his sport of four medals. Unusually, wrestler Imre Polyák (HUN) finally won gold in his fourth Games after an unprecedented three silvers. Of the two new sports, the other was volleyball, judo had been included at the express wish of the host country. It was considered to be a Japanese monopoly, and the country suffered a terrible shock when the Open class judo title went to the big (1.98m *6ft 6in*) Dutchman Anton Geesink. Leading the United States basketball team to its sixth consecutive victory was Bill Bradley, a Rhodes scholar and later a member of the US Senate.

The oldest gold medallist in Tokyo was Australian 5.5m yachtsman William Northam aged 59yr 23days, and the youngest was swimmer 'Pokey' Watson (USA) aged 14yr 96days in the freestyle relay. The oldest female winner was Katalin Juhász Nagy (HUN), a member of the foil team at 31yr 328days, while the youngest male champion was swimmer Richard Roth

(USA) in the 400m medley 18 days past his 17th birthday. Teammate 1500m freestyler John Nelson was the youngest male medallist at 16yr 131days.

1964 Medals

	G	S	B
United States	36	26	28
Soviet Union	30	31	35
Japan	16	5	8
Germany	10	22	18
Italy	10	10	7
Hungary	10	7	5
Poland	7	6	10
Australia	6	2	10
Czechoslovakia	5	6	3
Great Britain	4	12	2
Bulgaria	3	5	2
Finland	3	-	2
New Zealand	3	-	2
Romania	2	4	6
Netherlands	2	4	4
Turkey	2	3	1
Sweden	2	2	4
Denmark	2	1	3
Yugoslavia	2	1	2
Belgium	2	-	1
France	1	8	6
Canada	1	2	1
Switzerland	1	2	1
Bahamas	1	-	-
Ethiopia	1	-	-
India	1	-	-
Korea	-	2	1
Trinidad	-	1	2
Tunisia	-	1	1
Argentina	-	1	-
Cuba	-	1	-
Pakistan	-	1	-
Philippines	-	1	-
Iran	-	-	2
Brazil	-	-	1
Ghana	-	-	1
Ireland	-	-	1
Kenya	-	-	1
Mexico	-	-	1
Nigeria	-	-	1
Uruguay	-	-	1

GRENOBLE 1968

Xth Winter Games. 6 – 18 February
Attended by representatives of 37 countries, comprising 1158 competitors, of which 211 were women.

THERE WERE COMPLAINTS that venues at Grenoble were very widespread, with some 40km distant, but the new 12,000 seat indoor ice stadium delighted everyone. For the first time gender tests for female competitors were held. The political split between East and West Germany was finally acknowledged, and separate teams accepted. Morocco made its debut, and the official opening was performed by the President of France, Charles de Gaulle. The last relay runner was Alain Calmat, the 1964 skating silver medallist, and the oath was taken by Léo Lacroix, a 1964 skiing silver medal winner. The IOC attempted to control the exploitation of the Games by commercial interests by banning the use of trade names on competitors' equipment. Following the threat of a withdrawal by some leading skiers, who relied very heavily on ski company sponsorship, it was finally agreed that they need only remove the equipment before appearing in photographs or on television.

The undoubted star of these Games was Jean-Claude Killy (FRA), who emulated Toni Sailer's 1956 record by winning all three Alpine skiing events. However, in the last of the three, the slalom, Karl Schranz (AUT) claimed that in his second round run he had been distracted by a policeman cutting across the course in front of him. He was allowed another run, which he accomplished in a faster time to become the overall winner. Then it was decided that on his first attempt he had already missed a gate before the policeman incident, and his rerun was disqualified. He was to be even more unlucky four years later. The best of the women Alpinists was Canada's Nancy Greene with a gold in the giant slalom and a silver in the slalom. The latter was won by Marielle Goitschel (FRA) to keep the title in the family – her sister had won it in 1964.

The most successful Nordic skier was Finnish-born Toini Gustafsson (SWE) with two gold and a silver in the women's events. By winning the 30km race Franco Nones (ITA) became the first ever non-Scandinavian winner in cross-country skiing. Another shock to Scandinavian sensibilities occurred in the two jumps and the combination event, when they only won a single bronze from the nine medals available. Yet another upset was in the women's luge, where the GDR women, in first, second and fourth places were disqualified for illegally heating their sled runners. The bob run at Alpe d'Huez, which was badly sited and considered to be very dangerous, was the scene of total triumph for the good sport of Innsbruck, four years previously, Eugenio Monti. The Italian, nine times a world champion bobsledder, won both Olympic gold medals. In the 2-man event the total times after four runs for Monti's bob and that of the German bob were equal. The tie was decided in the Italian's favour as he had the fastest single run. Aged 40yr 24days, Monti was the oldest gold medallist at Grenoble.

The youngest champion was skater Peggy Fleming (USA) aged 19yr 198days. The youngest male gold medallist was Wolfgang Schwarz, winning Austria's first skating title since 1936, aged 20yr 155days. Ludmila and Oleg Protopopov (URS) retained their pairs title, with Ludmila the oldest female champion at 32yr 84days. In 26th place in the men's figure skating was Jan Hoffmann (GDR) aged 12y 110days – the youngest ever male competitor in Olympic Winter Games.(Twelve years later he won the silver medal). The oldest female medallist was Nordic skier Alevtina Koltschina (URS) with a bronze in her 4th Games at 37yr 97days.

For the only time to date no speed skater gained more than one victory. The women's 500m was reminiscent of the men's event of 1948 and 1964 as three women tied for the silver medal. Making this occasion unique was the fact that all three of them were from the same country, the United States. For the last time Norway topped the medal table.

Grenoble 1968 Medals

	G	S	B
Norway	6	6	2
Soviet Union	5	5	3
France	4	3	2
Italy	4	-	-
Austria	3	4	4
Netherlands	3	3	3
FRG	2	2	3
United States	1	5	1
Finland	1	2	2
GDR	1	2	2
Czechoslovakia	1	2	1
Canada	1	1	1
Switzerland	-	2	4
Romania	-	-	1

MEXICO CITY 1968

XIXth Olympic Games. 12 – 27 October
Attended by representatives of 112 countries, comprising 5555 competitors, of which 784 were women.

FROM 1963, WHEN these Games were awarded to Mexico City, there was a gradually increasing furore about the effects of its altitude, 2240m *7347ft* above sea level, on competitors in events which required endurance. Some medical authorities even forecast possible deaths. This extreme view was, thankfully, overly pessimistic, but many cases of severe exhaustion occurred. When Australian distance runner Ron Clarke developed serious heart problems in 1981, there was speculation that his condition had been aggravated by his efforts in Mexico City in 1968. Certainly standards were low in events which required over three minutes of continuous effort. However, the same conditions contributed to some startling performances in

the 'explosive' events. Outstanding was the 8.90m *29ft 2½in* long jump by Bob Beamon (USA) – a performance of 21st-century quality. The world records set in that long jump, and the 4x400m relay, lasted for over 22 years.

The thin air was not the only complaint raised prior to these Games. Some felt that the traditional 'mañana' attitude attributed to the Mexicans would result in incomplete facilities. In fact all were ready in good time. There was a threat of a boycott by Black African nations over the readmission of South Africa earlier in the year. After 40 countries had indicated that they would withhold their teams, the IOC reversed its decision and South Africa was barred again, permanently. In August the Soviet Union and its allies invaded Czechoslovakia, and international tension mounted. A few weeks before the Games began, serious student riots erupted at the University of Mexico which were ruthlessly suppressed, with dozens killed and hundreds injured. Some of the foreign press sports reporters became 'war' correspondents for their newspapers. In America there was a move to get black athletes to boycott the US team to protest the alleged bad treatment of Afro-Americans in general in the United States. When this appeared to get little support, the organizers implied that some sort of dramatic demonstration would be held at the Games. Despite all these problems President Gustavo Diaz Ordaz declared the formal opening to a record number of teams and athletes. Enriqueta Basilio, a hurdler, became the first woman to light the Olympic flame in the stadium.

Due to conditions the distance running events were dominated by athletes who lived and trained at high altitude, such as the Kenyans and Ethiopians. Exceptional performances abounded in the sprints and jumps. Beamon's jump (see above) was beyond the limits of the measuring device in use at the pit, and a steel tape had to be used. In the triple jump the existing Olympic record was beaten by seven men, and the world mark was improved on five occasions. The high jump winner, Dick Fosbury (USA), used the 'flop' style which he popularized and which was to revolutionize the event. Al Oerter (USA) won his record fourth consecutive discus title, and Wyomia Tyus (USA) was the first sprinter successfully to defend an Olympic 100m crown, other than Archie Hahn (USA) in the 1906 Intercalated Games. The men's 100m final was unique, up to that time, in that all eight finalists were black. A more heralded expression of black power was the demonstration by the Black Power supporters, Tommie Smith and John Carlos (USA), in the 200m victory ceremony. The Americans, who had come first and third respectively, raised black-gloved, clenched fists, with heads bowed, during the playing of the American anthem. For this action they were suspended and expelled from the Olympic village. Some oldtimers noted that their action was no more, no less, insulting than that of the numerous medallists who had given the Nazi salute in 1936. The marathon was won, for the third consecutive time, by an Ethiopian, but this time by Mamo Wolde, after two-time champion Abebe Bikila withdrew at 17km with a bone fracture to his leg. Tragically he was paralysed in a car accident the following year, and died in 1973 at the age of 41.

Most medals were won, as usual, by gymnasts. Although Mikhail Voronin (URS) won seven medals (two gold, four silver, one bronze), the star of the sport was Vera Cáslavská (TCH) with four golds and two silvers. Her floor exercises routine, to the music of the *Mexican Hat Dance*, was immensely popular. Soon after her events were over, but still during the Games, she married her countryman, Josef Odlozil, the 1964 1500m silver medallist. Incidentally, Voronin's wife, Sinaida, won a gold, a silver, and two bronze medals in the Soviet women's gymnastic team. The outstanding swimmers were Charles Hickcox (USA) with three gold and a silver, and Debbie Meyer (USA), who won three individual events. Six other swimmers won two gold medals each, including an eighteen-year-old American named Mark Spitz. Mexico's first ever swimming gold medal was won by Felipe Muñoz in the 200m breaststroke. He was nicknamed 'Tibio', which means lukewarm in English. This was no reflection on his determination, but was the result of his father coming from a town named Aguascalientes ('hot water'), and his mother from Rio Frio ('cold river').

Although eliminated in the fencing, Janice Romary (USA) became the first woman to compete in six consecutive Games, and because of this also became the first woman to carry the flag for the United States in a Games Opening Ceremony. The 5.5m class sailing, held at the resort city of Acapulco, produced the unique result of triple gold medal siblings. The Swedish brothers, Ulf, Peter and Jörgen Sundelin crewed *Wasa IV* to an easy victory. Behind them, skippering the second placed Swiss boat *Toucan* was Louis Noverraz, at 66yr 154days, the oldest medallist at these Games.

The oldest gold medallist was Josef Neckarmann (FRG) in the dressage team aged 56yr 141days, while the youngest was Günther Tiersch (GDR), cox of the winning eight aged 14yr 172days. The oldest female champion was Liselott Linsenhoff (FRG), also in the dressage team aged 41yr 58days, while the youngest female gold medallist was swimmer Susan Pedersen (USA) in the medley relay the day after her 15th birthday. The oldest competitor at Mexico City was Roberto Soundy, a trapshooter from El Salvador aged 68yr 229days, and the same country had the youngest male competitor in Ruben Guerrero, a medley relay swimmer, aged 13yr 351days. However, the youngest competitor of all was Liana Vicens, of Puerto Rico, only 11yr 328days in the women's 100m breaststroke. The oldest woman was Britain's Lorna Johnstone, who was 13th in the dressage at 66yr 51days.

For the first time since they had entered the hockey competition in 1928 India failed to reach the final. In soccer, won for a record third time by Hungary, the surprise bronze medallist was Japan. They were the first, and to date the only, Asian team to win a soccer medal, and the first non-European team to do so for 40 years.

Mexico City 1968 Medals

	G	S	B
United States	45	28	34
Soviet Union	29	32	30
Japan	11	7	7
Hungary	10	10	12
GDR	9	9	7
France	7	3	5
Czechoslovakia	7	2	4
FRG	5	11	10
Australia	5	7	5
Great Britain	5	5	3
Poland	5	2	11
Romania	4	6	5
Italy	3	4	9
Kenya	3	4	2
Mexico	3	3	3
Yugoslavia	3	3	2
Netherlands	3	3	1
Bulgaria	2	4	3
Iran	2	1	2
Sweden	2	1	1
Turkey	2	-	-
Denmark	1	4	3
Canada	1	3	1
Finland	1	2	1
Ethiopia	1	1	-
Norway	1	1	-
New Zealand	1	-	2
Tunisia	1	-	1
Pakistan	1	-	-
Venezuela	1	-	-
Cuba	-	4	-
Austria	-	2	2
Switzerland	-	1	4
Mongolia	-	1	3
Brazil	-	1	2
Belgium	-	1	1
Korea	-	1	1
Uganda	-	1	1
Cameroon	-	1	-

Jamaica	-	1	-
Argentina	-	-	2
Greece	-	-	1
India	-	-	1
Taiwan (Taipei)	-	-	1

SAPPORO 1972

XIth Winter Games. 3 – 13 February
Attended by representatives of 35 countries, comprising 1008 competitors, of which 206 were women

THE GAMES FINALLY came to Sapporo 32 years after they were first awarded to the city but cancelled due to World War II. It was the most populous city, with one million inhabitants, ever to host the Winter Games. Some $555 million was spent on facilities over a five year period, not least for the enormous number of media personnel who outnumbered competitors by two to one. Arguments between the IOC and sponsored skiers, which had caused problems in 1968, came to a head, and resulted in Austria's star skier, Karl Schranz, being expelled. Although there was a list of 40 competitors apparently under threat of suspension, only he was banned. This led to an initial threat of withdrawal by the Austrian team, but at Schranz's urging this was averted. Another aspect of the amateur/professional debate was highlighted by Canada's refusal to compete in ice hockey due to the state-sponsored players from the Eastern bloc. Their call for 'open' Olympic ice hockey was ignored.

The Games were formally opened by Emperor Hirohito. The flame was delivered by Hideki Takada, a speed skater, and another, Keichi Suzuki, took the oath. Teams from Taiwan and the Philippines competed for the first time. First ever Winter gold medals were won by Poland (ski jumping), Spain (slalom) and the host country (ski jumping). In the latter event, on the 70m hill, Japan had a unique grand slam of all three medals. To win his title, Spanish skier Francisco Fernandez-Ochoa beat the Italian cousins Gustav and Roland Thöni. The women's slalom was won by Barbara Cochran (USA) by the smallest margin ever, 0.02sec, in an Olympic Alpine event. Her sister Marilyn and brother Bob were also in the US team.

Galina Kulakova (URS) won three gold medals in Nordic skiing, and this total was matched in the speed skating by Ard Schenk of Holland. The Dutchman might have had more but he fell in the 500m event and finished 34th out of 37 competitors. East Germany (GDR) returned to total domination of the luge competitions. The women's event was won by Anna-Maria Müller, one of the three girls who had been disqualified for heating their runners at the previous Games. Austria's Trixi Schuba took the women's figure

skating title despite a comparatively poor (7th placed) free skating segment – her compulsory figures were excellent and at the time the two segments scored on a 50-50 basis. Soon after the Games this method was changed in favour of free skating ability. An *'affaire de coeur'* involving Alexei Ulanov (URS), who with Irina Rodnina won the skating pairs, and Ludmila Smirnova, his teammate who placed second with her partner Andrei Suraikin, titillated the skating world. Later they married and competed internationally as partners, but never with the success they had attained with their original partners.

The oldest gold medallist was Jean Wicki (SUI) in the 4-man bob aged 38yr 239days. The youngest was Anne Henning (USA) who won the 500m speed skating title aged 16yr 157days. The oldest female winner was Christina Baas-Kaiser (NED) with her 3000m speed skating victory at 33yr 268days, and the youngest male champion was Wojciech Fortuna (POL) who won the 90m ski jump aged 19yr 189days. The youngest medallist was skater Manuela Gross (GDR), bronze in the pairs aged 15yr 10days. Overall, medals were won by a record 17 countries, with 14 of them gaining gold.

Sapporo 1972 Medals

	G	S	B
Soviet Union	8	5	3
GDR	4	3	7
Switzerland	4	3	3
Netherlands	4	3	2
United States	3	2	3
FRG	3	1	1
Norway	2	5	5
Italy	2	2	1
Austria	1	2	2
Sweden	1	1	2
Japan	1	1	1
Czechoslovakia	1	-	2
Poland	1	-	-
Spain	1	-	-
Finland	-	4	1
France	-	1	2
Canada	-	1	-

MUNICH 1972

XXth Olympic Games. 26 August – 10 September
Attended by representatives of 121 countries, comprising 7116 competitors, of which 1059 were women.

AWARDED THE GAMES in 1966, Munich built a magnificent complex on the rubble of World War II bombing. Total costs were estimated at $650 million. Just prior to the opening day, the IOC expelled Rhodesia under intense pressure from

Black African nations. A number of new electronic devices were used in the conduct of the Games, including a triangulation device to measure distances in the athletics throwing events. Archery and men's handball returned to the Olympic programme, and there were additions to other sports, making a total of 195 gold medals available – and the Soviet Union took over a quarter of them. It became the most widely covered sports occasion in history with over 4000 representatives of the world's media on hand. When the German President Gustav Heinemann opened the Games in a colourful ceremony there was a television audience estimated at an all-time live viewing record of 1000 million. The oath was taken by athlete Heidi Schüller, the first woman ever to do so. The record number of countries taking part included first timers, Albania, Dahomey (later Benin), Lesotho, Malawi, Upper Volta (later Burkina Faso), Somalia, Swaziland, Togo and North Korea (South Korea sent a separate team).

The first week was dominated by swimmer Mark Spitz (USA) who smashed all records for a single Games by winning seven gold medals, four individual and three relays – there were world records in each of his events. With his medals from Mexico City he had a total of nine golds, one silver and a bronze. His female equivalent, Shane Gould (AUS) won three golds, a silver and a bronze, swimming in 12 races, itself a record for a female swimmer in the Games. The closest win in Olympic history came in the men's 400m medley when Gunnar Larsson (SWE) was given the decision over Tim McKee (USA) by two thousandth of a second. This led to a change in the rules so that, in future, times and places would be decided in hundredths. Valeri Borzov (URS) became the first European to win a men's sprint double on the track. In 1994 he became the IOC member for the Ukraine. Ulrike Meyfarth (FRG) equalled the world high jump record to win the gold medal aged 16yr 123days, the youngest ever individual athletics event champion. In hockey, for the first time since 1920, a team, Germany, from outside the Indian sub-continent won the title. However, the outstanding attraction of the first few days was gymnast Olga Korbut (URS) whose gamine qualities stole the show from her more illustrious colleague, Ludmilla Tourischeva (who later married sprint champion Borzov). Virtually overnight, with blanket media coverage, Korbut became a 'superstar', although she only finished seventh in the all-around competition.

On the morning of 5 September all the euphoria evaporated when a band of eight Arab terrorists broke into the Israeli team headquarters at 31 Connollystrasse in the Olympic village. Two Israelis were killed immediately, and nine others held hostage, as German police and the world's press surrounded the area. After lengthy negotiations the terrorists and their hostages were allowed to go to the airport, where an abortive rescue attempt resulted in the murder of all nine Israelis and the death of some of their captors. The following morning the Games were suspended for a memorial service in a packed stadium, but with the agreement of most of the parties involved, including the Israelis, competitions were resumed later in the day. The overall feeling seemed to be that the Games should go on, although some individuals, notably from The Netherlands, Norway and the Philippines decided to withdraw. The Israeli team returned home immediately.

The Games continued with the United States suffering a unusual number of misfortunes and reverses. Two prospective medallists had missed the 100m second round heats due to a misreading, by their coach, of the starting time. The world 1500m record holder, Jim Ryun, did not get seeded as he should have done, because his entry performance, a fast mile time, was mistakenly interpreted by the computerised seeding system as a slow 1500m time. Then, to add to his misfortunes, he fell in his heat and was eliminated. A pre-Games banning of the poles used by the American vaulters probably ended a 13-Games winning streak. Their gold and silver medallists in the 400m were banned from further competition for a 'Black Power' protest which meant that the United States, the favourites, could not field a 4x400m relay team. Since 1920 teams from the USA had always won a medal. In swimming, Rick DeMont, won the 400m freestyle but was disqualified after a dope test proved positive. If the US team officials had notified the IOC beforehand that he had to take a certain drug, containing the prohibited substance, to alleviate an asthma condition, he would have retained his title. Then to cap it all, the American basketball team were controversially defeated by the Soviet Union – ending a remarkable 63 consecutive victories in the Games since 1936. Another incident, with a happier conclusion, occurred when the 800m champion, Dave Wottle, in his excitement at the victory ceremony forgot to remove his lucky cap during the American national anthem. He was very embarrassed and proffered apologies to everyone who would listen.

On the track Kipchoge Keino (KEN) added the 3000m steeplechase title to the 1500m that he had won four years earlier. This made him the first runner since James Lightbody (USA) in 1904 to win Olympic titles at those two distances. Lasse Virén (FIN) won the 5000m/10,000m double, setting a world record in the latter, despite falling over early in the race, and America's Frank Shorter won the marathon in the city of his birth. Romanian discus thrower Lia Manoliu competed in her record sixth Games (placing ninth with a performance superior to that which won her the gold medal in Mexico City). In the women's pentathlon silver medallist, Heide Rosendahl (FRG) theoretically held the Olympic and world records for the event for 1.12sec, the difference between her winning time in the last discipline, the 200m, and that of the eventual overall champion Mary Peters (GBR).

By winning the five-sport modern pentathlon individual title Hungary's András Balczó brought his total medal haul since 1960 to an event record of three golds and two silvers. For the second consecutive Games the three medallists in skeet shooting all achieved the same score, the tie being broken by shooting another 25-bird round. Double cycling gold medallist from 1968, Daniel Morelon (FRA), added a third by retaining the sprint title, and Aleksandr Medved (URS) won his third wrestling title in a row (and his tenth world championship) after a disputed decision over the giant American Chris Taylor. Taylor, reportedly weighing 182kg *401lb* or more, was the heaviest known man to have competed in the Olympic Games. Among serious doping disqualifications at these Games were those of Bakhaavaa Buidaa who had won a wrestling silver medal for Mongolia, Jaime Huelamo (ESP) the bronze medallist in the cycling road race, and the Dutch four who had gained third place in the cycling team race.

The oldest gold medallist at Munich was Hans Günter Winkler (FRG) aged 46yr 49days in the show-jumping team, and the youngest Deana Deardurff (USA) aged 15yr 118days in the swimming medley relay. The oldest female champion was Liselott Linsenhoff (FRG) in the dressage at 45yr 13days, and she was also the first woman to win an individual equestrian event. In that competition Britain's Lorna Johnstone became the oldest ever female competitor in the Olympics when she reached the last 12 five days past her 70th birthday. A bronze medallist in this event was Maud Van Rosen (SWE), the oldest female medallist at these Games 46yr 258days. The youngest male gold medallist at Munich was Uwe Benter (FRG), cox of the winning fours at 16yr 276days, although it should be noted that the unfortunate Rick DeMont was 143 days younger. The youngest medallist was swimmer Kornelia Ender (GDR) at 13yr 308days.

The tallest competitor at the Games, and the tallest medallist ever in the Olympics, was Tom Burleson (USA) the 2.23m *7ft 4in* basketball player. One of the runners in the torch relay bringing the Olympic flame to Munich, was Edgar Fried, a former secretary-

general of the Austrian Olympic Committee, who had been in the original torch relay in 1936, and was the only one to repeat in that of 1972, in his 78th year. At the end of the XXth Games a record 48 countries had won at least one medal.

Munich 1972 Medals

	G	S	B
Soviet Union	50	27	22
United States	33	31	30
GDR	20	23	23
FRG	13	11	16
Japan	13	8	8
Australia	8	7	2
Poland	7	5	9
Hungary	6	13	16
Bulgaria	6	10	5
Italy	5	3	10
Sweden	4	6	6
Great Britain	4	5	9
Romania	3	6	7
Cuba	3	1	4
Finland	3	1	4
Netherlands	3	1	1
France	2	4	7
Czechoslovakia	2	4	2
Kenya	2	3	4
Yugoslavia	2	1	2
Norway	2	1	1
North Korea (PRK)	1	1	3
New Zealand	1	1	1
Uganda	1	1	-
Denmark	1	-	-
Switzerland	-	3	-
Canada	-	2	3
Iran	-	2	1
Belgium	-	2	-
Greece	-	2	-
Austria	-	1	2
Colombia	-	1	2
Argentina	-	1	-
Korea	-	1	-
Lebanon	-	1	-
Mexico	-	1	-
Mongolia	-	1	-
Pakistan	-	1	-
Tunisia	-	1	-
Turkey	-	1	-
Brazil	-	-	2
Ethiopia	-	-	2
Ghana	-	-	1
India	-	-	1
Jamaica	-	-	1
Niger Republic	-	-	1
Nigeria	-	-	1
Spain	-	-	1

INNSBRUCK 1976

XIIth Winter Games. 4 – 15 February
Attended by representatives of 37 countries, comprising 1129 competitors, of which 231 were women.

THESE GAMES WERE originally awarded to Denver, Colorado, in 1970, but two years later a State referendum decided against providing the necessary finance. So, in February 1973, Innsbruck became the first centre to be awarded the Winter Games for a second time. Most facilities were still available from 1964, and 'only' $44 million was required to refurbish and update. The Games were opened by the President of Austria, Dr Rudolf Kirchschläger, and, uniquely, two Olympic flames were lit, by Christl Haas, 1964 gold medal skier, and Josef Feistmantl, 1964 gold medal luger. The oath was taken by Werner Delle-Karth, a bobsledder. A total of 1.5 million spectators watched the 37-event schedule. There were also 600 million television viewers around the world. Unfortunately an influenza outbreak affected some of the competitors. Two of the smallest States in the world, Andorra and San Marino, made their Winter Games debuts.

The outstanding competitor was Rosi Mittermaier (FRG) who, by winning the downhill and slalom races, and taking second place in the giant slalom, set up the best series of performances ever by a female Alpine skier. She failed by a mere 0.13 sec, in the giant slalom, to match the male record of three golds held by Sailer and Killy. In taking the men's downhill on the Patscherkofel course Austria's Franz Klammer achieved the then highest speed recorded in an Olympic downhill race, 102.828km/h *63.894mph*. In Nordic skiing Galina Kulakova (URS) was disqualified from third place in the 5000m event when a banned drug was found present in a nasal spray she was using to combat influenza, but she was allowed to compete in other events and won a gold and another bronze. Her teammate Raisa Smetanina won two golds and a silver to be the most successful Nordic skier. Particular attention, and some ridicule, was given to Bill Koch (USA) who used his newly developed 'skating' style of skiing. Rather more attention, and less ridicule, came when he won a silver medal in the 30km race, the only Nordic skiing medal ever won by an American. However, the greatest tally of medals at these Games was two gold and two bronze by Tatyana Averina (URS) in speed skating. Preventing a clean sweep of those titles by the Soviet women was Sheila Young (USA) who took the 500m title, and later in the year won her second world cycling championship.

In figure skating, the 'jilted' Irina Rodnina (URS)

successfully defended her pairs skating title, but this time with a different partner, her new husband Aleksandr Zaitsev. The US pair were only fifth, but Tai Babilonia became the first black competitor in the Winter Games. The men's champion John Curry (GBR) brought balletic art to his event, just as the Protopopovs had to the pairs in 1964 and 1968. His Italian/American coach, Carlo Fassi, became the first to train both individual champions at a single Games when Dorothy Hamill (USA) won the women's title. In the new ice dancing event Soviet couples were placed first, second and fourth. All five luge and bobsled events were won by GDR competitors.

The oldest gold medallist was Meinhard Nehmer (GDR) in the 2-man bob aged 35yr 25days, and the youngest was skater Hamill aged 19yr 201days. The youngest male gold medallist was Boris Aleksandrov (URS) in the champion ice hockey team aged 20yr 93days, while the oldest female champion was Galina Kulakova (see above) in the Nordic relay aged 33yr 289days. Toni Innauer (AUT) won a silver in ski jumping aged 17yr 320days, while the oldest medallist was Marjatta Kajosmaa (FIN) with a Nordic relay silver nine days after her 38th birthday. The oldest competitor at these Games was 46-year-old Carl Erik Eriksson (SWE) in the bob events, while the youngest was figure skater Yelena Voderzova (URS), some three months away from her 13th birthday.

Innsbruck 1976 Medals

	G	S	B
Soviet Union	13	6	8
GDR	7	5	7
United States	3	3	4
Norway	3	3	1
FRG	2	5	3
Finland	2	4	1
Austria	2	2	2
Switzerland	1	3	1
Netherlands	1	2	3
Italy	1	2	1
Canada	1	1	1
Great Britain	1	-	-
Czechoslovakia	-	1	-
Lichtenstein	-	-	2
Sweden	-	-	2
France	-	-	1

MONTREAL 1976

XXIst Olympic Games. 17 July – 1 August
Attended by representatives of 92 countries, comprising 6073 competitors, of which 1262 were women.

WHEN THE GAMES were initially awarded to Montreal, mainly due to the efforts of Mayor Jean Drapeau, it was estimated that they would cost

$310 million. Because of planning errors, strikes, slowdowns, and, it has been suggested, widespread corruption, the final bill amounted to $1400 million – the stadium alone cost $485 million, and the projected 160m high tower and suspended roof were never completed. In 1994 it was stated that the total debt remaining to the citizens of Quebec was $304 million. After the Munich disaster, security arrangements involving 16,000 police and soldiers cost $100 million. Six months before it seemed that the main facilities would not be finished in time, but by the official opening performed by Queen Elizabeth II, all that was necessary was ready. The expected record number of entries was well down due to a last minute boycott by 20 Third World, mainly African, nations, protesting against the inclusion of New Zealand, whose rugby union team had visited South Africa. Also withdrawing was Taiwan because Canada refused to recognize them under the title of Republic of China, a situation which owed much, it was suggested, to Canada's grain-trading relations with mainland China. The withdrawals, mostly only two days prior to the start of competitions, caused some problems with seeding arrangements, and particularly affected the quality of boxing and some running events.

Efforts had been made by the IOC to prune the programme, and to this end the 50km walk, tandem cycling, slalom canoeing, the free rifle and three swimming events had been eliminated. However, with the addition of women's basketball and handball, four canoeing races and seven rowing events, of which six were for women, the total number of gold medals available was now 198 – three more than at Munich. The torch was brought into the stadium by two 15 year olds, a girl and a boy; Sandra Henderson of English descent and Stéphane Prefontaine of French stock, each with a hand on the torch, signifying Canada's joint heritage. In true storybook fashion the pair were married some years later.

The star of Munich, gymnast Olga Korbut, was at Montreal, but she was overshadowed by a 14-year-old Romanian, Nadia Comaneci, who scored the first-ever maximum 10.00 marks achieved at the Olympics on the first day, and ended the Games with a total of seven maximums, having drawn a world record crowd for gymnastics of 18,000 to the finals of the women's events. Nelli Kim (URS) also scored two maximums. The men's individual champion, Nikolai Andrianov (URS) won the most medals at Montreal with four gold, two silver and a bronze. In the swimming pool, Kornelia Ender (GDR) and John Naber (USA) each won four golds and a silver, with Ender and her teammates only failing to win two of the thirteen women's swimming titles. The American

men did better, only losing one of their thirteen events – David Wilkie won Britain's first men's swimming gold since 1908. Incidentally, Ender later married her teammate, backstroke specialist Roland Matthes, giving them a family total of eight gold, six silver and two bronze medals from three Games. In highboard diving the Austrian-born Italian, Klaus Dibiasi, competing in his fourth Games, became the first diver to gain three consecutive gold medals. A member of the Hungarian water polo team, which won their country's record sixth victory in the sport, was István Szivós, whose father had been in the winning 1952 and 1956 teams.

In the main stadium Lasse Virén, the latest 'Flying Finn', completed his double 'double' by successfully defending his 5000m and 10,000m titles. He attempted to emulate Zátopek's 1952 feat, but finished fifth in the marathon. The Cuban Alberto Juantorena, nicknamed *El Caballo* – 'The Horse' – won a rare 400m/800m double (only America's Paul Pilgrim had previously achieved it in the 1906 Games). Irena Szewinska (POL), now aged 30, won the 400m in her fourth games, to equal the record total of seven medals in athletics. The winner of the men's javelin with a new world record, Miklós Németh (HUN), was the son of the 1948 hammer winner. They remain the only father and son in track and field to win gold medals.

Three sets of brothers did very well in the Montreal rowing events. Frank and Alf Hansen (NOR) won the double sculls, while the Landvoigt twins, Jörg and Bernd (GDR) took the coxless pairs. Another set of GDR twins, Walter and Ullrich Diessner, were in the silver medal coxed four crew. Elsewhere the Flying Dutchman class yachting was won by another set of brothers, Jörg and Eckart Diesch (FRG). In women's fencing Elena Novikova-Belova (URS) won her record fourth gold medal in the team contest, while Hungary's Ildikó Ságiné-Retjö set an all-medal record of seven, comprising two gold, three silver and two bronzes collected at five Games. America's Margaret Murdock became the first woman to win a shooting medal, and was unlucky not to win the gold. Initially she was declared the winner of the small-bore rifle (three positions) event, but an error was discovered which gave her a tie with her teammate, Lanny Bassham. A closer examination of targets then relegated her down a place. Although unplaced, show jumpers Raimondo and Piero D'Inzeo (ITA) set an unprecedented record by competing in their eighth Games 1948-76. Alwin Schockemöhle (FRG) became only the third rider in Games history to win the jumping title without any faults.

The new Olympic sport of women's basketball produced the tallest known woman ever to compete in the Games. She was Iuliana Semenova (URS), who was unofficially 2.18m *7ft 2in* tall (See 'Tallest') and weighed 129kg *284lb*. Her team won the title, and she is one of tallest, including men, to win an Olympic gold medal. In weightlifting, two Bulgarians and a Pole, all medallists, were later disqualified for failing dope tests. A far greater scandal occurred in the modern pentathlon when one of the favourites, Boris Onischenko (URS), was discovered to have tampered with his epee in the fencing segment of the competition. His disqualification eliminated the Soviet team and the team gold medal went to Great Britain. The revenge basketball match between the USA and USSR never materialized as the Soviets were beaten by Yugoslavia in the semifinals. Thus the United States regained the title, making their Olympic match record – played 70, won 69.

The oldest gold medallist at Montreal was Harry Boldt (FRG) in the winning dressage team aged 46yr 157days. The youngest was gymnast Nadia Comaneci who won her first gold medal aged 14yr 252days. The youngest male champion/medallist was Brian Goodell (USA) aged 17yr 109days when he won the 1500m freestyle, while the oldest female gold medallist was Ivanka Khristova (BUL) in the shot aged 34yr 255days. The youngest female medallist was Canadian swimmer, Robin Corsiglia, in the medley relay aged 13yr 341days. The oldest medallist was Australian 3-day eventer Bill Roycroft aged 61yr 131days. One of the youngest competitors ever in the Olympics was Spanish swimmer Antonia Real aged 12yr 310days. In 1904 a Montreal policeman, Etienne Desmarteau, had won Canada's first Olympic gold medal. At these Games Canada gained the unhappy distinction of being the only host country of a Summer Olympics not to win a single gold medal.

Montreal 1976 Medals

	G	S	B
Soviet Union	49	41	35
GDR	40	25	25
United States	34	35	25
FRG	10	12	17
Japan	9	6	10
Poland	7	6	13
Bulgaria	6	9	7
Cuba	6	4	3
Romania	4	9	14
Hungary	4	5	13
Finland	4	2	-
Sweden	4	1	-
Great Britain	3	5	5
Italy	2	7	4
France	2	3	4
Yugoslavia	2	3	3
Czechoslovakia	2	2	4
New Zealand	2	1	1
Korea	1	1	4
Switzerland	1	1	2
Jamaica	1	1	-
North Korea (PRK)	1	1	-
Norway	1	1	-
Denmark	1	-	2
Mexico	1	-	1
Trinidad	1	-	-
Canada	-	5	6
Belgium	-	3	3
Netherlands	-	2	3
Portugal	-	2	-
Spain	-	2	-
Australia	-	1	4
Iran	-	1	1
Mongolia	-	1	-
Venezuela	-	1	-
Brazil	-	-	2
Austria	-	-	1
Bermuda	-	-	1
Pakistan	-	-	1
Puerto Rico	-	-	1
Thailand	-	-	1

LAKE PLACID 1980

XIIth Winter Games. 13–24 February
Attended by representatives of 37 countries, comprising 1072 competitors, of which 235 were women.

LAKE PLACID HAD been applying for the Games unsuccessfully since 1962 when they were finally rewarded in 1974. Most of the facilities used in 1932 had to be rebuilt, and new ones constructed, so that the budget for these Games was nearly 80 times the $1.1 million spent in 1932. Some complaints were voiced about the 'village', a building later to be used as a penal institution, but as a report noted 'at least security would not be a problem'. Once the Games were under way the accommodation was found to be quite suitable and acceptable. One pre-Games worry which turned into a major problem was transport for the spectators and Press. At times it was virtually impossible to reach and/or return from venues. The official opening was undertaken by Walter Mondale, the Vice-President of the United States. The last relay runner was Dr Charles Morgan Kerr, a psychiatrist, and the oath was taken, with outstanding foresight, by speed skater Eric Heiden. The People's Republic of China and Cyprus made their debuts in the Winter Games.

The afore-mentioned Heiden (USA) stole all the headlines by gaining an unprecedented sweep of all five speed skating gold medals, all in Olympic record times. His sister, Beth, also won a bronze in the women's events. Her teammate Leah Poulos-

Mueller won two silver medals but could not match her husband Peter's gold performance of 1976. Peter Mueller, who coached Bonnie Blair (USA), Dan Jansen (USA) and Marianne Timmer (NED) to their gold medals, later married the latter. In Nordic skiing Nikolai Simyatov (URS) won a unique three golds in one Games, while teammate Galina Kulakova, now over 37, raised her record total of medals over four Games to eight. Ulrich Wehling (GDR) won his third consecutive gold medal in the Nordic combination, and Aleksandr Tikhonov (URS) won a fourth consecutive gold in the biathlon relay. The closest ever result in Olympic Nordic skiing came in the men's 15km cross-country event when Thomas Wassberg (SWE) beat Juha Mieto (FIN) by 0.01sec. Eight years previously the unlucky Finn had lost a bronze by only 0.06sec. However, he did win a gold in the 1976 relay.

Slalom specialist Ingemar Stenmark (SWE) won both of his races to became the most successful male Alpine skier at these Games, but Hanni Wenzel from tiny Liechtenstein won both women's slaloms and the silver medal in the downhill. Her brother Andreas added a silver to put their country in sixth place on the unofficial medal table.(Another sister Petra was also in the team of seven). In winning the 90m ski jump Jouko Törmänen (FIN) made the longest jump attained to that time in Olympic competition when he cleared 117m *383ft*. In the 70m event, there was an unfortunate incident when after nine competitors had taken their jumps the judges ruled that conditions were too dangerous. The start point was moved lower down, to reduce take-off speed, and the competition begun again. Irina Rodnina (URS) equalled the record of three gold medals by a figure skater when she and her husband, Aleksandr Zaitsev retained the pairs title. By successfully defending the men's singles for Great Britain Robin Cousins won his country's only medal of these Games. The bobsledding was a virtual replay of the 1976 rivalry between the Swiss and GDR teams. In the American 12th-placed 4-man bob was Willie Davenport, who had competed in the Summer Games from 1964 to 1976 and had won the 110m hurdles in 1968. By far the most popular win was that of the United States ice hockey team over the Soviet Union (their first defeat since 1964) on the way to the final. The celebrations which followed were described on American television as the biggest since the end of World War II. In the final they then beat Finland.

The oldest gold medallist was Meinhard Nehmer (GDR) in the 4-man bob aged 39yr 42days, and the youngest was his teammate Karin Enke who won the 500m speed skating title aged 18yr 240days. The youngest male winner was Mike Ramsey of the victorious US ice hockey team aged 19yr 83days. The oldest female champion was Irina Rodnina (see above) aged 30yr 159days. Special mention must be made of Marina Tcherkasova (URS), a silver medallist in pair skating only 93 days past her 15th birthday.

Lake Placid 1980 Medals

	G	S	B
Soviet Union	10	6	6
GDR	9	7	7
United States	6	4	2
Austria	3	2	2
Sweden	3	-	1
Liechtenstein	2	2	-
Finland	1	5	3
Norway	1	3	6
Netherlands	1	2	1
Switzerland	1	1	3
Great Britain	1	-	-
FRG	-	2	3
Italy	-	2	-
Canada	-	1	1
Hungary	-	1	-
Japan	-	1	-
Bulgaria	-	-	1
Czechoslovakia	-	-	1
France	-	-	1

MOSCOW 1980

XXIInd Olympic Games. 19 July – 1 August
Attended by representatives of 80 countries, comprising 5252 competitors, of which 1120 were women.

THERE HAD BEEN only a little dissent when the IOC awarded these Games to Moscow in 1974. Tsarist Russia had competed in 1900 and from 1906 to 1912. Athletes from Lithuania, Estonia and Latvia, which had been provinces of Russia prior to 1918 and were taken over by the Soviet Union in 1940, had competed independently between 1920 and 1936. The Soviet Union had entered the Olympics in force in 1952, and was now the second highest medal scorer of all time – a remarkable achievement. However, in December 1979 the Soviet Union invaded Afghanistan, and much of the non-Communist world, led by the United States, tried to impose a boycott on the Games – although not, it should be noted, on trade or other economic activity. Not all countries supported the boycott, although sports within those countries sometimes did. Because a number of countries, which were unlikely to go to Moscow anyway for financial reasons, found it politic to 'jump on the bandwagon', it is difficult to complete a list of boycotting nations. The most reliable estimate is 45-50, of which the most important in sporting terms were the United States, the Federal Republic of Germany and Japan. When the Games were officially opened by Leonid Brezhnev, President of the USSR, there were eight first time entries, not including Zimbabwe which had previously competed as Rhodesia.

Facilities in Moscow were excellent, including the 103,000 capacity Lenin stadium, and large crowds attended most sports. It must be stated that though, in the main, the Soviet spectators were very knowledgeable, they left something to be desired in their treatment of foreign competitors, particularly those from other Eastern bloc countries. New competitions, such as women's hockey, two extra judo classes, one extra weightlifting class, and various reintroduced events, brought the total of gold medals available to a record 203 (barring ties). The heroine of Montreal, Nadia Comaneci (ROM), returned but was no longer the force she had been, and for the first time for many years the star of gymnastics was a male, Aleksandr Dityatin (URS). He won the greatest number of medals, eight, ever won by a competitor at any sport at one Games, and was also awarded a 10.00 in the horse vault, the first maximum ever to a male gymnast in the Olympics. His teammate, Nikolai Andrianov, brought his total of medals to a male record of 15, in three Games. This total has only ever been exceeded by Larissa Latynina, also a Soviet gymnast.

East African athletes dominated the distance runs, led by Miruts Yifter (ETH) with a 5000m/10,000m double. The 100m was the closest for 28 years with Britain's Allan Wells given the verdict over Silvio Leonard of Cuba. Two other Britons each won the 'wrong' event, Steve Ovett and Sebastian Coe taking the 800m and 1500m respectively. Waldemar Cierpinski (GDR) became only the second man to successfully defend the marathon title, although he was over a minute slower than in 1976. In the triple jump Viktor Saneyev (URS) ended his remarkable career with a silver to add to his three gold medals since 1968. By repeating her Montreal gold medals in the 200m and relay Barbel Wöckel (GDR) equalled the female track and field record of four. In that relay, Ludmila Maslakova of the silver medal Soviet team was running in her fourth consecutive relay final since 1968. Although only winning the pentathlon silver medal, Olga Rukavishnikova (URS) theoretically held the world record, albeit for only 0.4 sec, as she finished first in the last discipline, 800m. That gave her the shortest reign of any world record holder ever.

Once more the GDR women dominated the swimming events, winning 26 of the available 35 medals. Highest medal scorers were Caren Metschuck

with three golds and a silver, and Ines Diers with two golds, two silvers and a bronze. More unusually, their teammate Rica Reinisch won three gold medals all in world record times. In the inaugural women's hockey competition, Zimbabwe gained a gold medal in its debut at the Games, while India was back to its former winning ways by taking a record eighth title in the men's competition. At Tallinn, in the sailing events, the Finn class dinghy event was won appropriately enough by a Finn, Esko Rechardt.

Vladimir Parfenovich (URS) was the first canoeist to win three gold medals at the same Games, and the Cuban heavyweight, Teofilo Stevenson, became the only boxer to win the same event in three Games. Note that the great Hungarian László Papp had won three golds at two different weights. In rowing the Landvoigt twins, Jörg and Bernd (GDR) retained their coxless pairs title by beating the Soviet Pimenov twins, Yuri and Nikolai. The other GDR twins, Ulrich and Walter Diessner, went one better than four years previously and won gold medals in the coxed fours. Yet another pair of twins won titles in wrestling when Anatoli and Sergei Beloglasov (URS) won the 52kg and 57kg freestyle events respectively.

The oldest gold medallist at Moscow, or rather Tallinn, was Valentin Mankin (URS) in the Star sailing, in his fourth Games, aged 41yr 346days, while the youngest champion at these Games was swimmer Rica Reinisch (GDR) winning the first of her three golds aged 15yr 105days. The oldest female winner was Anthea Stewart (ZIM) at 35yr 253days in the hockey, while the youngest male gold medallist was the Hungarian backstroker Sándor Wladár, seven days over his seventeenth birthday. The youngest medallist was Zirvard Emirzyan (URS) with a silver in women's diving aged 14yr 52days, while the oldest medallist was Petre Rosca (ROM) in the dressage at 57yr 283days. The youngest competitor of all was Polish gymnast Anita Jokiel aged 13yr 232days. In the same competition was Myong Hui Choe of North Korea, the smallest competitor of all at 1.35m 4ft 5in tall and weighing 25kg 55lb. At the other end of the scale was Soviet basketball player Vladimir Tkachenko, standing 2.20m 7ft 2½in tall, and Greco-Roman wrestler Roman Codreanu (ROM) who weighed 170kg 374lb. Despite the unfillable losses and gaps caused by the boycott, the standard of performances was very high throughout the Games.

Moscow 1980 Medals

	G	S	B
Soviet Union	80	69	46
GDR	47	37	42
Bulgaria	8	16	17
Cuba	8	7	5

Italy	8	3	4
Hungary	7	10	15
Romania	6	6	13
France	6	5	3
Great Britain	5	7	9
Poland	3	14	15
Sweden	3	3	6
Finland	3	1	4
Czechoslovakia	2	3	9
Yugoslavia	2	3	4
Australia	2	2	5
Denmark	2	1	2
Brazil	2	-	2
Ethiopia	2	-	2
Switzerland	2	-	-
Spain	1	3	2
Austria	1	2	1
Greece	1	-	2
Belgium	1	-	-
India	1	-	-
Zimbabwe	1	-	-
North Korea (PRK)	-	3	2
Mongolia	-	2	2
Tanzania	-	2	-
Mexico	-	1	3
Netherlands	-	1	2
Ireland	-	1	1
Uganda	-	1	-
Venezuela	-	1	-
Jamaica	-	-	3
Guyana	-	-	1
Lebanon	-	-	1

SARAJEVO 1984

XIVth Winter Games. 8 – 19 February
Attended by representatives of 49 countries, comprising 1273 competitors, of which 277 were women.

THE FIRST WINTER Games held in eastern Europe was awarded to Sarajevo in 1978. With a population of 500,000 it was the second largest city to host the Winter Games, and was previously famous only as the site of the assassination of Archduke Ferdinand on 28 June 1914 – an act which historians argue contributed to the start of the First World War. There were a record 49 countries attending, including debuts by the British Virgin Islands, Egypt, Costa Rica, Puerto Rico and perhaps most unlikely, Senegal. The Games were opened by Mika Špiljak, the President of the Presidency of the Socialist Federal Republic of Yugoslavia. The flame was lit by Sanda Dubravcic after running up 94 steps in the Kosovo stadium. She later placed tenth in the women's figure skating. The oath was taken by skier Bojan Krizaj, later seventh in the slalom. Actually the competitions had started the day before, with preliminary rounds of the ice hockey tournament. Prior to the Games much had been made of the

wolf mascot, Vucko, being depicted with its claws crossed – as though hoping for the best. In fact, although the weather caused various problems, the enthusiasm of the organisers and the local populace overcame most difficulties. Even the transport system worked. One of the few things that did cause hackles to rise was outside the control of the host city. This was the highly questionable, or at the least confusing, judging of the figure skating – a problem not unique to Sarajevo in recent years. One *cause celebre* just prior to the Games was the banning, as professionals, of the two defending champions in the men's and women's slalom races, Ingemar Stenmark (SWE) and Hanni Wenzel (LIE). There was only one new event in the programme, a 20km Nordic skiing race for women.

For the first time the GDR won more gold medals than the Soviet Union, although not total medals. However, in the men's luge, in which they had won seven gold, two silver and four bronze medals in the last four Games, they only took a single bronze. The outstanding competitor, unusually, was a female Nordic skier, Marja-Liisa Hämäläinen (FIN), who won all three individual events and a bronze in the relay. However, Britain's Jayne Torvill and Christopher Dean gained the most media attention with their superb ice dancing – their artistic interpretation of Ravel's *Bolero* was awarded an unprecedented nine perfect sixes, with another three for technical merit. The women's singles winner, Katarina Witt (GDR), was trained by Jutta Müller, who had not only coached her daughter, Gabriele Seyfert, to a silver in 1968, but had also been the driving force behind the 1980 champion, Anett Pötzsch.

Alpine skiers from the United States made a major impact with three titles. Bill Johnson, hardly a retiring personality, proved he was as good as he had been saying he was, to anyone and everyone who would listen, and won the first Olympic downhill title by an American, in a record average speed of 104.532km/h *64.593mph*. His team-mates, twins Phil and Steve Mahre took the gold and silver medals in the slalom. By winning the women's downhill race Michaela Figini (SUI) became the youngest ever Alpine skiing gold medallist aged 17yr 314days, as well as being the youngest champion at Sarajevo. Unusually, in Alpine skiing, only one skier, Perrine Pelen (FRA) won more than one medal, and few begrudged the silver gained by Jure Franko in the giant slalom, the first Winter Games medal ever by Yugoslavia.

In speed skating, Tomas Gustafson (SWE) and Igor Malkov (URS) swapped medals over 5000m and 10,000m, in two of the closest races ever skated in the Games, unique over such distances. The Swede won the shorter race by 0.02sec, and the Soviet won the longer by 0.05sec. The Soviet ice hockey team equalled Canada's record with a sixth gold medal. Just prior to the Games another ice hockey eligibility controversy had arisen with the decision that an amateur for Olympic purposes was someone who had not played in the National Hockey League of North America. One other bone of contention had been resolved before competitions began when the revolutionary rocket-shaped Soviet bobs were barred. The 90m ski jump was won by a young Finn, Matti Nykänen, by a record margin of 18.5 points, but he was to make a far greater impression four years later.

The oldest gold medallist at Sarajevo was the Soviet ice hockey goalminder Vladyslav Tretyak, in his fourth Games, aged 31yr 299days. The youngest was Michela Figini (see above). The youngest male champion was speed skater Igor Malkov (URS) just nine days past his 19th birthday, while the oldest female gold medallist was Marja-Liisa Hämäläinen (see above) aged 28yr 161days. The oldest competitor was Carl-Erik Eriksson (SWE) at 53yr 289days, competing in his record sixth successive Olympic bobsleigh competition. The youngest was Babette Preussler (GDR) in pair skating aged 15yr 143days. One of the victorious German pair in the luge, Hans Stanggassinger, had another distinction. He was reportedly the heaviest champion weighing 111kg *244lb*.

Sarajevo 1984 Medals

	G	S	B
GDR	9	9	6
Soviet Union	6	10	9
United States	4	4	-
Finland	4	3	6
Sweden	4	2	2
Norway	3	2	4
Switzerland	2	2	1
Canada	2	1	1
FRG	2	1	1
Italy	2	-	-
Great Britain	1	-	-
Czechoslovakia	-	2	4
France	-	1	2
Japan	-	1	-
Yugoslavia	-	1	-
Liechtenstein	-	-	2
Austria	-	-	1

LOS ANGELES 1984

XXIIIrd Olympic Games. 28 July – 12 August
Attended by representatives of 140 countries, comprising 6799 competitors, of which 1575 were women.

THE IOC AWARDED the Games to Los Angeles (in 1978) only after protracted negotiations about the financial guarantees usually required from a host city. Various innovations to protect the city from a Montreal-like deficit were implemented – not least, widespread sponsorship by private corporations. Television rights alone amounted to $287 million – one of the largest TV audiences in history, some 2500 million, watched the Games – of which the great bulk came from the ABC network for US rights. The programme was expanded to 221 events, including an extra 12 for women, while baseball and tennis were demonstration sports. The Memorial Coliseum, main site for the 1932 Games, was fully refurbished and had a seating capacity of 92,607, and many other venues, often famous in their own right, were utilized. There were complaints that some of these venues were too far-flung, but the overall good weather and the enthusiasm, at times overwhelming, of the American crowds offset most problems.

The one, albeit major, disaster suffered by these Games was the last-minute boycott by the Soviet Union, which announced its non-participation on the very day, 8 May 1984, that the Olympic flame arrived in the United States to begin a nationwide torch relay. Within a week or so most of the Soviet bloc had also pulled out – with the notable exception of Romania. Additionally, but not surprisingly, Iran and Libya did not appear. However, of 159 invitations sent out, 140 countries accepted – beating the Munich record. Nevertheless, a number of sports were very seriously affected, although standards were still generally high. In particular, canoeing, fencing, gymnastics, weightlifting, wrestling and women's athletics were diminished, both in numbers and quality.

The Games were formally opened by President Ronald Reagan, the first incumbent ever to do so. The final runner on the torch relay was Gina Hemphill, a granddaughter of the great Olympian Jesse Owens. Interestingly, she had also run the first leg on American soil, jointly with Jim Thorpe's grandson, Bill. Some years after the Games she married Henry Tillman who won the heavyweight boxing title at Los Angeles. In the stadium she handed over the torch to 1960 Olympic decathlon champion Rafer Johnson, who, by means of a gantry, lit the flame on the top of the stadium peristyle. Apparently in rehearsals Johnson had developed a leg injury, and 1976 champion Bruce Jenner, one of the Olympic flag's escorts, stood by in case he had to replace Johnson. The oath was taken, somewhat stumblingly, by the 1976 400m hurdle champion Edwin Moses, who went on to win a second gold medal. There followed a three-hour Hollywood-style extravaganza featuring, among other things, marching bands and 85 pianos, which was produced by film producer David Wolper.

Smog and traffic congestion did not materialize to anything like the degree predicted, although one unfortunate phenomenon, however, was the orgy of American chauvinism displayed – especially by the media. Attendances at all sports were quite remarkable, with a final attendance figure of 5.7 million, and a highest single figure, 101,799, for the final of the soccer tournament (France beat Brazil 2-0) in the famed Rose Bowl at Pasadena. One particular feature of these Games was the tremendous outlay made on security – some 7000 personnel and ancillary equipment costing as much as $100 million.

The first gold medal of the Games was won by shooter Xu Haifeng with China's first ever Olympic title. Aided enormously by the absence of Soviet and East German opposition, the United States gained by far the lion's share of the medals. Leading their gold rush was sprinter/jumper Carl Lewis, who exactly duplicated Jesse Owens's feat of 1936, with four gold medals in the 100m, 200m, long jump and relay. Another athlete, Valerie Brisco-Hooks, and five swimmers, all won three golds each. However, the most successful competitors were gymnasts Ecaterina Szabó (ROM) with four golds and a silver, and China's Li Ning with three golds, two silvers and a bronze.

The introduction of consolation finals in swimming, for non-qualifiers to the regular finals, led to the unusual situation of an Olympic record being set in the men's 400m freestyle 'B' final, faster than the gold medallist had attained. The judo Open champion Yasuhiro Yamashita (JPN) extended his winning streak to 198, despite being handicapped by a foot injury. A number of families were particularly successful: twins Mark and David Schultz (USA), and Lou and Ed Banach (USA), all won wrestling gold medals; William Buchan (USA) and his son William Jr won sailing titles, but not together; British husband and wife Garry (silver, 4x400m) and Kathy Cook (bronze, 400m & 4x100m) won medals; Al Joyner (USA) and his sister Jackie won gold (triple jump) and silver (heptathlon) medals respectively; brothers Carmine and Giuseppe Abbagnale (ITA) won the coxed pairs rowing event.

In the dressage event 48yr old Reiner Klimke (FRG) won two gold medals in his fourth Games over a 20-year period, equalling his countryman Hans-Günter Winkler's equestrian record of five golds and seven medals. One of the few negative things at Los Angeles was the disqualification for doping offences of 12 competitors from weightlifting, wrestling, volleyball and athletics. Probably the most well-known of these was Martti Vainio (FIN) who finished second in the 10,000m on the track.

The oldest gold medallist at Los Angeles was William Buchan (USA) in the Star yachting aged 49yr 91days (see above). The youngest was Romanian gymnast Simona Pauca in the team event aged 14yr 317days, and who won the individual beam title four days later. The youngest male champion was Perica Bukic (YUG) in water polo aged 17yr 264days, while the oldest female gold medallist was Linda Thom (CAN) winning the women's pistol aged 40yr 212days. The oldest female medallist was the lady who finished third in that competition, Patricia Dench (AUS) at 52yr 143days. The oldest male medallist was another shooter Ragnar Skanaker (SWE) aged 50yr 52days. At the other end of the scale was Belgian coxswain Philippe Cuelenaere, the youngest competitor at Los Angeles, a month short of his 13th birthday.

At the end of the Games – after another closing extravaganza featuring one of the greatest firework displays ever seen – the organizers reported a profit of $215 million, prompting the suggestion that perhaps the pendulum had swung too far the other way since Montreal. The whole thing was a triumphant vindication of the leadership of Peter Ueberroth, President of the Los Angeles Olympic Organizing Committee. Coincidentally, Ueberroth was born on the very day, 2 September 1937, that Baron de Coubertin had died. A sour note was added some time later when it was reported that a number of drug test samples had been unaccountably lost.

Los Angeles 1984 Medals

	G	S	B
United States	83	61	30
Romania	20	16	17
FRG	17	19	23
China	15	8	9
Italy	14	6	12
Canada	10	18	16
Japan	10	8	14
New Zealand	8	1	2
Yugoslavia	7	4	7
Korea	6	6	7
Great Britain	5	11	21
France	5	7	16
Netherlands	5	2	6
Australia	4	8	12
Finland	4	2	6
Sweden	2	11	6
Mexico	2	3	1
Morocco	2	-	-
Brazil	1	5	2
Spain	1	2	2
Belgium	1	1	2
Austria	1	1	1
Kenya	1	-	2
Portugal	1	-	2

Pakistan	1	-	-
Switzerland	-	4	4
Denmark	-	3	3
Jamaica	-	1	2
Norway	-	1	2
Greece	-	1	1
Nigeria	-	1	1
Puerto Rico	-	1	I
Colombia	-	1	-
Egypt	-	1	-
Ireland	-	1	-
Ivory Coast	-	1	-
Peru	-	1	-
Syria	-	1	-
Thailand	-	1	-
Turkey	-	-	3
Venezuela	-	-	3
Algeria	-	-	2
Cameroon	-	-	1
Dominican Republic	-	-	I
Iceland	-	-	1
Taiwan (Taipei)	-	-	1
Zambia	-	-	1

CALGARY 1988

XVth Winter Games. 13 – 28 February
Attended by representatives of 57 countries, comprising 1425 competitors, of which 315 were women.

HAVING HAD THREE unsuccessful bids previously, Calgary was finally awarded these Games in 1981. Most of the venues were close together except for Mount Allan and Kenmore, some 90km away, where the Alpine and Nordic skiing took place. The programme was stretched to 16 days to include three weekends, particularly favourable for television coverage – for which ABC paid $309 million for the North American rights, over three times the sum for the Sarajevo 1984 coverage. There were a number of new events; Nordic Combination for teams, Team Ski Jumping, Alpine Combination, Super Giant Slaloms for men and women, and a 5000m speed skating event for women. In all there were 46 events, as well as the demonstration sports of curling, short track speed skating and freestyle skiing. Five teams made their Winter Games debuts; Fiji, Guam, Guatemala, Ireland and Jamaica. The official opening was performed by the Governor-General of Canada, Jeanne Sauvé, on behalf of Queen Elizabeth II. The torch was brought into the stadium by a couple, speed skater Cathy Priestner and skier Ken Read, and then handed to a 12-year-old girl skater, Robyn Perry, who lit the flame. Incidentally, that flame was easily the highest ever as it was set at the top of the Calgary Tower, which is 191m *616ft* high. The oath was taken by Pierre Harvey, a Nordic skier who had also represented Canada at cycling in the 1984 Olympics.

The facilities in the main were excellent, and the expected local transport problems were few and far between. Accommodation was at a premium with so many teams and competitors, and some officials were based in an establishment which had previously been a 'house of ill-repute'. However, one unforeseen occurrence caused real problems, and that was a dramatic climatic change caused by the 'chinook' wind, which gave springlike weather, and strong winds, which caused havoc to the timetable. These conditions, which primarily affected the bob, luge and ski jumping events, resulted in some unexpected results. The exposed ski jumps were very dangerous at times, and caused the Nordic Combination event, comprising jumping and cross-country skiing, to be contested on the one day.

Nevertheless, there were many excellent performances, although the 'star' of these Games was an unknown British ski jumper. Despite, or more likely because of, being totally inept by world standards Michael 'Eddie the Eagle' Edwards stole the media attention from the great and famous, to the amusement of many and the chagrin of some. Britain's first Olympic entrant ever in this sport, he finished last in both jumps, albeit with a British record of 71m, over 20m behind the rest of the competitors.

The most successful competitors were Yvonne van Gennip (HOL) who won three speed skating titles, and Matti Nykänen (FIN), who won all three gold medals open to him. The Finn totally dominated his sport and leapt to 118.5m on the 90m hill, the greatest distance ever achieved in the Games. In Alpine skiing both Vreni Schneider (SUI) and Alberto Tomba (ITA) won the slalom and giant slalom events. Frank-Peter Roetsch (GDR) became the first man to win both individual biathlon races in a single Games, while the Soviet Union won the relay for the sixth consecutive time. The Soviet women hardly made an error in the Nordic skiing taking seven of the nine individual medals as well as the relay. Although not in that relay, 35-year-old Raisa Smetanina gained a silver and a bronze to raise her total from four Games to a record nine medals for the sport.

After the shocks of Sarajevo the GDR lugers were back winning all three golds, two silvers and a bronze. Steffi Walter (née Martin) was the first luger to retain an individual title, and led her teammates to a clean sweep. Incidentally, one of the British competitors in this sport was Nick Ovett, whose older brother Steve won the 1980 Olympic 800m. The bobsleigh course was likened to sandpaper as the winds had blown so much dirt on the track, and many of the top crews were upset. There was bitter rivalry between the Swiss and GDR 4-man crews, with officials of both teams checking the legality of each others sleds. The coach of the Swiss team was 1980 gold medallist Erich Schärer, while the GDR coach was Horst Hörnlein who had won gold in the 2-man luge in 1972. After the fourth and final run the Swiss were triumphant by 0.07 of a second, the smallest margin ever in the event. The drama was heightened even further when the rather unlikely crew from Jamaica, who had never been on ice before, crashed badly, but happily no one was seriously hurt. Some years later a film was made about their efforts. Bogdan Musiol (GDR) with two silver medals raised his total to a record equalling six. Placed 25th (of 41) in the 2-man bob was Albert Grimaldi, otherwise known as Prince Albert of Monaco, partnered by a croupier from the Principality's Casino. Himself a Member of the IOC, Prince Albert's grandfather and uncle, both named Jack Kelly, had won Olympic rowing medals.

Katarina Witt (GDR) was the first individual skater since 1952 to retain a figure skating title, amid some criticism – not shared by the spectators – about her skimpy costumes. In third place Debbie Thomas (USA) was the first black skater to win an Olympic skating medal. Speed skating was held indoors for the first time at the Olympics, in the superb $39 million Olympic Oval. It proved to be the fastest circuit in the world with world records in seven of the nine events, and as many as 29 skaters bettering the world mark in the men's 5000m. Karin Kania (née Enke) (GDR) added two silvers and a bronze for a record medal haul of eight since 1980. Monika Pflug-Holzner (FRG), the 1972 1000m champion competed in her fifth Games, then a record number of appearances for a female Winter Olympics competitor. The Soviet Union moved past Canada in ice hockey with its seventh title, while the host nation and the United States, who won in 1980, failed to gain a medal. A small consolation prize for Canada was that the most prolific goalscorer, with seven, in the tournament was Serge Boisvert. There was only one competitor in Calgary who failed a dope test – a Polish ice hockey player.

The youngest gold medallist was Ekaterina Gordiyeva (URS) in the pairs skating aged 16yr 264days, while the oldest was Ekkehard Fasser (SUI) in the 4-man bob aged 35yr 178days. The youngest male champion was Ari Pekka Nikkola (FIN) in the 90m team ski jump at 18yr 284days, and the oldest female gold medallist was Christa Rothenburger (GDR) who won the 1000m speedskating aged 28yr 84days. Competitors ages ranged from a 14yr old Seba Johnson of the US Virgin Islands, the first black Olympic skier, to her countryman, 52-year-old Harvey Hook, a bobsledder.

Calgary 1988 Medals

	G	S	B
Soviet Union	11	9	9
GDR	9	10	6
Switzerland	5	5	5
Finland	4	1	2
Sweden	4	-	2
Austria	3	5	2
Netherlands	3	2	2
FRG	2	4	2
United States	2	1	3
Italy	2	1	2
France	1	-	1
Norway	-	3	2
Canada	-	2	3
Yugoslavia	-	2	1
Czechoslovakia	-	1	2
Japan	-	-	1
Liechtenstein	-	-	1

SEOUL 1988

XXIVth Olympic Games. 17 September – 2 October
Attended by representatives of 159 countries, comprising 8447 competitors, of which 2196 were women.

THE CAPITAL OF Korea, Seoul, has one of the largest populations of any city on earth – an estimated 9,000,000. Nearly all facilities for the Games were in situ by the end of 1986 when the Asian Games were held there. Most major installations were part of the sports complex on the banks of the Han River, and included a 90,000 spectator stadium. Once again the programme was expanded, with the reintroduction of tennis (for the first time since 1924), the addition of table tennis, and the inclusion of a number of extra events, which brought the total to a record 237. Baseball, taekwondo and women's judo were the demonstration sports. American television companies offered incredible sums (up to $750 million) for the US rights, providing the major sports finals took place during the American prime time viewing. That would have required that athletics finals be held between 9.00 – 11.00am Korean time. This was opposed by the International Amateur Athletic Federation, and indeed by the IOC, although some compromise was finally agreed. The income from television sources was still immense, NBC acquiring the American rights alone for $300 million. There were an estimated 16,000 media personnel at these Games.

Prior to the Opening Ceremony the most tenacious problem was the claim of North Korea to host half the Games. Against IOC rules, but with their blessing, some sports were offered to them, but they continued to be intransigent. They finally refused to attend and attempted to get the Eastern bloc to support them. However, only the hard line Communist countries backed them, and the other absentees were; Albania, Cuba, Ethiopia, Madagascar, Nicaragua and the Seychelles. Against that there were a number of first-timers including; American Samoa, Aruba, Burkina Faso (which had competed as Upper Volta in 1972), Cook Islands, Guam, the Maldives, St Vincent, Vanuatu and the Democratic Republic of Yemen. Also attending was Brunei, but only with an official, so that the officially claimed figure of 160 countries participating is not correct.

The Opening Ceremony began on the Han River and transferred to the main stadium. The President of Korea, Roh Tae-Woo, declared the Games open, and the oath was taken jointly by Huh Jae, a basketball player, and Son Mi-Na, a handball player. One unusual feature of the ceremony was that as the Korean alphabet began with the letter 'G', the traditional first team, Greece, was then followed by Gabon and Ghana. A more entertaining occurrence in that march-past was the inclusion in the Thailand contingent of the reigning Miss Universe, Porntip 'Pui' Nakhirunkanok, a beautiful Thai girl, which delighted the spectators. Because the original 1920 Olympic flag had been fading away, a new one, made of Korean silk, had been presented to the IOC by the Seoul Organizing Committee and was flown for the first time on the 17 September 1988. The torch was carried for part of the distance on the track by 76-year-old Sohn Kee-Chung (better known as Kitei Son), the 1936 marathon champion – a Korean who had been forced to run for Japan, the occupying power at the time. He passed it to the final runner, a female athlete Lim Chun-Ae. The torch was raised to the top of the cauldron tower, and the flame was lit by three representatives of Science, Art and Sport (whose names were Ching Sun-Man, Kim Won-Tuk and Sohn Mi-Chung). It is feared that some of the pigeons which had been released during part of the ceremony, and had perched on the cauldron, were caught in the rush of flame.

The athlete who gained most attention at these Games was undoubtedly the Canadian sprinter Ben Johnson, initially for the best of reasons and then for the worst. Having looked somewhat out of form in the preliminary rounds of the 100m, he blasted away in the final to destroy a talented field, including arch-rival Carl Lewis, and record an almost unbelievable world record of 9.79 sec. Three days later it was revealed that he had failed a drug test and was disqualified, with Lewis moving up to the gold medal with a very respectable 9.92sec. Another nine competitors, from weightlifting (four), modern pentathlon (two), judo, wrestling and shooting were disqualified for drug-related offences. Although

African men won everything on the track over 400m, the outstanding athlete at the Games was a woman, Florence Griffith Joyner (USA), wife of the 1984 triple jump winner, who won three golds and a silver in the sprints and relays, running a total of 11 races. Her sister-in-law, Jackie Joyner-Kersee won the heptathlon, as expected, and the long jump. Continuing the Olympic tradition of successful families, Viktor Bryzgin (4x100m) and his wife Olga Bryzgina (400m, 4x400m) both won gold medals. In rowing Carmine and Giuseppe Abbagnale (ITA) retained their coxed pair title from 1984, and a third brother, Agostino, was a member of the winning quadruple sculls crew.

The most successful competitor in Seoul was Kristin Otto (GDR), who not only won six gold medals (a record by any woman, in any sport at any Games), but also became the first swimmer to win titles at three different strokes at the same Games. America's Matt Biondi, saddled before the Games with an impossible Mark Spitz-like scenario, nevertheless ended the Games with seven medals (5g, 1s, 1b). Vladimir Salnikov (URS) became the only swimmer to regain a title eight years after winning it the first time. Greg Louganis (USA) gained the first double 'double' by a male diver when he successfully defended his two titles from Los Angeles, despite hitting his head on the board during a dive in the springboard preliminaries. Also in the pool, Anthony Nesty of Surinam became the first black competitor, and the first South American, to win a swimming gold medal by taking the 100m butterfly. Similarly Kenny Monday (USA) was the first black wrestler to win a gold medal.

A number of 'old-timers' reappeared on the Olympic scene. Fifty-two-year-old Reiner Klimke (FRG) won his sixth dressage gold medal, and his eighth medal in five Games, over a 24 year period, all records for his sport. His horse *Ahlerich* also set a record. One of Klimke's compatriots in the winning team was Ann-Kathrin Linsenhoff – remarkably her mother had been his teammate in the gold medal team of 1968. Britain's David Broome returned after three Games out as a 'professional', 28 years after he first competed. The sailing events, held at Pusan, had two of the greatest Olympians of all time. Quadruple gold medallist Paul Elvstrøm (DEN), partnered by his daughter Trine, was competing in a record-equalling eighth Games, over a 40 year span. This was matched by yachtsman Durward Knowles (BAH), a 1964 gold medallist, also in his eighth celebration over a similar span.

By winning the silver medal in women's sprint cycling, the GDR's Christa Luding (née Rothenburger) became the first competitor in

Olympic history to win medals at a Summer and Winter celebration in the same year. She had won a speed skating gold and silver at Calgary. Because of a record number of entries in boxing, two rings were used simultaneously. Not surprisingly, this caused some confusion. Also, not for the first time, the boxing competitions witnessed some 'bizarre', often home-town, decisions. One of the most scandalous decisions in Olympic boxing history occurred when Roy Jones Jr (USA) was judged to have lost his light-middleweight bout against Park Si Hun of Korea. Pointedly, the International Amateur Boxing Association awarded Jones the Val Barker Cup as the best stylist at the Games. In early 2003 Jones made further history, when, as a middleweight, he won the WBA heavyweight title. There were other disputed decisions and some of the judges were suspended. One of the Korean boxers, Byun Jong-Il, refused to leave the ring after the decision went against him in his bantamweight bout, and remained there, a solitary figure, for over an hour.

The oldest gold medallist at Seoul was Reiner Klimke (see above) aged 52yr 255days. The youngest was swimmer Krisztina Egerszegi (HUN) at 14yr 41days. The oldest female champion was hockey player Elspeth Clement (AUS) aged 32yr 103days, while the youngest male winner was Soviet cyclist Dmitri Nelyubin aged 17yr 229days. The oldest medallist at Seoul was Romanian cox Ladislau Lovrenski aged 56yr 65days. The youngest medallist was Egerszegi three days before her gold, while the youngest male medallist was Xiong Ni (CHN) with a silver in diving aged 14yr 247days. The oldest competitor was Durward Knowles (see above) in Star class yachting aged 70yr 331days, while the youngest was swimmer Nadia Cruz of Angola aged 13yr 73days. The oldest female competitor was Inoue Kikuko (JPN) in the dressage aged 63yr 297days.

Thus, despite threats, of boycotts, of North Korean terror, of student riots etc, the Games on the whole went very well. The good humour, flexibility and courtesy of the hosts overcame most minor problems. A record 52 countries won medals, and some time after the Games ended it was reported that a record profit of $288 million had been made.

Seoul 1988 Medals

	G	S	B
Soviet Union	55	31	46
GDR	37	35	30
United States	36	31	27
Korea	12	10	11
FRG	11	14	15
Hungary	11	6	6
Bulgaria	10	12	13
Romania	7	1	6
France	6	4	6
Italy	6	4	4
China	5	11	12
Great Britain	5	10	9
Kenya	5	2	2
Japan	4	3	7
Australia	3	6	5
Yugoslavia	3	4	5
Czechoslovakia	3	3	2
New Zealand	3	2	8
Canada	3	2	5
Poland	2	5	9
Norway	2	3	-
Netherlands	2	2	5
Denmark	2	1	1
Brazil	1	2	3
Finland	1	1	2
Spain	1	1	2
Turkey	1	1	-
Morocco	1	-	2
Austria	1	-	-
Portugal	1	-	-
Surinam	1	-	-
Sweden	-	4	7
Switzerland	-	2	2
Jamaica	-	2	-
Argentina	-	1	1
Chile	-	1	-
Costa Rica	-	1	-
Indonesia	-	1	-
Iran	-	1	-
Netherlands Antilles	-	1	-
Peru	-	1	-
Senegal	-	1	-
Virgin Islands	-	1	-
Belgium	-	-	2
Mexico	-	-	2
Colombia	-	-	1
Djibouti	-	-	1
Greece	-	-	1
Mongolia	-	-	1
Pakistan	-	-	1
Philippines	-	-	1
Thailand	-	-	1

ALBERTVILLE 1992

XVIth Winter Games. 8 – 23 February
Attended by representatives of 64 countries, comprising 1801 competitors of which 488 were women.

IN OCTOBER 1986 the IOC awarded the Games to Albertville, in the Savoie region of France, ahead of six other sites in six other countries. The 1968 triple gold medallist, Jean-Claude Killy, was co-president of the organising committee. With a population of less than 20,000, Albertville was the smallest place ever to host an Olympic Games. The 13 different venues were very widespread, which gave rise to complaints that 'atmosphere and spirit' were lacking when compared to previous celebrations. Nevertheless, the Games were highly successful, with a record number of competitors and participating countries. These included newcomers such as Swaziland and Ireland. The political upheavals in eastern Europe manifested themselves in various ways: there was a combined German team for the first time since 1964; Latvia, Estonia and Lithuania competed independently again after 56 years, having been incorporated into the Soviet Union in 1940; competing under the title of the Unified Team (EUN) were the National Olympic Committees (NOCs) of Russia, Belarus, Ukraine, Kazakhstan and Uzbekistan – they used the Olympic flag, and Beethoven's *Ode to Joy* for victory ceremonies. The break-up of Yugoslavia meant that Croatia and Slovenia competed separately for the first time, too.

As usual the world's media attended in force, trying to cope with the logistical problems caused by the multi-venued sports facilities. CBS paid some $243 million for the American TV rights. There was a remarkable opening ceremony with the Games declared open by François Mitterand, the President of France. The flame was lit by soccer star Michel Platini and a local child, François-Syrille Grange, and figure skater Surya Bonaly (later placed fifth) took the oath.

A record 57 events included the newly accepted sports of short-track speed skating and freestyle skiing. Overall, there were nine extra events since the previous Games, as well as demonstration sports of curling, speed skiing, and two forms of freestyle skiing not in the Games proper. Another change was that in figure skating compulsory exercises had been eliminated.

Unusually, the Alpine skiers did not produce the stars of this Games, as in the past. Italy's Alberto Tomba gained a lot of attention by becoming the first Alpinist to successfully defend a title, but no skier really dominated. Indeed, only Petra Kronberger of Austria won more than one event, and the 30 available medals in the sport were spread among 25 skiers. Surprisingly, the Swiss won only a single bronze, while female skiers from Sweden and New Zealand won the first such medals from their areas.

Nordic Skiing made a big impact, and, with good television coverage, some of the cross-country competitors became stars. The Norwegians, Vegard Ulvang and Bjørn Daehlie, got their due recognition for winning three golds and a silver each. They made good media copy too, especially Daehlie, who deliberately skied backwards over the line for his last gold medal, in the relay. But the most successful competitor at Albertville was their female equivalent, Lyubov Yegorova of the Unified Team, who won three golds and two silvers – a record total of medals in one

winter Games. That was matched by her teammate, Yelena Valbe, with four individual bronzes and a gold in the relay. The inclusion of women's biathlon events enabled Anfissa Reztsova (URS/EUN) to become the first winter Olympian to win gold medals in two separate sports – she had previously gained a gold in the 1988 cross-country relay.

Austrian ski jumpers put up a surprising challenge to the Finns, especially in the team event, and it was mainly the superb jumping of the young Toni Nieminen that won the day. Another closely fought contest involving Austria came in the 4-man bob, when their team beat Germany by a mere 2/100ths of a second after four rounds, the smallest margin of victory ever. In lugeing, the Neuner sisters, also from Austria, took first and second places, matching the feat of the French Goitschel sisters in the 1964 Alpine skiing. By winning the ice hockey the Unified Team, in effect, extended the Soviet Union's victory run to eight since first entering the Games in 1956.

Despite the new rules most of the favourites won the medals in figure skating, with Viktor Petrenko (EUN) taking his country's first individual skating gold since 1908. In speed skating both sprint titles were retained by the 1988 champions, Bonnie Blair (USA) and Uwe-Jens Mey (GER) respectively. However, the surprise here, and in the new short-track events, was the rise of Asia, whose skaters, from China, Japan and the Koreas, won 13 medals.

Toni Nieminen, the Finnish gold medallist in the 120m ski -jump individual and team events, was only 16yr 259days of age when he gained his first title, thereby becoming the youngest ever male winter Olympics champion. A member of the Unified Team, Raisa Smetanina, was the oldest ever female gold medallist as a member of the 4x5km relay team, just twelve days short of her 40th birthday. She set another record by winning medals in five consecutive Games, from 1976 to 1992. She said her secret was that she was really only ten years old – being born on 29th February. The oldest male champion was Fritz Fischer (GER) in the biathlon aged 35yr 146days, while the oldest medallist was Maurilio De Zolt (ITA) with a silver in the 50km cross-country aged 41yr 150days. The youngest medallist was Nikki Ziegelmeyer (USA) with a silver in the women's short-track speed skating relay at 16yr 149days, while the youngest competitor was figure skater Krisztina Czakó (HUN), aged 13yr 66days, whose father/coach Gyorgy had skated in the 1952 Games.

These were the last Winter Games to be held in the same year as the Summer celebration. In future the Winter Games would be held on the even-numbered years between the editions of the Summer Games.

Albertville 1992 Medals

	G	S	B
Germany	10	10	6
Unified Team	9	6	8
Norway	9	6	5
Austria	6	7	8
United States	5	4	2
Italy	4	6	4
France	3	5	1
Finland	3	1	3
Canada	2	3	2
Korea	2	1	1
Japan	1	2	4
Netherlands	1	1	2
Sweden	1	-	3
Switzerland	1	-	2
China	-	3	-
Luxembourg	-	2	-
New Zealand	-	1	-
Czechoslovakia	-	-	3
North Korea (PRK)	-	-	1
Spain	-	-	1

NB Two silvers and no bronze in Women's Giant Slalom

BARCELONA 1992

XXVth Olympic Games. 25 July – 9 August
Attended by representatives of 169 countries, comprising 9385 competitors, of which 2723 were women.

AFTER INTENSE 'POLITICKING' the 1992 Summer Games were awarded to Barcelona, Spain in October 1986. The city, the birthplace of the then President of the IOC, Juan Antonio Samaranch, had been promised the Games in 1924 but Baron de Coubertin had changed his mind and opted for Paris. Barcelona was then suggested for the 1936 celebration, but by then the spectre of civil war decided the IOC in favour of Berlin. The stadium intended for those Games, built in 1929 on Montjuic, was completely refurbished, and was the main venue. Most of the other venues were within city limits, with only football (preliminary games), rowing, canoeing and road cycling sites at any great distance. Television revenue set what was then a record with NBC paying $401 million for the American rights. As well as two new sports, baseball and badminton, being added to the official programme there were also a number of extra events. These included seven for women in judo, a women's 10km walk, a dinghy sailing competition for women, and four canoe-slalom contests. There were 26 sports and the total number of medal events was 259 (with the distribution of 815 medals in all). An outbreak of African equine plague in Spain in 1989 originally cast considerable doubt as to whether the equestrian events would be held, but it was curtailed in time. There were three demonstration sports; pelota Basque, taekwondo, and rink hockey.

Prior to the Games, as always, there were the familiar cries from media doom-mongers that the Olympics were finished, and that there was no point in holding them again. It was stated that most sports had their own world championships and thus the importance of the Olympic Games was diluted. What these critics seem never to understand is that the world's sportsmen and women still consider an Olympic medal as the pinnacle of sporting achievement. For the first time in many Olympiads not a single nation boycotted the occasion, and there were a record number of countries and competitors, which caused the IOC to discuss the need for 'quotas' to limit numbers in future Games. The Baltic states were independent again and Germany competed as one team. However, Yugoslavia was split into Bosnia-Herzegovina, Croatia and Slovenia, with competitors from Serbia and Macedonia competing as Independent Olympic Participants (IOP). South Africa returned to the Olympic fold after 32 years. In total 170 countries marched in the parade, but Afghanistan actually had no competitors. Media representatives, including the critics, outnumbered the competitors.

The Barcelona Games were a tremendous success overall – many thought it one of the best ever. The one sour note was caused by transport shortcomings for fans billeted a long way out of town. Happily, fears of terrorist activity proved to be unfounded, but security arrangements were reported to have cost $90 million. Tennis professionals were joined by others in basketball, and the US 'Dream Team', containing Earvin 'Magic' Johnson, Michael Jordan, Larry Bird and Charles Barkley, was one of the highlights of the Games. Because of their presence these sports were given greatly increased television coverage, even outside the United States. The disintegrating Soviet Union, known here as the Commonwealth of Independent States (CIS) or Unified Team (UT), made its last appearance. King Juan Carlos, an Olympic yachtsman in 1972, declared the Games open during a colourful ceremony, and the oath was taken by Luis Doreste Blanco, who later won a gold medal in the Flying Dutchman class. He had won gold in the 1984 470 class, while his brother José-Luis had won the 1988 Finn event. Incidentally the King's son, Felipe placed 6th in the Barcelona Soling, and his daughter, Christina, had been in the 1988 Tornado class. Their uncle, Constantine of Greece, had been a sailing gold medallist in 1960. The flame on the stadium pedestal was spectacularly lit by paraplegic archer Antonio Rebollo symbolically shooting an arrow at the torch tower. Recent research indicates that Spain's first Olympic champion, Lucius

Minicius, winner of the chariot race in 129 AD, was born in Barcelona, and his ghost must have been smiling as Spain gained a record number of medals, nearly doubling its total from the 16 previous Games. In all, 64 countries won a medal, another record to that time, and of these 37 won a gold.

Although the heat did affect a number of sports adversely, the overall standard was very high, with perhaps the outstanding individual performances of the Games being the 1500m freestyle of 14min 43.48sec by Kieren Perkins (AUS), and the 400m hurdles in 46.78sec by Kevin Young (USA). In the swimming pool there was a fine swansong by the Unified Team as Alexander Popov won two gold and two silver, and Yevgeni Sadovyi took three golds. The most successful competitor was their compatriot gymnast Vitali Scherbo who won six gold medals. Although he only placed 20th in the Star yacht class Hubert Raudaschl (AUT) equalled a record, of competing in eight Games, 1964-92 – he has since added another. Indonesian-born Chrisilor Hanson-Boylen (CAN), 12th in the dressage competition, set a new record for women, also in her eighth Games, and also equalled the 28yr span of competition.

The youngest gold medallist/medallist was the diver Fu Mingxia (CHN) aged 13yr 345days, while the youngest male winner was her diving teammate Sun Shuwei at 16yr 185days. The oldest gold medallist was Klaus Balkenhol (GER) in the dressage team aged 52yr 243days, with the oldest female champion Gillian Rolton (AUS) in the 3-Day Event team at 36yr 88days. The oldest medallist was the 1972 gold medallist Swedish shooter Ragnar Skanåker in his sixth Games at 58yr 48days, while the oldest female medallist was Carol Lavell (USA) in the dressage aged 49yr 118days. The youngest competitor was rowing cox Carlos Barrera of Spain aged 11yr 256days. The youngest female competitor was Hungarian swimmer Judit Kiss at 12yr 184days.

Barcelona 1992 Medals

	G	S	B
Unified Team	45	38	29
United States	37	34	37
Germany	33	21	28
China	16	22	16
Cuba	14	6	11
Spain	13	7	2
Korea	12	5	12
Hungary	11	12	7
France	8	5	16
Australia	7	9	11
Canada	7	4	7
Italy	6	5	8
Great Britain	5	3	12
Romania	4	6	8
Czechoslovakia	4	2	1
North Korea (PRK)	4	-	5
Japan	3	8	11
Bulgaria	3	7	6
Poland	3	6	10
Netherlands	2	6	7
Kenya	2	4	2
Norway	2	4	1
Turkey	2	2	2
Indonesia	2	2	1
Brazil	2	1	-
Greece	2	-	-
Sweden	1	7	4
New Zealand	1	4	5
Finland	1	2	2
Denmark	1	1	4
Morocco	1	1	1
Ireland	1	1	-
Ethiopia	1	-	2
Algeria	1	-	1
Estonia	1	-	1
Lithuania	1	-	1
Switzerland	1	-	-
Jamaica	-	3	1
Nigeria	-	3	1
Latvia	-	2	1
Austria	-	2	-
Namibia	-	2	-
South Africa	-	2	-
Belgium	-	1	2
Croatia	-	1	2
IOP	-	1	2
Iran	-	1	2
Israel	-	1	1
Chinese Taipei	-	1	-
Mexico	-	1	-
Peru	-	1	-
Slovenia	-	-	2
Mongolia	-	-	2
Argentina	-	-	1
Bahamas	-	-	1
Colombia	-	-	1
Ghana	-	-	1
Malaysia	-	-	1
Pakistan	-	-	1
Philippines	-	-	1
Puerto Rico	-	-	1
Qatar	-	-	1
Surinam	-	-	1
Thailand	-	-	1

LILLEHAMMER 1994

XVIIth Winter Games. 12 – 27 February
Attended by representatives of 67 countries, comprising 1738 competitors, of which 522 were women.

IT WAS DURING the 1988 Olympic Games at Seoul, in September 1988, that the IOC decided to award these Games to Lillehammer, a town of 23,000 people some 180km *111 miles* north of Oslo. Three other cities had made bids but the Norwegian town, which had lost out to Albertville in the 1992 vote, won the IOC's approval this time. This was the first winter Games not held in the same year as a summer celebration. Lillehammer held one of the most successful Games, summer or winter, of all time, with excellent weather, eye-catching facilities, firm and deep snow, good organisation, and enthusiastic but non-chauvinistic spectators. The only adverse items were extremely cold temperatures, often below minus 20 degrees C, and the high cost of food and drink.

A spectacular opening ceremony, embodying traditional themes such as the mythical Vetter people, involved actress Liv Ullmann and Kon-Tiki anthropologist Thor Heyerdahl. The Games were officially opened by King Harald V, himself a former Olympian. The torch was brought into the stadium by Stein Gruben, who leaped from the ski jump before handing it to Catherine Nottingnes. She, in turn, passed it to Crown Prince Haakon, who lit the flame. The oath was taken by triple gold medallist skier Vegard Ulvang. There was a minute's silence for the plight of Sarajevo – a former Olympic site.

The record number of countries, including 14 first-timers, was boosted by the break-up of the former Soviet Union, and led to a then record 22 countries winning medals. In ice hockey and figure skating, professionals were allowed to compete. In the latter, stricter rules were in force governing skimpy clothing, and there were a number of controversial judging decisions which drew strong criticisms. Prior to the Games, excessive media interest had been generated by the vicious attack on US skater Nancy Kerrigan, and the alleged involvement of her teammate Tonya Harding.

A reported 83% sale of event tickets was evidenced by enormous crowds, particularly at the Nordic skiing, despite intense cold. There were a number of new events including aerials in the freestyle skiing, and men's 500m and women's 1000m in the short-track speed skating. A reported $295 million was paid by CBS for the American television rights. After the Games it was announced that a profit of $63.5 million had been made.

The most successful competitor at Lillehammer was Manuela di Centa (ITA) who won five medals (2g, 2s, 1b) in cross-country skiing, equalling a single Games best ever total. However, fellow Nordic skier Lyubov Yegorova (RUS) won 3g and 1s, thus equalling the winter Games record total of six gold medals. In bobsledding, Gustave Weder (SUI) became the only man to successfully defend the 2-man title, while Wolfgang Hoppe (GER) was the first to be a medallist in four Games. Alpine skier Vreni Schneider (SUI) was the first woman to total three gold medals in her sport, as well as setting an all-time record of five medals. Alberto Tomba (ITA) uniquely made it medals at three consecutive Games in Alpine skiing, which sport also featured some very small margins of victory. Remarkably, for the first time ever, no Alpine nation gained a medal in the men's downhill race.

American speed skaters, Bonnie Blair, with a record third consecutive 500m title, and Dan Jansen, a very popular emotional winner after a series of disasters in the previous three Games, could not take the spotlight away from Norway's Johann Olav Koss. He won three gold medals, all in world record times. The ice hockey competition witnessed shock bad results by the United States and, even more surprisingly, Russia, and resulted in the first win by Sweden.

The youngest ever gold medallist at a winter Games was Kim Yoon-Mi (KOR), in the short-track skating women's relay, aged 13yr 83days. She was also the youngest ever female Olympic champion in either winter or summer Games. The youngest male gold medallist/medallist at these Games was Maurizio Carnino (ITA) in the short-track relay aged 18yr 356days. The winner of the women's figure skating, Oksana Baiul (UKR) was the youngest, at 16yr 101days, to win that title since Sonja Henie (NOR) in 1928. The oldest gold medallist/medallist was Maurilio De Zolt (ITA) in the Nordic relay aged 43yr 150days, competing in his fifth Games. The oldest female medallist was Marja-Liisa Kirvesniemi (FIN) at 38yr 167days, in her record -equalling sixth Games.

Lillehammer was also the scene for the greatest sibling performance in a winter Games, by the four Huber brothers of Italy. Wilfried and Norbert won gold and silver, separately in the luge pairs; Gunther got a bronze in the 2-man bob; and Arnold placed fourth in the luge singles.

Lillehammer 1994 Medals

	G	S	B
Russia	11	8	4
Norway	10	11	5
Germany	9	7	8
Italy	7	5	8
United States	6	5	2
Korea	4	1	1
Canada	3	6	4
Switzerland	3	4	2
Austria	2	3	4
Sweden	2	1	-
Japan	1	2	2
Kazakstan	1	2	-
Ukraine	1	-	1
Uzbekistan	1	-	-
Belarus	-	2	-

Finland	-	1	5
France	-	1	4
Netherlands	-	1	3
China	-	1	2
Slovenia	-	-	3
Great Britain	-	-	2
Australia	-	-	1

ATLANTA 1996

XXVIth Olympic Games. 19 July – 4 August
*Attended by representatives of 197 countries, comprising
10327 competitors, of which 3510 were women.*

THE 1996 GAMES celebrated the 100th anniversary of the rebirth of the Modern Olympics, and Athens was thought by many to be the obvious venue. The somewhat surprising decision, in September 1990, was in favour of Atlanta. It was immediately suggested that many in the IOC were swayed by the financial support that the city would receive from American TV and other corporate sponsors.(American TV rights were sold for a record $456 million). In the event there was much criticism of the chauvinistic coverage by NBC, with the excessive emphasis on American performances reaching ludicrous levels. However, it was reported that the television company received some $700 million in advertising revenue for the Games period. It was expected that Atlanta would provide the model of top-flight organisation and excellent technology – but it didn't. There was much criticism of the extreme commercialisation and of the organisational failures, particularly in the field of transportation. The cost of hotels and the high price of tickets was another area of foreign concern. On the plus side was the undoubted goodwill and friendliness of the city's inhabitants, and the generally good, albeit hot and humid, weather. Also, it was one of the most centralized Games of recent years with most of the sports held within the periphery of the city, although sailing was held on the Georgia coast at Savannah. Although cut-backs to the number of sports and events in the Games have been mooted for years, there were a record 29 sports and 271 events. Newcomers included softball, beach volleyball, mountain bike racing, and soccer for women. However, it had been agreed that demonstration sports would no longer be held as part of this and future Games. Other changes included the holding of the modern pentathlon on only one day, and the replacement of the Flying Dutchman 2-man yachting class by a single-handed Laser class. Many new, excellent, facilities were built, including an 85,000 seat stadium and a remarkable equestrian centre.

The Games were officially opened by President William Jefferson Clinton, and the overlong opening ceremony witnessed, for the first time, a full turnout of all 197 countries then affiliated to the Olympic movement. New countries, in addition to those coming from the breakup of the former Soviet Union and Czechoslovakia, included Burundi, Guinea-Bissau, Nauru and Palestine. Other debuts included the first female competitor ever from Iran, in the shooting events. Entries exceeded 10,000 for the first time, and there were over 17,000 representatives of the world media. The American team numbered 697, the largest ever national contingent since the enormous French team (884) at Paris in 1900.

An unusual scenario for the end of the traditional Olympic torch run had representatives of, white and black, male and female, and current and first Olympic hosts. Thus, in the last few changeovers, Al Oerter (four-time champion) passed to Evander Holyfield (bronze 1984), he was joined by Paraskevi Patoulidou (1992 women's 100mH gold for Greece), and then the torch was handed to Janet Evans (four-time swimming gold medallist), who took it up the stairs in the stadium. There she gave it to the one-time boxing champion, Muhammad Ali, sadly a shadow of his former self, who finally lit the stadium flame, an exceptionally moving moment. The oath, on behalf of all the competitors, was taken by American basketball player Teresa Edwards.

In all, 79 countries won medals, of which a record 53 won gold, including the first ever medal (a gold) for Hong Kong, in board sailing, on what was thought to be its last appearance as a separate entity on the Olympic stage. The most successful competitor was Amy Van Dyken (USA), who won four gold medals in swimming, while Alexei Nemov of Russia won six gymnastic medals (2g, 1s, 3b). Over 32,000 packed the gymnastics hall to see injured US gymnast Kerri Strug complete her final vault to guarantee the hosts the team gold medal. In general there were excellent attendances at all venues, with an unprecedented 8.6 million tickets sold for the 17 days competitions. In the athletics stadium, later to be converted for baseball, Michael Johnson set an astounding time of 19.32sec for 200m, while teammate Carl Lewis won his fourth consecutive long jump title to take his career total to nine Olympic golds. The star of the swimming pool was the Irishwoman Michelle Smith, who was not only her country's first ever swimming finalist, but won three gold medals and a bronze. She was the target of much innuendo about drug-taking, especially from some of the US swimming team and American press. In rowing Britain's Steve Redgrave took his fourth gold medal in as many Games; France's Jeannie Longo won the cycling women's road race, improving on her Barcelona silver, at the age of 37yr; and yachtsman Hubert Raudaschl of land-locked Austria competed in a record breaking, for any sport, ninth Olympic Games. The first Australian Aboriginal athlete to gain a gold medal was Nova Peris-Kneebone in the winning Australian women's hockey team. Primarily a sprinter she was in the athletics team in 2000. Appallingly, halfway through the Games a bomb went off in Centennial Park, a popular place for fans and general public alike, which thankfully resulted only in two deaths, although over 100 others were injured. This happened despite an enormous outlay on security, which involved some 30,000 operatives, yet another record.

The youngest gold medallist was swimmer Amanda Beard (USA) at 14yr 269days as a member of the winning medley relay squad. She was the youngest medallist three days earlier when she took silver in the 100m breaststroke. The youngest male champion was Michal Martikan (SVK) aged 17yr 70days winning the C1 slalom event, while individual pursuit cyclist Alexei Markov (RUS) won a bronze just eight days younger. The oldest gold medallist and medallist at Atlanta was Klaus Balkenhol (GER) taking gold in the dressage team event aged 56yr 235days. The oldest female champion was Jeannie Longo (FRA) aged 37yr 264days when she won the cycling road race. Softball player Jocelyn Lester (AUS) was the oldest female medallist at 38yr 130days. The oldest competitor at Atlanta was Faustino Puccini (ITA) in the dressage event aged 63yr 267days.

Atlanta 1996 Medals

	G	S	B	Total
United States	44	32	25	101
Germany	20	18	27	65
Russia	26	21	16	63
China	16	22	12	50
Australia	9	9	23	41
France	15	7	15	37
Italy	13	10	12	35
Korea	7	15	5	27
Cuba	9	8	8	25
Ukraine	9	2	12	23
Canada	3	11	8	22
Hungary	7	4	10	21
Romania	4	7	9	20
Netherlands	4	5	10	19
Poland	7	5	5	17
Spain	5	6	6	17
Bulgaria	3	7	5	15
Brazil	3	3	9	15
Great Britain	1	8	6	15
Belarus	1	6	8	15
Japan	3	6	5	14
Czech Republic	4	3	4	11
Kazakhstan	3	4	4	11
Greece	4	4	-	8
Sweden	2	4	2	8
Kenya	1	4	3	8
Switzerland	4	3	-	7
Norway	2	2	3	7
Denmark	4	1	1	6
Turkey	4	1	1	6
New Zealand	3	2	1	6
Belgium	2	2	2	6
Nigeria	2	1	3	6
Jamaica	1	3	2	6
South Africa	3	1	1	5
North Korea	2	1	2	5
Ireland	3	-	1	4
Finland	1	2	1	4
Indonesia	1	1	2	4
Yugoslavia	1	1	2	4
Algeria	2	-	1	3
Ethiopia	2	-	1	3
Iran	1	1	1	3
Slovakia	1	1	1	3
Argentina	-	2	1	3
Austria	-	1	2	3
Armenia	1	1	-	2
Croatia	1	1	-	2
Portugal	1	-	1	2
Thailand	1	-	1	2
Namibia	-	2	-	2
Slovenia	-	2	-	2
Malaysia	-	1	1	2
Moldova	-	1	1	2
Uzbekistan	-	1	1	2
Georgia	-	-	2	2
Morocco	-	-	2	2
Trinidad & Tobago	-	-	2	2
Burundi	1	-	-	1
Costa Rica	1	-	-	1
Ecuador	1	-	-	1
Hong Kong	1	-	-	1
Syria	1	-	-	1
Azerbaijan	-	1	-	1
Bahamas	-	1	-	1
Latvia	-	1	-	1
Philippines	-	1	-	1
Taiwan	-	1	-	1
Tonga	-	1	-	1
Zambia	-	1	-	1
India	-	-	1	1
Israel	-	-	1	1
Lithuania	-	-	1	1
Mexico	-	-	1	1
Mongolia	-	-	1	1
Mozambique	-	-	1	1
Puerto Rico	-	-	1	1
Tunisia	-	-	1	1
Uganda	-	-	1	1

NAGANO 1998

XVIIIth Winter Games. 7 – 22 February
Attended by representatives of 72 countries, comprising 2180 competitors, of which 789 were women

NAGANO IN JAPAN was awarded these Games

in 1991 winning the IOC vote against Val d'Aosta (Italy), Jaca (Spain), Ostersund (Sweden), and Salt Lake City (USA). It was the most southerly venue ever for a Winter games. In 1994 CBS paid a record $375 million for the US TV rights, while the EBU paid another record $72 million for the European rights. Curling and women's ice hockey brought the number of events to a record 68. There were a record number of competitors from a record number of countries. Winter Games debuts were made by Kenya, Uruguay and Venezuela. The 10,300 media representatives was yet another record for a Winter celebration. Curling, snowboarding and women's ice hockey made their Olympic debuts.

The Games were officially opened by Emperor Akihito, whose father had done the honours at Sapporo in 1972. Part of the opening ceremony consisted of a multi continental concert, via TV satellite, with Beethoven's *9th Symphony Ode to Joy* conducted by the renowned Seiji Ozawa. The Olympic flame was lit by Midori Ito, the 1992 figure skating silver medallist, after the torch had been run up the steps to the cauldron by Hiromi Suzuki, the women's world marathon champion. The oath on behalf of the competitors was taken by Kenji Ogiwara, who had won gold in the 1992 Nordic Combination.

Bad weather caused serious disruption to the Alpine skiing events – the programme lost five days of competition and the organisers had to schedule an unprecedented three events for the same day. The weather also caused severe transportation problems. Many competitors were badly affected by a 'flu' epidemic. Nevertheless there was a very high standard of competition. In Alpine skiing Katja Seizinger (GER) was the most successful with two gold medals and a bronze, while the biggest surprise was the poor showing of the Swiss skiers. The Austrian, Hermann Maier, suffered a bad fall in the downhill race, but returned to win popular golds in the giant slalom and the super giant slalom. In the Nordic events Larissa Lazutina (RUS) became the most bemedalled competitor at the Games with three golds, one silver and a bronze, her total of five equalling the record for medals at a single Winter games. Even more of a record breaker was Norway's Bjørn Daehlie, whose three golds and a silver, raised his total medal hauls to a record eight golds and 12 medals overall, 1992-1998.

The youngest gold medallist/medallist at Nagano was Tara Lipinski (USA) who won the women's figure skating aged 15yr 255days, the youngest ever to win that title, and the youngest ever to win an individual gold medal at the winter Games. The youngest male champion, and medallist, was Kim Dong-Sung (KOR) who took the 1000m short

track speed skating event aged eight days past his 18th birthday. The oldest gold medallist was Patrik Loertscher, a member of the Swiss curling team, at 37yr 333days, while the oldest female champion was Jan Betker of the winning Canadian curling team aged 37yr 211days. A member of the Danish silver medal women's curling team, Jane Bidstrup, was 42 years 178days old, while Paul Savage (CAN) also won a silver in the men's curling at 50yr 235days. Both Bidstrup and Savage are the oldest ever medallists, respectively, in Winter Games history.

Perhaps the most startling of upsets was the failure of the teams from the United States or Canada, which included the legendary Wayne Gretzky, to win medals in men's ice hockey. An agreement had been reached to allow players from the professional National Hockey League in Canada and America to attend. The NHL suspended its season to allow players to compete for their national teams, and 125 such players were present in nine of the teams. In snowboarding there was a minor furore when the winner of the men's slalom event, Ross Rebagliati of Canada, was initially disqualified after a doping test. After an appeal he was reinstated.

Nagano 1998 Medals

	G	S	B	Total
Germany	12	9	8	29
Norway	10	10	5	25
Russia	9	6	3	18
Austria	3	5	9	17
Canada	6	5	4	15
United States	6	3	4	13
Finland	2	4	6	12
Netherlands	5	4	2	11
Japan	5	1	4	10
Italy	2	6	2	10
France	2	1	5	8
China	-	6	2	8
Switzerland	2	2	3	7
Korea	3	1	2	6
Czech Republic	1	1	1	3
Sweden	-	2	1	3
Belarus	-	-	2	2
Kazakstan	-	-	2	2
Bulgaria	1	-	-	1
Denmark	-	1	-	1
Ukraine	-	1	-	1
Australia	-	-	1	1
Belgium	-	-	1	1
Great Britain	-	-	1	1

SYDNEY 2000

XXVIIth Olympic Games. 15 September – 1 October
*Attended by representatives of 199 countries, comprising
10,647 competitors, of which 4068 were women.*

IN 1994, SYDNEY, Australia was awarded the
first Games of the second millenium. It beat bids
from Beijing, Brasilia, Istanbul, Manchester,
and, tentatively, Berlin. There were 28 sports on
the programme, including, new to the Games,
taekwondo (with four classes each for men
and women), the triathlon, trampolining and
synchronized diving. Additionally, for the first time,
there were women's events in modern pentathlon,
weightlifting and water polo. In all there was a
record total of 300 medal events, including 23 new
events for women. It was announced in August
1995 that NBC had paid a staggering $1.27 billion
for the US TV rights for Sydney ($705 million) and
for the Winter Games of 2002.

Records were set for the number of countries
and number of competitors, and there were some
15,000 accredited representatives of the world's
media. The opening ceremony was watched by an
estimated 115,000 spectators in the stadium – well
over the stated capacity of 110,000, itself a record for
an Olympic stadium – and an estimated television
audience of 3.7 billion people worldwide. The official
opening was by Sir William Deane, the Governor-
general of Australia, and the competitor's oath was
taken by Rechelle Hawkes, a double gold medallist in
hockey who won another in Sydney. After the longest
torch relay ever, 51 184km *31,811 miles* involving
over 11,000 runners, the Olympic flame in the
stadium was lit, by Cathy Freeman, later to win the
400m. In a moving tribute to women's participation
in the Olympics, six former Australian Olympic stars,
Betty Cuthbert, Raelene Boyle, Dawn Fraser, Shirley
de la Hunty, Shane Gould and Debbie Flintoff-
King, were the last carriers, on the track, prior to
the torch being handed to Freeman. The march past
of countries indicated that Palau, Palestine and the
Federated States of Micronesia were making their
debuts at the Games, while East Timor competed
as an IOP (Independent Olympic Participant). The
two Koreas, North and South, marched under one
flag, but competed separately.

The Games at Sydney were praised by all and sundry
as the best there have ever been, although there were
a number of minor glitches, mostly overcome by the
good nature of the 47,000 volunteer helpers. There
was an error with one of the illustrations on the
medals, with a depiction of the Colosseum (Roman),
instead of something Greek, as intended. At the
opening ceremony, which was overly long, there was
a heart-stopping moment or two when the Olympic
flame cauldron refused to move as it was supposed to.
Strong winds affected archery, athletics and rowing,
and much media coverage was given to the possibility
of sharks attacking the competitors in the swimming
section of the triathlon, held in Sydney harbour –
they didn't! Unfortunately, as is becoming common,
there were a number of drug-related disqualifications,
particularly in weightlifting and wrestling. Prior to
the Games, it was announced that in addition to the
normal drug tests, there would also be testing for
EPO (Erythropoietin), the 'endurance' drug.

The most successful competitors were swimmers
Inge de Bruijn (NED) and Ian Thorpe (AUS) with
three gold medals and a silver, a haul equalled by
Leontien Zijlaard (NED) in cycling. However, it
should be noted that the latter's medals were all won
in individual events. The greatest number of medals
was won by Russia's Alexei Nemov with a total of
six (2g,1s,3b). Arguably the most popular winner
at Sydney was Cathy Freeman, who won the 400m
on the track in front of an officially stated Olympic
stadium record crowd of 112,524.

The youngest gold medallist at Sydney was Xue Sang
of China in the women's synchronized diving event
aged 15yr 286days, while the oldest champion was
the Swedish-born American sailor, Magnus Liljedahl,
in the Star class at 46yr 119days. The youngest male
gold medallist was Australian swimmer Ian Thorpe,
who won two gold medals aged 17yr 339days; while
the oldest female champion was Ellina Zvereva of
Belarus, who won the discus aged 39yr 316days.
The oldest competitor in Sydney was Francois Latil
of Vanuatu, in archery aged 62yr 98days, while the
youngest was Fatema Gerashi of Bahrein, a 12-year-
old swimmer. Probably, the oldest spectator at these
Games was an 103-year-old American, Haig Prieste,
who had won a bronze medal in the 1920 diving
competitions.

At the end of the Games, some 80 countries had
won a medal, of which 51 had won a gold. However,
it was one of the also-rans, or to be exact also-swims,
who got the most attention from media. Eric 'the Eel'
Moussambani, from Equatorial Africa, won the first
heat of the 100m freestyle in the slowest time ever
recorded for the distance in the Olympics. The other
two competitors in his heat had been disqualified for
anticipating the gun, and there was serious concern
that not only would he not finish, but that he might
drown. To vociferous support from the crowd he
made it, and overnight became famous, or notorious,
worldwide. It was reported that 93% of all available
tickets, covering all sports, had been sold.

Sydney 2000 Medals

	G	S	B	Total
United States	40	24	33	97
Russia	32	28	28	88
China	28	16	15	59
Australia	16	25	17	58
Germany	13	17	26	56
France	13	14	11	38
Italy	13	8	13	34
Cuba	11	11	7	29
Great Britain	11	10	7	28
Korea	8	10	10	28
Romania	11	6	9	26
Netherlands	12	9	4	25
Ukraine	3	10	10	23
Japan	5	8	5	18
Hungary	8	6	3	17
Belarus	3	3	11	17
Poland	6	5	3	14
Canada	3	3	8	14
Bulgaria	5	6	2	13
Greece	4	6	3	13
Sweden	4	5	3	12
Brazil	-	6	6	12
Spain	3	3	5	11
Norway	4	3	3	10
Switzerland	1	6	2	9
Ethiopia	4	1	3	8
Czech Republic	2	3	3	8
Kazakstan	3	4	-	7
Kenya	2	3	2	7
Jamaica	-	4	3	7
Denmark	2	3	1	6
Indonesia	1	3	2	6
Mexico	1	2	3	6
Georgia	-	-	6	6
Turkey	3	-	2	5
Lithuania	2	-	3	5
Slovakia	1	3	1	5
Algeria	1	1	3	5
Belgium	-	2	3	5
South Africa	-	2	3	5
Morocco	-	1	4	5
Taiwan	-	1	4	5
Iran	3	-	1	4
Finland	2	1	1	4
Uzbekistan	1	1	2	4
New Zealand	1	-	3	4
Argentina	-	2	2	4
North Korea (PRK)	-	1	3	4
Austria	2	1	-	3
Azerbaijan	2	-	1	3
Latvia	1	1	1	3
Yugoslavia	1	1	1	3
Estonia	1	-	2	3
Thailand	1	-	2	3
Nigeria	-	3	-	3
Slovenia	2	-	-	2
Bahamas	1	1	-	2
Croatia	1	-	1	2
Moldova	-	1	1	2
Saudia Arabia	-	1	1	2
Trinidad/Tobago	-	1	1	2
Costa Rica	-	-	2	2
Portugal	-	-	2	2
Cameroon	1	-	-	1
Colombia	1	-	-	1
Mozambique	1	-	-	1
Ireland	-	1	-	1
Uruguay	-	1	-	1
Vietnam	-	1	-	1
Armenia	-	-	1	1
Barbados	-	-	1	1
Chile	-	-	1	1
Iceland	-	-	1	1
India	-	-	1	1
Israel	-	-	1	1
Kirghizstan	-	-	1	1
Kuwait	-	-	1	1
Macedonia	-	-	1	1
Qatar	-	-	1	1
Sri Lanka	-	-	1	1

SALT LAKE CITY 2002

XIXth Winter Game.– 9-24 February
Attended by representatives of 77 countries, comprising 2399 competitors, of which 886 were women.

THERE WERE NINE original applicants. After four previous bids, the first in 1966 for the 1972 Games, Salt Lake City was finally chosen by the IOC in June 1995. At the end of 1998 there was a scandal about several IOC members having taken bribes relating to the selection of various Games venues. Salt Lake City one was of the places involved, and a number of local and international officials resigned. The city was the largest to host the Winter Games, its population being over a million. Despite the oft stated desire of the IOC to scale down the Games, there were ten events added, resulting in a record total of 78 events contested. Despite the fact that Puerto Rico didn't actually compete after marching in the opening ceremony, there were a record number of countries, of which there were Winter Games debuts by five countries; Cameroon, Hong Kong (China), Nepal, Tadjikistan, and Thailand. Participation figures, male, female and total, were also records for a Winter Games. The official opening was by President George W Bush, and the oath on behalf of the competitors was taken by a third generation Olympian, Jim Shea, who later won the skeleton sled event. Uniquely, the Olympic flag was brought in by a multi-national, multi-cultural group who represented all the continents, and included Jean-Claude Killy (FRA), Lech Walensa (POL), Archbishop Desmond Tutu (RSA), Jean-Michael Cousteau (FRA), John Glenn (USA), Cathy Freeman (AUS), Steven Spielberg

(USA), and Fazuyoshi Funaki (JPN). The ceremony was watched by a TV audience estimated at 3.5 billion, and there were over 8000 media representatives from all over the world reporting the occasion.

The altitude of Salt Lake City made it one of the highest places ever to hold the Games, and the Utah Olympic indoor ice oval at 1424m *4675ft*, and of a highly technical design, guaranteed Olympic and/or world records in every speed skating event. After the terrorist attack in New York in the previous September, security was a prime concern, with some $310 million being expended on the operation. There were some transportation problems for fans, and the weather caused the postponement of a few events. As has become almost the norm for major sports occasions, there were a number of drug abuse disqualifications, and there were complaints about poor standards of judging, particularly in the pairs skating final. This latter, in which a French judge was reportedly pressured by her federation into voting for the Russian pair over the Canadians, caused the governing body of the sport to decide on a new format of judging panels in future.

The most successful competitor was Ole Einar Bjørndalen of Norway, who won four gold medals in the biathlon, while the best by a woman was Janica Kostelic of Croatia who won three golds and a silver in Alpine skiing. In the luge, Georg Hackl of Germany became the first Winter Olympian to win medals in five consecutive Games. The youngest gold medallist was Gi-Hyun Ko (KOR) who won the women's 1500m short track speed skating aged 15yr 278days. She was also the youngest female medallist. The youngest male winner was Stephan Hocke (GER) in the 120m ski jumping team at 18yr 121days, while Veli-Metti Lindström (FIN) was in the second placed team when 26 days younger. The oldest gold medallists was Christoph Langen in the German 2-man bob aged 39yr 327days, the oldest female champion was Danielle Goyette of the victorious Canadian ice hockey team at 36yr 22days. The oldest male medallist was Ken Trainberg of the silver medal Canadian curling squad aged 45yr 209days, while his female equivalent was his teammate Cheryl Noble in the bronze curling team at 45yr 135days. Vonetta Flowers (USA), in the two-women bobsled event, became the first black gold medallist in a Winter Games, and Jarome Iginla was the first black male to win gold as a member of the winning Canadian ice hockey team.

Salt Lake City 2002 Medals

	G	S	B	Total
Germany	12	16	8	36
United States	10	13	11	34
Norway	13	5	7	25
Canada	7	3	7	17
Austria	3	4	10	17
Russia	5	4	4	13
Italy	4	4	5	13
France	4	5	2	11
Switzerland	3	2	6	11
Netherlands	3	5	-	8
China	2	2	4	8
Finland	4	2	1	7
Sweden	-	2	5	7
Croatia	3	1	-	4
Korea	2	2	-	4
Czech Republic	1	2	-	3
Estonia	1	1	1	3
Bulgaria	-	1	2	3
Australia	2	-	-	2
Great Britain	1	-	1	2
Japan	-	1	1	2
Poland	-	1	1	2
Belarus	-	-	1	1
Slovenia	-	-	1	1

ATHENS 2004

XXVIIIth Olympic Games. 13 – 29 August
Attended by representatives of 201 countries, comprising 10,558 competitors, of which 4302 were women.

THERE WAS PRELIMINARY interest shown by 14 cities around the world, but in September 1997 the IOC decided on Athens, the site of the inaugural modern Games in 1896. However, construction work did not start until 2000 and with two years to go serious concerns were expressed as to the ability of the city to be ready in time, with suggestions that the Games be transferred elsewhere. In addition to an ongoing pollution problem, transport, construction and accommodation shortfalls were just some of the sectors worrying the IOC hierarchy. Finally, the organisation committee was taken over by Gianna Angelopoulos-Daskalaki and things started to improve drastically. The cost of the Games was put at $12 million, of which $1.5 million was allocated for security purposes. There had been a strong move in 2002, by the IOC, to remove baseball, softball and modern pentathlon from the Games programme, but, though the idea was strongly supported by the new President, Jacques Rogge, it was defeated, and the sports remain on the roster. However, there were a number of minor changes to other sports. These included wrestling events for women, and the introduction of further 50m swimming events. Despite the long-term ongoing discussions to reduce the size of the Games, the total of events was a record 301 in the 29 sports held. There was a new record of 201 countries competing and a record total of women. The number of media representatives, 21,500, also reached a new high.

Two of the host country's top athletes were involved in a missed drugs tests scandal, which created a tremendous furore, following which they were withdrawn from the Games. There was a spectacular 3½ hour opening ceremony, consisting of a mixture of tradition and modern technology. The parade of countries was slightly confusing to most foreign observers, as they entered alphabetically, but according to the Greek (cyrillic) alphabet. Thus St Lucia was first, and Hong Kong the penultimate before the host. There was an estimated TV audience for the Games of 3.9 billion. The official opening was by Greek President Kostic Stephanopoulos, with the oath taken by Zoe Dimoschaki, and the flame lit by Nikolaos Kaklamanakis, the Sydney windsurfing gold medallist. The flame had been on a 78,000 km 48,467 miles journey, taking 78 days and involving 11,000 torch bearers in five continents. The men's and women's shot were held at Olympia itself. Kristin Heaston (USA) became the first athlete to compete there for some 1611 years when she took the first putt in the women's event, and was also the first female contestant ever allowed on the hallowed site. During the Games there were 2800 drug tests, with 24 cases of doping violations.

The most successful competitor was swimmer Michael Phelps (USA) with six gold medals and two bronzes, swimming a remarkable 17 races in seven days. The youngest gold medallist was his swimming teammate, Dana Vollmer in the 4x200m relay aged 16yr 279days, while the youngest male winner was Ilias Iliadis (GRE) taking the 81kg class in judo at 17 yr 281days. The oldest gold medallist and medallist was Jean Teulere (FRA) in the 3-day equestrian team aged 50yr 173days, with the oldest female champion Ulla Salzgeber (GER) in the dressage team at 46yr 16days. The youngest medallist was Daniel Gyurta (HUN) with a silver in the 200m breaststroke at 15yr 106days, with the youngest female being Yue Guo (CHN) in the table tennis doubles aged 16yr 33days.

The oldest competitor was Canadian show jumper Ian Millar, at 57yr 236days, in his eighth Games over a period of 32 years, 1972-2004. The oldest woman was Annette Woodward (AUS) in the 25m pistol event, seven days past her 57th birthday. The youngest competitor was Rubab Raza (PAK) In the women's 50m freestyle aged 13yr 218days, while the youngest male was diver Nickson Bryan (MAS) at 14yr 58days. He was also probably the smallest competitor at 1.38m *4ft 6¼in* tall and 30kg *66lb* in weight. By contrast, the tallest ever Olympian, Yao Ming, played in the Chinese basketball team at 2.26m

7ft 5in. The former Jamaican sprinter, Merlene Ottey, now representing Slovenia, remarkably reached the semi-final of the 200m in her 45th year, competing in her seventh Olympic Games.

A total of 74 countries won medals, of which a record 56 won gold medals. Despite the initial problems and fears, the Games went off quite smoothly, and, thankfully, there were no security problems.

Athens 2004 Medals

	G	S	B	Total
United States	36	39	27	102
Russia	27	27	38	92
China	32	17	14	63
Australia	17	16	16	49
Germany	13	16	20	49
Japan	16	9	12	37
France	11	9	13	33
Italy	10	11	11	32
Korea	9	12	9	30
Great Britain	9	9	12	30
Cuba	9	7	11	27
Ukraine	9	5	9	23
Netherlands	4	9	9	22
Romania	8	5	6	19
Spain	3	11	5	19
Hungary	8	6	3	17
Greece	6	6	4	16
Belarus	2	6	7	15
Canada	3	6	3	12
Bulgaria	2	1	9	12
Brazil	5	2	3	10
Turkey	3	3	4	10
Poland	3	2	5	10
Thailand	3	1	4	8
Denmark	2	-	6	8
Kazakhstan	1	4	3	8
Czech Republic	1	4	3	8
Sweden	4	2	1	7
Austria	2	4	1	7
Ethiopia	2	3	2	7
Kenya	1	4	2	7
Norway	5	-	1	6
Iran	2	2	2	6
Slovakia	2	2	2	6
Argentina	2	-	4	6
South Africa	1	3	2	6
New Zealand	3	2	-	5
Taipei	2	2	1	5
Jamaica	2	1	2	5
Uzbekistan	2	1	2	5
Croatia	1	2	2	5
Egypt	1	1	3	5
Switzerland	1	1	3	5
Azerbaijan	1	-	4	5
North Korea (PKR)	-	4	1	5
Georgia	2	2	-	4
Indonesia	1	1	2	4

Latvia	-	4	-	4
Mexico	-	3	1	4
Slovenia	-	1	3	4
Morocco	2	1	-	3
Chile	2	-	1	3
Lithuania	1	2	-	3
Zimbabwe	1	1	1	3
Belgium	1	-	2	3
Portugal	-	2	1	3
Estonia	-	1	2	3
Bahamas	1	-	1	2
Israel	1	-	1	2
Finland	-	2	-	2
Serbia/Montenegro	-	2	-	2
Colombia	-	-	2	2
Nigeria	-	-	2	2
Venezuela	-	-	2	2
Cameroon	1	-	-	1
Dominican Republic	1	-	-	1
United Arab Emirates	1	-	-	1
Hong Kong	-	1	-	1
India	-	1	-	1
Paraguay	-	1	-	1
Eritrea	-	-	1	1
Mongolia	-	-	1	1
Syria	-	-	1	1
Trinidad & Tobago	-	-	1	1

TURIN 2006

XXth Winter Games. 11-26 February
Attended by representatives of 79 countries, comprising 2494 competitors, of which 954 were women.

IN JUNE 1999 the Italian city of Turin was selected as the venue for the 2006 Winter Olympics. Other places in contention had been Sion, Klagenfurt, Poprad-Tatry, Zakopane, and Helsinki. Turin was the second largest city ever to host the Winter Games, with a population of some 900,000. A spectacular opening ceremony featured world-famous singer Luciano Pavarotti performing *Nessun Dorma*, and the Olympic flag was brought into the stadium by a group of women who included film stars Sophia Loren and Susan Sarandon. Actually, a record 80 countries were represented in the march-past, with North and South Korea entering as one, but the sole representative of the US Virgin Islands did not eventually compete due to injury. Albania, Ethiopia and Madagascar made their first appearance at the Winter Olympics. Both the total number of competitors and the number of women were records. The Olympic flame covered a route of 11,400km before being delivered to what was claimed as the highest ever Olympic cauldron, at 57m tall. That flame was lit by former Olympic champion Nordic skier Stefania Belmondo, and the oath was taken by Alpine skier Giorgio Rocca. The Games were officially opened by the President of Italy, Carlo Azaglio Ciampi. It has been estimated that the cost of staging the Games was $3.6 billion, of which a large sum went towards the massive and costly security arrangements.

There were a record 84 events, with two extra each in Nordic skiing, biathlon, snowboarding and speed skating, and more countries than ever before, 26, won medals, with the first ever for Latvia and Slovakia. The USA achieved its oft-stated target of gaining more medals than Norway, but was topped by Germany. After the 2002 furore in figure skating, a new scoring system was used in Turin. Television coverage went to 200 countries and an estimated 3.2 billion viewers. Just before the Games started, twelve athletes were suspended for five days after tests showed abnormally high red blood cell counts. During the Games, however, there was only one medallist disqualified for doping. The biggest field was in the men's 15km cross country with 99 competitors. Shani Davis (USA) became the first black male to win an individual event gold medal in the Winter Olympics with his victory in the 1000m speed skating event. There was a surprise in men's ice hockey, when, for the first time ever, neither Canada, the USA nor Russia gained a medal, and, despite taking a total of 150 medals in the Winter Games since 1920, Finland won its first ever in Alpine skiing.

The most successful competitor was Hyun-Soo Ahn (KOR) with three golds and a bronze in short track speed skating, while his teammate, Sun-Yu Jin, was the most successful woman with three golds. Michael Greis (GER) also won three golds in the biathlon. However, speed skater Cindy Klassen (CAN) won a total of five medals (1g, 2s, 2b). Scott Baird became the oldest ever Winter Olympian as a member of the USA curling team, aged 54yr 293days, but did not actually play, so making the 52-year-old Venezuelan luger Werner Höger the oldest competitor at Turin. Anne Abernathy of the US Virgin Islands, already the oldest ever female competitor from 2002, was entered in the luge aged 52, but had to withdraw due to an injury suffered in training. The youngest competitor was Zhifeng Sun of China in the women's snowboarding halfpipe at 14yr 211days. The oldest gold medallist/medallist at Turin was the skip of the Canadian curling team, Russ Howard at five days past his 50th birthday, and the oldest female champion was his countrywoman Danielle Goyette in ice hockey 21 days past her 40th. The youngest gold medallist was Sun-Yu Jin (KOR) in short-track speed skating at 17yr 67days, and the male equivalent was Shaun White (USA) with the snowboard halfpipe title aged 19yr 162days. The oldest female medallist was Sandra Jenkins (CAN) taking a curling bronze at 44yr 217days. The youngest medallist in Turin was Arianna Fontana (ITA) with a short track speed skating bronze aged 15yr 283days, and the youngest male medal was won by Anssi Koivuranta (FIN) with a Nordic Combination bronze aged 17yr 228days.

Turin 2006 Medals

	G	S	B	Total
Germany	11	12	6	29
United States	9	9	7	25
Canada	7	10	1	24
Austria	9	7	7	23
Russia	8	6	8	22
Norway	2	8	9	19
Sweden	7	2	5	14
Switzerland	5	4	5	14
Korea	6	3	2	11
Italy	5	-	6	11
China	2	4	5	11
France	3	2	4	9
Netherlands	3	2	4	9
Finland	-	6	3	9
Czech Republic	1	2	1	4
Estonia	3	-	-	3
Croatia	1	2	-	3
Australia	1	-	1	2
Poland	-	1	1	2
Ukraine	-	-	2	2
Japan	1	-	-	1
Belarus	-	1	-	1
Bulgaria	-	1	-	1
Great Britain	-	1	-	1
Slovakia	-	1	-	1
Latvia	-	-	1	1

BEIJING 2008

XXIXth Olympic Games, 8-24 August

BEIJING WAS SELECTED over Paris, Osaka, Istanbul and Toronto. It is the most populous venue to host the Games, with a population of over 13 million. Cost estimates of new construction and renovations have been put at over $3.2 billion.

VANCOUVER 2010

XXIst Winter Games

CANDIDATES ORIGINALLY INCLUDED Andorra, Harbin, Jaca, and Sarajevo, but a short list was decided in 2002 which comprised; Berne, Salzburg, Vancouver and Pyeong Chang in Korea. It was eventually given to the Canadian city of Vancouver.

LONDON 2012

XXXth Olympic Games. 27 July – 12 August

THERE WERE ELEVEN cities which showed some interest in applying for these Games, Berlin, Budapest, Istanbul, London, Madrid or Seville, Moscow, New York, Paris, Rio de Janeiro, Rome, and Toronto. In 2005, to a certain amount of surprise, the winning city was London. The main stadia will be built on the eastern side of the city, and road and rail infrastructure will be improved and/or built. As always, estimates of final cost have varied widely, depending on what items are included, but the latest figures seem to suggest that it may reach £9 billion.

SOCHI 2014

XXIInd Winter Games

In July 2007, the Black Sea resort of Sochi in Rissia was chosen over Pyeongchang (Korea) and Salzburg (Austria) to host these Games. Years of campaigning and millions of dollars were spent in an unprecedented volume of lobbying by sportin g and political leaders on behalf of the various applicants.

THE FUTURE

DESPITE CONTINUING SCEPTICISM, and even downright hostility at times, from sections of the world's press, numerous cities and countries still show great interest in hosting future summer and winter celebrations of the Games.

ABBREVIATIONS

ALL MEMBER COUNTRIES, present and past, have an official Olympic three-letter abbreviation, used in results. These can be found under the entry for 'Participation, by country'.

ALPINE SKIING

SEPARATE ALPINE SKIING events were first introduced into the Games in 1948, but this style had been contested in 1936 as an Alpine combination event consisting of an aggregate of points scored in a downhill and a slalom race. Kjetil André Aamodt (NOR) has won most gold medals with four 1992-2006. Toni Sailer (AUT) in 1956 and Jean-Claude Killy (FRA) in 1968 both won a record three gold medals in the same Games. This was matched by Janica Kostelic of Croatia in 2002, when she also won a silver to become the first Alpine skier to win four medals in one Games. She won a fourth gold in 2006 to equal Aamodt's record, and she also holds the female record of six medals (4g, 2s) 2002-06. The men's record is eight medals by Aamodt 1992-2006 (4g, 2s, 2b). Alberto Tomba (ITA) was the first Alpine skier to win medals in three consecutive Games 1988-94 (Tomba's coach, Gustav Thöni, won the 1972 giant slalom). However, Deborah Compagnoni (ITA) became the first Alpine skier to win gold medals in three Games (1992-1998). There were a record 131 competitors in the 1992 giant slalom, representing a record 47 countries. Uniquely, in 1998, Lasse Kjus of Norway won two silver medals on the same day, firstly in the postponed downhill race, and then, four hours later, in the combined event. Graham Bell (GBR)

was the first Alpine skier to compete in five Olympic Games, 1984-98. In 2006 Tanja Poutiainen (FIN) won her country's 150th Winter Games medal by taking silver in the giant slalom – but it was Finland's first ever Alpine skiing medal.

The oldest gold medallist/medallist was Kjetil André Aamodt (NOR) who won the 2006 super giant slalom aged 34yr 169days, while the youngest to win a gold was Michaela Figini (SUI) aged 17yr 314days when winning the 1984 downhill. The youngest male winner was Sailer (see above) aged 20yr 73days in the 1956 slalom, and the youngest male medallist was Alfred Matt (AUT) with the 1968 slalom bronze aged 19yr 281days. The oldest female champion and medallist was Michaela Dorfmeister (AUT) winning the 2006 super giant slalom aged 32yr 271days. Incidentally, Dorfmeister was the granddaughter of 1948 downhill champion, Hedy Schlunneger. The youngest ever medallist was Gertraud 'Traudl' Hecher (AUT) aged 16yr 145days with the bronze in the 1960 downhill race.

Speeds of 145km/h *90mph* are reached by men, and 130km/h *80mph* by women, in the downhill events at the Games. However, the highest average speed recorded in an Olympic downhill race was 109.158km/h *67.827mph* by Antoine Deneriaz in 2006. The highest by a woman was 101.977km/h *63.365mph* by Katja Seizinger in the 1998 main event, although she achieved 102.403km/h *63.630mph* in the downhill segment of the combined event.

The greatest margin of victory in downhill was 4.7sec by Madeleine Berthod (FRA) in 1956, while the best in the male race was 4.1sec by Henri Oreiller (FRA) in 1948. However, Birger Ruud (NOR), the reigning Olympic ski jump champion, won the

Average speeds in Olympic downhill races since 1936

		Men			Women
Year	km/h	Winner	km/h		Winner
1936	47.599	Ruud (NOR)	39.031		Schou-Nilsen (NOR)
1948	66.034	Oreiller (FRA)	43.695		Schlunegger (SUI)
1952	57.629	Colò (ITA)	50.420		Jochum-Beiser (AUT)
1956	72.356	Sailer (AUT)	55.484		Berthod (SUI)
1960	88.429	Vuarnet (FRA)	67.426		Biebl (GER)
1964	81.297	Zimmermann (AUT)	74.496		Haas (AUT)
1968	86.808	Killy (FRA)	77.080		Pall (AUT)
1972	85.291	Russi (SUI)	78.568		Nadig (SUI)
1976	102.828	Klammer (AUT)	85.286		Mittermaier (FRG)
1980	102.677	Stock (AUT)	99.598		Moser-Pröll (AUT)
1984	104.532	Johnson (USA)	96.428		Figini (SUI)
1988	94.702	Zurbriggen (SUI)	93.836		Kiehl (FRG)
1992	99.418	Ortlieb (AUT)	88.600		Lee-Gartner (CAN)
1994	103.319	Moe (USA)	99.109		Seizinger (GER)
1998	107.532	Cretier (FRA)	101.977		Seizinger (GER)
2002	103.880	Strobl (AUT)	97.420*		Montillet (FRA)
2006	109.158	Deneriaz (FRA)	94.504		Dorfmeister (AUT)

* In downhill segment of combined event Renate Götschl (AUT) achieved 106.990 km/h

Alpine Skiing Medals (Not including Freestyle skiing)

	Men			Women			
	G	*S*	*B*	*G*	*S*	*B*	*Total*
Austria	19	18	24	11	16	13	101
Switzerland	6	11	11	10	8	7	53
France	11	6	7	4	8	7	43
United States	4	6	1	8	9	3	31
Italy	7	5	2	5	3	5	27
Germany	3	2	1	7	5	7	25
Norway	8	7	6	-	-	1	22
Sweden	2	-	3	3	2	4	14
Canada	-	-	2	4	1	3	10
FRG	-	1	-	3	4	1	9
Liechtenstein	-	1	3	2	1	2	9
Croatia	-	1	-	4	2	-	7
Slovenia	-	-	1	-	-	2	3
Luxembourg	-	2	-	-	-	-	2
Spain	1	-	-	-	-	1	2
Yugoslavia	-	1	-	-	1	-	2
Finland	-	-	-	-	1	-	1
Japan	-	1	-	-	-	-	1
New Zealand	-	-	-	-	1	-	1
Russia	-	-	-	-	1	-	1
Australia	-	-	-	-	-	1	1
Czechoslovakia	-	-	-	-	-	1	1
Soviet Union	-	-	-	-	-	1	1
	61	62[1]	61[2]	61	63[3]	59	367

[1]Two silvers in 1998 Super Giant Slalom; [2]two bronzes in 1948 Downhill; [3]Two silvers in 1964 1964 and 1992 Giant Slalom

downhill segment of the 1936 combination by 4.4sec. The smallest margin was 0.04sec in the 1994 men's race, while that for women was 0.05sec in the 1984 event. The greatest margin in slalom was 11.3sec by Cristl Cranz (GER) in the 1936 combination event, while that in the men's equivalent was 5.9sec by Franz Pfnür (GER). Since then Toni Sailer (AUT) won by 4.0sec in 1956 and Anne Heggtveit (CAN) the 1960 women's race by 3.3sec. The smallest margin was 0.02sec in the 1972 women's event, and in the men's race it was 0.06sec by Alberto Tomba (ITA) in 1988.

In the giant slalom the biggest margin was 6.2 sec by Sailer in 1956, while for women it was 2.64sec by Nancy Greene (CAN) in 1968. The smallest margin was 0.1sec (before electronic timing) by Yvonne Ruegg (SUI) in 1960, and 0.12sec by Kathy Kreiner (CAN) in 1976. The smallest for men was 0.02sec by Markus Wasmeier (GER) in 1994. The tie for silver in the 1992 women's giant slalom was the first such tie since the introduction of automatic timing.

The greatest margin in the super giant slalom was 1.30sec by Franck Piccard (FRA) in 1988, and for women it was 1.41sec by Deborah Compagnoni (ITA) in 1992. The smallest for men was 0.08sec by Markus Wasmeier (GER) in 1994, and for women it was 0.01sec by Picabo Street (USA) in 1998 – the latter being the smallest margin of victory in any Olympic Alpine skiing event.

AMERICAN FOOTBALL

A DEMONSTRATION SPORT at Los Angeles in 1932. Two teams representing the East and West of America played an exhibition which the West won 7-6.

ARCHERY

THE SPORT MADE its first appearance in the 1900 Games in Paris with six events on the programme. Some Olympic historians consider that another, live pigeon shooting, was an official event, but the majority think not, and this book follows that opinion. The contests were held in Continental style, with each archer shooting a single arrow at a time in competition order (as opposed to the British method of three arrows at each turn). The eligibility of the 1904 archery competitions is also disputed by some, particularly as only American archers took part. However, the majority of historians, and the author, accept them as Olympic events. The competitors in the 1904 women's contests were among the first women to compete in the Olympics, with only the tennis players in 1900 having a prior claim. The competitions of 1908 were accorded a much higher status than before despite only three nations taking part. The men's York Round was won by William Dod (GBR), and his remarkable sister, Charlotte, took

ARCHERY MEDALS

	Men			Women			
	G	S	B	G	S	B	Total
United States	9	6	5	4	2	3	29
Korea	3	3	1	11	4	3	25
France	6	10	6	-	-	-	22
Belgium	10	6	3	-	-	-	19
Great Britain	1	1	3	1	1	2	9
Soviet Union	-	1	1	1	2	4	9
Italy	1	1	3	-	-	-	5
Finland	1	1	1	-	-	1	4
China	-	-	-	-	4	-	4
Japan	-	2	1	-	-	-	3
Ukraine	-	-	1	-	1	1	3
Australia	1	-	1	-	-	-	2
Netherlands	1	-	1	-	-	-	2
Sweden	-	2	-	-	-	-	2
Germany	-	-	-	-	1	1	2
Poland	-	-	-	-	1	1	2
Taipei	-	1	-	-	-	1	2
Spain	1	-	-	-	-	-	1
Indonesia	-	-	-	-	1	-	1
	34[1]	34	27[2]	17	17	17	146

[1]Only a gold medal awarded in two 1920 events; [2]No bronze medals in one 1900 and six 1920 events

the silver behind Queenie Newall in the women's event. Lottie Dod, then over 36 years old, was one of the greatest sportswomen of her, or, indeed, of any generation. She had won the Wimbledon tennis singles five times, the British Ladies golf crown in 1904, and had represented England at hockey. She also excelled at skating and tobogganing. She and William were also the first brother and sister, in any sport, to win medals at the Olympic Games.

Archery was not included in the 1912 Games but, reflecting Belgium's great interest in the sport, there were ten events at Antwerp in 1920, all in the Belgian style of shooting. With only three countries present again, Hubert van Innis (BEL), now 54, brought his total medals to a record six gold and three silver. The most successful woman has been Kim Soo-Nyung (KOR) with three gold medals and a silver in 1988-92. The sport was dropped from the Games until 1972. In 1988 a team competition was introduced.

Archery appears to be a sport at which competitors can continue at the highest level until well advanced in years. Thus, the oldest gold medallist was the Rev Galen Spencer (USA) in the winning 1904 team two days past his 64th birthday. A fellow team member, Robert Williams Jr, a youngster of 63yr, was uniquely the only known Olympic gold medallist to have fought in the American Civil War – that time on the losing side. The youngest champion was Yun Young-Sooh (KOR) aged 17yr 21days in the winning 1988 women's team. The youngest male winner was Park Sung-Soo (KOR) in the 1988 team aged 18yr 135days, while the oldest female champion was Queenie Newall (GBR)

in 1908 aged 53yr 275days. The oldest ever medallist was Samuel Harding Duvall (USA) aged 68yr 194days winning a silver in the 1904 team contest, while the youngest medallist was Denise Parker (USA) with a team bronze in 1988 aged 14y 294days. The youngest male medallist was Henry Richardson (USA) with a team bronze in 1904 aged 15yr 126days. Hubert van Innis (BEL) won gold medals over a record span of 20 years (1900-20). The first paraplegic to compete in a standard Olympic event was Neroli Fairhall (NZL) who, from her wheelchair, finished 35th in the 1984 women's archery event. In 2000, the Korean women equalled their clean sweep of 1988

ATHLETICS

(See also 'Tug-of-War')

THE TRACK AND field events have been the centre-piece of every Olympic Games since 1896. From 1920 until the International Amateur Athletics Federation (IAAF) inaugurated their first world title meeting in 1983, the Olympic events were also official world championships. In the early Games quite large numbers of entries per country were allowed in an event, e.g. 12 in 1908, but in 1928 that was limited to four and in 1932 to three. After Barcelona in 1992 a suggestion was made to reduce the number to two, but has not been acted on to date. The first champion in modern Olympic history was James Connolly (USA) who won the triple jump (then called the hop, step and jump) on 6 April 1896. He also won medals in the high and long jumps, and went on to become a

OLYMPIC ATHLETICS RECORDS

(There has always been some confusion as to whether wind-assisted performances should be considered as Games records. Both are given here).

Men

100m	9.84	Donovan Bailey (CAN)	1996
200m	19.32	Michael Johnson (USA)	1996
400m	43.49	Michael Johnson (USA)	1996
800m	1:42.58	Vebjørn Rodal (NOR)	1996
1500m	3:32.07	Noah Ngeny (KEN)	2000
5000m	13:05.59	Said Aouita (MAR)	1984
10,000m	27:05.10	Kenenisa Bekele (ETH)	2004
Marathon	2:09:21	Carlos Lopes (POR)	1984
110m Hurdles	12.91	Liu Xiang (CHN)	2004
400m Hurdles	46.78	Kevin Young (USA)	1992
3000m St	8:05.51	Julius Kariuki (KEN)	1988
20km Walk	1:18:59	Robert Korzeniowski (POL)	2000
50km Walk	3:38:29	Vyacheslav Ivanenko (URS)	1988
4x100m	37.40	United States	1992
4x400m	2:55.74	United States	1992
High Jump	2.39	Charles Austin (USA)	1996
Pole Vault	5.95	Tim Mack (USA)	2004
Long Jump	8.90	Bob Beamon (USA)	1968
Triple Jump	18.09	Kenny Harrison (USA	1996
	(18.17w	*Mike Conley (USA)*	*1992)*
Shot	22.47	Ulf Timmermann (GDR)	1988
Discus	69.89	Virgilijus Alekna (LTU)	2004
Hammer	84.80	Sergei Litvinov (URS)	1988
Javelin	90.17	Jan Zelezny (TCH)	2000
Decathlon	8893	Roman Sebrle (CZE)	2004

Women

100m	10.62*	Florence Griffith Joyner (USA)	1988
	(10.54w	*Florence Griffith Joyner (USA)*	*1988)*
200m	21.34	Florence Griffith Joyner (USA)	1988
400m	48.25	Marie-José Pérec (FRA)	1996
800m	1:53.43	Nadyezda Olizarenko (URS)	1980
1500m	3:53.96	Paula Ivan (ROM)	1988
5000m	14:40.79	Gabriela Szabo (ROM)	2000
10,000m	30:17.49	Derartu Tulu (ETH)	2000
Marathon	2:23:14	Naoko Takahashi (JPN)	2000
100m Hurdles	12.37	Joanna Hayes (USA)	2004
400m Hurdles	52.77	Fania Halkia (GRE)	2004
4x100m	41.60	GDR	1980
4x400m	3:15.17	USSR	1988
20,000 Walk	1:29:05	Wang Liping (CHN)	2000
High Jump	2.06	Yelena Slesarenko (RUS)	2004
Pole Vault	4.91	Yelena Isinbayeva (RUS)	2004
Long Jump	7.40	Jackie Joyner-Kersee (USA)	1988
Triple Jump	15.33	Inessa Kravets (UKR)	1996
Shot	22.41	Ilona Slupianek (GDR)	1980
Discus	72.30	Martina Hellmann (GDR)	1988
Hammer	75.02	Olga Kuzenkova (RUS)	2004
Javelin	71.53	Osleidys Menendez (CUB)	2004
(new implement)			
Heptathlon	7291	Jackie Joyner-Kersee (USA)	1988

* In preliminary round

novelist and war correspondent. The first winner of an Olympic event was Francis Lane (USA), who won the first heat of the 100m earlier the same day. Women's events were introduced in 1928, and the first female gold medallist was Halina Konopacka (POL) in the discus. As with the men, the first winner of an Olympic women's event was Anni Holdmann (GER) who took the first heat of the 100m the day before.

YOUNGEST AND OLDEST MEDALLISTS, BY EVENT

Men

Event	Medal	Yr/Dy	Youngest Name/Country/Date	Yr/Dy	Oldest Name/Country/Date
100m	G	19-128	Reggie Walker (RSA) 1908	32-121	Linford Christie (GBR) 1992
	M	18-234	Donald Lippincott (USA) 1912	32-121	Linford Christie (GBR) 1992
200m	G	20-47	Percy Williams (CAN) 1928	29-323	Michael Johnson (USA) 1996
	M	17-287	Dwayne Evans (USA) 1976	30-170	Barney Ewell (USA) 1948
400m	G	19-135	Steve Lewis (USA) 1988	33-12	Michael Johnson (USA) 2000
	M	19-135	Steve Lewis (USA) 1988	33-12	Michael Johnson (USA) 2000
800m	G	20-237	Ted Meredith (USA) 1912	31-147	Albert Hill (GBR) 1920
	M	20-035	Earl Jones (USA) 1984	33-260	Wilson Kipketer (DEN) 2004
1500m	G	21-62	Peter Rono (KEN) 1988	31-149	Albert Hill (GBR) 1920
	M	21-62	Peter Rono (KEN) 1988	31-149	Albert Hill (GBR) 1920
5000m	G	20-321	Joseph Guillemot (FRA) 1920	36-78[1]	Miruts Yifter (ETH) 1980
	M	19-237	Fita Bayissa (ETH) 1992	36-78[1]	Miruts Yifter (ETH) 1980
10,000m	G	21-42	Brahim Boutayeb (MAR) 1988	36-73[1]	Miruts Yifter (ETH) 1980
	M	20-104	Richard Chelimo (KEN) 1992	36-73[1]	Miruts Yifter (ETH) 1980
Marathon	G	20-301	Juan Zabala (ARG) 1932	37-176	Carlos Lopes (POR) 1984
	M	19-178	Ernst Fast (SWE) 1900	40-90	Mamo Wolde (ETH) 1972
3km St	G	20-33	Matthew Birir (KEN) 1992	32-211	Kip Keino (KEN) 1972
	M	19-24	Brimin Kipruto (KEN) 2004	32-211	Kip Keino (KEN) 1972
110m H	G	20-304	Fred Kelly (USA) 1912	30-237	Mark McKoy (CAN) 1992
	M	20-304	Fred Kelly (USA) 1912	33-50	Willie Davenport (USA) 1976
400m H	G	20-329	Ed Moses (USA) 1976	29-207	Roy Cochran (USA) 1948
	M	18-325	Eddie Southern (USA) 1956	33-252	Kriss Akabusi (GBR) 1992
4x100m	G	18-118	Johnny Jones (USA) 1976	32-21	John Drummond (USA) 2000
	M	17-229	Ture Persson (SWE) 1912	33-292	Jocelyn Delecour (FRA) 1968
4x400m	G	19-100	Edgar Ablowich (USA) 1932	33-17	Michael Johnson (USA) 2000
	M	17-+	Pál Simon (HUN) 1908	33-254	Kris Akabusi (GBR) 1992
20km Walk	G	22-25	Jefferson Perez (ECU) 1996	33-110	Peter Frenkel (GDR) 1972
	M	21-253	Noel Freeman (AUS) 1960	37-71	Peter Frenkel (GDR) 1976
50km Walk	G	25-103	Norman Read (NZL) 1956	38-128	Thomas Green (GBR) 1932
	M	24-32	Denis Nizhegorodov (RUS) 2004	48-115	Tebbs Lloyd Johnson (GBR) 1948
High Jump	G	19-214	Jacek Wszola (POL) 1976	30-3	Con Leahy (GBR) 1906
	M	18-140	Valeri Brumel (URS) 1960	32-347	Javier Sotomayor (CUB) 2000
Pole Vault	G	17-360	Lee Barnes (USA) 1924	31-347	Tim Mack (USA) 2004
	M	17-360	Lee Barnes (USA) 1924	31-347	Tim Mack (USA) 2004
Long Jump	G	19-17	Randy Williams (USA) 1972	35-28	Carl Lewis (USA) 1996
	M	19-17	Randy Williams (USA) 1972	35-28	Carl Lewis (USA) 1996
Triple Jump	G	20-225	Gustaf Lindblom (SWE) 1912	34-141	Jonathan Edwards (GBR)2000
	M	20-38	Arnoldo Devonish (VEN) 1952	34-296	Viktor Saneyev (URS) 1980
Shot	G	19-167[2]	Ralph Rose (USA) 1904	32-151	Wladyslaw Komar (POL) 1972
	M	19-167[2]	Ralph Rose (USA) 1904	37-59	Denis Horgan (GBR) 1908
Discus	G	20-69	Al Oerter (USA) 1956	35-240	Ludvik Danek (TCH) 1972
	M	19-170	Ralph Rose (USA) 1904	37-46	John Powell (USA) 1984
Hammer	G	20-161	József Csermák (HUN) 1952	35-187	John Flanagan (USA) 1908
	M	19-165	Ralph Rose (USA) 1904	45-205	Matt McGrath (USA) 1924
Javelin	G	20-34	Erik Lundkvist (SWE) 1928	34-99	Jan Zelezny (CZE) 2000
	M	20-34[3]	Erik Lundkvist (SWE) 1928	38-332	József Várszegi (HUN) 1948
Decathlon	G	17-263	Bob Mathias (USA) 1948	30-102[4]	Helge Løvland (NOR) 1920
	M	17-263	Bob Mathias (USA) 1948	30-166	Chris Huffins (USA) 2000

Women

Event	Medal	Yr/Dy	Youngest Name/Country/Date	Yr/Dy	Oldest Name/Country/Date
100m	G	16-343	Elizabeth Robinson (USA) 1928	30-98	Fanny Blankers-Koen (NED) 1948
	M	16-343	Elizabeth Robinson (USA) 1928	36-78	Merlene Ottey (JAM) 1996
200m	G	18-254	Betty Cuthbert (AUS) 1956	30-102	Fanny Blankers-Koen (NED)1948
	M	17-116	Raelene Boyle (AUS) 1968	36-83	Merlene Ottey (JAM) 1996
400m	G	19-340	Monika Zehrt (GDR) 1972	30-66	Irena Szewinska (POL) 1976
	M	18-152	Christina Brehmer (GDR) 1976	30-66	Irena Szewinska (POL) 1976
800m	G	20-251	Madeline Manning (USA) 1968	34-126	Kelly Holmes (GBR) 2004
	M	20-100	Inge Gentzel (SWE) 1928	34-126	Kelly Holmes (GBR) 2004
1500m	G	24-29	Hassiba Boulmerka (ALG) 1992	34-131	Kelly Holmes (GBR) 2004
	M	19-227	Qu Yunxia (CHN) 1992	35-188	Violeta Szekely (ROM) 2000
3000/5000m	G	20-278	Meseret Defar (ETH) 2004	34-12	Maricica Puica (ROM) 1984
	M	19-82	Tirunesh Dibaba (ETH) 2004	34-12	Maricica Puica (ROM) 1984
10,000m	G	20-139	Derartu Tulu (ETH) 1992	28-193	Derartu Tulu (ETH) 2000
	M	20-139	Derartu Tulu (ETH) 1992	32-159	Derartu Tulu (ETH) 2004

Event		Age	Youngest		Age	Oldest	
Marathon	G	22-223	Fatuma Roba (ETH) 1996		30-86	Rosa Mota (POR) 1988	
	M	22-223	Fatuma Roba (ETH) 1996		37-61	Lorraine Moller (NZL) 1992	
80m/100m H	G	17-19	Maureen Caird (AUS) 1968		32-101	Ludmila Engquist (SWE) 1996	
	M	17-19	Maureen Caird (AUS) 1968		34-95	Karin Balzer (GDR) 1972	
400m H	G	22-115	Nawal El Moutawakel (MAR)1984		31-310	Irina Privalova (RUS) 2000	
	M	22-115	Nawal El Moutawakel (MAR)1984		314-319	Tatyana Tereshchuk (UKR) 2004	
4x100m	G	15-123	Barbara Jones (USA) 1952		35-115	Evelyn Ashford (USA) 1992	
	M	15-123	Barbara Jones (USA) 1952		40-143	Merlene Ottey (JAM) 2000	
4x400m	G	18-154	Christina Brehmer (GDR) 1976		34-26	Jearl Miles-Clark (USA) 2000	
	M	17-236⁵	Mabel Fergerson (USA) 1972		34-26	Jearl Miles-Clark (USA) 2000	
20km Walk	G	22-234	Athanasia Tsoumeléka (GRE) 2004		24-82	Wang Liping (CHN) 2000	
	M	22-234	Athanasia Tsoumeléka (GRE) 2004		34-110	Olimpiada Ivanova (RUS) 2004	
High Jump	G	16-123	Ulrike Meyfarth (FRG) 1972		31-131	Stefka Kostadinova (BUL) 1996	
	M	16-115	Dorothy Odam-Tyler (GBR) 1936		31-131	Stefka Kostadinova (BUL) 1996	
Pole Vault	G	22-82	Yelena Isinbayeva (RUS) 2004		29-184	Stacy Dragila (USA) 2000	
	M	22-82	Yelena Isinbayeva (RUS) 2004		29-194	Stacy Dragila (USA) 2000	
Long Jump	G	20-256	Tatyana Kolpakova (URS) 1980		29-67	Viorica Viscopoleanu (ROM) 1968	
	M	17-332	Willye White (USA) 1956		35-288	Heike Drechsler (GER) 2000	
Triple Jump	G	23-19	Tereza Marinova (BUL) 2000		29-300	Inessa Kravets (UKR) 1996	
	M	23-19	Tereza Marinova (BUL) 2000		29-300	Inessa Kravets (UKR) 1996	
Shot	G	21-186	Galina Zybina (URS) 1952		34-255	Ivanka Khristova (BUL) 1976	
	M	21-186	Galina Zybina (URS) 1952		36-212	Larisa Peleshenko (RUS) 2000	
Discus	G	20-121	Evelin Schlaak (GDR) 1976		39-318	Ellina Zvereva (BLR) 2000	
	M	20-100	Ruth Osborn (USA) 1932		39-318	Ellina Zvereva (BLR) 2000	
Hammer	G	17-361	Kamila Skolimowski (POL) 2000		33-326	Olga Kuzenkova (RUS) 2004	
	M	17-361	Kamila Skolimowski (POL) 2000		33-326	Olga Kuzenkova (RUS) 2004	
Javelin	G	17-86	Mihaela Penes (ROM) 1964		31-165	Trine Hattestad (NOR) 2000	
	M	17-86	Mihaela Penes (ROM) 1964		37-348	Dana Zátopková(TCH) 1960	
Heptathlon	G	21-201	Carolina Kluft (SWE) 2004		30-152	Jackie Joyner-Kersee (USA) 1992	
	M	21-201	Carolina Kluft (SWE) 2004		30-344	Sabine John (GDR) 1988	

¹Questionable date of birth would result in revised age of 20 days less; ²Mickel Dorizas (GRE) was third in the 1906 stone throw reputedly aged 16-11, but this age is in doubt; ³Michel Dorizas (GRE) was second in the 1908 javelin(freestyle) aged 18-90, but his age is in doubt; ⁴Thomas Kiely (GBR) won the 1904 all-round title aged 34-134; ⁵Grit Breuer (GDR) only ran in heats of 1988 event, but received a bronze medal aged 16-228

A record ten gold medals were won by Ray Ewry (USA) in the standing jumps from 1900 to 1908. It is a feat unsurpassed in any sport – Ewry had contracted polio as a child – and included a unique three titles on a single day in 1900. The Finnish distance runner Paavo Nurmi won a total of 12 medals from 1920 to 1928, comprising nine golds and three silvers. He won them in an unmatched seven different events, and his five golds in 1924 is a record for a single Games. Carl Lewis (USA) equalled Nurmi's nine gold medals, 1984-96, as a sprinter/long jumper, adding a silver as well. However, the most individual titles at one Games is four by Alvin Kraenzlein (USA), who won the 60m, 110mH, 200mH, and long jump in 1900. Incidentally, in the 200mH final he was penalised by one metre for a false start. His total of four golds was equalled by Jesse Owens (USA) in 1936 and Carl Lewis (USA) in 1984, but they only gained three individual events – 100m, 200m and long jump – with the fourth gold medal in the relay. Fanny Blankers-Koen of Holland matched them in 1948 with golds in the 100m, 200m, 80mH and relay. Nurmi's teammate, Ville Ritola, won a record six medals in 1924, consisting of four golds and two silvers, incurring eight distance races in eight days. Nurmi himself, when winning his five golds in 1924, had won seven races in six days. The forerunner of all 'Flying Finns', Hannes Kohlemainen, had won six such races within nine days in 1912.

Four gold medals have been won by four women: Fanny Blankers-Koen (NED) in 1948, a female record for one Games, as is the three individual titles included; Betty Cuthbert (AUS) in 1956 and 1964; Bärbel Wöckel (née Eckert) (GDR) in 1976 and 1980; and Evelyn Ashford (USA) from 1984 to 1992.

When Merlene Ottey (JAM) competed at Sydney in 2000, she set or equalled a number of records for a woman. She won her eighth medal, in her 13th Olympic final, at her sixth Games, over a period of 20 years. (In 2004 Ottey, representing Slovenia) attended her seventh Games over a period of 24 years). Shirley Strickland (later de la Hunty) (AUS) won an official total of seven medals from 1948 to 1956, comprising three golds, one silver and three bronzes. However, a 1975 study of photo evidence indicates that Strickland also came third, not fourth, in the 1948 200m, but no official move has been made to change the result. Irina Szewinska (née Kirszenstein) (POL), is the only woman to win medals at four successive Games – Ottey's medals were won at five Games, but not consecutive ones.

A further remarkable track and field achievement was the four successive gold medals in the discus

ATHLETICS MEDALS

(Excluding Tug-of-War)

Men				Women			
	G	S	B	G	S	B	Total
United States [1]	273	207	166	45	27	22	740
Soviet Union	37	37	42	34	29	35	214
Great Britain	44	63	43	8	20	17	195
Finland	48	33	30	1	2	-	114
GDR	14	14	14	24	23	21	110
Germany	8	24	26	10	14	16	98
Sweden	19	25	41	2	-	4	91
Australia	6	11	13	12	10	13	65
France	8	20	19	6	1	5	59
Italy	15	8	21	3	7	3	57
Kenya	16	20	14	-	3	1	54
Canada	12	10	17	2	5	7	53
Poland	14	8	5	8	8	8	51
FRG	4	8	12	8	6	5	43
Hungary	7	14	16	3	1	2	43
Jamaica [2]	4	12	7	3	9	8	43
Russia	2	4	7	10	13	6	42
Greece	4	7	14	3	6	1	35
Romania	-	1	1	10	13	9	34
Cuba	5	8	6	4	3	6	32
Ethiopia	10	3	8	4	2	4	31
Czechoslovakia [3]	8	7	3	3	2	2	25
South Africa	5	6	6	1	4	1	23
Japan	5	5	6	1	2	1	20
New Zealand	7	1	7	1	-	2	18
Bulgaria	1	-	1	4	7	5	18
Norway	5	2	7	1	2	1	18
Morocco	5	3	5	1	1	1	16
Netherlands	-	-	5	6	2	1	14
China	1	-	1	4	3	4	13
Brazil	3	3	7	-	-	-	13
Belarus	-	2	2	3	1	4	12
Spain	2	4	4	-	-	1	11
Nigeria	-	2	3	1	2	3	11
Mexico	3	4	2	-	1	-	10
Belgium	2	6	2	-	-	-	10
Ukraine	1	1	3	1	1	3	10
Portugal	1	2	2	2	-	2	9
Trinidad & Tobago	1	2	5	-	-	-	8
Switzerland	-	6	2	-	-	-	8
Czech Republic	3	1	2	-	-	1	7
Austria	-	-	-	1	2	4	7
Denmark	1	2	3	-	-	1	7
Ireland	4	1	-	-	1	-	6
Algeria	1	1	2	2	-	-	6
Bahamas	-	-	1	2	2	1	6
Argentina	2	2	-	-	1	-	5
Lithuania	3	-	-	-	1	-	4
Tunisia	1	2	1	-	-	-	4
Estonia	1	1	2	-	-	-	4
Namibia	-	4	-	-	-	-	4
Latvia	-	2	1	-	-	-	3
Korea	1	1	-	-	-	-	2
Mozambique	-	-	-	1	-	1	2
Uganda	1	-	1	-	-	-	2
Chile	-	1	-	-	1	-	2
Tanzania	-	2	-	-	-	-	2
Yugoslavia	-	2	-	-	-	-	2
Iceland	-	1	-	-	-	1	2
Kazakhstan	-	-	1	1	-	-	2
Slovenia	-	-	-	-	1	1	2
Sri Lanka	-	1	-	-	-	1	2

Taipei	-	1	-	-	-	1	2
Barbados[2]	-	-	2	-	-	-	2
Panama	-	-	2	-	-	-	2
Philippines	-	-	2	-	-	-	2
Turkey	-	-	2	-	-	-	2
Burundi	1	-	-	-	-	-	1
Cameroon	-	-	-	1	-	-	1
Dominican Republic	1	-	-	-	-	-	1
Ecuador	1	-	-	-	-	-	1
Luxembourg	1	-	-	-	-	-	1
Syria	-	-	-	1	-	-	1
Haiti	-	1	-	-	-	-	1
Ivory Coast	-	1	-	-	-	-	1
Saudia Arabia	-	1	-	-	-	-	1
Senegal	-	1	-	-	-	-	1
Zambia	-	1	-	-	-	-	1
Colombia	-	-	-	-	-	1	1
Djibouti	-	-	1	-	-	-	1
Eritrea	-	-	1	-	-	-	1
Qatar	-	-	1	-	-	-	1
Venezuela	-	-	1	-	-	-	1
	622	623	621	238	239	237[4]	2580

[1]Includes 2 extra golds when Jim Thorpe reinstated to 1912 decathlon/pentathlon titles; [2]Two bronzes counted for joint British West Indies 4x400m relay team in 1960; [3]Split into Czech Republic and Slovakia from 1996; [4]Two bronzes in high jump in 2000

won by Al Oerter (USA) 1956-1968. This was matched by Carl Lewis (USA) in the long jump 1984-1996. Almost as worthy were the three golds and one silver won by Viktor Saneyev (URS) in the injury-prone triple jump event 1968-80. Mildred Didrikson (USA) – who later achieved golf fame as 'Babe' Zaharias – achieved a unique triple in 1932, when she won medals in a run (80m hurdles -gold), a jump (high jump-silver) and a throw (javelin – gold). Another unusual spread of medals was by Micheline Ostermeyer (FRA) in 1948 with golds in the shot and discus and a bronze in the high jump. Perhaps even more surprising was the fact that she was a concert pianist. The foremost male equivalent was Robert Garrett (USA) with golds in the shot and discus, and silvers in the high and long jumps, in 1896 Stanley Rowley won bronze medals in the 60m, 100m and 200m in 1900 representing Australasia (he was an Australian), and then was drafted into the British team for the 5000m team event, and won a gold medal although he did not actually finish the race.

The oldest gold medallist was Patrick 'Babe' McDonald (USA) winning the 56lb weight throw in 1920 aged 42yr 23days. The youngest gold medallist was Barbara Pearl Jones (USA) in the 1952 sprint relay aged 15yr 123days, while the youngest individual event champion was Ulrike Meyfarth (FRG) who won the high jump in 1972 aged exactly one year older. The youngest male champion was Robert Mathias (USA) who won the 1948 decathlon aged 17yr 263days, and later (1966), after a brief movie career, became a US Congressman. The oldest female champion was Ellina Zvereva (BLR) in the 2000 discus aged 39yr 316days. Sprinter Merlene Ottey (JAM/SLO) (1980-2004), holds the record of attending seven Games. The male record, for athletes, of five Games, is held by eleven men. Ottey's 24-year span matches the male record of competition in Olympic athletics by discus thrower Frantisek Janda-Suk of Bohemia and Czechoslovakia, 1900-24. The oldest medallist was Tebbs Lloyd Johnson (GBR) in the 50km walk of 1948 aged 48yr 115days, and the oldest female medallist was Merlene Ottey (JAM) winning a silver in the 2000 relay aged 40yr 143days. Barbara Jones (see above) was also the youngest medallist. The youngest male medallist was thought to be Mikhel Dorizas (GRE) in the 1906 stone throw aged 16yr 11days, but some doubts have arisen about his age, and thus Frank Castleman (USA), silver in the 1904 200mH takes the title aged 17yr 167days. The oldest competitor ever in Olympic athletics was Percy Wyer (CAN) aged 52yr 199days when 30th in the 1936 marathon. The oldest female competitor was Lourdes Klitzkie of Guam aged 48yr 234days when placing 63rd in the 1988 marathon. The youngest ever competitor was Celestine N'Drin (CIV) in the 800m in 1976 when three days past her 13th birthday. The youngest male was Vahram Papazian (TUR) who was in the 800m in 1906 aged 13yr 256days.

The first brothers to win medals were Richard and Lewis Sheldon (USA) in the 1900 throws and jumps respectively. The first to gain medals in the same event were Platt and Ben Adams (USA) who won gold and silver in the 1912 standing high jump. Brothers Commodore and Leroy Cochran both won gold medals in the 4x400m relay, but in 1924 and 1948 respectively, 'Roy' also winning the 400mH in London. The most successful siblings were the Press sisters (URS), Tamara with three golds and a silver, and Irina, with two golds, in 1960 and 1964. The only twins to win medals were Patrick and Pascal Barré (FRA) in the bronze medal sprint relay of 1980. Father and son gold medallists are represented by two families. Werner Järvinen (FIN) won the 1906 Greek style discus, his son Matti won the javelin in 1932, and another son Akilles, gained silver medals in the 1928 and 1932 decathlons. In 1948 Imre Németh (HUN) won the hammer, and 28 years later his son Miklós won the javelin with a world record throw. The only father/daughter medal combination was Lennox Miller (JAM), with a 1968 100m silver, and Inger Miller (USA), with a gold in the 1996 sprint relay.

The most successful mother/daughter combination was Elisabeta Bagriantseva (URS), with a silver in the 1952 discus, and Irina Nazarova, with a gold in the 4x400m relay of 1980. Uniquely, Violet Webb (GBR) and her daughter, Janet Simpson, both won bronze medals in the 4x100m relay, in 1932 and 1964 respectively. One of the more poignant Olympic stories relates to Marie Dollinger, who was one of the women involved in dropping the baton in the 1936 sprint relay when the German women 'couldn't lose'. One imagines the thoughts of her daughter, Brunhilde Hendrix, in the 1960 relay final – happily she won a silver medal to match that of her father, Friedrich, in the 1932 sprint relay. Incidentally, it has recently been suggested that the disaster to the usual machine-like precision exchanges of the 1936 German team was due to a last-minute change in their order to match similar changes to the American team's order. Remarkably, Dollinger had first run in the Olympics in 1928, in the inaugural 800m, and in 1931 had equalled the world 800m record – not the usual CV of a world class sprinter.

The first married couple to win gold medals were Emil and Dana Zátopek (TCH). Even more coincidental is the fact that Dana won her javelin title on the same afternoon as one of Emil's victories in 1952 – remarkably, both of them were also born on the same day. The only other couple have been Victor Bryzgin (URS), 4x100m in 1988, and his wife, Olga, gold medallist in the 400m and 4x400m. Frank Wykoff (USA) was the only sprinter to win gold medals in three Games, in relay teams from 1928 to 1936, until he was equalled by Evelyn Ashford (USA), also in relay teams, 1984-92, and Carl Lewis (USA) 1984-92.

The first Olympic athlete to be disqualified for contravening the drug regulations was Danuta Rosani (POL) in the 1976 discus. By far the biggest uproar occurred with the positive testing of Ben Johnson (CAN) after he had won the 1988 100m title in an apparently fabulous new world record of 9.79sec. The repercussions on world attitudes to drug

testing were immense. The scrutiny of 'sex testing' of women was introduced into the Games in 1968, many years too late in the opinion of many. They had in mind the case of Dora Ratjen (GER) who placed fourth in the 1936 high jump and was later found to be a man posing as a woman. There was also the case of Stella Walasiewicz (later Walsh), Polish-born but later an American citizen, who won gold and silver in the 100m of 1932 and 1936 respectively, and was reported, after her violent death in 1980, to have 'primary male characteristics'.

The shortest time that an athlete has held an Olympic record was 0.4sec by Olga Rukavishnikova (URS) in the 1980 pentathlon. That is the difference between her second place time of 2m 04.8sec in the final 800m event of the five-event contest, and the time of the third-placed Nadyezda Tkachenko (URS), whose overall points score exceeded her teammate's by 146. Only three athletes have lost, actually lost, a title and then won it back. Nina Romashkova-Ponomareva (URS) won the discus in 1952, came third in 1956, then won again in 1960. Similarly, Ulrike Meyfarth (FRG) won the high jump in 1972, did not make the final in 1976, but won again in 1984. The only man was Vladimir Golubnichi (URS) in the 20km walk, winning in 1960, third in 1964 and first again in 1968. (Incidentally he also placed second in 1972). Meyfarth's twelve years between gold medals is matched by only Al Oerter, Carl Lewis and Irina Szewinska. Martin Sheridan (USA) competed in 15 events from 1904 to 1908, winning 5g, 3s, and 1b.

The largest number of competitors in a single event was the 124 runners in the 1996 men's marathon – 111 finished. The largest women's field was also in the 1996 marathon, with 86 starters of which 65 finished. The use of starting blocks was allowed in the Games for the first time in 1948. (See also 'Automatic Timing').

A number of Olympic athletics medallists have later made their mark in Hollywood films. In particular, they have come from the ranks of the decathletes – Jim Thorpe, Glenn Morris, Bob Mathias, Rafer Johnson, C K Yang, Floyd Simmons and Bruce Jenner. The 1924 pole vault champion, Lee Barnes, doubled for Buster Keaton for a vault sequence in his excellent film *College*. The 1928 silver medallist in the shot, Herman Brix, changed his name to Bruce Bennett, and had many serious roles after an initial 'Tarzan' appearance. Norman Pritchard an Indian-born 1900 medallist, but representing Great Britain, reportedly made many silent films, while more recent additions to the Hollywood scene have been 1952 sprint relay gold winner Dean Smith (USA) and 1968 pole vault champion Bob Seagren (USA). The film industries of other countries have welcomed

Tapio Rautavaara (FIN), the 1948 javelin champion, Giuseppe Tosi (ITA) the 1948 discus silver medallist, Giuseppe Gentile (ITA) 1968 triple jump bronze, and Adhemar Ferreira da Silva (BRA) the 1952 and 1956 triple jump champion.

The 2004 women's marathon champion, Mizuki Noguchi (JPN), at 1.50m *4ft 11 ins* tall and weighing 41kg *90lb*, is the smallest ever Olympic athletics gold medallist. The 1996 marathon champion, Josiah Thugwane (RSA), is thought to be the smallest male gold medallist in athletics, at 1.58m *5ft 2¹/₂ins* tall and weighing 45kg *99lb*. The above mentioned Merlene Ottey (JAM) is the only athlete to be a finalist in the same event, the 200m in her case, at five Games, 1984-00. At Sydney, Marla Runyan (USA) became the first legally blind athlete to run in an Olympic final. Only able to see nearby blurred shapes, she nevertheless placed 8th in a 12-woman field in the 1500m.

AUSTRALIAN RULES FOOTBALL

A DEMONSTRATION SPORT at Melbourne in 1956. Two amateur Australian teams played an exhibition that resulted in a 250-135 score.

AUTOMATIC TIMING

THE FIRST TIME electrical/photo timing equipment was tried out for the athletic events at the Games was at Stockholm in 1912. The photograph produced by the system was used to determine second and third placings in the 1500m. However, the first use of 'modern' photo-timing was at Los Angeles in 1932, with the film made available to the Jury of Appeal, but times not officially given. In 1948, at London, photo-finish equipment used for horse-racing was employed at the athletic events, but only to help the judges decide on placings, not for timings. At these Games, in at least one event, the women's 200m final, an incorrect result was allowed to stand (see 'Athletics' section). Although automatic timing devices were in use from 1952, they were not officially recognised and hand timings were given. (However,

those automatic timings have been published after research by statistician Bob Sparks). Timings in athletics, to two decimal places in the short races, were first given officially in 1972 at Munich.

BADMINTON

INTRODUCED AS A medal sport for the first time in 1992, badminton had been a demonstration sport in 1972, when the men's singles was won by Rudy Hartono of Indonesia. Because it was felt necessary to control the number of entries a mixed doubles competition was not included until 1996.

The most successful players have been the women's doubles pair of Fei Ge and Jun Gu (CHN) who won gold in 1996 and 2000. The most successful male has been Joo-Bong Park (KOR) with a gold in 1992 and a silver in 1996. The Chinese mixed pair of Jun Zhang and Ling Gao were the first players to retain a title, 2000-04.

The youngest gold medallist was Fei Ge (CHN) in the 1996 women's doubles aged 20yr 175days, while the youngest male champion was Dong Moon Kim (KOR) in the 1996 mixed doubles aged 20yr 314days. The oldest champion was Poul-Erik Hoyer-Larsen (DEN) the 1996 singles champion aged 30yr 316days, and the oldest female winner was Ning Zhang (CHN) taking the 2004 singles title at 29yr 92days. The youngest medallist was Mia Audina (INA) taking the silver in the 1996 women's singles at 16yr 345days, while the youngest male medallist was Sori Dwi Kuncoro (INA) with the 2006 singles bronze aged 20yr 45days.

The oldest male medallist was Jens Eriksen (DEN) with a mixed doubles bronze in 2006 aged 34yr 233days, while the oldest female medallist was Minarti Timur (INA) 32yr 181days in the Sydney mixed doubles. Barcelona female gold medallist Susi Susanti, Indonesia's first ever Olympic champion, later married her countryman, the male singles winner Alan Budi Kusuma. Brothers Razif and Jalani Sidek won the bronze in the 1992 men's doubles, for Malaysia's first ever Olympic medal, and in 1996 another brother, Rashid, won a bronze in the singles.

BADMINTON MEDALS

	Men[1]			Women			
	G	S	B	G	S	B	Total
China	3	1	3	5	3	7	22
Indonesia	4	4	4	1	1	1	15
Korea	3	4	1	2	2	2	14
Denmark	1	-	2	-	1	-	4
Malaysia	-	1	2	-	-	-	3
Great Britain	-	1	1	-	-	-	2
Netherlands	-	-	-	-	1	-	1

[1]Including mixed doubles

BANDY

A DEMONSTRATION SPORT at the Oslo Winter games in 1952, bandy is similar to ice hockey, but played with a ball instead of a puck. A tournament was held, and final placings were decided on goal average with Sweden winning from Norway and Finland.

BASEBALL

THERE WERE SIX occasions when American baseball was demonstrated, plus an exhibition of Finnish baseball in 1952. In 1912 the USA team, containing many track and field medallists, beat Sweden 13-3. In 1936 a 'World Amateurs' team beat an American 'Olympic' team in front of 100,000 spectators in the Berlin Olympic Stadium. In 1956 an American Services team beat an Australian team 11-5 before an estimated 114,000 people, then a record crowd for any baseball game anywhere. At Tokyo in 1964 an USA team beat two Japanese teams, and in 1984 Japan won an eight-nation tournament. In 1988 the USA also won an eight-nation tournament, beating Japan in the final. Finally, in 1992, baseball became an official medal sport.

The greatest margin of victory, and the highest score, was the 20-0 victory by Chinese Taipei (Taiwan) over Spain in the 1992 competition. In 1996 Cuba beat Italy 20-6 to equal the highest score, and set an aggregate record of 27 when beating Australia 19-8. Orestes Kindelan (CUB) scored a record nine home runs in 1996, and a total of 11 home runs in the 1996/2000 competitions. Luigi Carrozza (ITA) has had the best batting average with .571 at Atlanta, while Jan Rauch (USA) achieved 21 strikeouts at Sydney in 2000. In 2006 Cuba made it three golds and a silver since 1992.

The oldest gold medallist/medallist was Antonio Scull (CUB) aged 38yr 349days in 2004, while the youngest winner was his teammate, pitcher Frank Montieth (CUB), at 19yr 226days. Jong Yeu-Jeng (TPE) played for the 1992 silver medal team aged 18yr 217days. Scull has been the most successful player winning golds in 1996 and 2004, and a silver in 2000. A member of the second placed Australian team in 2004 was Graeme Lloyd, who, at 2.00m 6ft 7in, was pobably the tallest ever baseball Olympian.

Baseball Medals

	G	S	B	Total
Cuba	3	1	-	4
Japan	-	1	2	3
United States	1	-	1	2
Australia	-	1	-	1
Chinese Taipei	-	1	-	1
Korea	-	-	1	1

BASKETBALL

THE GAME MADE its official Olympic debut in 1936, although it was demonstrated in 1904, and the analogous Dutch game Korfball was demonstrated in 1928. The 1936 tournament was uniquely played outdoors, and the final score was very low due to a downpour which made the ground slippery and the ball slimy. Interestingly, one of the referees in that tournament was Avery Brundage (USA), later to become President of the IOC, while the man who had devised the modern game, Dr James Naismith, was among those who presented the medals. The tournament was won by the United States, beginning a winning streak of seven titles and 63 victories. The run began with a walkover against Spain, whose team had returned home to fight in the Spanish Civil War, and ended when they were beaten by the Soviet Union 51-50 in the 1972 final. That final was much disputed, with the Americans claiming that too much overtime was played during which the Soviet Aleksandr Belov (who tragically died six years later) scored the winning basket. With one second to go, and the USA in the lead 50-49, the Soviet inbounds pass had been deflected and everyone thought the game was over. However, the Soviet team was given another chance, but did not score. Again the game seemed to be over. But Dr William Jones (GBR), Secretary-General of FIBA (Fédération Internationale de Basketball Amateur), stated that play was incorrectly restarted at one second and that there should have been three seconds allowed. The clock was reset to three seconds and the Soviet team scored. The US team protested vigorously and refused to accept the silver medals.

After various changes and qualifying conditions since 1976, the IOC accepted 12 teams in both the men's and women's competitions at Atlanta. Eleven US players have won two gold medals each, but only David Robinson (1988-96) additionally won a bronze. Two men have won medals at four Games; Gennadi Volnov (URS) with a gold, two silvers and a bronze 1960-72, and Sergei Belov (URS) with a gold and three bronzes 1968-80. In April 1989 it was decided to allow professional players to compete in the Olympic tournaments. Thus the American 'Dream Team' for 1992, included all-time NBA greats Earvin 'Magic' Johnson, Larry Bird, Michael Jordan, Patrick Ewing, Charles Barkley, and David Robinson. This team averaged 117.25 points per game.

The oldest male gold medallist was Larry Bird (USA) in 1992 aged 35yr 245days, while the

Basketball Medals

| | Men | | | Women | | | |
	G	S	B	G	S	B	Total
United States	12	1	2	5	1	1	22
Soviet Union	2	4	3	3	-	1	13
Yugoslavia	1	4	1	-	1	1	8
Brazil	-	-	3	-	1	1	5
Australia	-	-	-	-	2	1	3
Lithuania	-	-	3	-	-	-	3
France	-	2	-	-	-	-	2
Bulgaria	-	-	-	-	1	1	2
China	-	-	-	-	1	1	2
Italy	-	2	-	-	-	-	2
Uruguay	-	-	2	-	-	-	2
Argentina	1	-	-	-	-	-	1
Canada	-	1	-	-	-	-	1
Croatia	-	1	-	-	-	-	1
Korea	-	-	-	-	1	-	1
Spain	-	1	-	-	-	-	1
Cuba	-	-	1	-	-	-	1
Mexico	-	-	1	-	-	-	1
Russia	-	-	-	-	-	1	1
	16	16	16	8	8	8	72

youngest was Spencer Haywood (USA) aged 19yr 186days in 1968. The oldest medallist was Sergejus Jovaisa (LTU) in 1992 aged 37yr 235days, while the youngest medallist was Vladimir Tkachenko (URS) in 1976 aged 18yr 311days. The highest aggregate score in a game is 238 points when Brazil beat China 130-108 in 1988. In that same tournament Brazil also scored the highest ever by a team in Olympic contests when they beat Egypt 138-85. The biggest margin of victory is 100 points, when Korea beat Iraq 120-20, and when China beat Iraq 125-25, both in 1948. The highest score by an individual in a single game is 55 points by Oscar Schmidt (BRA) in a 1988 qualifying round encounter in which Spain beat Brazil 118-110. In Seoul he scored 338 points and averaged a record 42.2 points a game. Schmidt, 1980-96, and Teofilo Cruz (PUR), 1960-76, have competed in a record five Olympic basketball tournaments. In 1996 Schmidt for the third time was the highest scorer in the tournament, aged 38y 171days, and brought his total points in Olympic competition to a remarkable 1093. In 2004 Jose Ortiz (PUR) played when two months short of his 41st birthday.

In the women's game Japan beat Canada 121-89 for an aggregate record of 210 points in 1976, while the highest total was 122 by the Soviet Union against Bulgaria (83) in 1980. The biggest margin was 66 points when the Soviet Union beat Italy 119-53 in 1980. Yevladia Stefanova (BUL) scored a record 39 points against Korea in 1988. The most successful female player has been Teresa Edwards (USA) with four gold medals and a bronze 1984-2000. She is also the only woman to play in five Games, and only player,

male or female, to win four gold medals. Edwards became the oldest gold medallist, male or female, in 2000 aged 36yr 73days, and she was also the youngest in 1984 aged 20yr 19days. The oldest medallist was a member of the silver medal Brazilian team in 1996, Hortencia Marcan Oliva, at 36yr 315days, while the youngest medallist was Zheng Haixia (CHN) in 1984 at 17yr 151days. When the Soviet men's team beat the USA at Seoul their coach was Alexander Gomelsky, and when the Unified women's team beat the American women in Barcelona their coach was his brother Yevgeni. A member of the winning American men's team in 1996, Reggie Miller, was a brother of the star of the 1984 gold medal women's team, Cheryl Miller.

The tallest ever player in Olympic basketball, was Yao Ming, in the unplaced Chinese team of 2004, at 2.26m 7ft 5in. He was also probably the tallest ever Olympian. However, the tallest ever medallist in any sport, was Tommy Burleson (USA), silver in 1972, at 2.23m 7ft 4in. Also reported in some quarters as the same height, but actually some 2cm less, was Arvidas Sabonis, who won gold in the 1988 Soviet team, and bronze in the 1992 Lithuanian team. The tallest female player, and the tallest Olympic female gold medallist ever, was Iuliana Semenova (URS) at 2.18m 7ft 2in in 1976 and 1980. She was also the heaviest female gold medallist ever at 129kg 284lb. Margorzata 'Margo' Dybek (POL), who played for the Polish team at Sydney in 2000 was also 2.18m tall, but didn't win a medal. One of her teammates was Katarzyna, her older sister, but she was only 1.98m 6ft 6in tall. Incidentally, during the first tournament

Beach Volleyball Medals

| | Men | | | Women | | | |
	G	S	B	G	S	B	Total
Brazil	1	1	-	1	3	1	7
United States	2	1	-	1	-	1	5
Australia	-	-	-	1	-	1	2
Spain	-	1	-	-	-	-	1
Canada	-	-	1	-	-	-	1
Germany	-	-	1	-	-	-	1
Switzerland	-	-	1	-	-	-	1

in 1936 there was a move to ban all players taller than 1.90m *6ft 2¾in*, but happily this was withdrawn. In the 1996 tournament an Olympic basketball record of 34,447 spectators watched the US men's team beat China 133-70 in the Georgia Dome, and the women's semi-final between USA and Australia (93-71) drew a female match record of 33,952.

BEACH VOLLEYBALL

THE SPORT APPEARS to have originated in Santa Monica, California in the early 1930s. In 1996, at Atlanta, beach volleyball became an Olympic sport. Special sand courts were built within the city's Olympic complex and the separate contests for men and women gained much spectator and media support.

The most successful beach volleyball player has been Ricardo Santos (BRA) with a gold and a silver in the 2000/2004 competitions. The most successful female players have been Sandra Pires (BRA), Natalie Cook (AUS) and Kerri Pottharst (AUS), who all won a gold and a bronze in the 1996/2000 competitions. The oldest gold medallist was Karch Kiraly (USA) aged 35yr 268days in 1996. He had won two gold medals in the standard indoor sport in 1984 and 1988, and thus becomes the most successful volleyball player, either sort, with three golds.

The oldest medallist was Michael Dodd (USA) who won a silver medal at 38yr 343days at Atlanta. The oldest female gold medallist was Kerri Pottharst (AUS) at 35yr 92days in 2000, and the oldest medallist was Adrianna Behar (BRA) in 2004 at 35yr 193days. The youngest winner was Sandra Pires (BRA) aged 23yr 41days in 1996 and the youngest medallist was Natalie Cook (AUS) aged 21yr 190days winning the bronze at Atlanta. The youngest male champion was Kent Steffes (USA) at 28yr 35days in 1996 and the youngest male medallist was Pablo Herrara (ESP) with the silver aged 22yr 57days in 2004. Chris St John 'Sinjin' Smith (USA) whose pair finished equal 5th in 1996 was 39yr 80days old.

BIATHLON

THE COMBINATION OF skiing and shooting was introduced for men in 1960, and for women in 1992. Aleksandr Tikhonov (URS) set a Winter Games record by winning a gold medal in the relay on four successive occasions 1968-1980. However, Ole Einar Bjørndalen (NOR) won an unprecedented four gold medals at the one Games, at Salt Lake City in 2002, and holds the overall records of five golds and nine medals (5g, 3s, 1b) 1998-2006. The most successful woman has been Ursula 'Uschi' Disl (GER) who has also won nine medals (2g, 4s, 3b), 1992-2006. Kati Wilhelm (GER) has a record three gold medals, 2002-06.

The oldest gold medallist was Rico Gross (GER) in the 2006 relay aged 35yr 183days. The oldest female champion was Svetlana Ishmouratova (RUS) in the 15km in 2006 aged 33yr 299days, while the oldest female medallist was Disl with a bronze in the 2006 12.5km race at 35yr 102days. The oldest male medallist was Sergei Tchepikov (RUS), competing in his sixth Games, with a silver in the 2006 relay aged 22 days past his 39th birthday. The youngest winner and medallist was Corinne Niogret (FRA) in the 1992 relay at 19yr 86days, while the youngest male winner was Yuri Kachkarov (URS) in the 1984 relay aged 20yr 75days. Frank Peter Roetsch (GDR) was the youngest male medallist when he won a silver in the 20km event in 1984 aged only 19yr 298days.

BICYCLE POLO

A DEMONSTRATION SPORT at London in 1908. Consisted of a match between a German team and one from the Irish Bicycle Polo Association.

BIGGEST FIELDS

THE LARGEST ENTRY in any Olympic event was the 183 competitors in the 1996 cycling road race. The female best is the 86 runners in the 1996 marathon race. The 124 competitors in the men's marathon that year is the record for an Olympic athletics event. In boxing there was a record entry of

Biathlon Medals

	Men			Women			
	G	S	B	G	S	B	Total
Germany	8	7	3	6	10	4	38
Soviet Union	10	6	5	1	1	2	25
Norway	9	7	5	-	2	1	24
Russia	2	2	3	5	1	3	16
GDR	3	4	4	-	-	-	11
France	1	1	3	2	1	2	10
Sweden	1	-	4	1	1	2	9
Finland	-	4	2	-	-	-	6
FRG	1	2	2	-	-	-	5
Canada	-	-	-	2	-	1	3
Italy	-	1	2	-	-	-	3
Ukraine	-	-	-	-	1	2	3
Bulgaria	-	-	-	1	-	1	2
Belarus	-	-	1	-	1	-	2
Austria	-	-	1	-	-	-	1
Poland	-	1	-	-	-	-	1
	35	35	35	18	18	18	159

441 in the 1988 tournament, while in sailing there was an unsurpassed 239 boats (plus 73 sailboards) in the 1996 regatta. In the Winter Games, the greatest single field was the 131 competitors in the 1992 men's giant slalom.

BOBSLEDDING

AN OLYMPIC BOB competition for 4-man sleds was first held in 1924. The rules allowed for 4 or 5-men teams in 1924 and 1928. The 2-man event was introduced in 1932. Both competitions have been held ever since except for 1960 when the Squaw Valley Organizing Committee refused to build a run. In 1952 a situation arose which led to changes in the rules governing the overall weight of teams and bobs.

The Germans combined their heaviest men from their two 2-man vehicles into one 4-man sled averaging 117kg *258lb* per man, and won easily. Resulting complaints led to rules currently stipulating that the maximum weight of the bobs, with crews, must not exceed 390kg *860lb* (2-man) and 630kg *1389lb* (4-man), but that extra weights may be added within those limits.

In 1994 Gustave Weder (SUI) was the first to retain a 2-man title, and Wolfgang Höppe (GER) became the first man to win medals in four winter Games. The most gold medals won by an individual is three by Bernhard Germeshausen (GDR) and Meinhard Nehmer (GDR) both 1976-80, and André Lange (GER) 2002-06. The most medals won is seven by Bogdan Musiol (GDR), comprising

Bobsledding Medals

	Men			Women			
	G	S	B	G	S	B	Total
Switzerland	9	10	11	-	-	-	30
Germany	8	2	5	1	1	1	18
United States	5	5	6	1	1	-	18
GDR	5	5	3	-	-	-	13
Italy	4	4	3	-	-	1	12
FRG	1	3	2	-	-	-	6
Great Britain	1	1	2	-	-	-	4
Canada	2	1	-	-	-	-	3
Austria	1	2	-	-	-	-	3
Soviet Union	1	-	2	-	-	-	3
Belgium	-	1	1	-	-	-	2
Russia	-	1	-	-	-	-	1
France	-	-	1	-	-	-	1
Romania	-	-	1	-	-	-	1
	37[1]	35	37[2]	2	2	2	115

[1]Tie in 1998 2-man; [2]Tie in 1998 4-man

one gold, five silver and one bronze 1980-92. The oldest gold medallist was Jay O'Brien (USA) in the 4-man in 1932 aged 48yr 359days, which also makes him the oldest gold medallist in Winter Games history. The youngest champion was William Fiske (USA) who piloted the winning 5-man bob in 1928 aged 16yr 260days. The youngest medallist was Thomas Doe Jr (USA) aged 15yr 127days in the 1928 silver medal bob. The oldest medallist was Max Houben (BEL) aged 49yr 278days in the 1948 4-man event. He had been a member of the athletics sprint relay squad at Antwerp in 1920.

That 1932 American 4-man team had unusually eventful lives outside bobsledding. Fiske had the distinction of being the first American to join the RAF in the Second World War – he was killed in the Battle of Britain. Jay O'Brien married silent film star Mae Murray. British-born Clifford 'Tippy' Gray was a songwriter, and Eddie Eagan, a Rhodes scholar, lawyer and wartime colonel, was the only man to win gold medals in both Summer and Winter Games. The tallest gold medallist was Edy Hubacher (SUI) in the 1972 4-man bob at 2.01m *6ft 7in*. He also competed in the 1968 Summer Games shot put event. Carl-Erik Eriksson (SWE) was the first Winter Olympic competitor to compete in six Games, 1964-84. The first brothers to win bob gold medals were Alfred and Heinrich Schläppi (SUI) in the 4-man of 1924, while the inaugural 2-man event of 1932 was won by siblings Hubert and Curtis Stevens (USA). Prince Albert of Monaco became the first bobsledder to compete in five Games at Salt Lake City in 2002.

The closest finishes in Olympic bobsledding have occurred in the 2-man events of 1968 and 1998. In 1968, at Grenoble, Italy I and FRG I had identical aggregate times after the four runs. The title went to Italy, driven by the 40-year-old Eugenio Monti, as they had the fastest single run. In 1998, at Nagano, the same thing happened with Italy I and Canada I tieing after four runs. However, this time they were both awarded joint first place. Incidentally, the Canadian pair had the fastest single run. The greatest margin of victory was in 1924 when the Swiss 4-man won by 3.29sec, and the smallest margin in 4-man was 0.02sec between Austria and Germany after four runs in 1992. The fastest speed attained (average for a run) was by the 2002 USA I 4-man team of 103.12km/h *64.08mph*, although a momentary speed of 143km/h *88.8mph* was recorded by the Swiss team at Calgary in 1988.

In 2002, a bob event for women was introduced, and the fastest speed (average for a run) was by the winning USA II team with 98.47km/h *61.19mph*. In that team, Vonetta Flowers became the first ever black gold medallist at a Winter Games. The oldest gold medallist was Sandra Kiriasis (née Prokoff) at

30yr 326days in 2006. Jill Bakken (USA), in 2002, was the youngest gold medallist aged 25yr 25days. The oldest medallist was Gerda Weissensteiner (ITA) at 49 days past her 37th birthday in 2006 – she had won gold in the 1994 luge.

BOXING

CONTESTS WERE INCLUDED in the ancient Games in 688 BC, when competitors wore leather straps on their hands. As the status of the Games deteriorated in Roman times, metal studs were added. Later still boxers wore metal 'knuckledusters'. One of the earliest known champions was Onomastos of Smyrna. The last known champion before the Games were abolished was Varazdetes (or Varastades), the winner in AD 369, who later became King of Armenia. This type of boxing should not be confused with the pankration event, which was a brutal combination of boxing and wrestling in which virtually anything was permitted. It is recorded that Arrachion of Phigalia was awarded that title in 564 BC, as his opponent 'gave up' – although Arrachion himself was by then lying dead in the arena. Boxing was included in the modern Games in 1904 when the USA won all the titles. A pattern was set by the first heavyweight champion, Samuel Berger, when he turned professional after his victory. Incidentally, he was a member of the San Francisco Olympic Club that had also produced 'Gentleman Jim' Corbett who had won the world title in 1892. Over the years the weight limits for the various classes have changed, and new classes added. Bronze medals for losing semi-finalists were not awarded until 1952.

Three men have won three golds. László Papp (HUN), a southpaw, won the middleweight division in 1948 and the light-middleweight class in 1952 and 1956; Teofilo Stevenson (CUB) won the same class, heavyweight, 1972-1980; his countryman, Felix Savon, matched him, also at heavyweight, 1992-2000. In 1904 Oliver Kirk (USA) won two events at the same Games, also unique (but he only fought one bout in each class). The first boxer to defend a title successfully was middleweight Harry Mallin (GBR) in 1920 and 1924. In those latter Games the standard of refereeing was highly suspect, not least because the European custom of seating the referees outside the ring was followed. Mallin was continually fouled by his French opponent in a preliminary bout, and ended the fight with teeth marks on his chest. Despite this, the outclassed Frenchman was declared the winner of the bout. An immediate appeal, backed by a threat of withdrawal of all English-speaking countries, was upheld. A strange occurrence was the disqualification of Ingemar Johansson (SWE) in the

The Val Barker Cup

presented by the International Amateur Boxing Association (AIBA) – Val Barker was a former President – to the competitor adjudged the best stylist at the Games. First awarded in 1936, the winners have been:

1936	Louis Lauria (USA)	bronze	flyweight
1948	George Hunter (SAF)	gold	light-heavyweight
1952	Norvel Lee (USA)	gold	light-heavyweight
1956	Dick McTaggart (GBR)	gold	lightweight
1960	Giovanni Benvenuti (ITA)	gold	welterweight
1964	Valeri Popentschenko (URS)	gold	middleweight
1968	Philip Waruinge (KEN)	bronze	featherweight
1972	Teofilo Stevenson (CUB)	gold	heavyweight
1976	Howard Davis (USA)	gold	lightweight
1980	Patrizio Oliva (ITA)	gold	light-welterweight
1984	Paul Gonzales (USA)	gold	light-flyweight
1988	Roy Jones Jr (USA)	silver	light-middleweight
1992	Roberto Balado (CUB)	gold	super-heavyweight
1996	Vasili Jirov (KZK)	gold	light-heavyweight
2000	Alexander Lebziak (RUS)	gold	light-heavyweight
2004	Bakhtiyar Artayev (KZK)	gold	welterweight

1952 heavyweight final, and the withholding of the silver medal, due to 'inactivity in the ring'. In 1959 he won the world professional title, and thirty years after the Games, on his 50th birthday, he was finally presented with his medal.

The oldest gold medallist/medallist was Richard Gunn (GBR), the 1908 featherweight champion, aged 37yr 254days. The youngest was Jackie Fields (né Jacob Finkelstein) (USA) winning the 1924 featherweight crown aged 16yr 162days. Neither of these records can be broken as current rules specify that boxers must be over 17 and under 37 prior to the start of the particular Games. Floyd Patterson (USA) won the 1952 middleweight title aged 17yr 211days, and four years later became the youngest ever world professional heavyweight champion. The first black African to win a gold medal was Robert Wangila (KEN) in 1988. A number of brothers have won medals, but the only known father and son medallists are Jose Villanueva (PHI), bronze bantamweight in 1932, and Anthony Villanueva (PHI), silver featherweight in 1964.

Many Olympic boxing champions, and even more minor medallists, have won world professional titles. Only two, Joe Frazier (USA 1964) and George Foreman (USA-1968), won the Olympic heavyweight title and then became undisputed professional heavyweight champions. Note also that the 1988 super-heavyweight champion, Lennox Lewis, then of Canada, won the undisputed world professional heavyweight title in 1999, representing Great Britain. Perhaps more unusually the 1908 middleweight champion, John Douglas (GBR), later, in 1911, captained the England cricket team against Australia. Just as unusual was the fact that his opponent in the 1908 final, Reg 'Snowy' Baker, also competed in springboard diving and was a member of the Australian 4x200m swimming team which place fourth. Incidentally, over the years there has been an unsubstantiated story that their final bout was refereed by Douglas's father. Recent research indicates that the official in charge was Eugene Corri.

In the 1988 tournament, because of a record 441 entries, two rings were used, simultaneously. In 1992 elimination contests were held to limit entries to 32 per class. Despite pressure to drop boxing from the Olympic programme, the introduction of new gloves, safer protective helmets and three rounds of three minutes, seems to have reprieved the sport, at least for the foreseeable future. In Sydney 2000, contests of four rounds of 2mins each were introduced. In 1992 an electronic scoring system was introduced, in which the judges had to simultaneously push a button to record a scoring point. Despite this innovation there was still considerable criticism of the scoring during the tournament, especially in the early bouts. The 1992 tournament was also noteworthy for the virtual eclipse of American boxers, with only one medal of each colour – their worse ever showing – and the domination of the Cubans, with seven golds and two silvers out of nine finals reached. In 2006, at Athens, the USA gained only a single medal, a gold. Since 1972 Cuban boxers have won the heavyweight title seven times – they were not present in 1984-88.

Boxing Medals

	G	S	B	Total
United States	48	23	38	109
Cuba	32	16	8	56
Soviet Union	14	20	19	53
Great Britain	13	11	21	45
Poland	8	9	26	43
Italy	14	12	15	41
Germany	5	12	11	28

Country			
Romania	1	9	15	25
Argentina	7	7	10	24
Hungary	10	2	8	20
South Africa	6	4	9	19
Korea	3	6	10	19
Russia	6	2	9	17
Bulgaria	4	5	8	17
Canada	3	7	7	17
France	4	5	6	15
Finland	2	1	11	14
GDR	5	2	6	13
Mexico	2	3	7	12
Denmark	1	5	6	12
Kazakhstan	4	4	3	11
Yugoslavia	3	2	6	11
Sweden	-	5	6	11
Thailand	3	2	5	10
Ireland	1	3	5	9
North Korea (PRK)	2	3	2	7
Ukraine	1	2	4	7
Kenya	1	1	5	7
Czechoslovakia	3	1	2	6
Netherlands	1	1	4	6
Algeria	1	-	5	6
FRG	1	-	5	6
Uzbekistan	1	-	5	6
Nigeria	-	3	3	6
Puerto Rico	-	1	5	6
Norway	1	2	2	5
Venezuela	1	2	2	5
Australia	-	2	3	5
Philippines	-	2	3	5
Belgium	1	1	2	4
Uganda	-	3	1	4
Turkey	-	2	2	4
Egypt	-	1	3	4
New Zealand	1	1	1	3
Japan	1	-	2	3
Chile	-	1	2	3
Ghana	-	1	2	3
Spain	-	1	2	3
Azerbaijan	-	-	3	3
Colombia	-	-	3	3
Morocco	-	-	3	3
Belarus	-	2	-	2
Cameroon	-	1	1	2
Mongolia	-	-	2	2
Tunisia	-	-	2	2
Czech Republic	-	1	-	1
Estonia	-	1	-	1
Tonga	-	1	-	1
Bermuda	-	-	1	1
Brazil	-	-	1	1
Dominican Rep.	-	-	1	1
China	-	-	1	1
Georgia	-	-	1	1
Guyana	-	-	1	1
Moldova	-	-	1	1
Niger	-	-	1	1
Pakistan	-	-	1	1
Syria	-	-	1	1
Tunisia	-	-	1	1
Uruguay	-	-	1	1
Zambia	-	-	1	1
	215	214	369[1]	798

[1]The official 1908 report only notes a single bronze medal awarded

BROTHERS

MANY BROTHERS HAVE competed together in the Games, especially in fencing, rowing and yachting. The first gold medallists were John and Sumner Paine (USA) who won the military pistol and free pistol events respectively in 1896. However, the first to win gold medals together were Reggie and Laurie Doherty (GBR) in the men's tennis doubles in 1900. The three Gossler brothers, Oscar, Gustav and Carl, were in the winning German rowing four in 1900, the latter as cox, and the French Thubé brothers, Amédée, Gaston and Jacques won golds in the 1912 6m class yachting. At the next Games, in 1920, they were eclipsed by Henrik, Jan, Ole and Kristian Østervold, of Norway, who crewed the winning 12m (1907 rating) yacht.

Probably the most successful brothers were two sets of sibling fencers. Nedo and Aldo Nadi (ITA) won a total of nine golds and one silver in 1912 and 1920, while their countrymen, Edoardo and Dario Mangiarotti amassed seven golds, seven silvers and two bronzes between 1936 and 1960. Also worthy of note are; Dhyand Chand Bais and Roop Singh Bais of India in hockey, with the former gaining three gold medals 1928-1936, and the latter two, 1932-1936; and the rowing Abbagnale brothers of Italy, Carmine and Giuseppe won the coxed pairs in 1984-88 and a silver in 1992, and Agostino won gold in the 1992 quadruple sculls and 1996 double sculls. In the Winter Games, Andreas and Wolfgang Linger (AUT) won the 2006 doubles luge event.

BUDO

A DEMONSTRATION SPORT at Tokyo in 1964, when exhibitions of Japanese archery, wrestling and fencing were given.

CANOEING

OFFICIAL CANOEING COMPETITIONS were first held in 1936, although kayak and Canadian events were demonstrated in 1924. In 1972, at Munich, four slalom events were held, and after a gap of 20 years slalom racing was reintroduced at Barcelona. The most successful canoeist has been Birgit Fischer-Schmidt, first representing the GDR and then Germany, over a record 24 year period 1980-2004, during which she has won a record eight gold medals, and four silvers to total another record of twelve medals. Had the GDR not boycotted Los Angeles in 1984 she would have assuredly won even more. The most successful male has been Gert Fredriksson (SWE) with six golds, one silver and one bronze from 1948 to 1960, all in kayaks. Two men, Vladimir Parfenovich (URS) in 1980, and Ian Ferguson (NZL) in 1984, have won three gold medals at one Games. The best by a woman at one Games is two golds and a silver, by Agneta Andersson (SWE) in 1984 and Birgit Fischer-Schmidt (GDR) in 1988.

The highest speed achieved in the Games over the standard 1000m course is 21.05km/h *13.08mph* when the Hungarian K4 clocked 2min 51.010 sec in a heat in 2004. Also in a heat at Athens the Belarus K4 team achieved an average speed of 22.38km/h *13.91mph* over the first 250m. The fastest by a female crew over the 500m course is 19.76km/h *12.27mph* when the German K4 clocked 1min 31.07sec in 1996. In that race the German K4 achieved an average speed of 20.20km/h *12.55mph* over the first 250m. The closest finish in an Olympic canoeing final occurred in the 1952 K2 1000m when the timekeepers were unable to separate the first and second placed pairs. The closest finish in women's canoeing was in the 1988 K1 500m when the winning margin was 0.12sec. This was equalled in the 1992 K2 final.

The oldest ever canoeing male gold medallist/medallist was Gert Fredriksson (SWE) aged 40yr 292days in the 1960 K2 over 1000m. The youngest was Bent Peder Rasch (DEN) in the 1952 C2 at 1000m aged 18yr 58days. However, Michal Martikan

Canoeing Medals

	Men			Women			
	G	S	B	G	S	B	Total
Hungary	13	19	18	4	7	5	66
Germany	18	13	15	8	7	1	62
Soviet Union	22	18	0	8	2	3	53
Romania	9	9	10	1	1	4	34
GDR	8	5	8	6	2	1	30
Sweden	12	9	2	3	2	2	30
France	5	6	15	-	1	2	29
Canada	4	5	5	-	3	2	19
Bulgaria	3	3	7	1	2	1	17
Poland	-	5	7	-	-	5	17
United States	5	2	4	-	3	2	16
Australia	1	5	6	-	1	2	15
Italy	4	4	3	1	1	-	13
Austria	3	4	4	-	1	1	13
Czechoslovakia	7	4	1	-	-	-	12
Norway	5	3	4	-	-	-	12
Denmark	2	4	4	1	-	1	12
Finland	4	2	3	1	-	-	10
New Zealand	5	2	1	-	-	-	8
Czech Republic	2	2	2	2	-	-	8
Slovakia	3	2	2	1	-	-	8
Netherlands	-	1	3	-	2	2	8
FRG	1	1	1	1	2	1	7
Spain	1	3	2	-	-	-	6
Great Britain	-	3	2	-	-	1	6
Yugoslavia	2	2	1	-	-	-	5
Russia	-	2	3	-	-	-	5
Cuba	-	3	-	-	-	-	3
Latvia	-	2	-	-	-	-	2
Slovenia	-	2	-	-	-	-	2
China	1	-	-	-	-	-	1
Moldova	-	1	-	-	-	-	1
Switzerland	-	-	-	-	1	-	1
Israel	-	-	1	-	-	-	1
Belarus	-	-	1	-	-	-	1
Ukraine	-	-	-	-	-	1	1
	140	140	140	38	38	38	534

CELEBRATIONS OF THE GAMES

(New research by Bill Mallon has resulted in revised figures for participation in medal events)

SUMMER

	Year	Venue	Date	Nations	Women	Men	Total
I	1896	Athens, Greece	6–15 April[1]	14	–	246	246
II	1900	Paris, France	20 May–28 October	25	22	1591	1613
III	1904	St Louis, USA	1 July–23 November	13	6	643	649
*	1906	Athens, Greece	22 April–2 May	20	6	835	841
IV	1908	London, England	27 April–31 October	22	37	1965	2002[2]
V	1912	Stockholm, Sweden	5 May–22 July	28	53	2328	2381
VI	1916	Berlin, Germany	Not held due to war	–	–	–	–
VII	1920	Antwerp, Belgium	20 April–12 September	29	65	2517	2582[3]
VIII	1924	Paris, France	4 May–27 July	44	135	2932	3067
IX	1928	Amsterdam, Holland	17 May–12 August	46	274	2595	2869
X	1932	Los Angeles, USA	30 July–14 August	37	126	1200	1326
XI	1936	Berlin, Germany	1–16 August	49	329	3625	3954
XII	1940	Tokyo, then Helsinki	Not held due to war	–	–	–	–
XIII	1944	London	Not held due to war	–	–	–	–
XIV	1948	London, England	29 July–14 August	59	393	3678	4071
XV	1952	Helsinki, Finland	19 July–3 August	69	521	4398	4919
XVI	1956	Melbourne, Australia[4]	22 Nov–8 December	67	370	2812	3182
XVII	1960	Rome, Italy	25 Aug–11 September	83	612	4726	5338
XVIII	1964	Tokyo, Japan	10–24 October	93	680	4454	5134
XIX	1968	Mexico City, Mexico	12–27 October	112	784	4771	5555
XX	1972	Munich, FRG	26 Aug–10 September	121	1059	6057	7116
XXI	1976	Montreal, Canada	17 July–1 August	92	1262	4811	6073
XXII	1980	Moscow, Soviet Union	19 July–3 August	80	1120	4132	5252
XXIII	1984	Los Angeles, USA	28 July–12 August	140	1575	5224	6799
XXIV	1988	Seoul, Korea	17 Sep–2 October	159	2196	6251	8447
XXV	1992	Barcelona, Spain	25 July–9 August	169	2723	6662	9385
XXVI	1996	Atlanta, USA	19 July–4 August	197	3510	6817	10327
XXVII	2000	Sydney, Australia	15 Sep–1 October	199	4068	6579	10647
XXVIII	2004	Athens, Greece	13–29 August	201	4302	6256	10558
XXIX	2008	Beijing, China	8–24 August	–	–	–	–
XXX	2012	London, England	27 July – 12 August	–	–	–	–

*This celebration (to mark the tenth anniversary of the modern Games) was officially intercalated, but not numbered; [1]Actually 25 March – 3 April by the Julian Calendar then in use in Greece; [2]Including 21 competitors (of which 7 were women) in the ice skating events; [3]Including 86 competitors (of which 12 were women) in the ice skating events; [4]Equestrian events held in Stockholm, 10–17 June, with 158 competitors, of which 13 were women.

WINTER

	Year	Venue	Date	Nations	Women	Men	Total
I	1924	Chamonix, France	25 Jan–4 February	16	13	278	291
II	1928	St Moritz, Switzerland	11–19 February	25	28	436	464
III	1932	Lake Placid, USA	4–15 February	17	21	231	252
IV	1936	Garmisch–Partenkirchen, Germany	6–16 February	28	80	588	668
–	1940	Sapporo, then St Moritz, then Garmisch–P Not held due to war		–	–	–	–
–	1944	Cortina d'Ampezzo, Italy	Not held due to war	–	–	–	–
V	1948	St Moritz, Switzerland	30 Jan–8 February	28	77	591	668
VI	1952	Oslo, Norway	14–25 February	30	109	584	693
VII	1956	Cortina d'Ampezzo, Italy	26 Jan–5 February	32	132	689	821
VIII	1960	Squaw Valley, USA	18–28 February	30	144	520	664
IX	1964	Innsbruck, Austria	29 Jan–9 February	36	199	894	1093
X	1968	Grenoble, France	6–18 February	37	211	947	1158
XI	1972	Sapporo, Japan	3–13 February	35	206	802	1008

XII	1976	Innsbruck, Austria	4–15 February	37	231	898	1129
XIII	1980	Lake Placid, USA	13–24 February	37	235	837	1072
XIV	1984	Sarajevo, Yugoslavia	8–19 February	49	277	996	1273
XV	1988	Calgary, Canada	13–28 February	57	315	1110	1425
XVI	1992	Albertville, France	8–23 February	64	488	1313	1801
XVII	1994	Lillehammer, Norway	12–27 February	67	522	1216	1738
XVIII	1998	Nagano, Japan	7–22 February	72	789	1391	2180
XIX	2002	Salt Lake City, USA	9–24 February	77	886	1513	2399
XX	2006	Turin, Italy	11–26 February	79	054	1540	2494
XXI	2010	Vancouver, Canada	–	–	–	–	–

(SVK) won the C1 slalom event in 1996 aged 17yr 70days, making him easily the youngest ever champion in Olympic canoeing events. The youngest female champion was Birgit Fischer-Schmidt (GDR/GER) aged 18y 158days in 1980, and she was also the oldest ever canoeing champion/medallist at Athens in 2004 aged 42yr 184days. The youngest female medallist was Francine Fox (USA), with a silver in the 1964 K2 at 15y 220days. (Incidentally, her partner was 20 years older). The youngest male medallist was Gábor Novák (HUN) in 1952 aged 17yr 348days. Ivar Patzaichin (ROM) won gold medals over a 16 year period, 1968-84, in the Canadian events. This has been exceeded by Birgit Fischer-Schmidt (GDR/GER) 1980-04.

When Philippe Renaud (FRA) won a bronze in the 1988 C2 500m, he was the latest success of an Olympic family – his brother, Eric, won a canoe bronze in 1984, their father, Marcel gained a canoe silver in 1956, and a great-uncle won a cycling bronze in 1924. The first brothers, indeed twins, to win gold medals were Pavol and Peter Hochschorner (SVK) in the slalom C2 at Sydney, and they retained their title in 2004. In 1996, the bronze medal in the women's K2 500m was won for Australia by Katrin Borchert and Anna Wood. Interestingly, Borchert had won a silver in the 1992 German K4, and Wood had taken a bronze in the 1988 Dutch K2.

CONSECUTIVE MEDALS

THE ONLY COMPETITOR to win six consecutive gold medals in the Olympic Games is Aladár Gerevich (HUN) who was a member of the winning sabre fencing team 1932-1960. His teammate, Pál Kovács, won five golds consecutively 1936-1960. Hans-Günter Winkler (FRG) also won medals in six consecutive Games in show jumping, but they were not all gold. A countryman, Reiner Klimke, won gold medals at five Games between 1964 and 1988, but they were not consecutive. The canoeist Birgit Fischer-Schmidt (GDR/GER) is the only woman to win gold medals in six Games, between 1980 and 2006, but she missed 1984. However, she is the only woman to win gold medals at five consecutive Games.

Fencer Ildikó Ságiné-Uljakiné-Rejtő (HUN),

1960-1976, also won medals at five consecutive Games, but they were not all gold. In the Winter Games, biathlete Rico Gross (GER) 1992-2006 is the only man to win medals in five consecutive Games, but only gold on four occasions. Two women have won medals in five consecutive Winter Games, cross-country skier Raisa Smetanina (URS/EUN) 1976-1992 and speed skater Claudia Pechstein (GER) 1992-2006, but Pechstein won gold on the last four occasions.

CREED

THE OLYMPIC CREED has been displayed on the scoreboard at every opening ceremony since the 1932 Games at Los Angeles. The words are: "The most important thing in the Olympic Games is not to win but to take part, just as the most important thing in life is not the triumph but the struggle. The essential thing is not to have conquered but to have fought well'. They are attributed usually to Baron de Coubertin, but were actually based on words used by Ethelbert Talbot, the Bishop of Central Pennsylvania, in a sermon at St Paul's Cathedral in London on the 19 July 1908.

CRICKET

ON THE ONLY occasion that cricket was played at the Games, in 1900, Great Britain, represented by the Devon Wanderers CC, beat a French team, consisting of mainly expatriate Britons, in a 12-a-side match scoring 117 and 145 for five declared, against the French score of 78 and 26.

CROQUET

IT WAS ONLY contested in 1900 when all the competitors were French. There were two singles competitions, and a doubles in which only a gold medal was awarded.

CURLING

CURLING, MADE MANY appearances as a demonstration sport before it finally became a medal

Curling Medals

(including 1924)

| | Men | | | Women | | | |
	G	S	B	G	S	B	Total
Canada	1	2	-	1	-	2	6
Switzerland	1	-	1	-	2	-	4
Sweden	-	1	-	1	-	1	3
Great Britain	1	-	-	1	-	-	2
Norway	1	-	1	-	-	-	2
Denmark	-	-	-	-	1	-	1
Finland	-	1	-	-	-	-	1
France	-	-	1	-	-	-	1
United States	-	-	1	-	-	-	1

sport at Nagano in 1998. However, in 2006 it was confirmed by the IOC that curling's first appearance in 1924, which also had been considered for years as a demonstration event, was actually a medal sport, and that the gold, silver and bronze medals were won by Great Britain, Sweden and France respectively. In 1932 there were four Canadian Provincial and four American club teams. The Canadians took the first four places with the title won by Manitoba. In 1936 eight teams from Austria (three), Germany (three) and Czechoslovakia (two) competed in a specialized version of the game, German curling, with the Austrian number one team from the Tyrol, winning. The Austrians demonstrated the game in 1964 at Innsbruck, and it was a demonstration sport again in 1988 and 1992.

The curling events in 1998 were held at the Kazakoshi Park, Karuizawa, which had been the site for the show jumping contests in the 1964 Summer Games, thus making it the first venue to host both Winter and Summer Games events. In the men's competition the highest score was when Canada beat USA 11-5, and USA beat Norway 11-5, both in 2006. The biggest margin of victory, was when the German team beat New Zealand 10-1 in 2006. The greatest aggregate score was when Norway beat Canada 10-8 in 1998. The youngest gold medallist was Dominic Andres (SUI) aged 25yr 132days in 1998, while the oldest was Russ Howard (CAN) in 2006 at 50yr 5days. The oldest medallist was Paul Savage (CAN) in the 1998 silver winning team at 50yr 235days, while the youngest was his teammate Mike Harris aged 20yr 251days. It should be noted that Scott Baird was a member of the victorious Canadian team in 2006, aged 54yr 293days, but never actually played.

In the women's competition the biggest margin of victory came when the USA beat Norway 11-2 in 2002. The highest score was when Sweden beat Japan 12-6 in 1998, while the greatest aggregate was when Denmark beat Sweden 11-9 in 2002. The youngest gold medallist was Atina Ford (CAN) aged 26yr 126days in 2002. The oldest was Anette Norberg (SWE) in 2006 aged 39yr 103days – her younger sister, Cathrine Lindahl was a teammate. The youngest medallist was Valeria Spälty (SUI) with a silver in 2006 aged 22yr 244days, and the oldest was Cheryl Noble in the Canadian bronze medal squad at 45yr 145days. Mirjam Ott (SUI) has won the most medals with two silvers in 2002-06.

CYCLING

THE FIRST OLYMPIC cycling champion was Léon Flameng (FRA), winner of the 100km race in 1896, which was held on a 333.33m cement track and involved 300 circuits. Five men have won three gold medals: Paul Masson (FRA) in 1896, Francisco Verri (ITA) in 1906, Robert Charpentier (FRA) in 1936, Daniel Morelon (FRA) in 1968 (two) and 1972, and Florian Rousseau (FRA) in 1996 and 2000 (two). Of these only Rousseau won a silver as well. Initially, the seven 1904 cycling events were not considered official, as there were no foreign entries. However, recent thinking has 'reinstated' them. Thus it should be noted that Marcus Hurley (USA) won a record four titles, and a bronze medal, at that Games. His teammate, Burton Downing, also set a 'record' at St Louis with six medals, comprising two gold, three silver and a bronze.

However, Leontien Zijlaard-van Moorsel (NED) has won four golds 2000-04, of which three were at Sydney. Additionally she won a silver and a bronze to make a total of six medals. The first pair of brothers to win a medal were the Götze duo, Bruno and Max, of Germany with a tandem silver in 1906. The greatest family performance in Olympic cycling was achieved by the Pettersson brothers of Sweden, Gösta, Sture, Erik and Tomas. The first three with Sven Hamrin won a bronze in the 1964 team road race, and then, in 1968 with their younger brother, won the silver. Two extremes of sportsmanship have been highlighted in Games cycling. In 1936 Robert Charpentier beat his teammate Guy Lapébie by 0.2 sec at the end of the 100km, the latter inexplicably slowing down just before the line. A photograph showed that

Cycling Medals

	Men			Women			
	G	S	B	G	S	B	Total
France	33	18	23	5	4	1	84
Italy	31	15	7	4	-	-	57
Great Britain	12	23	18	-	-	1	54
United States [1]	12	11	15	1	4	3	46
Germany	11	11	14	1	3	2	42
Australia	10	11	11	3	4	2	41
Netherlands	9	14	5	5	2	4	39
Belgium	6	8	11	-	-	-	25
Soviet Union	10	4	8	1	-	1	24
Denmark	6	7	8	-	-	-	21
GDR	6	5	4	-	1	-	16
FRG	4	4	4	-	1	1	14
Sweden	3	2	8	-	-	-	13
Switzerland	2	5	3	-	1	1	12
Russia	2	2	1	2	2	2	11
Canada	-	3	3	1	2	2	11
Spain	3	4	2	-	-	1	10
South Africa	1	4	3	-	-	-	8
Poland	-	5	3	-	-	-	8
Czechoslovakia	2	2	2	-	-	-	6
Greece	1	3	1	-	-	-	5
Norway	1	-	1	1	-	-	3
Austria	1	-	2	-	-	-	3
Japan	-	1	2	-	-	-	3
New Zealand	1	-	1	-	-	-	2
Ukraine	-	1	-	-	-	1	2
China	-	-	-	-	1	1	2
Mexico	-	-	1	-	1	-	2
Estonia	-	-	-	1	-	-	1
Kazakstan	-	1	-	-	-	-	1
Jamaica	-	-	1	-	-	-	1
Latvia	-	-	1	-	-	-	1
Portugal	-	1	-	-	-	-	1
Uruguay	-	1	-	-	-	-	1
Belarus	-	-	-	-	-	1	1
Colombia	-	-	-	-	-	1	1
Lithuania	-	-	-	-	-	1	1
	167	166	163[2]	25	26	26	573

[1]Includes 7 events in 1904 formerly excluded
[2]No bronzes in 1896 100km,1972 road team trial and individual race

Cycling Records

Men

1000m Time-Trial	1:00.711	Chris Hoy (GBR)	2004
4000m Individual Pursuit	4:15.165	Bradley Wiggins (GBR)	2004
4000m Team Pursuit	3:56.610	Australia	2004

Women

500m Time-Trial	33.952s	Anna Meares (AUS)	2004
3000m Individual Pursuit	3:24.537s	Sarah Ulmer (NZL)	2004

Charpentier had pulled his rival back by his shirt. More credit-worthy was another Frenchman, Léon Flameng, who, when far ahead of his only opposition, a Greek, in 1896, stopped when the man's cycle broke down. After waiting for it to be replaced, Flameng still won by six laps. After the 1984 Games it was admitted that many of the US cycling team had indulged in 'blood-boosting' procedures – not illegal at the time. Those Games also witnessed numerous 'space-age' innovations, especially in the composition and construction of wheels. Of the many excellent facilities that have been built for Olympic cycling programmes, one of the most remarkable sites was the magnificent Hachioji velodrome in Tokyo 1964. Built at a cost of $840,000, it was used for only four days during the Games, and within a year was demolished. Track cycling was held indoors for the first time in 1976.

The greatest speed ever achieved in Olympic cycling was in the altitude of Mexico City in 1968 when Daniel Morelon and Pierre Trentin (FRA) clocked 9.83 sec for the last 200m in the tandem race, an average of 73.24km/h *45.50mph*. The greatest speed by an individual rider was 71.08km/h *44.16mph* by Gary Niewand (AUS) in the elimination rounds at Atlanta, 1996 when he clocked 10.129 sec for the last 200m in the 1000m sprint. The fastest by a female rider was 64.21km/h *39.89mph* by Michelle Ferris (AUS), also in 1996, when she clocked 11.212 sec. The longest race ever held in the Games, at any sport, was the 1912 cycling road race over a distance of 320km *198.8 miles*. The largest entry in any Olympic event came in the 1996 men's road race which had 183 competitors.

Few future top professionals competed at the Games successfully as amateurs, but now professionals are allowed to compete. Lance Armstrong (USA), who has won the Tour de France a record seven times, won only a single medal at the Games, a bronze at Sydney in 2000. Of the four men who have won the Tour de France five times, only Miguel Induráin (ESP) has won at the Games, in 1996. Eddy Merckx (BEL) and Jacques Anquetil (FRA), both finished twelfth in the Olympic race, in 1964 and 1952 respectively. However, the latter won a bronze in the team race. Interestingly, Axel Merckx, Eddy's son, achieved something his father never did when he took the bronze medal in the 2004 road race. The only other Olympic gold medallist to also win the Tour de France was Joop Zoetemelk (NED), a member of the winning quartet in the 1968 team time-trial. British rider Chris Boardman, riding a high-tech carbon-fibre machine with a revolutionary frame design, won the 1992 4km pursuit final by uniquely catching his opponent with a lap to go.

The youngest gold medallist was Dmitri Nelyubin (URS) in the 1988 team pursuit aged 17yr 229days, while the oldest was Maurice Peeters (NED) aged 38yr 99days in the 1920 1000m sprint. Winning a bronze four years later in the tandem, Peeters, at 42yr 83days, was the oldest ever medallist as well. The youngest medallist was Alexei Markov (RUS) in the silver medal team pursuit squad in 1996 at 17yr 62days. The oldest female champion was Lori-Ann Münzer (CAN) who won the 2004 sprint aged 38yr 91days. Jeannie Longo-Ciprelli (FRA) was the oldest female medallist when she placed third in the 2000 road time trial aged 41yr 335days. The winner of the 2004 500m time trial, Anna Meares (AUS), became the youngest ever female gold medallist aged 20yr 334days, while the youngest female medallist was Sandra Schumacher (FRG) in 1984 at 17yr 217days. In 1984, the first race for women, a road race, was won by Connie Carpenter-Phinney (USA), whose husband Davis won a bronze in the 100km team event. She had competed in the 1972 Winter Games as a 14-year-old speed skater.

In 1996 mountain bike events for men and women were introduced and at Sydney in 2000 there was the addition of three track events for men the Madison, Keirin and the Olympic sprint (a team event), and a 500m time trial for women.

DE COUBERTIN

THE ACCOLADE OF founder of the modern Olympic Games is universally given to Pierre de Fredi, Baron de Coubertin of France. He was born in Paris on 1 January 1863, and early on studied the impact that sport had, and could have, on society at large, particularly appreciating the Greek ideal of developing the body and mind at the same time. He was also influenced by the ideas of the British educationalist Thomas Arnold, and from a young age concentrated his energies on improving general education in France. He vigorously propounded the importance of exercise and fitness as a cornerstone of education. He was particularly interested in fencing, and was a rugby football referee.

In 1890, as part of a French government commission to study physical culture methods, he visited Dr William Penny Brookes and his Much Wenlock Olympic Society in Britain. Impressed on this and other visits, he developed his concept of a revived Games. He put forward his ideas publicly in a lecture at the Sorbonne, Paris, on 25 November 1892. They were received enthusiastically, and this encouraged him to meet with representatives of top American universities in the following year. In June 1894 he called an international conference, again at the Sorbonne, which was attended by 12 countries, and received messages of support from another 21. A resolution, dated 23 June, called for competitions along the lines of the ancient Olympic Games to be held every four years. An International Olympic Committee was formed with de Coubertin as secretary-general. Two years later he was appointed President, and retained that position until 1925, when he retired. He was then given then title of Honorary President until his death, at Geneva, Switzerland, on 2 September 1937. He was buried at Lausanne, but his heart was interred in a marble monument at Olympia in Greece. He wrote a number of books, and in 1912, under a pseudonym, won a gold medal in the Artistic Olympics for Ode to Sport.

DEMONSTRATION SPORTS

IT WAS DECIDED by the IOC that after 1992 there would no longer be any demonstration sports held at the Games. However, since 1904 there had been a variety of such demonstrations held but not as official events eligible for medals. Some of them later became official sports and they have been mentioned elsewhere. Other than those there have been the following:

American Football (1932); Australian Rules Football (1956); Bandy (1952); Bicycle Polo (1908); Budo (1964); Dog Sled Racing (1932); Gliding (1936); Jeu de Paume (1928); Korfball (1920); Lacrosse (1928, 1932, 1948); Military Patrol (1928, 1936, 1948); Pelota Basque (1924, 1968, 1992); Roller Hockey (1992); Speed Skiing (1992); Water Skiing (1972); Winter Pentathlon (1948). See under separate headings.

DISCONTINUED SPORTS

IN THE EARLY celebrations of the Games there were a number of sports included, often of a purely local interest to the host country. The last of these was polo which had its final outing in 1936. Below are listed all such sports, and the years they were held. Cricket (1900); Croquet (1900); Golf (1900, 1904); Jeu de Paume (1908); Lacrosse (1904,1908); Motorboating (1908); Polo (1900, 1908, 1920, 1924, 1936); Roque (1904); Rackets (1908); Rugby Union (1900, 1908, 1920, 1924); See under separate headings.

DIVING

PART OF THE aquatics programme, men's diving was introduced into the Games in 1904, and that for women in 1912. In 1996 new rules came into operation that provide for three rounds instead of two, but with fewer dives in each round. The most successful diver has been Greg Louganis (USA) with four golds (a double 'double') in 1984-88, and a silver in 1976. However, Dmitri Sautin (RUS) has won a record seven medals (2g, 1s, 4b) 1992-2004, including fur medals at a single Games (2000). Austrian-born Klaus Dibiasi

Diving Medals

(including synchronised diving)

	Men			Women			
	G	S	B	G	S	B	Total
United States	27	20	20	20	20	21	128
China	8	7	5	12	6	-	38
Germany	3	7	6	3	2	3	24
Sweden	4	5	4	2	3	3	21
Soviet Union	2	1	4	2	5	3	17
Russia	2	1	3	1	3	1	11
Italy	3	4	2	-	-	-	9
Australia	1	1	3	1	-	3	9
Mexico	1	4	4	-	-	-	9
GDR	1	-	-	1	2	3	7
Canada	-	1	-	1	1	4	7
Great Britain	-	1	2	-	1	2	6
Czechoslovakia	-	-	-	1	1	-	2
Denmark	-	-	-	1	-	1	2
Egypt	-	1	1	-	-	-	2
Greece	1	-	-	-	-	-	1
France	-	-	-	-	1	-	1
Austria	-	-	1	-	-	-	1
Ukraine	-	-	-	-	-	1	1
	53	53	55[1]	45	45	45	296

[1]*Two bronzes awarded in a 1904 and a 1908 event*

(ITA) has uniquely won the same event three times, and gained medals in four Games, 1964-1976. Ni Xiong (CHN) also won medals in four Games 1988-2000. Pat McCormick (USA) set a female record of four golds in 1952 and 1956, which was matched by Fu Mingxia (CHN) in 1992-00. However, Fu Mingxia also won a silver for a female record of five medals. (McCormick's daughter Kelly won a silver in 1984 and a bronze in 1988.) Dorothy Poynton-Hill (USA) 1928-1936, Paula Myers-Pope (USA) 1952-1960, Fu Mingxia (CHN) 1992-00, and Irina Lashko 1992-2004, all won medals in three separate Games. However, the latter, Lashko, represented EUN (1992), RUS (1996) and AUS (2004). Isabella White (GBR), 1912-28, Nicole Pellissard-Darrigrand (FRA), 1948-60, Juno Stover-Irwin (USA), 1948-60, and Irina Lashko (URS/EUN/RUS/AUS) 1988-96, 2004, all competed in four Games. Lashko was the most successful of these with two silvers and a bronze.

The oldest gold medallist was Hjälmar Johansson (SWE) aged 34yr 186days in the plain diving at London 1908, and also the oldest ever medallist four years later in Stockholm with a silver aged 38yr 173days. The oldest female champion was Micki King (USA) in 1972 aged 28yr 33days, while the oldest female medallist was Mary Ellen Clark (USA) with a bronze in 1996 at 34yr 215days. The youngest champion, and the youngest individual Olympic champion in any Summer Games sport, was Marjorie Gestring (USA) who won the 1936 springboard title aged 13yr 268days. The youngest male diving champion was Sun Shuwei (CHN) in 1992 aged 16yr 185days. Dorothy Poynton-Hill (USA) was the youngest medallist in 1928 aged 13yr 23days, while the youngest male medallist was Nils Skoglund (SWE) aged 14yr 10days, also in 1920. Greg Louganis (USA) won both diving titles in 1984 by the biggest margins ever recorded at the Games.

Five divers, four women and a man, have won medals at swimming as well as for diving. The most successful was Aileen Riggin (USA) with gold and silver diving medals in 1920 and 1924, and a bronze in the backstroke at Paris. Georg Hoffmann (GER) won silvers in 1904 at diving and the 100m backstroke; Helen Wainwright (USA) won a silver in the 1920 diving, and another silver in the 1924 400m freestyle; Katherine Rawls (USA) won a silver in the 1936 springboard and a bronze in the relay; Hjördis Töpel (SWE) won bronzes at diving and the relay in 1924.

The most successful husband and wife team were Clarence and Elizabeth (née Becker) Pinkston (USA), who between them won three golds, two silvers and two bronzes from 1920 to 1928. Elizabeth won her second gold medal, in 1928,

on the second birthday of her twin children. Two male divers, Giorgio Cagnotto (ITA), 1964-80, and Niki Stajkovic (AUT), 1972-80 and 1988-92, have competed at five Games. In 2000, at Sydney, male and female synchronized diving events were added.

DOG SLED RACING

A DEMONSTRATION SPORT held at the Lake Placid Winter Games in 1932. A race for twelve sled teams, seven dogs to a sled, was held There were two races of approximately 40km 25 miles each, with the aggregate times added together. Emile St Goddard (CAN) won easily finishing first both times in a combined 4hr 23min 12.5sec, nearly eight minutes ahead of Lennard Seppala (USA).

DOUBLES ACROSS SPORTS

THERE HAVE BEEN a number of multi-talented sports people who have won Olympic medals in different sports. The only one to win gold medals in both Summer and Winter Games was Eddie Eagan (USA) who won the 1920 light-heavyweight boxing title, and was a member of the 1932 winning 4-man bob. His closest rival has been Jacob Tullin Thams (NOR) who won the ski jump in 1924, and then took a silver in yachting in 1936. The most outstanding woman in this line of endeavour was Christa Rothenburger-Luding (GDR) who won a gold and a silver at speed skating at Calgary in 1988, and then came second in the sprint cycling at Seoul later the same year. Not quite of the same standard was Clara Hughes (CAN), who won two bronzes in the 1996 cycling events, and then won a gold, a silver and a bronze at speed skating in 2002-06. In the Summer Games the earliest double gold winner at two sports was Carl Schuhmann (GER), with three gymnastic events and the wrestling in 1896. At the same Games, Edwin Flack (AUS) won the 800/1500m double on the track, and joined with British discus thrower George Robertson to win the tennis doubles bronze medal on the morning of the 800m final. He also started the marathon two days later, but dropped out some 4km short of the finish. Also at Athens, Viggo Jensen (DEN) won a gold and silver in weightlifting, a silver and a bronze at shooting, and was fourth in the rope climb. Fritz Hofmann (GER) won the silver medal in the 1896 100m, and is also included in the gold medal gymnastics team in some sources. Morris Kirksey (USA) won gold medals in the 4x100m relay and as a member of the American Rugby team in 1920. Daniel Norling (SWE) won gymnastic golds in 1908 and 1912, and then an equestrian gold in 1920. John Derbyshire (GBR) and Paul Radmilovic (GBR) won golds at swimming and the allied sport of water polo in the early part of the century. In 1908/1912 Victor Boin (BEL) won a silver and a bronze medal in water polo, and then in 1920, after having taken the oath for competitors in the opening ceremony, gained a silver as a member of the épée team.

Examples of women excelling in two summer Olympic sports are rare, with the most outstanding being Roswitha Krause (GDR) who won a 1968 silver in the 4x100m freestyle, and then won silver and bronze in the 1976 and 1980 handball tournaments. Anfissa Reztsova (URS/EUN) was the first Winter Games Olympian to win gold medals at two sports, in cross-country skiing in 1988 and the biathlon in 1992.

One of the more unusual doubles was that of Fernand de Montigny (BEL), who won a gold, two silver and two bronze medals in fencing in five Games, 1906-1924, and another bronze on the hockey field in 1920. Although Otto Herschmann's double, of a bronze in the 1896 100m freestyle and a silver in the 1912 sabre fencing team, is not particularly outstanding, he was unique in that at the time of his fencing medal he was the President of the Austrian Olympic Committee, and is the only competitor holding such a position to win an Olympic medal. However, even more unique was Frank Kungler (USA), who has the unmatched distinction of winning medals at three sports at the same Games. (See 'Trebles').

DRUGS

DISTANCE RUNNERS AT the end of the 19th century took small doses of strychnine as a stimulant, and it is known that the winner of the 1904 Olympic marathon was administered a dose during the race. However, under the regulations of the time this was not illegal.

Although there are reports that evidence of drug use had been found after the Winter Games at Oslo in 1952, the first 'official' Olympic drug abuse scandal occurred in the 1960 100km cycling race when two Danish competitors collapsed. One of them, Knut Jensen, died from what was originally thought to be sunstroke. It transpired that they had both taken overdoses of a blood-circulation stimulant. Random testing was introduced at the 1964 Games at Tokyo for cycling, and then in 1968, at the Grenoble Winter Games and Mexico City, testing for all sports was instituted. At Munich in 1972, the American swimmer Rick DeMont lost the gold medal in the 400m freestyle after testing positive for a prohibited substance, though it should be stated that as an asthmatic DeMont apparently did not realise that the drug was in his regular medication. Also at Munich

came the first judo contestant to fail a drugs test, when Bakhaavaa Buidaa (MGL) was disqualified after taking the silver medal in his class. There was a spate of disqualifications in weightlifting at Montreal in 1976, and the first track and field athlete at the Olympics to fail a test was the Polish female discus thrower, Danuta Rosani in 1976. An even more high-profile case occurred in the 1984 10,000m, when the second placed finisher, Martti Vainio of Finland, was disqualified after a test. It was reported that as many as 17 'A' samples were found to be positive at Los Angeles, but as the athlete's code numbers mysteriously disappeared no 'B' samples were tested.

Without doubt the biggest drugs 'scandal' at the Games was when the Canadian sprinter Ben Johnson was disqualified after winning the 100m, in a sensational 9.79sec, at Seoul in 1988. However, in 2004, at Athens, the 'Johnson' incident was rivalled by the farcical events involving the Greek sprinters Konstadinos Kedéris and Ekaterini Thánou relating to missed out-of competition drug tests. In 1992 the International Weightlifting Federation changed all weight categories after the Olympic Games of that year, thus eliminating all existing world records, in a move to counter marks made during a period of suspected excessive drug abuse. In the 1990s there surfaced irrefutable evidence that the East German (GDR) state sponsored the supply of drugs to East German sportsmen and women, especially the latter. It should be noted that there is also strong evidence that the drugs 'culture' was, and is, very prevalent in the western democracies. National and international governing bodies are working hard to counter this cheating, and foremost in this fight has been the IAAF (International Association of Athletics Federations).

EQUESTRIANISM

IN THE ANCIENT Games the first known event using horses was a chariot race in 680BC. Horses with riders came into the Games in 648BC. The first equestrian gold medallist of the modern Olympics was Aimé Haegeman (BEL) on *Benton II* in the 1900 show jumping. In 1956 the equestrian events were held separately, at Stockholm, from the main Games due to the strict Australian quarantine laws. The most gold medals won by a rider is six (one individual and five team events) by Reiner Klimke (FRG) 1964-1988. Klimke's total of eight medals, comprising the six golds and two bronzes, also constitutes a record for equestrianism, as does his feat of winning golds in five separate Games over a 24 year period. The medals won by Gustav-Adolf Boltenstern Jr (SWE) over a similar 24-year period, 1932-1956, were not both gold.

The oldest gold medallist was Josef Neckarmann

(FRG) in the 1968 dressage team aged 56yr 141days. The oldest individual event winner was Ernst Linder (SWE) in the 1924 dressage aged 56yr 91days. The youngest individual champion was Edmund Coffin (USA) in the 1976 three-day event aged 21yr 77days. However, Mary Tauskey (USA) won a gold medal in the three-day team event in 1976 aged 20yr 235days. The d'Inzeo brothers of Italy, Raimondo and Piero, competed in a record eight Games, 1948-1976. Raimondo won a gold, two silver and three bronze medals, while Piero gained two silvers and four bronze. Ian Millar (CAN) also competed at show jumping in eight Games, but over a period of 32 years, 1972-2004. A Bulgarian, Kroum Lekarski, competed in the three-day event over a record period of 36 years between 1924 and 1960, but only competed in four Games. The female record is competition in six Games by Christilot Hansen-Boylen (CAN), over a record period of 28 years, 1964-92. This 28-year span was first achieved by British-born Anne Jessica Ransehousen (née Newberry) (USA) 1960-88. Women first competed in 1952, and Lis Hartel (DEN) won the first female medal with a silver in the dressage, and repeated the feat in 1956. The most successful women have been Nicole Uphoff (GER) with four golds in 1988-92, and Isabell Werth (GER) with four golds in 1992-2000. However, Werth also won two silvers. Since 1984 equestrianism has been the only Olympic sport in which men and women compete against each other in individual events.

The only horse to be ridden to gold medals in three Games was *Gigolo* under Isabell Werth (GER) 1992-2000 when they won four golds and two silvers. Liselott Linsenhoff (FRG) won two dressage golds and a silver in 1968-72, and her daughter Ann-Kathrin won a gold in 1988. The most successful father and son have been Gustav-Adolf Boltenstern senior and junior (SWE), with the former winning a dressage individual bronze in 1912, and the latter two golds a silver and a bronze, also in dressage, 1932-56. A unique equestrian participation record is that held by the family of William Roycroft (AUS), himself the oldest medallist in the sport at 61yr 130days in 1976. His son Wayne won a bronze in the same team, as he also had in 1968, while two other sons, Clarke (1972) and Barry (1976 & 1988) also competed well. In addition, Wayne's wife Vicki competed in 1984 and 1988, so that a Roycroft was in Australian teams from 1960 to 1988, and Wayne coached the winning Australian 3-Day team in 1996-2000.

In 1936 Germany completed the only six gold medal 'clean sweep' in Games equestrian history. In the 1912 and 1920 individual dressage Sweden took the first three places both times, a unique occurrence.

Show Jumping

This was the first equestrian event to be included in the Games, along with high and long jumping contests, in 1900. From 1924 until 1968 teams comprised three members, all counting for the final score. This led to many teams not finishing, as in 1932 when no team medals were awarded at all, and in 1948 when only four of the 14 competing teams finished. Since 1972 teams have consisted of four riders with the best three scoring. The most gold medals won are five by Hans-Günter Winkler (FRG) 1956-72. His total of seven medals, including a silver and bronze, is also a record for the discipline, as is his feat of winning medals in six Games. Only Pierre Jonquères d'Oriola (FRA) has won the individual title twice. The first woman to win a medal was Pat Smythe (GBR) in the 1956 team event, while the first individual medallist was Marion Coakes (GBR) in 1968.

The oldest gold medallist was Winkler in 1972 aged 46yr 49days, while the oldest individual champion was Jonquères d'Oriola aged 44yr 266days in 1964. Bill Steinkraus (USA) won medals over a twenty-year period 1952-1972, a record matched by Winkler 1956-1976. The youngest gold medallist was Jim Day (CAN) in the 1968 team aged 22yr 117days. The lowest score obtained by a winner is no faults, by Frantisek Ventura (TCH) on *Eliot* in 1928, Jonquères d'Oriola (FRA) on *Ali Baba* in 1952, Alwin Schockemöhle (FRG) on *Warwick Rex* in 1976, and Ludger Beerbaum (GER) on *Classic Touch* in 1992. The most successful horse was *Winkler's Halla* with three golds in 1956 and 1960.

Dressage

The most successful rider was Reiner Klimke (see above), but Henri St Cyr (SWE), 1952-56, and Nicole Uphoff (GER), 1988-92, won the individual title twice. Remarkably, when Reiner Klimke (GER) won his last gold, it was in the 1988 team event which included Ann-Kathrin Linsenhoff, the daughter of his gold-winning team partner of twenty years before. In all St Cyr won a record four golds, as did Nicole Uphoff. Undoubtedly St Cyr's total would have been more but his team was disqualified in 1948, having finished first, because one of its members, Gehnäll Persson, was not a fully commissioned officer – a requirement at that time. With the rules changed Persson was in the 1952 and 1956 winning teams. This Swedish team of St Cyr, Persson, and Gustav-Adolf Boltenstern Jr, uniquely finished in first place three times in a row, and can claim to be the most successful combination in Olympic history. Isabell Werth (GER) won four golds and two silvers 1992-2000, including a unique, for women, golds in three Games.

The first woman to win a medal was Lis Hartel (see

above). Amazingly she was a polio victim who had to be helped on and off her horse. The first female gold medallist was Liselott Linsenhoff (FRG) in 1972. The silver medallist that year, Yelena Petushkova (URS), won gold in the team event, and was, for a time, married to Valeri Brumel, the 1964 Olympic high jump champion. The oldest gold medallist was Josef Neckarmann (see above), who was also the oldest medallist in 1972 aged 60yr 96days. Incidentally the oldest competitor in Olympic equestrian history was General Arthur von Pongracz (AUT) who began his Olympic career in 1924 aged 60yr and finished it in 1936, just missing a bronze medal, aged 72 – one of the oldest ever Olympians. The oldest woman ever to compete in the Olympic Games, at any sport, was Lorna Johnstone (GBR) who placed twelfth in the 1972 dressage five days after her 70th birthday. The youngest rider to win a gold medal was Nicole Uphoff (FRG) in the 1988 team event aged 22y 244days. The most successful horse has been *Gigolo* ridden by Isabell Werth 1992-2000 to four golds and two silvers. *Rembrandt* ridden by Nicole Uphoff (GER) also won four golds in 1988 and 1992, including, uniquely, the individual title twice. They competed again in 1996 but failed to reach the final.

Three-Day Event

Competitions actually last four days as the dressage segment now occupies two days. Charles Pahud de Mortanges (NED) won the individual title twice, in 1928 and 1932, as did Mark Todd (NZL) in 1984 and 1988. However, the Dutchman also won a record total of four golds and a silver from 1924 to 1932. His Dutch team, including Gerard de Kruijff and Adolph van der Voort van Zijp, uniquely won two team titles with the same team members. The most appearances and the longest span of competition is seven Games and 28 years by Mickey Plumb (USA) 1964-1992. (His Games total would have been a record-equalling eight except for the US boycott of Moscow in 1984). The first female competitor was Helena Dupont (USA), 33rd in 1964, while the first female gold medallists were Mary Gordon-Watson and Bridget Parker (both GBR) in 1972. The first individual medals won by women were in 1984 by Karen Stives (USA) and Virginia Holgate (GBR).

The oldest gold medallist was Derek Allhusen (GBR) aged 54yr 286days in 1968, while the youngest was Mary Takey (USA) in 1976 aged 20yr 235days. The oldest medallist is William Roycroft (AUS) with a bronze in 1976 aged 61yr 130days in the same team as his son, Wayne. The youngest medallist was Charles Hough (USA) aged 18yr 92days in 1952. The most successful horse was *Marcroix* ridden by Charles Pahud de Mortange (NED) to three golds

and a silver in 1928 and 1932. Both *Silver Piece*, ridden by Voort van Zijp (NED), 1924 and 1928, and *Charisma*, ridden by Mark Todd (NZL), 1984 and 1988, also won three golds. Two members of the 1996 winning US team were husband and wife David and Karen O'Connor, and David won the individual title in 2000. Twice (2000-04) placed fourth in the team event was Ingrid Klimke, daughter and pupil of the legendary Reiner (see above).

The 1936 cross-country course was so tough that only four teams out of 14 finished. One of the members of that fourth placed team, Otomar Bureš of Czechoslovakia, had over 18,000 penalty points against him at the finish, having taken over 2¾ hours to catch his horse after a fall. Britain's Capt Richard Fanshawe, with a similar problem with his horse, *Bowie Knife*, gained over 8,000 penalty points, but had the satisfaction of finishing with a team bronze. In 1920 the dressage was excluded, with two cross-country runs, at 20km *12.4 miles* and 50km *31.06 miles*, added to the jumping.

Equestrianism Medals

	G	S	B	Total
Germany	23	14	14	51
United States	10	19	17	46
Sweden	17	9	14	40
France	12	12	11	35
FRG	11	5	9	25
Great Britain	6	9	10	25
Italy	7	9	7	23
Switzerland	4	10	7	21
Netherlands	9	9	2	20
Soviet Union	6	5	4	15
Belgium	4	2	5	11
Australia	6	2	2	10
New Zealand	3	2	4	9
Mexico	2	1	4	7
Poland	1	3	2	6
Denmark	-	4	1	5
Spain	1	2	1	4
Canada	1	1	2	4
Austria	1	1	1	3
Brazil	1	-	2	3
Portugal	-	-	3	3
Chile	-	2	-	2
Romania	-	1	1	2
Czechoslovakia	1	-	-	1
Japan	1	-	-	1
Argentina	-	1	-	1
Bulgaria	-	1	-	1
Norway	-	1	-	1
Hungary	-	-	1	1
Saudi Arabia	-	-	1	1
	127[1]	125	125[2]	377

[1]*Two golds in 1900 high jump*
[2]*No bronze in 1932 Three-Day team event*

EVER PRESENT

Countries

ONLY FIVE COUNTRIES have never failed to be represented at celebrations of the Summer Games since 1896 (including 1906): Australia, France, Greece, Great Britain and Switzerland. (It should be noted that prior to 1924 Irish competitors were members of the United Kingdom of Great Britain and Ireland team, and did not then represent Ireland. In 1956 Switzerland only competed in the Stockholm segment of the Games). Of those five, only France, Great Britain and Switzerland have been present at all Winter Games as well. Of these only Great Britain competed in the skating and ice hockey events of 1908 and 1920, the 'winter' events included in those Summer Games.

Events

THERE HAVE BEEN 15 individual events that have been contested at every modern Olympic Games. In the athletics programme they are: 100m, 400m, 800m, 1500m, Marathon, 110m hurdles, high jump, pole vault, long jump, triple jump (originally the hop, step and jump), shot and discus. In fencing there have been the individual foil and sabre contests. In swimming the 1500m freestyle may be included although the event was actually 1200m in 1896, 1000m in 1900, and one mile in 1904 and 1906.

Sports

ONLY FIVE SPORTS have been contested at every modern Games since 1896. They are athletics, cycling, fencing, gymnastics and swimming. Rowing would have been included, but rough seas caused the cancellation of the programmed rowing events in 1896.

FAMILIES

THERE HAVE BEEN some remarkable family achievements in the Olympic Games.(See also under 'Brothers' and 'Sisters'). Outstanding among them have been the Gyarmati family of Hungary. The patriarch was Dezső, who won three golds, one silver and a bronze in water polo 1948-64; his wife Éva Székely won one gold and a silver as a breaststroke swimmer 1952-56; their daughter Andrea won a silver and a bronze in 1972 at backstroke and butterfly; and Andrea married Mihály Hesz who had won a gold and a silver at canoeing 1964-68. Also noteworthy were the yachting Lunde family of Norway. Eugen Lunde won a gold in the 1924 6m class; his son Peder, daughter-in-law Vibeke, and Vibeke's brother, won a silver in the 1952 5.5m class; and grandson Peder Jr won a gold in the 1960 Flying Dutchman

class. A similar impact was made on fencing by the Gerevich family of Hungary: Aladár won a record seven golds, one silver and two bronzes 1932-60; his wife Erna Bogen won a bronze in 1932; her father Albert Bogen (AUT) won a silver in 1912; and Aladár and Erna's son, Pál, won two bronze medals in 1972 and 1980. The latest high-flying family are the hockey playing Kellers of Germany. Grandfather Erwin won a silver back in 1936, in the era of the all-conquering Indians; his son Carsten took gold in 1972; Grandson Andreas won gold in 1996; and his granddaughter Natascha gained gold in 2004. Many other father/son, mother/daughter, brother/sister, and husband/wife combinations have enriched the Games – they are noted under the various sports.

FENCING

UNDOUBTEDLY BECAUSE OF de Coubertin's personal interest, fencing was of the original sports held in 1896, when the first Olympic champion was Eugène-Henri Gravelotte (FRA) in the foil. Until recently it was the only sport in which professionals had openly competed in the Games, as special events for fencing masters were held in 1896 and 1900. At the latter Games they even competed against amateur competitors, so that Albert Ayat (FRA) beat his pupil Ramón Fonst (CUB) in the épée. When Leon Pyrgos won the foil contest for fencing masters in 1896 he became the first Greek Olympic champion of modern times. A foil competition for women was introduced in 1924, and a team contest for them in 1960. Team and individual épée events for women were introduced in 1996. In 2004 an individual sabre event for women was added, but the foil team event was dropped. Electronic scoring equipment was used for épée in 1936, for foil in 1956, and for the sabre in 1992.

Aladár Gerevich (HUN) won a record seven gold medals in the sabre between 1932 and 1960. The record for most medals is 13 by Edoardo Mangiarotti (ITA) in foil and épée 1936-1960, comprising six golds, five silvers and two bronzes. His elder brother Dario won a gold and two silvers in 1948 and 1952. Nedo Nadi (ITA) won an unequalled five golds at one Games in 1920, and his younger brother Aldo added three more golds and a silver – a family record total at a Games. The most individual event gold medals is three achieved by Ramón Fonst (CUB) in 1900 and 1904 (two), and by Nedo Nadi (ITA) in 1912 and 1920 (two). The only man, in any sport, to win Olympic gold medals at six consecutive Games was Aladár Gerevich (see above); his medal winning span of 28 years is also a record. Britain's Bill Hoskyns also competed at six Games, 1956-1976, but won only two silver medals, while Norman Armitage (USA) attended six celebrations, 1928-56, and gained a bronze in 1948. The equal longest span of competition by any Olympic competitor is 40 years by Ivan Osiier (DEN) who fenced from 1908 to 1948, in a record seven Games, during which time he won a silver medal in 1912, and became the oldest Olympic fencer in 1948 aged 59yr 240days. His fencer wife Ellen won a gold medal in 1924.

Four fencers have won individual medals in all three disciplines at one Games. Both Nedo Nadi and his brother Aldo won golds in each of the team events in 1920. Roger Ducret (FRA) won foil and épée golds and a sabre silver in 1924. In the sparsely supported 1904 events American-born Albertson Van Zo Post (CUB) won a foil silver and bronzes in the other two disciplines. The oldest gold medallist was Aladár Gerevich (HUN) in 1960 aged 50yr 178days, while the youngest was Ramón Fonst (CUB) aged 16yr 289days in 1900. The family of Gerevich has a unique position in Olympic fencing as he won seven golds, one silver and two bronzes; his wife Erna Bogen won a bronze in 1932, her father-in-law Albert Bogen won a silver in 1912, and Aladár's son Pál won bronze medals in 1972 and 1980.

Foil

ONLY NEDO NADI (ITA) in 1912 and 1920, and Christian d'Oriola (FRA) in 1952 and 1956 have won two individual titles. In addition, d'Oriola won two team golds and two silvers for a record six medals. The oldest gold medallist was Henri Jobier (FRA) who was over 44 years old in the winning 1924 team, while the youngest was Nedo Nadi (ITA) in 1912 aged 18yr 29days. In the 15 Games from 1920 to 1984 France only failed once to gain a team competition medal.

Epée

RAMÓN FONST (CUB) was the only double winner of the individual title, but the most successful was Edoardo Mangiarotti (ITA) with five gold, one silver and two bronze medals 1936-1960. The oldest gold medallist was Fiorenzo Marini (ITA) aged 46yr 179days in the 1960 team, and the youngest was Fonst (see above). Charles Newton-Robinson, a member of the silver winning British team in 1906 was 52yr 197days, the oldest ever Olympic fencing medallist.

Fencing Medals

	Men			Women			
	G	S	B	G	S	B	Total
France	38	36	30	4	3	5	116
Italy	35	34	22	8	5	5	109
Hungary	27	16	20	7	6	6	82
Soviet Union	14	14	15	5	3	3	54
Germany	4	4	6	2	5	4	25
Poland	4	7	7	-	1	2	21
United States[1]	2	6	11	1	-	1	21
FRG	4	6	-	3	2	1	16
Russia	6	2	4	2	-	1	15
Belgium	5	3	5	-	-	-	13
Romania	2	-	2	1	3	4	12
Cuba[1]	5	3	3	-	-	-	11
Great Britain	-	6	-	1	3	-	10
Greece	3	3	2	-	-	-	8
Switzerland	1	2	3	-	2	-	8
Netherlands	-	1	7	-	-	-	8
Sweden	2	3	2	-	-	-	7
China	-	3	-	1	2	1	7
Austria	-	1	3	1	-	2	7
Denmark	-	1	1	1	1	2	6
Korea	1	-	1	-	-	-	2
Bohemia(Czech)	-	-	2	-	-	-	2
GDR	-	1	-	-	-	-	1
Mexico	-	-	-	-	1	-	1
Argentina	-	-	1	-	-	-	1
Portugal	-	-	1	-	-	-	1
Ukraine	-	-	1	-	-	-	1
	153	152	149	37	37	37	565

[1]Double counting for 1904 team gold medal

Sabre

JEAN GEORGIADIS (GRE), Jenő Fuchs (HUN), Rudolf Kárpáti (HUN), Viktor Krovopouskov (URS) and Jean François Lamour (FRA) have all won two individual titles. Gerevich (see above) won a record seven gold medals (only one individual) and was also the oldest gold medallist. The youngest was Mikhail Burtsev (URS) aged 20yr 36days in the 1976 team event. Hungarians have dominated the discipline to an unparalleled extent, winning 12 gold, six silver and eight bronze individual medals. They won the individual title every year from 1908 to 1964, except in 1920 when they were not invited. They have won the team title 11 times, placed second once, and third on three occasions, and won 46 consecutive contests from 1924 to 1964. Their 1960 team included Gerevich, Rudolf Kárpáti and Pál Kovács, who between them amassed a total of 19 gold medals. The winning Hungarian teams of 1948 and 1952 comprised the same members. An interesting coincidence is that Kárpáti and former IOC President Juan Antonio Samaranch were born on the same day. In 2004 Aldo Montano (ITA), won the individual sabre title – his father, Mario, had won golds in the team events in 1972-76, and his grandfather, also Aldo, had won silvers in the team events of 1936 and 1948.

Women's Foil

ONLY ILONA ELEK (HUN) 1936-48 and Valentina Vezzali (ITA) 2000-04 have won two individual titles. However, Yelena Novikova-Belova (URS) 1968-76, Vezzali and Giovanna Trillini (ITA) 1992-04, all won a record four golds. However, Trillini also won a silver and two bronzes, matching the record for most medals, seven. This was held by Ildikó Ságiné-Rejtó (formerly Ujlakiné-Rejtó) of Hungary who won medals in a record five Games, 1960-1976. Perhaps surprisingly she was born deaf. Ellen Müller-Preis (AUT) competed over a record 24 year period 1932-1956. This was matched by Kerstin Palm (SWE) from 1964-88, but she notched up a record seven Games – the most attended by any female Olympic competitor, in any sport. It is noteworthy that both Vezzali and Trillini came from the same small town, Jesi, in Italy.

Elek was the oldest gold medallist in 1948 aged 41yr 77days, and the oldest medallist four years later with a silver aged 45yr 71days. The youngest champion/medallist was Helene Mayer (GER) in 1928 aged 17yr 225days. When Gillian Sheen (GBR) won her gold medal in 1956 there were hardly any members of the British press corps on hand as they considered that fencing was a 'minor' sport, and anyway she had not been expected to achieve anything of note.

Women's Épée

FIRST HELD IN 1996, with individual and team competitions. The most successful has been Laura Flessel-Colovic (FRA) with two golds a silver and a bronze 1996-2004. The youngest gold medallist was Anna Sivkova, in the winning Russian team in 2004 aged 22yr 130days, while the oldest gold medallist/medallist was Sophie Moresee-Pichot (FRA) in the winning team in 1996 aged 34yr 112days. The youngest medallist was Sophie Lamon (SUI) in the Sydney silver medal épée team aged 15yr 224days.

Women's Sabre

FIRST HELD IN 2004. The oldest/youngest gold medallist was Mariel Zagunis (USA) aged 19yr 167days She was also the youngest medallist. The oldest medallist was her teammate Sada Jacobson aged 21yr 185days.

FIGURE SKATING

ICE SKATING HAD been included in the original programme of events for the 1900 Games, but was not held. Thus, the first Olympic title at a winter Games event was won by Ulrich Salchow (SWE) in 1908 at the Prince's Ice Rink, London. Salchow gave his name to one of the most popular jumps. Also in the 1908 Games there was a special figures event that was won by a Russian (Czarist variety), Nikolai Panin, who had been too ill to compete in the main event. The first women's title went to Madge Syers (GBR), who six years previously had entered the World Championships, ostensibly for men only, and had placed second to Salchow. The most gold medals won by a figure skater is three achieved by Gillis Grafström (SWE) 1920-1928, Sonja Henie (NOR) 1928-1936, and Irina Rodnina (URS) in the pairs 1972-1980. Of these only Grafström also won a silver, in 1932 aged 38, and thus is the only skater to win medals in four Games. No skater has doubled completely successfully in singles and pairs at the Games. The best have been Ernst Baier (GER) with the pairs gold and a singles silver in 1936, and Madge Syers (GBR) with a singles gold and a pairs bronze in 1908.

The oldest gold medallist was Walter Jakobsson (FIN) who won the 1920 pairs with his German-born wife Ludowika aged 38yr 80days. Ludowika became the oldest ever female winner aged 35yr 276days. The youngest was Maxi Herber (GER) aged 15yr 128days in the 1936 pairs with Baier, whom she later married. The youngest individual event champion was Tara Lipinski (USA) in 1998 aged 15yr 255days. The youngest male champion was Richard Button (USA) aged 18yr 202days winning the 1948 singles. The youngest medallist was Scott Allen (USA) two days short of his 15th birthday taking the 1964 singles bronze, while the youngest female medallist was Manuela Gross (GDR) just ten days past her 15th birthday in the 1972 bronze-winning pair. The oldest medallist was Martin Stixrud (NOR) with the 1920 singles bronze aged 44yr 78days, while the oldest female medallist was Ludowika Jacobsson (FIN) with a pairs silver in 1924 aged 39yr 189days. The youngest ever Winter Games competitor was Cecilia Colledge (GBR), who was 11yr 73days at the 1932 Games – she gained the silver medal in 1936 behind Sonja Henie. The youngest male competitor was Jan Hoffmann (GDR) aged 12yr 110days in 1968 – twelve years later he gained the silver medal.

Sonja Henie won three Olympic, six European and ten World titles before turning professional and making an estimated $47 million in ice shows and films. The film world attracted a number of other Olympic skaters. Down the field (16th) in 1936 was Gladys Jepson-Turner (GBR) who had a Hollywood career as Belita, and Vera Hruba (TCH), one place behind the British girl, married the head of Republic Pictures and starred in many films as Vera Hruba Ralston. Sonja Henie is usually credited with introducing jumps into the women's event, but in 1920, Theresa Weld (USA), the bronze medal winner, included a salchow in her programme, which brought a reprimand from the judges and a threat that she would be penalized if she continued with such 'unfeminine behaviour'. In the 1992 Games Surya Bonaly (FRA) attempted the first ever quadruple jump, in competition, by a woman.

A change of marking in the sport was brought about by Trixi Schuba (AUT) winning the 1972 title primarily on the basis of her excellent set figures (she was only placed seventh in free skating). At that time the marks had been divided 50-50 between sections, but they were changed to give greater emphasis to free skating. Set figures were skated for the last time at Calgary in 1988, and are no longer included in Olympic competition. On the subject of marks, Jayne Torvill and Christopher Dean (GBR) were awarded a maximum nine sixes for their artistic impression in the 1984 ice dancing event, as well as another three sixes for technical merit – unsurpassed marking at the Games. In 1994 stricter rules governing skimpy clothing were introduced, but have not always been enforced. The sport has always been plagued by the accusations – often thought to be merited – that many of the judges indulge in so-called 'protocol judging', or judging on reputation rather than actual performance. In 2002 at Salt Lake City there were accusations that a French judge in the pairs event had 'done a deal' – her marking was so blatantly incorrect that the result was revised to give the Canadian pair a joint gold medal with the Russians. A new scoring system has since been introduced,

In 1972, although Irina Rodnina and Aleksey Ulanov (URS) won the pairs it was the latter's dalliance with Ludmila Smirnova, silver medallist with Andrei Suraikin, which caught the media interest. The result was a break-up of the top Soviet pair. Rodnina then teamed with Aleksandr Zaitsev, while Ulanov and Smirnova got married. In the World Championships the Rodnina/Zaitsev partnership beat the other pair and, getting married themselves in 1975, they went on to win two Olympic titles, the second less than a year after the birth of a son. Artur Dmitriyev (EUN/RUS), with Natalya Mishkutienok, won the 1992 pairs title. At Nagano in 1998 he appeared with a new partner, Oksana Kazakova, and won the gold again, In 2006, the pairs title went to Russian (i.e. URS, EUN, RUS) pairs for the twelfth consecutive time. There was high drama in the 2006 pairs event when Zhang Dan (CHN) crashed to the ice after attempting a quadruple Salchow. After resting a few minutes, she resumed with her partner, Zhang Hao, and, remarkably, won the silver medal. In 1998, Yevgeni Platov and Oksana Grischuk became the first couple to successfully defend the ice dance title.

Figure Skating Medals

	G	S	B	Total
United States	13	15	16	44
Soviet Union	13	10	6	29
Russia	12	7	1	20
Austria	7	9	4	20
Canada	3	7	10	20
Great Britain	5	3	7	15
France	3	2	7	12
Sweden	5	3	2	10
GDR	3	3	4	10
Germany	4	4	1	9
Norway	3	2	1	6
Hungary	-	2	4	6
Czechoslovakia	1	1	3	5
Netherlands	1	2	-	3
Switzerland	-	2	1	3
China	-	-	3	3
Finland	1	1	-	2
Japan	1	1	-	2
Belgium	1	-	1	2
Ukraine	1	-	1	2
China	-	1	1	2
FRG	-	-	2	2
Italy	-	-	1	1
	77[1]	75[1]	76	228

[1]In 2002 there were two gold medals in the pairs event

FIRSTS

THE FIRST PERSON to win an event in the Modern Olympics was Francis Lane (USA), who won heat one of the 100m in 1896. The first gold medallist was James Brendan Connolly (USA) the winner of the 1896 hop, step and jump (now known as the triple jump). See also under 'Women'.

FLAG

THE OLYMPIC FLAG was devised by Baron de Coubertin, based on a design depicted on an ancient Greek symbol found at Delphi. It consists of five interlaced rings in two rows, coloured blue, yellow, black, green and red, from left to right. The rings are meant to symbolize the friendship of mankind, with the colours, including the white background of the flag itself, representing all nations – every national flag contains at least one of the colours.

There is an erroneous idea that the colours themselves represent the continents: blue – Europe; yellow – Asia; black – Africa; Green – the Americas; Red – Australasia. It was originally presented to the IOC in 1912, and was to be flown for the first time at the 1916 Games, but Antwerp had the honour in 1920. In 1984 Korea presented a new flag to the IOC and it was first flown at the Seoul Games in 1988. At the end of a Games the flag is placed in the safe keeping of the host city of the next celebration.

FLAME

IT SEEMS THAT the original idea to have an Olympic flame in an Olympic stadium was by Jan Wils, the Dutch architect of the 1928 Amsterdam stadium, who included in his design a tower specifically for that purpose, topped by a cauldron. Since then has always burned throughout the duration of a Games. It symbolizes the endeavour for perfection and struggle for victory. It is first lit by the rays of the sun in an enactment of an ancient ceremony at Olympia, the site of the original Games. (See also Torch Relay). The following have lit the Olympic flame in the stadium:

Summer

1936	Fritz Schilgen
1948	John Mark
1952	Paavo Nurmi (Hannes Kolehmainen on tower)
1956	Ron Clarke
1960	Giancarlo Peris
1964	Yoshinori Sakai
1968	Enriqueta Basilio
1972	Gunter Zahn
1976	Stephane Prefontaine & Sandra Henderson
1980	Sergei Belov
1984	Rafer Johnson
1988	Sun-Man Chung, Won-Tuk Kim & Mi-Chung Sohn
1992	Antonio Rebollo
1996	Muhammad Ali
2000	Cathy Freeman
2004	Nikos Kaklamanakis

The first flame to burn at a Winter Games was at Oslo in 1952. It was lit at the home of Sondre Nordheim, the founder of modern skiing, at Morgedal in southern Norway, and brought by a relay of skiers to the Bislett stadium at Oslo. Thereafter the flame came from Olympia.

Winter

1952	Eigil Nansen
1956	Guido Caroli
1960	Ken Henry
1964	Joseph Rieder
1968	Alain Calmat
1972	Hideki Takada
1976	Christl Haas/Josef Feistmantl
1980	Dr Charles Morgan Kerr
1984	Sandra Dubravcic
1988	Robyn Perry
1992	Michel Platini/François-Cyrille Grange
1994	Crown Prince Haakon
1998	Midori Ito
2002	1980 USA Ice Hockey Team
2006	Stefania Belmondo

FOOTBALL

(See under separate headings for American, Australian Rules.)

SOME SOURCES REFER to two exhibition matches at Athens in the first Games of 1896, when after two Greek towns had played an eliminator, the winner, Smyrna, was defeated by a Danish side 15-0. However, the Swedish Olympic expert Ture Widlund, after considerable research, considers these reports to be spurious. Although sometimes considered unofficial, the tournaments of 1900, 1904 and 1906 are usually counted in medal tables.

Therefore soccer was the first team game to be included in the Olympics. The first goal was scored by Great Britain (represented by Upton Park FC) versus France (4-0) in 1900. The 1904 tournament only had three entries, one Canadian and two American teams, while in 1906 a Danish team beat Smyrna (representing Greece). In that latter team were five Britons named Whittal, of which three were one set of brothers and the other two another set, the two lots being cousins. This must be some sort of Olympic record for a family.

With the founding of FIFA in 1904 Olympic soccer came under their control, and from 1908 the competition grew in stature. In 1920, Egypt, the first non-European country – excepting the North Americans of 1904 – entered, and by 1924 there were 22 countries competing. That tournament and the next was won by Uruguay – who surprisingly never took part in Olympic soccer again. Two years after their Amsterdam victory Uruguay won the inaugural World Cup of 1930 with nine of their Olympic team playing. Only three other players, all Italian, have been in both Olympic (1936) and World Cup (1938) winning sides. The most successful teams have been Great Britain, winners in 1900, 1908 &

1912, and Hungary, with gold medals in 1952, 1964 & 1968. However, Hungary have also won a silver and a bronze.

There was considerable disillusionment with the interpretation of the term 'amateur' as applied to soccer at the Games, similar to the troubles in ice hockey. These arguments about pseudo-amateurs were exacerbated with the entry of the eastern European powers into the game after 1948. Great Britain, after three gold medals in the early days, did not enter in 1924 and 1928 due to disagreements between the Football Association (FA) and FIFA about broken time payments to amateurs. It re-entered Olympic competition in 1936, but after a series of poor results, Britain has not taken part since 1972. In 1952, as entries increased, qualifying rounds were introduced to decide on final 16 teams. In 1984 professionals

Football Medals

	Men			Women			
	G	S	B	G	S	B	Total
Hungary	3	1	1	-	-	-	5
United States	-	1	1	2	1	-	5
Soviet Union	2	-	3	-	-	-	5
Denmark	1	3	1	-	-	-	5
Yugoslavia	1	3	1	-	-	-	5
Brazil	-	2	1	-	1	-	4
Great Britain	3	-	-	-	-	-	3
Argentina	1	2	-	-	-	-	3
Poland	1	2	-	-	-	-	3
Spain	1	2	-	-	-	-	3
GDR	1	1	1	-	-	-	3
Italy	1	-	2	-	-	-	3
Norway	-	-	1	1	-	1	3
Sweden	1	-	2	-	-	-	3
Germany	-	-	1	-	-	2	3
Netherlands	-	-	3	-	-	-	3
Uruguay	2	-	-	-	-	-	2
Czechoslovakia	1	1	-	-	-	-	2
France	1	1	-	-	-	-	2
Belgium	1	-	1	-	-	-	2
Austria	-	1	-	-	1	-	2
Bulgaria	-	1	1	-	-	-	2
Greece	-	1	1	-	-	-	2
Cameroon	1	-	-	-	-	-	1
Canada	1	-	-	-	-	-	1
Nigeria	1	-	-	-	-	-	1
Paraguay	-	1	-	-	-	-	1
Switzerland	-	1	-	-	-	-	1
Chile	-	-	1	-	-	-	1
FRG	-	-	1	-	-	-	1
Ghana	-	-	1	-	-	-	1
Japan	-	-	1	-	-	-	1
	24	24	25[1]	3	3	3	82

[1]Third place tie in 1972

were allowed to take part, but only those who had not yet participated in World Cup competition were eligible. Currently the only restriction on players is that they must be under 23 years of age, except for three players per squad.

The highest team score in Olympic soccer was the 17-1 defeat of France by Denmark in 1908, during which the Danish centre-forward Sophus Nielsen scored a record ten goals. This mark was equalled by Gottfried Fuchs for Germany when they beat Russia 16-0 in 1912. The most goals scored by an individual in one tournament is 12 by Ferenc Bene (HUN) in 1964. The most scored in Olympic competition is 13 by Sophus Nielsen (DEN) 1908-1912, and by Antal Dunai (HUN) 1968-1972. The highest score in a final since the institution of 'proper' tournaments in 1908 has been the 4-2 defeat of Denmark by Great Britain in 1912. France's victory in 1984 was the first win by a Western European side since the outstanding Swedish team of 1948, and the first medal since the Swedish bronze of four years later. The 1968 final ended with only 18 players on the field, as three Bulgarians and an Hungarian had been sent off. In 2004 Argentina became the first team, in modern times, to go through the competition without conceding a goal (17-0).

Highest scoring individuals in Olympic tournaments

Men

1908	11	Sophus Nielsen (DEN)
1912	10	Gottfried Fuchs (GER)
1920	7	Herbert Karlsson (SWE)
1924	8	Pedro Petrone (URU)
1928	11	Domingo Tarasconi (ARG)
1936	7	Annibale Frossi (ITA)
1948	7	Gunnar Nordahl (SWE) and Karl Aage Hansen (DEN)
1952	7	Branko Zebec (YUG) and Rajko Mitic (YUG)
1956	4	Dimiter Milanov (BUL) and Neville d'Souza (IND)
1960	7	Milan Galic (YUG) and Borivoje Kostic (YUG)
1964	12	Ferenc Bene (HUN)
1968	7	Kunishige Kamamoto (JPN)
1972	9	Kazimiercz Deyna (POL)
1976	6	Andrzej Szarmach (POL)
1980	5	Sergei Andreyev (URS)
1984	5	Borislav Cvetkovic (YUG), Stjepan Deveric (YUG) and Daniel Xuereb (FRA)
1988	7	Romario Farias (BRA)
1992	7	Andrzej Juskowiak (POL)
1996	6	Hernán Crespo (ARG) and Bebeto (BRA)
2000	6	Ivan Zamorano (CHI)
2004	8	Carlos Tevez (ARG)

Women

1996	4	Linda Medalen (NOR), Pretinha (BRA), Ann Kristin Aarønes (NOR)
2000	4	Wen Sun (CHN)
2004	5	Birgit Prinz (GER)

THERE HAS ONLY been one draw in an Olympic final. That was in 1928 between Uruguay and Argentina (1-1), and the replay was won by the defending champions Uruguay 2-1. The Hungarian team which won in Helsinki in 1952 was virtually the same team that 16 months later inflicted the first home defeat on England's professionals at Wembley stadium. The most successful player has been Dezsö Nowák (HUN) who added gold medals in 1964 and 1968 to the bronze he won in 1960. Of the ten other players to win two gold medals only Arthur Berry and Vivian Woodward (both GBR) were not Uruguayans. Two of those latter, Antonio and Santos Urdinaran became the first brothers to win soccer gold medals in 1924. This feat was surpassed by the Nordahl brothers, Bertil, Knut and Gunnar, in 1948. In 1908 the Danish silver medal team included mathematician Harald Bohr, the brother of the famous nuclear physicist Niels.

The oldest gold medallist was Rostislav Václavícek (TCH) aged 33yr 239days in the 1980 final. The youngest was Idriss Carlos Kameni (CMR) aged 16yr 225days at Sydney in 2000. The youngest medallist was Osei Kuffour (GHA) in 1992 at 15yr 339days, and the oldest Fyodor Cherenkov (URS) aged 41yr 92days in 1980.

A women's competition was instituted in 1996, which proved popular with media and fans. There were 76,481 spectators for the final when the USA beat China 2-1, reportedly the largest crowd to watch any women only sporting event. The greatest aggregate was when Germany beat China 8-0 in a preliminary game in 2004, with Germany's score the highest ever achieved. The greatest winning margin was also in that match. The youngest gold medallist was Cindy Parlow (USA) aged 18yr 85days in 2000. The oldest gold medallist/medallist was Joy Fawcett (USA) in 2004 aged 36yr 200days. The youngest medallist as Renata Cota (BRA) at 18yr 49days at Athens. Twins Anne and Nina Andersen of Norway won bronze medals in 1996. The most successful players have been Mia Hamm, Julie Foudy, Joy Fawcett, Kristine Lilly and Brandi Chastain all of USA, who have each won a two golds and a silver in 1996/2004.

One of the most remarkable goals in international football involved the Swedish centre-forward Gunnar Nordahl in the 1948 semi-final against Denmark. Unexpectedly caught offside by a quick reversal of play, Nordahl realized that his team were attacking again. With lightning presence of mind he leapt into the back of the Danish goal, thus taking himself off the field of play, and duly caught the goal scoring header from his teammate Henry Carlsson with the goalkeeper on the ground five metres away. In the 1920 final between Belgium and Czechoslovakia, the latter team walked off the field, in protest against the referee, before half-time when they were 2-0 down. The match was abandoned and the Czechs disqualified. The 1936 tournament resulted in many incidents, not least the withdrawal of the Peruvian team when its win over Austria in the second round was ordered to be re-played. Austria went on to reach the final.

After many years in the doldrums, Olympic soccer had a revival in 1980 when the 56 games of the tournament, played in Moscow, Leningrad, Minsk and Kiev, attracted nearly two million spectators – more than a third of all spectators for the 1980 Games. This revival was reinforced, somewhat surprisingly, in Los Angeles in 1984, when nearly 1.5 million watched the matches, including a record 101,799 audience for the final.

FREESTYLE SKIING

FREESTYLE SKIING, FOR men and women, was a demonstration sport in 1988, comprising ballet, aerials and mogul events. Mogul events became an Olympic medal sport in 1992, with aerials added in 1994. Marking is complicated but can best be compared to diving as each manoeuvre has a degree of difficulty which affects the final marks.

The most successful competitor has been Kari Traa (NOR) with a gold, a silver and a bronze,

1998-2006. The most successful male, with a gold and a silver, has been Janne Lahtela (FIN) 1998-2002. The oldest winner and male medallist was Aleš Valenta (CZE) who won the 2002 aerials at 29yr 13days, while the oldest female gold medallist was Evelyne Leu (SUI) who won the 2006 aerials at 29yr 230days. The youngest winner, of the 2006 moguls, was Dale Begg-Smith (AUS) aged 21yr 28days, while the youngest female champion was Tae Satoya (JPN) aged 21yr 244days taking the 1998 moguls. The youngest medallist was Yelizaveta Kozhevnikova (EUN-RUS) in the 1992 moguls aged 19yr 48days, and the youngest male to win a medal was Dimitri Daschinsky (BLR) with an aerials bronze in 1998 at 20yr 101days. Elizabeth McIntyre (USA) was the oldest medallist in the 1998 moguls aged 33yr 229days. When Satoya won the 1998 moguls title she became the first Japanese women to win a Winter Olympics gold medal. At Salt Lake City in 2002 Aleš Valenta achieved the first ever 5-twist jump at the Games.

GLIDING

A DEMONSTRATION SPORT at Berlin in 1936. Fourteen countries took part in an exhibition, but the main participants were German gliders.

GOLF

PLAYED TWICE IN the Games, in 1900 and 1904. George Lyon, a former Canadian pole vault record holder, was 46yr 59days when he won the 1904 title. The most successful player was Chandler Egan (USA) who won a team gold and individual silver in

Freestyle Skiing Medals

| | Men | | | Women | | | |
	G	S	B	G	S	B	Total
United States	2	2	2	2	2	-	10
Norway	-	-	-	2	1	3	6
Canada	1	1	1	1	1	1	6
France	1	2	2	-	-	1	6
Finland	1	2	1	-	-	-	4
Australia	2	-	-	-	-	1	3
Switzerland	1	-	-	1	-	1	3
China	1	-	-	-	2	-	3
Russia	-	1	1	-	-	1	3
Belarus	-	1	2	-	-	-	3
Japan	-	-	-	1	-	1	2
Czech Republic	1	-	-	-	-	-	1
Uzbekistan	-	-	-	1	-	-	1
Germany	-	-	-	-	1	-	1
Soviet Union	-	-	-	-	1	-	1
Sweden	-	-	-	-	1	-	1
	9	9	9	9	9	9	54

1904. Sharing also in that gold medal team was his brother Walter. Charles Sands (USA), who won the inaugural competition in 1900, was one of the few people to compete in three sports at the Games, as he had played in the tennis tournament in 1900, and took part in Jeu de Paume in 1908. The winner of the only women's competition, in 1900, was Margaret Abbott, aged 20yr 110days, who became the first American woman to win an Olympic gold medal. Her mother, Mary, placed seventh in a rare case of mother and daughter competing in the same event at a Games. Currently, there have been suggestions of bringing golf back into the Games.

GYMNASTICS

IN ARTISTIC GYMNASTICS there are eight interlinked events for men and six for women. A team competition comes first, comprising one compulsory and one optional exercise for each separate discipline. For men these are: floor exercises, pommel horse, rings, horse vault, parallel bars and horizontal bar. For women they are: floor exercises, asymmetrical bars, horse vault and balance beam. Each competitor is marked out of 10.00 for both the compulsory and optional exercises at each discipline. The best total of five gymnasts per country decides the team competition. The best 36 individuals (but only a maximum of three per country) then qualify for the individual all-round competition. They each complete a further optional exercise for each discipline, and are awarded new marks. Prior to 1992 these were added to the average of their previous best total from the team competition, but since then they start from scratch. The best eight in each discipline go forward to the individual final for that event. With the exception of 1948, when scores were marked out of 20.00, points since 1936 are of some comparative value. After 1996 there were no compulsory exercises. In 1984 an individual modern rhythmic event for women was introduced, and in 1996 there was a team event. At Sydney, in 2000, trampolining for men and women was introduced. (See separate entry on Trampolining).

The first gymnastics gold medal was won by the German team on the parallel bars event in 1896, and the first individual champion was Carl Schuhmann of that team in the vault. Due to the large number of disciplines, each with their own medals awarded, gymnasts are foremost among the greatest collectors of Olympic medals. The most successful was Larissa Latynina (URS) who won a record 18 medals from 1956 to 1964, comprising nine golds (the most by any female Olympian), five silvers and four bronzes – unsurpassed in any sport. The most individual gold

medals is seven won by Vera Cáslavská (TCH) in 1964 and 1968, an Olympic record in any sport by a woman. The most gold medals won by a man is eight by Sawao Kato (JPN) 1968-76, but the male record for individual golds is six by Boris Shakhlin (URS) 1956-64 and Nikolai Andrianov (URS) 1972-80. The latter also holds the absolute Olympic record for most medals by a male competitor, in any sport, with a total of fifteen. In 1980 Aleksandr Ditiatin (URS) became the only male gymnast to gain medals in all eight events at one Games, while in 1992 Vitali Scherbo (EUN) uniquely won six gold medals at the one Games.

Gymnastics multi-medal winners

	G	S	B
Larissa Latynina (URS) 1956-64	9	5	4
Sawao Kato (JPN) 1968-76	8	3	1
Nikolai Andrianov (URS) 1972-80	7	5	3
Boris Shakhlin (URS) 1956-64	7	4	2
Vera Cáslavská (TCH) 1960-68	7	4	0
Viktor Chukarin (URS) 1952-56	7	3	1

IN RECENT YEARS the sport has caught the imagination of the public due to a tremendous increase in media, especially television, coverage. In 1968 it was the attractive blonde Czech Vera Cáslavská who drew the attention, by defeating the Soviet women only two months after the invasion of her country. At Munich, it was elfin Olga Korbut (URS) who was the focus of all, even though she was outshone, technically, by her illustrious teammate Ludmila Tourischeva. In 1976 the unsmiling Nadia Comaneci (ROM) deserved all the adulation as she scored the ultimate 10.00 on seven occasions, while the photogenic Nelli Kim (URS) attained that score twice. Aleksandr Ditiatin stole the show from the women in 1980, and also gained the first Olympic 10.00 by a man, in the horse vault. In 1984 the television cameras made a superstar of Mary Lou Retton (USA) in the absence of the East Europeans. The television pictures of the injured Kerri Strug (USA) successfully vaulting to clinch the American's team gold at Atlanta in 1996, were beamed around the world.

The oldest gold medallist was Masao Takemoto (JPN) aged 40yr 344days in the 1960 team event. Only 24 days younger was Heikki Savolainen (FIN) in the 1948 team event, who competed in a record five Games over a record span of 24 years from 1928 to 1952. The oldest male medallist was Lucien Démanet (FRA) at 45yr 266days in 1920. The youngest champion was Nadia Comaneci (ROM) aged 14yr 252days in 1976, while the oldest female champion was Àgnes Keleti (HUN) in 1956 aged 35yr 331days. The oldest female medallist has been Ethel Seymour (GBR) in 1928 aged 46yr 222days.

Gymnastics Medals

Excluding trampolining

	Men			Women			
	G	S	B	G	S	B	Total
Soviet Union	45	42	19	38	30	30	204
Japan	28	29	32	-	-	1	90
United States [1]	23	19	19	5	10	10	86
Romania	1	4	4	22	16	20	67
Switzerland	15	19	13	-	-	-	47
Hungary	7	6	4	7	6	10	40
China	11	10	6	3	4	5	39
GDR	3	3	10	3	10	7	36
Czechoslovakia	3	7	9	9	6	1	35
Russia	4	3	6	8	7	6	34
Germany	12	7	11	1	1	-	32
Italy	14	7	10	-	1	-	32
Finland	8	5	12	-	-	-	25
France	4	9	9	1	-	-	23
Bulgaria	2	2	5	-	2	2	13
Greece	5	3	3	-	-	1	12
Ukraine	2	1	3	3	1	2	12
Yugoslavia	5	2	4	-		-	11
Sweden	4	1	-	1	1	1	8
Korea	-	3	4	-	-	-	7
Belarus	-	-	4	-	2	-	6
Spain	2	-	-	1	1	1	5
Norway	2	2	1	-	-	-	5
Denmark	1	3	1	-	-	-	5
Austria[1]	2	1	-	-	-	-	3
Great Britain	-	1	1	-	-	1	3
Poland	-	1	1	-	-	1	3
Latvia	1	1	-	-	-	-	2
Belgium	-	1	1	-	-	-	2
FRG	-	-	1	-	-	1	2
Canada	1	-	-	1	-	-	2
Netherlands	-	-	-	1	-	-	1
North Korea (PRK)	1	-	-	-	-	-	1
	206	192	192	104	99	100	893

[1]*Double counting for 1904 men's team title*

The youngest male to win a gold medal was Harald Eriksen (NOR) in 1906 aged 17yr 292days. The youngest medallist was Dimitrios Loundras (GRE) who gained a bronze in the parallel bars team event of 1896 aged 10yr 218days. However, it should be noted that some doubt exists about his exact age. The youngest ever female medallist was Luigina Giavotti (ITA) in 1928 aged 11yr 303days. In 1984 it was decided that male competitors had to be a minimum of 16 years and females 15years, but in 2000 at Sydney the minimum age for all was fixed at 16years. Recent revelations suggest that in the past some countries in the Eastern bloc faked the ages of their young female performers, presenting them as older than in fact they were.

The closest margin of victory in the individual all-round contest for men was 0.012 of a point in 2004 when Paul Hamm (USA) beat Dae Eun Kim (KOR). However, the International Gymnastics Federation (FIG) has since acknowledged that a scoring error meant that the title should have gone to Yang Tae Young (KOR), who was placed third. In 1992 there was a tremendous duel for the women's all-around title between Tatyana Gutsu (EUN) and Shannon Miller (USA) which resulted in the Ukrainian girl winning by the equal smallest ever margin of 0.012p. There had been some controversy over the inclusion of Gutsu, who had failed to make the cut-off after the team competition, but was a replacement for an injured (allegedly) teammate. On two occasions there has been a triple tie for a gold medal – both times in the pommel horse event, in 1948 and 1988. Since the Soviet Union entered Olympic competition in 1952 they have won the women's team title nine times (They were not present in 1984). In 1992 they (in the guise of the Unified Team) not only won for the tenth time, but, as their swansong, took the men's and women's

Handball Medals

	Men			Women			
	G	S	B	G	S	B	Total
Soviet Union	3	1	-	2	-	2	8
Korea	-	1	-	2	3	-	6
Yugoslavia	2	-	1	1	1	-	5
Romania	-	1	3	-	-	-	4
Denmark	-	-	-	3	-	-	3
GDR	1	-	-	-	1	1	3
Norway	-	-	-	-	2	1	3
Sweden	-	3	-	-	-	-	3
Hungary	-	-	-	-	1	2	3
Croatia	2	-	-	-	-	-	2
Germany	1	1	-	-	-	-	2
Russia	1	-	1	-	-	-	2
Spain	-	-	2	-	-	-	2
Austria	-	1	-	-	-	-	1
Czechoslovakia	-	1	-	-	-	-	1
FRG	-	1	-	-	-	-	1
China	-	-	-	-	-	1	1
France	-	-	1	-	-	-	1
Poland	-	-	1	-	-	-	1
Switzerland	-	-	1	-	-	-	1
Ukraine	-	-	-	-	-	1	1
	10	10	10	8	8	8	54

individual and team titles plus the rhythmic crown. With the Soviet Union broken up, it was Russia which took the 1996 men's title.

One of the most amazing competitors in Olympic history must be the American gymnast George Eyser, who won six medals, including three golds, in the 1904 Games. He was well over 30 years of age, but, even more remarkably, had a wooden leg. Despite this he also competed in the all-round contest (the forerunner of the decathlon) in the track and field programme. In 1988 Vladimir Gogoladze (URS) performed a triple somersault in the team floor exercises – the first achieved in the Olympics. In the 1988 modern rhythmic competition, Marina Lobatch (URS) scored the maximum possible 60.00 points.

The largest crowd to watch an Olympic gymnastic event was the 32,600 at the Georgia Dome in 1996 for the final of the women's team contest. Prior to 1928 it has been suggested that there were no individual medal events, merely competitors as part of the all-round title. However, the author has shown these in the tables of results and added them in the medal lists until more evidence comes to light to indicate otherwise. In 1996 Nadia Comaneci (ROM), who had won five golds, three silvers and a bronze (1976-80), married two-time Olympic gold medallist (1984) Bart Conner (USA).

HANDBALL

THE SPORT WAS INTRODUCED in 1936, appropriately since it was a German invention, and was played as an outdoor eleven-a-side game. When reintroduced in 1972 it was as an indoor seven-a-side competition. The most successful player has been goalie Andrei Lavrov (URS/EUN/RUS), who has won a record four gold medals, competing in a record five Games. The most successful women have been Zinaida Tourchina (URS) and her teammate Larissa Karlova, who won gold medals in 1976 and 1980, and then a bronze in 1988.

The oldest gold medallist was Andrei Lavrov (RUS) aged 38yr 188 day in 2000, while the oldest female winner was Ludmila Poradnik (URS) in 1980 aged 34yr 200days. Lavrov's bronze in 2004 came at the age of 42yr 155days, while Tourchina's bronze in 1988 was achieved at the age of 42yr 135days. The youngest gold medallist/medallist was Larissa Karlova (URS) aged 17yr 356days in 1976, while the youngest male winner was Günther Ortmann (GER) aged 19yr 257days in 1936. Willy Hufschmid (SUI) won a bronze medal in 1936 aged 17yr 310days.

The greatest margin of victory was 34 when Yugoslavia beat Kuwait 44-10 in 1980. The comparable margin among the women was 30 when Yugoslavia beat Congo 39-9 also in 1980. The greatest aggregate score was 71 in Sydney, when the Austrian women beat Brazil 45-26. In the same competition this was matched when Romania also beat Brazil 38-33. The comparable men's figure is 69, in 2004, when Spain beat Slovenia 41-28. The record score by an individual in one game was 17 by Jasna Kolar-Merdan for the Yugoslavian women when they beat USA 33-20 in 1984. The male record is 13, by István Varga (HUN) against the United States in 1972, and by Kenji Tamamura (JPN) against Hungary in 1988.

Hockey Medals

	Men			Women			Total
	G	S	B	G	S	B	
Netherlands	2	3	3	1	1	3	13
India	8	1	2	-	-	-	11
Australia	1	3	3	3	-	-	10
Great Britain	3	2	4	-	-	1	10
Pakistan	3	3	2	-	-	-	8
Germany	1	1	3	1	1	-	7
FRG	1	2	-	-	-	1	4
Spain	-	2	1	1	-	-	4
Korea	-	1	-	-	2	-	3
Argentina	-	-	-	-	1	1	2
Soviet Union	-	-	1	-	-	1	2
United States	-	-	1	-	-	1	2
New Zealand	1	-	-	-	-	-	1
Zimbabwe	-	-	-	1	-	-	1
Czechoslovakia	-	-	-	-	1	-	1
Denmark	-	1	-	-	-	-	1
Japan	-	1	-	-	-	-	1
Belgium	-	-	1	-	-	-	1
	20	20	21[1]	7	7	7	82

[1] Two bronzes in 1908

A member of the GDR winning team in 1980 was Hans-Georg Beyer, the brother of 1976 shot put champion Udo (who also won a bronze in 1980). To complete an outstanding family trio, their sister Gisela narrowly missed a bronze medal in the women's discus in Moscow. Their countrywoman, Roswitha Krause, a member of the silver medal handball team of 1976, and of the bronze medal team in 1980, had been a silver medallist in the 4x100m freestyle swimming quartet in 1968.

HEAVIEST

THE HEAVIEST PERSON to win an Olympic medal, and indeed the heaviest known to have competed in the Games, was probably Chris Taylor (USA), the 1972 super-heavyweight wrestling bronze medallist. He weighed between 182kg *401lb* and 190kg *419lb*. One other contender for the 'title' is the American weightlifter Mark Henry who weighed in at 184.92kg *407½lb* in the 1996 Games. The heaviest woman to win a gold medal at the Games was Iuliana Semenova, a member of the Soviet gold medal basketball teams in 1976 and 1980.(See also 'Tallest'). She weighed 129kg *284lb*.

However, at Sydney in the 2000 inaugural women's weightlifting tournament, 17yr old Cheryl Haworth (USA) weighed 138kg *304lb* when she took the heavyweight bronze medal. Perhaps it should be noted that the famed sumo wrestler, Akebono, (actually born Chad Rowan in Hawaii), who played a prominent part in the opening ceremony of the 1998 Winter games at Nagano, weighed in at 234kg *516lb*. The heaviest gold medallist, and indeed competitor, at the Winter Games was Friedrich Kuhn (GER), a member of the winning 4-man bob at Oslo in 1952, who weighed 140kg *308lb*. The team totalled 468kg *1032lb* – an average of 117kg *258lb* – leading to a change in the rules limiting the overall weight of the manned bob.

HOCKEY

THE FIRST OLYMPIC hockey game was won by Scotland who beat Germany 4-0 in 1908, with the first goal scored by Ivan Laing only two minutes after the start. In those Games, four of the six teams competing represented England, Ireland, Scotland, and Wales. From 1928 until 1984 Olympic hockey tournaments were dominated by teams from the Indian sub-continent, with India winning eight times and Pakistan three. However, it should be noted that Great Britain, probably the world's strongest team at the time, did not participate in 1932 and 1936. The long-awaited meeting between them, the masters, and India, the pupils, came in the 1948 final, which India won 4-0. In 1988, for the first time for 60 years, no team from the sub-continent won a medal. Interestingly, after years of decline, in 1984 the Great Britain team was a last-minute replacement for the boycotting Soviet Union, and they won the bronze – their first medal for 32 years. Then in 1988 the British team won the gold medal again, after 68 years.

Several members of Indian teams have won a record three gold medals: Dhyan Chand 1928-36, Richard Allen 1928-36, Randhir Singh 1948-56, Balbir Singh 1948-56, Leslie Claudius 1948-56, Ranganandhan Francis 1948-56, and Udham Singh 1952-1956 and 1964. Of these only Claudius and Udham Singh also each won a silver in 1960. The most successful female player is Rechelle Hawkes (AUS) with three golds 1988-2000. The oldest gold medallist/medallist was Dharam Singh (IND) in 1964 aged 45yr 278days. The youngest winner was Russell Garcia (GBR) in 1988 aged 18yr 103days, and the youngest medallist was Haneef Khan (PAK) at 17yr 26days in 1976. The youngest female champion was Maider Goni (ESP) in 1992 aged 19yr 24days, although Arlene Boxhall was under 19 as a member of the 1980 Zimbabwe women's team but she did not actually play in the tournament. The oldest female gold medallist was the Zimbabwe coach/player Anthea Stewart aged 35yr 253days. Iveta Sramkova (TCH), in the 1980 silver medal team, was only 16yr 304days of age.

The highest score ever achieved in international hockey was when India beat the United States 24-1 in 1932. The highest score in a final was also in 1932 when India beat Japan 11-1. Roop Singh (IND), the brother of the team captain Dhyan Chand, scored a record 12 goals in the above mentioned match against the United States in 1932. In their six successive wins 1928-1956, India scored 178 goals and conceded only seven. They did not concede a single goal during the 1928 tournament (five games). The longest game in Olympic hockey lasted 2hr 25min (into the sixth period of extra time) when the Netherlands beat Spain 1-0 in Mexico in 1968.

The biggest margin of victory in the women's contests came in 1980 when the Soviet Union beat Poland 6-0. This was matched by Australia in 1996 beating Argentina 7-1, and in 2000 when Argentina beat New Zealand also by 7-1. Those winning scores are the highest ever in the women's competitions. The greatest aggregate was in 1988 when Korea and Australia tied 5-5.

Natascha Keller's gold medal in Germany's 2004 team added to her amazing family's achievements. Her brother Andreas won gold in Germany's 1992 team, their father, Carsten, won gold in 1972, and their grandfather, Erwin, silver in 1936. The 1988 Olympic competitions were particularly noteworthy for family achievements. Twin sisters Lee and Michelle Capes gained gold medals in the Australian women's team, and the Dutch siblings Marc and Carina Benninga gained bronze medals in their country's respective third placed teams.

ICE HOCKEY

THE GAME WAS introduced in 1920 as part of the Summer Games. The tournament was won by Canada, the first of a run of six victories only interrupted by Great Britain in 1936. Incidentally, although most of that team was Canadian-based, ten of the twelve members were actually born in

Britain. However, the record number of wins is eight by the Soviet Union/EUN between 1956 and 1992. However, in 1994 they did not win a medal for the first time since they entered in 1956. In the early days the Canadians were always represented by a club side, not a national one, so that the first Olympic champions were actually the Winnipeg Falcons. Since 1948, the tournament has been decided on a championship format and not, as previously, on a knock-out basis – thus there is no Olympic final as such. The game has been the centre of much bitter argument about amateur/professional status, and in 1972 Canada withdrew in protest against alleged 'professionalism' of the eastern European teams in particular. Happily they returned in 1980. In 1994 professionals were allowed to compete, and in 1998, the National Hockey League, in Canada and America, agreed to a 'hiatus' of the regular season in Winter Olympics years to allow players to compete for their national teams – well over 100 players do so. The major surprise of the 1998 tournament was that neither the United States nor Canadian men's teams gained a medal. The latter were beaten in a semi-final by the Czech Republic in the first ever Olympic game decided by a penalty shootout. In 2002 the Canadian men's team won their first gold for 50 years and added the women's title for the icing on the cake. In 2006, for the first time in 86 years of Olympic ice hockey, neither Canada, the USA nor Russia/Soviet Union won a medal in the men's event.

In 1948 there was a strange situation when two teams turned up to represent the United States, one from the Amateur Hockey Association (AHA) and the other picked by the US Olympic Committee (USOC). The AHA, while not affiliated to the USOC, was a member of the International Hockey Federation (IHF), the governing body of most of the other teams present in St Moritz. The IHF threatened to withdraw all the other teams if the AHA team did not play, while the USOC threatened to withdraw the whole Olympic team if the AHA team did play. Initially the IOC barred both teams, but then agreed to allow the AHA team to compete. They eventually finished fourth, but a year later were disqualified for non-affiliation to the Olympic movement. Strangely the USOC hockey team members marched in the opening ceremony.

Six Soviet players have won a record three gold medals, but only goalminder Vladislaw Tretyak, 1972-1984, also won a silver. Richard 'Bibi' Torriani (SUI) won a bronze in 1928 and another in 1948, for a record 20 year span. The oldest gold medallist was Carl Erhardt (GBR) in 1936 on the day after his 39th birthday. The youngest was John Kilpatrick (GBR) in 1936 aged 18yr 224days, while the

Ice Hockey Medals

	Men			Women			
	G	S	B	G	S	B	Total
Canada	7	4	2	2	1	-	16
United States	2	7	1	1	1	1	13
Soviet Union	8	1	1	-	-	-	10
Sweden	2	2	4	-	1	1	10
Czechoslovakia	-	4	4	-	-	-	8
Finland	-	2	2	-	-	1	5
Czech Republic	1	-	1	-	-	-	2
Great Britain	1	-	1	-	-	-	2
Russia	-	1	1	-	-	-	2
Switzerland	-	-	2	-	-	-	2
FRG	-	-	1	-	-	-	1
Germany	-	-	1	-	-	-	1
	21	21	21	3	3	3	72

youngest medallist was Richard Torriani (SUI) at 16yr 141days in 1928. The oldest medallist was Igor Larionov in the bronze medal Russian team of 2002 aged 41yr 82days. The first brothers to win gold were Herbert, Hugh and Roger Plaxton along with Frank and Joseph Sullivan in the 1928 Canadian team. The first twins were Boris and Yevgeni Maiorov (URS) in 1964, and they were matched by Daniel and Henrik Sedin of Sweden in 2006. The only known father and son gold medallists were Bill and David Christian (USA) who won in 1960 and 1980 respectively. Another distinction for Bill is that he and his brother Roger, were one of two sets of brothers. The other was Bill and Bob Cleary, who helped the USA to win its first ice hockey gold in 1960. Pavel and Valeri Bure, who won silver medals in the Russian team in 1998 (and bronzes in 2002), are the sons of Vladimir Bure (URS) who won a silver and two bronze medals in swimming at Munich in 1972. Martin Brodeur won a gold as a member of the 2002 Canadian team, whereas his father Denis had only gained a bronze in 1956. Jarome Iginla, a member of the winning Canadian team in 2002, became the first black male to win a gold medal in a Winter Games.

The highest score and aggregate in Olympic ice hockey was the 33-0 victory by Canada over Switzerland in 1924. In that tournament the Canadians totalled 110 goals in five matches with only three against. In the 1980 tournament the American goalminder, James Craig, stopped 163 of 178 shots at his goal (91.6%), including 39 in the match against the Soviet Union. When the Czechs won the 1948 silver medal, a member of the team was 1954 Wimbledon tennis champion Jaroslav Drobny. Vladimir Ruzicka of the Czech Republic, who won a gold medal in 1998, had won silver in the Czechoslovakian team 14 years previously. Raimo Helminen (FIN) played in a record six Olympic tournaments, 1984-02, winning a silver and a bronze.

A women's tournament was instituted in 1998. The highest score, margin of victory, and aggregate came when Canada beat Italy 16-0 in Turin – the gold medal Canadian team had a 46-2 overall score in the 2006 tournament. The youngest gold medallist was Angela Ruggerio (USA) aged 18yr 45days in 1998, while Kim Martin of the 2002 bronze medal Swedish team was aged only 15yr 358days. The oldest gold medallist/medallist was Danielle Goyette (CAN) in 2006 at 40yr 21days. Cammi Granato of the winning 1998 USA squad did considerably better than her older brother, Tony, who was a member of the seventh placed American team at Calgary in 1988. Six Canadian players have won two golds and one silver each 1998-2006.

ICE SKATING

SEE SEPARATE ENTRIES for Figure Skating, Speed Skating, and Short-Track Speed Skating

IOC

INTERNATIONAL OLYMPIC COMMITTEE

INAUGURATED ON 23 June 1894 under the presidency of Demetrius Vikelas of Greece, and with Baron de Coubertin as its first Secretary-General. On 23 June 1994 the IOC celebrated its centenary, noting that the advances of Olympianism had extended competition to all continents, and given access for all races, religions and languages. Its headquarters have been in Lausanne, Switzerland since 1915. The IOC co-opts and elects its members, and they are the IOC's representatives in their respective countries, and not delegates from those countries. The Executive Board consists of the President, four Vice Presidents and six other members. In 1996 here were a number of resignations and expulsions following a bribery scandal to do with the selection of certain host cities. In 2007 there were 122 members of the IOC. There is a current total of 203 National Olympic Committees

Judo Medals

	Men			Women			
	G	S	B	G	S	B	Total
Japan	24	7	8	7	7	5	58
France	6	4	14	4	2	3	33
Korea	6	9	9	2	2	4	32
Soviet Union	7	5	14	-	-	1	27
Cuba	1	3	4	4	5	9	26
Great Britain	-	5	7	-	2	2	16
China	-	-	-	5	2	8	15
Netherlands	4	-	6	-	1	4	15
Germany	1	1	7	1	-	4	14
Brazil	2	3	6	-	-	-	11
Italy	2	2	2	-	1	4	11
GDR	1	2	6	-	-	-	9
United States	-	3	6	-	-	-	9
Poland	3	2	2	-	1	-	8
FRG	1	4	3	-	-	-	8
Hungary	1	2	4	1	-	-	8
Belgium	1	-	2	-	1	4	8
Russia	-	2	4	-	1	1	8
Spain	-	1	-	3	-	2	6
North Korea (PRK)	-	1	1	1	1	1	5
Austria	2	-	1	-	1	-	4
Georgia	1	1	2	-	-	-	4
Canada	-	2	2	-	-	-	4
Mongolia	-	1	3	-	-	-	4
Switzerland	1	1	1	-	-	-	3
Bulgaria	-	1	2	-	-	-	3
Israel	-	-	2	-	1	-	3
Estonia	-	-	3	-	-	-	3
Romania	-	-	2	-	-	1	3
Belarus	1	-	1	-	-	-	2
Turkey	1	-	-	-	-	1	2
Australia	-	-	1	-	-	1	2
Ukraine	-	1	1	-	-	-	2
Yugoslavia	-	-	2	-	-	-	2
Greece	1	-	-	-	-	-	1
Egypt	-	1	-	-	-	-	1
Slovakia	-	1	-	-	-	-	1
Uzbekistan	-	1	-	-	-	-	1
Czechoslovakia	-	-	1	-	-	-	1
Iceland	-	-	1	-	-	-	1
Kirghizstan	-	-	1	-	-	-	1
Latvia	-	-	1	-	-	-	1
Portugal	-	-	1	-	-	-	1
Slovenia	-	-	-	-	-	1	1
	67	66[1]	133	28	28	56	378

[1] 1972 silver withheld due to disqualification

(NOCs) affiliated to the IOC. Presidents of the organisation are listed below.

1894 – 1896	Demetrius Vikelas (Greece)
1896 – 1925	Baron Pierre de Coubertin (France)
1925 – 1942	Comte Henri de Baillet-Latour (Belgium)
1942 – 1952	J Sigfrid Edström (Sweden)
1952 – 1972	Avery Brundage (USA)
1972 – 1980	Lord Killanin (Ireland)
1980 – 2001	Juan Antonio Samaranch (Spain)
2001 –	Jacques Rogge (Belgium)

JEU DE PAUME

A MEDAL SPORT only at London in 1908. Held at Queen's Club, Kensington, it was also a demonstration sport at Amsterdam in 1928. The winner in London was Jay Gould Jr, son of the American railroad tycoon of the same name, who had tried to corner the gold market in 1869, causing the infamous 'Black Friday' panic.

JUDO

THIS SPORT WAS introduced in 1964, and appropriately the first gold medal was won by Japan's Takehide Nakatani in the lightweight class. However, one of the greatest upsets to a nation's sporting pride occurred in Tokyo's Nippon Budokan Hall in 1964 when the giant Dutchman Anton Geesink (1.98m *6ft 6in*) beat the Japanese favourite for the Open category title in front of 15,000 home supporters. Another Dutchman, Wilhelm Ruska, is the only man to win two gold medals at a single Games, with the over 93kg and Open classes in 1972. Tadahiro Nomura (JPN) is the only man to win three gold medals, all consecutive, 1996-2004, in the under 60kg class. His uncle Toyokazu Nomura won the light-middleweight title in 1972. Angelo Parisi won a record four medals, with a bronze in 1972 representing Great Britain, and then gold and two silvers in 1980 and 1984 representing France. The winning of medals for two different countries at the Olympic Games is rare, but not unique. Parisi was born in Italy, went to Britain as a child, became a citizen, then married a French girl in 1973 and changed his nationality again. This total of four medals was also achieved by Ryoko Tamura-Tani (JPN) in the women's competitions with two golds and two silvers 1992-2004. She is the only judoka to have won medals in four Games, although Robert Van de Walle (BEL) did compete in a record five Olympic judo competitions 1976-1992.

The oldest gold medallist was Ruska when he won the 1972 Open class aged 32yr 11days. The youngest, and the youngest ever medallist, was Ilias Iliadis (GRE) in the 2004 light-middleweight division aged 17yr 281days. The oldest medallis at was Arthur Schnabel (FRG) with a bronze in the 1984 Open class aged 35yr 329days. The youngest female gold medallist was Kye Sun (KOR) aged 16yr 359days winning the 48kg class in 1996, while the oldest was Ryoko Tamura-Tani (JPN) at 28yr 343days in 2004. The oldest medallist was Laetitia Meignan (FRA) aged 32yr 33days at Barcelona, and the youngest was Ryoko Tamura (JPN) at 16yr 331days, also in 1992. The fastest throw in Olympic competition was in 4 sec by Akio Kaminaga (JPN) against Thomas Ong (PHI) in 1964

The biggest of many big men in Olympic judo was Jong Gil Pak (PRK) who was 2.13m *7ft* tall and weighed 163kg *359lb* in the 1976 Games. In 1972 the Mongolian lightweight silver medallist, Bakhaavaa

Buidaa, became the first competitor ever disqualified for failing a dope test in any international judo competition. An amusing sidelight was provided by the 1976 lightweight gold medal winner, Hector Rodriguez (CUB), who said that he took up the sport as a child in order to defend himself against his six older brothers.

Women's events were contested as a demonstration sport in Seoul, and were added to the official programme in 1992. In 1996 a total limit of 400 competitors for the sport was imposed.

KORFBALL

A DEMONSTRATION EVENT at Antwerp in 1920 when a team representing South Holland beat Amsterdam 2-0.

LACROSSE

HELD AS A medal sport at St Louis in 1904 and London in 1908, both competitions were won by Canada. In 1904 a Mohawk Indian team, representing Canada, won the bronze, but in 1908 only two teams competed. The highest score was when Canada beat Great Britain 14-10 in 1908. Demonstrations were held in 1928, 1932 and 1948.

LAUSANNE

IN 1915 IT was agreed that the administrative headquarters of the IOC were to be set up in Lausanne, Switzerland, a town popular with Baron de Coubertin. In 1922 he and the IOC moved into a house in the centre of the town. By 1968 the premises had become too small, and the Chateau de Vidy, on the outskirts, was made available by the Town Council as the headquarters of the IOC. Lausanne also houses the ultra modern Olympic museum, on the Quai d'Ouchy.

LONGEST

THE LONGEST RACE ever held at the Olympic Games, in any sport, was the cycling road race in 1912, which measured 320km *198.8 miles*. The longest equestrian event ever held at the Games was the 55km *34.1 miles* distance riding discipline at Stockholm in 1912. Athletics and nordic skiing both share the upper limit of 50km *31 miles* – in athletics it is a walk and in skiing a cross-country event. The furthest a swimming race has ever been is 4000m *2.48 miles* in 1900, while in rowing there was a 3000m *1.86 miles* race in 1906 for coxed 16-man naval rowing boats. The longest sailing event seems to have been the 12m class race in 1908 which was over a 26 mile *41.8km* course.

Timewise, the longest single contest in Olympic history was the semifinal of the 1912 Greco-Roman middleweight wrestling tournament. It went on for 11hr 40min, in very hot weather, between Martin Klein, an Estonian representing Russia, and Alfred Asikainen of Finland, with brief breaks allowed every 30min. Klein eventually won, but was so exhausted that he had to miss the final. The longest final contest was the same year in the Greco-Roman light-heavyweight class, when Anders Ahlgren (SWE) struggled for nine hours with Ivar Böhling (FIN), without a result – both men were awarded silver medals.

LUGEING

LUGE RACING, IN which contestants lie back, was introduced in 1964. The most successful luger has been Georg Hackl (GER), with three golds and two silvers in 1988-2002. Hackl was the first man to successfully defend the singles title – he did it twice – and he was matched by Armin Zöggeler (ITA) in 2002-06. Hackl is also the only luger to win five medals in five Games. The most successful women, with two golds, were Steffi Martin-Walter (GDR), 1984-88, and Sylke Otto (GER), 2002-06.

The oldest gold medallist was Armin Zöggeler (ITA) aged 33yr 39days in the 2006 singles, while the youngest was Manfred Stengl (AUT) in the 2-man in 1964 aged 17yr 310days. The youngest female winner/medallist was Ortrun Enderlein (GER) aged 20yr 65days in 1964, and the oldest was Sylke Otto (GER) in 2006 aged 36yr 225days. The youngest medallist has been Ute Ruhrold (GDR) aged 17yr 60days gaining the silver in 1972. The oldest medallist was Fritz Nachmann (FRG) in 1968 aged 38yr 186days. The oldest female medallist was Sylke Otto. Anne Abernathy of the US Virgin Is was the oldest ever female Winter Olympian when she competed in

the 2002 luge aged 48yr 307days – she may well have been the oldest luger, male or female, ever to compete at the Games. Four years later she was in Turin and entered in the event, but was injured and did not start. Probably the heaviest winner of a luge title was Hans Stanggassinger (FRG) in the 2-man of 1984 at a weight of 111kg *244lb*. At Salt Lake City in 2002, Werner and Christopher Hoeger of Venezuela became the first father and son in Winter Games history to compete against one another, with son Christopher finishing nine places ahead of his father. In 2006 the doubles was won by Andreas and Wolfgang Linger (AUT), the first brothers to win the event.

The smallest winning margin ever was in the women's singles in 1998, when Silke Krausshaar (GER) beat teammate Barbara Niedernhuber by 0.002sec. The closest in the men's contests was in the 1994 men's singles when Georg Hackl (GER) beat Markus Prock (AUT), for the second successive Games, by only 0.013sec. In contrast, Ortrun Enderlein (GDR) won the inaugural women's event in 1964 by the remarkable margin of 2.75sec. At the following Games in 1968, a scandal shook the Games when the first, second and fourth placed women from the GDR were all disqualified for illegally heating the runners of their sleds. The leading girl was Enderlein. While speeds of over 139km/h *86mph* are attained briefly, the greatest average speed for a single run was 107.02km/h *66.50mph* by Markus Prock (AUT) in 2002. The equivalent fastest by a female luger (average for a single run) was 95.58km/h *59.39mph* by Sylke Otto (GER) in 2002. Optimum speeds in the female event have been in excess of 128km/h *79.53mph*.

MASCOTS

THE VARIOUS SYMBOLS and emblems used to publicise the Olympic Games over the years have generally been very successful. In 1932 there was an unofficial live mascot, a dog named Smoky, but it was only in 1968 that the first official Olympic mascot made

Luge Medals

Excluding 1928, 1948 & 2002 Skeleton Sled events

	Men			Women			
	G	S	B	G	S	B	Total
GDR	9	4	5	5	6	4	33
Germany	7	3	3	3	4	2	22
Austria	3	4	4	1	1	3	16
Italy	5	4	4	2	-	-	15
FRG	1	3	3	-	1	2	10
Soviet Union	-	2	2	1	-	1	6
United States	-	2	2	-	-	-	4
Russia	-	1	-	-	-	-	1
Latvia	-	-	1	-	-	-	1
	25*	23	24	12	12	12	108

* Two golds in the 1972 2-man event

its appearance. For the Mexico City Games it was a Red Jaguar, selected because of its cultural and geographical associations. However, it was not given a name, and was not marketed with any particular enthusiasm. Since then, however, the mascot has become an institution.

Summer

Year	Character	Name
1968	–	Red Jaguar
1972	Waldi	Dachshund
1976	Amik	Beaver
1980	Misha	Bear
1984	Sam	Eagle
1988	Hodori/Hosuni	Tigers
1992	Cobi	Dog
1996	Izzy	Cartoon
2000	Olly	Kookaburra
	Syd	Platypus
	Millie	Anteater
	Coal	Bear

2004	Athena	Doll
	Phevos	Doll
2008	Beibei	Fish
	Jingjing	Panda
	Nini	Swallow
	Yingying	Antelope
	Ituanhuen	Olympic Flame Creature

Winter

Year	Character	Name
1968	Schuss	Man
1972	–	–
1976	Schneemanner	Snowman
1980	Roni	Raccoon
1984	Vucko	Wolf
1988	HidyHowdy	Polar bears
1992	Magique	Man/Star
1994	Haakon/Kristin	Children
1998	The Snowlets	Owls
2002	Powder	Hare
	Copper	Coyote
2006	Neve	Snow
	Gliz	Ice
	Ituanhuen	Olympic Flame Creature

MEDAL WINNERS BY NATION 1896-2006

THESE FIGURES SOMETIMES differ from official sources for a number of reasons, some given below. However, one of the main causes is that official sources have prevaricated over various issues, sometimes for nearly 100 years. Thus, I have made my own independent decisions – based on the best evidence currently available.

These totals include all first, second and third places, including those events no longer on the current schedule. The 1906 Games, which were officially staged by the International Olympic Committee (IOC), have also been included, although, unaccountably, some historians choose to ignore them. However, medals won in the Art Competitions 1912-1948, have not been included.

Medals won in 1896, 1900, 1904, 1908 and 1912 by mixed teams from two countries have been counted twice, ie for both countries involved. The Unified teams(EUN) of 1992 have been included in the Soviet Union figures. Medals won by IOP designated competitors in 1992 have been included in Yugoslavia figures.

Since the birth of the modern Olympics 125 countries have won medals in the Summer and/or the Winter Games – of these, 90 have won at least one gold medal.

This unique table indicates a country's position in the medal tables three ways. Mainly it shows its position overall, but also gives that for the Summer and Winter Games respectively.

Overall		Summer				Winter				Total
		G	S	B	Total	G	S	B	Total	Total
1	United States	912	700	612	2224 (1)	78	81	59	218 (2)	2442
2	Soviet Union[1]	440	357	325	1122 (2)	87	63	67	217 (3)	1339
3	Germany[2]	178	214	231	623 (5)	69	64	45	178 (5)	801
4	Great Britain	197	254	244	695 (3)	9	5	14	28 (19)	723
5	France	200	204	230	634 (4)	25	24	34	83 (12)	717
6	Italy	189	154	167	510 (6)	36	31	34	101 (11)	611
7	Sweden	142	159	177	478 (7)	46	33	45	124 (7)	602
8	GDR[3]	153	130	127	410 (9)	39	36	35	110 (10)	520
9	Hungary	158	140	160	441 (8)	-	2	4	6 (=25)	464
10	Finland	101	83	114	298 (12)	42	58	52	152 (6)	450
11	Norway	55	43	42	140 (28)	98	100	85	283 (1)	423
12	Australia	121	126	154	401 (10)	3	-	3	6 (=25)	407
13	Japan	114	106	115	335 (11)	9	10	13	32 (17)	367
14	Canada	55	86	102	243 (17)	39	37	44	120 (8)	363
15	Russia[6]	85	80	85	250 (16)	34	26	18	78 (=13)	328
16	China	112	96	78	286 (13)	4	16	13	33 (16)	319
17	Netherlands	65	75	94	234 (18)	25	30	23	78 (=13)	312
18	Switzerland	49	77	65	191 (21)	38	37	43	118 (9)	309
19	Romania	82	88	114	284 (14)	-	-	1	1 (=38)	285

20	Austria	23	36	37	96 (29)	51	64	70	185 (4)	**281**
21	Poland	59	74	118	251 (15)	1	3	4	8 (23)	**259**
22	FRG[4]	56	64	80	200 (20)	11	17	14	42 (15)	**242**
23	Korea	55	64	65	184 (22)	17	8	6	31 (18)	**215**
24	Bulgaria	50	83	74	207 (19)	1	2	3	6 (=25)	**213**
25	Czechoslovakia[5]	49	50	51	150 (25)	2	8	16	26 (20)	**176**
26	Denmark	43	63	64	170 (23)	-	1	-	1 (=38)	**171**
27	Cuba	65	51	49	165 (24)	-	-	-	-	**165**
28	Belgium	38	52	53	143 (=26)	1	1	3	5 (=30)	**148**
29	Greece	38	54	51	143 (=26)	-	-	-	-	**143**
30	Yugoslavia	28	32	33	93 (31)	-	3	1	4 (=33)	**97**
31	Spain	28	39	27	94 (30)	1	-	1	2 (=35)	**96**
32	New Zealand	34	14	32	80 (32)	-	1	-	1 (=38)	**81**
33	Brazil	17	21	38	76 (33)	-	-	-	-	**76**
=34	Turkey	36	19	19	74 (34)	-	-	-	-	**74**
=34	Ukraine	21	17	31	69 (35)	1	1	3	5 (=30)	**74**
36	South Africa	20	23	25	68 (36)	-	-	-	-	**68**
37	Kenya	17	24	20	61 (37)	-	-	-	-	**61**
38	Argentina	15	23	22	60 (38)	-	-	-	-	**60**
39	Belarus	6	15	26	47 (40)	-	3	3	6 (=25)	**53**
40	Mexico	10	18	23	51 (39)	-	-	-	-	**51**
41	Iran	10	15	21	46 (41)	-	-	-	-	**46**
42	Jamaica	7	21	16	44 (42)	-	-	-	-	**44**
43	North Korea (PRK)	8	11	16	35 (43)	-	1	1	2 (=35)	**37**
44	Czech Republic	7	9	11	27 (46)	3	4	2	9 (=21)	**36**
45	Estonia	8	7	14	29 (45)	4	1	1	6 (=25)	**35**
=46	Ethiopia	14	5	12	31 (44)	-	-	-	-	**31**
=46	Kazakhstan	7	12	7	26 (47)	1	2	2	5 (=30)	**31**
48	Egypt	7	7	9	23 (48)	-	-	-	-	**23**
=49	Ireland	8	6	6	20 (=49)	-	-	-	-	**20**
=49	Portugal	3	6	11	20 (=49)	-	-	-	-	**20**
=49	Indonesia	5	8	7	20 (=49)	-	-	-	-	**20**
=52	Nigeria	2	8	9	19 (=52)	-	-	-	-	**19**
=52	Morocco	6	4	9	19 (=52)	-	-	-	-	**19**
=52	Croatia	3	4	5	12 (=60)	4	3	-	7 (24)	**19**
55	Thailand	5	2	10	17 (54)	-	-	-	-	**17**
=56	India	8	2	5	15 (=55)	-	-	-	-	**15**
=56	Mongolia	-	5	10	15 (=55)	-	-	-	-	**15**
=56	Latvia	1	10	3	14 (=58)	-	-	1	- (=38)	**15**
=56	Taipei (Taiwan)	2	6	7	15 (=55)	-	-	-	-	**15**
=56	Slovakia[5]	4	6	4	14 (=58)	-	1	-	1 (=38)	**15**
61	Slovenia	2	3	5	10 (=67)	-	-	4	4 (=33)	**14**
=62	Algeria	4	1	7	12 (=60)	-	-	-	-	**12**
=62	Trinidad & Tobago	1	3	8	12 (=60)	-	-	-	-	**12**
=62	Chile	2	6	4	12 (=60)	-	-	-	-	**12**
=62	Georgia	2	2	8	12 (=60)	-	-	-	-	**12**
=62	Uzbekistan	3	3	5	11 (=65)	-	-	-	-	**11**
67	Lithuania	4	2	5	11 (=65)	-	-	-	-	**11**
=68	Pakistan	3	3	4	10 (=67)	-	-	-	-	**10**
=68	Uruguay	2	2	2	10 (=67)	-	-	-	-	**10**
=68	Venezuela	1	2	7	10 (=67)	-	-	-	-	**10**
=71	Liechtenstein	-	-	-	-	2	2	5	9 (=21)	**9**
=71	Philippines	-	2	7	9 (=71)	-	-	-	-	**9**
=71	Colombia	1	2	6	9 (=71)	-	-	-	-	**9**
=71	Azerbaijan	3	1	5	9 (=71)	-	-	-	-	**9**
75	Bahamas	3	2	3	8 (74)	-	-	-	-	**8**
=76	Uganda	1	3	2	6 (=75)	-	-	-	-	**6**
=76	Tunisia	1	2	3	6 (=75)	-	-	-	-	**6**
=76	Puerto Rico	-	1	5	6 (=75)	-	-	-	-	**6**
=76	Israel	1	1	4	6 (=75)	-	-	-	-	**6**
=80	Peru	1	3	-	4 (=79)	-	-	-	-	**4**

=80	Luxembourg	1	1	-	2 (=91)	-	2	-	2 (=35)	4
=80	Costa Rica	1	1	2	4 (=79)	-	-	-	-	4
=80	Namibia	-	4	-	4 (=79)	-	-	-	-	4
=80	Lebanon	-	2	2	4 (=79)	-	-	-	-	4
=80	Moldova	-	2	2	4 (=79)	-	-	-	-	4
=80	Ghana	-	1	3	4 (=79)	-	-	-	-	4
=80	Cameroon	2	1	1	4 (=79)	-	-	-	-	4
=80	Zimbabwe	2	1	1	4 (=79)	-	-	-	-	4
=89	Armenia	1	1	1	3 (=87)	-	-	-	-	3
=89	Iceland	-	1	2	3 (=87)	-	-	-	-	3
=89	Malaysia	-	1	2	3 (=87)	-	-	-	-	3
=89	Syria	1	1	1	3 (=87)	-	-	-	-	3
=93	Mozambique	1	-	1	2 (=91)	-	-	-	-	2
=93	Surinam	1	-	1	2 (=91)	-	-	-	-	2
=93	Serbia/Montenegro	-	2	-	2 (=91)	-	-	-	-	2
=93	Tanzania	-	2	-	2 (=91)	-	-	-	-	2
=93	Haiti	-	1	1	2 (=91)	-	-	-	-	2
=93	Saudi Arabia	-	1	1	2 (=91)	-	-	-	-	2
=93	Sri Lanka	-	1	1	2 (=91)	-	-	-	-	2
=93	Zambia	-	1	1	2 (=91)	-	-	-	-	2
=93	Barbados	-	-	2	2 (=91)	-	-	-	-	2
=93	Panama	-	-	2	2 (=91)	-	-	-	-	2
=93	Qatar	-	-	2	2 (=91)	-	-	-	-	2
=93	Hong Kong	1	1	-	2 (=91)	-	-	-	-	2
=93	Dominican Rep	1	-	1	2 (=91)	-	-	-	-	2
=106	Burundi	1	-	-	1 (=105)	-	-	-	-	1
=106	Ecuador	1	-		1 (=105)	-	-	-	-	1
=106	United Arab Emirates	1	-	-	1 (=105)	-	-	-	-	1
=106	Ivory Coast	-	1	-	1 (=105)	-	-	-	-	1
=106	Netherlands Antilles-		1	-	1 (=105)	-	-	-	-	1
=106	Paraguay	-	1	-	1 (=105)	-	-	-	-	1
=106	Senegal	-	1	-	1 (=105)	-	-	-	-	1
=106	Singapore	-	1	-	1 (=105)	-	-	-	-	1
=106	Tonga	-	1	-	1 (=105)	-	-	-	-	1
=106	Vietnam	-	1	-	1 (=105)	-	-	-	-	1
=106	Virgin Islands	-	1	-	1 (=105)	-	-	-	-	1
=106	Bermuda	-	-	1	1 (=105)	-	-	-	-	1
=106	Djibouti	-	-	1	1 (=105)	-	-	-	-	1
=106	Eritrea	-	-	1	1 (=105)	-	-	-	-	1
=106	Guyana	-	-	1	1 (=105)	-	-	-	-	1
=106	Iraq	-	-	1	1 (=105)	-	-	-	-	1
=106	Kirghizstan	-	-	1	1 (=105)	-	-	-	-	1
=106	Kuwait	-	-	1	1 (=105)	-	-	-	-	1
=106	Macedonia	-	-	1	1 (=105)	-	-	-	-	1
=106	Niger Republic	-	-	1	1 (=105)	-	-	-	-	1

[1]Including Unified Team of 1992; [2]Germany 1896-1964,1992-98; [3]GDR, East Germany,1968-198; [4]FRG, West Germany,1968-1988; [5]Czechoslovakia includes Bohemia; Split into Czech Rep & Slovakia in 1992; [6]Includes Czarist Russia

MEDALS, MOST BY INDIVIDUALS – SUMMER GAMES

Men

15	Nikolai Andrianov (URS)	1972-80	Gymnastics
13	Edoardo Mangiarotti (ITA)	1936-60	Fencing
13	Takashi Ono (JPN)	1952-64	Gymnastics
13	Boris Shakhlin (URS)	1956-64	Gymnastics
12	Sawao Kato (JPN)	1968-76	Gymnastics
12	Paavo Nurmi (FIN)	1920-28	Athletics
12	Alexei Nemov (RUS)	1996-2000	Gymnastics
11	Matt Biondi (USA)	1984-92	Swimming
11	Viktor Chukarin (URS)	1952-56	Gymnastics
11	Carl Osburn (USA)	1912-24	Shooting
11	Mark Spitz (USA)	1968-72	Swimming
10	Alexander Dityatin (URS)	1976-80	Gymnastics
10	Ray Ewry (USA)	1900-08	Athletics
10	Aladár Gerevich (HUN)	1932-60	Fencing
10	Akinori Nakayama (JPN)	1968-72	Gymnastics
10	Carl Lewis (USA)	1984-96	Athletics
10	Vitali Shcherbo (EUN/BLR)	1992-96	Gymnastics
9	Zoltán Halmay (HUN)	1900-08	Swimming
9	Hubert Van Innis (BEL)	1900-20	Archery
9	Alfred Swahn (SWE)	1908-24	Shooting
9	Giulio Gaudini (ITA)	1928-36	Fencing
9	Heikki Savolainen (FIN)	1920-52	Gymnastics
9	Eizo Kenmotsu (JPN)	1968-76	Gymnastics
9	Martin Sheridan (USA)	1904-08	Athletics
9	Yuri Titov (URS)	1956-64	Gymnastics
9	Mitsuo Tsukahara (JPN)	1968-76	Gymnastics
9	Mikhail Voronin (URS)	1968-72	Gymnastics
9	Alexander Popov (RUS)	1992-2000	Swimming
9	Gary Hall Jr (USA)	1994-2004	Swimming

Women

18	Larissa Latynina (URS)	1956-64	Gymnastics
12	Birgit Fischer-Schmidt (GDR/GER)	1980-2004	Canoeing
12	Jenny Thompson (USA)	1992-2004	Swimming
11	Vera Cáslavská (TCH)	1960-68	Gymnastics
10	Polina Astakhova (URS)	1956-64	Gymnastics
10	Agnes Keleti (HUN)	1952-56	Gymnastics
10	Franziska van Almsick (GER)	1992-2004	Swimming
9	Nadia Comaneci (ROM)	1976-80	Gymnastics
9	Ludmila Turischeva (URS)	1968-76	Gymnastics
9	Dara Torres (USA)	1984-2000	Swimming
8	Shirley Babashoff (USA)	1972-76	Swimming
8	Kornelia Ender (GDR)	1972-76	Swimming
8	Dawn Fraser (AUS)	1956-64	Swimming
8	Margit Korondi (HUN)	1952-56	Gymnastics
8	Sofia Muratova (URS)	1956-60	Gymnastics
8	Merlene Ottey (JAM)	1980-2000	Athletics
8	Elisabeta Lipa (ROM)	1984-2004	Rowing
8	Inge de Bruijn (NED)	2000-04	Swimming
7	Maria Gorokhovskaya (URS)	1952	Gymnastics
7	Karin Janz (GDR)	1968-72	Gymnastics
7	Ildikó Ságiné-Ujlakiné-Rejtó (HUN)	1960-76	Fencing
7	Shirley Strickland (AUS)	1948-56	Athletics
7	Irena Szewinska (POL)	1964-76	Athletics
7	Shannon Miller (USA)	1992-96	Gymnastics
7	Simona Amanar (ROM)	1996-2000	Gymnastics
7	Petria Thomas (AUS)	2000-04	Swimming

MEDALS, MOST BY INDIVIDUALS – WINTER GAMES

Men

12	Bjørn Daehlie (NOR)	1992-98	Nordic Skiing
9	Sixten Jernberg (SWE)	1956-64	Nordic Skiing
9	Ole Einar Bjørndalen (NOR)	1998-2006	Biathlon
8	Kjetil André Aamodt (NOR)	1992-2006	Alpine Skiing
8	Rico Gross (GER)	1992-2006	Biathlon
8	Sven Fischer (GER)	1994-2006	Biathlon
7	Clas Thunberg (FIN)	1924-28	Speed Skating
7	Ivar Ballangrud (NOR)	1928-36	Speed Skating
7	Veikko Hakulinen (FIN)	1952-60	Nordic Skiing
7	Eero Mäntyranta (FIN)	1960-68	Nordic Skiing
7	Bogdan Musiol (GDR/GER)	1980-92	Bobsledding
7	Vladimir Smirnov (URS/EUN/KZK)	1988-98	Nordic Skiing

Women

10	Raisa Smetanina (URS/EUN)	1976-92	Nordic Skiing
10	Stefania Belmondo (ITA)	1992-02	Nordic Skiing
9	Lyubov Yegorova (EUN/RUS)	1992-94	Nordic Skiing
9	Claudia Pechstein (GER)	1992-2006	Speed Skating
9	Uschi Disl (GER)	1992-2006	Biathlon
8	Galina Kulakova (URS)	1968-76	Nordic Skiing
8	Karin Kania-Enke (GDR)	1980-88	Speed Skating
8	Marja-Liisa Hämäläinen-Kirvesniemi (FIN)	1980-94	Nordic Skiing
8	Gunda Kleemann-Niemann-Stirnemann (GDR/GER)	1992-94	Speed Skating
7	Andrea Mitscherlich-Schöne-Ehrig (GDR)	1976-88	Speed Skating
7	Manuela Di Centa (ITA)	1988-98	Nordic Skiing
7	Larisa Lazutina (EUN/RUS)	1992-98	Nordic Skiing
7	Yelena Valbe (EUN/RUS)	1992-98	Nordic Skiing

MEDIA

DURING THE FIRST modern Games at Athens in 1896 there was very little coverage in the world's press. Throughout its 100 year history the Games have constantly been written off and rubbished by some of the media, prophets of doom who predicted their demise, especially at the time of boycotts and financial and drugs scandals. Despite this the Games have gone from strength to strength, and indeed there has been tremendous coverage of each celebration. Thus, at Atlanta in 1996 there were over 17,000 representatives of the world media, far in excess of the number of competitors, and at the Winter Games at Nagano in 1998 there were over 10,000.

The Games at Berlin in 1936 witnessed the first major radio coverage of the event, with broadcasts going to some 40 countries. At those Games there was limited television coverage with a closed circuit system to special halls, operated by the Reich Rundfunkgesellschaft, and watched by a reported 150,000 people at 28 venues around Berlin. By 1996 television pictures were beamed to some 220 countries, with a global cumulative audience of 19.6 billion, and it has been estimated nine out of ten people in the developed world watched part of the Atlanta Games.

The money from TV rights has now become the prime source of income for the IOC, and the hosts. In August 1995 the American TV company NBC paid $1.27 billion for the exclusive US rights to the Games at Sydney in 2000, and the Winter Games at Salt Lake City in 2002. A few months later they paid $2.3 billion for the US rights to the Games of 2004, 2006 and 2008.

MEMBER COUNTRIES

FOR MEMBER COUNTRIES of the IOC, see under 'Participation, by Country'.

MILITARY PATROL

PREVIOUSLY ALWAYS THOUGHT to have been a demonstration sport, held at four Winter Games, in 2006 the 1924 competition was 'reinstated' as a medal sport, with the medals allocated to Switzerland (gold), Finland (silver) and France (bronze). It is significant that the host country of those Games, France, used a member of their military patrol team to take the oath on behalf of all competitors during the opening ceremony. The event is considered to be the forerunner of the official biathlon contests introduced in 1960. Norway finished first in the demonstration in 1928, Italy in 1936, and Switzerland again in 1948.

MODERN PENTATHLON

THIS SPORT, CURRENTLY under threat of being dropped from the Games, was invented by Baron de Coubertin. The five events constituting the modern pentathlon are: riding (formerly over an 800m course, now a 12-fence show jumping test); fencing (with épée); swimming (formerly 300m freestyle, now 200m); shooting; and cross-country running (formerly over 4000m, now 3000m). Shooting until 1992 was with a rapid-fire pistol over 25m, but since then it has been with an air pistol over 10m. In 1996 the team event was eliminated and the individual competition has to be completed in one day. In 2000 a modern pentathlon event for women was added.

The order of events has differed over the years, as has the points system. Prior to 1956, competitors were given points according to their placings in each event, i.e., one point for first place, two points for second etc. Since 1956 points have been allocated according to an international scoring table. It is difficult therefore to compare performers under the two systems, but it is generally accepted that the margin of victory by Willie Grut (SWE) in 1948 was the greatest ever. In that competition, Grut, later the Secretary-General of the sport's governing body, the Union Internationale de Pentathlon Moderne (UIPMB), placed first in riding, fencing and swimming, fifth in shooting, and eighth in running.

The most gold medals have been won by András Balczó (HUN) with three in 1960 (team), 1968 (team) and 1972 (individual). Only Lars Hall (SWE) has won two individual gold medals, in 1952 and 1956. Pavel Lednev (URS) won a record seven medals (two gold, two silver, three bronze) from 1968 to 1980.

Lednev was also the oldest gold medallist/medallist in 1980 aged 37yr 121days, while the youngest gold medallist/medallist was Aladár Kovacsi (HUN) in 1952 aged 19yr 227days. Peter Macken of Australia competed in a record five Olympic contests 1960-76. In the women's competition, the oldest gold medallist/medallist was Stephanie Cook (GBR) in Sydney aged 28yr 237days, while the youngest winner was Zsuzsanna Vörös HUN) in 2004 aged 27yr 115days. The youngest medallist was Emily de Riel (USA) at 25yr 312days in 2000. The youngest ever competitor was Aya Medany (EGY) in 2004 when she was only 15yr 281days of age.

Gustaf Dyrssen (SWE), who won the gold medal in 1920, and a silver in 1924, and Sven Thofelt (SWE), who won the gold in 1928, both won silver medals as members of the 1936 Swedish épée fencing team. Thofelt also won a bronze in the Swedish fencing team in 1948, while his son competed in the 1960 modern pentathlon. Dyrssen later became Sweden's IOC representative, and Thofelt became president of the UIPMB.

George Patton (USA), later the famous World War II general, was fifth in 1912, with results that indicated he was not very good at shooting. Two men have scored maximums of 200 hits in shooting; Charles Leonard (USA) in 1936 and George Horvath (SWE) in 1980. The fastest time ever recorded in the 300m swimming event was 3min 10.47sec by Gintaras Staskevicius (LTU) in 1992. The other three disciplines are either not measurable or comparable. However, it is noteworthy that the fastest time recorded for the 4000m cross-country run was 12min 09.50sec by Adrian Parker (GBR) in 1976. With the amendment of event distances in 2000, the current

Modern Pentathlon Medals

	Men			Women			
	G	S	B	G	S	B	Total
Hungary	8	8	4	1	-	-	21
Sweden	9	7	5	-	-	-	21
Soviet Union	5	6	6	-	-	-	17
United States	-	5	3	-	1	-	9
Italy	2	2	3	-	-	-	7
Great Britain	1	-	1	1	-	2	5
Finland	-	1	4	-	-	-	5
Poland	3	-	-	-	-	-	3
Russia	2	1	-	-	-	-	3
Germany	1	-	1	-	-	-	2
Czechoslovakia	-	1	1	-	-	-	2
France	-	-	2	-	-	-	2
Kazakstan	1	-	-	-	-	-	1
Latvia	-	-	-	-	1	-	1
Lithuania	-	1	-	-	-	-	1
Belarus	-	-	1	-	-	-	1
Czech Republic	-	-	1	-	-	-	1
	32	32	32	2	2	2	102

best performances are: 200m swimming – 1:58.88 by Andrei Moiseyev (RUS) in 2004 ; 3000m running – 9:10.69 Sebastien Deleigne (FRA) in 2000. The best by women are: 200m swimming – 2:14.44 Amélie Cazé (FRA) in 2004; 3000m running – 10:03.16 Stephanie Cook (GBR) in 2000.

One of the biggest scandals in Olympic history occurred in the fencing segment of the 1976 competition when Boris Onischenko (URS), previous winner of a gold and two silver medals, was disqualified for using an illegal weapon. It transpired that he had tampered with his epee so that it registered a hit even when contact with an opponent had not taken place. The incident has caused speculation about whether he had used the implement in the 1972 Games, where his fencing victory over Jim Fox cost the Briton the individual bronze medal. By coincidence Onischenko was fencing against Fox when the Montreal incident came to light.

MOST GAMES

PERHAPS NOT SURPRISINGLY, towns and cities in the United States have been the venues of the greatest number of celebrations of the Olympics. There have been four editions of the Summer Games: St Louis 1904; Los Angeles 1932 & 1984; and Atlanta 1996. The Winter Games have been hosted by Lake Placid 1932 & 1980, Squaw Valley 1960, and Salt Lake City 2002.

MOTOR BOATING

A MEDAL SPORT only held at London in 1908, when only one boat finished in each of the three classes. The competitions were held over a distance of 40 miles. Thomas Thornycroft (GBR) was in the crew of two of the winning boats, winning his second aged 44yr 281days. He was a reserve for the 1952 British Olympic sailing team when in his 71st year.

MOTTO

THE OLYMPIC MOTTO, *Citius, Altius, Fortius* (faster, higher, stronger), was a Latin phrase used by Father Henri Didon, of Paris, which was apparently carved over the entrance to his school. His use of the words to illustrate the sporting achievements of the scholars of another college in 1895, was noted by de Coubertin, who instituted them at the 1924 Games.

MULTI-REPRESENTATION

NOT COUNTING COMPETITORS who had won for the Soviet Union, and then when repres-

enting the new entities formed after the break up, only two people have won gold medals representing totally different countries. Rugby player Daniel Carroll won a gold in the 1908 winning Australian team, and then won again as a member of the 1920 USA team. Kakhi Kakhiashvili won for his native Georgia at weightlifting in 1992, and then won again in 1996, but was then representing Greece.

MULTI-SPORTS

THERE HAVE BEEN a number of Olympians who have competed at a number of different sports (see Doubles and Trebles) but perhaps the most outstanding was Launceston Eliot (GBR) in the very first modern Games in 1896. Winning gold and silver medals in his main sport of weightlifting, he also placed fourth in wrestling, fifth in rope-climbing, and ran in a heat of the 100m, thus competing in four different sports.

NORDIC COMBINATION

THE EVENT WAS the 'blue riband' of Nordic skiing in the early Games. The all-round title, comprising a cross-country race and a jump, was won three successive times by Ulrich Wehling (GDR) 1972-80. Samppa Lajunen (FIN) also won three golds, but all in 2002. Felix Gottwald (AUT) has won a record six medals (2g, 1, 3b) 2002-06. The oldest winner and medallist was Simon Slåttvik (NOR) who won the title in 1952 aged 34yr 209days. The youngest champion and medallist was Anssi Koivuranta (FIN) aged 17yr 228days in the 2006 relay. Up until 1952 the cross-country segment was held first, but at Oslo the order of events was reversed, and has remained so. In 2002 a 'sprint' race was added.

Nordic Combination Medals

	G	S	B	Total
Norway	11	8	7	26
Finland	4	8	2	14
Austria	2	2	6	10
GDR	3	-	4	7
Germany	2	3	2	7
Switzerland	1	2	1	4
FRG	2	1	-	3
Japan	2	1	-	3
France	1	1	1	3
Soviet Union	-	1	2	3
Sweden	-	1	1	2
Poland	-	-	1	1
Russia	-	-	1	1
	28	28	28	84

NORDIC SKIING

(See also Nordic Combination, Biathlon and
Ski-jumping)

NORDIC, OR CROSS-COUNTRY, skiing
was the first form of skiing in the Olympics. Bjørn
Daehlie (NOR) won a record 12 medals, 1992-98,
comprising another record eight golds and four
silvers. The most successful female competitor was
Raisa Smetanina (URS/EUN) with four golds, five
silvers and a bronze, making a female record of ten
medals) between 1976 and 1992. She is also the only
competitor to win medals in five Games. Stefania
Belmondo (ITA) also won ten medals (2g, 3s, 5b)
1992-2002. Only Sixten Jernberg (SWE), 1956-64,
and Daehlie, have won individual titles in three
successive Games, Jernberg doing it over an eight-year
period. Lyubov Yegorova (EUN/RUS) equalled the
winter Games record by a woman of six gold medals
with three in 1992, and three in 1994. Yegorova,
teammate Yelena Valbe, both in 1992, Manuela di
Centa (ITA) in 1994, and Larissa Lazutina (RUS) in
1998, have all set a female record of five medals in a
single Games. Lazutina won a gold and two silvers in
2002 to equal Smetanina's record of ten medals, but
was then disqualified from all three events. Marja-
Liisa Hämäläinen (later Kirvesniemi) of Finland
won a record three individual gold medals at one
Games in 1984. She competed in a record six Games,
1976-94. Her husband, Harri Kirvesniemi (FIN) also

competed in six Games 1980-98, winning six bronze
medals, during which period he raced an unmatched
aggregate record of 450km *279 miles*. Daehlie raced
345km *214 miles* in his three Games. The record
aggregate distance raced by a woman is 275km *171
miles* by Stefania Belmondo (ITA) 1988-2002.

The oldest gold medallist/medallist was Maurilo
De Zolt (ITA), aged 43yr 150days in the 1994 relay,
and the youngest champion was Gunde Svan (SWE)
who won the 15km race in 1984 aged 22yr 32days.
The youngest medallist was Ivar Formo (NOR) in the
1972 relay aged 20yr 234days. The oldest female gold
medallist was Smetanina as a member of the 1992
relay team aged 39yr 354days. The youngest female
champion was Carola Anding (GDR) aged 19yr
54days in the 1980 relay, while the youngest female
medallist was Marjo Matikainen (FIN) in the 1984
relay aged 19yr 12days. Bente Skari (NOR), who
won the 10km in 2002 is the daughter of 1968 relay
gold medallist Odd Martinsen. In 1994, a brother
and sister won medals when Giorgio Vanzetta (ITA)
took gold in the 4x10km relay and Bice gained a
bronze in the 4x5km. At Salt Lake City Manuela
Henkel (GER) won a gold in the Nordic relay, while
her sister Andrea won two golds in the biathlon. The
50km race in 1928 was won by Per Erik Hedlund
(SWE) with a remarkable margin of 13min 27sec
over the second man, whereas in the 1980 15km a
mere 0.01sec separated first and second. Perhaps as
significant was the 0.8sec margin of victory by Giorgio

Nordic Skiing Medals

	Men			Women			
	G	S	B	G	S	B	Total
Norway	25	27	12	3	8	9	85
Soviet Union	11	8	12	17	16	13	77
Finland	11	13	19	8	9	11	71
Sweden	20	13	14	4	2	2	55
Italy	4	6	7	5	5	5	32
Russia	2	1	1	11	7	5	27
Germany	-	2	2	1	3	-	8
Estonia	2	1	1	2	-	-	6
Czech Republic	-	1	-	1	2	2	6
Austria	-	2	3	-	-	-	5
Czechoslovakia	-	-	1	-	1	3	5
GDR	-	1	-	2	-	1	4
Kazakstan	1	2	1	-	-	-	4
Switzerland	-	-	3	-	-	1	4
Canada	-	-	-	1	1	1	3
Spain	2	-	-	-	-	-	2
Bulgaria	-	-	1	-	-	-	1
France	-	1	-	-	-	-	1
United States	-	1	-	-	-	-	1
Poland	-	-	-	-	-	1	1
	78	79[1]	77	55	55	55	399

[1]*Two silvers in 2002 combined pursuit*

di Centa (ITA) in the 2006 50km event. Incidentally, his sister Manuela won two golds in 1994. Certain of the races are designated as freestyle events i.e. the 'skating' technique may be used. Otherwise, only the classical 'stride and glide' is allowed. The shock silver medal won by Bill Koch (USA) in the 1976 50km was credited to his development of the former style.

In 2002 a 'sprint' race was introduced. The fastest time was achieved in 2006, over a course of 1.325km, by Björn Lind (SWE) in the heats with 2:13.53, representing an average speed of 35.72km/h *22.19mph*. The fastest by a woman, also in 2006, over 1.145m, was 2:12.3 by Chandra Crawford (CAN) in the final, representing an average speed of 31.15km/h *19.35mph*.

OLDEST COMPETITORS/ WINNERS

THE OLDEST EVER competitor at the Olympic Games was Oskar Swahn of Sweden who was in the shooting contests in 1920 at the age of 72y 280days (when he won a silver medal in a team event). He had won a gold medal eight years earlier, at Stockholm, in the running deer team, to become the oldest ever gold medallist 107 days short of his 65th birthday. Incidentally, his son, Alfred, also won gold in the team. He actually qualified for the 1924 Games in his 77th year but illness prevented him making the trip. In 1904 the Rev Galen Spencer (USA) had won an archery team gold just two days past his 64th birthday, while a fellow American, Samuel Duvall, won a team silver at 68y 194days. The oldest winner of an individual event was Joshua 'Jerry' Millner (GBR), who was four days past his 61st birthday winning the free rifle (1000y) event at London in 1908. The oldest woman to compete in the Games was Britain's Lorna Johnstone, who was five days past her 70th birthday when she took part in the dressage competition at Munich in 1972. The oldest female gold medallist was Queenie Newall, also of Britain, who won the archery contest in 1908 at 53y 275days.

In October 1994, Hjalmari Kivenheimo (FIN), silver medallist in the 1912 gymnastics team competition, died aged 105yr 34days – the greatest known age ever reached by an Olympic medallist. Not a medallist, but Dirk Janssen, of the Netherlands, also a gymnast, in 1908, held the Olympian longevity record when he died in November 1986 aged 105yr 114days.

At Turin in 2006, Anne Abernathy of the US Virgin Islands was listed in the luge when over 52 years of age, but was unable to start due to injury. Nevertheless, she can claim to be the oldest ever woman entered in the Winter Games.

OLYMPIC OATH

IT WAS INSTITUTED in 1920. At the opening ceremony a representative of the host country, usually a veteran of previous Games, mounts the rostrum, holds a corner of their national flag and, with the flag bearers of all the other countries drawn up in a semi-circle, pronounces the oath: 'In the name of all competitors, I promise that we shall take part in these Olympic Games, respecting and abiding by the rules which govern them, in the true spirit of sportsmanship, for the glory of sport and the honour of our teams'.(A similar oath is taken on behalf of all the judges). The following have taken the Olympic oath on behalf of the athletes:

Summer

1920	Victor Boin	Fencer
1924	Georges André	Athlete
1928	Harry Denis	Footballer
1932	George Calnan	Fencer
1936	Rudolf Ismayr	Weightlifter
1948	Donald Finlay	Athlete
1952	Heikki Savolainen	Gymnast
1956	John Landy	Athlete
	Henri Saint Cyr	Equestrian (Stockholm)
1960	Adolfo Consolini	Athlete
1964	Takashi Ono	Gymnast
1968	Pablo Garrido	Athlete
1972	Heidi Schüller	Athlete
1976	Pierre St Jean	Weightlifter
1980	Nikolai Andrianov	Gymnast
1984	Edwin Moses	Athlete
1988	Huh Jae/Son Mi-Na	Basketballer/ Handballer
1992	Luis Doreste Blanco	Yachtsman
1996	Teresa Edwards	Basketballer
2000	Rechelle Hawkes	Hockey
2004	Zoe Dimoschaki	Swimming

Winter

1924	Camille Mandrillon	Military Patrol
1928	Hans Eidenbenz	Skier
1932	Jack Shea	Speed skater
1936	Wilhelm Bogner	Skier
1948	Richard Torriani	Ice hockey player
1952	Torbjörn Falkanger	Ski jumper
1956	Guiliana Chenal-Minuzzo	Skier
1960	Carol Heiss	Figure skater
1964	Paul Aste	Bobsledder
1968	Leo Lacroix	Skier
1972	Keichi Suzuki	Speed skater
1976	Werner Delle-Karth	Bobsledder
1980	Eric Heiden	Speed skater
1984	Bojan Krizaj	Skier
1988	Pierre Harvey	Skier
1992	Surya Bonaly	Figure skater

1994	Vegard Ulvang	Skier
1998	Kenji Ogiwara	Skier
2002	Jim Shea	Skeleton
2006	Giorgio Rocca	Skier

OPENINGS

TRADITIONALLY, THE OLYMPIC Games are opened by a member of the reigning Royal Family or a senior representative of the national government of the host country. They have included:

Summer

1896	King George I
1900	–
1904	Mr David Francis (President of the World's Fair)
1906	King George I
1908	King Edward VII
1912	King Gustaf V
1920	King Albert
1924	President Gaston Doumergue
1928	HRH Prince Hendrik
1932	Vice President Charles Curtis
1936	Chancellor Adolf Hitler
1948	King George VI
1952	President Juho Paasikivi
1956	HRH The Duke of Edinburgh
	King Gustav VI (Stockholm)
1960	President Giovanni Gronchi
1964	Emperor Hirohito
1968	President Gustavo Diaz Ordaz

1972	President Gustav Heinemann
1976	Queen Elizabeth II
1980	President Leonid Brezhnev
1984	President Ronald Reagan
1988	President Roh Tae-Woo
1992	King Juan Carlos I
1996	President William Clinton
2000	Sir William Deane (Governor-General)
2004	President Kostis Stefanopoulos

Winter

1924	Under Secretary Gaston Vidal
1928	President Edmund Schulthess
1932	Governor Franklin D Roosevelt
1936	Chancellor Adolf Hitler
1948	President Enrico Celio
1952	HRH Princess Ragnhild
1956	President Giovanni Gronchi
1960	Vice President Richard Nixon
1964	President Adolf Schärf
1968	President Charles de Gaulle
1972	Emperor Hirohito
1976	President Rudolf Kirchschläger
1980	Vice President Walter Mondale
1984	President Mika Špiljak
1988	Governor-General Jeanne Sauvé
1992	President Francois Mitterand
1994	King Harald V
1998	Emperor Akihito
2002	President George W Bush
2006	President Carlo Azeglio Ciampi

OUTSTANDING ACHIEVEMENTS

Most Summer Golds

Men	10 Ray Ewry (USA) 1900-1908	Athletics
Women	9 Larissa Latynina (URS) 1956-64	Gymnastics
Men, in one Games	7 Mark Spitz (USA) 1972	Swimming
Women, in one Games	6 Kristin Otto (GDR) 1988	Swimming

Most Summer Medals

Men	15 Nikolai Andrianov (URS) 1972-80	Gymnastics
Women	18 Larissa Latynina (URS) 1956-64	Gymnastics
Men, in one Games	8 Alexander Dityatin (URS) 1980	Gymnastics
	8 Michael Phelps (USA) 2004	Swimming
Women, in one Games	7 Maria Gorokhovskaya (URS) 1952	Gymnastics

Most Winter Golds

Men	8 Bjørn Daehlie (NOR) 1992-98	Nordic Skiing
Women	6 Lydia Skoblikova (URS) 1960-64	Speed Skating
	6 Lyubov Yegorova (EUN-RUS) 1992-94	Nordic Skiing
Men, in one Games	5 Eric Heiden (USA) 1980	Speed Skating
Women, in one Games	4 Lydia Skoblikova (URS) 1964	Speed Skating

Most Winter Medals

Men	12 Bjørn Daehlie (NOR) 1992-98	Nordic Skiing
Women	10 Raisa Smetanina (URS) 1976-92	Nordic Skiing
Men, in one Games	5 Clas Thunberg (FIN) 1924	Speed Skating
	5 Roald Larsen (NOR) 1924	Speed Skating
	5 Eric Heiden (USA) 1980	Speed Skating
Women, in one Games	5 Lyubov Yegorova (EUN-RUS) 1992	Nordic Skiing
	5 Yelena Valbe (EUN-RUS) 1992	Nordic Skiing

	5 Manuela di Centa (ITA) 1994		Nordic Skiing
	5 Larissa Lazutina (RUS) 1998		Nordic Skiing

Summer Age Records

Oldest

Male Gold	64y 258d	Oscar Swahn (Swe) 1912	Shooting
Female Gold	53y 275d	Queenie Newall (GBR) 1908	Archery
Male Medallist	72y 280d	Oscar Swahn (Swe) 1920	Shooting
Female Medallist	53y 277d	Queenie Newall (GBR) 1908	Archery
Competitor Male	72y 280d	Oscar Swahn (SWE) 1920	Shooting
Competitor Female	70y 5d	Lorna Johnstone (GBR) 1972	Equestrianism

Youngest

Male Gold	7-10y	Unknown French boy* 1900	Rowing
Female Gold	13y 268d	Marjorie Gestring (USA) 1936	Diving
Male Medallist	7-10y	Unknown French boy 1900	Rowing
Female Medallist	11y 302d	Luigina Giavotti (ITA) 1928	Gymnastics
Competitor Male	7-10y	Unknown boy (FRA)* 1900	Rowing

There is an unsubstantiated report that his name was Marcel Depaillé

Competitor Female	11y 328d	Liana Vicens (PUR) 1968	Swimming

Winter Age Records

Oldest

Male Gold	48y 359d	Jay O'Brien (USA) 1932	Bobsledding
Female Gold	39y 354d	Raisa Smetanina (EUN-RUS) 1992	Nordic Skiing
Male Medallist	50y 235d	Paul Savage (CAN) 1998	Curling
Female Medallist	42y 178d	Jane Bidstrup (DEN) 1998	Curling
Competitor Male	53y 297d	James Coates (GBR) 1948	Tobogganing
Competitor Female	40y 307d	Anne Abernathy (ISV) 2002	Lugeing

Youngest

Male Gold	16y 259d	Toni Nieminen (FIN) 1992	Ski Jumping
Female Gold	13y 83d	Kim Yoon-Mi (KOR) 1994	Short-Track Speed Skating
Male Medallist	14y 363d	Scott Allen (USA) 1964	Figure Skating
Female Medallist	13y 83d	Kim Yoon-Mi (KOR) 1994	Short-Track Speed Skating
Competitor Male	12y 110d	Jan Hoffmann (GDR) 1968	Figure Skating
Competitor Female	11y 73d	Cecilia Colledge (GBR) 1932	Figure Skating

Most Summer Games/Longest Span

Men

9 Games	Hubert Raudaschl (AUT) 1964-96	Yachting
40 yr	Ivan Osiier (DEN) 1908-48	Fencing
40 yr	Magnus Konow (NOR) 1908-48	Yachting
40 yr	Durward Knowles (GBR/BAH) 1948-88	Yachting
40 yr	Paul Elvstrøm (DEN) 1948-88	Yachting

Most Summer Games/Longest Span

Women

7 Games*	Kerstin Palm (SWE) 1964-88	Fencing
	Merlene Ottey (JAM/SLO) 1980-2004	Athletics
28 yr	Anne Newberry-Ransehousen (USA) 1960-88	Equestrianism
	Christilot Hanson-Boylen (CAN) 1964-92	Equestrianism

Most Winter Games/Longest Span

Men

6 Games	Carl-Erik Eriksson (SWE) 1964-84	Bobsledding
6 Games	Colin Coates (AUS) 1968-88	Speed Skating
6 Games	Alfred Eder (AUT) 1976-94	Biathlon
6 Games	Jochen Behle (FRG/GER) 1980-98	Nordic Skiing
6 Games	Harri Kirvesniemi (FIN) 1980-98	Nordic Skiing
6 Games	Raimo Helminen (FIN) 1984-02	Ice Hockey
6 Games	Michael Dixon (GBR) 1984-02	Nordic Skiing/Biathlon
6 Games	Sergei Tchepikov (RUS) 1988-2006	Biathlon/Nordic skiing

20 yr	John Heaton (USA) 1928-48		Tobogganing
20 yr	Max Houben (BEL) 1928-48		Bobsledding
20 yr	Richard Torriani (SUI) 1928-48		Ice Hockey
20 yr	Frank Stack (CAN) 1932-52		Speed Skating
20 yr	Stanislaw Marusarz (POL) 1932-52		Nordic Skiing
20 yr	James Bickford (USA) 1936-56		Bobsledding
20 yr	Sepp Bradl (AUT) 1936-56		Ski Jumping
20 yr	Carl-Erik Eriksson (SWE) 1964-84		Bobsledding
20 yr	Colin Coates (AUS) 1968-88		Speed Skating

Most Winter Games/Longest Span

Women

6 Games*	Marja-Liisa Hämäläinen-Kirvesniemi (FIN) 1976-94	Nordic Skiing
6 Games*	Emese Hunyadi (HUN/AUT) 1984-02	Speed Skating
18yr	Marja-Liisa Hämäläinen-Kirvesniemi (FIN) 1976-94	Nordic Skiing
18yr	Emese Hunyadi (HUN/AUT) 1984-02	Speed Skating

*Seiko Hashimoto (JPN) has also competed in seven Games, comprising four in the Winter at speed skating 1984-94 and three in the Summer at cycling 1988-96.

PARTICIPATION

By competitors

It has been calculated that well over 100,000 sportsmen and women have competed in the Olympic Games, summer and winter, since 1896. Figures for the Summer Games are 93,984, of which 19,536 were women, and for the Winter Games a total of 15,914, of which 3938 were women. Aditionally there were 113 who competed in both, of which 20 were women. There is always some confusion about definitive totals due to the problem of double counting of those who compete in more than one event and/or one sport , and the fact that so-called official figures invariably include numbers of entries, and not just of those who actually competed. Also such figures often include administrators and coaches, thus exacerbating discrepances. Figures used in this book are based on the detailed research done by Wolf Lyberg of Sweden and, more recently, Bill Mallon of the United States.

By country

(The three-character country abbreviations used here are those used officially by the IOC at the Games. Individual sports' governing bodies sometimes use different abbreviations at other times.)

		Summer Games		Winter Games	
	Country	Debut	Number attended	Debut	Number attended
AFG	Afghanistan	1936	11	–	
AHO	Netherlands Antilles	1952	12	1988	2
ALB	Albania	1972	5	2006	1
ALG	Algeria	1964	10	1992	2
AND	Andorra	1976	8	1976	9
ANG	Angola	1980	6	–	
ANT	Antigua/Barbuda	1976	7	–	
ARG	Argentina	1920	19	1908	17
ARM	Armenia	1996	3	1994	4
ARU	Aruba	1988	5	–	
ASA	American Samoa	1988	5	1994	1
AUS	Australia[1]	1896	26	1936	16
AUT	Austria[2]	1896	25	1924	20
AZE	Azerbaijan	1996	3	1998	3
BAH	Bahamas	1952	13	–	
BAN	Bangladesh	1984	6	–	
BAR	Barbados[10]	1960	10	–	
BDI	Burundi	1996	3	–	
BEL	Belgium	1900	24	1920	19
BEN	Benin (ex Dahomey)	1972	8	–	
BER	Bermuda	1936	15	1992	5
BHU	Bhutan	1984	6	–	
BIH	Bosnia & Herzegovina	1992	4	1994	4
BIZ	Belize (ex Brit Honduras)	1968	9	–	
BLR	Belarus	1996	3	1994	4
BOH	Bohemia[3]	–			
BOL	Bolivia	1936	11	1956	5
BOT	Botswana	1980	7	–	

BRA	Brazil	1920	19	1992	5
BRN	Bahrain	1984	6	–	
BRU	Brunei	1996	3	–	
BUL	Bulgaria	1896	17	1936	17
BUR	Burkina Faso (ex Upper Volta)	1972	6	–	
CAF	Central African Republic	1968	7	–	
CAM	Cambodia[4]	1956	6	–	
CAN	Canada	1900	24	1920	21
CAY	Cayman Islands	1976	7	–	
CGO	Congo	1964	9	–	
CHA	Chad	1964	9	–	
CHI	Chile	1896	20	1948	14
CHN	China	1932	10	1980	8
CIV	Ivory Coast	1964	10	–	
CMR	Cameroon	1964	11	2002	1
COD	Democratic Republic of the Congo (ex Zaire)	1968	7	–	
COK	Cook Islands	1988	5	–	
COL	Colombia	1932	16	–	
COM	Comoros Islands	1996	3	–	
CPV	Cape Verde Islands	1996	3	–	
CRC	Costa Rica	1936	12	1984	6
CRO	Croatia	1992	4	1992	4
CUB	Cuba	1900	17	–	
CYP	Cyprus	1980	7	1980	8
CZE	Czech Republic[3]	1996	3	1994	4
DEN	Denmark	1896	25	1948	11
DJI	Djibouti	1984	5	–	
DMA	Dominica	1996	3	–	
DOM	Dominican Republic	1964	11	–	
ECU	Ecuador	1924	11	–	
EGY	Egypt[5]	1906	20	1984	1
ERI	Eritrea	2000	2	–	
ESA	El Salvador	1968	8	–	
ESP	Spain	1900	20	1936	17
EST	Estonia[6]	1920	9	1928	7
ETH	Ethiopia	1956	10	2006	1
FIJ	Fiji	1956	11	1988	3
FIN	Finland	1906	23	1920	21
FRA	France	1896	26	1920	21
FRG	Federal Republic of Germany[7]	1968	5	1968	6
FSM	Federated States of Micronesia	2000	2	–	
GAB	Gabon	1972	7	–	
GAM	Gambia	1984	6	–	
GBR	Great Britain	1896	26	1908	22
GBS	Guinea–Bissau	1996	3	–	
GDR	German Democratic Republic[7]	1968	5	1968	6
GEO	Georgia	1996	3	1994	4
GEQ	Equatorial Guinea	1984	6	–	
GER	Germany[8]	1896	17	1908	13
GHA	Ghana (Ex-Gold Coast)	1952	11	–	
GRE	Greece	1896	26	1936	16
GRN	Grenada	1984	6	–	
GUA	Guatemala	1952	11	1988	1
GUI	Guinea	1968	8	–	
GUM	Guam	1988	5	1988	1
GUY	Guyana (ex British Guiana)	1948	14	–	
HAI	Haiti	1900	13	–	
HKG	Hong Kong	1952	13	2002	2
HON	Honduras	1968	8	1992	1
HUN	Hungary	1896	24	1924	20
INA	Indonesia	1952	12	–	
IND	India	1920	20	1964	7
IRI	Iran	1948	13	1956	7
IRL	Ireland[9]	1924	18	1992	4
IRQ	Iraq	1948	11	–	
ISL	Iceland	1908	18	1948	15
ISR	Israel	1952	13	1994	4

ISV	Virgin Islands	1968	9	1984	6[22]
ITA	Italy	1900	24	1924	20
IVB	British Virgin Islands	1984	6	–	
JAM	Jamaica[10]	1948	15	1988	5
JOR	Jordan	1980	7	–	
JPN	Japan	1912	19	1928	17
KAZ	Kazakhstan	1996	3	1994	4
KEN	Kenya	1956	11	1998	3
KGZ	Kirghizstan	1996	3	1994	4
KIR	Kiribat	2004	1	–	
KOR	Korea[11]	1948	14	1948	15
KSA	Saudi Arabia	1972	8	–	
KUW	Kuwait	1968	10	–	
LAO	Laos	1980	6	–	
LAT	Latvia[6]	1924	8	1924	8
LBA	Libya	1968	8	–	
LBR	Liberia	1956	9	–	
LCA	St Lucia	1996	3	–	
LES	Lesotho	1972	8	–	
LIB	Lebanon	1948	14	1948	14
LIE	Liechtenstein	1936	14	1936	16
LTU	Lithuania[6]	1924	6	1928	6
LUX	Luxembourg	1912	20	1928	7
MAD	Madagascar	1964	9	2006	1
MAR	Morocco	1960	11	1968	4
MAS	Malaysia[12]	1956	12	–	
MAW	Malawi	1972	7	–	
MDA	Moldova	1996	3	1994	4
MDV	Maldives	1988	5	–	
MEX	Mexico	1924	19	1928	6
MGL	Mongolia	1964	10	1964	11
MKD	Macedonia	1996	3	1998	3
MLI	Mali	1964	10	–	
MLT	Malta	1928	13	–	
MON	Monaco	1920	17	1984	7
MOZ	Mozambique	1980	7	–	
MRI	Mauritius	1984	6	–	
MTN	Mauretania	1984	6	–	
MYA	Myanmar (ex Burma)	1948	14	–	
NAM	Namibia	1992	4	–	
NAU	Nauru	1996	3	–	
NCA	Nicaragua	1968	9	–	
NED	Netherlands	1900	24	1928	18
NEP	Nepal	1964	10	2002	2
NGR	Nigeria	1952	13	–	
NIG	Niger	1964	9	–	
NOR	Norway	1900	24	1920	21
NZL	New Zealand	1908	22	1952	13
OMA	Oman	1984	6	–	
PAK	Pakistan	1948	14	–	
PAN	Panama	1928	14	–	
PAR	Paraguay	1968	9	–	
PER	Peru	1936	15	–	
PHI	Philippines	1924	18	1972	3
PLE	Palestine	1996	3	–	
PLW	Palau	2000	2	–	
PNG	Papua New Guinea	1976	7	–	
POL	Poland	1924	18	1924	20
POR	Portugal	1912	21	1952	5
PRK	Democratic People's Republic of Korea[11]	1972	7	1964	7
PUR	Puerto Rico	1948	15	1984	5[21]
QAT	Qatar	1984	6	–	
ROM	Romania	1924	17	1928	18
RSA	South Africa[13]	1904	17	1960	5
RUS	Russia[14]	1900	6	1908	5
RWA	Rwanda	1984	6	–	
SAM	Western Samoa	1984	6	–	

SAR	Saar[15]	1952	1	–	
SCG	Serbia/Montenegro	1912	4	1992	4
SEN	Senegal	1964	11	1984	4
SEY	Seychelles	1980	6	–	
SIN	Singapore	1948	14	–	
SKN	St Kitts & Nevis	1996	3	–	
SLE	Sierra Leone	1968	8	–	
SLO	Slovenia	1992	4	1992	5
SMR	San Marino	1960	10	1976	7
SOL	Solomon Islands	1984	6	–	
SOM	Somalia	1972	6	–	
SRI	Sri Lanka (ex Ceylon)	1948	14	–	
STP	São Tomé & Príncipe	1996	3	–	
SUD	Sudan	1960	9	–	
SUI	Switzerland[16]	1896	26	1920	21
SUR	Surinam	1968	9	–	
SVK	Slovakia	1996	3	1994	4
SWE	Sweden	1896	25	1908	22
SWZ	Swaziland	1972	7	1992	1
SYR	Syria	1948	10	–	
TAN	Tanzania	1964	10		
TCH	Czechoslovakia[3]	1900	20	1920	18
TGA	Tonga	1984	0		
THA	Thailand	1952	13	2002	2
TJK	Tadjikistan	1996	3	2002	2
TKM	Turkmenistan	1996	3	–	
TLS	East Timor	2000	2		
TOG	Togo	1972	7	–	
TPE	Chinese Taipei (ex Formosa/Taiwan)	1956	11	1972	9
TRI	Trinidad & Tobago[10]	1948	15	1994	3
TUN	Tunisia	1960	101	–	
TUR	Turkey	1908	19	1936	14
UAE	United Arab Emirates	1984	6	–	
UGA	Uganda	1956	12	–	
UKR	Ukraine	1996	3	1994	4
URS	Soviet Union[17]	1952	10	1956	10
URU	Uruguay	1924	18	1998	1
USA	United States	1896	25	1908	22
UZB	Uzbekistan	1996	3	1994	4
VAN	Vanuatu	1988	5	–	
VEN	Venezuela	1948	15	1998	3
VIE	Vietnam[18]	1952	12	–	
VIN	St Vincent/Grenadines	1988	5	–	
YEM	Yemen[19]	1992	4	–	
YUG	Yugoslavia[20]	1920	16	1924	13
ZAM	Zambia (ex N Rhodesia)	1964	10	–	
ZIM	Zimbabwe (ex Rhodesia)	1928	10	–	

[1]Australia and New Zealand combined as Australasia 1908–12; [2]Not invited in 1920; [3]Czechoslovakia was represented by Bohemia up to 1912; [4]Provisional recognition of current regime in Cambodia; [5]As United Arab Republic 1960–68; [6]Annexed by the Soviet Union in 1940; Independent again from 1992; [7]Separate teams 1968–88; GDR part of combined German team 1956–64; [8]Not invited 1920,1924 and 1948; [9]Part of the United Kingdom until 1922; [10]Jamaica, Barbados and Trinidad combined as Antilles in 1960; [11]Country partitioned in 1945, and separate regimes established in 1948 [12]Prior to 1964 Malaya and North Borneo later Sabah competed separately. In 1964 they combined with Sarawak and Singapore. In 1965 Singapore left the Federation; [13]Not invited 1960–88; [14]As Czarist Russia 1900–12; Separate entity again in 1994; [15]Independent 1947–57, then incorporated into Germany; [16]Switzerland attended only Stockholm in 1956 [17]A combined team of the NOCs of the former Soviet republics excluding the Baltic States competed in the 1992 Summer and Winter Games as the Unified Team EUN or Commonwealth of Independent States CIS; [18]From 1952–72 only a South Vietnamese team competed; [19]The Republic of Yemen was formed in 1960 of the Yemen Arab Republic which competed 1984–88 and the Yemen People's Democratic Republic which competed in 1988
[20]Representatives of the Yugoslavia Serbs competed as Independent Olympic Participants IOP in the 1992 Games. In 1912 Serbia had competed as a separate entity
[21]Puerto Rico marched in the opening ceremony of 2002, but had no actual competitors in the Games.
[22]The US Virgin Islands marched in the opening ceremony of 2006, but had no actual competitors in the Games

PELOTA BASQUE

IT WAS A demonstration sport at Paris in 1924, with teams from Spain and France. It was seen again at Mexico City in 1968, and at Barcelona in 1992.

POLO

A MEDAL SPORT on five occasions. Only Sir John Wodehouse (GBR), the 3rd Earl of Kimberley, won a silver (1908) to add to a gold (1920). The oldest gold medallist was Manuel Andrada (ARG) in 1936 aged 46yr 211days, and the youngest was his teammate Roberto Cavanagh aged 21yr 269days. The biggest winning margin was 16-2 by Argentina v Spain and Great Britain v France, both in 1924, and by Mexico v Hungary in 1936. In 1900, in a remarkable display of unchauvinistic behaviour, there was an American in the British gold medal team, an American and a Spaniard in the British silver medal team, and a Briton in the French bronze team.

PRESS

SEE UNDER 'MEDIA'

RACKETS

A MEDAL SPORT only at London in 1908, with all competitors from Great Britain. The most successful were Evan Noel and American-born John Jacob Astor. Noel won the singles gold and a bronze in the doubles, while Astor won a gold in the doubles and a bronze in the singles. Later he became an MP, and, in 1956, he was made Baron Astor of Hever.

ROLLER HOCKEY

THIS WAS DEMONSTRATED for the first time at Barcelona in 1992.

ROQUE

A VARIATION OF croquet, played on a hard-surfaced court. Only a medal sport at St Louis in 1904 with all competitors from the United States. The gold medallist, Charles Jacobus, was aged 45yr 41days.

ROWING

ROWING FOR MEN was first held in the 1900 Games over a 1750m course on the river Seine in Paris. In 1904 the course measured 2 miles *3219m*, in 1908 it was 1.5 miles *2414m*, and in 1948 1 mile 300 yards *1883m*. Women's rowing was introduced in 1976 over a 1000m course, but since 1988 both men and women race over a standard 2000m 1.24 miles course. Even though recent Games rowing has been held on still water, as opposed to flowing rivers as in the past, water and weather conditions vary too much to allow official Olympic records. However, it is worthy of note that the fastest average speed achieved by a men's eight over the full course was 22.51km/h *13.98mph*, when the United States crew clocked 5min 19.85sec in a heat in 2004. In a that race the USA crew averaged 23.01km/h *14.29mph* for the first 500m. The 2004 USA women's eight won their heat in 5min 56.55sec averaging 20.19km/h *12.54mph*. They averaged 20.94 km/h *13.01mph* for the first 500m in that race. Since automatic timing was introduced in 1960, the narrowest winning margin has been 0.01sec in the women's single sculls at Sydney in 2000, and the smallest in the men's events was 0.08sec in the 2004 men's coxless fours. However, it is thought that the 1932 coxed fours may have been as close.

One of the first winning crews in the Games, the 1900 German four, contained three brothers, Oskar, Gustav and Carl Gossler, the latter as coxswain. This was the beginning of a tradition of sibling participation and success which reached a landmark at Moscow in 1980 when the Landvoigt twins (GDR) beat the Pimenov twins (URS) in the coxless pairs final – and caused problems at the medal ceremony. Similarly, in the 1992 coxed pairs, Jonathan and Greg Searle of Great Britain beat the Italian defending champions, Carmine and Giuseppe Abbagnale. When the latter pair won in 1988 their younger brother Agostino also won a gold in the quadruple sculls event. Fathers and sons have had great success in the sport, but usually independently of each other. The most famous are: the Beresfords (GBR), Julius with a silver in 1912, and Jack with five medals (see below) in the next five Games; the Costellos (USA), Paul winning three golds in the 1920s and son Bernard a silver in 1956; the Kellys (USA), John Sr winning three gold medals (see below) and John Jr a bronze in 1956; the Nickalls (GBR) with Guy Sr winning a gold in the 1908 eight and Guy Jr gaining two silvers in the 1920 and 1928 crews. However, the Burnells (GBR), Charles (1908) and Richard (1948), are the only father and son in Olympic rowing to both win gold medals.

Steve Redgrave (GBR) won a record five successive gold medals 1984-00, plus a bronze in 1988. Jack Beresford (GBR) also won medals (3g, 2s) at five Games. Vyacheslav Ivanov (URS) and Pertti Karppinen (FIN) are the only men to win three individual golds, in the single sculls. Ivanov had an unfortunate experience after his first title win in Melbourne. He excitedly threw his medal into the air and lost it in the waters of Lake Wendouree. It was never recovered and later the IOC gave him a replacement. John Kelly (USA), whose daughter Grace won an Academy Award in 1954, won gold medals in both the single and double sculls in 1920 within an hour.

The oldest gold medallist was Róbert Zimonyi who coxed the United States eight in 1964 aged 46yr 180days. In 1948 he had won a bronze coxing a pair from his native Hungary. The oldest actual oarsman to win a gold medal was Guy Nickalls (GBR) in the 1908 eight aged 41yr 261days. His compatriot Julius Beresford won his silver medal (see above) aged

44yr 20days. The youngest gold medal oarsman was Giliante D'Este (ITA) in 1928 aged 18yr 141days, while the youngest medallist oarsman was Australian Walter Howell in 1956 at 16yr 346days. The youngest gold medallist was the unknown French boy who coxed the winning Dutch pair in 1900. In 2006 a name, Marcel Depaillé, surfaced, but currently it is unsubstantiated. Believed to have been under ten years of age, he was recruited at the last moment out of the spectators to replace Hermanus Brockmann, their cox in the heats, who was considered to be too heavy. Incidentally, Brockmann coxed the Dutch fours to a silver medal and the eight to a bronze. Of the many other young medal winning coxes over the

Rowing Medals

| | Men | | | Women | | | |
	G	S	B	G	S	B	Total
United States	29	22	16	1	8	4	80
Germany	16	11	11	7	4	3	52
GDR	20	4	7	13	3	1	48
Great Britain	22	15	7	-	3	1	48
Soviet Union	11	14	6	1	6	5	43
Italy	13	13	13	-	-	-	39
Romania	2	4	2	16	6	5	35
France	7	15	12	-	-	1	35
Canada	4	9	9	4	4	4	34
Australia	7	8	9	1	1	3	29
Netherlands	5	7	6	-	3	4	25
Switzerland	6	8	9	-	-	-	23
Denmark	5	3	6	-	-	2	16
New Zealand	5	2	5	1	-	1	14
FRG	4	4	4	-	-	2	14
Norway	2	6	6	-	-	-	14
Bulgaria	-	-	2	2	4	5	13
Poland	2	1	9	-	1	-	13
Czechoslovakia	2	2	7	-	-	-	11
Belgium	-	6	1	-	1	1	9
Finland	3	-	3	-	-	-	6
Belarus	-	-	-	2	1	2	5
Greece	1	2	2	-	-	-	5
Yugoslavia	1	1	3	-	-	-	5
Austria	-	3	2	-	-	-	5
Argentina	1	1	2	-	-	-	4
Slovenia	1	1	2	-	-	-	4
Russia	1	-	2	-	-	1	4
China	-	-	-	-	2	2	4
Uruguay	-	1	3	-	-	-	4
Hungary	-	1	2	-	-	-	3
Sweden	-	2	-	-	-	-	2
Croatia	-	1	1	-	-	-	2
Ukraine	-	-	1	-	1	-	2
South Africa	-	-	2	-	-	-	2
Czech Republic	-	1	-	-	-	-	1
Estonia	-	1	-	-	-	-	1
Spain	-	1	-	-	-	-	1
Lithuania	-	-	-	-	-	1	1
	170	170	172	48	48	48	656

years, the youngest known for certain was another French boy, Noël Vandernotte, in the 1936 pairs and fours aged 12yr 232days. The latter crew included his father and uncle.

In women's rowing the youngest gold medal oarswoman was Andrea Kurth (GDR) in 1976 aged 18yr 298days, while the youngest medallist was Rodica Puscatu (ROM) at 18yr 83days in 1980. The youngest female coxswain of a winning crew was Sabine Hess (GDR) in the 1976 coxed four aged 17yr 297days, and Lynn Silliman was 17yr 92days old when she coxed the US eight to a bronze in 1976. The oldest female gold medallist/medallist oarswoman was Elisabeta Oleniuc-Lipa (ROM) in the 2004 eights aged 39yr 301days, although her teammate, Elena Georgescu, the cox of the eights, was aged 40yr 134days. However, Lesley Thompson was four days past her 41st birthday when she coxed the Canadian eight to a bronze medal in 2000. The most successful female rower, and arguably the most successful male or female, has been Elisabeta Oleniuc-Lipa (ROM) with five golds, two silvers and a bronze, 1984-2004, for a unmatched total of eight medals in six Games, over a record 20 year period. Oleniuc-Lipa and Kathrin Boron (GER) won gold medals in four consecutive Games, both in 1992-2004. The sibling tradition continues in the women's events, the German twins, Manja and Kerstin Kowalski, in the winning quadruple sculls in Sydney, and the Evers-Swindell twins, Georgina and Caroline, of New Zealand, taking the double sculls in 2004.

The US oarsman, Conn Findlay, winner of two golds and a bronze in coxed pairs 1956-64, also won a sailing bronze medal in 1976 in the Tempest class. In 1996 several changes to the programme included the deletion of men's coxed pairs and fours, and women's coxless fours. In 2000 new events included men's and women's lightweight double sculls and men's lightweight coxless fours.

ROYALTY

IN 1896 TWO princes of the Greek royal house escorted the marathon winner into the stadium at Athens. Since then a number of members of the royal families of Europe have actually competed, now and again with great success, in the Olympic Games. The first winner of a gold medal was Crown Prince Olav of Norway, later King Olav V, who was a member of the winning crew of the 6m sailing class in 1928. His son Crown Prince Harald, later Harald V, competed in the same sport from 1964-1972, gaining his best placing of 8th in the 5.5m class in 1964. The only other royal winner was the then Prince Constantine of Greece, later Constantine II, who won gold in the Dragon class in 1960. His brother-in-law, Juan Carlos

of Spain, was in the 1972 sailing, while his niece Princess Christina competed in the 1988 Tornado class, and his nephew, Prince Felipe, placed 6th in the Soling class of 1992. To add to the Spanish royal family's Olympic credentials, Princess Christina later married two-time Spanish bronze medal winning handballer Inaki Urdangarin.

Britain's Princess Anne finished 24th in the 3-day equestrian event in 1976. Her husband-to-be, Capt Mark Phillips had been a member of the gold medal winning 3-day team in 1972. In more recent years, in the Winter Games, Prince Albert of Monaco has competed, as Albert Grimaldi, for the principality in the 2-man and 4-man bob events from 1988 to 1998.

RUGBY UNION

THE FACT THAT Baron de Coubertin was a rugby referee probably lay behind it being a medal sport on four occasions; at Paris in 1900, London in 1908, Antwerp in 1920 and Paris again in 1924. Only six countries competed in the four tournaments held – Australia, France, Germany, Great Britain, Romania and the United States. The 1908 title was won by Australia while the Wallabies were on their first tour of Britain. The team they beat in the final was Cornwall, the English County champions. Five American players won two gold medals in 1920 and 1924: Charles Doe, John O'Neil, Colby Slater, John Patrick and Rudolph Scholz. Additionally, Daniel Carroll became the only Olympian to win gold medals for different countries when he won his second gold with the 1920 US team, having been on the 1908 Australian squad when only 16yr 245days. Thus he is the youngest ever rugby international, although 'purists' have never considered the Olympic matches to be 'full' internationals. The highest score was when France beat Romania 61-3 in 1924. In 1920, sprint relay gold medallist Morris Kirksey, also runner-up in the 100m, won another gold in the winning US rugby team. It always comes as a shock to enthusiasts to realize that the United States is the reigning Olympic rugby champion. Incidentally, before their Paris victory, they had played in Britain and were beaten by the Harlequins and Blackheath club teams.

SAILING

THE FIRST OLYMPIC regatta in 1896 should have been on the Bay of Salamis, but it was cancelled due to bad weather. Since 1900 the classes have been changed regularly until very recently when some measure of standardization was imposed. The results in each class are based on the aggregate positions in each of a set number of races – the number of races and the ones allowed to be discarded have changed over time. Currently all classes contest 11 races except for the 49ers which have 16. The only event which has been a permanent fixture is the Olympic monotype, i.e. one-man dinghy, albeit represented by different classes of boat prior to 1952 (now the Finn).

The most successful yachtsman is Paul Elvstrøm (DEN) who won four successive Olympic monotype titles from 1948-1960 – the first man to achieve such a run in any sport. He competed again in the 1968 Star (fourth), 1972 Soling (thirteenth), 1984 Tornado (fourth), and 1988 Tornado (fifteenth) – in the last two partnering his daughter Trine. Frances Clytie Rivett-Carnac (GBR) and her husband Charles, in the winning 7m yacht Heroine in 1908, were the first married couple to win gold medals in Olympic sailing, but not in the Games as is sometimes reported. The oldest gold medallist was Everard Endt (USA) in the 1952 6m class aged 59yr 112days, while the oldest in a single-handed event was Léon Huybrechts (BEL) aged 47yr 215days in 1924. The oldest female gold medallist was Virginie Hériot (FRA) in the 1928 8m class at the age of 38yr 16days, while the oldest female medallist was Pease Glaser (USA) in the Sydney women's 470 class aged 38yr 314days. The youngest gold medallist/medallist was Franciscus Hin (NED), in the 1920 12-foot dinghy event with his brother Johannes, aged 14yr 163days. The youngest female champion was Kristine Roug (DEN) in the 1996 Europe class aged 21yr 141days, while the youngest female medallist was Natalia Via Dufresne Perena (ESP), second in the same event in 1992 at 19yr 54days. The oldest medallist was Louis Noverraz (SUI) in the 5.5m category in 1968 aged 66yr 154days.

Outstanding family achievements have occurred in Olympic sailing. In 1920 four Norwegian brothers, Henrik, Jan, Ole and Kristian Østervold won gold medals in the 12m (1907 rating) class. The full crew of the winning 5.5m in 1968 were brothers Ulf, Jörgen and Peter Sundelin (SWE), and the winning 6m in 1912 was crewed by Amédée, Gaston and Jacques Thubé (FRA). The only twins to win gold were Sumner and Edgar White (USA) in the 5.5m of 1952. The first father and son to win together were Emile and Florimond Cornellie (BEL) in the 6m (1907 rating) in 1920. However, the greatest Olympic sailing family must be the Norwegians Lunde: Eugen won a gold in the 1924 6m class, his son Peder and daughter-in-law Vibeke along with Vibeke's brother won a silver in the 5.5m in 1952, and grandson Peder Jr won a gold in the 1960 Flying Dutchman contest. The winner of the women's sailboard title in 1992,

Barbara Kendall (NZL), was the sister of the 1988 men's winner, Bruce Kendall.

Rodney Pattisson and Iain Macdonald-Smith (GBR) scored the lowest number of penalty points (three) ever achieved in Olympic sailing when they won the 1968 Flying Dutchman class with five wins, a second place and a disqualification (finished first) in their seven starts. Their boat Superdocius is now in the National Maritime Museum, Greenwich. The only boat to win two gold medals in the same Games was Scotia, crewed by Lorne Currie and John Gretton for Great Britain, in the ½-1 ton and Open classes in 1900. The United States yacht Llanoria won the 6m class in 1948 and 1952, skippered both times by Herman Whiton.

In 1948 Magnus Konow (NOR) equalled the longest span of Olympic competition when he took part in the 6m event 40 years after his debut in the 8m class of 1908. He won two golds and a silver in 1912, 1920 and 1936, the only other Games he attended. Durward Knowles competed in a record eight Games, all in the Star class, from 1948 when he competed for Great Britain. He represented the Bahamas in the next six celebrations, and then again in 1988 (aged 71, and probably the oldest Olympic sailor ever). The afore-mentioned Paul Elvstrøm (DEN) also made it eight Games in 1988, and both he and Knowles matched the 40-year span record. In 1996 Hubert Raudaschl (AUT) outclassed them all, and competed in his ninth Games, 1964-96, which is a record for any sport. This could have been even more remarkable, as he had been a reserve for the Austrian Olympic team in 1960. Tore Holm (SWE) won medals over a record span of 28 years (1920-48), and, more unusual, Hans Fogh won medals 24 years apart (1960-84), firstly for Denmark and then for Canada.

Harry Melges (USA) won a gold medal in the 1972 Soling class, and then co-skippered the winning US yacht in the 1992 America's Cup. This achievement was matched by Russell Coutts (NZL), who won the 1984 Finn event, and was the skipper of Black Magic I which won the America's Cup for New Zealand in 1995. The helmsman of the third placed Tempest in 1976 was Dennis Conner (USA), who had won the America's Cup for the United States in 1980, lost it in 1983, and regained it in 1987. His Montreal partner, Conn Findlay, had won rowing golds in 1956 and 1964, and then was a crew member of successful Cup defender Courageous in 1977. A number of other Olympic yachtsmen have also competed, sometimes successfully, in the America's Cup competitions.

In the 1984 Games all thirteen members of the United States team won either gold or silver medals, a unique team achievement. The greatest number of boats in an Olympic regatta was the 239 (plus

73 sailboards) at Atlanta (Savannah) in 1996. The greatest entry in just one event was 56 in the 1996 Laser competition. When Lai Shan Lee won the women's sailboard title in 1996, she gained the first, and what was thought to be the last, Olympic gold medal ever for her country, as it was accepted that from 2000 Hong Kong would then be part of China, both politically and sportingly. However, Hong Kong has continued to compete as a separate entity.

An attempt has been made to bring some method of comparison to the Olympic results, made particularly difficult due to the wide variety of classes and types of boat used over the years. Where classes have been superseded by those of similar type, they have been listed in the same table. Purists may be unhappy but the general reader will find it easier to follow.

Olympic Yachting Venues

1900	River Seine at Meulan (10-20 tonners at Le Havre)
1908	Cowes, Isle of Wight, and the River Clyde
1912	Nyhashamn
1920	Ostend
1924	River Seine at Meulan (6m and 8m at Le Havre)
1928	Zuider-Zee
1932	San Pedro Bay
1936	Kiel
1948	Torbay, Devon
1952	Harmaja
1956	Port Phillip Bay
1960	Bay of Naples
1964	Sagami Bay
1968	Acapulco
1972	Kiel
1976	Kingston, Lake Ontario
1980	Tallinn
1984	Long Beach
1988	Pusan
1992	Barcelona
1996	Savannah
2000	Sydney Harbour
2004	Saronic Gulf

Yachting Medals

	G	S	B	Total
United States	17	19	16	52
Great Britain	19	15	12	46
Sweden	9	12	12	32
Norway	17	11	3	31
France	13	6	10	29
Denmark	11	8	6	25
Australia	5	3	8	16
Netherlands	4	6	6	16
Spain	10	4	1	15
New Zealand	6	4	5	15
Brazil	6	2	6	14
Soviet Union	4	5	3	12
Germany	3	5	4	12
Italy	3	2	7	12
Finland	2	1	6	9
Canada	-	3	6	9
Greece	3	3	2	8
Belgium	2	4	2	8
Austria	3	4	-	7
FRG	2	2	3	7
Argentina	-	4	3	7
Ukraine	1	2	2	5
Greece	2	1	1	4
Portugal	-	2	2	4
Switzerland[1]	1	1	1	3
Bahamas	1	-	1	2
Israel	1	-	1	2
Poland	1	-	1	2
China-	-	2	-	2
Japan	-	1	1	2
Russia	-	1	1	2
Estonia	-	-	2	2
Hong Kong	1	-	-	1
Cuba	-	1	-	1
Czech Republic	-	1	-	1
Ireland	-	1	-	1
Netherlands Antilles	-	1	-	1
Virgin Islands	-	1	-	1
Hungary[1]	-	-	1	1
Slovenia	-	-	1	1
	147	138[2]	135[2]	420

[1]It is perhaps worth noting that Austria, Hungary and Switzerland have no direct access to the sea
[2]Some events in the early Games had no silver and/or bronze medals

SHOOTING

BARON DE COUBERTIN, the founder of the modern Olympic Games, was a pistol shot of note in his youth, and this undoubtedly led to the sport being included in the first Games held in 1896. The first champion was Pantelis Karasevdas (GRE) who won the free rifle event over 200m on 9 April 1896. The number of events has varied considerably, especially in the early celebrations of the Games, from 21 in 1920 to only two in 1932. There were none at all in 1928. Since 1952 there has been some standardization. In 1984 three events for women were introduced, with another added in 1988, and two more in 2000. In 1996 mixed competition in the skeet and trap events was abolished, and at the same time double trap events for men and women were inaugurated. Currently there are ten events for men and seven for women. New regulations were introduced in 1988, in accordance with International Shooting Union rules.

The most successful competitor has been Carl Osburn (USA) who won a record eleven medals (five gold, four silver, two bronze) from 1912 to 1924. Six other men have won five gold medals: Konrad Stäheli (SUI) 1900-06; Louis Richardet

Shooting Medals

	Men[1]			Women			
	G	S	B	G	S	B	Total
United States	43	26	21	5	1	2	98
Soviet Union	18	16	15	4	1	3	57
Sweden	14	23	19	1	–	–	57
Great Britain	14	15	18	–	–	–	47
France	14	16	13	–	1	–	44
Norway	16	9	12	–	·	–	37
Switzerland	11	12	12	–	–	–	35
China	9	6	6	5	3	5	34
Italy	9	5	11	–	3	–	28
Russia	5	5	5	2	4	2	23
Greece	5	7	7	–	–	–	19
Finland	3	7	9	–	–	·	19
Germany	8	5	3	–	2	–	18
Hungary	6	3	6	1	–	1	17
Denmark	3	9	5	–	–	–	17
Bulgaria	2	2	3	2	4	3	16
GDR	3	8	5	–	–	–	16
Romania	5	4	5	–	–	–	14
Poland	2	2	3	2	1	2	12
FRG	3	2	0	1	2	·	11
Australia	3	1	3	1	–	3	11
Canada	3	3	2	1	–	–	9
Czechoslovakia	4	3	2	–	–	–	9
Yugoslavia	1	–	1	2	2	3	9
Belgium	2	3	3	–	–	–	8
Austria	1	2	4	–	–	–	7
Korea	1	1	–	1	2	1	6
Japan	1	1	3	–	1	–	6
Belarus	–	2	3	–	–	1	6
Brazil	1	1	1	–	–	–	3
Peru	1	2	–	–	–	–	3
North Korea (PRK)	1	1	1	–	–	–	3
Azerbaijan	–	–	–	1	–	2	3
Kazakhstan	–	2	1	–	–	–	3
Spain	–	1	1	–	1	–	3
Czech Republic	–	1	2	–	–	–	3
Ukraine	1	–	–	1	–	–	2
Slovenia	1	–	1	–	–	–	2
Colombia	–	2	–	–	–	–	2
Czech Republic	–	–	–	–	–	1	2
Netherlands	–	1	1	–	–	–	2
Cuba	–	–	2	–	–	–	2
Lithuania	–	–	–	1	–	–	1
United Arab Emirates	1	–	–	–	–	–	1
Argentina	–	1	–	–	–	–	1
Chile	–	1	–	–	–	–	1
India	–	1	–	–	–	–	1
Latvia	–	1	–	–	–	–	1
Mexico	–	1	–	–	–	–	1
Moldova	–	1	–	–	–	–	1
Portugal	–	1	–	–	–	–	1
Serbia/Montenegro	–	–	–	–	1	–	1
South Africa	–	1	–	–	–	–	1
Haiti	–	–	1	–	–	–	1
Kuwait	–	–	1	–	–	–	1
New Zealand	–	–	1	–	–	–	1
Mongolia	–	–	–	–	–	1	1
Slovakia	–	–	1	–	–	–	1
Venezuela	–	–	1	–	–	–	1
	215	217	217	31[2]	30	30	740

[1]Including female medallists prior to 1984; [2]Including female winner of 1992 open Skeet competition

(SUI) 1900-06; Alfred Lane (USA) 1912-20; Ole Lilloe-Olsen (NOR) 1920-24; Morris Fisher (USA) 1920-24; Willis Lee (USA) all in 1920, a record for the sport. However, the only man to win three individual gold medals at one Games was Gudbrand Skatteboe (NOR) in 1906. Lloyd Spooner (USA) competed in 12 events at the 1920 Games, a record in any sport in Olympic history. Lars Jorgen Madsen (DEN) won gold medals over a record 20 year span, 1900-20. Francois La Fortune (BEL) 1952-76, and Ragnar Skanåker (SWE) 1972-96, both competed in a record seven Games over a record 24 year period. Skanåkar won medals over a 20-year period, 1972 (gold)–1992 (bronze), both in the free pistol event. The most successful female shooter has been Marina Logvinenko-Dobrancheva (URS/EUN/RUS) who won two golds, one silver and two bronzes 1988-96.

Women first competed, in men's events, in 1968 when three countries, Mexico, Peru and Poland, entered one each. Eulalia Rolinska (POL) and Gladys de Seminario (PER) were the first to compete, finishing 22nd and 31st respectively in the small-bore rifle, prone, event. The first medallist was Margaret Murdock (USA) in the 1976 small-bore rifle, three positions. Initially listed as the winner, an error was discovered which placed her equal with her teammate, Lanny Bassham. Then on the count-back rule she was placed second, to the embarrassment of Bassham, who pulled her up to the top of the victory rostrum at the medal ceremony. The only woman to win an Olympic mixed shooting event is Zhang Shan (CHN) in the 1992 skeet contest.

The oldest gold medallist in Olympic history, in any sport, was the remarkable Oscar Swahn (SWE) in the 1912 running deer team aged 64yr 258days (his son Alfred was also in the team). At Antwerp in 1920 he became the oldest medallist (72yr 280days) and, indeed, the oldest competitor at any sport in the Olympics ever, when he was again a member of the Swedish running deer silver medal team. He qualified for the 1924 Games in his 77th year, but illness prevented him from competing. He died three years later. However, it should be noted that very recent research has discovered that the winner of the 1908 free rifle (1000y) event, Joshua 'Jerry' Millner (GBR) was some years older than originally thought, and at four days past his 61st birthday was the oldest ever Olympic gold medallist in an individual event. The youngest winner of a shooting gold medal was Konstantin Lukachik of the Unified Team in the 1992 free pistol aged 16yr 312days. The oldest female champion was Linda Thom (USA) aged 40yr 212days when winning the sport pistol in 1984. The youngest woman to win a gold was Kim Rhode (USA) in the Double Trap event in 1996 seven days after her 17th birthday. The youngest medallists were Marcus Dinwiddie (USA), silver in the 1924 small-bore rifle, prone, event, and Ulrike Holmer (FRG), silver in the 1984 standard rifle, both at 16yr 301days.

John and Sumner Paine (USA) were the first brothers to win gold medals at the Olympic Games, in 1896, while the first twins to do so were Vilhelm and Eric Carlberg (SWE) in 1912. Károly Takács (HUN) was a European pistol champion in the 1930s using his right hand. In 1938 while on army training a grenade blew up in his hand destroying his right arm. After the war he won the rapid fire pistol event with his left hand at the 1948 and 1952 Games. Walter Winans (USA), who had won a gold medal in the 1908 running deer event, became the only man to win gold medals in both sport and artistic events at the same Games in 1912 when he gained a silver in shooting and another gold at sculpture. Winans was born in Russia to Dutch-American parents, and lived most of his life in England – he never set foot in America.

Gerald Ouellette (CAN) won the 1956 small-bore, prone, gold medal with a world record maximum possible score of 600, but it was not accepted as such as the range was found to be 1.5m short of the regulation 50m distance. Miroslav Varga (TCH) also scored 600 in the 1988 event. When Li Ho Jun (PRK) won the same event in 1972 with a score of 599 he was asked how he concentrated so well. He answered that he pretended that he was 'aiming at a capitalist'. In 1992 Zhang Shan (CHN) became the first woman to win a gold medal in a mixed event and scored a maximum possible 200 in the preliminary round of skeet shooting. Francois La Fortune Jr

Short-Track Speed Skating Records

Men

500m	41.802	Marc Gagnon (CAN)	2002
1000m	1m 26.739	Hyun-Soo Ahn KOR)	2006
1500m	2m 15.942	Dong-Sung Kim (KOR)	2002
5000m Relay	6m 43.376	KOREA	2006

Women

500m	44.118	Yang Yang (A) (CHN)	2002
1000m	1m 31.235	Yang Yang (A) (CHN)	2002
1500m	2m 21.069	Eun-Kyung Choi (KOR)	2002
3000m Relay	4m 12.793	KOREA	2002

Short-Track Speed Skating Medals

	Men			Women			
	G	S	B	G	S	B	Total
Korea	8	4	2	9	3	3	29
Canada	3	5	4	2	3	3	20
China	-	3	3	3	7	4	20
United States	2	2	3	2	1	2	12
Italy	1	2	-	-	-	1	4
Japan	1	-	2	-	-	-	3
Bulgaria	-	-	-	-	2	1	3
Australia	1	-	1	-	-	-	2
Great Britain	-	-	1	-	-	-	1
North Korea (PRK)	-	-	-	-	-	1	1
Soviet Union	-	-	-	-	-	1	1
	16	16	16	16	16	16	96

(BEL) competed in a record seven Games, 1952-76, while his father, Francois Sr, competed over a 36 year span, 1924-1960. Philip Neame (GBR) is the only holder of the Victoria Cross to win an Olympic gold medal (1924 running deer, team), although another holder, Noel Chavasse had run in the 1908 400m prior to posthumously being awarded a bar to add to his VC in WWI.

One of the oddest occurrences in Olympic shooting was in the 1976 trap shooting event, when 65-year-old Paul Cerutti of Monaco was disqualified for using drugs, even though he had finished 43rd out of 44 competitors – he is the oldest competitor ever penalised in this way.

SHORT-TRACK SPEED SKATING

IN 1988 SHORT-TRACK speed skating was a demonstration sport, but four years later it became a medal sport with two events each for men and women. In 1994 another event each was added, and then in 2002 the 1500m for men and women were included. Despite the tight bends in the sport, speeds of 40km/h 25mph are reached. Indicative of the problems associated with short-track racing was the result in the 2002 men's 1000m race. Just short of the finish line, three of the four finalists fell, leaving the trailing fourth man, Steven Bradbury (AUS), to come through and win his country's first ever Winter Games gold medal.

So far the only person to gain a medal in both styles of speed skating is Eric Flaim (USA) with silvers in the 1988 1500m and the 1994 short-track relay. The most successful competitor has been Chun Lee-Kyung (KOR) with a record four gold medals and a bronze in the women's events, 1994-98, while the best by a man has been by Hyun-Soo Ahn (KOR) with three gold medals and a bronze, all in 2006. The youngest ever winner of a winter Games gold medal was Kim Yoon-Mi (KOR) in the 1998 women's relay aged 13yr 83days. (There is now a minimum age limit of 15 on 1 July of the Olympic year). She was also the youngest ever female Olympic winner in either winter or summer Games. The oldest champion/medallist in short-track was Cathy Turner who won the 1994 500m title aged 31yr 320days. The youngest male gold medallist was Jae Kun Song (KOR) aged 18yr 7days in the 1992 relay, only one day younger than countryman Dong-Sung Kim who won the 1000m individual event in 1998. The oldest male champion was Jae's teammate Ji Soo Mo aged 30yr 264days. It is noteworthy that the average age of the winning Korean women's relay team in 1994 was about 15¾yr.

SISTERS

THE FIRST SISTERS to take part in Olympic competition were Marion and Georgina Jones (USA) in the 1900 tennis events. Marion finished third in the singles, and was fourth in the mixed doubles. Her sister was eliminated in the first round of both contests. The most successful sisters in Olympic competition have been Irina and Tamara Press (URS) in athletics. Irina won the 80m hurdles title in 1960 and then the pentathlon in 1964. Tamara won the shot in 1960 and 1964, the discus in 1964 and a discus silver in 1960. However, there have been questions asked since they disappeared from competition when sex tests were introduced in 1966. In 2000, at Sydney, sisters Hazel and Joetta Clark, and their sister-in-law, Jearl Miles-Clark, all competed in the track 800m event, with all three reaching the semi-finals, but only Hazel making it to the final. (See also 'Twins').

SKELETON SLEDDING

THERE WERE ONE-MAN skeleton sled races held on the famous Cresta Run at St Moritz in 1928 and 1948. In this event the contestants lay face down, as compared to luge racers who lie back. The event was reintroduced in 2002 at Salt Lake City, and an event for women was inaugurated.

The youngest gold medallist was Jennison Heaton (USA) aged 24yr 307days in 1928, while his brother John was only 19yr 161days taking silver behind him. The oldest gold medallist was Duff Gibson (CAN) in 2006 aged 39yr 190days, and the oldest medallist has been John Crammond (GBR) who was aged 41yr 213days when he took the bronze medal in 1948. Gibson was the oldest ever winner of an individual event in the Winter Games. In the women's event, the oldest winner was Maya Pedersen (SUI) in 2006, aged 33yr 81days. The oldest gold medallist/medallist was Tristan Gale (USA) in 2002 at 21yr 194days, while the oldest female medallist was Lea Ann Parsley (USA), also in 2002, aged 33yr 253days.

The Heaton brothers (USA), unusually, competed successfully at skeleton and luge. Jennison won the 1928 skeleton event and was a member of the silver medal 5-man bob that year. Brother John was second in the 1928 skeleton, won a bronze in the 1932 2-man bob, and then, in his 40th year, won another skeleton silver in 1948. Seventh in that 1948 competition was Lt Col James Coates (GBR), holder of the Military Cross, and at 53yr 297days, the oldest ever competitor in the Winter Olympic Games. The winner of the event in Salt Lake City, Jim Shea, was the grandson of Jack Shea who won two speed skating golds in 1932, while his father, Jim Sr, was an Olympian in Nordic skiing in 1964 – such a three-generation competitive span is probably unique in the Winter Games. In 1928 a representative of one of the oldest British Earldoms, David, Earl of Northesk, took the bronze medal.

Speeds approaching 130km/h *80mph* are sometimes reached. However, the fastest average speed for a single run has been 94.44km/h *58.68mph* by Jim Shea in 2002, while the female record is 91.97kmh/*57.15mph* by Tristan Gale also at Salt Lake City.

SKIING

See separate entries under 'Alpine Skiing', 'Freestyle Skiing', and 'Nordic Skiing'.

SKI-JUMPING

FIRST CONTESTED IN 1924 with one hill. In 1964 two hills (70m and 90m) were introduced, which were changed to 90m and 120m in 1992. The controversial 'V' style was introduced by Jan Boklöv (SWE) in 1988, and was initially frowned on, and penalised, by the judges. However, by 1994 virtually all the competitors were using it. The most successful jumper has been Matti Nykänen (FIN) with four golds and one silver medal in 1984 and 1988, including three golds in one Games. However, his successes include the team competition, not introduced until 1988. Prior to him the most successful had been Birger Ruud (NOR) with two golds and a silver medal from 1932 to 1948. He also came fourth in the Alpine Combination event of 1936, winning the downhill segment. His brother Sigmund won a silver in 1928, while a third brother, Asbjørn, was seventh in 1948. In 1994 Jens Weissflog (GER) became only the third man to win at two Games, in his case, remarkably, with a ten-year gap, having competed in four Games. Only Nykänen in 1988 and Simon Ammann (SUI) in 2002 have won both 90m and 120m individual titles at the same Games.

Speeds of over 90km/h *56mph* are attained down the take-off ramp. The longest jump achieved in Olympic competition was 141m *462ft* by Roar Ljøkelsøj (NOR) in the bronze medal winning team on the 120m hill at Turin in 2006. The longest jump ever on a 90m hill was 118.5m *388ft* by Matti

Skeleton Sledding Medals

| | Men | | | Women | | | |
	G	S	B	G	S	B	Total
United States	2	2	-	1	1	-	6
Great Britain	-	-	2	-	1	1	4
Canada	1	1	-	-	-	1	3
Switzerland	-	-	2	-	1	-	3
Italy	1	-	-	-	-	-	1
Austria	-	1	-	-	-	-	1
	4	4	4	2	2	2	18

Nykänen (FIN) in 1988. The oldest gold medallist was Masahiko Harada in 1998 aged 29yr 284days, while the youngest was Toni Nieminen (FIN) in the 1992 team event aged 16yr 259days – also the youngest ever winter Games winner. The youngest medallist was also Nieminen when he won an individual bronze five days earlier than his gold, while the oldest was Birger Ruud in 1948 aged 36yr 168days. Sepp Bradl (AUT) – the first man ever to jump over 100m *328ft* – competed over a period of 20 years, 1936-1956, but never won a medal.

Ski-Jumping Medals

	G	S	B	Total
Norway	9	9	10	28
Finland	10	8	4	22
Austria	5	7	8	20
Japan	3	4	2	9
Germany	4	2	2	8
GDR	2	3	2	7
Czechoslovakia	1	2	4	7
Switzerland	2	1	-	3
Poland	1	1	11	3
Sweden	-	1	1	2
Yugoslavia	-	1	1	2
Soviet Union	1	-	-	1
Slovenia	-	-	1	1
United States	-	-	1	1
	38	39[1]	37	114

[1]Tie for silver in 1980 70m event

SMALLEST

THE SMALLEST EVER Olympic champion is gymnast Lu Li (CHN) who won the gold medal in the asymmetrical bars event at Barcelona in 1992. She stood only 1.36m *4ft 5½in* tall and weighed 36kg *79lb* The 1920 springboard diving champion, Aileen Riggin (USA), weighed less 31.5kg *70lb* but was taller. Perhaps the smallest ever competitor in the Games was the North Korean gymnast Choe Myong-

hui, at Moscow in 1980, who was only 1.35m *4ft 5in* tall and she weighed a mere 25kg *55lb*.

SNOWBOARDING

THE SPORT EVOLVED in the middle 1960s, and made its debut at the Olympic Games in 1998. Initially there were two events, the giant slalom, and the halfpipe. In 2002 the slalom was raced in parallel, in which two competitors compete side by side on identical courses. In 2006 a snowboard cross event was added. The halfpipe is a freestyle discipline down a 120m U-shaped course, on which a series of leaps, twists, rotations and flips are performed. The first winner of an Olympic title, the men's giant slalom, Ross Rebagliati of Canada, initially was disqualified after testing positive for marijuana – apparently a much-used substance by the sport's devotees. On appeal he was reinstated.

Philipp Schoch (SUI) became the first to successfully defend a snowboard title by taking the slalom in 2002-06. In the latter event his brother Simon placed second. The most successful woman has been Karine Ruby (FRA) with a gold in 1998 and a silver in 2002. The youngest gold medallist was Kelly Clark (USA) who won the 2002 women's halfpipe aged 18yr 199days. The youngest male champion was Shaun White (USA) in the 2006 halfpipe aged 19yr 162days. The oldest gold medallist was Seth Westcott (USA) in the 2006 cross at 29yr 233days, while the oldest female winner was Tanja Frieden (SUI) in the 2006 cross aged 30yr 11days. The youngest medallist was Amelie Kober (GER) with silver in the women's slalom in 2006, while the youngest male medallist was Ross Powers (USA) who won the 1998 halfpipe bronze two days after his 19th birthday. The oldest medallist was Siegfried Grabner (AUT) with a bronze in the 2006 slalom aged 31yr 18days and Rosey Fletcher (USA) was the oldest female medallist with a bronze in the 2006 slalom aged 30yr 85days.

Snowboarding Medals

	Men			Women			
	G	S	B	G	S	B	Total
United States	3	2	3	2	2	2	14
Switzerland	3	1	1	2	-	1	8
France	-	-	1	2	2	-	5
Germany	-	-	-	1	2	-	3
Norway	-	1	-	-	1	1	3
Canada	1	-	-	-	-	1	2
Italy	-	1	-	-	-	1	2
Austria	-	-	1	-	-	1	2
Slovakia	-	1	-	-	-	-	1
Sweden	-	1	-	-	-	-	1
Finland	-	-	1	-	-	-	1
	7	7	7	7	7	7	42

SOFTBALL

INVENTED AS AN indoor version of baseball in 1887, it did not become known as softball until 1920. Originally a ten-a-side game, it is now played with nine per side, and is governed by the International Softball Federation (ISF), formed in 1950. Pitching is done underarm, and there are fast-pitch and slow-pitch forms. A game lasts for seven innings. The fast-pitch variety for women was introduced as an official Olympic medal sport in 1996 – surprisingly never having been a demonstration sport – with eight teams.

The highest score achieved by a team is ten attained in 1996 by the USA v Puerto Rico (10-0), China v Puerto Rico (10-0), Australia v Japan (10-0), Chinese Taipei v Puerto Rico (10-2), in 2000 by China v New Zealand (10-0), and in 2004 by USA v Australia. The Chinese Taipei v Puerto Rico match in 1996, and Italy v China (7-5) in 2004, totalled the highest aggregate of 12. In the 2004 tournament the USA team's overall score was 51-1. Lisa Fernandez (USA) has had he best batting average of 0.545 in 2004.

The youngest gold medallist/medallist was Christa Lee Williams (USA) aged 18yr 173days in Atlanta, while the oldest champion was Dorothy Richardson (USA) at 39yr 4days in 2000. The oldest medallist was Reika Utsugi (JPN) aged 41yr 82days in 2004. Laura Berg, Lisa Fernandez, Leah O'Brien-Amico and Lori Harrigan, all of the USA team, won their third consecutive gold medal at Athens. In 1996 Gillian Boxx won a gold medal as part of the USA softball team, and eight years later, at Athens, her younger sister, Shannon, won gold as part of the USA football squad.

Softball Medals

	G	S	B	Total
United States	3	-	-	3
Australia	-	1	2	3
Japan	-	1	1	2
China	-	1	-	1

SPEED

THE FASTEST SPEED achieved by an athlete without mechanical aid at the Olympic Games is 43.56km/h *27.06mph*, by 1996 100m champion Donovan Bailey (CAN), recorded reaching his peak speed at 60m in the stadium at Atlanta. The fastest of all Olympians are the bobsledders, who have been recorded at 143km/h *88.8mph*. Downhill skiers and lugers attain over 130km/h *80mph* at times.

The fastest Summer Games Olympians were Daniel Morelon and Pierre Trentin (FRA) when they attained a speed of 73.24km/h *45.50mph* in their 1968 cycling tandem event, clocking 9.83sec for the last 200m of their race. The fastest individual cyclist was Gary Niewand (AUS) in 1996 when he clocked 10.219sec for 200m – 71.08km/h *44.16mph*. The fastest female cyclist was Michelle Ferris (AUS), also at Atlanta, with 11.212sec – 64.21km/h *39.90mph*. Speed skater Gerard van Velde (NED) set a record 1min 07.18sec for 1000m at Salt Lake City in 2002, which is an average of 53.59km/h *33.30mph*, while on the distaff side, Chris Witty (USA), also at Salt Lake City, did 1000m in 1m13.83sec to average 48.76km/h *30.30mph*. (See also Speed Skiing).

SPEED SKATING

THE SPORT WAS introduced into the Olympics in 1924, with the first official events for women in 1960. There have been two major controversies over the years. In 1928, the 10km event was cancelled by the Norwegian referee due to bad weather. That caused much ill-feeling in the American camp because at the time Irving Jaffee (USA) was the surprise leader, and as all the best skaters had competed the medal positions seemed assured. Despite vigorous protests by all nationalities no medals were awarded. The other occasion was in 1932 when the American 'mass start' system was used, for the only time in Olympic competition. This undoubtedly gave the

Speed Skating Olympic Records

Men			
500m	34.42s	Casey FitzRandolph (USA)	2002
1000m	1m 07.18s	Gerard van Velde (NED)	2002
1500m	1m 43.95s	Derek Parra (USA)	2002
5000m	6m 14.66s	Jochen Uytehaage (NED)	2002
10,000m	12m 58.92s	Jochen Uytehaage (NED)	2002
Team Pursuit	3m 43.64s	ITALY	2006
Women			
500m	37.30s	Catriona LeMay-Doan (CAN)	2002
1000m	1m 13.83s	Chris Witty (USA)	2002
1500m	1m 54.02s	Anni Friesinger (GER)	2002
3000m	3m 57.70s	Claudia Pechstein (GER)	2002
5000m	6m 46.91s	Claudia Pechstein (GER)	2002
Team Pursuit	3m 01.24s	CANADA	2006

Americans and Canadians a tremendous advantage as the Europeans were completely unfamiliar with the tactics involved – only two medals were won by European skaters. Since 1998 the 500m events are decided on the aggregate of two runs – interestingly, both male and female winners at Nagano would have won under the old system. A new type of skate, the clap skate, was used at Nagano, and the Dutch introduced aerodynamic silicon 'stripes' on their racing suits. At Salt Lake City in 2002, the facility was the highest enclosed ice track in the world at 1424m *4675ft* above sea level, thus virtually ensuring that the record book would be re-written. In 2006 new false start rules were in force with only one false start allowed

Lydia Skoblikova (URS) won a record six gold medals in 1960 and 1964, which is also a record for any sport in the Winter Games for a female competitor. The most by a man is five by Clas Thunberg (FIN) in 1924 and 1928, and by Eric Heiden (USA) with all five in 1980. Incidentally, there is a story that Thunberg deliberately let his teammate Julius Skutnabb win the 10km in 1924, thus denying himself even greater fame. There have been five individual events for men only since 1976, while a fifth event was added for women in 1988. In 2006 team pursuit events were added for men and women. The most medals won is nine by Claudia Pechstein (GER) with five golds, two silvers and two bronzes from 1992 to 2006. Eight of them were in individual events, a Winter Games record. The most

medals by a male skater is seven by Thunberg, who added a silver and a bronze to his golds, and by Ivar Ballangrud (NOR) who won four golds, two silvers and a bronze from 1928 to 1936. Skoblikova won her four golds in 1964 on four successive days. In 1994 Bonnie Blair (USA) uniquely won the same title (500m) for the third consecutive time.

The oldest gold medallist was Thunberg aged 35yr 315days in the 1928 1500m, while the oldest female champion was Christina Baas-Kaiser (NED) in the 1972 3000m aged 33yr 268 days. The youngest winner was Anne Henning (USA) in the 500m in 1952 aged 16yr 157days. The youngest male champion was Igor Malkov (URS) winning the 10km in 1984 aged 19yr 9days. The youngest ever medallist was Andrea Mitscherlich (later Schöne and then Ehrlich) (GDR) who won the 3000m silver in 1976 when only 15yr 69days. The youngest male medallist was Alv Gjestvang (NOR) in 1956 aged 18yr 147days. The oldest medallist was Julius Skutnabb (FIN) in 1928 at 38yr 246days, while the oldest female medallist was Eevi Huttunen (FIN) in the 1960 3000m aged 37yr 184days. Frank Stack (CAN) competed over a 20 year period from 1932 to 1952 (when he was 46) winning a bronze in 1932, while Colin Coates (AUS) also competed for 20 years, in six Games 1968-1988, but his best placing was 6th in the 10km in 1976.

The greatest average speed achieved is by Gerard van Velde (NED) in the 1000m at Salt Lake City with 53.59km/h *33.30mph*. The fastest by a woman is

Speed Skating Medals

| | Men | | | Women | | | |
	G	S	B	G	S	B	Total
Norway	24	28	25	1	-	1	79
Netherlands	13	21	18	11	7	5	75
United States	19	11	6	9	9	9	63
Soviet Union	12	10	9	12	7	10	60
Germany	2	-	1	11	13	9	36
GDR	2	1	2	6	11	7	29
Finland	6	6	7	1	2	2	24
Canada	2	4	7	4	6	5	28
Sweden	7	4	5	-	-	-	16
Japan	1	3	5	-	-	3	12
Russia	1	2	1	2	1	1	8
Austria	-	1	2	1	1	1	6
China	-	-	-	-	3	2	5
FRG	2	-	-	1	-	-	3
Italy	2	-	1	-	-	-	3
Korea	-	1	1	-	-	-	2
Poland	-	-	-	-	1	1	2
Belarus	-	1	-	-	-	-	1
North Korea (PRK)	-	-	-	-	1	-	1
Belgium	-	-	1	-	-	-	1
Kazakhstan	-	-	-	-	-	1	1
	93	93	91	59	62	57	455

48.76km/h 30.30mph by Chris Witty (USA), also in the 1000m in 2002. Unusually, Bart Veldkamp won medals in 1992-94 representing the Netherlands, and then won another in 1998 representing Belgium. In 2006, Shani Davis (USA) became the first black male to win a Winter Olympics gold medal in an individual event.

A number of speed skaters have found a happy affinity with cycle racing. One of the most successful at both roles has been Sheila Young (USA), who won the 500m Olympic skating title in 1976 and the world amateur sprint cycle championship in 1973 and 1976. However, Christa Rothenburger-Luding (GDR) possibly surpassed that in 1988. Having won the 1984 Olympic 500m gold and the 1986 world cycling sprint title in 1986, she then won the skating 1000m at Calgary and gained a cycling silver in Seoul, to become the first competitor to win medals at Summer and Winter games in the same year. This achievement can no longer be equalled. Clara Hughes (CAN), winner of the 2006 5000m, had won two bronze medals in the 1996 Olympic cycling events. Eric Flaim (USA) who had won a silver in the 1988 speed skating 1500m, became the first to also gain a medal at short track skating in 1994 with another silver in the relay.

SPEED SKIING

A DEMONSTRATION SPORT at Albertville in 1992, when world records were set in both men's, 229.299km/h *142.479mph* by Mickaël Prüfer (FRA), and women's, 219.245km/h *136.232mph* by Tarja Mulari (FIN), events. Second in the men's competition was Philippe Goitschel (FRA) nephew of the sisters who had won golds in the 1964 Alpine events. Davina Galica (GBR) competed in the women's event 28 years after her first Olympic appearance as an Alpine skier, aged 47yr 189days.

SPORTS

ONLY FIVE SPORTS have been on the programme of every Modern Games since 1896 – cycling, fencing, gymnastics, swimming, track and field athletics. Rowing should have been included with them, but although actually on the 1896 programme of events, rough seas caused its cancellation. To become an Olympic sport, recognised by the IOC but not necessarily contested at the Games, it must be widely practised in 75 countries on four continents (men's sports), and in 40 countries on three continents (women's sports). For a Winter Games sport it must be widely practised in 25 countries on three continents.

STADIA

THE LARGEST MAIN stadium used in the Olympics has been that at Sydney in 2000, nominally capable of holding 110,000, but it was reported that there were 112,524 to watch Cathy Freeman win her 400m title. Other large stadia include Melbourne Cricket Ground in 1956, which had its capacity increased to 104,000 for the Games. This was closely followed by the Lenin Stadium in Moscow in 1980, which had a capacity of 103,000 at the time. The Berlin stadium in 1936 actually held 100,000, and not 110,000 as was reported by some sources, and the Los Angeles Memorial Stadium, as used for the 1932 Games, could then seat 101,000.

STAMPS

THE FIRST OLYMPIC stamps were issued on 6 April 1896 in Greece to raise funds for the first Games, and to publicize the occasion. There were 12 stamps in the set, designed by Professor Gillieron and engraved by Eduard Mouchon, and they were produced by the French Government Printing Office for the Greek Post Office. The designs included ancient boxers, the stadium, and Myron's famous statue 'The Discus Thrower'. Because Greece was still using the Julian calendar, the cancelling postmark was dated 25 March. The first issue of Olympic stamps to use representations of modern sportsmen was that for the 1928 Games at Amsterdam. The first Winter Games to stimulate an issue of stamps was that at Lake Placid in 1932. After World War II many countries began to produce stamps with an Olympic theme, sometimes to commemorate them, but usually to raise funds for future participation. In 1980, in connection with the Games at Moscow, the Soviet Union produced a record of 74 stamps for the occasion. Well over 100 countries have issued stamps relating to the Games.

STOCKHOLM 1956

IN 1956, DUE to Australian quarantine regulations, the equestrian events of the Melbourne Olympic Games were held in the city of Stockholm. For data and medals see 'Melbourne 1956'.

SUMMER GAMES

FOR LIST OF Games, venues, dates and numbers of competitors, see 'Celebrations'.

SWIMMING

(See also Synchronized Swimming, Diving, and Water Polo)

THE SPORT HAS been an integral part of the Games since 1896 when the swimming was held in the Bay of Zea near Piraeus. The first champion was Alfréd Hajós (né Guttmann) (HUN) who won the 1896 100m freestyle in freezing water. Later, he became the first Olympian to win medals in a sport and in the artistic Games, when he took the 1924 silver medal in the Architecture category The first female champion (women's events were introduced in 1912) was Australia's Fanny Durack, also in the 100m freestyle. The first Olympic competition in a pool was in 1908, in a 100m long tank constructed inside the track at the Stadium (later called the White City), London. The first 50m pool was in 1924, outdoors, and the first one indoors was at Wembley, London in 1948. Emil Rausch (GER), in 1904, was the last to win an Olympic title using the side-stroke.

The most successful swimmer was Mark Spitz (USA) with nine gold medals plus a silver and a bronze in 1968 and 1972. His seven golds at one Games (1972) is unmatched in any sport. Almost as noteworthy was Michael Phelps (USA) in 2004 when he won a total of eight medals (6g, 2b), equalling the most ever won in a single Games in any sport. The most individual event golds won is five by Krisztina Egerszegi (HUN) 1988-96. Kristin Otto (GDR) won six golds at Seoul and set a female record for most at a single Games. Otto is also the only swimmer to win Olympic titles in three different strokes – freestyle, backstroke and butterfly. Dawn Fraser (AUS) in the 100m freestyle, and Krisztina Egerszegi (HUN) in the 200m backstroke, are the only swimmers, male or female, to win the same event three times. Matt Biondi (USA) equalled the record of 11 medals by Spitz, but his comprised 'only' eight golds, two silvers and a bronze 1984-92. Jenny Thompson (USA) won eight golds, three silver and a bronze for an overall record of 12 medals 1992-2004. Unusually, all Thompson's gold medals were won in relays. Michael Phelps (USA) set an endurance record of sorts in 2004 when he took part in eight different events comprising 17 races in seven days. On the distaff side, Shirley Babashoff (USA) competed in 13 races within eight days in 1976.

Swimming Olympic Records

Men

50m free	21.91s	Alexander Popov (EUN)	1992
100m free	47.84s	Pieter van den Hoogenband (NED)	2002
200m free	1:44.71s	Ian Thorpe (AUS)	2004
400m free	3:40.59s	Ian Thorpe (AUS)	2002
1500m free	14:43.40	Grant Hackett (AUS)	2004
4x100m free	3:13.17s	South Africa	2004
4 x 200m free	7:07.05s	Australia	2002
100m breast	1:00.01s	Brendan Hansen (USA)	2004
200m breast	2:09.44s	Kosuke Kitajima (JPN)	2004
100m back	53.45s	Aaron Peirsol (USA)	2004
200m back	1:54.95s	Aaron Peirsol (USA)	2004
100m butterfly	51.25s	Michael Phelps (USA)	2004
200m butterfly	1:54.04s	Michael Phelps (USA)	2004
200m medley	1:57.14s	Michael Phelps (USA)	2004
400m medley	4:08.26s	Michael Phelps (USA)	2004
4x100m medley	3:30.68s	United States	2004

Women

50m free	24.13s	Inge de Bruijn (NED)	2002
100m free	53.52s	Jodie Henry (AUS)	2004
200m free	1:57.65s	Heike Friedrich (GDR)	1988
400m free	4:03.85s	Janet Evans (USA)	1988
800m free	8:19.67s	Brooke Bennett (USA)	2002
4x100m free	3:35.94s	Australia	2004
4 x 200m free	7:53.42s	United States	2004
100m breast	1:06.64s	Xuejuan Luo (CHN)	2004
200m breast	2:23.37s	Amanda Beard (USA)	2004
100m back	59.68s	Natalie Coughlin (USA)	2004
200m back	2:07.06s	Krisztina Egerzegi (Hun)	1992
100m butterfly	56.61s	Inge de Bruijn (NED)	2002
200m butterfly	2:05.88s	Misty Hyman (USA)	2002
200m medley	2:10.68s	Jana Klochkova (UKR)	2002
400m medley	4:33.59s	Jana Klochkova (UKR)	2002
4x100m medley	3:57.32	Australia	2004

The first swimmer to defend successfully an Olympic swimming title was Charles Daniels (USA) in the 100m freestyle in 1908. The first woman to do so was Martha Norelius (USA) in 1928 in the 400m freestyle. She was born in Sweden and her father, Charles, had been a member of the 1906 Swedish Olympic swimming team, while an uncle, Benkt, had won gold in the 1912 gymnastics. Later, her first husband was the 1928 Canadian silver medallist oarsman Joseph Wright. Perhaps particularly noteworthy is the eleven gold medals in eleven attempts by the American 4x100m medley relay team 1960-2004 – they didn't compete in 1980 due to the boycott. In 1996 Claudia Poll (CRC) won the 200m freestyle to gain her country's first ever swimming gold medal – Costa Rica's only previous swimming medal, a silver in the same event, was won by her sister, Silvia, in 1988. Also in 1996 Michelle Smith (IRL) not only became the first Irish swimmer to reach an Olympic final, but she won three gold medals and a bronze. Gary Hall Jr (USA) won four gold and three silvers and two bronzes in 1996-2004 – his father had won two silvers and a bronze 1968-76.

The oldest gold medallist/medallist was Inge de Bruijn (NED) in the 2004 50m freestyle aged 30yr 363days. The oldest male champion was Cecil Healy (AUS) in the 1912 800m relay team aged 30yr 229days. The oldest medallist was William Henry (GBR), a last minute replacement in the 1906 relay, aged 46yr 301days. The youngest gold medallist was Kyoko Iwasaki (JPN) in the 1992 women's 200m breaststroke in 1964 at 14yr 6days. The youngest male champion/ medallist was Kusuo Kitamura (JPN) in the 1500m in 1932 aged 14yr 309days, while the youngest known individual event medallist in any sport at the Games was Inge Sörensen (DEN) aged 12yr 24days winning a bronze in the 200m breaststroke of 1936.

The first dead heat in Games swimming came in the 1984 women's 100m freestyle final when Carrie Steinseifer and Nancy Hogshead (both USA) gained a gold medal each. Also in those Games there was a strange situation when the winner of the 400m freestyle 'B' final, Thomas Fahrner (FRG), set an Olympic record faster than the winner of the 'A' final. The closest to a dead heat in the men's events was in the 1972 400m medley when Gunnar Larsson (SWE) was given the decision over Tim McKee (USA). The margin was 0.002 of a second or about three millimetres (estimated to be the length grown by a fingernail in three weeks). Happily timings and placings are now decided to hundredths only, and the above would now be given as a dead heat. Another controversial decision occurred in the 1960 100m freestyle when Lance Larson (USA) was timed (manually, and by the unofficial automatic system) faster than John Devitt (AUS), but the judges placed the Australian first – and

that is how the result remained despite protests. In 1968 poolside touch panels were introduced. Since 1984 only two competitors per country per individual event are allowed.

In the 1912 100m freestyle competition, the three best American swimmers missed the semi-finals because they had been told that there would not be any. Following protests it was agreed that if they were timed, in a special race, at faster than the slowest qualifier from those semis then they would go forward to the final. The outstanding Hawaiian swimmer Duke Kahanamoku was so incensed that he broke the world record, and then won the final. At the next Games, in 1920, the final was re-swum after the Australian, William Herald, complained that he was impeded by Norman Ross (USA) – this was before lane dividers were used. The original winner, once again Duke Kahanamoku (USA), won again but in a slower time than before, but his first time of 60.4 secs was recognized as a world record. Kahanamoku, the first of the great Hawaiian swimmers, was born into the Hawaiian Royal Family, and was named 'Duke' after the Duke of Edinburgh, Queen Victoria's second son, who was visiting the Palace at the time. He was a pioneer of surfing, and made many movies in Hollywood. He was the oldest individual event champion in 1920 when five days past his 30th birthday, until 1956 when Ursula Happe (GDR), 36days older, won the 200m breaststroke. His brother Sammy won a bronze in the 1924 100m freestyle. The first brothers to win swimming gold medals at the same Games were Pua and Warren Kealoha (USA) in 1920, with the latter winner of the 100m backstroke and the former in the 4x200m relay.

Hollywood has attracted a number of Olympian swimmers: Romanian-born Johnny Weissmuller (USA) who won five gold medals 1924-1928 and then became the most famous 'Tarzan' of them all; Clarence 'Buster' Crabbe (USA), the 1932 400m champion, played 'Flash Gordon' and 'Buck Rogers' in children's serials; Aileen Riggin (USA), the 1920 diving champion, and Eleanor Holm (USA), the 1932 backstroke champion, both took their good looks into movies. Holm was also in a Tarzan movie, in 1938, as Jane to the hero played by 1936 decathlon champion Glenn Morris.

Gertrude Ederle (USA) and Greta Andersen (DEN), gold medallists in 1924 and 1948 respectively, both later set Channel swimming records. As a matter of interest, the first Olympian to swim the Channel, and the first person to swim it both ways, in 1927 and 1934, was Edward Temme (GBR), who was in the fourth-placed British water polo team in 1928. Mexico's first ever swimming gold medallist, Felipe Muñoz, who won the 1968

YOUNGEST AND OLDEST MEDALLISTS, BY EVENT – MEN

Event		Age	Name	Year
50m Free	G	19-119	Anthony Ervin (USA)	2000
		29-329	Gary Hall Jr (USA)	2004
	M	19-119	Anthony Ervin (USA)	2000
		27-298	Tom Jager (USA)	1992
100m Free	G	15-297	Yasukji Miyazaki (JPN)	1932
		30-5	Duke Kahanamoku (USA)	1920
	M	15-297	Yasuji Miyazaki (JPN)	1932
		33-330	Duke Kahanamoku (USA)	1924
200m Free	G	18-342	Mike Wenden (AUS)	1968
		22-201	Mark Spitz (USA)	1972
	M	17-345	Ian Thorpe (AUS)	2000
		26-155	Pieter van den Hoogenband (NED)	2004
400m Free	G	16-134	Otto Scheff (AUT)	1906
		24-118	Norman Ross (USA)	1920
	M	16-134	Otto Scheff (AUT)	1906
		34-61	John Jarvis (GBR)	1906
1500m Free	G	14-309	Kusuo Kitamura (JPN)	1932
		28-127	Vladimir Salnikov (URS)	1988
	M	14-309	Kusuo Kitamura (JPN)	1932
		34-59	John Jarvis (GBR)	1906
4x100m Free	G	17-343	Ian Thorpe (AUS)	2000
		27-297	Tom Jager (USA)	1992
	M	16-338	Peter Bruch (GDR)	1972
		29-324	Gary Hall Jr (USA)	2004
4x200m Free	G	15-299	Yasuji Miyazaki (JPN)	1932
		30-229	Cecil Healy (AUS)	1912
	M	15-299	Yasuji Miyazaki (JPN)	1932
		46-301	William Henry (GBR)	1906[1]
100m Breast	G	21-73	Nobutaka Taguchi (JPN)	1972
		24-117	Adrian Moorhouse (GBR)	1988
	M	18-93	John Hencken (USA)	1972
		26-156	Mark Warnecke (GER)	1996
200m Breast	G	17-226	Ian O'Brien (AUS)	1964
		28-286	Yoshiyuki Tsoruta (JPN)	1932
	M	15-106	Daniel Gyurta (HUN)	2004
		38-25	William Robinson (GBR)	1908
100m Back	G	16-173	Warren Kealoha (USA)	1920
		26-172	Jeff Rouse (USA)	1996
	M	16-173	Warren Kealoha (USA)	1920
		28-15	Herbert Haresnape (GBR)	1908
200m Back	G	17-7	Sándor Wladár HUN)	1980
		24-359	Lenny Krayzelburg (USA)	2000
	M	17-7	Sándor Wladár (HUN)	1980
		24-359	Lenny Krayzelburg (USA)	2000
100m Butt	G	19-48	Matt Vogel (USA)	1976
		27-235	Pablo Morales (USA)	1992
	M	18-254	Mark Spitz (USA)	1968
		27-235	Pablo Morales (USA)	1992
200m Butt	G	17-345	Jon Sieben (AUS)	1984
		24-97	Michael Gross (FRG)	1988
	M	16-275	Neville Hayes (AUS)	1960
		27-324	György Tumpek (HUN)	1956
200m Med	G	19-50	Michael Phelps (USA)	2004
		25-58	Tamás Darnyi (HUN)	1992
	M	18-41	Attila Czene (HUN)	1992
		25-58	Tamás Darnyi (HUN)	1992
400m Med	G	17-18	Richard Roth (USA)	1964
		25-54	Tamás Darnyi (HUN)	1992
	M	16-166	András Hargitay (HUN)	1972
		25-349	Eric Namesnik (USA)	1996
4x100m Med	G	18-2	Neil Brooks (AUS)	1980
		28-327	Lenny Krayzelburg (USA)	2004
	M	16-274	Neville Hayes (AUS)	1960
		30-94	Horst-Günter Gregor (GDR)	1968

Youngest and Oldest medallists, by event – Women

Event		Age	Name	Year
50m Free	G	20-202	Yang Wenyi (CHN)	1992
		30-363	Inge de Bruijn (NED)	2004
	M	15-252	Katrin Meissner (GDR)	1988
		29-86	Angel Martino (USA)	1996
100m Free	G	16-162	Sandra Nielson (USA)	1972
		27-39	Dawn Fraser (AUS)	1964
	M	14-112	Franziska Van Almsick (GER)	1992
		33-159	Dara Torres (USA)	2000
200m Free	G	15-283	Shane Gould (AUS)	1972
		27-48	Susie O'Neill (AUS)	2000
	M	14-113	Franziska Van Almsick (GER)	1992
		25-72	Solenne Figues (FRA)	2004
400m Free	G	15-281	Shane Gould (AUS)	1972
		22-1219	Dagmar Hase (GER)	1992
	M	14-156	Sylvia Ruuska (USA)	1956
		27-271	Claudia Poll (CRC)	2000
800m Free	G	15-190	Keena Rothhammer (USA)	1972
		20-337	Janet Evans (USA)	1992
	M	15-70	Maria Teresa Ramirez (MEX)	1968
		26-216	Dagmar Hase (GER)	1996
4x100m Free	G	14-96	Lilian 'Pokey'Watson (USA)	1964
		33-176	Dara Torres (USA)	2000
	M	13-310	Kornelia Ender (GDR)	1972
		33-176	Dara Torres (USA)	2000
4 x 200m Free	G	16-279	Dana Vollmer (USA)	2004
		27-207	Jenny Thompson(USA)	2000
	M	16-152	Emma Johnson (AUS)	1996
		30-289	Kerstin Kielgass (GER)	2000
100m Breast	G	16-247	Megan Quann (USA)	2000
		24-85	Tonya Dangalakova (BUL)	1988
	M	14-266	Amanda Beard (USA)	1996
		26-151	Brooke Hanson (USA)	2004
200m Breast	G	14-6	Kyoko Iwasaki (JPN)	1992
		30-41	Ursula Happe (GER)	1956
	M	12-24	Inge Sörensen (DEN)	1936
		30-41	Ursula Happe (GER)	1956
100m Back	G	15-62	Beth Botsford (USA)	1996
		23-259	Karen Harup (DEN)	1948
	M	14-38	Krisztina Egerszegi (HUN)	1988
		25-135	Whitney Hedgepeth (USA)	1996
200m Back	G	14-41	Krisztina Egerszegi (HUN)	1988
		21-344	Krisztina Egerszegi (HUN)	1996
	M	14-41	Krisztina Egerszegi (HUN)	1988
		25-138	Whitney Hedgepeth (USA)	1996
100m Butt	G	15-342	Sharon Stouder (USA)	1964
		29-356	Petria Thomas (Aus)	2004
	M	15-75	Andrea Pollack (GDR)	1976
		33-155	Dara Torres (USA)	2000
200m Butt	G	15-72	Andrea Pollack (GDR)	1976
		22-274	Kathleen Nord (GDR)	1988
	M	15-72	Andrea Pollack (GDR)	1976
		29-359	Petria Thomas (AUS)	2004
200m Med	G	15-279	Shane Gould (AUS)	1972
		22-10	Yana Klochkova (UKR)	2004
	M	13-308	Kornelia Ender (GDR)	1972
		25-289	Lin Li (CHN)	1996
400m Med	G	17-29	Gail Neall (AUS)	1972
		22-7	Yana Klochkova (UKR)	2004
	M	16-99	Sabine Steinbach (GDR)	1968
		25-27	Beatrice Caslaru (ROM)	2000
4x100m Med	G	14-269	Amanda Beard (USA)	1996
		29-362	Petria Thomas (Aus)	2004
	M	13-314	Kornelia Ender (GDR)	1972
		33-161	Dara Torres (USA)	2000

[1]4x250m

200m breaststroke, was nicknamed 'Tibio' which means 'lukewarm' in English. This was no reflection on his determination, but was the result of his father coming from Aguascalientes ('hot water') and his mother from Rio Frio ('cold river'). A change in rules for 1992 allowed female swimmers to wear two-piece costumes in competition – only a few competitors took advantage of this at the time, most notably the Italians. In 2004, at Athens, Maritza Correia, a Puerto-Rican born member of the USA silver medal

4x100m freestyle team, became the first black woman to win an Olympic swimming medal. Anthony Nesty of Surinam became the first black swimmer to win a gold swimming medal at Seoul in 1988.

The swimming pool at the 2000 Sydney Games had a seating capacity of 17,000, which was claimed to be a record for an Olympics, but the 100m pool at the White City, London in 1908, was in the middle of the stadium, which could hold over 60,000 – although no actual attendance figures are known.

Swimming Medals

(Excluding diving, synchronized swimming and water polo)

	Men			Women			
	G	S	B	G	S	B	Total
United States	120	90	59	85	57	52	463
Australia[1]	32	29	36	20	22	18	157
GDR	6	7	5	32	25	17	92
Soviet Union	14	17	18	4	7	9	69
Germany	9	12	14	3	12	19	60
Great Britain	10	13	16	4	9	12	64
Hungary	14	15	12	10	6	5	62
Japan	14	18	13	4	3	5	57
Netherlands	3	2	4	13	15	14	51
Canada	6	7	9	1	6	10	39
Sweden	8	10	10	-	4	3	35
France	2	5	10	1	4	5	27
FRG	3	4	7	-	1	7	22
China	-	-	-	6	12	3	21
Italy	3	1	7	-	2	2	15
Austria	2	5	5	-	-	1	13
South Africa	1	2	1	3	-	5	12
Denmark	-	2	1	2	3	3	11
Russia	4	3	3	-	1	-	11
Romania	-	-	1	3	2	3	9
Brazil	-	3	6	-	-	-	9
Greece	1	4	3	-	-	-	8
New Zealand[1]	3	1	2	-	-	1	7
Poland	-	1	1	1	2	2	7
Ukraine	-	1	1	2	1	-	5
Ireland	-	-	-	3	-	1	4
Belgium	1	1	1	-	-	1	4
Costa Rica	-	-	-	1	1	2	4
Spain	1	-	2	-	-	1	4
Finland	-	1	3	-	-	-	4
Argentina	1	-	-	-	1	1	3
Bulgaria	-	-	-	1	1	1	3
Zimbabwe	-	-	-	1	1	1	3
Yugoslavia	-	-	-	1	1	-	2
Mexico	1	-	-	-	-	1	2
Surinam	1	-	1	-	-	-	2
Slovakia	-	-	-	-	2	-	2
Cuba	-	1	1	-	-	-	2
Philippines	-	-	2	-	-	-	2
Croatia	-	1	-	-	-	-	1
Switzerland	-	-	1	-	-	-	1
Trinidad & Tobago	-	-	1	-	-	-	1
Venezuela	-	-	1	-	-	-	1
	260[1/2]	256	257[3]	203[4]	201	204[5]	1381

[1]*Double counting of Australia/New Zealand relay team in 1912;* [2]*Two golds in 2000 50m freestyle;* [3]*Third place in 1896 100m freestyle not known;* [4]*Two golds in 1984 100m freestyle;* [5]*Two bronzes in 1988 50m freestyle, 2000 100m freestyle & 2006 200m backstroke*

SYNCHRONIZED DIVING

HELD FOR THE first time at the Games at Sydney in 2000. There were separate pairs events for men and women, in which they are judged on the synchronization of their movements and the execution of the dives. (See 'Diving' for medals).

SYNCHRONIZED SWIMMING

INTRODUCED IN THE Games in 1984, there were solo and duet events until 1996. At Atlanta they were replaced by a single team event, consisting of teams of eight women. Also compulsory figures were replaced with a technical programme. In 2000 the duet was reinstated.

The most successful women have been Olga Brusnikina (RUS) and Marja Kiselyeva (RUS), who have both won three gold medals 2000-04. The youngest gold medallist was Maria Gromova (RUS) in the 2004 team event aged 20yr 38days, while the youngest medallist was Valerie Hould-Marchand (CAN) with a silver in 1996 aged 16yr 65days. The oldest champions were Karen and Sarah Josephson (USA) in the 1992 duet aged 28yr 210days. The latter are among the most successful twins ever in Olympic aquatics with their gold medal in 1992 to add to the silver from 1988. The oldest medallist was Olga Kozlova (USA) with a bronze team medal at Athens aged 31yr 240days. Kozlova unusually placed fourth in 1992 as a member of the Russian duet, then placed fourth again in 2000 as a member of the USA pair, and then won two bronzes in 2004 in the US duet and team. In the 1992 solo event, a mistake by a judge deprived Sylvie Frechette (Can) from sharing the gold medal. In December 1993 the result was revised. The first ever 10.00 mark awarded in the Olympic Games was given to the winning Russian duet of Olga Brusnikina and Marija Kiselyeva in 2000.

Synchronised Swimming Medals

	G	S	B	Total
Japan	-	4	7	11
United States	5	2	2	9
Canada	3	4	1	8
Russia	4	-	-	4
France	-	-	1	1
	12[1]	10	11	33

[1]Tie for gold in 1992

TABLE TENNIS

RECOGNIZED AS AN Olympic sport by the IOC in 1977, table tennis was first included in the 1988 Seoul Games as a medal sport, never having been a demonstration sport. There are 64 men and 32 women, selected by an agreed international formula, competing in men's and women's singles and doubles events.

The most successful player has been Deng Yaping (CHN), only 1.50m *4ft 11*in tall, who successfully retained her singles and doubles titles from 1992 in 1996, thus totalling four gold medals in women's events. The most successful male was Guoliang Liu (CHN) with two golds in 1996, and a silver and a bronze in 2000 – Yoo Nam-Kyu (KOR) has also won four medals, comprising a gold and three bronzes 1988-96.

The youngest gold medallist was Hyun Jung-Hwa (KOR) in the 1988 women's doubles aged 18yr 360days, while the youngest male champion was Yoo Nam-Kyu (KOR) winning the 1988 singles aged 20yr 119days. The oldest gold medallist was Jan-Ove Waldner (SWE) winning the 1992 men's singles aged 26yr 308days, and the oldest female champion was Hong Qiao (CHN) in the 1996 women's doubles aged 27yr 251days. The youngest female medallist was Yue Guo (CHN) in the 2004 women's doubles aged 16yr 33days, and the youngest male medallist was Zoran Primorac (YUG) in 1988 at 19yr 143days. The oldest female medallist was

Table Tennis Medals

	Men			Women			
	G	S	B	G	S	B	Total
China	7	4	3	9	7	3	33
Korea	2	1	5	1	1	5	15
Sweden	1	1	1	-	-	-	3
North Korea (PRK)	-	-	-	-	1	2	3
Germany	-	1	1	-	-	-	2
Yugoslavia	-	1	-	-	-	1	2
France	-	1	1	-	-	-	2
Taipei	-	-	-	-	1	1	2
Hong Kong	-	1	-	-	-	-	1
Denmark	-	-	1	-	-	-	1
	10	10	12[1]	10	10	12[1]	64

[1]Two bronze medals in 1992

Taekwondo Medals

	Men			Women			
	G	S	B	G	S	B	Total
Korea	2	1	1	3	-	1	8
Taipei	1	1	1	1	-	1	5
China	-	-	-	3	-	-	3
United States	2	-	-	-	1	-	3
Greece	1	1	-	-	1	-	3
Cuba	1	-	-	-	2	-	3
Iran	1	-	2	-	-	-	3
France	-	-	2	-	1	-	3
Mexico	-	1	1	-	-	1	3
Australia	-	1	-	1	-	-	2
Turkey	-	1	-	-	-	1	2
Germany	-	1	-	-	-	-	1
Norway	-	-	-	-	1	-	1
Russia	-	-	-	-	1	-	1
Spain	-	1	-	-	-	-	1
Vietnam	-	-	-	-	1	-	1
Canada	-	-	-	-	-	1	1
Egypt	-	-	1	-	-	-	1
Japan	-	-	-	-	-	1	1
Thailand	-	-	-	-	-	1	1
Venezuela	-	-	-	-	-	1	1
	8	8	8	8	8	8	48

Yunping Giao (CHN) in the 1996 doubles aged 27yr 320days, and the oldest male medal winner was Jan-Ove Waldner (SWE) with the silver in the 2000 singles aged 34yr 358days.

TAEKWONDO

A DEMONSTRATION SPORT at Seoul in 1988 and at Barcelona in 1992, it was a medal sport at Sydney in the 2000 Games. The most successful competitors have been Steven Lopez (USA) who won the 68kg title in Sydney and the 80kg crown in 2004, and Zhong Chen (CHN) who took the women's 67kg+ gold medal in 2000 and 2004.

The youngest gold medallist was Zhong Chen (CHN) who won the women's 67kg+ class aged 17yr 313days, while the youngest male winner was Michael Mouroutsos (GRE) in the 58kg category aged 20yr 211days. The oldest champion was Hadi Saei Bonehkohal (IRI) with the 2004 68kg title aged 28yr 78days, while the oldest female gold medallist was Lauren Burns (AUS) aged 26yr 111days when taking the 49kg title in Sydney. The oldest medallist was Adriana Carmona (VEN) with the 2004 women's 67kg+ bronze aged 31yr 270days, and the oldest male medallist was Pascal Gentil (FRA) aged 31yr 106days in the Athens 80kg+ class The youngest medallist was Shu-Ju Chi (TPE) in the 2000 women's 49kg class aged 17yr 308days, with the youngest male medallist was Myeong Seob Song (KOR) in the 2004 68kg event aged 20yr 59days. At Athens in 2004 Mexican brother and sister, Oscar (silver) and Iridia (bronze) Salazar Blanco both won medals.

TALLEST

THE TALLEST PERSON ever to win an Olympic medal was Tony Burleson (USA) in the silver medal team at Munich in 1972. He was 2.23m *7ft 4in* tall. A member of the 1988 winning Soviet basketball team in 1988, Arvidas Sabonis, who also won a bronze in the Lithuanian team in 1992, was reported to be as tall, but was actually 2.21m *7ft 3in,* and is the tallest ever Olympic gold medallist. A member of the unplaced Chinese basketball team in 2004, Yao Ming, was reportedly 2.26m *7ft 5in,* the tallest ever Olympian. The tallest ever gold medal winner of an individual athletics event at the Games was Walt Davis (USA), who was 2.04m *6ft 8¼in* tall when he won the 1952 high jump title.

The tallest female gold medallist was the Soviet basketball player Iuliana Semenova in the winning 1976 and 1980 teams. Although officially given as 2.10m (perhaps a misprint), this was obviously ridiculous, and closer investigation indicates that her correct height was 2.18m *7ft 2in.* At the same height was Malgorzata Dydek in the Polish basketball team in 2000, but she didn't win a medal.

The tallest competitor in the Winter Games was Sam Guss (AUS) who competed in the 1984 Alpine events at Sarajevo. He was 2.08m *6ft 10in* tall.

Tennis Medals[3]

	Men[1]			Women			
	G	S	B	G	S	B	Total
Great Britain	11	9	11	5	5	5	46
United States	7	6	6	9	-	4	32
France	6	5	6	2	3	1	23
Germany	3	3	2	-	2	-	10
Greece	-	4	2	1	1	1	9
Spain	-	3	1	-	3	2	9
Czechoslovakia[2]	1	-	5	-	1	1	8
Sweden	-	2	4	-	-	1	7
Australia	1	1	1	-	-	3	6
South Africa	3	2	-	-	-	-	5
Chile	2	-	1	-	-	-	3
Argentina	-	-	1	-	1	1	3
Croatia	-	-	3	-	-	-	3
Russia	1	-	-	-	1	-	2
Belgium	-	-	-	1	-	1	2
FRG	-	-	-	1	-	1	2
Japan	-	2	-	-	-	-	2
Czech Republic	-	-	-	-	1	1	2
Netherlands	-	-	1	-	1	-	2
Soviet Union	-	-	1	-	-	1	2
Canada	1	-	-	-	-	-	1
China	-	-	-	1	-	-	1
Switzerland	1	-	-	-	-	-	1
Austria	-	1	-	-	-	-	1
Denmark	-	-	-	-	1	-	1
Hungary	-	-	1	-	-	-	1
India	-	-	1	-	-	-	1
Italy	-	-	1	-	-	-	1
New Zealand	-	-	1	-	-	-	1
Bulgaria	-	-	-	-	-	1	1
Norway	-	-	-	-	-	1	1
	37	38	49	20	20	25	189

[1]Includes mixed doubles; [2]Includes Bohemia; [3]Two-country pairs counted as two medals

TELEVISION

(See also 'Media')

THOUGH TELEVISION PICTURES were beamed by closed circuit to special halls around Berlin in 1936, the first true public television pictures of the Games came in London in 1948, although to the very limited number of TV receivers, estimated at 80,000, within range of the Wembley stadium. The first live international coverage of the Games came from Rome in 1960, with the Tokyo 1964 pictures the first to be sent by satellite. Live colour TV pictures were first broadcast from Mexico City in 1968.

The major providers of television income to the IOC and host cities have been the American networks, whose rivalry has pushed the sums involved ever upwards, as the following table of the winners of US TV rights shows:

Summer		$ (million)	Winter		$ (million)
1960	CBS	0.394	1960	CBS	0.050
1964	NBC	1.5	1964	ABC	0.597
1968	ABC	4.5	1968	ABC	2.5
1972	ABC	7.5	1972	NBC	6.4
1976	ABC	25.0	1976	ABC	10.0
1980	NBC	87.0	1980	ABC	15.5
1984	ABC	225.0	1984	ABC	91.5
1988	NBC	300.0	1988	ABC	309.0
1992	NBC	401.0	1992	CBS	243.0
1996	NBC	456.0	1994	CBS	300.0
2000	NBC	705.0	1998	CBS	375.0
2004	NBC	793.0	2002	NBC	545.0
2008	NBC	894.0	2006	NBC	613.0

TENNIS

TENNIS WAS EXCLUDED from the Games 1924-1988, although it was a demonstration sport in 1968 and 1984. The first gold medallist was Irish-born John Pius Boland (GBR) in the 1896 singles. He was in Athens, visiting the famous German archaeologist Heinrich Schliemann, and entered the Games at the last minute. The women's singles champion in 1900, Charlotte Cooper (GBR), was until recently thought to be the first woman to win an Olympic title in any sport (see 'Women'). In the early years a number of medal winning pairs were composed of players from two countries, thus Boland combined with a German to win the first mixed doubles title. The most successful player was Max Decugis (FRA) with a total of six medals comprising four golds, one silver and a bronze between 1900 and 1920. Britain's Kitty McKane won a record total for a woman of five (one gold, two silvers and two bronzes) in 1920 and 1924. At Sydney, in 2000, Venus Williams (USA) became only the second woman to win two gold medals at one Games, matching the feat of her countrywoman, Helen Wills in 1924.

The oldest gold medallist was George Hillyard (GBR) in the 1908 men's doubles aged 44yr 160days. The oldest female champion was Winifred McNair (GBR) aged 43yr 14days in the women's doubles of 1920. She was also the oldest British female competitor to win a gold medal in any sport. The youngest gold medallist/medallist in tennis was Jennifer Capriati (USA), winner of the 1992 singles aged 16yr 132days, while the youngest male was Fritz Traun (GER), Boland's partner in 1896, aged 20yr 13days. The youngest male medallist was Max Decugis (FRA) in 1900 aged 17yr 290days. Six years later, he and his wife Marie won the mixed title, becoming the first married couple to win gold medals in the Olympic Games. Brothers Reggie and Laurie Doherty (GBR) added the 1900 Olympic title to the eight Wimbledon doubles championships they won. At Sydney in 2000, the American sisters Serena and Venus Williams took the women's doubles title, after the latter had won the singles.

Many of the greatest names in tennis have played in the Games and there have been over 30 gold medal winners who also were successful at Wimbledon. One of the most remarkable of these was Swiss-born Norris Williams (USA), who survived the sinking of the *Titanic* in 1912 – swimming in icy water for over an hour – and won the Croix de Guerre and the Legion d'Honneur in the First World War, a Wimbledon title in 1920, an Olympic gold medal in 1924 (mixed doubles). He died aged 77.

Both 1996 singles winners had fathers who were ex-Olympians; Andre Agassi's father, Emanoul Aghassian, boxed for Iran in 1948-52; Lindsay Davenport's father, Winthrop Davenport, played volleyball for the United States in 1968. Additionally, Indian bronze medallist Leander Paes's father won a bronze medal at hockey in 1972, the last medal in that sport won by India. Ivo Karlovic (CRO), who played in the 2004 singles, was probably the tallest player, at 2.08m *6ft 10in*, ever to take part in the Olympic Games.

TOBOGGANING

SEE UNDER 'LUGEING' and 'Skeleton sledding'.

TORCH RELAY

IN THE ANCIENT Games a flame would burn at the altar of the statue of Zeus (one of the Seven Wonders of the World) during the period of the Games. In 1928, at Amsterdam, this was commemorated by a flame burning in the stadium throughout the competitions. The chairman of the organizing committee of the Berlin Games in 1936, Carl Diem, had the idea of lighting the Olympic flame at Olympia in Greece, and then bringing it, by a series of relay runners, across Europe, to the Olympic stadium in Berlin. It has been done ever since, including transportation by sea and air where necessary. The planned Olympic torch relay for the 2008 Games at Beijing will be the longest ever at 137,000km 85,000 miles, visiting all five continents.

TRAMPOLINING

AT SYDNEY, IN 2000, two events were added as part of the gymnastics programme. They were individual events for men and women. Competitions consist of compulsory and optional routines.

The most successful competitor was Alexander Moskalenko ((RUS) who won a gold medal in 2000 and a silver at Athens. On the female side, Karen Cockburn (CAN) took the bronze in Sydney and the silver in 2004. The oldest male champion was Moskalenko aged 30yr 323days in 2000. His female

Trampolining Medals

	Men			Women			
	G	S	B	G	S	B	Total
Russia	1	1	-	1	-	-	3
Canada	-	-	1	-	1	1	3
Ukraine	1	-	-	-	1	-	2
Germany	-	-	1	1	-	-	2
Australia	-	1	-	-	-	-	1
China	-	-	-	-	-	1	1

equivalent was Anna Dogonadze (GER) at Athens aged 31yr 187days. Moskalenko was also the oldest medallist with a silver in 2004 aged 33yr 291days, and Dogonadze was the oldest female medallist. The youngest winner was Irina Karayeva (RUS) at Sydney aged 25yr 127days, and the youngest male champion was Yuri Nikitin (UKR) in 2004 aged 26yr 37days. Shanshan Huang (CHN) was the youngest medallist at 16yr 215days in 2004, while Mathieu Turgeon (CAN) was the youngest male medallist at 21yr 52days at Sydney.

TREBLES

FRANK KUNGLER (USA) uniquely won medals at three sports at the same Games. At St Louis in 1904 he won a silver at wrestling, a bronze at tug-of-war, and two bronzes at weightlifting. Another excellent treble attempt was by Viggo Jensen (DEN) at Athens in 1896 when he won a gold and silver in weightlifting, a silver and bronze in shooting, and placed fourth in the rope climb. Possibly the greatest treble in Olympic history, albeit all in the same sport, was that by the Czech distance runner, Emil Zátopek, who won the 5000m, 10,000m and marathon at Helsinki in 1952, all within eight days, including running a heat of the shorter distance.

TRIATHLON

CONTESTED AT THE Games for the first time at Sydney in 2000. There were contests for men and women, and both consisted of a 1500m swim, a 40km cycle and a 10km run. Though times are not strictly comparable, the fastest for the swim was 17:43.89 by Craig Walton (AUS) in 2000, and in the women's race 18:37 in 2004 by Loretta Harrop (AUS).

The most successful competitor was Brigitte McMahon (SUI) who won the gold medal in 2000, and then placed 10th at Athens. The male equivalent was Simon Whitfield (CAN) who took the gold at Sydney and then placed 11th in 2004. The oldest gold medallist/medallist was Hamish Carter (NZL) in 2004 aged 33yr 120days, and youngest gold

medallist/medallist was Whitfield who was aged 25yr 124days at Sydney. The oldest female winner was Kate Allen (AUT) aged 34yr 122days at Athens, while the oldest medallist was Susan Williams (USA) aged 35yr 69days in 2004. The youngest female medallist was Magali Messmer (SUI), aged 29yr 6days at Sydney.

TUG OF WAR

THIS SPORT WAS part of the athletics programme 1900-1920. Three men won a record two golds and one silver from 1908 to 1920: John Shepherd, Frederick Humphreys and Edwin Mills, all from Great Britain. Edward Barrett, another member of the winning 1908 team, also won a bronze medal in the heavyweight wrestling class in London. The oldest gold medallist was Humphreys aged 42yr 204days in 1920, while the youngest was Karl Staaf (SWE) aged 19yr 101days in 1900. There were some strange team compositions in the early days: the winning 1900 team was composed of three Swedes and three Danes; the 1904 competition was between American clubs; and the 1908 tournament was between British Police Clubs with London City police beating their colleagues from Liverpool.

Tug of War Medals

	G	S	B	Total
Great Britain	2	2	1	5
Sweden	2	-	1	3
United States	1	1	1	3
Denmark	1	-	-	1
Germany	1	-	-	1
France	-	1	-	1
Greece	-	1	-	1
Netherlands	-	1	-	1
Belgium	-	-	1	1
	7[1]	6	4[2]	17

[1] Joint Denmark/Sweden team in 1900, counted as two medals
[2] No bronze medals in 1900 or 1912

Triathlon Medals

	Men			Women			
	G	S	B	G	S	B	Total
Switzerland	-	-	1	1	-	1	3
New Zealand	1	1	-	-	-	-	2
Australia	-	-	-	-	2	-	2
Austria	-	-	-	1	-	-	1
Canada	1	-	-	-	-	-	1
Germany	-	1	-	-	-	-	1
Czech Republic	-	-	1	-	-	-	1
United States	-	-	-	-	-	1	1

Volleyball Medals

	Men			Women			
	G	S	B	G	S	B	Total
Soviet Union	3	2	1	4	3	-	13
Japan	1	1	1	2	2	1	8
Cuba	-	-	1	3	-	1	5
United States	2	-	1	-	1	1	5
Brazil	2	1	-	-	-	2	5
China	-	-	-	2	1	1	4
Russia	-	1	1	-	2	-	4
Italy	-	2	2	-	-	-	4
Poland	1	-	-	-	-	2	3
Netherlands	1	1	-	-	-	-	2
Yugoslavia	1	-	1	-	-	-	2
GDR	-	1	-	-	1	-	2
Bulgaria	-	1	-	-	-	1	2
Czechoslovakia	-	1	1	-	-	-	2
Peru	-	-	-	-	1	-	1
Argentina	-	-	1	-	-	-	1
Korea	-	-	-	-	-	1	1
North Korea (PRK)	-	-	-	-	-	1	1
Romania	-	-	1	-	-	-	1
	11	11	11	11	11	11	66

TWINS

THE FIRST TWINS to win Olympic medals were Eric and Vilhelm Carlberg (SWE) in the 1908 shooting events. Four years later, at Stockholm, they became the first twins to win gold medals, in the duelling pistol-30m team event. The most successful have been the rowing twins, Bernd and Jörg Landvoigt (GDR), who won the coxless pairs in 1976 and 1980. Among women, the most successful are Karen and Sarah Josephson (USA) who won a silver and then gold in the synchronized duet swimming events in 1988 and 1992.

VOLLEYBALL

(See also Beach Volleyball)

INTRODUCED INTO THE Games in 1964 for men and women, volleyball was initially dominated by Soviet teams. The most successful female players have been Regla Torres and Mireya Luis, both of Cuba, with three gold medals each, 1992-2000. It should be noted that Inna Ryskal (URS) won two gold and two silver medals 1964-1976. The best by a male player was two golds and a silver by Yuri Poyarkov (URS) 1964-1972. The tallest player has been Alexei Kazakov (RUS) at 2.17m 7ft 1½in when he won a silver in 2000 and a bronze in 2004.

The oldest gold medallist was Mauricio Lima (BRA) aged 36yr 215days in 2004, and the oldest female winner/medallist was Ludmila Buldakova (URS) aged 34yr 105days in 1972. The youngest gold medallist was Regla Herrera (CUB) in 1992 aged 17yr 177days, and the youngest male champion was Marcelo Negrao (BRA) aged 19yr 303days in 1992. The oldest medallist was Paolo Tofili (ITA) winning a silver at Athens aged 38yr 15days, while the youngest was Yevgeniya Artamonova of the Unified Team in 1992 at 17yr 22days. The youngest male medallist was Alexander Savin (URS) in 1976 aged 19yr 29days.

In 1996 beach volleyball tournaments for men and women were introduced.(See separate entry).

WATER POLO

THE FIRST OLYMPIC contest was won by the Osborne Swimming Club, Manchester, representing Great Britain in 1900. Five players have won three gold medals each; George Wilkinson (GBR) 1900, 1908 and 1912; Paul Radmilovic and Charles Smith (both GBR) 1908-1920; Dezsö Gyarmati and György Kárpáti (HUN) 1952, 1956 and 1964. Of these Radmilovic, Welsh-born of a Greek father and Irish mother, also won a gold in the 4x200m team in 1908. He, 1908-28, Gyarmati, 1948-64, and Gianni De Magistris (ITA), 1968-84, competed in a record five Olympic tournaments. However, the Hungarian is the most successful player, adding a silver in 1948 and a bronze in 1960, and becoming one of the few Olympians in any sport to win medals in five Games. Gyarmati also heads a fine Olympic family, as his wife Éva Székely won a gold (1952) and a silver (1956) in the 200m breaststroke, and their daughter Andrea won silver and bronze medals in the 1972 backstroke and butterfly events respectively. She then added to

Water Polo Medals

	Men			Women			
	G	S	B	G	S	B	Total
Hungary	8	3	3	-	-	-	14
United States	1	4	4	-	-	1	10
Soviet Union	2	2	4	-	-	-	8
Yugoslavia	3	4	1	-	-	-	8
Italy	3	1	2	1	-	-	7
Belgium	-	4	2	-	-	-	6
Great Britain	4	-	-	-	-	-	4
France	1	-	3	-	-	-	4
Germany	1	2	-	-	-	-	3
Sweden	-	1	2	-	-	-	3
Spain	1	1	-	-	-	-	2
Russia	-	1	2	-	-	-	3
Netherlands	-	-	2	-	-	-	2
Australia	1	-	-	-	-	-	1
Croatia	-	1	-	-	-	-	1
Greece	-	-	-	-	1	-	1
Seria/Montenegro	-	1	-	-	-	-	1
FRG	-	-	1	-	-	-	1
	25	25[1]	26[1]	1	1	1	79

[1]Two bronzes in 1900; two silvers and no bronze in 1904

the family total of medals by marrying Mihály Hesz (HUN), a canoeist with a gold (1968 K1) and a silver (1964 K1).

The oldest gold medallist was Charles Smith (GBR) aged 41yr 217days in 1920, while the youngest was György Kárpáti (HUN) in 1952 aged 17yr 40days. The oldest medallist was also Smith, while the youngest was Paul Vasseur (FRA) in 1900 aged 15yr 305days. The first brothers to win gold medals in the same team were Ferenc and Alajos Keserü (HUN) in 1932, and they were matched by Tulio and Franco Pandolfini (ITA) in 1948. Georgi Mshvenieradze (URS) won a gold medal in 1980, going one better than his father Piotr, who had gained a silver (1960) and a bronze (1956). Similarly, Tamás Kásás (HUN) won gold in 2000/2004, while is father Zoltán had only won a silver in 1972. A number of men have won medals at both swimming and water polo, the most notable being Johnny Weissmuller (USA) who gained a bronze in 1924 on the same day that he won two freestyle golds. Tim Shaw (USA) who won a silver medal in the 1976 400m freestyle won another in the 1984 water polo competition.

The highest score by any team was in 2000 when Russia beat Slovakia 21-5. In 1996 Italy beat Hungary 20-18 to set an aggregate record of 38. The biggest margin of victory came when the GDR beat UAE 19-2 in 1968. The most goals scored by an individual in one game is nine, by Zoran Jankovic of Yugoslavia against Japan in 1968, and by Manuel Estiarte for Spain against Brazil in 1984. Estiarte played in his record sixth consecutive Olympic Games in Sydney, having finally won a gold medal in 1996. In the winning Hungarian teams of 1932 and 1936, Olivér Halassy, had a leg amputated below the knee as a child.

There had been an exhibition match in 1920 between two Dutch women's teams, but it wasn't until 2000, at Sydney, that there was an inaugural tournament for women. The highest score in the women's game was when Russia beat Kazakstan 15-6, the victory margin of nine also a record. The youngest gold medallist/medallist was Elena Gigli (ITA) aged 19yr 48days in 2004. The oldest gold medallist was Debbie Watson (AUS) aged 34yr 361days, and the oldest medallist was Maureen O'Toole (USA) at 39yr 183days. A member of the winning Australian team at Sydney, Taryn Woods, had her brother, Gavin, in the men's squad in 2000/2004, and their father, David, had played for Australia in the 1968, 1972 and 1976 tournaments. Seven members of the USA team won a silver medal in 2000 and a bronze at Athens.

WATER SKIING

A DEMONSTRATION SPORT, held at Kiel in 1972, with 36 competitors from 20 countries, with many of the best skiers in the world. Events were won by Roby Zucchi (ITA), Ricky McCormick (USA), Willy Stähle (HOL), Liz Allan-Shetter (USA) and Sylvie Maurial (FRA).

WEIGHTLIFTING

TWO EVENTS WERE held in 1896, consisting of one-arm and two-arm lifts. The first Olympic weightlifting champion was Viggo Jensen (DEN)

Weightlifting Medals

| | Men | | | Women | | | |
	G	S	B	G	S	B	Total
Soviet Union	44	25	2	-	-	-	71
United States	15	16	9	1	-	1	42
Bulgaria	12	16	8	-	-	-	36
China	9	9	8	7	1	-	34
Poland	4	4	19	-	1	1	29
Germany	5	7	10	-	-	-	22
Hungary	2	7	9	-	2	-	20
Greece	7	5	3	-	-	1	16
France	9	2	4	-	-	-	15
Italy	5	5	5	-	-	-	15
Russia	3	2	5	-	2	2	14
Iran	4	3	5	-	-	-	12
Japan	2	2	8	-	-	-	12
Austria	4	5	2	-	-	-	11
Romania	2	6	3	-	-	-	11
GDR	1	4	6	-	-	-	11
Turkey	7	-	1	1	-	-	9
Egypt	5	2	2	-	-	-	9
Czechoslovakia	3	2	3	-	-	-	8
Great Britain	1	3	4	-	-	-	8
Korea	1	2	4	-	1	-	8
FRG	2	2	3	-	-	-	7
Estonia	1	3	3	-	-	-	7
North Korea (PRK)	-	2	3	-	2	-	7
Thailand	-	-	-	2	-	3	5
Belarus	-	1	2	-	1	1	5
Cuba	2	1	1	-	-	-	4
Ukraine	1	1	1	1	-	-	4
Belgium	1	2	1	-	-	-	4
Australia	1	1	2	-	-	-	4
Indonesia	-	-	-	-	2	2	4
Switzerland	-	2	2	-	-	-	4
Sweden	-	-	4	-	-	-	4
Denmark	1	2	-	-	-	-	3
Taipei	-	-	1	-	1	1	3
Finland	1	-	2	-	-	-	3
Trinidad	-	1	2	-	-	-	3
Netherlands	-	-	3	-	-	-	3
Colombia	-	-	-	1	-	1	2
Croatia	1	-	1	-	-	-	2
Georgia	1	-	1	-	-	-	2
Canada	-	2	-	-	-	-	2
Kazakhstan	-	2	-	-	-	-	2
Argentina	-	1	1	-	-	-	2
Mexico	-	-	-	1	-	-	1
Norway	1	-	-	-	-	-	1
Lebanon	-	1	-	-	-	-	1
Luxembourg	-	1	-	-	-	-	1
Nigeria	-	-	-	-	1	-	1
Singapore	-	1	-	-	-	-	1
Armenia	-	-	1	-	-	-	1
India	-	-	-	-	-	1	1
Iraq	-	-	1	-	-	-	1
Latvia	-	-	1	-	-	-	1
Qatar	-	-	1	-	-	-	1
Venezuela	-	-	1	-	-	-	1
	158[1]	154	157[234]	14	14	14	511

[1]Tie for gold in 1928 and 1936 lightweight class; [2]Four-way tie for bronze in 1896; [3]Triple tie for bronze in 1906 heavyweight class; [4]No bronze in 1992 light-heavyweight class

who won the two-arm competition from Launceston Eliot (GBR); both had lifted the same weight but the Briton had moved one of his feet. The positions were reversed in the other event. An amusing incident occurred when an attendant was having great trouble moving one of the weights. Prince George of Greece, a member of the organizing committee and an immensely big and strong man, bent down and easily lifted it aside. Jensen and Eliot were among the first of the great all-rounders, as the Dane won silver and bronze medals at pistol and rifle shooting, and placed fourth in the rope climb, and Eliot competed in wrestling, rope climbing and the 100m run.

The sport was not included in the Games of 1900, 1908 or 1912. In 1920 the contests were decided in the aggregate of a one-hand snatch, a one-hand jerk, and a two-hands jerk. In 1924 an additional two lifts were included, two-hands press and snatch. From 1928 to 1972 the result depended on the aggregate of three two-handed lifts: the press, snatch, and clean and jerk. In 1976 the press was eliminated, owing to difficulty in judging it correctly, and the total now is for the snatch, and the clean and jerk. At the suggestion of the IOC the forerunner of the International Weightlifting Federation was formed in 1920 to control the sport.

Four men have won three gold medals: Naim Suleymanoglu (TUR) 1988-96, all in the feather-weight category; Pyrros Dimas (GRE) 1992-00, at light-heavyweight; Kakhi Khakiashvili (EUN/GRE) 1992-00, at middle heavyweight and first heavyweight, and Halil Mutlu (TUR) 1996-2004 at flyweight and bantamweight. However, Dimas also won a bronze medal, in 2004. His record total of four medals matches that of Norbert Schemansky (USA) who won a gold, a silver and two bronzes 1948-64; Ronny Weller (GER) with a gold, two silvers and a bronze 1988-2000; and Nikolay Pechalov with a gold, one silver and two bronzes 1992-2004. Pechalov competed for Bulgaria in his first two Games, and for Croatia in the next two. Tommy Kono (USA), Norair Nurikyan (BUL), Kakhi Kakhiashvili (EUN/GRE), and Halil Mutlu (TUR) have won gold medals in different categories. Kono won the 67.5 kg (1952) and the 82.5kg (1956); Kakhiashvili won the 91kg (1992)/94kg (2000), and the 99kg (1996); more unusually Nurikyan moved down from the 60kg (1972) to the 56kg (1976); Mutlu took the now-defunct 54kg category (1996) and the 56kg (2000-04).

The oldest gold medallist was Rudolf Plukfelder (URS) in the 82.5kg class of 1964 aged 36yr 40days, while Schemansky was the oldest medallist in 1964 aged 40yr 141days. The youngest gold medallist was Zeng Guoqiang (CHN) who won the 52kg class

in 1984 aged 19yr 133days, and the youngest ever medallist was Andrei Socaci (ROM) who won a 1984 silver in the 67.5kg category aged 18yr 43days. The oldest known competitor was 56-year-old Teunist Jonck (SAF) in 1952. It was originally reported that Mehmet Djemal (TUR), who competed in 1924, was only 13 years of age – this has proved to be untrue. Imre Földi (HUN) and Ronny Weller (GER) competed in five Games, 1960-76 and 1988-2004 respectively. The heaviest weightlifter ever at the Games was Mark Henry (USA) in 1996 when he weighed in at 184.92kg 407½lbs. The greatest single weight lifted at the Games has been a clean and jerk of 263.5kg 580¾lb by Hossein Reza Zadeh (IRI), in a record attempt after winning the 105Kg+ title at Athens in 2004. He is acknowledged as the strongest man in the world. The greatest margin of victory was the 37.5kg advantage by Stanley Stanczyk (USA) in the 1948 light-middleweight class. The silver medallist in that competition, Harold Sakata (USA), later gained fame portraying 'Oddjob' in the James Bond film Goldfinger.

The only brothers to win medals in the same event at the same Games were Yoshinobu and Yoshiyuki Miyake (JPN) who won gold and bronze medals respectively in the 60kg in 1968. Yoshinobu also won another gold and a silver, but Peter and James George (USA) hold the family record for medals with one gold, three silvers and a bronze from 1948 to 1960. In the 1988 featherweight class (up to 60kg) Naim Suleymanoglu (TUR) – for whose emigration the Turkish government is reported to have paid $1 million to Bulgaria – set an Olympic record, equalling that for the next weight class.

Disqualification due to use of drugs has affected this sport more than most with the first cases, gold medallist Zbigniew Kaczmarek (POL) and silver medallist Blagoi Blagoyev (BUL), being disqualified in 1976. At the end of 1992 the old weight classes were abolished by the IWF and replaced by new ones, in an attempt to replace any of the old records which may have been set by drug users prior to the introduction of strict controls. At Sydney, in 2000, there were further changes to the weight classes. In 2004 once again there were a rash of doping disqualifications.

In 2000 events for women were introduced. The greatest single weight lifted was a clean and jerk of 182.5kg 402¼lb by Gonghong Tang (CHN) at Athens. The heaviest competitor, and also the heaviest female competitor in Olympic Games history, was Cheryl Haworth (USA) who won a bronze in the Sydney heavyweight class weighing in at 138kg 304lb. The oldest winner was Tara Nott (USA) in the 48kg class aged 28yr 130days in 2000, while the youngest winner was Chunhong Li (CHN) in the Athens 69kg class aged 19yr 203days. The youngest medallist was Cheryl Haworth (USA) aged 17yr 156days in 2000, and the oldest medallist was Mabel Mosquera (COL) bronze in the 53kg class aged 35yr 45days at Athens. The biggest margin of victory was the 12.5kg *27lb* by Xia Yang (CHN) in the Sydney 53kg category, which was matched by Udomporn Polsak (THA) in the same class in Athens.

WINTER GAMES

THE FIRST WINTER Olympic Games were held at Chamonix, France in 1924. At first it was only called the 'The International Winter Sports Week', in deference to the Scandinavian countries who worried that a Winter Olympic meeting would detract from the importance of their Nordic Games. It was only in 1926 that, retrospectively, it was accorded Olympic status. Prior to this there had been figure skating in London in 1908, and figure skating and ice hockey at Antwerp in 1920, both times as part of the Summer Games programme. (For details of venues, dates, and numbers of competitors, see 'Celebrations').

WINTER PENTATHLON

A DEMONSTRATION SPORT held at St Moritz in 1948 and comprising a 10km cross-country skiing race, a pistol shoot, fencing, downhill skiing and horse-riding over a distance of 3500m. Gustaf Lindh (SWE) came first, with his teammate Willie Grut second. Grut later that year won the modern pentathlon in the Summer Games by a record margin. In sixth-place was Derek Allhusen (GBR), who 20 years later in his 55th year won an equestrian gold medal at Mexico City.

WOMEN

Participation in the Olympic Games

IN THE ANCIENT Games women were banned, under threat of death, from even attending as spectators. The only exceptions being made for the high priestesses of the most important gods. Nevertheless, it was possible for a woman to gain an Olympic prize – as the owner of a winning chariot. One of the first to win in such a way was Belistike of Macedonia, the owner of the champion 2-horse chariot in 268 BC. Some women defied the rules and disguised themselves, but were found out and thrown over a cliff on discovery. It is recorded that Pherenice of Rhodes acted as a second to watch her son, Pisidores, win his event. In her excitement she gave herself away, but when it was realised that not only her son, but also her father and brothers had all been Olympic victors, she was pardoned.

The founder of the Modern Games, Baron de Coubertin, was not in favour of women competing at the Games, but in 1900, at Paris, women were allowed in specified events. It has always been thought that the first female Olympic champion was Charlotte Cooper (GBR), the winner of the women's tennis singles at Paris in 1900, but new evidence now gives that honour to Helen, Countess de Pourtalès, a crew member of the Swiss gold medal yacht *Lerina* in the 1-2 Tonnes class at the same Games. She also becomes the first ever female Olympic competitor.

Women's swimming events were included for the first time at Stockholm in 1912, and athletics events came in at Amsterdam in 1928. Soccer was added, and proved very popular, in 1996. By the Sydney Games in 2000, there were 120 events for women, compared to 168 for the men, and another 12 which are mixed. In 2004 more events for women came in, including at wrestling. In the Winter Games, female skaters were competing from the beginning, and Alpine Skiing events for women began, alongside the men, in 1936. In 1998 there was a women's ice hockey tournament, and in 2002 a two-woman bob event was introduced.

WRESTLING

WRESTLING WAS THE most popular sport in the ancient Games with victors recorded from 708 BC. The most famous was Milon of Kroton, a five-time winner. Greco-Roman wrestling was included in the 1896 Games and freestyle in 1904 Basically, holds are unlimited in freestyle, but in the Greco-Roman style holds below the waist are barred. There was no bodyweight limit in Athens and it was won, surprisingly, by gymnastics triple gold medallist Carl Schuhmann (GER), who was only 1.63m *5ft 4in* tall, and who defeated Games weightlifting champion Launceston Eliot (GBR) in the preliminaries. Until a time limit was set in 1924 bouts often lasted for remarkable lengths of time. The most extreme was when Martin Klein, an Estonian representing Russia, and Alfred 'Alpo' Asikainen of Finland, in the 1912 Greco-Roman middleweight class, wrestled for 11 hours 40 minutes. Klein won, but was too exhausted to challenge for the gold medal. In the light-heavy final that year Anders Ahlgren (SWE) and Ivar Böhling (FIN) were declared equal second after nine hours without a decision, and no gold medal was awarded.

Four men have won three gold medals: Carl Westergren (SWE), 1920-32; Ivar Johansson (SWE) 1932-36, Alexander Medved 1964-72, and Alexander

Wrestling Medals

Men

	Freestyle			Greco-Roman			
	G	S	B	G	S	B	Total
Soviet Union	31	17	15	37	19	13	132
United States	46	36	24	3	6	4	119
Finland	8	7	11	19	22	19	86
Sweden	8	10	8	2	17	19	82
Bulgaria	7	17	9	9	14	7	64
Turkey	16	11	8	11	5	5	56
Hungary	3	4	7	16	10	11	51
Japan	16	9	10	4	5	2	46
Korea	4	9	7	6	2	5	33
Romania	1	-	4	6	8	13	32
Germany	1	3	3	4	13	8	32
Iran	5	11	13	-	1	1	31
Russia	10	2	2	5	5	4	28
Poland	-	1	3	5	8	6	23
Italy	1	-	-	5	4	9	19
Great Britain	3	4	10	-	-	-	17
Cuba	2	1	4	3	4	2	16
Yugoslavia	1	1	2	3	5	4	16
Czechoslovakia	-	1	3	1	6	4	15
France	2	2	4	1	2	2	13
Switzerland	4	4	3	-	-	1	12
Denmark	-	-	-	2	3	7	12
Canada	1	5	5	-	-	-	11
Greece	-	-	2	1	3	5	11
Estonia	2	1	-	3	-	4	10
FRG	-	1	3	1	3	1	9
North Korea (PRK)	3	2	3	-	-	1	9
Mongolia	-	4	4	-	-	-	8
GDR	-	2	1	2	1	1	7
Ukraine	1	1	2	1	1	1	7
Egypt (UAR)	-	-	-	2	2	2	6
Kazakhstan	-	2	1	1	1	1	6
Austria	-	-	1	1	2	2	6
Norway	-	1	-	2	1	1	5
Belarus	-	-	-	-	2	3	5
Georgia	-	-	2	-	1	2	5
Uzbekistan	1	2	-	1	-	-	4
Belium	-	3	-	-	-	1	4
Azerbaijan	1	1	-	1	-	-	3
Australia	-	1	2	-	-	-	3
Lebanon	-	-	-	-	1	2	3
China	-	-	-	-	-	3	3
Armenia	-	1	-	1	-	-	2
Latvia	-	-	-	-	1	-	1
Mexico	-	-	-	-	1	-	1
Syria	-	1	-	-	-	-	1
India	-	-	1	-	-	-	1
Macedonia	-	-	1	-	-	-	1
Moldova	-	-	-	-	-	1	1
Pakistan	-	-	1	-	-	-	1
	178	178	179[1]	177[2]	179	178[3]	1069

Women

	Freestyle			
	G	S	B	Total
Japan	2	1	1	4
United States	-	1	1	2
France	-	-	2	2
China	1	-	-	1
Ukraine	1	-	-	1
Canada	-	1	-	1
Russia	-	1	-	1

[1]Two bronzes in 1920 heavyweight class, [2]No gold in 1912 light-heavyweight class, [3]No bronze in 1906 all-around class

Karelin (URS/EUN/RUS) 1988-96. The latter also won a silver in 2000 (thus suffering his first defeat for 14 years). Karelin is also the only man to win three successive titles in the same event, Greco-Roman superheavyweight. Johansson, 1932, and Kristjan Palusala (EST), 1936, are the only men to win titles in both styles at the same Games, although Kaarle Antila (FIN) had achieved this distinction previously over a two Games period 1920-24. Wilfried Dietrich (GER/FRG) won most medals with one gold, two silvers and two bronzes at both styles from 1956 to 1968, and competed in a record seven tournaments, both styles, 1956-72. Dietrich, 1956-72; Mario Tovar Gonzalez (MEX), 1952-68; Khorloo Baianmunkh (MGL), 1964-80; Czeslaw Kwiecinski (POL), 1964-80, and George Mackenzie (GBR), 1908-28, competed at a record five Games in the one style. Mackenzie also competed over a record span of 20 years. Although a number of brothers have each won gold medals, uniquely, two pairs of brothers, Ed and Lou Banach and Dave and Mark Schultz, all from the United States, won titles in 1984. The only twins to win gold medals were Anatoli and Sergei Beloglazov (URS) in 1980, and Ed and Lou Banach (USA) in 1984. Kustaa and Hermanni Pihlajamäki (FIN), who won three golds, one silver and a bronze between 1924 and 1936, were not brothers, as often indicated, but cousins. What is thought to be a unique situation occurred in the freestyle 82kg class in 1996, when Elmadi Zhabrailov (KZK) beat his brother Lucman representing Moldova. The first black champion was Kenny Monday (USA) in the 1988 freestyle welterweight division.

The oldest gold medallist/medallist was Adolf Lindfors (FIN) in 1920 aged 41yr 199days. The youngest champion was Saban Trstena (YUG) in 1984 aged 19yr 222days, and the youngest medallist was Nasser Givechi (IRN) in 1952 aged 16yr 254days. The heaviest competitor ever in any Olympic event was the 1972 super-heavyweight bronze medallist Chris Taylor (USA) who weighed between 182kg *401lb* and 190kg *419lb*. When Osamu Watanabe (JPN) won the 1964 freestyle featherweight title it was his 186th successive victory in the sport. After gaining the silver medal in the 1920 unlimited class, Nat Pendleton first turned professional, and then went to Hollywood and appeared in many films, usually playing 'dumb ox' roles.

At Athens in 2004, four freestyle events for women were added to the programme. The oldest gold medallist was Irina Merleni (UKR) in the 48kg class aged 22yr 197days, while the youngest was Xu Wang (CHN) winning her 72kg title at 18yr 331days. She was also the youngest medallist. The oldest medallist was Anna Gomis (FRA) taking the bronze in the 55kg category aged 30yr 332days. In 2004 Kaori Icho won a gold medal while her sister Chiharu won a silver.

YOUNGEST

THE YOUNGEST COMPETITOR, and indeed medallist, in the Olympic Games, except for the unconfirmed report of a an even younger rowing cox in 1900, was gymnast Dimitrios Loundras (GRE) in the bronze medal team in 1896, aged 10yr 218days. The youngest female participant was the British skater Cecilia Colledge in 1932 aged 11yr 73days. (Four years later she won a silver medal). The youngest female competitor, and medallist, in any Summer Games sport was Luigina Giavotti (ITA) in the 1928 silver medal gymnastic team at 11yr 302days. The youngest to win a medal in an individual event was Inge Sorensen (DEN) in 1936 with a 200m breaststroke bronze aged 12yr 24days, while the youngest male medallist in an individual event was Nils Skoglund (SWE) in the 1920 diving aged 14yr 11days. At Berlin in 1936 diver Marjorie Gestring (USA) became the youngest ever female gold medallist aged 13yr 267days. The youngest known male gold medallist was Klaus Zerta, cox of the winning German pair in 1960 aged 13yr 283days. The youngest male to win an individual event gold medal was swimmer Kusuo Kitamura (JPN) in the 1932 1500m freestyle aged 14yr 309days.

The youngest ever Winter Games competitor was figure skater Cecilia Colledge (GBR) aged 11yr 73days at the 1932 Games, while the youngest male competitor figure skater was Jan Hoffmann (GDR), aged 12yr 110days in 1968. The youngest ever medallist/gold medallist at the Winter Games was Kim Yoon-Mi (KOR) in the women's short track speed skating relay in 1994 aged 13yr 83days. In 1964 Scott Allen (USA) became the youngest male Winter medallist with a figure skating bronze aged 14yr 363days. The youngest male gold medallist was Finnish ski-jumper Toni Nieminen in 1992 aged 16yr 259days.

MEDALLISTS

SUMMER GAMES

ARCHERY 1972-2004

Gold	Silver	Bronze

Men

	Gold	Silver	Bronze
1972	John Williams (USA) 2528pts	Gunnar Jarvil (SWE) 2481	Kyösti Lassonen (FIN) 2467
1976	Darrell Pace (USA) 2571pts	Hiroshi Michinaga (JPN) 2502	Giancarlo Ferrrari (ITA) 2495
1980	Tomi Poikolainen (FIN) 2455pts	Boris Isachenko (URS) 2452	Giancarlo Ferrari (ITA) 2449
1984	Darrell Pace (USA) 2616pts	Richard McKinney (USA) 2564	Hiroshi Yamamoto (JPN) 2563
1988	Jay Barrs (USA) 338pts (2605)	Park Sung-Soo (KOR) 336 (2614)	Vladimir Yecheyev (URS) 335 (2600)
1992	Sebastien Flute (FRA)	Chung Jae-Hun (KOR)	Simon Terry (GBR)
1996	Justin Huish (USA)	Magnus Petersson (SWE)	Oh Kyun-Moon (KOR)
2000	Simon Fairweather (AUS)	Victor Wonderle (USA)	Wietse van Alten (NED)
2004	Marco Galiazzo (ITA)	Hiroshi Yamamoto (JPN)	Tim Cuddihy (AUS)

Team

	Gold	Silver	Bronze
1988	KOREA	UNITED STATES	GREAT BRITAIN
1992	SPAIN	FINLAND	GREAT BRITAIN
1996	UNITED STATES	KOREA	ITALY
2000	KOREA	ITALY	UNITED STATES
2004	KOREA	TAIPEI	UKRAINE

Women

	Gold	Silver	Bronze
1972	Doreen Wilber (USA) 2424pts	Irena Szydlowska (POL) 2407	Emma Gapchenko (URS) 2403
1976	Luann Ryon (USA) 2499pts	Valentina Kovpan (URS) 2460	Zebeniso Rustamova (URS) 2407
1980	Keto Losaberidze (URS) 2491pts	Natalya Butuzova (URS) 2477	Päivi Meriluoto (FIN) 2449
1984	Seo Hyang-Soon (KOR) 2568pts	Li Lingjuan (CHN) 2559	Kim Jin-Ho (KOR) 2555
1988	Kim Soo-Nyung (KOR) 344pts (2683)	Wang Hee-Kyung (KOR) 332 (2612)	Yung Young-Sook (KOR) 327 (2603)
1992	Cho Youn-Jeong (KOR)	Kim Soo-Nyung (KOR)	Natalia Valeyeva (EUN)
1996	Kim Kyung-Wook (KOR)	He Ying (CHN)	Olena Sadovnycha (UKR)
2000	Mi-Jin Yun (KOR)	Nam-Soon Kim (KOR)	Soo-Nyung Kim (KOR)
2004	Sung-Hyun Park (KOR)	Sung-Jin Lee (KOR)	Alison Williamson (GBR)

Team

	Gold	Silver	Bronze
1988	KOREA	INDONESIA	UNITED STATES
1992	KOREA	CHINA	UNIFIED TEAM
1996	KOREA	GERMANY	POLAND
2000	KOREA	UKRAINE	GERMANY
2004	KOREA	CHINA	TAIPEI

DISCONTINUED

1900

Gold	Silver	Bronze
Au cordon doré-50m		
Henri Hérouin (FRA)	Hubert van Innis (BEL)	Emile Fisseux (FRA)
Au cordon doré-33m		
Hubert van Innis (BEL)	Victor Thibaud (FRA)	Charles Petit (FRA)
Au chapelet-50m		
Eugène Mougin (FRA)	Henri Helle (FRA)	Emile Mercier (FRA)
Au chapelet-33m		
Hubert van Innis (BEL)	Victor Thibaud (FRA)	Charles Petit (FRA)
Sur la perche à la herse		
Emmanuel Foulon (FRA)	Pierre Serrurier (FRA)	Emile Druart Jr (BEL)
Sur la perche à la pyramide		
Emile Grumiaux (FRA)	Auguste Serrurier (FRA)	Louis Glineaux (BEL)

1904

Men
Double York Round
| Phillip Bryant (USA) | Robert Williams (USA) | William Thompson (USA) |

Double American Round
| Phillip Bryant (USA) | Robert Williams (USA) | William Thompson (USA) |

Team Round
| Potomac Archers (USA) | Cincinnati Archery Club (USA) | Boston AA (USA) |

Women
Double National Round
| Lida Howell (USA) | Jessie Pollack (USA) | Emma Cooke (USA) |

Double Columbia Round
| Lida Howell (USA) | Emma Cooke (USA) | Jessie Pollack (USA) |

1908

Men
York Round
| William Dod (GBR) | Reginald Brooks-King (GBR) | Henry Richardson (USA) |

Continental Style
| Eugène Grisot (FRA) | Louis Vernet (FRA) | Gustave Cabaret (FRA) |

Women
National Round
| Queenie Newall (GBR) | Charlotte Dod (GBR) | Beatrice Hill-Lowe (GBR) |

1920

Fixed bird target-small birds-individual
| Edmond van Moer (BEL) | Louis van de Perck (BEL) | Joseph Hermans (BEL) |

Fixed bird target-small birds-team
| BELGIUM | - | - |

Fixed bird target-large birds-individual
| Edouard Cloetens (BEL) | Louis van der Perck (BEL) | Firmin Flamand (BEL) |

Fixed bird target-large birds-team
| BELGIUM | - | - |

Moving bird target-28m-individual
| Hubert van Innis (BEL) | Léone Quentin (FRA) | - |

Moving bird target-team
| NETHERLANDS | BELGIUM | FRANCE |

Moving bird target-33m-individual
| Hubert van Innis (BEL) | Julien Brulé (FRA) | - |

Moving bird target-33m-team
| BELGIUM | FRANCE | - |

Moving bird target-50m-individual
| Julien Brulé (FRA) | Hubert van Innis (BEL) | - |

Moving bird target-50m-team
| BELGIUM | FRANCE | - |

ATHLETICS

Men

100 Metres

Year	Gold	Silver	Bronze
1896	Thomas Burke (USA) 12.0	Fritz Hofmann (GER) 12.2e	Alajos Szokolyi (HUN) 12.6e
1900	Frank Jarvis (USA) 11.0	Walter Tewksbury (USA) 11.1	Stanley Rowley (AUS) 11.2
1904	Archie Hahn (USA) 11.0	Nathaniel Cartmell (USA) 11.2	William Hogenson (USA) 11.2
1906	Archie Hahn (USA) 11.2	Fay Moulton (USA) 11.3	Nigel Barker (AUS) 11.3
1908	Reginald Walker (RSA) 10.8	James Rector (USA) 10.9	Robert Kerr (CAN) 11.0
1912	Ralph Craig (USA) 10.8	Alvah Meyer (USA) 10.9	Donald Lippincott (USA) 10.9
1920	Charles Paddock (USA) 10.8	Morris Kirksey (USA) 10.8	Harry Edward (GBR) 11.0
1924	Harold Abrahams (GBR) 10.6	Jackson Scholz (USA) 10.7	Arthur Porritt (NZL) 10.8
1928	Percy Williams (CAN) 10.8	Jack London (GBR) 10.9	Georg Lammers (GER) 10.9
1932	Eddie Tolan (USA) 10.3 (10.38)	Ralph Metcalfe (USA) 10.3 (10.38)	Arthur Jonath (GER) 10.4 (10.50)
1936	Jesse Owens (USA) 10.3	Ralph Metcalfe (USA) 10.4	Martinus Osendarp (NED) 10.5
1948	Harrison Dillard (USA) 10.3	Norwood Ewell (USA) 10.4	Lloyd La Beach (PAN) 10.4
1952	Lindy Remigino (USA) 10.4 (10.79)	Herb McKenley (JAM) 10.4 (10.80)	Emmanuel McDonald Bailey (GBR) 10.4 (10.83)
1956	Bobby Joe Morrow (USA) 10.5 (10.62)	Thane Baker (USA) 10.5 (10.77)	Hector Hogan (AUS) 10.6 (10.77)

1960	Armin Hary (GER) 10.2 (10.32)	David Sime (USA) 10.2 (10.35)	Peter Radford (GBR) 10.3 (10.42)
1964	Bob Hayes (USA) 10.0 (10.06)[1]	Enrique Figuerola (CUB) 10.2 (10.25)	Harry Jerome (CAN) 10.2 (10.27)
1968	James Hines (USA) 9.9 (9.95)	Lennox Miller (JAM) 10.0 (10.04)	Charles Greene (USA) 10.0 (10.07)
1972	Valeri Borzov (URS) 10.14	Robert Taylor (USA) 10.24	Lennox Miller (JAM) 10.33
1976	Hasely Crawford (TRI) 10.06	Don Quarrie (JAM) 10.08	Valeri Borzov (URS) 10.14
1980	Allan Wells (GBR) 10.25	Silvio Leonard (CUB) 10.25	Petar Petrov (BUL) 10.39
1984	Carl Lewis (USA) 9.99	Sam Graddy (USA) 10.19	Ben Johnson (CAN) 10.22
1988	Carl Lewis (USA) 9.92[2]	Linford Christie (GBR) 9.97	Calvin Smith (USA) 9.99
1992	Linford Christie (GBR) 9.96	Frankie Fredericks (NAM) 10.02	Dennis Mitchell (USA) 10.04
1996	Donovan Bailey (CAN) 9.84	Frankie Fredericks (NAM) 9.89	Ato Boldon (TRI) 9.90
2000	Maurice Greene (USA) 9.87	Ato Boldon (TRI) 9.99	Obadele Thompson (BAR) 10.04
2004	Justin Gatlin (USA) 9.85	Francis Obikwelu (POR) 9.86	Maurice Greene (USA) 9.87

[1]Hayes ran a wind-assisted 9.91 in the semi-final; [2]Ben Johnson (CAN) won in 9.79 but was later disqualified

200 Metres

1900	Walter Tewksbury (USA) 22.2	Norman Pritchard (GBR) 22.8	Stanley Rowley (AUS) 22.9
1904[1]	Archie Hahn (USA) 21.6	Nathaniel Cartmell (USA) 21.9	William Hogenson (USA) dna
1908	Robert Kerr (CAN) 22.6	Robert Cloughen (USA) 22.6	Nathaniel Cartmell (USA) 22.7
1912	Ralph Craig (USA) 21.7	Donald Lippincott (USA) 22.1	Willie Applegarth (GBR) 22.0
1920	Allen Woodring (USA) 22.0	Charles Paddock (USA) 22.1	Harry Edward (GBR) 22.2
1924	Jackson Scholz (USA) 21.6	Charles Paddock (USA) 21.7	Eric Liddell (GBR) 21.9
1928	Percy Williams (CAN) 21.8	Walter Rangeley (GBR) 21.9	Helmut Kornig (GER) 21.9[2]
1932	Eddie Tolan (USA) 21.2 (21.12)	George Simpson (USA) 21.4	Ralph Metcalfe (USA) 21.5[3]
1936	Jesse Owens (USA) 20.7	Mack Robinson (USA) 21.1	Martinus Osendarp (NED) 21.3
1948	Mel Patton (USA) 21.1	Norwood Ewell (USA) 21.1	Lloyd La Beach (PAN) 21.2
1952	Andrew Stanfield (USA) 20.7 (20.81)	Thane Baker (USA) 20.8 (20.97)	James Gathers (USA) 20.8 (21.08)
1956	Bobby Joe Morrow (USA) 20.6 (20.75)	Andrew Stanfield (USA) 20.7 (20.97)	Thane Baker (USA) 20.9 (21.05)
1960	Livio Berruti (ITA) 20.5 (20.62)	Lester Carney (USA) 20.6 (20.69)	Abdoulaye Seye (FRA) 20.7 (20.83)
1964	Henry Carr (USA) 20.3 (20.36)	Paul Drayton (USA) 20.5 (20.58)	Edwin Roberts (TRI) 20.6 (20.63)
1968	Tommie Smith (USA) 19.8 (19.83)	Peter Norman (AUS) 20.0 (20.06)	John Carlos (USA) 20.0 (20.10)
1972	Valeri Borzov (URS) 20.00	Larry Black (USA) 20.19	Pietro Mennea (ITA) 20.30
1976	Don Quarrie (JAM) 20.23	Millard Hampton (USA) 20.29	Dwayne Evans (USA) 20.43
1980	Pietro Mennea (ITA) 20.19	Allan Wells (GBR) 20.21	Don Quarrie (JAM) 20.29
1984	Carl Lewis (USA) 19.80	Kirk Baptiste (USA) 19.96	Thomas Jefferson (USA) 20.26
1988	Joe DeLoach (USA) 19.75	Carl Lewis (USA) 19.79	Robson da Silva (BRA) 20.04
1992	Mike Marsh (USA) 20.01	Frankie Fredericks (NAM) 20.13	Michael Bates (USA) 20.38
1996	Michael Johnson (USA) 19.32	Frankie Fredericks (NAM) 19.68	Ato Boldon (TRI) 19.80
2000	Konstadinos Kederis (GRE) 20.09	Darren Campbell (GBR) 20.14	Ato Boldon (TRI) 20.20
2004	Shawn Crawford (USA) 19.79	Bernard Williams (USA) 20.01	Jutin Gatlin (USA) 20.03

1896, 1906 Event not held
[1]Race over straight course. Hahn's three opponents were all given 2yd handicaps for false starting; [2]Awarded bronze medal when Scholz (USA) refused to re-run after tie; [3]Metcalfe's lane was later found to be 1.5m too long

400 Metres

1896	Thomas Burke (USA) 54.2	Herbert Jamison (USA) 55.2	Charles Gmelin (GBR) 55.6
1900	Maxey Long (USA) 49.4	William HJolland (USA) 49.6	Ernst Schultz (DEN) 15m
1904	Harry Hillman (USA) 49.2	Frank Waller (USA) 49.9	Herman Groman (USA) 50.0
1906	Paul Pilgrim (USA) 53.2	Wyndham Halswelle (GBR) 53.8	Nigel Barker (AUS) 54.1
1908[1]	Wyndham Halswelle (GBR) 50.0	–	–
1912	Charles Reidpath (USA) 48.2	Hanns Braun (GER) 48.3	Edward Lingberg (USA 48.4
1920	Bevil Rudd (RSA) 49.6	Guy Butler (GBR) 49.9	Nils Engdahl (SWE) 50.0
1924	Eric Liddell (GBR) 47.6	Horatio Fitch (USA) 48.4	Guy Butler (GBR) 48.6
1928	Ray Barbuti (USA) 47.8	James Ball (CAN) 48.0	Joachim Büchner (GER) 48.2
1932	William Carr (USA) 46.2 (46.28)	Ben Eastman (USA) 46.4 (46.50)	Alexander Wilson (CAN) 47.4
1936	Archie Williams (USA) 46.5 (46.66)	Godfrey Brown (GBR) 46.7 (46.68)	James LuValle (USA) 46.8 (46.84)
1948	Arthur Wint (JAM) 46.2	Herb McKenley (JAM) 46.4	Mal Whitfield (USA) 46.6
1952	George Rhoden (JAM) 45.9 (46.09)	Herb McKenley (JAM) 45.9 (46.20)	Ollie Matson (USA) 46.8 (46.94)
1956	Charles jenkinsd (USA) 46.7 (46.85)	Karl-Friedrich Haas (GER) 46.8 (47.12)	Voitto Hellsten (FIN) 47.0 (47.15) Ardalion Ignatyev (URS) 47.0 (47.15)
1960	Otis Davis (USA) 44.9 (45.07)	Carl Kaufmann (GER) 44.9 (45.08)	Mal Spence (RSA) 45.5 (45.60)
1964	Mike Larrabee (USA) 45.1 (45.15)	Wendell Mottley (TRI) 45.2 (45.24)	Andrzej Badenski (POL) 45.6 (45.64)
1968	Lee Evans (USA) 43.8 (43.86)	Lawrence James (USA) 43.9 (43.97)	Ron Freeman (USA) 44.4 (44.41)
1972	Vince matthews (USA) 44.66	Wayne Collett (USA) 44.80	Julius Sang (KEN) 44.92
1976	Alberto Juantorena (CUB) 44.26	Fred Newhouse (USA) 44.40	Herman Frazier (USA) 44.95
1980	Viktor Markin (URS) 44.60	Rick Mitchell (AUS) 44.84	Frank Schaffer (GDR) 44.87
1984	Alonzo Babers (USA) 44.27	Gabriel Tiacoh (CIV) 44.54	Antonio McKay (USA) 44.71

1988	Steve Lewis (USA) 43.87	Butch Reynolds (USA) 43.93	Danny Everett (USA) 44.09
1992	Quincy Watts (USA) 43.50	Steve Lewis (USA) 44.21	Samson Kitur (KEN) 44.24
1996	Michael Johnson (USA) 43.49	Roger Black (GBR) 44.41	Davis Kamoga (UGA) 44.53
2000	Michael Johnson (USA) 43.84	Alvin Harrison (USA) 44.40	Greg Haughton (JAM) 44.70
2004	Jeremy Wariner (USA) 44.00	DERRICK Brew (USA) 44.16	Otis Harris (USA) 44.42

[1]Re-run ordered after John Carpenter (USA) disqualified in first final. Only Halswelle showed up and 'walked over' for the title

800 Metres

1896	Edwin Flack (AUS) 2:11.0	Nándor Dáni (HUN) 2:11.8	Dimitrios Golemis (GRE) 2:28.0
1900	Alfred Tysoe (GBR) 2:01.2	John Cregan (USA) 2:03.0	David Hall (USA) dna
1904	James Lightbody (USA) 1:56.0	Howard Valentine (USA) 1:56.3	Emil Breitkreutz (USA) 1:56.4
1906	Paul Pilgrim (USA) 2:01.5	James Lightbody (USA) 2:01.6	Wyndham Halswelle (GBR) 2:03.0
1908	Mel Sheppard (USA) 1:52.8	Emilio Lunghi (ITA) 1:54.2	Hanns Braun (GER) 1:55.2
1912	James Meredith (USA) 1:51.9	Mel Sheppard (USA) 1:52.0	Ira Davenport (USA) 1:52.0
1920	Albert Hill (GBR) 1:53.4	Earl Eby (USA) 1:53.6	Bevil Rudd (RSA) 1:54.0
1924	Douglas Lowe (GBR) 1:52.4	Paul Martin (SUI) 1:52.6	Schuyler Enck (USA) 1:53.0
1928	Douglas Lowe (GBR) 1:51.8	Erik Byléhn (SWE) 1:52.8	Hermann Engelhardt (GER) 1:53.2
1932	Thomas Hampson (GBR) 1:49.7	Alexander Wilson (CAN) 1:49.9	Phil Edwards (CAN) 1:51.5
1936	John Woodruff (USA) 1:52.9	Mario Lanzi (ITA) 1:53.3	PhilEdwards (CAN) 1:53.6
1948	Mal Whitfield (USA) 1:49.2	Arthur Wint (JAM) 1:49.5	Marcel Hansenne (FRA) 1:49.8
1952	Mal Whitfield (USA) 1:49.2	Arthur Wint (JAM) 1:49.4	Heinz Ulzheimer (GER) 1:40.7
1956	Tom Courtney (USA) 1:47.7	Derek Johnson (GBR) 1:47.8	Audun Boysen (NOR) 1:48.1
1960	Peter Snell (NZL) 1:46.3	Roger Moens (BEL) 1:46.5	George Kerr (BWI)[1] 1:47.1
1964	Peter Snell (NZL) 1:45.1	Bill Crothers (CAN) 1:45.6	Wilson Kiprugut (KEN) 1:45.9
1968	Ralph Doubell (AUS) 1:44.3	Wilson Kiprugut (KEN) 1:44.5	Tom Farrell (USA) 1:45.4
1972	Dave Wottle (USA) 1:45.9	Yevgeni Arzhanov (URS) 1:45.9	Mike Boit (KEN) 1:46.0
1976	Alberto Juantorena (CUB) 1:43.5	Ivo Van Damme (BEL) 1:43.9	Richard Wohlhuter (USA) 1:44.1
1980	Steve Ovett (GBR) 1:45.4	Sebastian Coe (GBR) 1:45.9	Nikolai Kirov (URS) 1:46.0
1984	Joachim Cruz (BRA) 1:43.00	Sebastian Coe (GBR) 1:43.64	Earl Jones (USA) 1:43.83
1988	Paul Ereng (KEN) 1:43.45	Joachim Cruz (BRA) 1:43.90	Saïd Aouita (MAR) 1:44.06
1992	William Tanui (KEN) 1:43.66	Nixon Kiprotich (KEN) 1:43.70	Johnny Gray (USA) 1:43.97
1996	Vebjörn Rodal (NOR) 1:42.58	Hezekiel Sepeng (RSA) 1:42.74	Fred Onyancha (KEN) 1:42.79
2000	Nils Schumann (GER) 1:45.08	Wilson Kipketer (DEN) 1:45.14	Aissa Saïd-Guerni (ALG) 1:45.16
2004	Yuri Borzakovski (RUS) 1:44.45	Mbulaeni Mulaudzi (RSA) 1:44.61	Wilson Kipketer (DEN) 1:44.65

[1]Kerr was a Jamaican in the combined Antilles team

1500 Metres

1896	Edwin Flack (AUS) 4:33.2	Arthur Blake (USA) 4:34.0	Albin Lermusiaux (FRA) 4:36.0
1900	Charles bennett (GBR) 4:06.2	Henri Deloge (FRA) 4:06.6	John Bray (USA) 4:07.2
1904	James Lightbody (USA) 4:05.4	William Verner (USA) 4:06.8	Lacey Hearn (USA) dna
1906	James Lightbody (USA) 4:12.0	John McGough (GBR) 4:12.6	Kristian Hellström (SWE) 4:13.4
1908	Mel Sheppard (USA) 4:03.4	Harold Wilson (GBR) 4:03.6	Norman Hallows (GBR) 4:04.0
1912	Arnold Jackson (GBR) 3:56.8[1]	Abel Kiviat (USA) 3:56.9	Norman Taber (USA) 3:56.9
1920	Albert Hill (GBR) 4:01.8	Philip Baker (GBR) 4:02.4[2]	Lawrence Shields (USA) 4:03.1
1924	Paavo Nurmi (FIN) 3:53.6	Willy Schärer (SUI) 3:55.0	Henry Stallard (GBR) 3:55.6
1928	Harri Larva (FIN) 3:53.2	Jules Ladoumègue (FRA) 3:53.8	Eino Purje (FIN) 3:56.4
1932	Luigi Beccali (ITA) 3:51.2	John Cornes (GBR) 3:52.6	Phil Edwards (CAN) 3:52.8
1936	Jack Lovelock (NZL) 3:47.8	Glenn Cunningham (USA) 3:48.4	Luigi Beccali (ITA) 3:49.2
1948	Henry Eriksson (SWE) 3:49.8	Lennart Strand (SWE) 3:50.4	Willem Slijkhuis (NED) 3:50.4
1952	Josef Barthel (LUX) 3:45.1	Bob McMillen (USA) 3:45.2	Werner Lueg (GER) 3:45.4
1956	Ron Delany (IRL) 3:41.2	Klaus Richtzenhain (GER) 3:42.0	John Landy (AUS) 3:42.0
1960	Herb Elliott (AUS) 3:35.6	Michel Jazy (FRA) 3:38.4	István Rózsavölgyi (HUN) 3:39.2
1964	Peter Snell (NZL) 3:38.1	Josef Odlozil (TCH) 3:39.6	John Davies (NZL) 3:39.6
1968	Kipchoge Keino (KEN) 3:34.9	Jim Ryun (USA) 3:37.8	Bodo Tümmler (FRG) 3:39.0
1972	Pekka Vasala (FIN) 3:36.3	Kipchoge Keino (KEN) 3:36.8	Rod Dixon (NZL) 3:37.5
1976	John Walker (NZL) 3:39.2	Ivo Van Damme (BEL) 3:39.3	Paul-Heinz Wellmann (FRG) 3:39.3
1980	Sebastian Coe (GBR) 3:38.4	Jürgen Straub (GDR) 3:38.8	Steve Ovett (GBR) 3:39.0
1984	Sebastian Coe (GBR) 3:32.53	Steve Cram (GBR) 3:33.40	José Abascal (ESP) 3:34.30
1988	Peter Rono (KEN) 3:35.96	Peter Elliott (GBR) 3:36.15	Jens-Peter Herold (GDR) 3:36.21
1992	Fermin Cacho (ESP) 3:40.12	Rachid El Basir (MAR) 3:40.62	Mohamed Suleiman (QAT) 3:40.69
1996	Noureddine Morceli (ALG) 3:35.78	Fermin Cacho (ESP) 3:36.40	Stephen Kipkorir (KEN) 3:36.72
2000	Noah Ngeny (KEN) 3:32.07	Hicham El Guerrouj (MAR) 3:32.32	Bernard Lagat (KEN) 3:32.44
2004	Hicham El Guerrouj (MAR) 3:34.18	Bernard Lagat (KEN) 3:34.30	Rui Silva (POR) 3:34.68

[1]Jackson later changed his name to Strode-Jackson, and [2]Baker changed to Noel-Baker

5000 Metres

| 1912 | Hannes Kolehmainen (FIN) 14:36.6 | Jean Bouin (FRA) 14:36.7 | George Hutson (GBR) 15:07.6 |

Year	Gold	Silver	Bronze
1920	Joseph Guillemot (FRA) 14:55.6	Paavo Nurmi (FIN) 15:00.0	Erik Backman (SWE) 15:13.0
1924[1]	Paavo Nurmi (FIN) 14:31.2	Ville Ritola (FIN) 14:31.4	Edvin Wide (SWE) 15:01.8
1928	Ville Ritola (FIN) 14:38.0	Paavo Nurmi (FIN) 14:40.0	Edvin Wide (SWE) 14:41.2
1932	Lauri Lehtinen (FIN) 14:30.0	Ralph Hill (USA) 14:30.0	Lauri Virtanen (FIN) 14:44.0
1936	Gunnar Höckert (FIN) 14:22.2	Lauri Lehtinen (FIN) 14:25.8	Henry Jonsson (SWE) 14:29.0[2]
1948	Gaston Reiff (BEL) 14:17.6	Emil Zátopek (TCH) 14:17.8	Willem Slijkhuis (NED) 14:26.8
1952	Emil Zátopek (TCH) 14:06.6	Alain Mimoun (FRA) 14:07.4	Herbert Schade (GER) 14:08.6
1956	Vladimir Kuts (URS) 13:39.6	Gordon Pirie (GBR) 13:50.6	Derek Ibbotson (GBR) 13:54.4
1960	Murray Halberg (NZL) 13:43.4	Hans Grodotzki (GDR) 13:44.6	Kazimierz Zimny (POL) 13:44.8
1964	Bob Schul (USA) 13:48.8	Harald Norpoth (GER) 13:49.6	Bill Dellinger (USA) 13:49.8
1968	Mohamed Gammoudi (TUN) 14:05.0	Kipchoge Keino (KEN) 14:05.2	Naftali Temu (KEN) 14:06.4
1972	Lasse Viren (FIN) 13:26.4	Mohamed Gammoudi (TUN) 13:27.4	Ian Stewart (GBR) 13:27.6
1976	Lasse Viren (FIN) 13:24.8	Dick Quax (NZL) 13:25.2	Klaus-Peter Hildenbrand (FRG) 13:35.4
1980	Miruts Yifter (ETH) 13:21.0	Suleiman Nyambui (TAN) 13:21.6	Kaarlo Maaninka (FIN) 13:22.0
1984	Saïd Aouita (MAR) 13:05.59	Markus Ryffel (SUI) 13:07.54	Antonio Leitao (POR) 13:09.20
1988	John Ngugi (KEN) 13:11.70	Dieter Baumann (FRG) 13:15.52	Hansjörg Kunze (GDR) 13:15.73
1992	Dieter Baumann (GER) 13:12.52	Paul Bitok (KEN) 13:12.71	Fita Bayissa (ETH) 13:13.03
1996	Venuste Niyongabo (BDI) 13:07.96	Paul Bitok (KEN) 13:08.16	Khalid Boulami (MAR) 13:08.37
2000	Million Wolde (ETH) 13:35.49	Ali Said-Sief (ALG) 13:36.20	Brahim Lahlafi (MAR) 13:36.47
2004	Hicham El Guerrouj (MAR) 13:14.39	Kenenisa Bekele (ETH) 13:14.59	Eliud Kipchoge (KEN) 13:15.10

1896-1908 Event not held
[1]*Nurmi won the 5000m only 90 minutes after winning the 1500m;* [2]*Jonsson later changed his name to Kälarne*

10,000 Metres

Year	Gold	Silver	Bronze
1906[1]	Henry Hawtrey (GBR) 26:11.8	John Svanberg (SWE) 26:19.4	Edward Dahl (SWE) 26:26.2
1908[1]	Emil Voigt (GBR) 25:11.2	Edward Owen (GBR) 25:24.0	John Svanberg (SWE) 25:37.2
1912	Hannes Kolehmainen (FIN) 31:20.8	Louis Tewanima (USA) 32:06.6	Albin Stenroos (FIN) 32:21.8
1920	Paavo Nurmi (FIN) 31:45.8	Joseph Guillemot (FRA) 31:47.2	James Wilson (GBR) 31:50.8
1924	Ville Ritola (FIN) 30:23.2	Edvin Wide (SWE) 30:55.2	Eero Berg (FIN) 31:43.0
1928	Paavo Nurmi (FIN) 30:18.8	Ville Ritola (FIN) 30:19.4	Edvin Wide (SWE) 31:00.8
1932	Janusz Kusocinski (POL) 30:11.4	Volmari Iso-Hollo (FIN) 30:12.6	Lauri Virtanen (FIN) 30:35.0
1936	Ilmari Salminen (FIN) 30:15.4	Arvo Askola (FIN) 30:15.6	Volmari Iso-Hollo (FIN) 30:20.2
1948	Emil Zátopek (TCH) 29:59.6	Alain Mimoun (FRA) 30:47.4	Bertil Albertsson (SWE) 30:53.6
1952	Emil Zátopek (TCH) 29:17.0	Alain Mimoun (FRA) 29:32.8	Alexander Anufriyev (URS) 29:48.2
1956	Vladimir Kuts (URS) 28:45.6	József Kovács (HUN) 28:52.4	Allan Lawrence (AUS) 28:53.6
1960	Pyotr Bolotnikov (URS) 28:32.2	Hans Grodotzki (GDR) 28:37.0	David Power (AUS) 28:38.2[2]
1964	Billy Mills (USA) 28:24.4	Mohamed Gammoudi (TUN) 28:24.8	Ron Clarke (AUS) 28:25.8
1968	Naftali Temu (KEN) 29:27.4	Mamo Wolde (ETH) 29:28.0	Mohamed Gammoudi (TUN) 29:34.2
1972	Lasse Viren (FIN) 27:38.4	Emiel Puttemans (BEL) 27:39.6	Miruts Yifter (ETH) 27:41.0
1976	Lasse Viren (FIN) 27:44.4	Carlos Lopes (POR) 27:45.2	Brendan Foster (GBR) 27:54.9
1980	Miruts Yifter (ETH) 27:42.7	Kaarlo Maaninka (FIN) 27:44.3	Mohammed Kedir (ETH) 27:44.7
1984	Alberto Cova (ITA) 27:47.54	Mike McLeod (GBR) 28:06.22[3]	Mike Musyoki (KEN) 28:06.46
1988	Brahim Boutayeb (MAR) 27:21.46	Salvatore Antibo (ITA) 27:23.55	Kipkemboi Kimeli (KEN) 27:25.16
1992	Khalid Skah (MAR) 27:46.70	Richard Chelimo (KEN) 27:47.72	Adiis Abebe (ETH) 28:00.07
1996	Haile Gebrselassie (ETH) 27:07.34	Paul Tergat (KEN) 27:08.17	Salah Hissou (MAR) 27:24.67
2000	Haile Gebrselassie (ETH) 27:18.20	Paul Tergat (KEN) 27:18.29	Assefa Mezgebu (ETH) 27:19.75
2004	Kenenisa Bekele (ETH) 27:05.10	Sileshi Sihine (ETH) 27:09.39	Zersenay Tadesse (ERI) 27:22.57

1896-1908 Event not held
[1]*Held over 5 miles (8046m);* [2]*Recent investigation suggests 28:37.7;* [3]*Martti Vainio (FIN) finished second but failed a drug test*

Marathon

The length of the marathon was standardized from 1924 at the 1908 distance of 26 miles 385 yards (42,195m). Previously the distances had been: 1896 & 1904 – 40,000m, 1900 – 40,260m, 1906 – 41,860m, 1912 – 40,200m, 1920 – 42,750m

Year	Gold	Silver	Bronze
1896	Spyridon Louis (GRE) 2:58:50	Charilaos Vasilakos (GRE) 3:06:03	Gyula Kellner (HUN) 3:09:35
1900	Michel Theato (FRA)[1] 2:59:45	Emile Champion (FRA) 3:04:17	Ernst Fast (SWE) 3:36:14
1904	Thomas Hicks (USA) 3:28:35	Albert Coray (FRA)[2] 3:34:52	Arthur Newton (USA) 3:47:33
1906	William Sherring (CAN) 2:51:23.6	John Svanberg (SWE) 2:58:20.8	William Frank (USA) 3:00:46.8
1908[3]	John Hayes (USA) 2:55:18.4	Charles Hefferon (RSA) 2:56:06.0	Joseph Forshaw (USA) 2:57:10.4
1912	Kennedy McArthur (RSA) 2:36:54.8	Christian Gitsham (RSA) 2:37:52.0	Gaston Strobino (USA) 2:38:42.4
1920	Hannes Kolehmainen (FIN) 2:32:35.8	Jüri Lossman (EST) 2:32:48.6	Valerio Arri (ITA) 2:36:32.8
1924	Albin Stenroos (FIN) 2:41:22.6	Romeo Bertini (ITA) 2:47:19.6	Clarence DeMar (USA) 2:48:14.0
1928	Mohamed El Ouafi (FRA) 2:32:57	Miguel Plaza (CHI) 2:33:23	Martti Marttelin (FIN) 2:35:02
1932	Juan Carlos Zabala (ARG) 2:31:36	Sam Ferris (GBR) 2:31:55	Armas Toivonen (FIN) 2:32:12
1936	Sohn Kee-Chung (JPN)[4] 2:29:19.2	Ernest Harper (GBR) 2:31:23.2	Nam Seong-Yong (JPN)[4] 2:31:42:0
1948	Delfo Cabrera (ARG) 2:34:51.6	Tom Richards (GBR) 2:35:07.6	Etienne Gailly (BEL) 2:35:33.6

1952	Emil Zátopek (TCH) 2:23:03.2	Reinaldo Gorno (ARG) 2:25:35.0	Gustaf Jansson (SWE) 2:26:07.0
1956	Alain Mimoun (FRA) 2:25:00	Franjo Mihalic (YUG) 2:26:32	Velkko Karvonen (FIN) 2:27:47
1960	Abebe Bikila (ETH) 2:15:16.2	Rhadi Ben Abdesselem (MAR) 2:15:41.6	Barry Magee (NZL) 2:17:18.2
1964	Abebe Bikila (ETH) 2:12:11.2	Basil Heatley (GBR) 2:16:19.2	Kokichi Tsuburaya (JPN) 2:16:22.8
1968	Mamo Wolde (ETH) 2:20:26.4	Kenji Kimihara (JPN) 2:23:31.0	Michael Ryan (NZL) 2:23:45.0
1972	Frank Shorter (USA) 2:12:19.8	Karel Lismont (BEL) 2:14:31.8	Mamo Wolde (ETH) 2:15:08.4
1976	Waldemar Cierpinski (GDR) 2:09:55.0	Frank Shorter (USA) 2:10:45.8	Karel Lismont (BEL) 2:11:12.6
1980	Waldemar Cierpinski (GDR) 2:11:03	Gerard Nijboer (NED) 2:11:20	Satymkul Dzhumanazarov (URS) 2:11:35
1984	Carlos Lopes (POR) 2:09:21	John Treacy (IRL) 2:09:56	Charles Spedding (GBR) 2:09:58
1988	Gelindo Bordin (ITA) 2:10:32	Douglas Wakiihuri (KEN) 2:10:47	Ahmed Saleh (DJI) 2:10:59
1992	Hwang Young-cho (KOR) 2:2:13:23	Koichi Morishita (JPN) 2:13:45	Stephan Freigang (GER) 2:14:00
1996	Josiah Thugwane (RSA) 2:12:36	Bong-ju Lee (KOR) 2:12:39	Eric Wainaina (KEN) 2:12:44
2000	Gezahegne Abera (ETH) 2:10:11	Eric Wainaina (KEN) 2:10:31	Tesfaye Tola (ETH) 2:11:10
2004	Stefano Baldini (ITA) 2:10:55	Menbrahtom Keflezeghi (USA) 2:11:29	Vanderlei de Lima (BRA) 2:12:11

[1]Recently found to be of Luxembourg origin; [2]Usually shown incorrectly as American; [3]Dorando Pietri (ITA) finished first but was disqualified due to assistance by officials on last lap of the track; [4]Then known as Kitei Son and Shoryu Nan – both from Korea

3000 Metres Steeplechase

1900[1]	George Orton (CAN) 7:34.4	Sidney Robinson (GBR) 7:38.0	Jean Chastanié (FRA) 7:41.0
1900[2]	John Rimmer (GBR) 12:58.4	Charles Bennett (GBR) 12:58.6	Sidney Robinson (GBR) 12:58.8
1904[3]	James Lightbody (USA) 7:00.0	John Daly (GBR) 7:40.6	Arthur Newton (USA) 25m
1908[4]	Arthur Russell (GBR) 10:47.8	Archie Robertson (GBR) 10:48.4	John Eisele (USA) 11:00.8
1920	Percy Hodge (GBR) 10:00.4	Patrick Flynn (USA) 100m	Ernesto Ambrosini (ITA) 50m
1924	Ville Ritola (FIN) 9:33.6	Elias Katz (FIN) 9:44.0	Paul Bontemps (FRA) 9:45.2
1928	Tolvo Loukola (FIN) 9:21.8	Paavo Nurmi (FIN) 9:31.2	Ove Andersen (FIN) 9:35.6
1932[5]	Volmari Iso-Hollo (FIN) 10:33.4	Tom Evenson (GBR) 10:46.0	Joseph McCluskey (USA) 10:46.2
1936	Volmari Iso-Hollo (FIN) 9:03.8	Kaarlo Tuominen (FIN) 9:06.8	Alfred Dompert (GER) 9:07.2
1948	Tore Sjöstrand (SWE) 9:04.6	Erik Elmsäter (SWE) 9:08.2	Göte Hagström (SWE) 9:11.8
1952	Horace Ashenfelter (USA) 8:45.4	Vladimir Kazantsev (URS) 8:51.6	John Disley (GBR) 8:51.8
1956	Chris Brasher (GBR) 8:41.2	Sándor Rozsnói (HUN) 8:43.6	Ernst Larsen (NOR) 8:44.0
1960	Zdzslaw Krzyszkowiak (POL) 8:34.2	Nikolai Sokolov (URS) 8:36.4	Semyon Rzhischin (URS) 8:42.2
1964	Gaston Roelants (BEL) 8:30.8	Maurice Herriott (GBR) 8:32.4	Ivan Belyayev (URS) 8:33.8
1968	Amos Biwott (KEN) 8:51.0	Benjamin Kogo (KEN) 8:51.6	George Young (USA) 8:51.8
1972	Kipchoge Keino (KEN) 8:23.6	Benjamin Jipcho (KEN) 8:24.6	Tapio Kantanen (FIN) 8:24.8
1976	Anders Garderud (SWE) 8:08.0	Bronislaw Malinowski (POL) 8:09.1	Frank Baumgartl (GDR) 8:10.4
1980	Bronislaw malinowski (POL) 8:09.7	Filbert Bayi (TAN) 8:12.5	Eshetu Tura (ETH) 8:13.6
1984	Julius Korir (KEN) 8:11.80	Joseph Mahmoud (FRA) 8:13.31	Brian Diemer (USA) 8:14.06
1988	Julius Kariuki (KEN) 8:05.51	Peter Koech (KEN) 8:06.79	Mark Rowland (GBR) 8:07.96
1992	Matthew Birir (KEN) 8:08.84	Patrick Sang (KEN) 8:09.55	William Mutwol (KEN) 8:10.74
1996	Joseph Keter (KEN) 8:07.12	Moses Kiptanui (KEN) 8:08.33	Alessandro Lambruschini (ITA) 8:11.28
2000	Reuben Kosgei (KEN) 8:21.43	Wilson Boit Kipketer (KEN) 8:21.77	Ali Ezzine (MAR) 8:22.15
2004	Ezekiel Kemboi (KEN) 8:05.81	Brimin Kipruto (KEN) 8:06.11	Paul Koech (KEN) 8:06.64

1896, 1906, 1912 Event not held
[1]2500m, [2]4000m, [3]2590m, [4]3200m, [5]3460m in final due to lap scoring error. Iso-Hollo ran 9:14.6 in a heat

110 Metres Hurdles

1896	Thomas Curtis (USA) 17.6	Grantley Goulding (GBR) 18.0	– [1]
1900	Alvin Kraenzlein (USA) 15.4	John McLean (USA) 15.5	Fred Moloney (USA) 15.6
1904	Frederick Schule (USA) 16.0	Thadeus Shideler (USA) 16.3	Lesley Ashburner (USA) 16.4
1906	Robert Leavitt (USA) 16.2	Alfred Healoy (GBR) 16.2	Vincent Duncker (GER) 16.3[2]
1908	Forrest Smithson (USA) 15.0	John Garrels (USA) 15.7	Arthur Shaw (USA) 15.8
1912	Frederick Kelly (USA) 15.1	James Wendell (USA) 15.2	Martin Hawkins (USA) 15.3
1920	Earl Thomson (CAN) 14.8	Harold Barron (USA) 15.1	Frederick Murray (USA) 15.2
1924	Daniel Kinsey (USA) 15.0	Sydney Atkinson (RSA) 15.0	Sten Pettersson (SWE) 15.4
1928	Sydney Atkinson (RSA) 14.8	Stephen Anderson (USA) 14.8	John Collier (USA) 15.0
1932	George Saling (USA) 14.6 (14.57)	Percy Beard (USA) 14.7	Don Finlay (GBR) 14.8
1936	Forrest Towns (USA) 14.2	Don Finlay (GBR) 14.4	Fred Pollard (USA) 14.4
1948	William Porter (USA) 13.9	Clyde Scott (USA) 14.1	Craig Dixon (USA) 14.1
1952	Harrison Dillard (USA) 13.7 (13.91)	Jack Davis (USA) 13.7 (14.00)	Art Barnard (USA) 14.1 (14.40)
1956	Lee Calhoun (USA) 13.5 (13.70)	Jack Davis (USA) 13.5 (13.73)	Joel Shankle (USA) 14.1 (14.25)
1960	Lee Calhoun (USA) 13.8 (13.98)	Willie May (USA) 13.8 (13.99)	Hayes Jones (USA) 14.0 (14.17)
1964	Hayes Jones (USA) 13.6 (13.67)	Blaine Lindgren (USA) 13.7 (13.74)	Anatoli Mikhailov (URS) 13.7 (13.78)
1968	Willie Davenport (USA) 13.3 (13.33)	Ervin Hall (USA) 13.4 (13.42)	Eddy Ottoz (ITA) 13.4 (13.46)
1972	Rod Milburn (USA) 13.24	Guy Drut (FRA) 13.34	Tom Hill (USA) 13.48

1976	Guy Drut (FRA) 13.30	Alejandro Casanas (CUB) 13.33	Willie Davenport (USA) 13.38
1980	Thomas Munkelt (GDR) 13.39	Alejandro Casanas (CUB) 13.40	Alexander Puchkov (URS) 13.44
1984	Roger Kingdom (USA) 13.20	Greg Foster (USA) 13.23	Arto Bryggare (FIN) 13.40
1988	Roger Kingdom (USA) 12.98	Colin Jackson (GBR) 13.28	Tonie Campbell (USA) 13.38
1992	Mark McKoy (CAN) 13.12	Tony Dees (USA) 13.24	Jack Pierce (USA) 13.26
1996	Allen Johnson (USA) 12.95	Mark Crear (USA) 13.09	Florian Schwarthoff (GER) 13.17
2000	Anier Garcia (CUB) 13.00	Terrence Trammell (USA) 13.16	Mark Crear (USA) 13.22
2004	Liu Xiang (CHN) 12.91	Terrence Trammell (USA) 13.18	Anier Garcia (CUB) 13.20

[1]There were only two finallists; [2]Duncker often incorrectly shown as South African

400 Metres Hurdles

1900[1]	Walter Tewksbury (USA) 57.6	Henri Tauzin (FRA) 58.4e	George Orton (CAN) 58.9e
1904[2]	Harry Hillman (USA) 53.0	Frank Waller (USA) 53.2	George Poage (USA) 30m
1908	Charles Bacon (USA) 55.0	Harry Hillman (USA) 55.3	Leonard Tremeer (GBR) 57.0
1920	Frank Loomis (USA) 54.0	John Norton (USA) 54.3	August Desch (USA) 54.5
1924	Morgan Taylor (USA) 52.6[3]	Erik Vilén (FIN) 53.8	Ivan Riley (USA) 54.2
1928	Lord Burghley (GBR) 53.4	Frank Cuhel (USA) 53.6	Morgan Taylor (USA) 53.6
1932	Bob Tisdall (IRL) 51.7 (51.67)[3]	Glenn Hardin (USA) 51.9 (51.85)	Morgan Taylor (USA) 52.0 (51.96)
1936	Glenn Hardin (USA) 52.4	John Loaring (CAN) 52.7	Miguel White (PHI) 52.8
1948	Roy Cochran (USA) 51.1	Duncan White (SRI) 51.8	Rune Larsson (SWE) 52.2
1952	Charlie Moore (USA) 50.8 (51.06)	Yuri Lituyev (URS) 51.3 (51.51)	John Holland (NZL) 52.2 (52.26)
1956	Glenn Davis (USA) 50.1 (50.29)	Eddie Southern (USA) 50.8 (50.94)	Josh Culbreath (USA) 51.6 (51.74)
1960	Glenn Davis (USA) 49.3 (49.51)	Cliff Cushman (USA) 49.6 (49.77)	Dick Howard (USA) 49.7 (49.90)
1964	Rex Cawley (USA) 49.6	John Cooper (GBR) 50.1	Salvatore Morale (ITA) 50.1
1968	David Hemery (GBR) 48.1 (48.12)	Gerhard Hennige (FRG) 49.0 (49.02)	John Sherwood (GBR) 49.0 (49.03)
1972	John Akii-Bua (UGA) 47.82	Ralph Mann (USA) 48.51	David Hemery (GBR) 48.52
1976	Edwin Moses (USA) 47.64[4]	Mike Shine (USA) 48.69	Yevgeni Gavrilenko (URS) 49.45
1980	Volker Beck (GDR) 48.70	Vasili Arkhipenko (URS) 48.86	Gary Oakes (GBR) 49.11
1984	Edwin Moses (USA) 47.75	Danny Harris (USA) 48.13	Harald Schmid (FRG) 48.19
1988	Andre Phillips (USA) 47.19	Amadou Dia Ba (SEN) 47.23	Edwin Moses (USA) 47.56
1992	Kevin Young (USA) 46.78	Winthrop Graham (JAM) 47.66	Kriss Akabusi (GBR) 47.82
1996	Derrick Adkins (USA) 47.54	Samuel Matete (ZAM) 47.78	Calvin Davis (USA) 47.96
2000	Angelo Taylor (USA) 47.50	Hadi Al-Somaily (KSA) 47.53	Llewellyn Herbert (RSA) 47.81
2004	Felix Sanchez (DOM) 47.63	Danny McFarlane (JAM) 48.11	Naman Keita (FRA) 48.26

1896,1906,1912 Event not held
[1]Tenth barrier was a water jump; [2]Hurdles 2ft 6in (76.2cm) high instead of usual 3ft (91.4cm); [3]Record not allowed because hurdle knocked down; [4]Recent rescrutiny of the photo-finish film indicates that the time was 47.63

4x100 Metres Relay

1912	Great Britain 42.4	Sweden 42.6[1]	—
1920	United States 42.2	France 42.6	Sweden 42.9
1924	United States 41.0	Great Britain 41.2	Netherlands 41.8
1928	United States 41.0	Germany 41.2	Great Britain 41.8
1932	United States 40.0 (40.10)	Germany 40.9	Italy 41.2
1936	United States 39.8	Italy 41.1	Germany 41.2
1948	United States 40.6[2]	Great Britain 41.3	Italy 41.5
1952	United States 40.1 (40.26)	Soviet Union 40.3 (40.58)	Hungary 40.5 (40.83)
1956	United States 39.5 (39.60)	Soviet Union 39.8 (39.92)	Germany 40.3 (40.34)
1960	Germany 39.5 (39.66)[3]	Soviet Union 40.1 (40.24)	Great Britain 40.2 (40.32)
1964	United States 39.0 (39.06)	Poland 39.3 (39.36)	France 39.3 (39.36)
1968	United States 38.2 (38.24)	Cuba 38.3 (38.40)	France 38.4 (38.43)
1972	United States 38.19	Soviet Union 38.50	FRG 38.79
1976	United States 38.33	GDR 38.66	Soviet Union 38.78
1980	Soviet Union 38.26	Poland 38.33	France 38.53
1984	United States 37.83	Jamaica 38.62	Canada 38.70
1988	Soviet Union 38.19	Great Britain 38.28	France 38.40
1992	United States 37.40	Nigeria 37.98	Cuba 38.00
1996	Canada 37.69	United States 38.05	Brazil 38.41
2000	United States 37.61	Brazil 37.90	Cuba 38.04
2004	Great Britain 38.07	United States 38.08	Nigeria 38.23

1896-1908 Event not held
[1]Germany finished second but was disqualified; [2]United States originally disqualified but later reinstated; [3]United States finished first (39.60) but was disqualified

4x400 Metres Relay

1908[1]	United States 3:29.4	Germany 3:32.4	Hungary 3:32.5

1912	United States 3:16.6	France 3:20.7	Great Britain 3:23.2
1920	Great Britain 3:22.2	South Africa 3:24.2	France 3:24.8
1924	United States 3:16.0	Sweden 3:17.0	Great Britain 3:17.4
1928	United States 3:14.2	Germany 3: 14.8	Canada 3:15.4
1932	United States 3:08.2 (3:08.14)	Great Britain 3:11.2	Canada 3:12.8
1936	Great Britain 3:09.0	United States 3:11.0	Germany 3:11.8
1948	United States 3:10.4	France 3:14.8	Sweden 3:16.3
1952	Jamaica 3:03.9 (3:04.04)	United States 3:04.0 (3:04.21)	Germany 3:06.6 (3:06.78)
1956	United States 3:04.8 (3:04.81)	Australia 3:06.2 (3:06.19)	Great Britain 3:07.2 (3:07.19)
1960	United States 3:02.2 (3:02.37)	Germany 3:02.7 (3:02,84)	BWI² 3.04.0 (3:04.13)
1964	United States 3:00.7	Great Britain 3:01.6	Trinidad & Tobago 3:01.7
1968	United States 2:56.1 (2:56.16)	Kenya 2:59.6 (2:59.64)	FRG 3:5 (3:00.57)
1972	Kenya 2:59.83	Great Britain 3:00.46	France 3:00.65
1976	United States 2:58.65	Poland 3:01.43	FRG 3:01.98
1980	Soviet Union 3:01.08	GDR 3:01.26	Italy 3:04.3
1984	United States 2:57.91	Great Britain 2:59.13	Nigeria 2:59.32
1988	United States 2:56.16	Jamaica 3:00.30	FRG 3:00.56
1992	United States 2:55.74	Cuba 2:59.51	Great Britain 2:59.73
1996	United states 2:55.99	Great Britain 2:56.60	Jamaica 2:59.42
2000	United States 2:56.35³	Nigeria 2:58.68	Jamaica 2:58.78
2004	United States 2:55.91	Australia 3:00.60	Nigeria 3:00.90

1896-1906 Event not held
¹Medley relay – 200m, 200m, 400m, 800m; ²British West Indies team, comprising three from Jamaica and one from Barbados; ³The USA was later disqualified, due to one of their runners in a preliminary round having failed a drug test earlier, but on appeal the final team was reinstated

20,000 Metres Road Walk

1956	Leonid Spirin (URS) 1:31.27.4	Antonas Mikenas (URS) 1:32:03.0	Bruno Junk (URS) 1:32:12.0
1960	Vladimir Golubnichi (URS) 1:34:07.2	Noel Freeman (AUS) 1:34:16.4	Stan Vickers (GBR) 1:34:56.4
1964	Ken Matthews (GBR) 1:29:34 0	Dieter Lindner (GER) 1:31:13.2	Vladimir Golubnichi (URS) 1:31:59.4
1968	Vladimir Golubnichi (URS) 1:33:58.4	José Pedraza (MEX) 1:34:00.0	Nikolai Smaga (URS) 1:34:03.4
1972	Peter Frenkel (GDR) 1:26:42.4	Vladimir Golubnichi (URS) 1:26:55.2	Hans Reimann (GDR) 1:27:16.6
1976	Daniel Batista (MEX) 1:24:40.6	Hans Reimann (GDR) 1:25:13.8	Peter Frenkel (GDR) 1h:25:29.4
1980	Maurizio Damilano (ITA) 1:23:35.5	Pyotr Pochenchuk (URS) 1:24:45.4	Roland Wieser (GDR) 1:25:58.2
1984	Ernesto Canto (MEX) 1:23:13	Raul Gonzalez (MEX) 1:23:20	Maurizio Damilano (ITA) 1:23:26
1988	Jozef Pribilinec (TCH) 1:19:57	Ronald Weigel (GDR) 1:20:00	Maurizio Damilano (ITA) 1:20:14
1992	Daniel Plaza (ESP) 1:21:45	Guillaume Leblanc (CAN) 1:22:25	Giovanni de Benedictis (ITA) 1:23:11
1996	Jefferson Perez (ECU) 1:20:07	Ilya Markov (RUS) 1:20:16	Bernardo Segura (MEX) 1:20:23
2000	Robert Korzeniowski (POL) 1:18:59	Noé Hernandez (MEX) 1:19:03	Vladimir Andreyev (RUS)1:19:27
2004	Ivano Brugnetti (ITA) 1:19:40	Francisco Hernandez (ESP) 1:19:45	Nathan Deakes (AUS) 1:20:02

1896-1952 Event not held

50,000 Metres Road Walk

1932	Thomas Green (GBR) 4:50:10	Janis Dalinsh (LAT) 4:57:20	Ugo Frigerio (ITA) 4:59:06
1936	Harold Whitlock (GBR) 4:30:41.1	Arthur Schwab (SUI) 4:32:09.2	Adalberts Bubenko (LAT) 4:32:42.2
1948	John Ljunggren (SWE) 4:41:52	Gaston Godel (SUI) 4:48:17	Tebbs Lloyd Johnson (GBR) 4:48:31
1952	Giuseppe Dordoni (ITA) 4:28:07.8	Josef Dolezal (TCH) 4:30:17.8	Antal Róka (HUN) 4:31:27.2
1956	Norman Read (NZL) 4:30:42.8	Yevgeni Maskinskov (URS) 4:32:57.0	John Ljunggren (SWE) 4:35:02.0
1960	Don Thompson (GBR) 4:25:30.0	John Ljunggren (SWE) 4:25:47.0	Abdon Pamich (ITA) 4:27:55.4
1964	Abdon Pamich (ITA) 4:11:12.4	Paul Nihill (GBR) 4:11:31.2	Ingvar Pettersson (SWE) 4:14:17.4
1968	Christoph Höhne (GDR) 4:20:13.6	Antal Kiss (HUN) 4:30:17.0	Larry Young (USA) 4:31:55.4
1972	Bernd Kannenberg (FRG) 3:56:11.6	Venjamin Soldatenko (URS) 3:58:24.0	Larry Young (USA) 4:00:46.0
1980	Hartwig Gauder (GDR) 3:49:24	Jorge Llopart (ESP) 3:51:25	Yevgeni Ivchenko (URS) 3:56:32
1984	Raul Gonzalez (MEX) 3:47:26	Bo Gustafsson (SWE) 3:53:19	Sandro Bellucci (ITA) 3:53:45
1988	Vyacheslav Ivanenko (URS) 3:38:29	Ronald Weigel (GDR) 3:38:56	Hartwig Gauder (GDR) 3:39:45
1992	Andrei Perlov (EUN) 3:50:13	Carlos Mercenario (MEX) 3:52:09	Ronald Weigel (GER) 3:53:45
1996	Robert Korzeniowski (POL) 3:43:30	Mikhail Shchennikov (RUS) 3:43:46	Valentin Massana (ITA) 3:44:19
2000	Robert Korzeniowski (POL) 3:42:21	Aigars Fadejevs (LAT) 3:43:40	Joel Sanchez (MEX) 3:44:35
2004	Robert Korzeniowski (POL) 3:38:46	Denis Nizhegorodov (RUS) 3:42:50	Alexei Voyevodin (RUS) 3:43:34

1896-1928, 1976 Event not held

High Jump

1896	Ellery Clark (USA) 1.81	James Connolly (USA) 1.65	–
	Robert Garrett (USA) 1.65		
1900	Irving Baxter (USA) 1.90	Patrick Leahy (GBR) 1.78	Lajos Gönczy (HUN) 1.75
1904	Samuel Jones (USA) 1.80	Garrett Serviss (USA) 1.77	Paul Weinstein (GER) 1.77

Year	Gold	Silver	Bronze
1906	Con Leahy (GBR) 1.77 Themistoklis Diakidis (GRE) 1.72	Lajos Gönczy (HUN) 1.75	Herbert Kerrigan (USA) 1.72
1908	Harry Porter (USA) 1.905 István Somodi (HUN) 1.88 Georges André (FRA) 1.88	Con Leahy (GBR) 1.88	–
1912	Alma Richards (USA) 1.93	Hans Liesche (GER) 1.91	George Horine (USA) 1.89
1920	Richmond Landon (USA) 1.94	Harold Muller (USA) 1.90	Bo Ekelund (SWE) 1.90
1924	Harold Osborn (USA) 1.98	Leroy Brown (USA) 1.95	Pierre Lewden (FRA) 1.92
1928	Robert King (USA) 1.94	Ben Hedges (USA) 1.91	Claude Ménard (FRA) 1.91
1932	Duncan MacNaughton (CAN) 1.97	Robert Van Osdel (USA) 1.97	Simeon Toribio (PHI) 1.97
1936	Cornelius Johnson (USA) 2.03	David Albritton (USA) 2.00	Delos Thurber (USA) 2.00
1948	John Winter (AUS) 1.98	Björn Paulsen (NOR) 1.95	George Stanich (USA) 1.95
1952	Walt Davis (USA) 2.04	Ken Wiesner (USA) 2.01	Jose Telles da Conceicao (BRA) 1.98
1956	Charlie Dumas (USA) 2.12	Chilla Porter (AUS) 2.10	Igor Kashkarov (URS) 2.08
1960	Robert Shavlakadze (URS) 2.16	Valeri Brumel (URS) 2.16	John Thomas (USA) 2.14
1964	Valeri Brumel (URS) 2.18	John Thomas (USA) 2.18	John Rambo (USA) 2.16
1968	Dick Fosbury (USA) 2.24	Ed Caruthers (USA) 2.22	Valentin Gavrilov (URS) 2.20
1972	Jüri Tarmak (URS) 2.23	Stefan Junge (GDR) 2.21	Dwight Stones (USA) 2.21
1976	Jacek Wszola (POL) 2.25	Greg Joy (CAN) 2.23	Dwight Stones (USA) 2.21
1980	Gerd Wessig (GDR) 2.36	Jacek Wszola (POL) 2.31	Jörg Freimuth (GDR) 2.31
1984	Dietmar Mögenburg (FRG) 2.35	Patrik Sjöberg (SWE) 2.33	Zhu Jianhua (CHN) 2.31
1988	Gennadi Avdeyenko (URS) 2.38 Patrik Sjöberg (SWE) 2.36	Hollis Conway (USA) 2.36	Rudolf Povarnitsin (URS) 2.36
1992	Javier Sotomayor (CUB) 2.34 Tim Forsythe (AUS) 2.34 Artur Partyka (POL) 2.34	Patrik Sjöberg (SWE) 2.34	Hollis Conway (USA) 2.34
1996	Charles Austin (USA) 2.39	Artur Partyka (POL) 2.37	Steve Smith (GBR) 2.35
2000	Sergei Klyugin (RUS) 2.35	Javier Sotomayor (CUB) 2.32	Abderahmane Hammad (ALG) 2.32
2004	Stefan Strand (SWE) 2.36	Matt Hemingway (USA) 2.34	Jarislav Baba (CZE) 2.34

Pole Vault

Year	Gold	Silver	Bronze
1896	William Hoyt (USA) 3.30 Vasilios Xydas (GRE) 2.60 Evangelos Damaskos (GRE) 2.60	Albert Tyler (USA) 3.20	Ioannis Theodoropoulos (GRE) 2.60
1900	Irving Baxter (USA) 3.30	Meredith Colkett (USA) 3.25	Carl-Albert Andersen (NOR) 3.20
1904	Charles Dvorak (USA) 3.50	LeRoy Samse (USA) 3.43	Louis Wilkins (USA) 3.43
1906	Fernand Gonder (FRA) 3.50	Bruno Söderstrom (SWE) 3.40	Edward Glover (USA) 3.35
1908	Edward Cooke (USA) 3.70 Alfred Gilbert (USA) 3.70	– Bruno Söderstrom (SWE) 3.58 Charles Jacobs (USA) 3.58	Edward Archibald (CAN) 3.58
1912	Harry Babcock (USA) 3.95	Frank Nelson (USA) 3.85 Marcus Wright (USA) 3.85	Bertil Uggla (SWE) 3.80 William Hapenny (CAN) 3.80 Frank Murphy (USA) 3.80
1920	Frank Foss (USA) 4.09	Henry Petersen (DEN) 3.70	Edwin Meyers (USA) 3.60
1924	Lee Barnes (USA) 3.95	Glenn Graham (USA) 3.95	James Brooker (USA) 3.90
1928	Sabin Carr (USA) 4.20	William Droegemuller (USA) 4.10	Charles McGinnis (USA) 3.95
1932	William Miller (USA) 4.31	Shuhei Nishida (JPN) 4.30	George Jefferson (USA) 4.20
1936	Earle Meadows (USA) 4.35	Shuhei Nishida (JPN) 4.25[1]	Sueo Oe (JPN) 4.25m[1]
1948	Guinn Smith (USA) 4.30	Erkki Kataja (FIN) 4.20	Bob Richards (USA) 4.20
1952	Bob Richards (USA) 4.55	Don Laz (USA) 4.50	Ragnar Lundberg (SWE) 4.20
1956	Bob Richards (USA) 4.56	Bob Gutowski (USA) 4.53	Georgios Roubanis (GRE) 4.50
1960	Don Bragg (USA) 4.70	Ron Morris (USA) 4.60	Eeles Landstrom (FIN) 4.55
1964	Fred Hansen (USA) 5.10	Wolfgang Reinhardt (GER) 5.05	Klaus Lehnertz (GER) 5.00
1968	Bob Seagren (USA) 5.40	Claus Schiprowski (FRG) 5.40	Wolfgang Nordwig (GDR) 5.40
1972	Wolfgang Nordwig (GDR) 5.50	Bob Seagren (USA) 5.40	Jan Johnson (USA) 5.35
1976	Tadeusz Slusarski (POL) 5.50	Antti Kalliomaki (FIN) 5.50	David Roberts (USA) 5.50
1980	Wladislaw Kozakiewicz (POL) 5.78 Konstantin Volkov (URS) 5.65	Tadeusz Slusarski (POL) 5.65	–
1984	Pierre Quinon (FRA) 5.75	Mike Tully (USA) 5.65	Earl Bell (USA) 5.60 Thierry Vigneron (FRA) 5.60
1988	Sergei Bubka (URS) 5.90	Rodion Gataullin (URS) 5.85	Grigori Yegorov (URS) 5.80
1992	Maksim Tarasov (EUN) 5.80	Igor Trandenkov (EUN) 5.80	Javier Garcia (CUB) 5.75
1996	Jean Galfione (FRA) 5.92	Igor Trandenkov (RUS) 5.92	Andrei Tivontchik (GER) 5.92
2000	Nick Hysong (USA) 5.90	Lawrence Johnson (USA) 5.90	Maksin Tarasov (RUS) 5.90
2004	Timothy Mack (USA) 5.95	Toby Stevenson (USA) 5.90	Giuseppe Gibilisco (ITA) 5.85

[1]Nishida and Oe refused to jump-off and decided places by lot

Long Jump

1896	Ellery Clark (USA) 6.35	Robert Garrett (USA) 6.18	James Connolly (USA) 6.11
1900	Alvin Kraenzlein (USA) 7.18	Myer Prinstein (USA) 7.17	Patrick Leahy (GBR) 6.95
1904	Myer Prinstein (USA) 7.34	Daniel Frank (USA) 6.89	Robert Stangland (USA) 6.88
1906	Myer Prinstein (USA) 7.20	Peter O'Connor (GBR) 7.02	Hugo Friend (USA) 6.96
1908	Francis Irons (USA) 7.48	Daniel Kelly (USA) 7.09	Calvin Bricker (CAN) 7.08
1912	Albert Guttersson (USA) 7.60	Calvin Bricker (CAN) 7.21	Georg Aberg (SWE) 7.18
1920	William Pettersson (SWE) 7.15	Carl Johnson (USA) 7.09	Erik Abrahamsson (SWE) 7.08
1924	William DeHart Hubbard (USA) 7.44	Ed Gourdin (USA) 7.27	Sverre Hansen (NOR) 7.26
1928	Edward Hamm (USA) 7.73	Silvio Cator (HAI) 7.58	Alfred Bates (USA) 7.40
1932	Ed Gordon (USA) 7.63	Lambert Redd (USA) 7.60	Chuhei Nambu (JPN) 7.44
1936	Jesse Owens (USA) 8.06	Luz Long (GER) 7.87	Naoto Tajima (JPN) 7.74
1948	Willie Steele (USA) 7.82	Theodore Bruce (AUS) 7.55	Herbert Douglas (USA) 7.54
1952	Jerome Biffle (USA) 7.57	Meredith Gourdine (USA) 7.53	Odön Földessy (HUN) 7.30
1956	Greg Bell (USA) 7.83	John Bennett (USA) 7.68	Jorma Valkama (FIN) 7.48
1960	Ralph Boston (USA) 8.12	Irvin Roberson (USA) 8.11	Igor Ter-Ovanesian (URS) 8.04
1964	Lynn Davies (GBR) 8.07	Ralph Boston (USA) 8.03	Igor Ter-Ovanesian (URS) 7.99
1968	Bob Beamon (USA) 8.90	Klaus Beer (GDR) 8.19	Ralph Boston (USA) 8.16
1972	Randy Williams (USA) 8.24	Hans Baumgartner (FRG) 8.18	Arnie Robinson (USA) 8.03
1976	Arnie Robinson (USA) 8.35	Randy Williams (USA) 8.11	Frank Wartenberg (GDR) 8.02
1980	Lutz Dombrowski (GDR) 8.54	Frank Paschek (GDR) 8.21	Valeri Podluzhni (URS) 8.18
1984	Carl Lewis (USA) 8.54	Gary Honey (AUS) 8.24	Giovanni Evangelisti (ITA) 8.24
1988	Carl Lewis (USA) 8.72	Mike Powell (USA) 8.49	Larry Myricks (USA) 8.27
1992	Carl Lewis (USA) 8.67	Mike Powell (USA) 8.64	Joe Greene (USA) 8.34
1996	Carl Lewis (USA) 8.50	James Beckford (JAM) 8.29	Joe Greene (USA) 8.24
2000	Ivan Pedroso (CUB) 8.55	Jai Taurima (AUS) 8.49	Roman Shchurenko (UKR) 8.31
2004	Dwight Phillips (USA) 8.59	John Moffitt (USA) 8.47	Joan Lino Martinez (ESP) 8.32

Triple Jump

Formerly known as the Hop, Step and Jump

1896[1]	James Connolly (USA) 10.71	Alexandre Tuffere (FRA) 12.70	Ioannis Persakis (GRE) 12.52
1900	Myer Prinstein (USA) 14.47	James Connolly (USA) 13.97	Lewis Sheldon (USA) 13.64
1904	Myer Prinstein (USA) 14.35	Frederick Englehardt (USA) 13.90	Robert Stangland (USA) 13.36
1906	Peter O'Connor (GBR) 14.07	Con Leahy (GBR) 13.98	Thomas Cronan (USA) 13.70
1908	Tim Ahearne (GBR) 14.92	Garfield McDonald (CAN) 14.76	Edvard Larsen (NOR) 14.39
1912	Gustaf Lindblom (SWE) 14.76	Georg Aberg (SWE) 14.51	Erik Amlöf (SWE) 14.17
1920	Vilho Tuulos (FIN) 14.50	Folke Jansson (SWE) 14.48	Erik Amlöf (SWE) 14.27
1924	Anthony Winter (AUS) 15.52	Luis Brunetto (ARG) 15.42	Vilho Tuulos (FIN) 15.37
1928	Mikio Oda (JPN) 15.21	Levi Casey (USA) 15.17	Vilho Tuulos (FIN) 15.11
1932	Chuhei Nambu (JPN) 15.72	Erik Svensson (SWE) 15.32	Kenkichi Oshima (JPN) 15.12
1936	Naoto Tajima (JPN) 16.00	Masao Harada (JPN) 15.66	John Metcalfe (AUS) 15.50
1948	Arne Ahman (SWE) 15.40	George Avery (AUS) 15.36	Ruhi Sarialp (TUR) 15.02
1952	Adhemar Ferreira de Silva (BRA) 16.22	Leonid Shcherbakov (URS) 15.98	Arnoldo Devonish (VEN) 15.52
1956	Adhemar Ferreira da Silva (BRA) 16.35	Vilhjalmur Einarsson (ISL) 16.26	Vitold Kreyer (URS) 16.02
1960	Jozef Schmidt (POL) 16.81	Vladimir Goryayev (URS) 16.63	Vitold Kreyer (URS) 16.43
1964	Jozef Schmidt (POL) 16.85	Oleg Fedoseyev (URS) 16.58	Viktor Kravchenko (URS) 16.57
1968	Viktor Saneyev (URS) 17.39	Nelson Prudencio (BRA) 17.27	Giuseppe Gentile (ITA) 17.22
1972	Viktor Saneyev (URS) 17.35	Jörg Drehmel (GDR) 17.31	Nelson Prudencio (BRA) 17.05
1976	Viktor Saneyev (URS) 17.29	James Butts (USA) 17.18	João de Oliveira (BRA) 16.90
1980	Jaak Uudmae (URS) 17.35	Viktor Saneyev (URS) 17.24	João de Oliveira (BRA) 17.22
1984	Al Joyner (USA) 17.26	Mike Conley (USA) 17.18	Keith Connor (GBR) 16.87
1988	Khristo Markov (BUL) 17.61	Igor Lapshin (URS) 17.52	Alexander Kovalenko (URS) 17.42
1992	Mike Conley (USA) 18.17	Charles Simkins (USA) 17.60	Frank Rutherford (BAH) 17.36
1996	Kenny Harrison (USA) 18.09	Jonathan Edwards (GBR) 17.88	Yoelbi Quesada (CUB) 17.44
2000	Jonathan Edwards (GBR) 17.71	Yoel Garcia (CUB) 17.47	Denis Kapustin (RUS) 17.46
2004	Christian Olsson (SWE) 17.79	Marian Oprea (ROM) 17.55	Danila Burkenya (RUS) 17.48

[1]Winner took two hops with his right foot, contrary to present rules

Shot

1896[1]	Robert Garrett (USA) 11.22	Miltiades Gouskos (GRE) 11.15	Georgios Papasideris (GRE) 10.36
1900[1]	Richard Sheldon (USA) 14.10	Josiah McCracken (USA) 12.85	Robert Garrett (USA) 12.37
1904[1]	Ralph Rose (USA) 14.81	Wesley Coe (USA) 14.40	Leon Feuerbach (USA) 13.37
1906	Martin Sheridan (USA) 12.32	Mihály Dávid (HUN) 11.83	Eric Lemming (SWE) 11.26
1908	Ralph Rose (USA) 14.21	Dennis Horgan (GBR) 13.61	John Garrels (USA) 13.18
1912	Patrick McDonald (USA) 15.34	Ralph Rose (USA) 15.25	Lawrence Whitney (USA) 13.93
1920	Ville Pörhölä (FIN) 14.81	Elmer Niklander (FIN) 14.155	Harry Liversedge (USA) 14.15

1924	Clarence Houser (USA) 14.99	Glenn Hartranft (USA) 14.89	Ralph Hills (USA) 14.64
1928	John Kuck (USA) 15.87	Herman Brix (USA) 15.75	Emil Hirschfield (GER) 15.72
1932	Leo Sexton (USA) 16.00	Harlow Rothert (USA) 15.67	Frantisek Douda (TCH) 15.60
1936	Hans Woellke (GER) 16.20	Sulo Bärlund (FIN) 16.12	Gerhard Stöck (GER) 15.66
1948	Wilbur Thompson (USA) 17.12	Jim Delaney (USA) 16.68	Jim Fuchs (USA) 16.42
1952	Parry O'Brien (USA) 17.41	Darrow Hooper (USA) 17.39	Jim Fuchs (USA) 17.06
1956	Parry O'Brien (USA) 18.57	Bill Nieder (USA) 18.18	Jiri Skobla (TCH) 17.65
1960	Bill Nieder (USA) 19.68	Parry O'Brien (USA) 19.11	Dallas Long (USA) 19.01
1964	Dallas Long (USA) 20.33	Randy Matson (USA) 20.20	Vilmos Varju (HUN) 19.39
1968	Randy Matson (USA) 20.54	George Woods (USA) 20.12	Eduard Gushchin (URS) 20.09
1972	Wladyslaw Komar (POL) 21.18	George Woods (USA) 21.17	Hartmut Briesenick (GDR) 21.14
1976	Udo Beyer (GDR) 21.05	Yevgeni Mironov (URS) 21.03	Alexander Baryshnikov (URS) 21.00m
1980	Volodomir Kiselyev (URS) 21.25	Alexander Baryshnikov (URS) 21.08	Udo Beyer (GDR) 21.06
1984	Alessandro Andrei (ITA) 21.26	Michael Carter (USA) 21.09	Dave Laut (USA) 20.97
1988	Ulf Timmermann (GDR) 22.47	Randy Barnes (USA) 22.39	Werner Günthör (SUI) 21.99
1992	Mike Stulce (USA) 21.70	James Doehring (USA) 20.96	Vyacheslav Lykho (EUN) 20.94
1996	Randy Barnes (USA) 21.62	John Godina (USA) 20.79	Alexander Bagach (UKR) 20.75
2000	Arsi Harju (FIN) 21.29	Adam Nelson (USA) 21.21	John Godina (USA) 21.20
2004	Yuri Bilinog (UKR) 21.16	Adam Nelson (USA) 21.16	Joachim Olsen (DEN) 21.07

[1]In 1896, 1900 & 1904 competition was from a 7ft (2.13m) square

Discus

1896[1]	Robert Garrett (USA) 29.15	Pan. Paraskevopoulos (GRE) 28.95	Sotirios Versis (GRE) 28.78
1900[1]	Rudolf Bauer (HUN) 36.04	Frantisek Janda-Suk (BOH) 35.25	Richard Sheldon (USA) 34.60
1904[2]	Martin Sheridan (USA) 39.28	Ralph Rose (USA) 39.28	Nicolaos Georgantas (GRE) 37.68
1906	Martin Sheridan (USA) 41.46	Nicolaos Georgantas (GRE) 38.06	Werner Järvinen (FIN) 36.82
1908	Martin Sheridan (USA) 40.89	Merritt Griffin (USA) 40.70	Marquis Horr (USA) 39.44
1912	Armas Taipale (FIN) 45.21	Richard Byrd (USA) 42.32	James Duncan (USA) 42.28
1920	Elmer Niklander (FIN) 44.68	Armas Taipale (FIN) 44.19	Augustus Pope (USA) 42.13
1924	Clarence Houser (USA) 46.15	Vilho Niittymaa (FIN) 44.95	Thomas Lieb (USA) 44.83
1928	Clarence Houser (USA) 47.32m	Antero Kivi (FIN) 47.23	James Corson (USA) 47.10
1932	John Anderson (USA) 49.49	Henri Laborde (USA) 48.47	Paul Winter (FRA) 47.85
1936	Ken Carpenter (USA) 50.48	Gordon Dunn (USA) 49.36	Giorgio Oberweger (ITA) 49.23
1948	Adolfo Consolini (ITA) 52.78	Giuseppe Tosi (ITA) 51.78	Fortune Gordien (USA) 50.77
1952	Sim Iness (USA) 55.03	Adolfo Consolini (ITA) 53.78	James Dillion (USA) 52.38
1956	Al Oerter (USA) 56.36	Fortune Gordien (USA) 54.81	Des Koch (USA) 54.40
1960	Al Oerter (USA) 59.18	Rink Babka (USA) 58.02	Dick Cochran (USA) 57.16
1964	Al Oerter (USA) 61.00	Ludvik Danek (TCH) 60.52	Dave Weill (USA) 59.49
1968	Al Oerter (USA) 64.78	Lothar Milde (GDR) 63.08	Ludvik Danek (TCH) 62.92
1972	Ludvik Danek (TCH) 64.40	Jay Silvester (USA) 63.50	Ricky Bruch (SWE) 63.40
1976	Mac Wilkins (USA) 67.50	Wolfgang Schmidt (GDR) 66.22	John Powell (USA) 65.70
1980	Viktor Rashchupkin (URS) 66.64	Imrich Bugár (TCH) 66.38	Luis Delis (CUB) 66.32
1984	Rolf Danneberg (FRG) 66.60	Mac Wilkins (USA) 66.30	John Powell (USA) 65.46
1988	Jürgen Schult (GDR) 68.82	Romas Ubartas (URS) 67.48	Rolf Danneberg (FRG) 67.38
1992	Romas Ubartas (LTU) 65.12	Jürgen Schult (GER) 64.94	Roberto Moya (CUB) 64.12
1996	Lars Riedel (GER) 69.40	Vladimir Dubrovchik (BLR) 66.60	Vasili Kaptyukh (BLR) 65.80
2000	Virgilijus Alekna (LTU) 69.30	Lars Riedel (GER) 68.50	Frantz Kruger (RSA) 68.19
2004	Virgilijus Alekna (LTU) 69.89m[3]	Zoltán Kövágó (HUN) 67.94	Alexander Tammert (EST) 66.66

[1]1896-1900 competitions from 2.50m circle; [2]First place decided by throw-off; [3]Robert Fazekas (HUN) threw 70.93m but was disqualified

Hammer

1900[1]	John Flanagan (USA) 49.73	Truxton Hare (USA) 49.13	Josiah McCracken (USA) 42.46
1904	John Flanagan (USA) 51.23	John De Witt (USA) 50.26	Ralph Rose (USA) 45.73
1908	John Flanagan (USA) 51.92	Matt McGrath (USA) 51.18	Con Walsh (CAN) 48.50
1912	Matt McGrath (USA) 54.74	Duncan Gillis (CAN) 48.39	Clarence Childs (USA) 48.17
1920	Patrick Ryan (USA) 52.87	Carl Lind (SWE) 48.43	Basil Bennett (USA) 48.25
1924	Fred Tootell (USA) 53.29	Matt McGrath (USA) 50.84	Malcolm Nokes (GBR) 48.87
1928	Patrick O'Callaghan (IRL) 51.39	Ossian Skjöld (SWE) 51.29	Edmund Black (USA) 49.03
1932	Patrick O'Callaghan (IRL) 53.92	Ville Pörhöla (FIN) 52.27	Peter Zaremba (USA) 50.33
1936	Karl Hein (GER) 56.49	Erwin Blask (GER) 55.04	Fred Warngard (SWE) 54.83
1948	Imre Németh (HUN) 56.07	Ivan Gubijan (YUG) 54.27	Bob Bennett (USA) 53.73
1952	József Csermák (HUN) 60.34	Karl Storch (GER) 58.86	Imre Németh (HUN) 57.74
1956	Harold Connolly (USA) 63.19	Mikhail Krivonosov (URS) 63.03	Anatoli Samotsvetov (URS) 62.56
1960	Vasili Rudenkov (URS) 67.10	Gyula Zsivótzky (HUN) 65.79	Tadeusz Rut (POL) 65.64
1964	Romuald Klim (URS) 69.74	Gyula Zsivótzky (HUN) 69.09	Uwe Beyer (GER) 68.09

1968	Gyula Zsivótzky (HUN) 73.36	Romuald Klim (URS) 73.28	Lázár Lovász (HUN) 69.78
1972	Anatoli Bondarchuk (URS) 75.50	Jochen Sachse (GDR) 74.96	Vasili Khmelevski (URS) 74.04
1976	Yuri Sedykh (URS) 77.52	Alexei Spriridonov (URS) 76.08	Anatoli Bondarchuk (URS) 75.48
1980	Yuri Sedykh (URS) 81.80	Sergei Litvinov (URS) 80.64	Juri Tamm (URS) 78.96
1984	Juha Tiainen (FIN) 78.08	Karl-Hans Riehm (FRG) 77.98	Klaus Ploghaus (FRG) 76.68
1988	Sergei Litvinov (URS) 84.80	Yuri Sedykh (URS) 83.76	Juri Tamm (URS) 81.16
1992	Andrei Abduvalyev (EUN) 82.54	Igor Astapkovich (EUN) 81.96	Igor Nikulin (EUN) 81.38
1996	Balázs Kiss (HUN) 81.24	Lance Deal (USA) 81.12	Alexander Krykun (UKR) 80.02
2000	Szymon Ziolkowski (POL) 80.02	Nicola Vizzoni (ITA) 79.64	Igor Astapkovich (BLR) 79.17
2004	Koji Murofushi (JPN) 82.91[2]	Ivan Tikhon (BLR) 79.81	Esref Apak (TUR) 79.51

1896, 1906 Event not held
[1]*Competition from a 9ft (2.74m) circle;* [2]*Adrian Annus (HUN) threw 83.19m but was disqualified*

Javelin

1906	Eric Lemming (SWE) 53.90	Knut Lindberg (SWE) 45.17	Bruno Söderström (SWE) 44.92
1908	Eric Lemming (SWE) 54.82	Arne Halse (NOR) 50.57	Otto Nilsson (SWE) 47.09
1912	Eric Lemming (SWE) 60.64	Juho Saaristo (FIN) 58.66	Mór Kóczán (HUN) 55.50
1920	Jonni Myyrä (FIN) 65.78	Urho Peltonen (FIN) 63.50	Pekka Johansson (FIN) 63.09
1924	Jonni Myyrä (FIN) 62.96	Gunnar Lindström (SWE) 60.92	Eugene Oberst (USA) 58.35
1928	Erik Lundkvist (SWE) 66.60	Béla Szepes (HUN) 65.26	Olva Sunde (NOR) 63.97
1932	Matti Järvinen (FIN) 72.71	Matti Sippala (FIN) 69.79	Eino Penttila (FIN) 68.69
1936	Gerhard Stock (GER) 71.84	Yrjö Nikkanen (FIN) 70.77	Kalervo Toivonen (FIN) 70.72
1948	Tapio Rautavaara (FIN) 69.77	Steve Seymour (USA) 67.56	József Várszegi (HUN) 67.03
1952	Cyrus Young (USA) 73.78	Bill Miller (USA) 72.46	Toivo Hyytiäinen (FIN) 71.89
1956	Egil Danielsen (NOR) 85.71	Janusz Sidlo (POL) 79.98	Viktor Tsibulenko (URS) 79.50
1960	Viktor Tsibulenko (URS) 84.64	Walter Krüger (GER) 79.36	Gergely Kulcsár (HUN) 78.57
1964	Pauli Nevala (FIN) 82.66	Gergely Kulcsár (HUN) 82.32	Janis Lusis (URS) 80.57
1968	Janis Lusis (URS) 90.10	Jorma Kinnunen (FIN) 88.58	Gergely Kulcsár (HUN) 87.06
1972	Klaus Wolfermann (FRG) 90.48	Janis Lusis (URS) 90.46	Bill Schmidt (USA) 84.42
1976	Miklos Németh (HUN) 94.58	Hannu Siitonen (FIN) 87.92	Gheorghe Megelea (ROM) 87.16
1980	Dainis Kula (URS) 91.20	Alexander Makarov (URS) 89.64	Wolfgang Hanisch (GDR) 86.72
1984	Arto Härkonen (FIN) 86.76	David Ottley (GBR) 85.74	Kenth Eldebrink (SWE) 83.72
1988	Tapio Korjus (FIN) 84.28	Jan Zelezny (TCH) 84.12	Seppo Räty (FIN) 83.26
1992[1]	Jan Zelezny (TCH) 89.66	Seppo Räty (FIN) 86.60	Steve Backley (GBR) 83.38
1996	Jan Zelezny (CZE) 88.16	Steve Backley (GBR) 87.44	Seppo Räty (FIN) 86.98
2000	Jan Zelezny (CZE) 90.17	Steve Backley (GBR) 89.85	Sergei Makarov (RUS) 88.67
2004	Andreas Thorkildsen (NOR) 86.50	Vadims Vasilevski (RUS) 84.95	Sergei Makarov (RUS) 84.84

1896-1904 Event not held
[1]*New javelin introduced*

Decathlon

[1,2]*New points calculations made by Bob Sparks*

1904[3]	Thomas Kiely (GBR) 6036	Adam Gunn (USA) 5907	Truxton Hare (USA) 5813
1912[4]	Hugo Wieslander (SWE) 5966	Charles Lomberg (SWE) 5721	Gösta Holmer (SWE) 5768
1920	Helge Lövland (NOR) 5803	Brutus Hamilton (USA) 5739	Bertil Ohlsson (SWE) 5640
1924	Harold Osborn (USA) 6476	Emerson Norton (USA) 6117	Alexander Klumberg (EST) 6056
1928	Paavo Yrjölä (FIN) 6587	Akilles Järvinen (FIN) 6645	Ken Doherty (USA) 6428
1932	Jim Bausch (USA) 6736	Akilles Järvinen (FIN) 6879	Wolrad Eberle (GER) 6661
1936	Glenn Morris (USA) 7254	Robert Clark (USA) 7063	Jack Parker (USA) 6760
1948	Bob Mathias (USA) 6628	Ignace Heinrich (FRA) 6559	Floyd Simmons (USA) 6531
1952	Bob Mathias (USA) 7592	Milt Campbell (USA) 6995	Floyd Simmons (USA) 6945
1956	Milt Campbell (USA) 7614	Rafer Johnson (USA) 7457	Vasili Kuznetsov (URS) 7337
1960	Rafer Johnson (USA) 7926	Yang Chuan-Kwang (TPE) 7839	Vasili Kuznetsov (URS) 7557
1964	Willi Holdorf (GER) 7794	Rein Aun (URS) 7744	Hans-Joachim Walde (GER) 7735
1968	Bill Toomey (USA) 8144	Hans-Joachim Walde (FRG) 8094	Kurt Bendlin (FRG) 8071
1972	Nikolai Avilov (URS) 8466	Leonid Litvinenko (URS) 7970	Ryszard Katus (POL) 7936
1976	Bruce Jenner (USA) 8634	Guido Kratschmer (FRG) 8407	Nikolai Avilov (URS) 8378
1980	Daley Thompson (GBR) 8522	Yuri Kutsenko (URS) 8369	Sergei Zhelanov (URS) 8135
1984	Daley Thompson (GBR) 8847	Jürgen Hingsen (FRG) 8695	Siegfried Wentz (FRG) 8416
1988	Christian Schenk (GDR) 8488	Torsten Voss (GDR) 8399	Dave Steen (CAN) 8328
1992	Robert Zmelik (TCH) 8611	Antonio Penalver (CUB) 8412	Dave Johnson (USA) 8309
1996	Dan O'Brien (USA) 8824	Frank Busemann (GER) 8706	Tomas Dvorak (CZE) 8664
2000	Erki Nool (EST) 8641	Roman Sebrle (CZE) 8606	Chris Huffins (USA) 8595
2004	Roman Sebrle (CZE) 8893	Bryan Clay (USA) 8820	Dmitri Karpov (KAZ) 8725

1896-1900, 1906-1908 Event not held
[1]*The decathlon consists of 100m, long jump, shot put, high jump, 400m, 110m hurdles, discus, pole vault, javelin and*

1500m. The competition occupies two days, although in 1912 it took three days; [2]The scores since 1912 given above have been recalculated on the current, 1984, scoring tables, for purposes of comparison. Note that in 1912, 1928, 1932 and 1948 the original medal order would have been different if these tables had been in force
[3]Consisted of 100yd, 1 mile, 120yd hurdles, 880yd walk, high jump, long jump, pole vault, shot put, hammer and 56lb weight; [4]Jim Thorpe (USA) finished first with 6564pts, but was later disqualified for a breach of the then amateur rules. He was reinstated posthumously by the IOC in 1982, but only as joint first

Women

(Women's events first contested in 1928)

100 Metres

1928	Elizabeth Robinson (USA) 12.2	Fanny Rosenfeld (CAN) 12.3	Ethel Smith (CAN) 12.3
1932	Stanislawa Walasiewicz (POL) 11.9	Hilda Strike (CAN) 11.9	Wilhelmina von Bremen (USA) 12.0
1936	Helen Stephens (USA) 11.5	Stanislawa Walasiewicz (POL) 11.7	Kathe Krauss (GER) 11.9
1948	Fanny Blankers-Koen (NED) 11.9	Dorothy Manley (GBR) 12.2	Shirley Strickland (AUS) 12.2
1952	Marjorie Jackson (AUS) 11.5 (11.67)	Daphne Hasenjager (RSA) 11.8 (12.05)	Shirley Strickland (AUS) 11.9 (12.12)
1956	Betty Cuthbert (AUS) 11.5 (11.82)	Christa Stubnick (GER) 11.7 (11.92)	Marlene Matthews (AUS) 11.7 (11.94)
1960	Wilma Rudolph (USA) 11.0 (11.18)	Dorothy Hyman (GBR) 11.3 (11.43)	Giuseppina Leone (ITA) 11.3 (11.48)
1964	Wyomia Tyus (USA) 11.4 (11.49)	Edith Maguire (USA) 11.6 (11.62)	Ewa Klobukowska (POL)[1] 11.6 (11.64)
1968	Wyomia Tyus (USA) 11.0 (11.08)	Barbara Ferrell (USA) 11.1 (11.15)	Irena Szewinska (POL) 11.1 (11.19)
1972	Renate Stecher (GDR) 11.07	Raelene Boyle (AUS) 11.23	Silvia Chivas (CUB) 11.24
1976	Annegret Richter (FRG) 11.08	Renate Stecher (GDR) 11.13	Inge Helten (FRG) 11.17
1980	Ludmila Kondratyeva (URS) 11.06	Marlies Göhr (GDR) 11.07	Ingrid Auerswald (GDR) 11.14
1984	Evelyn Ashford (USA) 10.97	Alice Brown (USA) 11.13	Merlene Ottey-Page (JAM) 11.16
1988	Florence Griffith-Joyner (USA) 10.54[2]	Evelyn Ashford (USA) 10.83	Heike Drechsler (GDR) 10.85
1992	Gail Devers (USA) 10.82	Juliet Cuthbert (JAM) 10.83	Irina Privalova (EUN) 10.84
1996	Gail Devers (USA) 10.94	Merlene Ottey (JAM) 10.94	Gwen Torrence (USA 10.96
2000	Marion Jones (USA) 10.75	Ekaterini Thanou (GRE) 11.12	Tanya Lawrence (JAM) 11.18
2004	Yuliya Nesterenko (BLR) 10.93	Lauryn Williams (USA) 10.96	Veronica Campbell (JAM) 10.97

[1]Three years later Klobukowska failed a sex test and was banned from competition; [2]Final was wind-assisted; 10.62 in preliminary round

200 Metres

1948	Fanny Blankers-Koen (NED) 24.4	Audrey Williamson (GBR) 25.1	Audrey Patterson (USA) 25.2[1]
1952	Marjorie Jackson (AUS) 23.7 (23.89)	Bertha Brouwer (NED) 24.2 (24.25)	Nadyezda Khnykina (URS) 24.2 (24.37)
1956	Betty Cuthbert (AUS) 23.4 (23.55)	Christa Stubnick (GER) 23.7 (23.89)	Marlene Matthews (AUS) 23.8 (24.10)
1960	Wilma Rudolph (USA) 24.0 (24.13)	Jutta Heine (GER) 24.4 (24.58)	Dorothy Hyman (GBR) 24.7 (24.82)
1964	Edith Maguire (USA) 23.0 (23.05)	Irena Kirszenstein (POL) 23.1 (23.13)	Marilyn Black (AUS) 23.1 (23.18)
1968	Irena Szewinska (POL) 22.5 (22.58)	Raelene Boyle (AUS) 22.7 (22.74)	Jennifer Lamy (AUS) 22.8 (22.88)
1972	Renate Stecher (GDR) 22.40	Raelene Boyle (AUS) 22.45	Irena Szewinska (POL) 22.74
1976	Bärbel Eckert (GDR) 22.37	Annegret Richter (FRG) 22.39	Renate Stecher (GDR) 22.47
1980	Bärbel Wöckel (GDR) 22.03	Natalya Bochina (URS) 22.19	Merlene Ottey (JAM) 22.20
1984	Valerie Brisco-Hooks (USA) 21.81	Florence Griffith (USA) 22.04	Merlene Ottey-Page (JAM) 22.09
1988	Florence Giffith-Joyner (USA) 21.34	Grace Jackson (JAM) 21.72	Heike Drechsler (GDR) 21.95
1992	Gwen Torrence (USA) 21.81	Juliet Cuthbert (JAM) 22.02	Merlene Ottey (JAM) 22.09
1996	Marie-José Pérec (FRA) 22.12	Merlene Ottey (JAM) 22.24	Mary Onyali (NGR) 22.38
2000	Marion Jones (USA) 21.84	Pauline Davis-Thompson (BAH) 22.27	Susanthika Jayasinghe (SRI) 22.28
2004	Veronica Campbell (JAM) 22.05	Allyson Felix (USA) 22.18	Debbie Ferguson (BAH) 22.30

1928-1936 Event not held
[1]Photo-finish picture indicates that Shirley Strickland (AUS) was third

400 Metres

1964	Betty Cuthbert (AUS) 52.0 (52.01)	Ann Packer (GBR) 52.2 (52.20)	Judith Amoore (AUS) 53.4
1968	Colette Besson (FRA) 52.0 (52.03)	Lillian Board (GBR) 52.1 (52.12)	Natalya Burda (URS) 52.2 (52.25)
1972	Monika Zehrt (GDR) 51.08	Rita Wilden (FRG) 51.21	Kathy Hammond (USA) 51.64
1976	Irena Szewinska (POL) 49.29	Christina Brehmer (GDR) 50.51	Ellen Streidt (GDR) 50.55
1980	Marita Koch (GDR) 48.88	Jarmila Kratochvilová (TCH) 49.46	Christina Lathan (GDR) 49.66
1984	Valerie Brisco-Hooks (USA) 48.83	Chandra Cheeseborough (USA) 49.05	Kathy Cook (GBR) 49.43
1988	Olga Bryzgina (URS) 48.65	Petra Müller (GDR) 49.45	Olga Nazarova (URS) 49.90
1992	Marie-José Pérec (FRA) 48.83	Olga Bryzgina (EUN) 49.05	Ximena Restrepo (COL) 49.64
1996	Marie-José Pérec (FRA) 48.25	Cathy Freeman (AUS) 48.63	Falilat Ogunkoya (NGR) 49.10
2000	Cathy Freeman (AUS) 49.11	Lorraine Graham (JAM) 49.58	Katharine Merry (GBR) 49.72
2004	Tonique Williams (BAH) 49.41	Ana Guevera (MEX) 49.56	Natalya Antyukh (RUS) 49.89

1928-1960 Event not held

800 Metres

1928	Lina Radke (GER) 2:16.8	Kinuye Hitoml (JPN) 2:17.6	Inga Gentzel (SWE) 2:17.8
1960	Ludmila Shevtsova (URS) 2:04.3	Brenda Jones (AUS) 2:04.4	Ursula Donath (GER) 2:05.6
1964	Ann Packer (GBR) 2:01.1	Maryvonne Dupureur (FRA) 2:01.9	Marise Chamberlain (NZL) 2:02.8
1968	Madeline Manning (USA) 2:00.9	Ilona Silai (ROM) 2:02.5	Maria Gommers (NED) 2:02.6
1972	Hildegard Falck (FRG) 1:58.6	Niole Sabaite (URS) 1:58.7	Gunhild Hoffmeister (GDR) 1:59.2
1976	Tatyana Kazankina (URS) 1:54.9	Nikolina Shtereva (BUL) 1:55.4	Elfi Zinn (GDR) 1:55.6
1980	Nadyezda Olizarenko (URS) 1:53.5	Olga Mineyeva (URS) 1:54.9	Tatyana Providokhina (URS) 1:55.5
1984	Doina Melinte (ROM) 1:57.60	Kim Gallagher (USA) 1:58.63	Fita Lovin (ROM) 1:58.83
1988	Sigrun Wodars (GDR) 1:56.10	Christine Wachtel (GDR) 1:56.64	Kim Gallagher (USA) 1:56.91
1992	Ellen van Langen (NED) 1:55.54	Lilia Nurutdinova (EUN) 1:55.99	Ana Quirot (CUB) 1:56.80
1996	Svetlana Masterkova (RUS) 1:57.73	Ana Quirot (CUB) 1:58.11	Maria Mutola (MOZ) 1:58.71
2000	Maria Mutola (MOZ) 1:56.15	Stephanie Graf (AUT) 1:56.64	Kelly Holmes (GBR) 1:56.80
2004	Kelly Holmes (GBR) 1:56.38	Hasna Benhassi (MAR) 1:56.43	Jolanda Ceplak (SLO) 1:56.43

1932-1956 Event not held

1500 Metres

1972	Ludmila Bragina (URS) 4:01.4	Gunhild Hoffmeister (GDR) 4:02.8	Paola Cacchi-Pigni (ITA) 4:02.9
1976	Tatyana Kazankina (URS) 4:05.5	Gunhild Hoffmeister (GDR) 4:06.0	Ulrike Klapezynski (GDR) 4:06.1
1980	Tatyana Kazankina (URS) 3:56.6	Christiane Wartenberg (GDR) 3:57.8	Nadyezda Olizarenko (URS) 3:59.6
1984	Gabriella Dorio (ITA) 4:03.25	Doina Melinte (ROM) 4:03.76	Maricica Puica (ROM) 4:04.15
1988	Paula Ivan (ROM) 3:53.96	Laima Baikauskaite (URS) 4:00.24	Tatyana Samolenko (URS) 4:00.30
1992	Hassiba Boulmerka (ALG) 3:55.30	Ludmila Rogachova (EUN) 3:56.91	Qu Yunxia (CHN) 3:57.08
1996	Svetlana Masterkova (RUS) 4:00.83	Gabriela Szabo (ROM) 4:01.54	Theresia Kiesl (AUT) 4:03.02
2000	Nouria Merah-Benida (ALG) 4:05.10	Violeta Szekely (ROM) 4:05.15	Gabriela Szabo (ROM) 4:05.27
2004	Kelly Holmes (GBR) 3:57.90	Tatyana Tomashovu (RUS) 3:58.12	Maria Cioncan (ROM) 3:58.39

1928-1968 Event not held

3000 Metres

Replaced by 5000m in 1996

1984	Maricica Puica (ROM) 8:35.96	Wendy Sly (GBR) 8:39.47	Lynn Williams (CAN) 8:42.14
1988	Tatyana Samolenko (URS) 8:26.53	Paula Ivan (ROM) 8:27.15	Yvonne Murray (GBR) 8:29.02
1992	Yelena Romanova (EUN) 8:46.04	Tatyana Dorovskikh (EUN) 8:46.85	Angela Chalmers (CAN) 8:47.22

1928-1980 Event not held

5000 Metres

1996	Wang Junxia (CHN) 14:59.88	Pauline Konga (KEN) 15:03.49	Roberta Brunet (ITA) 15:07.52
2000	Gabriela Szabo (ROM) 14:40.79	Sonia O'Sullivan (IRL) 14:41.02	Gete Wami (ETH) 14:42.23
2004	Meseret Defar (ETH) 14:45.65	Isabella Ochichi (KEN) 14:48.19	Tirunesh Dibaba (ETH) 14:51.83

1928-1992 Event not held

10,000 Metres

1988	Olga Bondarenko (URS) 31:05.21	Liz McColgan (GBR) 31:08.44	Yelena Zhupiyeva (URS) 31:19.82
1992	Derartu Tulu (ETH) 31:06.02	Elana Meyer (RSA) 31:11.75	Lynn Jennings (USA) 31:19.89
1996	Fernanda Ribeiro (POR) 31:01.63	Wang Junxia (CHN) 31:02.58	Gete Wami (ETH) 31:06.65
2000	Derartu Tulu (ETH) 30:17.49	Gete Wami (ETH) 30:22.48	Fernanda Ribeiro (POR) 30:22.88
2004	Xing Huina (CHN) 30:24.36	Ejagayehu Dibaba (ETH) 30:24.98	Derartu Tult (ETH) 30:26.42

1928-1984 Event not held

Marathon

1984	Joan Benoit (USA) 2:24:52	Grete Waitz (NOR) 2:26:18	Rosa Mota (POR) 2:26:57
1988	Rosa Mota (POR) 2:25:40	Lisa Martin (AUS) 2:25:53	Kathrin Dörre (GDR) 2:26:21
1992	Valentina Yegorova (EUN) 2:32:41	Yuko Arimori (JPN) 2:32:49	Lorraine Moller (NZL) 2:33:59
1996	Fatuma Roba (ETH) 2:26:05	Valentina Yegorova (RUS) 2:28:05	Yuko Arimori (JPN) 2:28:39
2000	Naoko Takahashi (JPN) 2:23:14	Lidia Simon (ROM) 2:23:22	Joyce Chepchumba (KEN) 2:24:45
2004	Mizuki Noguchi (JPN) 2:26:20	Catherine Ndereba (KEN) 2:26:32	Deena Kastor (USA) 2:27:20

1928-1980 Event not held

100 Metres Hurdles

(Held over 80 metres Hurdles 1932-1968)

1932	Mildred Didrikson (USA) 11.7	Evelyne Hall (USA) 11.7	Marjorie Clark (RSA) 11.8
1936	Trebisonda Valla (ITA) 11.7 (11.75)	Anny Steuer (GER) 11.7 (11.81)	Elizabeth Taylor (CAN) 11.7 (11.81)

1948	Fanny Blankers-Koen (NED) 11.2	Maureen Gardner (GBR) 11.2	Shirley Strickland (AUS) 11.4
1952	Shirley de la Hunty (AUS) 10.8 (11.01)	Maria Golubnichaya (URS) 11.1 (11.24)	Maria Sander (GER) 11.1 (11.38)
1956	Shirley de la Hunty (AUS) 10.7 (10.96)	Gisela Köhler (GER) 10.9 (11.12)	Norma Thrower (AUS) 11.0 (11.25)
1960	Irina Press (URS) 10.8 (10.93)	Carol Quinton (GBR) 10.9 (10.99)	Gisela Birkemeyer (GER) 11.0 (11.13)
1964	Karin Balzer (GER) 10.5 (10.54)	Teresa Ciepla (POL) 10.5 (10.55)	Pam Kilborn (AUS) 10.5 (10.56)
1968	Maureen Caird (AUS) (10.3 (10.39)	Pam Kilborn (AUS) 10.4 (10.46)	Chi Cheng (TPE) 10.4 (10.51)
1972	Annelie Ehrhardt (GDR) 12.59	Valeria Bufanu (ROM) 12.84	Karin Balzer (GDR) 12.90
1976	Johanna Schaller (GDR) 12.77	Tatyana Anisimova (URS) 12.78	Natalya Lebedyeva (URS) 12.80
1980	Vera Komisova (URS) 12.56	Johanna Klier (GDR) 12.63	Lucyna Langer (POL) 12.65
1984	Benita Fitzgerald-Brown (USA) 12.84	Shirley Strong (GBR) 12.88	Kim Turner (USA) 13.06
			Michele Chardonnet (FRA) 13.06
1988	Yordanka Donkova (BUL) 12.38	Gloria Siebert (GDR) 12.61	Claudia Zaczkiewicz (FRG) 12.75
1992	Paraskevi Patoulidou (GRE) 12.64	LaVonna Martin (USA) 12.69	Yordanka Donkova (BUL) 12.70
1996	Ludmila Engquist (SWE) 12.58	Brigita Bukovec (SLO) 12.59	Patricia Girard-Leno (FRA) 12.65
2000	Olga Shishigina (KAZ) 12.65	Gloria Alozie (NGR) 12.68	Melissa Morrison (USA) 12.76
2004	Joanna Hayes (USA) 12.37	Olena Krasovska (UKR) 12.45	Melissa Morrison (USA) 12.56

1928 Event not held

400 Metres Hurdles

1984	Nawal El Moutawakel (MAR) 54.61	Judi Brown (USA) 55.20	Cristina Cojocaru (ROM) 55.41
1988	Debbie Flintoff-King (AUS) 53.17	Tatyana Ledovskaya (URS) 53.18	Ellen Fiedler (GDR) 53.63
1992	Sally Gunnell (GBR) 53.23	Sandra Farmer-Patrick (USA) 53.69	Janeene Vickers (USA) 54.31
1996	Deon Hemmings (JAM) 52.82	Kim Batten (USA) 53.08	Tonja Buford-Bailey (USA) 53.22
2000	Irina Privalova (RUS) 53.02	Deon Hemmings (JAM) 53.45	Nezha Bidouane (MAR) 53.57
2004	K-Fani Halkia (GRE) 52.82	Ionela Tirlea (ROM) 53.38	Tatyana Tereshyuk (UKR) 53.44

1928-1980 Event not held

4x100 Metres Relay

1928	CANADA 48.4	UNITED STATES 48.8	GERMANY 49.2
1932	UNITED STATES 47.0 (46.86)	CANADA 47.0	GREAT BRITAIN 47.6
1936	UNITED STATES 46.9	GREAT BRITAIN 47.6	CANADA 47.8
1948	NETHERLANDS 47.5	AUSTRALIA 47.6	CANADA 47.8
1952	UNITED STATES 45.9 (46.14)	GERMANY 45.9 (46.18)	GREAT BRITAIN 46.2 (46.41)
1956	AUSTRALIA 44.5 (44.65)	GREAT BRITAIN 44.7 (44.70)	UNITED STATES 44.9 (45.04)
1960	UNITED STATES 44.5 (44.72)	GERMANY 44.8 (45.00)	POLAND 45.0 (45.19)
1964	POLAND 43.6 (43.69)	UNITED STATES 43.9 (43.92)	GREAT BRITAIN 44.0 (44.09)
1968	UNITED STATES 42.8 (42.88)	CUBA 43.3 (43.36)	SOVIET UNION 43.4 (43.41)
1972	FRG 42.81	GDR 42.95	CUBA 43.36
1976	GDR 42.55	FRG 42.59	SOVIET UNION 43.09
1980	GDR 41.60	SOVIET UNION 42.10	GREAT BRITAIN 42.43
1984	UNITED STATES 41.65	CANADA 42.77	GREAT BRITAIN 43.11
1988	UNITED STATES 41.98	GDR 42.09	SOVIET UNION 42.75
1992	UNITED STATES 42.11	UNIFIED TEAM (EUN) 42.16	NIGERIA 42.81
1996	UNITED STATES 41.95	BAHAMAS 42.14	JAMAICA 42.24
2000	BAHAMAS 41.95	JAMAICA 42.13	UNITED STATES 42.20
2004	JAMAICA 41.73	RUSSIA 42.27	FRANCE 42.54

4x400 Metres Relay

1972	GDR 3:22.95	UNITED STATES 3:25.15	FRG 3:26.51
1976	GDR 3:19.23	UNITED STATES 3:22.81	SOVIET UNION 3:24.24
1980	SOVIET UNION 3:20.12	GDR 3:20.35	GREAT BRITAIN 3:27.5
1984	UNITED STATES 3:18.29	CANADA 3:21.21	FRG 3:22.98
1988	SOVIET UNION 3:15.17	UNITED STATES 3:15.51	GDR 3:18.29
1992	UNIFIED TEAM (EUN) 3:20.20	UNITED STATES 3:20.92	GREAT BRITAIN 3:24.23
1996	UNITED STATES 3:20.91	NIGERIA 3:21.04	GERMANY 3:21.14
2000	UNITED STATES 3:22.62	JAMAICA 3:23.25	RUSSIA 3:23.44
2004	UNITED STATES 3:19.01	RUSSIA 3:20.16	JAMAICA 3:22.00

1928-1968 Event not held

10,000 Metres Walk

Replaced by a 20,000 metres walk in 2000

1992	Chen Yueling (CHN) 44:32	Yelena Nikoleyeva (EUN) 44:33	Li Chunxiu (CHN) 44:41
1996	Yelena Nikolayeva (RUS) 41:49	Elisabetta Perrone (ITA) 42:12	Wang Yan (CHN) 42:19

1928-1988 Event not held

20,000 Metres Walk

Introduced in 2000

2000	Wang Liping (CHN) 1:29:05	Kjersti Plätzer (NOR) 1:29:33	Maria Vasco (ESP) 1:30:23
2004	Athanasia Tsoumeléka (GRE) 1:29:12	Olimpiada Ivanova (RUS) 1:29:16	Jane Saville (AUS) 1:29:25

High Jump

1928	Ethel Catherwood (CAN) 1.59	Carolina Gisolf (NED) 1.56	Mildred Wiley (USA) 1.56
1932	Jean Shiley (USA) 1.657[1]	Mildred Didrikson (USA) 1.657[1]	Eva Dawes (CAN) 1.60
1936	Ibolya Csák (HUN) 1.60	Dorothy Odam (GBR) 1.60	Elfriede Kaun (GER) 1.60
1948	Alice Coachman (USA) 1.68	Dorothy Tyler (GBR) 1.68	Micheline Ostermeyer (FRA) 1.61
1952	Esther Brand (RSA) 1.67	Sheila Lerwill (GBR) 1.65	Alexandra Chudina (URS) 1.63
1956	Mildred McDaniel (USA) 1.76	Thelma Hopkins (GBR) 1.67	–
		Maria Pisaryeva (URS) 1.67	
1960	Iolanda Balas (ROM) 1.85	Jaroslawa Józwiakowska (POL) 1.71	–
		Dorothy Shirley (GBR) 1.71	
1964	Iolanda Balas (ROM) 1.90	Michelle Brown (AUS) 1.80	Taisia Chenchik (URS) 1.78
1968	Miloslava Rezková (TCH) 1.82	Antonina Okorokova (URS) 1.80	Valentina Kozyr (URS) 1.80
1972	Ulrike Meyfarth (FRG) 1.92	Yordanka Blagoyeva (BUL) 1.88	Ilona Gusenbauer (AUT) 1.88
1976	Rosemarie Ackermann (GDR) 1.93	Sara Simeoni (ITA) 1.91	Yordanka Blagoyeva (BUL) 1.91
1980	Sara Simeoni (ITA) 1.97	Urszula Kielan (POL) 1.94	Jutta Kirst (GDR) 1.94
1984	Ulrike Meyfarth (FRG) 2.02	Sara Simeoni (ITA) 2.00	Joni Huntley (USA) 1.97
1988	Louise Ritter (USA) 2.03	Stefka Kostadinova (BUL) 2.01	Tamara Dykova (URS) 1.99
1992	Heike Henkel (GER) 2.02	Galina Astafei (ROM) 2.00	Ioamnet Quintero (CUR) 1.97
1996	Stefka Kostadinova (BUL) 2.05	Niki Bakogianni (GRE) 2.03	Inga Babakova (UKR) 2.01
2000	Yelena Yelesina (RUS) 2.01	Hestrie Cloete (RSA) 2.01	Oana Pantelimon (ROM) 1.99
			Kajsa Bergqvist (SWE) 1.99
2004	Yelena Slesarenko (RUS) 2.06	Hestrie Cloete (RSA) 2.02	Victtoriya Styopina (UKR) 2.02

[1] *Some sources suggest 1.66*

Pole Vault

Introduced in 2000

2000	Stacy Dragila (USA) 4.60	Tatiana Grigorieva (AUS) 4.55	Vala Flosadottir (ISL) 4.50
2004	Yelena Isinbbayeva (RUS) 4.91	Svetlana Feofanova (RUS) 4.75	Anna Rogowska (POL) 4.70

Long Jump

1948	Olga Gyarmati (HUN) 5.69	N. Simonetta de Portela (ARG) 5.60	Ann-Britt Leyman (SWE) 5.57
1952	Yvette Williams (NZL) 6.24	Alexandra Chudina (URS) 6.14	Shirley Cawley (GBR) 5.92
1956	Elzbieta Krzesinska (POL) 6.35	Willye White (USA) 6.09	Nadyezda Dvalishvili (URS) 6.07
1960	Vera Krepkina (URS) 6.37	Elzbieta Krzesinska (POL) 6.27	Hildrun Claus (GER) 6.21
1964	Mary Rand (GBR) 6.76	Irena Kirszenstein (POL) 6.27	Tatyana Schelkanova (URS) 6.42
1968	Viorica Viscopoleanu (ROM) 6.82	Sheila Sherwood (GBR) 6.68	Tatyana Talysheva (URS) 6.66
1972	Heidemarie Rosendahl (FRG) 6.78	Diana Yorgova (BUL) 6.77	Eva Suranová (TCH) 6.67
1976	Angela Voigt (GDR) 6.72	Kathy McMillan (USA) 6.66	Lidia Alfeyeva (URS) 6.60
1980	Tatyana Kolpakova (URS) 7.06	Brigitte Wujak (GDR) 7.04	Tatyana Skatchko (URS) 7.01
1984	Anisoara Stanciu (ROM) 6.96	Vali Ionescu (ROM) 6.81	Susan Hearnshaw (GBR) 6.80
1988	Jackie Joyner-Kersee (USA) 7.40	Heike Drechsler (GDR) 7.22	Galina Chistiakova (URS) 7.11
1992	Heike Drechsler (GDR) 7.14	Inessa Kravets (EUN) 7.12	Jackie Joyner-Kersee (USA) 7.07
1996	Chioma Ajunwa (NGR) 7.12	Fiona May (ITA) 7.02	Jackie Joyner-Kersee (USA) 7.00
2000	Heike Drechsler (GER) 6.99	Fiona May (ITA) 6.92	Marion Jones (USA) 6.92
2004	Tatyana Lebedeva (RUS) 7.07	Irina Simagina (RUS) 7.05	Tatyana Kotova (RUS) 7.05

1928-1936 Event not held

Triple Jump

Introduced in 1996

1996	Inessa Kravets (UKR) 15.33	Inna Lasovskaya (RUS) 14.98	Sarka Kasparkova (CZE) 14.98
2000	Tereza Marinova (BUL) 15.20	Tatyana Lebedyeva (RUS) 15.00	Olena Govorova (UKR) 14.96
2004	Francoise Mbango (CMR) 15.30	Hrysopiyi Devetzki (GRE) 15.25	Tatyana Lebedeva (RUS) 15.124

1928-1992 Event not held

Shot

1948	Micheline Ostermeyer (FRA) 13.75	Amelia Piccinini (ITA) 13.09	Ina Schäffer (AUT) 13.08
1952	Galina Zybina (URS) 15.28	Marianne Werner (GER) 14.57	Klavdia Tochonova (URS) 14.50
1956	Tamara Tyshkevich (URS) 16.59	Galina Zybina (URS) 15.53	Marianne Werner (GER) 15.61

Year			
1960	Tamara Press (URS) 17.32	Johanna Lüttge (GER) 16.61	Earlene Brown (USA)16.42
1964	Tamara Press (URS) 18.14	Renate Garisch (GDR) 17.61	Galina Zybina (URS) 16.42
1968	Margitta Gummel (GDR) 19.61	Marita Lange (GDR) 18.78	Nadyezda Chizhova (URS) 18.19
1972	Nadyezda Chizhova (URS) 21.03	Margitta Gummel (GDR) 20.22	Ivanka Khristova (BUL) 19.35
1976	Ivanka Khristova (BUL) 21.16	Nadyezda Chizhova (URS) 20.96	Helena Fibingerová (TCH) 20.67
1980	Ilona Slupianek (GDR) 22.41	Svetlana Krachevskaya (URS) 21.42	Margitta Pufe (GDR) 21.20
1984	Claudia Losch (FRG) 20.48	Mihaela Loghin (ROM) 20.47	Gael Martin (AUS) 19.19
1988	Natalya Lisovskaya (URS) 22.24	Kathrin Neimke (GDR) 21.07	Li Meisu (CHN) 21.06
1992	Svetlana Krivelyova (EUN) 21.06	Huang Zhihong (CHN) 20.47	Kathrin Neimke (GER) 19.78
1996	Astrid Kumbernuss (GER) 20.56	Sui Xinmei (CHN) 19.88	Irina Khudorozhkina (RUS) 19.35
2000	Yanina Korolchik (BLR) 20.56	Larisa Peleshenko (RUS) 19.92	Astrid Kumbernuss (GER) 19.62
2004	Yumileidi Cumba (CUB) 19.59m[1]	Nadine Kleinert (GER) 19.55	Svetlana Krivelyova ((RUS) 19.49

1928-1936 Event not held
[1]Irina Korzhanenko (RUS) threw 21.06m but was disqualified

Discus

Year			
1928	Helena Konopacka (POL) 39.62	Lilian Copeland (USA) 37.08	Ruth Svedberg (SWE) 35.92
1932	Lilian Copeland (USA) 40.58	Ruth Osburn (USA) 40.11	Jadwiga Wajsówna (POL) 38.73
1936	Gisela Mauermayer (GER) 47.63	Jadwiga Wajsówna (POL) 46.22	Paula Mollenhauer (GER) 39.80
1948	Micheline Ostermeyer (FRA) 41.92	Edera Gentile (ITA) 41.17	Jacqueline Mazéas (FRA) 40.47
1952	Nina Romashkova (URS) 51.42	Elizaveta Bagryantseva (URS) 47.08	Nina Dumbadze (URS) 46.29
1956	Olga Fikotová (TCH) 53.69	Irina Beglyakova (URS) 52.54	Nina Ponomaryeva (URS) 52.02
1960	Nina Ponomaryeva (URS) 55.10	Tamara Press (URS) 52.59	Lia Manoliu (ROM) 52.36
1964	Tamara Press (URS) 57.27	Ingrid Lotz (GER) 57.21	Lia Manoliu (ROM) 56.97
1968	Lia Manoliu (ROM) 58.28	Liesel Westermann (FRG) 57.76	Jolán Kleiber (HUN) 54.90
1972	Faina Melnik (URS) 66.62	Argentina Menis (ROM) 65.06	Vasilka Stoyeva (BUL) 64.34
1976	Evelin Schlaak (GDR) 69.00	Maria Vergova (BUL) 67.30	Gabriele Hinzmann (GDR) 66.84
1980	Evelin Jahl (GDR) 69.96	Maria Petkova (BUL) 67.90	Tatyana Lesovaya (URS) 67.40
1984	Ria Stalman (NED) 65.36	Leslie Deniz (USA) 64.86	Florenta Craciunescu (ROM) 63.64
1988	Martina Hellmann (GDR) 72.30	Diane Gansky (GDR) 71.88	Tsvetanka Khristova (BUL) 69.74
1992	Maritza Marten (CUB) 70.06	Tsvetanka Khristova (BUL) 67.78	Daniela Costian (AUS) 66.24
1996	Ilke Wyludda (GER) 69.66	Natalya Sadova (RUS) 66.48	Ellina Zvereva (BLR) 65.64
2000	Ellina Zvereva (BLR) 68.40	Anastasia Kelesidou (GRE) 65.71	Irina Yatchenko (BLR) 65.20
2004	Natalya sadova (RUS) 67.02	Anastasia Kelesidou (GRE) 66.68	Irina Yatchenko (BLR) 66.17

Hammer

Introduced in 2000

Year			
2000	Kamila Skolimowska (POL) 71.16	Olga Kuzenkova (RUS) 69.77	Kirsten Munchow (GER) 69.28
2004	Olga Kuzenkova (RUS) 75.02	Yipsi Moreno (CUB) 73.36	Yunaika Crawford (CUB) 73.16

Javelin

Year			
1932	Mildred Didrikson (USA) 43.68	Ellen Braumüller (GER) 43.49	Tilly Fleischer (GER) 43.40
1936	Tilly Fleischer (GER) 45.18	Louise Krüger (GER) 43.29	Marja Kwasniewska (POL) 41.80
1948	Herma Bauma (AUT) 45.57	Kaisa Parviainen (FIN) 43.79	Lily Carlstedt (DEN) 42.08
1952	Dana Zátopková (TCH) 50.47	Alexandra Chudina (URS) 50.01	Yelena Gorchakova (URS) 49.76
1956	Inese Jaunzeme (URS) 53.86	Marlene Ahrens (CHI) 50.38	Nadyezda Konyayeva (URS) 50.28
1960	Elvira Ozolina (URS) 55.98	Dana Zátopková (TCH) 53.78	Birute Kalediene (URS) 53.45
1964	Mihaela Penes (ROM) 60.64	Márta Rudas (HUN) 58.27	Yelena Gorchakova (URS) 57.07
1968	Angéla Németh (HUN) 60.36	Mihaela Penes (ROM) 59.92	Eva Janko (AUT) 58.04
1972	Ruth Fuchs (GDR) 63.88	Jacqueline Todten (GDR) 62.54	Kathy Schmidt (USA) 59.94
1976	Ruth Fuchs (GDR) 65.94	Marion Becker (FRG) 64.70	Kathy Schmidt (USA) 63.96
1980	María Colón (CUB) 68.40	Saida Gunba (URS) 67.76	Ute Hommola (GDR) 66.56
1984	Tessa Sanderson (GBR) 69.56	Tiina Lillak (FIN) 69.00	Fatima Whitbread (GBR) 67.14
1988	Petra Felke (GDR) 74.68	Fatima Whitbread (GBR) 70.32	Beate Koch (GDR) 67.30
1992	Silke Renk (GER) 68.34	Natalya Shikolenko (EUN) 68.26	Karen Forkel (GER) 66.86
1996	Heli Rantanen (FIN) 67.94	Louise McPaul (AUS) 65.54	Trine Hattestad (NOR) 64.68
2000	Trine Hattestad (NOR) 68.91	Mirela Manjani-Tzelili (GRE) 67.51	Osleidys Menendez (CUB) 66.18
2004	Osleidys Menendez (CUB) 71.53	Steffi Nerius (GER) 65.82	Mirela Manjani (GRE) 64.29

1928 Event not held

Pentathlon[1]

Year			
1964	Irina Press (URS) 5246	Mary Rand (GBR) 5035	Galina Bystrova (URS) 4956
1968	Ingrid Becker (FRG) 5098	Liese Prokop (AUT) 4966	Annamaria Tóth (HUN) 4959
1972[2]	Mary Peters (GBR) 4801	Heidemarie Rosendahl (FRG) 4791	Burglinde Pollak (GDR) 4768
1976	Siegrun Siegl (GDR) 4745[3]	Christine Laser (GDR) 4745	Burglinde Pollak (GDR) 4740

1980   Nadyezda Tkachenko (URS) 5083   Olga Rukavishnikova (URS) 4937   Olga Kuragina (URS) 4875
1928-1960 Event not held
[1]The pentathlon consisted of 100 metres hurdles, shot, high jump, long jump and 200m, from 1964 to 1976. In 1980 the 200m was replaced by 800m; [2]New scoring tables were introduced in May 1971; [3]Siegl finished ahead of Laser in three events

Heptathlon[4]

Replaced Pentathlon in 1984
1984   Glynis Nunn (AUS) 6387[5]   Jackie Joyner (USA) 6363   Sabine Everts (FRG) 6388
1988   Jackie Joyner-Kersee (USA) 7291   Sabine John (GDR) 6897   Anke Behmer (GDR) 6858
1992   Jackie Joyner-Kersee (USA) 7044   Irina Belova (EUN) 6845   Sabine Braun (GER) 6649
1996   Ghada Shouaa (SYR) 6780   Natasha Sazanovich (BLR) 6563   Denise Lewis (GBR) 6489
2000   Denise Lewis (GBR) 6584   Yelena Prokhorova (RUS) 6531   Natalya Sazanovich (BLR) 6527
2004   Carolina Kluft (SWE) 6952   Austra Skujyte (LTU) 6435   Kelly Sotherton (GBR) 6424
[4]The heptathlon consists of 100 metres hurdles, high jump, shot, 200m on the first day; long jump, javelin and 800m on the second day; [5]Recalculated on current tables.

Women who have won medals under both their maiden and married names

Becker – Mickler (FRG)
Brehmer – Lathan (GDR)
Eckert – Wöckel (GDR)
Foulds – Paul (GBR)
Joyner – Kersee (USA)
Khnykina – Dvalishvili (URS)
Kirszenstein – Szewinska (POL)
Köhler – Birkemeyer (GDR)
Manning – Jackson (USA)

Odam – Tyler (GBR)
Ponomaryeva – Romashkova (URS)
Richter – Górecka (POL)
Samolenko – Dorovskikh (URS)
Schaller – Klier (GDR)
Schlaak – Jahl (GDR)
Vergova – Petkova (BUL)
Wieczorek – Ciepla (POL)
Zharkova – Maslakova (URS)

DISCONTINUED EVENTS

Men

60 metres

1900   Alvin Kraenzlein (USA) 7.0   Walter Tewksbury (USA) 7.1   Stanley Rowley (AUS) 7.2
1904   Archie Hahn (USA) 7.0   William Hogenson (USA) 7.2   Fay Moulton (USA) 7.2

3000 Metres Team Race

1912   United States 9pts   Sweden 13   Great Britain 23
1920   United States 10pts   Great Britain 20   Sweden 24
1924   Finland 8pts   Great Britain 14   United States 25

3 Miles Team Race

1908   Great Britain 6 pts   United States 19   France 32

5000 Metres Team Race

1900   Great Britain 26pts   France 29pts   –

4 Miles Team Race

1904   United States 27pts   United States 28pts   –

Individual Cross-Country

1912[1]   Hannes Kolehmainen (FIN) 45:11.6   Hjalmar Andersson (SWE) 45:44.8   John Eke (SWE) 46:37.6
1920[2]   Paavo Nurmi (FIN) 27:15.0   Erick Backman (SWE) 27:27.6   Heikki Liimatainen (FIN 27:37.4
1924[3]   Paavo Nurmi (FIN) 32:54.8   Ville Ritola (FIN) 34:19.4   Earle Johnson (USA) 35:21.0
[1]12,000 metres; [2]8,000 metres; [3]10,000 metres

Team Cross-Country

1912   Sweden 10pts   Finland 11   Great Britain 49
1920   Finland 10pts   Great Britain 21   Sweden 23
1924   Finland 11pts   United States 14   France 20

200 Metres Hurdles

| 1900 | Alvin Kraenzlein (USA) 25.4 | Norman Pritchard (GBR) 26.6 | Walter Tewksbury (USA) nta |
| 1904 | Harry Hillman (USA) 24.6 | Frank Castleman (USA) 24.9 | George Poage (USA) nta |

1500 Metres Walk

| 1906 | George Bonhag (USA) 7:12.6 | Donald Linden (CAN) 7:19.8 | Konstantin Spetsiosis (GRE) 7:22.0 |

3000 Metres Walk

| 1906 | György Szantics (HUN) 15:13.2 | Hermann Müller (GER) 15:20.0 | Georgios Saridakis (GRE) 15:33.0 |
| 1920 | Ugo Frigerio (ITA) 13:14.2 | George Parker (AUS) nta | Richard Remer (USA) nta |

3500 Metres Walk

| 1908 | George larner (GBR) 14:55.0 | Ernest Webb (GBR) 15:07.4 | Harry Kerr (NZL) 15:43.4 |

10,000 Metres Walk

1912	George Goulding (CAN) 46:28.4	Ernest Webb (GBR) 46:50.4	Fernando Altimani (ITA) 47:37.6
1920	Ugo Frigerio (ITA) 48:06.2	Joseph Pearman (USA) nta	Charles Gunn (GBR) nta
1924	Ugo Frigerio (ITA) 47:49.0	Gordon Goodwin (GBR) 200m	Cecil McMaster (RSA) 300m
1948	John Mikaelsson (SWE) 45:13.2	Ingemar Johansson (SWE) 45:43.8	Fritz Schwab (SUI) 46:00.2
1952	John Mikaelsson (SWE) 45:02.8	Fritz Schwab (SUI) 45:41.0	Bruno Junk (URS) 45:41.2

1928-1936 Event not held

10 Miles Walk

| 1908 | George Larner (GBR) 1:15:57.4 | Ernest Webb (GBR) 1:17:31.0 | Edward Spencer (GBR) 1:21:20.2 |

Standing High Jump

1900	Ray Ewry (USA) 1.655	Irving Baxter (USA) 1.525	Lewis Sheldon (USA) 1.50
1904	Ray Ewry (USA) 1.50[1]	James Stadler (USA) 1.45	Lawson Robertson (USA) 1.45
1906	Ray Ewry (USA) 1.565	Martin Sheridan (USA) 1.40	–
		Léon Dupont (BEL) 1.40	
		Lawson Robertson (USA) 1.40	
1908	Ray Ewry (USA) 1.57	Konstantin Tsiklitiras (GRE) 1.55	–
		John Biller (USA) 1.55m	
1912	Platt Adams (USA) 1.63	Benjamin Adams (USA) 1.60	Konstantin Tsiklitiras (GRE) 1.55

[1]Some reports suggest height was 1.60

Standing Long Jump

1900	Ray Ewry (USA) 3.21	Irving Baxter (USA) 3.135	Emile Torchebeouf (FRA) 3.03
1904	Ray Ewry (USA) 3.476	Charles King (USA) 3.28	John Biller (USA) 3.26
1906	Ray Ewry (USA) 3.30	Martin Sheridan (USA) 3.095	Lawson Robertson (USA) 3.05
1908	Ray Ewry (USA) 3.335	Konstantin Tsiklitiras (GRE) 3.23	Martin Sheridan (USA) 3.225
1912	Konstantin Tsiklitiras (GRE) 3.37	Platt Adams (USA) 3.36	Benjamin Adams (USA) 3.28

Standing Triple Jump

| 1900 | Ray Ewry (USA) 10.58 | Irving Baxter (USA) 9.95 | Robert Garrett (USA) 9.50 |
| 1904 | Ray Ewry (USA) 10.55 | Charles King (USA) 10.16 | James Stadler (USA) 9.53 |

Stone Put (6.40kg)

| 1906 | Nicolaos Georgantas (GRE) 19.925 | Martin Sheridan (USA) 19.035 | Michel Dorizas (GRE) 18.585 |

Shot (Both Hands)

Aggregate of throws with right and left hands

| 1912 | Ralph Rose (USA) 27.70 | Patrick McDonald (USA) 27.53 | Elmer Niklander (FIN) 27.14 |

Discus (Both Hands)

Aggregate of throws with right and left hands

| 1912 | Armas Taipale (FIN) 82.86 | Elmer Niklander (FIN) 77.96m | Emil Magnusson (SWE) 77.37 |

Discus (Greek Style)

1906	Werner Järvinen (FIN) 35.17	Nicolaos Georgantas (GRE) 32.80	István Mudin (HUN) 31.91
1908	Martin Sheridan (USA) 38.00	Marquis Horr (USA) 37.325	Werner Järvinen (FIN) 36.48

Javelin (Both Hands)

Aggregate of throws with right and left hands

1912	Juho Saaristo (FIN) 109.42	Väinö Siikamiemi (FIN) 101.13	Urho Peltonen (FIN) 100.24

Javelin (Free Style)

1908	Eric lemming (SWE) 54.445	Michel Dorizas (GRE) 51.36	Arne Halse (NOR) 49.73

56-Pound (25.4kg) Weight Throw

1904	Étienne Desmarteau (CAN) 10.465	John Flanagan (USA) 10.16	James Mitchell (USA) 10.135
1920	Patrick McDonald (USA) 11.265	Patrick Ryan (USA) 10.965	Carl Lind (SWE) 10.25

Pentathlon

1906[1]	Hjalmar Mellander (SWE) 24	István Mudin (HUN) 25	Eric Lemming (SWE) 29
1912[2]	Ferdinand Bie (NOR) 16[3]	James Donahue (USA) 24	Frank Lukeman (CAN) 24
1920[2]	Eero Lehtonen (FIN) 14	Everett Bradley (USA) 24	Hugo Lahtinen (FIN) 26
1924[2]	Eero Lehtonen (FIN) 14	Elemér Somfay (HUN) 16	Robert LeGendre (USA) 10

[1]Consisted of standing long jump, discus (Greek style), javelin, one-lap (100m) race, Greco-Roman wrestling; [2]Consisted of long jump, javelin, 200m, discus, 1500m, [3]Jim Thorpe (USA) finished first with 7 pts but was subsequently disqualified. He was reinstated posthumously in 1982, but only as joint first.

BADMINTON

Men

1992	Alan Budi Kusuma (INA)	Ardy Wiranata (INA)	Thomas Stuer-Lauridsen (DEN)
			Hermawan Susanto (INA)
1996	Poul-Erik Høyer-Larsen (DEN)	Jiong Dong (CHN)	Rashid Sidek (MAS)
2000	Ji Xinpeng (CHN)	Hendrawan (INA)	Xuanze Xia (CHN)
2004	Taufik Hidayat (INA)	Seung Mo Shon (KOR)	Soni Dwi Kuncoro (INA)

1896-1988 Event not held

Doubles

1992	KOREA	INDONESIA	MALAYSIA
			CHINA
1996	INDONESIA	MALAYSIA	INDONESIA
2000	INDONESIA	KOREA	KOREA
2004	KOREA	KOREA	INDONESIA

1896-1988 Event not held

Women

1992	Susl Susanti (INA)	Bang Soo-Hyun (KOR)	Huang Hua (CHN)
			Tang Jiuhong (CHN)
1996	Bang Soo-Hyun (KOR)	Mia Audina (INA)	Susi Susanti (INA)
2000	Gong Zhichao (CHN)	Camilla Martin (DEN)	Ye Zhaoying (CHN)
2004	Ning Zhang (CHN)	Mia Audina (NED)	Mi Zhou (CHN)

1896-1988 Event not held

Doubles

1992	KOREA	CHINA	KOREA
			CHINA
1996	CHINA	KOREA	CHINA
2000	CHINA	CHINA	CHINA
2004	CHINA	CHINA	KOREA

1896-1988 Event not held

Mixed Doubles

1996	KOREA	KOREA	CHINA
2000	CHINA	INDONESIA	GREAT BRITAIN
2004	CHINA	GREAT BRITAIN	DENMARK

1896-1992 Event not held

BASEBALL

1992	CUBA	TAIWAN	JAPAN
1996	CUBA	JAPAN	UNITED STATES
2000	UNITED STATES	CUBA	KOREA
2004	CUBA	AUSTRALIA	JAPAN

1896-1988 Event not held

BASKETBALL

Men

1936	UNITED STATES	CANADA	MEXICO
1948	UNITED STATES	FRANCE	BRAZIL
1952	UNITED STATES	SOVIET UNION	URUGUAY
1956	UNITED STATES	SOVIET UNION	URUGUAY
1960	UNITED STATES	SOVIET UNION	BRAZIL
1964	UNITED STATES	SOVIET UNION	BRAZIL
1968	UNITED STATES	YUGOSLAVIA	SOVIET UNION
1972	SOVIET UNION	UNITED STATES	CUBA
1976	UNITED STATES	YUGOSLAVIA	SOVIET UNION
1980	YUGOSLAVIA	ITALY	SOVIET UNION
1984	UNITED STATES	SPAIN	YUGOSLAVIA
1988	SOVIET UNION	YUGOSLAVIA	UNITED STATES
1992	UNITED STATES	CROATIA	LITHUANIA
1996	UNITED STATES	YUGOSLAVIA	LITHUANIA
2000	UNITED STATES	FRANCE	LITHUANIA
2004	ARGENTINA	ITALY	UNITED STATES

1896-1932 Event not held

Women

1976	SOVIET UNION	UNITED STATES	BULGARIA
1980	SOVIET UNION	BULGARIA	YUGOSLAVIA
1984	UNITED STATES	KOREA	CHINA
1988	UNITED STATES	YUGOSLAVIA	SOVIET UNION
1992	UNIFIED TEAM	CHINA	USA
1996	UNITED STATES	BRAZIL	AUSTRALIA
2000	UNITED STATES	AUSTRALIA	BRAZIL
2004	UNITED STATES	AUSTRALIA	RUSSIA

1896-1972 Event not held

BEACH VOLLEYBALL

Introduced in 1996

Men

Doubles

1996	UNITED STATES	UNITED STATES	CANADA
2000	UNITED STATES	BRAZIL	GERMANY
2004	BRAZIL	SPAIN	SWITZERLAND

Women

Doubles

1996	BRAZIL	BRAZIL	AUSTRALIA
2000	AUSTRALIA	BRAZIL	BRAZIL
2004	UNITED STATES	BRAZIL	UNITED STATES

BOXING

Light-Flyweight

Weight up to 48kg/105.8lb

1968	Francisco Rodriguez (VEN)	Yong-ju Jee (KOR)	Harlan Marbley (USA)
			Hubert Skrzypczak (POL)
1972	György Gedo (HUN)	U Gil Kim (PRK)	Ralph Evans (GBR)
			Enrique Rodriguez (ESP)

1976	Jorge Hernandez (CUB)	Byong Uk Li (PRK)	Payao Pooltarat (THA)
			Orlando Maladonado (PUR)
1980	Shamil Sabirov (URS)	Hipolito Ramos (CUB)	Byong Uk Li (PRK)
			Ismail Moustafov (BUL)
1984	Paul Gonzales (USA)	Saltore Todisco (ITA)	Keith Mwila (ZAM)
			Jose Bolivar (VEN)
1988	Ivailo Hristov (CUB)	Michael Carabajal (USA)	Robert Isaszegi (HUN)
			Leopoldo Serantes (PHI)
1992	Rogelio Marcelo (CUB)	Daniel Bojinov (BUL)	Roel Velasco (PHI)
			Jan Quast (GER)
1996	Daniel Petrov (BUL)	Mansueto Velsco (PHI)	Oleg Kuryukhin (UKR)
			Rafael Lozano (ESP)
2000	Brahim Asloum (FRA)	Rafael Lozano Munoz (CUB)	Un-Chol Kim (KOR)
			Maikro Romero (CUB)
2004	Yan Varela Bhartelemy (CUB)	Atagün Yalçinkaya (TUR)	Sergei Kazakov (RUS)
			Shiming Zou (CHN)

1896-1964 Event not held

Flyweight

From 1948 the weight limit has been 51kg/112^1/₂lb. In 1904 it was 105lb/47,6kg. From 1920 to 1936 112lb/50.8kg

1904	George Finnegan (USA)	Miles Burke (USA)	–[1]
1920	Frank Di Gennara (USA)	Anders Petersen (DEN)	William Cuthbertson (GBR)
1924	Fidel LaBarba (USA)	James McKenzie (GBR)	Raymond Fee (USA)
1928	Antal Kocsis (HUN)	Armand Appel (FRA)	Carlo Cavagnolli (ITA)
1932	István Enekes (HUN)	Francisco Cabanas (MEX)	Louis Sallca (USA)
1936	Willi Kaiser (GER)	Gavino Matta (ITA)	Louis Lauria (USA)
1948	Pascual Perez (ARG)	Spartaco Bandinelli (ITA)	Soo-Ann Han (KOR)
1952	Nathan Brooks (USA)	Edgar Basel (GER)	Anatoli Bulakov (URS)
			William Toweel (RSA)
1956	Terence Spinks (GBR)	Mircea Dobrescu (ROM)	John Caldwell (IRL)
			René Libeer (FRA)
1960	Gyula Török (HUN)	Sergei Sivko (URS)	Kyoshi Tanabe (JPN)
			Abdelmoncim Elguindi (EGY)
1964	Fernando Atzori (ITA)	Artur Olech (POL)	Robert Carmody (USA)
			Stanislav Sorokin (URS)
1968	Ricardo Delagdo (MEX)	Artur Olech (POL)	Servilio Oliveira (BRA)
			Leo Rwabwogo (UGA)
1972	Gheorghi Kostadinov (BUL)	Leo Rwabwogo (UGA)	Leszek Blazynski (POL)
			Douglas Rodriguez (CUB)
1976	Leo Randolph (USA)	Ramón Duvalon (CUB)	Leszek Blazynski (POL)
			David Torsyan (URS)
1980	Petar Lessov (BUL)	Viktor Miroschnicheko (URS)	Hugh Russel (IRL)
			Janos Varadi (HUN)
1984	Steve McCrory (USA)	Redzep Redzepovski (YUG)	Eyup Can (TUR)
			Ibrahim Bilali (KEN)
1988	Kim Kwang-Sun (KOR)	Andreas Tew (GDR)	Mario González (MEX)
			Timofey Skriabin (URS)
1992	Choi Chol-su (PRK)	Rául González (CUB)	Timothy Austin (USA)
			István Kovács (HUN)
1996	Maikro Romero (CUB)	Bulat Dzumadilov (KAZ)	Albert Pakeyev (RUS)
			Zoltan Lunka (GER)
2000	Wijan Ponlid (THA)	Bolat Dzumadilov (KAZ)	Jerôme Thomas (USA)
			Vladimir Sidorenko (UKR)
2004	Yuriorkis Gamboa Toledano (CUB)	Jerôme Thomas (FRA)	Rustamhodza Rahimov (GER)
			Fuad Aslanov (AZE)

1896-1900, 1906-1912 Event not held
[1]No third place

Bantamweight

From 1948 the weight limit has been 54kg/119lb. In 1904 it was 115lb/52.16kg. In 1908 it was 116lb/52.62kg. From 1920 to 1936 118lb/53.52kg.

1904	Oliver Kirk (USA)	George Finnegan (USA)	–[1]
1908	Henry Thomas (GBR)	John Condon (GBR)	William Webb (GBR)
1920	Clarence Walker (RSA)	Christopher Graham (CAN)	James McKenzie (GBR)
1924	William Smith (RSA)	Salvadore Tripoli (USA)	Jean Ces (FRA)
1928	Vittorio Tamagnini (ITA)	John Daley (USA)	Harry Isaacs (RSA)
1932	Horace Gwynne (CAN)	Hans Ziglarski (GER)	José Villanueva (PHI)
1936	Ulderico Sergo (ITA)	Jack Wilson (USA)	Fidel Ortiz (MEX)

1948	Tibor Csik (HUN)	Giovanni Zuddas (ITA)	Juan Venegas (PUR)
1952	Pentti Hämäläinen (FIN)	John McNally (IRL)	Gennadi Garbuzov (URS)
			Joon-Ho Kang (KOR)
1956	Wolfgang Behrendt (GER)	Soon Chun-Song (KOR)	Frederick Gilroy (IRL)
			Claudio Barrientos (CHI)
1960	Oleg Grigoriev (URS)	Primo Zamparini (ITA)	Brunoh Bendig (POL)
			Oliver Taylor (AUS)
1964	Takao Sakurai (JPN)	Shin Cho Chung (KOR)	Juan Fabila Mendoza (MEX)
			Washington Rodriguez (URU)
1968	Valeri Sokolov (URS)	Eridadi Mukwanga (UGA)	Eiji Morioka (JPN)
			Kyou-Chull Chang (KOR)
1972	Orlando Martinez (CUB)	Alfonso Zamora (MEX)	George Turpin (GBR)
			Ricardo Carreras (USA)
1976	Yong Jo Gu (PRK)	Charles Mooney (USA)	Pat Cowdell (GBR)
			Viktor Rybakov (URS)
1980	Juan Hernandez (CUB)	Bernando Pinango (VEN)	Dumitru Cipere (ROM)
			Michael Anthony Parris (GUY)
1984	Maurizio Stecca (ITA)	Hector Lopez (MEX)	Dale Walters (CAN)
			Pedro Nolasco (DOM)
1988	Kennedy McKinney (USA)	Alexandar Hristov (BUL)	Jorge Julio Rocha (COL)
			Phajol Moolsan (THA)
1992	Joel Casamayor (CUB)	Wayne McCullough (IRL)	Li Gwang-sik (PRK)
			Mohamed Achik (MAR)
1996	István Kovács (HUN)	Arnoldo Mesa (CUB)	Raimkul Malakhbekov (RUS)
			Khadpo Vichairachanun (THA)
2000	Guillermo Rigondeaux (CUB)	Raimkol Malakhbekov (RUS)	Sergei Danilchenko (UKR)
			Clarence Vinson (USA)
2004	Guillermo Rigondeaux (CUB)	Worapoj Petchkoom (THA)	Bahodirjon Soltonov (UZB)
			Aghasi Mammadov (AZE)

1896-1900, 1906, 1912 Event not held
[1]No third place

Featherweight

From 1952 the weight limit has been 57kg/126lb. In 1904 it was 125lb/56.70kg. From 1908 to 1936 it was 126lb/57.15kg. In 1948 it was 58kg

1904	Oliver Kirk (USA)	Frank Haller (USA)	Fred Gilmore (USA)
1908	Richard Gunn (GBR)	Charles Morris (GBR)	Hugh Roddin (GBR)
1920	Paul Fritsch (FRA)	Jean Gachet (FRA)	Edoardo Garzena (ITA)
1924	Jackie Fields (USA)	Joseph Salas (USA)	Pedro Quartucci (ARG)
1928	Lambertus van Klaveren (NED)	Victor Peralta (ARG)	Harold Devine (USA)
1932	Carmelo Robeldo (ARG)	Josef Schleinkofer (GER)	Carl Carlsson (SWE)
1936	Oscar Casanovas (ARG)	Charles Cattterall (RSA)	Josef Miner (GER)
1948	Ernesto Foremnti (ITA)	Denis Shepherd (RSA)	Alexei Antkiewicz (POL)
1952	Jan Zachara (TCH)	Sergio Caprari (ITA)	Joseph Ventaja (FRA)
			Leonard Leisching (RSA)
1956	Vladimir Safronov (URS)	Thomas Nicholls (GBR)	Henryk Niedzwiedzki (POL)
			Pentti Hämäläinen (FIN)
1960	Francesco Musso (ITA)	Jerzy Adamski (POL)	William Meyers (RSA)
			Jorma Limmonen (FIN)
1964	Stanislav Stepashkin (URS)	Anthony Villaneuva (PHI)	Charles Brown (USA)
			Heinz Schultz (GER)
1968	Antonio Roldan (MEX)	Albert Robinson (USA)	Philip Waruinge (KEN)
			Ivan Michailov (BUL)
1972	Boris Kuznetsov (URS)	Philip Waruinge (KEN)	Clemente Rojas (COL)
			András Botos (HUN)
1976	Angel Herrera (CUB)	Richard Nowakowski (GDR)	Juan Peredes (MEX)
			Leszek Kosedowski (POL)
1980	Rudi Fink (GDR)	Adolfo Horta (CUB)	Viktor Rybakov (URS)
			Krzysztof Kosedowski (POL)
1984	Meldrick Taylor (USA)	Peter Konyegwachie (NGR)	Turgut Aykac (TUR)
			Omar Peraza (VEN)
1988	Giovanni Parisi (ITA)	Daniel Dumitrescu (ROM)	Lee Jae-Hyuk (KOR)
			Abdelhak Achik (MAR)
1992	Andreas Tew (GER)	Faustino Reyes Lopez (ESP)	Hocine Soltani (ALG)
			Ramazi Paliani (EUN)
1996	Somluck Kamsing (THA)	Serafim Todorov (BUL)	Pablo Chacon (ARG)
			Floyd Mayweather (USA)

2000	Beksat Sattarkhanov (KAZ)	Ricardo Juarez (USA)	Tahar Tamsamani (MAR)
			Kamil Dzamalutdinov (RUS)
2004	Alexei Tichthenko ((RUS)	Song-Guk Kim (KOR)	Vitali Tajbert (GER)
			Seok-Hwan Jo (KOR)

1896-1900, 1906, 1912 Event not held

Lightweight

From 1952 the weight has been 60kg/132lb in 1904 and from 1920 to 1936 it was 135lb/61.24kg. In 1908 it was 140lb/63.50kg. In 1948 it was 62kg/136$\frac{1}{2}$lb

1904	Harry Springer (USA)	James Fagan (USA)	Russell Van Horn (USA)
1908	Frederick Grace (GBR)	Frederick Spiller (GBR)	Harry Johnson (GBR)
1920	Samuel Mosberg (RSA)	Gotfried Johansen (DEN)	Clarence Newton (CAN)
1924	Hans Nielsen (DEN)	Alfredo Coppello (ARG)	Frederick Boylstein (USA)
1928	Carlo Orlandi (ITA)	Stephen Halaiko (USA)	Gunnar Berggren (SWE)
1932	Lawrence Stevens (RSA)	Thure Ahlqvist (SWE)	Nathan Bor (RSA)
1936	Imre Harangi (HUN)	Nikolai Stepulov (EST)	Erik Agren (SWE)
1948	Gerald Dreyer (USA)	Joseph Vissers (BEL)	Svend Wad (DEN)
1952	Aureliano Bolognesi (ITA)	Alexei Antkiewicz (POL)	Gheorge Fiat (ROM)
			Erkki Pakkanen (FIN)
1956	Richard McTaggart (GBR)	Harry Kurschat (GER)	Anthony Byren (IRL)
			Anatoli Lagetko (URS)
1960	Kazimierz Pazdzior (POL)	Sandro Lopopoli (ITA)	Richard McTaggart (GBR)
			Abel Laudonio (ARG)
1964	Józef Grudzien (POL)	Velikton Barannikov (URS)	Ronald A Harris (USA)
			James McCourt (IRL)
1968	Ronald W Harris (USA)	Józef Grudzien (POL)	Calistrat Cutov (ROM)
			Zvonimir Vujin (YUG)
1972	Jan Szczepanksi (POL)	László Orban (HUN)	Samuel Mbugna (KEN)
			Alfonso Perez (COL)
1976	Howard Davis (USA)	Simion Cutov (ROM)	Ace Rusevski (YUG)
			Vasiliy Solomin (URS)
1980	Angel Horrara (CUB)	Viktor Demianenko (URS)	Kazimierz Adach (POL)
			Richard Nowakowski (GDR)
1984	Pernell Whitaker (USA)	Luis Ortiz (PUR)	Martin Mbanga (CMR)
			Chun Chi-Sung (KOR)
1988	Andreas Zülow (GDR)	George Cramme (SWE)	Nerguy Enkhbat (MGL)
			Romallis Ellis (USA)
1992	Oscar de la Hoya (CUB)	Marco Rudolph (USA)	Namjil Bayarsaikhan (MGL)
			Hong Sung-sik (KOR)
1996	Hocine Soltani (ALG)	Tontcho Tonchev (BUL)	Terrance Cauthen (USA)
			Leonard Doroftei (ROM)
2000	Mario Kindelan (CUB)	Andrei Kotelnyk (UKR)	Alexander Maletin (RUS)
	Christian Bejarano Benitez (MEX)		
2004	Mario Kindelan (CUB)	Amir Khan (GBR)	Serik Yeleuov (KAZ)
			Murat Krachev (RUS)

1896-1900, 1906, 1912 Event not held

Light-Welterweight

Weight up to 63.5kg/140lb

1952	Charles Adkins (USA)	Viktor Mednov (URS)	Errki Mallenius (FIN)
			Bruno Visintin (ITA)
1956	Vladimir Yengibarvan (URS)	Franco Nenci (ITA)	Henry Loubscher (RSA)
			Constantin Dumitrescu (ROM)
1960	Bohumil Nemecek (TCH)	Clement Quartey (GHA)	Quincy Daniels (USA)
			Marian Kasprzvk (POL)
1964	Jerzy Kulej (POL)	Yevgeni Frolov (URS)	Eddie Blay (GHA)
			Habib Galhia (TUN)
1968	Jerzy Kulej (POL)	Enrique Regueiforos (CUB)	Arto Nilsson (FIN)
			James Wallington (USA)
1972	Ray Seales (USA)	Anghel Anghelov (BUL)	Zvonimir Vujin (YUG)
			Issaka Daborg (NGR)
1976	Ray Leonard (USA)	Andres Aldama (CUB)	Vladimir Kolev (BUL)
			Kazimierz Szczerba (POL)
1980	Patrizio Oliva (ITA)	Serik Konakbeyev (URS)	Jose Aguilar (CUB)
			Anthony Willis (GBR)
1984	Jerry Page (USA)	Dhawee Umponmana (THA)	Mircea Fuger (ROM)
			Mirko Puzovic (YUG)

1988	Vycheslav Janovski (URS)	Grahame Cheney (AUS)	Lars Myrberg (SWE)
			Reiner Gies (FRG)
1992	Hector Vinent (CUB)	Marc Leduc (CAN)	Jyri Kjall (FIN)
			Leonard Doroftei (ROM)
1996	Hector Vinent (CUB)	Oktay Urkal (GER)	Bolat Niyazymbetov (KAZ)
			Fathi Missaoui (TUN)
2000	Mahamadkadis Abdullayev (UZB)	Ricardo Williams (USA)	Diogenes Luna Martinez (CUB)
			Mohamed Allalou (ALG)
2004	Manus Boonjumnong (THA)	Yudel Johnson Cedeno (CUB)	Boris Georgiev (BUL)
			Ionut Gheorghe (ROM

1896-1948 Event not held

Welterweight

From 1948 the weight limit has been 67kg/148lb. In 1904 it was 147^1/$_2$lb/65.27kg. From 1920 to 1936 it was 147lb/66.68kg

1904	Albert Young (USA)	Harry Springer (USA)	Joseph Lydon (USA)
			James Eagan (USA)
1920	Albert Schneider (CAN)[1]	Alexander Ireland (GBR)	Frederick Colberg (USA)
1924	Jean Delarge (BEL)	Héctor Mendez (ARG)	Douglas Lewis (CAN)
1928	Edward Morgan (NZL)	Raul Landini (ARG)	Raymond Smillie (CAN)
1932	Edward Flynn (USA)	Erich Campe (GER)	Bruno Ahlberg (FIN)
1936	Sten Suvio (FIN)	Michael Murach (GER)	Gerhard Petersen (DEN)
1948	Julius Torma (TCH)	Horace Herring (USA)	Alessandro D'Ottavio (ITA)
1952	Zygmunt Chycla (POL)	Sergei Schtsherbakov (URS)	Victor Jörgensen (DEN)
			Günther Heidemann (GER)
1956	Nicholae Lince (ROM)	Frederick Tiedt (IRL)	Kevin Hogarth (AUS)
			Nicholas Gargano (GBR)
1960	Giovanni Benvenutti (ITA)	Yuriy Radonyak (URS)	Leszek Drogosz (POL)
			James Lloyd (GBR)
1964	Marian Kasprzyk (POL)	Ritschardas Tamulis (URS)	Pertti Perhonen (FIN)
			Silvano Bertini (ITA)
1968	Manfred Wolfe (GDR)	Joseph Bessala (CMR)	Vladimir Musalinov (URS)
			Mario Guillot (ITA)
1972	Emilio Corea (CUB)	Janos Kajdi (HUN)	Dick Murunga (KEN)
			Jesse Valdez (USA)
1976	Jochen Bachfeld (GDR)	Pedro Gamarro (VEN)	Reinhard Skricek (FRG)
			Victor Zilberman (ROM)
1980	Andrew Aldama (CUB)	John Mugabi (UGA)	Karl-Heinz Krüger (GDR)
			Kazimierz Szczerba (POL)
1984	Mark Breland (USA)	An Young-Su (KOR)	Joni Nyman (FIN)
			Luciano Bruno (ITA)
1988	Robert Wanglia (KEN)	Laurent Boudouani (FRA)	Jan Dydak (POL)
			Kenneth Gould (USA)
1992	Michael Carruth (IRL)	Juan Hernandez (CUB)	Akrom Chenglai (THA)
			Anibal Acevedo (PUR)
1996	Oleg Saitov (RUS)	Juan Hernandez (CUB)	Marian Simion (ROM)
			Daniel Santos (PUR)
2000	Oleg Saitov (RUS)	Sergei Dotsenko (UKR)	Dorel Simion (ROM)
			Vitali Gusac (MOL)
2004	Bakhtiyar Artayev (KAZ)	Lorenzo Aragon Armenteros (CUB)	Jung-Joo Kim (KOR)
			Oleg Saitov (RUS)

1896-1900, 1906-1912 Event not held
[1]*Actually an American citizen*

Light-Middleweight

Weight up to 71kg/157lb

1952	László Papp (HUN)	Theunis van Schalkwyk (RSA)	Boris Tishin (URS)
			Eladio Herrera (ARG)
1956	László Papp (HUN)	José Torres (USA)	John McCormack (GBR)
			Zbigniew Pietrzkowski (POL)
1960	Wilbert McClure (USA)	Carmelo Bossi (ITA)	Boris Lagutin (URS)
			William Fisher (GBR)
1964	Boris Lagutin (URS)	Josef Gonzales (FRA)	Nohim Maivegun (NGR)
			Jozef Grzsiak (POL)
1968	Boris Lagutin (URS)	Rolondo Garbey (CUB)	John Baldwin (USA)
			Günther Meier (FRG)
1972	Dieter Kottysch (FRG)	Wieslaw Rudkowski (POL)	Alan Minter (GBR)
			Peter Tiepold (GDR)

1976	Jerzy Rybicki (POL)	Tadiji Kacar (YUG)	Rolando Garbey (CUB)
			Viktor Savchenko (URS)
1980	Armando Martinez (CUB)	Alexander Koshkin (URS)	Jan Franck (TCH)
			Detlef Kastner (GDR)
1984	Frank Tate (USA)	Shawn O'Sullivan (CAN)	Manfred Zielonka (FRG)
			Christophe Tiozzo (FRA)
1988	Park Si-Hun (KOR)	Roy Jones (USA)	Richard Woodhall (GBR)
			Raymond Downey (CAN)
1992	Juan Carlos Lemus (CUB)	Orhan Delibas (NED)	György Mizsei (HUN)
			Robin Reid (GBR)
1996	David Reid (USA)	Alfredo Duvergel (CUB)	Karim Tulaganov (UZB)
			Ezmouhan Ibzaimov (KAZ)
2000	Jermachan Ibraimov (KAZ)	Marian Simion (ROM)	Pornchai Thongburan (THA)
			Jermain Taylor (USA)

1896-1948, 2004 Event not held

Middleweight

From 1952 the weight has been 75kg/165lb. From 1904 to 1908 it was 158lb/71.68kg. From 1920 to 1936 it was 160lb/72.57kg. In 1948 it was 73kg/161lb

1904	Charles Mayer (USA)	Benjamin Spradley (USA)	–[1]
1908	John Douglas (GBR)	Reginald Baker (AUS/NZL)	William Philo (GBR)
1920	Harry Mallin (GBR)	Georges Prud'homme (CAN)	Moe Herscovich (CAN)
1924	Harry Mallin (GBR)	John Elliott (GBR)	Joseph Beecken (BEL)
1928	Piero Toscani (ITA)	Jan Hermandek (TCH)	Léonard Steyaert (BEL)
1932	Carmen Barth (USA)	Amado Azar (ARG)	Ernest Pierce (RSA)
1936	Jean Despeaux (FRA)	Henry Tiller (NOR)	Raúl Villareal (ARG)
1948	László Papp (HUN)	John Wright (GBR)	Ivano Fontana (ITA)
1952	Floyd Patterson (USA)	Vasile Tita (ROM)	Boris Nikolov (URS)
			Stig Sjolin (SWE)
1956	Gennadi Schatkov (URS)	Ramon Tapia (CHI)	Gilbert Chapron (FRA)
			Victor Zalazar (ARG)
1960	Edward Crook (USA)	Tadeusz Walasek (POL)	Ion Monea (ROM)
			Yovgeni Feofanov (URS)
1964	Valeri Popenchenko (URS)	Emil Schultz (GER)	Franco Valle (ITA)
			Tadeusz Walasek (POL)
1968	Christopher Finnegan (GBR)	Alexei Kisselyov (URS)	Agustin Zaragoza (MEX)
			Alfred Jones (USA)
1972	Vyatcheslav Lemechev (URS)	Reima Virtanen (FIN)	Prince Armartey (GHA)
			Marvin Johnston (USA)
1976	Michael Spinks (USA)	Rufat Riskiev (URS)	Alec Nastac (ROM)
			Luis Martinez (CUB)
1980	Jose Gomez (CUB)	Viktor Savchenko (URS)	Jerzy Rybicki (POL)
			Valentin Silaghi (ROM)
1984	Shin Joop-Sup (KOR)	Virgil Hill (USA)	Mohammed Zaoui (ALG)
			Aristides Gonzales (PUR)
1988	Henry Maske (GDR)	Egerton Marcus (CAN)	Chris Sande (KEN)
			Hussain Shaw Syed (PAK)
1992	Ariel Hernandez (CUB)	Chris Byrd (USA)	Chris Johnson (CAN)
			Lee Seung-Bae (KOR)
1996	Ariel Hernandez (CUB)	Malik Beyleroglu (TUR)	Mohamed Bahari (ALG)
			Roshii Wells (USA)
2000	Jorge Gutierrez (CUB)	Gaidarbek Gaidarbekov (RUS)	Vugar Alekperov (AZE)
			Zsolt Erdei (HUN)
2004	Gaydarbek Gaydarbekov (RUS)	Gennadi Golovkin (KAZ)	Andre Dirrell (USA)
			Suriya Prasathinphimai (THA)

1896-1900, 1906, 1912 Event not held
[1]No Third Place

Light-Heavyweight

From 1952 the weight limit has been 81kg/178 1/2lb. From 1920 to 1936 it was 175lb/79.38kg. In 1948 it was 80kg/186 1/4lb

1920	Edward Eagan (USA)	Sverre Sörsdal (NOR)	Harold Franks (GBR)
1924	Harry Mitchell (GBR)	Thyge Petersen (DEN)	Sverre Sörsdal (NOR)
1928	Victor Avendano (ARG)	Ernst Pistulla (GER)	Karel Miljon (NED)
1932	David Carstens (RSA)	Gino Rossi (ITA)	Peter Jörgensen (DEN)
1936	Roger Michelot (FRA)	Richard Vogt (GER)	Francisco Risiglione (ARG)
1948	George Hunter (RSA)	Donald Scott (GBR)	Maurio Cia (ARG)

1952	Norvel Lee (USA)	Antonio Pacenza (ARG)	Anotoli Perov (URS)
			Harri Siljander (FIN)
1956	James Boyd (USA)	Gheorghe Negrea (ROM)	Carlos Lucas (CHI)
			Romualdas Murauskas (URS)
1960	Cassius Clay (USA)	Zbigniew Pietrzykowski (POL)	Anthony Madigan (AUS)
			Giulio Saraudi (ITA)
1964	Cosimo Pinto (ITA)	Alexei Kisselyov (URS)	Alexander Nikolov (BUL)
			Zbigniew Pietrzykowski (POL)
1968	Dan Poznyak (URS)	Ion Monea (ROM)	Georgy Stankov (BUL)
			Stanislav Gragan (POL)
1972	Mate Petlov (YUG)	Gilberto Carrillo (CUB)	Issac Ikhouria (NGR)
			Janusz Gortat (POL)
1976	Leon Spinks (USA)	Sixto Soria (CUB)	Costica Danifoiu (ROM)
			Janusz Gortat (POL)
1980	Slobodan Kacar (YUG)	Pavel Skrzecz (POL)	Herbert Bauch (GDR)
			Ricardo Rojas (CUB)
1984	Anton Josipovic (YUG)	Kevin Barry (NZL)	Mustapha Moussa (ALG)
			Evander Holyfield (USA)
1988	Andrew Maynard (USA)	Nourmagomed Chanavazov (URS)	Damir Skaro (YUG)
			Henryk Petrich (POL)
1992	Torsten May (GER)	Rostislav Zaoulitchyni (EUN)	Wojciech Bartnik (POL)
			Zoltan Beres (HUN)
1996	Vasili Jirov (KAZ)	Lee Seung-Bae (KOR)	Antonio Tarver (USA)
			Thomas Ulrich (GER)
2000	Alexander Lebziak (RUS)	Rudolf Kraj (CZE)	Andrei Fedtchuk (UKR)
			Sergei Michailov (UZB)
2004	Andre Ward (USA)	Magomed Aripgadjiev (BLR)	Utkirbek Haydarov (UZB)
			Ahmed Ismail (EGY)

1896-1912 Event not held

Heavyweight

From 1984 the weight limit has been 91kg/200½lb. From 1904 to 1908 it was over 158lb/71.67kg. From 1920 to 1936 it was over 175lb/79.38kg. In 1948 it was over 80kg/176¼lb. From 1952 to 1980 it was over 81kg/178¼lb

1904	Samuel Berger (USA)	Charles Mayer (USA)	William Michaels (USA)
1908	Albert Oldman GBR)	Sydney Evans (GBR)	Frederick Parks (GBR)
1920	Ronald Lawton (GBR)	Sören Petersen (DEN)	Xavier Eluère (FRA)
1924	Otto von Porat (NOR)	Sören Petersen (DEN)	Alfredo Porzio (ARG)
1928	Arturo Rodriguez Jurado (ARG)	Nils Ramm (SWE)	Jacob Michaelsen (DEN)
1932	Santiago Lovell (ARG)	Luigi Rovati (ITA)	Frederick Feary (USA)
1936	Herbert Runge (GER)	Guillermo Lovell (ARG)	Erling Nilsen (NOR)
1948	Rafael Iglesias (ARG)	Gunnar Nilsson (SWE)	John Arthur (RSA)
1952	Hayes Edward Sanders (USA)	Ingemar Johansson[1] (SWE)	Andries Nieman (RSA)
			Ilkka Koski (FIN)
1956	Peter Rademacher (USA)	Lev Mukhin (URS)	Daniel Bekker (RSA)
			Giacomo Ros (ITA)
1960	Franco de Piccoli (ITA)	Daniel Bekker (RSA)	Josef Nemec (TCH)
			Günther Siegmund (GER)
1964	Joe Frazier (USA)	Hans Huber (GER)	Guiseppe Ros (ITA)
			Vadim Yemeynaov (URS)
1968	George Foreman (USA)	Ionas Tschepulis (URS)	Giorgio Bambini (ITA)
			Joaquim Rocha (MEX)
1972	Teofilio Stevenson (CUB)	Ion Alexe (ROM)	Peter Hussing (FRG)
			Hasse Thomsen (SWE)
1976	Teofilio Stevenson (CUB)	Mircea Simon (ROM)	Johnny Tate (USA)
			Clarence Hill (BER)
1980	Teofilio Stevenson (CUB)	Pyotr Zayev (URS)	Jürgen Fanghanel (GDR)
			István Levai (HUN)
1984	Henry Tillman (USA)	Willie Dewitt (CAN)	Angelo Musone (ITA)
			Arnold Vanderlijde (NED)
1988	Ray Mercer (USA)	Baik Hyun-Man (KOR)	Andrzej Golota (POL)
			Arnold Vanderlidje (NED)
1992	Félix Savón (CUB)	David Izonretei (NGR)	David Tua (NZL)
			Arnold Vanderlijde (NED)
1996	Félix Savón (CUB)	David Defiagbon (CAN)	Nate Jones (USA)
			Luan Krasniqui (GER)
2000	Félix Savón (CUB)	Sultanahmed Ibzagimov (RUS)	Vladimir Tchanturia (GEO)
			Sebastian Kober (GER)

2004   Odlanier Solis Fonte (CUB)   Viktor Zuyev (BLR)   Naser El Shami (SYR)
                                                                             Mohamed El Sayed (EGY)

1896-1900, 1906, 1912 Event not held
[1]Silver medal originally not awarded; Johansson disqualified but reinstated in 1982

Super-Heavyweight

From 1984 the class has been for those over 91kg/200[1]/₂lb

1984   Tyrell Biggs (USA)   Francesco Damiani (ITA)   Robert Wells (GBR)
                                                                            Salihu Azis (YUG)
1988   Lennox Lewis (CAN)   Riddick Bowe (USA)   Alexander Mirochnitchenko (URS)
                                                                            Jasz Zarenkiewicz (POL)
1992   Roberto Balado (CUB)   Richard Igbineghu (NGR)   Brian Nielsen (DEN)
                                                                            Svilen Roussinov (BUL)
1996   Vladimir Klichko (UKR)   Paea Wolfgram (TGA)   Alexei Lezin (RUS)
                                                                            Duncan Dokwari (NGR)
2000   Audley Harrison (GBR)   Muchtarchan Dildabekov (KAZ)   Rustam Saidov (UZB)
                                                                            Paolo Vidoz (ITA)
2004   Alexander Pvyetkin (RUS)   Mohamed Aly (EGY)   Roberto Cammarelle (ITA)
                                                                            Michel Lopez Nunez (CUB)

1896-1980 Event not held

CANOEING
Men

500 Metres Kayak Singles (K1)

1976   Vasile Diba (ROM) 1:46.41   Zoltán Szytanity (HUN) 1:46.95   Rüdiger Helm (GDR) 1:48.30
1980   Vladimir Parfenovich (URS) 1:43.43   John Sumegi (AUS) 1:44.12   Vasile Diba (ROM) 1:44.90
1984   Ian Ferguson (NZL) 1:47.84   Lars-Erik Möberg (SWE) 1:48.18   Bernard Bregeon (FRA) 1:48.41
1988   Zsolt Gyulay (HUN) 1:44.82   Andreas Stähle (GDR) 1:46.38   Paul McDonald (NZL) 1:46.46
1992   Mikko Kolehmainen (FIN) 1:40.34   Zsolt Gyulay (HUN) 1:40.64   Knut Holmann (NOR) 1:40.71
1996   Antonio Rossi (ITA) 1:37.423   Knut Holmann (NOR) 1:38.339   Piotr Markiewicz (POL) 1:38.615
2000   Knut Holmann (NOR) 1:57.847   Petar Markov (BUL) 1:58.393   Michael Kolganov (ISR) 1:59.563
2004   Adan van Koeverden (CAN) 1:37.919   Nathan Baggaley (AUS) 1:38.467   Ian Wynne (GBR) 1:38.547
1896-1972 Event not held

1000 Metres Kayak Singles (K1)

1936   Gregor Hradetsky (AUT) 4:22.9   Helmut Cämmerer (GER) 4:25.6   Jacob Kraaier (NED) 4:35.1
1948   Gert Fredriksson (SWE) 4:33.2   Johann Kobberup (DEN) 4:39.9   Henri Eberhardt (FRA) 4:41.4
1952   Gert Fredriksson (SWE) 4:07.9   Thorvald Strömberg (FIN) 4:09.7   Louis Gantois (FRA) 4:20.1
1956   Gert Fredriksson (SWE) 4:12.8   Igor Pissaryev (URS) 4:15.3   Lajos Kiss (HUN) 4:16.2
1960   Erik Hansen (DEN) 3:53.00   Imre Szöllösi (HUN) 3:54.02   Gert Fredriksson (SWE) 3:55.89
1964   Rolf Peterson (SWE) 3:57.13   Mihály Hesz (HUN) 3:57.28   Aurel Vernescu (ROM) 4:00.77
1968   Mihály Hesz (HUN) 4:02.63   Alexander Shaparenko (URS) 4:03.58   Erik Hansen (DEN) 4:04.39
1972   Aleksandr Shaparenko (URS) 3:48.06   Rolf Peterson (SWE) 3:48.35   Géza Csapó (HUN) 3:49.38
1976   Rüdiger Helm (GDR) 3:48.20   Géza Csapó (HUN) 3:48.84   Vasile Diba (ROM) 3:49.65
1980   Rüdiger Helm (GDR) 3:48.77   Alain Lebas (FRA) 3:50.20   Ion Birladeanu (ROM) 3:50.49
1984   Alan Thompson (NZL) 3:45.73   Milan Janic (YUG) 3:46.88   Greg Barton (USA) 3:47.38
1988   Greg Barton (USA) 3:55.27   Grant Davies (AUS) 3:55.28   Andre Wohliebe (GDR) 3:55.55
1992   Clint Robinson (AUS) 3:37.26   Knut Holmann (NOR) 3:37.50   Greg Barton (USA) 3:37.93
1996   Knut Holmann (NOR) 3:25.785   Beniamino Bonomi (ITA) 3:27.073   Clint Robinson (AUS) 3:29.713
2000   Knut Holmann (NOR) 3:33.269   Petar Markov (BUL) 3:34.649   Tim Brabants (GBR) 3:35.057
2004   Eirk Larsen (NOR) 3:25.897   Ben Fouhy (NZL) 3:27.413   Adam van Koeverden (CAN) 3:28.218
1896-1932 Event not held

10,000 Metres Kayak Singles (K1)

1936   Ernst Krebs (GER) 46:01.6   Fritz Landertinger (AUT) 46:14.7   Ernest Riedel (USA) 47:23.9
1948   Gert Fredriksson (SWE) 50:47.7   Kurt Wires (FIN) 51:18.2   Ejvind Skabo (NOR) 51:35.4
1952   Thorvald Strömberg (FIN) 47:22.8   Gert Fredriksson (SWE) 47:34.1   Michel Scheuer (GER) 47:54.5
1956   Gert Fredriksson (SWE) 47:43.4   Ferenc Hatlaczky (HUN) 47:53.3   Michel Scheuer (GER) 48.00.3
1896-1932, 1960-2004 Event not held

500 Metres Kayak Pairs (K2)

1976   GDR 1:35.87   SOVIET UNION 1:36.81   ROMANIA 1:37.43

1980	SOVIET UNION 1:32.38	SPAIN 1:33.65	GDR 1:34.00
1984	NEW ZEALAND 1:34.21	SWEDEN 1:35.26	CANADA 1:35.41
1988	NEW ZEALAND 1:33.98	SOVIET UNION 1:34.15	HUNGARY 1:34.32
1992	GERMANY 1:28.27	POLAND 1:29.84	ITALY 1:30.00
1996	GERMANY 1:28.697	ITALY 1:28.729	AUSTRALIA 1:29.409
2000	HUNGARY 1:47.055	AUSTRALIA 1:47.895	GERMANY 1:48.771
2004	GERMANY 1:27.897	AUSTRALIA 1:27.920	BELARUS 1:27.996

1896-1972 Event not held

1000 Metres Kayak Pairs (K2)

1936	AUSTRIA 4:03.8	GERMANY 4:08.9	NETHERLANDS 4:12.2
1948	SWEDEN 4:07.3	DENMARK 4:07.5	FINLAND 4:08.7
1952	FINLAND 3:51.1	SWEDEN 3:51.1	AUSTRIA 3:51.4
1956	GERMANY 3:49.6	SOVIET UNION 3:51.4	AUSTRIA 3:55.8
1960	SWEDEN 3:34.7	HUNGARY 3:34.91	POLAND 3:37.34
1964	SWEDEN 3:38.4	NETHERLANDS 3:39.30	GERMANY 3:40.69
1968	SOVIET UNION 3:37.54	HUNGARY 3:38.44	AUSTRIA 3:40.71
1972	SOVIET UNION 3:31.23	HUNGARY 3:32.00	POLAND 3:38.33
1976	SOVIET UNION 3:29.01	GDR 3:29.33	HUNGARY 3:30.56
1980	SOVIET UNION 3:26.72	HUNGARY 3:28.49	SPAIN 3:28.66
1984	CANADA 3:24.22	FRANCE 3:25.97	AUSTRALIA 3:26.80
1988	UNITED STATES 3:32.42	NEW ZEALAND 3:32.71	AUSTRALIA 3:33.76
1992	GERMANY 3:16.10	SWEDEN 3:17.70	POLAND 3:18.86
1996	ITALY 3:09.190	GERMANY 3:10.518	BULGARIA 3:11.206
2000	ITALY 3:14.461	SWEDEN 3:16.075	HUNGARY 3:16.357
2004	SWEDEN 3:18.420	ITALY 3:19.484	NORWAY 3:19.528

1896-1932 Event not held

10,000 Metres Kayak Pairs (K2)

1936	GERMANY 41:45.0	AUSTRIA 42:05.4	SWEDEN 43:06.1
1948	SWEDEN 46:09.4	NORWAY 46:44.8	FINLAND 46:48.2
1952	FINLAND 44:21.3	SWEDEN 44:21.7	HUNGARY 44:26.6
1956	HUNGARY 43:37.0	GERMANY 43:40.6	AUSTRALIA 43:43.2

1896-1932, 1960-2004 Event not held

1000 Metres Kayak Fours (K4)

1964	SOVIET UNION 3:14.67	GERMANY 3:15.39	ROMANIA 3:15.51
1968	NORWAY 3:14.38	ROMANIA 3:14.81	HUNGARY 3:15.10
1972	SOVIET UNION 3:14.38	ROMANIA 3:15.07	NORWAY 3:15.27
1976	SOVIET UNION 3:08.69	SPAIN 3:08.95	GDR 3:10.76
1980	GDR 3:13.76	ROMANIA 3:15.35	BULGARIA 3:15.46
1984	NEW ZEALAND 3:02.28	SWEDEN 3:02.81	FRANCE 3:03.94
1988	HUNGARY 3:00.20	SOVIET UNION 3:01.40	GDR 3:02.37
1992	GERMANY 2:54.18	HUNGARY 2:54.82	AUSTRALIA 2:56.97
1996	GERMANY 2:51.528	HUNGARY 2:53.184	RUSSIA 2:53.996
2000	HUNGARY 2:55.188	GERMANY 2:55.704	POLAND 2:57.192
2004	HUNGARY 2:56.919	GERMANY 2:58.659	SLOVAKIA 2:2:59.314

1896-1960 Event not held

500 Metres Canadian Singles (C1)

1976	Alexander Rogov (URS) 1:59.23	John Wood (CAN) 1:59.58	Matija Ljubek (YUG) 1:59.60
1980	Sergei Postrekhin (URS) 1:53.37	Lubomir Lubenov (BUL) 1:53.49	Olaf Heukrodt (GDR) 1:54.38
1984	Larry Cain (CAN) 1:57.01	Henning Jakobsen (DEN) 1:58.45	Costica Olaru (ROM) 1:59.86
1988	Olaf Heukrodt (GDR) 1:56.42	Mikhail Slivinski (URS) 1:57.26	Martin Marinov (BUL) 1:57.27
1992	Nikolai Boukhalov (BUL) 1:51.15	Mikhail Slivinski (EUN) 1:51.40	Olaf Heukrodt (GER) 1:53.00
1996	Martin Doktor (CZE) 1:49.934	Slavomir Knazovicky (SLO) 1:50.510	Imre Pulai (ITA) 1:50.758
2000	György Kolonics (HUN) 2:24.813	Maksim Opalyev (RUS) 2:25.809	Andreas Dittmer (GER) 2:27.591
2004	Andreas Dittmer (GER) 1:46.383	David Cal (ESP) 1:46.723	Maxim Opalyev ((RUS) 1:47.767

1896-1972 Event not held

1000 Metres Canadian Singles (C1)

1936	Francis Amyot (CAN) 5:32..1	Bohuslav Karlik (TCH) 5:36.9	Erich Koschik (GER) 5:39.0
1948	Josef Holocek (TCH) 5:42.0	Douglas Bennet (CAN) 5:53.3	Robert Boutigny (FRA) 5:55.9
1952	Josef Holocek (TCH) 4:56.3	János Parti (HUN) 5:03.6	Olavi Ojanpera (FIN) 5:08.5

1956	Leon Rotman (ROM) 5:05.3	István Hernek (HUN) 5:06.2	Gennadi Bukharin (URS) 5:12.7
1960	János Parti (HUN) 4:33.93	Alexsandr Silayov (URS) 4:34.41	Leon Rotman (ROM) 4:35.87
1964	Jürgen Eschert (GER) 4:35.14	Andrei Igorov (ROM) 4:37.89	Yevgeni Penyayev (URS) 4:38.31
1968	Tibor Tatai (HUN) 4:36.14	Detlef Lewe (FRG) 4:38.31	Vitali Galkov (URS) 4:40.42
1972	Ivan Patzaichin (ROM) 4:08.94	Tamas Wichmann (HUN) 4:12.42	Detlef Lewe (FRG) 4:13.36
1976	Matija Ljubek (YUG) 4:09.51	Vassili Urchenko (URS) 4:12.57	Tamas Wichmann (HUN) 4:14.11
1980	Lubomir Lubenov (BUL) 4:12.38	Sergei Postrekhin (URS) 4:13.53	Eckhard Leue (GDR) 4:15.02
1984	Ulrich Eicke (FRG) 4:06.32	Larry Cain (CAN) 4:08.67	Henning Jakobsen (DEN) 4:09.51
1988	Ivans Klementjevs (URS) 4:12.78	Jörg Schmidt (GDR) 4:15.83	Nikolai Boukhalov (BUL) 4:18.94
1992	Nikolai Boukhalov (BUL) 4:05.92	Ivans Klementjevs (LAT) 4:06.60	György Zala (HUN) 4:07.35
1996	Martin Doktor (CZE) 3:54.418	Ivans Klementjevs (LAT) 3:54.954	György Zala (HUN) 3:56.366
2000	Andreas Dittmer (GER) 3:54.379	Ledys Frank Balceiro (CUB) 3:56.071	Steve Giles (CAN) 3:56.437
2004	David Cal (ESP) 3:46.201	Andreas Dittmer (GER) 3:46.721	Attila Vajda (HUN) 3:49.025

1896-1932 Event not held

10,000 Metres Canadian Singles (C1)

1948	Frantisek Capek (TCH) 62:05.2	Frank Havens (USA) 62:40.4	Norman Lane (CAN) 64:35.3
1952	Frank Havens (USA) 57:41.1	Gabór Novák (HUN) 57:49.2	Alfréd Jindra (TCH) 57:33.1
1956	Leon Rotman (ROM) 56:41.0	János Parti (HUN) 57:11.0	Gennadi Bukharin (URS) 57:14.5

1896-1936, 1960-2004 Event not held

500 Metres Canadian Pairs (C2)

1976	SOVIET UNION 1.45.81	POLAND 1:47.77	HUNGARY 1:47.35
1980	HUNGARY 1:43.39	ROMANIA 1:44.12	BULGARIA 1:44.83
1984	YUGOSLAVIA 1:43.67	ROMANIA 1:45.68	SPAIN 1:47.71
1988	SOVIET UNION 1:41.77	POLAND 1:43.61	FRANCE 1:43.81
1992	UNIFIED TEAM 1:41.54	GERMANY 1:41.68	BULGARIA 1:41.94
1996	HUNGARY 1:40.42	MOLDOVA 1:40.45	ROMANIA 1:41.33
2000	HUNGARY 1:51.284	POLAND 1:51.536	ROMANIA 1:54.200
2004	CHINA 1:1:40.278	CUBA 1.40.350	RUSSIA 1:40.442

1896-1972 Event not held

1000 Metres Canadian Pairs (C2)

1936	CZECHOSLOVAKIA 4:50.1	AUSTRIA 4:53.8	CANADA 4:56.7
1948	CZECHOSLOVAKIA 5:07.1	UNITED STATES 5:08.2	FRANCE 5:15.2
1952	DENMARK 4:38.3	CZECHOSLOVAKIA 4:42.9	GERMANY 4:48.3
1956	ROMANIA 4:47.4	SOVIET UNION 4:48.6	HUNGARY 4:54.3
1960	SOVIET UNION 4:17.94	ITALY 4:20.77	HUNGARY 4:20.89
1964	SOVIET UNION 4:04.64	FRANCE 4:06.52	DENMARK 4:07.48
1968	ROMANIA 4:07.18	HUNGARY 4:08.77	SOVIET UNION 4:11.30
1972	SOVIET UNION 3:52.60	ROMANIA 3:52.63	BULGARIA 3:58.10
1976	SOVIET UNION 3:52.76	ROMANIA 3:54.28	HUNGARY 3:55.66
1980	ROMANIA 3:47.65	GDR 3:49.93	SOVIET UNION 3:51.28
1984	ROMANIA 3:40.60	YUGOSLAVIA 3:41.56	FRANCE 3:48.01
1988	SOVIET UNION 3:48.36	GDR 3:51.44	POLAND 3:54.33
1992	GERMANY 3:37.42	DENMARK 3:39.26	FRANCE 3:39.51
1996	GERMANY 3:31.870	ROMANIA 3:32.294	HUNGARY 3:32.514
2000	ROMANIA 3:37.355	CUBA 3:38.753	GERMANY 3:41.129
2004	GERMANY 3:41.802	RUSSIA 3:42.990	HUNGARY 3:43.106

1896-1932 Event not held

10,000 Metres Canadian Pairs (C2)

1936	CZECHOSLOVAKIA 50.33.5	CANADA 51:15.8	AUSTRIA 51:28.0
1948	UNITED STATES 55:55.4	CZECHOSLOVAKIA 57:38.5	FRANCE 58:00.8
1952	FRANCE 54:08.3	CANADA 54:09.9	GERMANY 54:28.1
1956	SOVIET UNION 54:02.4	FRANCE 54:48.3	HUNGARY 55:15.6

1896-1932, 1960-2004 Event not held

4x500 Metres Kayak Singles (K1) Relay

1960	GERMANY 7:39.43	HUNGARY 7:44.02	DENMARK 7:46.09

1896-1956, 1964-2004 Event not held

10,000 Metres Folding Kayak Singles (K1)

1936	Gregor Hradetzky (AUT) 50:01.2	Henri Eberhardt (FRA) 50:04.2	Xaver Hörmann (GER) 50:06.5

1896-1932, 1948-2004 Event not held

10,000 Metres Folding Kayak Pairs (K2)

| 1936 | SWEDEN 45:48.9 | GERMANY 45:49.2 | NETHERLANDS 46:12.4 |

1896-1932, 1948-2004 Event not held

SLALOM RACING

(Not held 1896-1968, 1976-88)

Kayak Singles (K1)

1972	Siegbert Horn (GDR) 268.56pts	Norbert Sattler (AUT) 270.76	Harald Gimpel (GDR) 277.95
1992	Pierpaolo Ferrazzi (ITA) 106.89pts	Sylvain Curinier (FRA) 107.06	Jochen Lettmann (GER) 108.52
1996	Oliver Fix (GER) 141.22pts	Andraz Vehovar (SLO) 141.65	Thomas Becker (GER) 142.79
2000	Thomas Schmidt (GER) 217.25pts	Paul Ratcliffe (GBR) 223.71	Pierpaolo Ferrazzi (ITA) 225.03
2004	Benoit Peschier (FRA) 187.96pts	Campbell Walsh (GBR) 190.17	Fabien Lefevre (FRA) 190.99

Canadian Singles (C1)

1972	Reinhard Eiben (GDR) 315.84pts	Reinhold Kauder (FRG) 327.89	Jamie McEwan (USA) 335.95
1992	Lukas Pollert (CZE) 113.69pts	Gareth Marriott (GBR) 116.48	Jacky Avril (FRA) 117.18
1996	Michal Martikan (SVK) 151.03pts	Lukás Pollert (CZE) 151.17	Patrice Estanguet (FRA) 152.84
2000	Tony Estanguet (FRA) 231.87pts	Michal Martikan (SVK) 233.76	Juraj Mincik (SVK) 234.22
2004	Tony Estanguet (FRA) 189.16pts	Michal Martikan (SVK) 189.28	Stefan Pfannmöller (GER) 191.56

Canadian Pairs (C2)

1972	GDR 310.68pts	FRG 311.90	FRANCE 315.10
1992	UNITED STATES 122.41pts	CZECHOSLOVAKIA 124.25	FRANCE 124.38
1996	FRANCE 158.82pts	CZECH REPUBLIC 160.16	GERMANY 163.72
2000	SLOVAKIA 237.74pts	POLAND 243.81	CZECH REPUBLIC 249.45
2004	SLOVAKIA 207.16pts	GERMANY 210.98	CZECH REPUBLIC 212.86

Women

500 Metres Kayak Singles (K1)

1948	Karen Hoff (DEN) 2:31.9	Alide Van de Anker-Doedans (NED) 2:32.8	Fritzi Schwingl (AUT) 2:32.9
1952	Slyvi Saimo (FIN) 2:18.4	Gertrude Liebhart (AUT) 2:18.8	Nina Savina (URS) 2:21.6
1956	Yelisaveta Demntyeva (URS) 2:18.9	Therese Zenz (GDR) 2:19.6	Tove Söby (DEN) 2:22.3
1960	Antonina Seredina (URS) 2:08.8	Therese Zenz (GDR) 2:08.22	Daniele Walkowiak (POL) 2:10.46
1964	Ludmila Khvedosyuk (URS) 2:12.87	Hilde Lauer (ROM) 2:15.35	Marcia Jones (USA) 2:15.68
1968	Ludmila Pinyeva (URS) 2:11.09	Renate Breuer (FRG) 2:12.71	Viorica Dumitru (ROM) 2:13.22
1972	Yulia Ryabchinskaya (URS) 2:03.17	Mieke Jaapies (NED) 2:04.03	Anna Pfeffer (HUN) 2:05.50
1976	Carola Zirzow (GDR) 2:01.05	Tatyana Korshunova (URS) 2:03.07	Klara Rajnai (HUN) 2:05.01
1980	Birgit Fischer (GDR) 1:57.96	Vanya Gheva (BUL) 1:59.48	Antonina Melnikova (URS) 1:59.66
1984	Agneta Andersson (SWE) 1:58.72	Barbara Schuttpelz (FRG) 1:59.93	Annemiek Derckx (NED) 2:00.11
1988	Vania Guecheva (BUL) 1:55.19	Birgit Schmidt (GDR) 1:55.31	Izabella Dylewska (POL) 1:57.38
1992	Birgit Schmidt (GER) 1:51.60	Rita Kõbán (HUN) 1:51.96	Izabella Dylewska (POL) 1:52.36
1996	Rita Kõbán (HUN) 1:47.655	Caroline Brunet (CAN) 1:47.891	Josefa Idem (ITA) 1:48.731
2000	Josefa Idem Guerrini (ITA) 2:13.848	Caroline Brunet (CAN) 2:14.646	Katrin Borchert (AUS) 2:15.138
2004	Natasa Janics (HUN) 1:47.741	Josefa Idem (ITA) 1:49.729	Caroline Brunet (CAN) 1:50.601

1896-1936 Event not held

500 Metres Kayak Pairs (K2)

1960	SOVIET UNION 1:54.76	GERMANY 1:56.66	HUNGARY 1:58.22
1964	GERMANY 1:56.95	UNITED STATES 1:59.16	ROMANIA 2:00.25
1968	FRG 1:56.44	HUNGARY 1:58.60	SOVIET UNION 1:58.61
1972	SOVIET UNION 1:53.50	GDR 1:54.30	ROMANIA 1:55.01
1976	SOVIET UNION 1:51.15	HUNGARY 1:51.69	GDR 1:51.81
1980	GDR 1:43.88	SOVIET UNION 1:46.91	HUNGARY 1:47.95
1984	SWEDEN 1:45.25	CANADA 1:47.13	FRG 1:47.32
1988	GDR 1:43.46	BULGARIA 1:44.06	NETHERLANDS 1:46.00
1992	GERMANY 1:40.29	SWEDEN 1:40.41	HUNGARY 1:40.81
1996	SWEDEN 1:39.329	GERMANY 1:39.589	AUSTRALIA 1:40.641
2000	GERMANY 1:56.996	HUNGARY 1:58.580	POLAND 1:58.784
2004	HUNGARY 3:38.101	GERMANY 3:3.533	POLAND 3:40.077

1896-1956 Event not held

500 Metres Kayak Fours (K4)

1984	ROMANIA 1:38.34	SWEDEN 1:38.87	CANADA 1:39.40
1988	GDR 1:40.78	HUNGARY 1:41.88	BULGARIA 1:42.63
1992	HUNGARY 1:38.32	GERMANY 1:38.47	SWEDEN 1:39.79
1996	GERMANY 1:31.077	SWITZERLAND 1:32.701	SWEDEN 1:32.917
2000	GERMANY 1:34.532	HUNGARY 1:34.946	ROMANIA 1:37.010
2004	GERMANY 1:34.340	HUNGARY 1:34.536	UKRAINE 1:36.192

1896-1980 Event not held

SLALOM RACING

Not held 1896-1968, 1976-88

Kayak Singles (K1)

1972	Angelika Bahmann (GDR) 364.50	Gisela Grothaus (FRG) 398.15	Magdelena Wunderlich (FRG) 400.50
1992	Elisabeth Micheler (GER) 126.41	Danielle Woodward (AUS) 128.27	Diana Chladek (USA) 131.75
1996	Stepanka Hilgertová (CZE) 169.49	Dana Chladek (USA) 169.49	Myriam Fox-Jerusalmi (FRA) 171.00
2000	Stepanka Hilgertová (CZE) 247.04	Brigitte Guibal (FRA) 251.88	Anne-Lise Bardet (FRA) 254.77
2004	Elena Kaliska (SVK) 210.03	Rebecca Giddens (USA) 214.62	Helen Reeves (GBR) 218.77

CYCLING

Men

1000 Metres Time Trial

1896[1]	Paul Masson (FRA) 24.0	Stamatios Nikolopoulos (GRE) 25.4	Adolf Schmal (AUT) 26.6
1906[1]	Francesco Verri (ITA) 22.8	Herbert Crowther (GBR) 22.8	Menjou (FRA) 23.2
1928	Willy Falck-Hansen (DEN) 1:14.4	Gerard Bosch van Drakestein (NED) 1:15.2	Edgar Gray (AUS) 1:15.6
1932	Edgar Gray (AUS) 1:13.0	Jacobus van Egmond (NED) 1:13.3	Charles Rampelberg (FRA) 1:13.4
1936	Arie van Vliet (NED) 1:12.0	Pierre Georget (FRA) 1:12.8	Rudolf Karsch (GER) 1:13.2
1948	Jacques Dupont (FRA) 1:13.5	Pierre Nihant (BEL) 1:14.5	Thomas Godwin (GBR) 1:15.0
1952	Russell Mockridge (AUS) 1:11.1	Marino Morettini (ITA) 1:12.7	Raymond Robinson (RSA) 1:13.0
1956	Leandro Faggin (ITA) 1:09.8	Ladislav Foucek (TCH) 1:11.4	J Alfred Swift (RSA) 1:11.6
1960	Sante Gaiardoni (ITA) 1:07.27	Dieter Giessler (GER) 1:08.75	Rotislav Vargshkin (URS) 1:08.86
1964	Patrick Sercu (BEL) 1:09.59	Giovanni Pettonella (ITA) 1:10.09	Pierre Trentin (FRA) 1:10.42
1968	Pierre Trentin (FRA) 1:03.91	Niels-Christian Fredborg (DEN) 1:04.61	Janusz Kierkowski (POL) 1:04.63
1972	Niels-Christian Fredborg (DEN) 1:06.44	Daniel Clark (AUS) 1:06.87	Jürgen Schütze (GDR) 1:07.02
1976	Klaus-Jürgen Grunke (GDR) 1:05.93	Michel Vaarten (BEL) 1:07.52	Niels-Christian Fredborg (DEN) 1:07.62
1980	Lothar Thomas (GDR) 1:02.955	Alexander Pantilov (URS) 1:04.845	David Weller (JAM) 1:05.241
1984	Fredy Schmidke (FRG) 1:06.10	Curtis Harnett (CAN) 1:06.44	Fabrice Colas (FRA) 1:06.65
1988	Alexander Kiritchenko (URS) 1:04.499	Martin Vinnicombe (AUS) 1:04.784	Robert Lechner (FRG) 1:05.114
1992	Jose Manuel Moreno (ESP) 1:03.342	Shane Kelly (AUS) 1:04.288	Erin Hartwell (USA) 1:04.753
1996	Florian Rousseau (FRA) 1:02.712	Erin Hartwell (USA) 1:02.940	Takandu Jumonji (JPN) 1:02.261
2000	Jason Queally (GBR) 1:01.689	Stefan Nimke (GER) 1:02.487	Shane Kelly (AUS) 1:02.818
2004	Chris Hoy (GBR) 1:00.711	Arnaud Tournant (FRA) 1:00.896	Stefan Nimke (GER) 1:01.186

1900-1904, 1908-1924 Event not held
[1]*Held over 333.33 metres*

1000 Metres Sprint

1896[1]	Paul Masson (FRA) 4:56.0	Stamatios Nikopoulos (GRE)	Léon Flameng (FRA)
1900[1]	Georges Taillandier (FRA) 2:52.0	Fernand Sanz (FRA)	John Lake (USA)
1906	Francesco Verri (ITA) 1:42.2	Herbert Bouffler (GBR)	Eugène Debougnie (BEL)
1908[2]	–	–	–
1920	Maurice Peeters (NED) 1:38.3	Horace Johnson (GBR)	Harry Ryan (GBR)
1924[3]	Lucien Michard (FRA) 12.8	Jacob Meijer (NED)	Jean Cugnot (FRA)
1928	René Beaufrand (FRA) 13.2	Antoine Mazairac (NED)	Willy Falck-Hansen (DEN)
1932	Jacobus van Egmond (NED) 12.6	Louis Chaillot (FRA)	Bruno Pellizzari (ITA)
1936	Toni Merkens (GER) 11.8	Arie van Vliet (NED)	Louis Chaillot (FRA)
1948	Mario Ghella (ITA) 12.0	Reginald Harris (GBR)	Axel Schandorff (DEN)
1952	Enzo Sacchi (ITA) 12.0	Lionel Cox (AUS)	Werner Potzernheim (GER)
1956	Michel Rousseau (FRA) 11.4	Guglielmo Presenti (ITA)	Richard Ploog (AUS)
1960	Sante Gaiardoni (ITA) 11.1	Leo Sterckz (BEL)	Valentina Gasparella (ITA)
1964	Giovanni Petternella (ITA) 13.69	Sergio Bianchetto (ITA)	Daniel Morelon (FRA)
1968	Daniel Morelon (FRA) 10.68	Giordano Turrini (ITA)	Pierre Trentin (FRA)
1972	Daniel Morelon (FRA) 11.25	John Nicholson (AUS)	Omar Pchakadze (URS)

1976 Anton Tkac (TCH) 10.78	Daniel Morelon (FRA)	Hans-Jürgen Geschke (GDR)
1980 Lutz Hesslich (GDR) 11.40	Yave Cahard (FRA)	Sergey Kopylov (URS)
1984 Mark Gorski (USA) 10.49	Nelson Vails (USA)	Tsutomu Sakamoto (JPN)
1988 Lutz Hesslich (GDR)	Nikolai Kovche (URS)	Gary Neiwand (AUS)
1992 Jens Fiedler (GER)	Gary Neiwand (AUS)	Curtis Harnett (CAN)
1996 Jens Fiedler (GER)	Marthy Nothstein (USA)	Curtis Harnett (CAN)
2000 Marty Nothstein (USA)	Florian Rousseau (FRA)	Jens Fiedler (GER)
2004 Ryan Bayley (AUS)	Theo Bos (NED)	Rene Wolff (GER)

1904,1912 Event not held

[1]*Held over 2000 metres. In 1900 Taillandier's last 200m was 13.0sec;* [2]*There was a 1000 metres sprint event in the 1908 Games, but it was declared void because the riders exceeded the time limit in spite of repeated warnings;* [3]*Since 1924 only times over the last 200 metres of the event have been recorded*

4000 Metres Individual Pursuit

Note: Bronze medal times are set in a third place race, so can be faster than those set in the race for first and second places.

1964 Jiri Daler (TCH) 5:04.75	Giorgio Utsi (ITA) 5:05.96	Preben Isaksson (DEN) 5:01.90
1968 Daniel Rebillard (FRA) 4:41.71	Mogens Frey Jensen (DEN) 4:42.43	Xaver Kurmann (SUI) 4:39.42
1972 Knut Knudsen (NOR) 4:45.74	Xaver Kurmann (SUI) 4:51.96	Hans Lutz (FRG) 4:50.80
1976 Gregor Braun (FRG) 4:47.61	Herman Ponsteen (NED) 4:49.72	Thomas Huschke (GDR) 4:52.71
1980 Robert Dilli-Bundi (SUI) 4:35.66	Alain Bondue (FRA) 4:42.96	Hans-Henrik Orsted (DEN) 4:36.54
1984 Steve Hegg (USA) 4:39.35	Rolf Gölz (FRG) 4:43.82	Leonard Nitz (USA) 4:44.03
1988 Gintaoutas Umaras (URS) 4:32.00	Dean Woods (AUS) 4:35.00	Bernd Dittert (GDR) 4:34.17
1992 Chris Boardman (GBR)[1]	Jens Lehmann (GER) –	Gary Anderson (NZL) 4:31.061
1996 Andrea Collinelli (ITA) 4:20.893	Philippe Ermenault (FRA) 4:22.714	Brad McGee (AUS) 4:26.121
2000 Robert Bartko (GER) 4:18.515	Jens Lehmann (GER) 4:23.824	Brad McGee (AUS) 4:19.250
2004 Bradley Wiggins (GBR) 4:16.304	Brad McGee (AUS) 4:20.436	Sergi Escobar (ESP) 4:17.947

1896-1960 Event not held

[1]*Lapped Lehmann in final*

4000 Metres Team Pursuit

Note: Bronze medal times are set in a third place race, so can be faster than those set in the race for first and second place

1908[1] GREAT BRITAIN 2:18.6	GERMANY 2:28.6	CANADA 2:29.6
1920 ITALY 5:14.2[2]	GREAT BRITAIN 5:13.8	SOUTH AFRICA 5:17.8
1924 ITALY 5:15.0	POLAND nta	BELGIUM nta
1928 ITALY 5:01.8	NETHERLANDS 5:06.2	GREAT BRITAIN nta
1932 ITALY 4:53.0	FRANCE 4:55.7	GREAT BRITAIN 4:56.0
1936 FRANCE 4:45.0	ITALY 4:51.0	GREAT BRITAIN 4:52.6
1948 FRANCE 4:57.8	ITALY 5:36.7	GREAT BRITAIN 4:55.8
1952 ITALY 4:46.1	SOUTH AFRICA 4:53.6	GREAT BRITAIN 4:51.5
1956 ITALY 4:37.4	FRANCE 4:39.4	GREAT BRITAIN 4:42.2
1960 ITALY 4:30.90	GERMANY 4:35.78	SOVIET UNION 4:34.05
1964 GERMANY 4:35.67	ITALY 4:35.74	NETHERLANDS 4:38.99
1968 DENMARK 4:22.44[3]	FRG 4:18.94	ITALY 4:18.35
1972 FRG 4:22.14	GDR 4:25.25	GREAT BRITAIN 4:23.78
1976 FRG 4:21.06	SOVIET UNION 4:27.15	GREAT BRITAIN 4:22.41
1980 SOVIET UNION 4:15.70	GDR 4:19.67	CZECHOSLOVAKIA[4]
1984 AUSTRALIA 4:25.99	UNITED STATES 4:29.85	FRG 4:25.60
1988 SOVIET UNION 4:13.31	GDR 4:14.09	AUSTRALIA 4:16.02
1992 GERMANY 4:08.791	AUSTRALIA 4:10.218	DENMARK 4:15.860
1996 FRANCE 4:05.930	RUSSIA 4:07.730	AUSTRALIA 4:07.570
2000 GERMANY 3:59.710	UKRAINE 4:04.520	GREAT BRITAIN 4:01.979
2004 AUSTRALIA 3:58.233	GREAT BRITAIN 4:01.760	SPAIN 4:05.523

1896-1906, 1912 Event not held.

[1]*Held over 1810.5 metres;* [2]*Great Britain finished first but were relegated to second for alleged interference;* [3]*Federal Republic of Germany (FRG) finished first but were disqualified for illegal assistance. After the Games ended the International Cycling Federation awarded them the silver medal;* [4]*Italy disqualified in third place*

Olympic Sprint

Introduced in 2000 – three man teams over three laps

2000 FRANCE 44.233s	GREAT BRITAIN 44.680s	AUSTRALIA 45.161s
2004 GERMANY 43.980	JAPAN 44.246	FRANCE 44.359

2000 Metres Tandem

1906 GREAT BRITAIN 2:57.0	GERMANY 2:57.2	GERMANY nta

1908	FRANCE 3:07.8	GREAT BRITAIN nta	GREAT BRITAIN nta
1920	GREAT BRITAIN 2:94.4	SOUTH AFRICA nta	NETHERLANDS nta
1924[1]	FRANCE 12.6	DENMARK	NETHERLANDS
1928	NETHERLANDS 11.8	GREAT BRITAIN	GERMANY
1932	FRANCE 12.0	GREAT BRITAIN	DENMARK
1936	GERMANY 11.8	NETHERLANDS	FRANCE
1948	ITALY 11.3	GREAT BRITAIN	FRANCE
1952	AUSTRALIA 11.0	SOUTH AFRICA	ITALY
1956	AUSTRALIA 10.8	CZECHOSLOVAKIA	ITALY
1960	ITALY 10.7	GERMANY	SOVIET UNION
1964	ITALY 10.75	SOVIET UNION	GERMANY
1968	FRANCE 9.83	NETHERLANDS	BELGIUM
1972	SOVIET UNION	GDR	POLAND

1896-1904, 1912, 1976-2004 Event not held
[1]*Since 1924 only times over the last 200m have been recorded*

Individual Points Race

1984	Roger Ilegems (BEL)	Uwe Messerschmidt (FRG)	Jose Youshimatz (MEX)
1988	Dan Frost (DEN)	Leo Peelen (NED)	Marat Ganeyev (URS)
1992	Giovanni Lombardi (ITA) 44	Leon van Bon (NED) 43	Cedric Mathy (BEL) 41
1996	Silvio Martinello (ITA) 37	Brian Walton (CAN) 29	Stuart O'Grady (AUS) 25
2000	Juan Llaneras (ESP) 14	Milton Wynants (URU) 18	Alexei Markov (RUS) 16
2004	Mikhail Ignatyev (RUS) 93	Joan Llaneras (ESP) 82	Guido Fulst (GER) 79

1896-1980 Event not held

Madison

Introduced in 2000 – two-man teams over 60km course

2000	AUSTRALIA 26	BELGIUM 22	ITALY 15
2004	AUSTRALIA 22	SWITZERLAND 15	GREAT BRITAIN 12

Keirin

Introduced in 2000. (An 8-lap race)

2000	Florian Rousseau (FRA)	Gary Niewand (AUS)	Jens Fiedler (GER)
2004	Ryan Bayley (AUS)	Jose Escuredo (ESP)	Shane Kelly (AUS)

Team Road Race

In 1912-1920 consisted of the combined times of the four best riders from each country in the individual race; in 1924-1952 the combined times of the best three; in 1956 based on placings of the best three
Raced over 320km – 1912; 175km – 1920; 168km – 1924-1928; 100km – 1932-1936; 194.63km – 1948; 190.4km – 1952

1912	SWEDEN 44:35:33.6	GREAT BRITAIN 44:44:39.2	UNITED STATES 44:47:55.5
1920	FRANCE 19:16:43.2	SWEDEN 19:23:10.0	BELGIUM 19:28:44.4
1924	FRANCE 19:30:14.0	BELGIUM 19:46:55.4	SWEDEN 19:59:41.6
1928	DENMARK 15:09:14.0	GREAT BRITAIN 15:14:49.0	SWEDEN 15:27:49.0
1932	ITALY 7:27:15.2	DENMARK 7:38:50.2	SWEDEN 7:39:12.6
1936	FRANCE 7:39:16.2	SWITZERLAND 7:39:20.4	BELGIUM 7:39:21.0
1948	BELGIUM 15:58:17.4	GREAT BRITAIN 16:03:31.6	FRANCE 16:08:19.4
1952	BELGIUM 15:20:46.6	ITALY 15:33:27.3	FRANCE 15:38:58.1
1956	FRANCE 22pts	GREAT BRITAIN 23pts	GERMANY 27pts

Road Team Time-Trial

Raced over 100km, except in 1964 (109.89km), 1968 (104km), 1980 (101km)

1960	ITALY 2:14:33.53	GERMANY 2:16:56.31	SOVIET UNION 2:18:41.67
1964	NETHERLANDS 2:26:31.19	ITALY 2:26:55.39	SWEDEN 2:27:11.52
1968	NETHERLANDS 2:07:49.06	SWEDEN 2:09:26.60	ITALY 2:10:18.74
1972	SOVIET UNION 2:11:17.8	POLAND 2:11:47.5	–[1]
1976	SOVIET UNION 2:08:53.0	POLAND 2:09:13.0	DENMARK 2:12:20.0
1980	SOVIET UNION 2:01:21.7	GDR 2:02:53.2	CZECHOSLOVAKIA 2:02:53.9
1984	ITALY 1:58:28.0	SWITZERLAND 2:02:38.0	UNITED STATES 2:02:46.0
1988	GDR 1:57:47.7	POLAND 1:57:54.2	SWEDEN 1:59:47.3
1992	GERMANY 2:01:39	ITALY 2:02:39	FRANCE 2:05:25

1896-1908, 1996-2004 Event not held
[1]*Netherlands finished in third place but their bronze medal was withdrawn following a drugs test*

Road Individual Time Trial

Held over 52km in 1996; 46.8km in 2000

1996	Miguel Induráin (ESP) 1:04:05	Abraham Olano (ESP) 1:04:17	Chris Boardman (GBR) 1:04:36
2000	Vyacheslav Ekimov (RUS) 57:40	Jan Ullrich (GER) 57:48	Lance Armstrong (USA) 58:14
2004	Tyler Hamilton (USA) 57:31.74	Vyacheslav Ekimov (RUS) 57:50.58	Bobby Julich (USA) 57:58.19

1896-1992 Event not held

Individual Road Race

1896	Aristidis Konstantinidis (GRE) 3:22:31.0	August Goedrich (GER) 3:42:18.0	F Battel (GBR) dna
1906	Fernand Vast (FRA) 2:41:28.0	Maurice Bardonneau (FRA) 2:41:28.4	Edmund Lugnet (FRA) 2:41:28.6
1912	Rudolp:Lewis (RSA) 10:42:39.0	Frederick Grubb (GBR) 10:51:24.2	Carl Schutte (USA) 10:52:38.8
1920	Harry Stenqvist (SWE) 4:40:01.8	Henry Kaltenbrun (RSA) 4:41:26.6	Fernand Canteloube (FRA) 4:42:54.4
1924	Armand Blanchonnet (FRA) 6:20:48.0	Henry Hoevenaers (BEL) 6:30:27.0	René Hamel (FRA) 6:40:51,6
1928	Henry Hansen (DEN) 4:47:18.0	Frank Southall (GBR) 4:56:06.0	Gösta Carlsson (SWE) 5:00:17.0
1932	Attilio Pavesi (ITA) 2h 28:05.6	Guglielmo Segato (ITA) 2:29:21.4	Bernhard Britz (SWE) 2:29:45.2
1936	Robert Charpentier (FRA) 2:33:05.0	Guy Lapébie (FRA) 2:33:05.2	Ernst Nievergeit (SUI) 2:33:05.8
1948	José Bevaert (FRA) 5:18:12.6	Gerardus Voorting (NED) 5:18:16.2	Lode Wouters (BEL) 5:18:16.2
1952	André Noyelle (BEL) 5:06:03.4	Robert Grondelaers (BEL) 5:06:51.2	Edi Ziegler (GER) 5:07:47.5
1956	Ercole Baldini (ITA) 5:21:17	Arnaud Gevre (FRA) 5:23:16	Alan Jackson (GBR) 5:23:16
1960	Viktor Kapitonov (URS) 4:20:37	Livio Trapé (ITA) 4:20:37	Willy van den Berghen (BEL) 4:20:57
1964	Mario Zanin (ITA) 4:39:51.63	Kjell Rodian (DEN) 4:39:51.65	Walter Godefroot (BEL) 4:39:51.74
1968	Pierfranco Vianelli (ITA) 4:41:25.24	Leif Mortensen (DEN) 4:42:49.71	Gösta Pettersson (SWE) 4:43:15.24
1972	Hennie Kuiper (NED) 4:14:37	Kevin Sefton (AUS) 4:15:04	–[1]
1976	Bernt Johansson (SWE) 4:46:52	Giuseppe Martinelli (ITA) 4:47:23	Mieczyslaw Nowicki (POL) 4:47:23
1980	Sergey Sukhoruchenkov (URS) 4:48:28.9	Czeslaw Lang (POL) 4:51:26.9	Yuri Barinov (URS) 4:51:26.9
1984	Alexi Grewal (USA) 4:59:57	Steve Bauer (CAN) 4:32:25	Dag Otto Lauritzen (NOR) 5:00:18
1988	Olaf Ludwig (GDR) 4:32:22	Bernd Gröne (FRG) 4:32:25	Christian Henn (FRG) 4:32:46
1992	Fabio Casartelli (ITA) 4:35:21	Hendrik Dekker (NED) 4:35:22	Dainis Ozols (LAT) 4:35:24
1996	Pascal Richard (SUI) 4:53:56	Rolf Sörensen (DEN) 4:53:56	Max Sciandri (GBR) 4:53:58
2000	Jan Ullrich (GER) 5:29:08	Alexander Vinokourov (KAZ) 5:29:17	Jens Voigt (GER) 5:29:20
2004	Paolo Bettini (ITA) 5:41:44	Sergio Paulinho (POR) 5:41:45	Axel Merckx (BEL) 5:41:52

1900-1904, 1908 Event not held
This event has been held over the following distances: 1896 – 87km; 1906 – 84km; 1912-329km; 1920-175km;
1924 – 188km; 1928-168km; 1932 and 1936 – 100km; 1948 – 194.63km; 1952 – 190.4km; 1956 – 187.73km; 1960
– 175.38km; 1964 – 194.83km 1968 – 196.2km; 1972 – 182.4km; 1976 – 175km; 1980 – 189km; 1984 – 190.2km;
1988 – 196.8km; 1992 – 194km; 1996 – 221.85km; 2000 – 239.4km; 2004 – 224.4km
[1]Jaime Huelano (ESP) finished third but medal withdrawn following a drug test

DISCONTINUED EVENTS

440 Yards Track (402.34m)

1904	Marcus Hurley (USA) 31.8	Burton Downing (USA)	Edward Billingham (USA)

0.33 Mile Track (536.45m)

1904	Marcus Hurley (USA) 43.8	Burton Downing (USA)	Edward Billingham (USA)

660 Yards Track (603.5m)

1908	Victor Johnson (GBR) 51.2	Emile Demangel (FRA) close	Karl Neumer (GER) 1 length

880 Yards Track (804.67m)

1904	Marcus Hurley (USA) 1:09.0	Edward Billingham (USA)	Burton Downing (USA)

1 Mile Track (1609.34m)

1904	Marcus Hurley (USA) 2:41.4	Burton Downing (USA)	Edward Billingham (USA)

2 Miles Track (3218.6m)

1904	Burton Downing (USA) 4:57.8	Oscar Goerke (USA)	Marcus Hurley (USA)

5000 MetresTrack

1906	Francesco Verri (ITA) 8:35.0	Herbert Crowther (GBR)	Fernand Vast (FRA)
1908	Benjamin Jones (GBR) 8:36.2	Maurice Schilles (FRA)	Andre Auffray (FRA)

5 Miles Track (8046.57m)

1904	Charles Schlee (USA) 13:08.2	George Wiley (USA)	Arthur Andrews (USA)

10,000 MetresTrack

1896	Paul Masson (FRA) 17:54.2	Léon Flameng (FRA)	Adolf Schmal (AUT)

20,000 MetresTrack

1906	William Pett (GBR) 29:00.0	Maurice Bardonneau (FRA) 29:30.0	Fernand Vast (FRA) 29:32.0
1908	Clarence Kingsbury (GBR) 34:13.6	Benjamin Jones (GBR)	Joseph Werbrouck (BEL)

25 Miles Track (40.225m)

1904	Burton Downing (USA) 1:10:55.4	Arthur Andrews (USA)	George Wiley (USA)

50,000 MetresTrack

1920	Henry George (BEL) 1:16:43.2	Cyril Alden (GBR)[1]	Petrus Ikelaar (NED)
1924	Jacobus Willems (NED) 1:18:24	Cyril Alden (GBR)	Frederick Wyld (GBR)

[1]Most eyewitnesses considered that Ikelaar finished second

100 Kilometres Track

1896	Leon Flameng (FRA) 3:08:19.2	Georgios Kolettis (GRE) 6 laps	–[1]
1908	Charles Bartlett (GBR) 2h 41:48.6	Charles Denny (GBR)	Octave Lapize (FRA)

[1]Only two riders finished

12 hours Track

1896	Adolf Schmal (AUT) 314.997km	Frank Keeping (GBR) 314.664km	Georgios Paraskevopoulous (GRE) 313.330km

Women

Sprint

1988	Erika Salumäe (URS)	Christa Röthenburger Luding (GDR)	Connie Young (USA)
1992	Erika Salumäe (EST)	Annett Neumann (GER)	Ingrid Haringa (NED)
1996	Felicia Ballanger (FRA)	Michelle Ferris (AUS)	Ingrid Haringa (NED)
2000	Felicia Ballanger (FRA)	Oksana Gritschina (RUS)	Irina Janovich (UKR)
2004	Lori-Ann Munzer (CAN)	Tamila Abassova (RUS)	Anna Meares (AUS)

1896-1984 Event not held

500 MetresTime Trial

Introduced in 2000

2000	Felicia Ballanger (FRA) 34.140s	Michelle Ferris (AUS) 34.696s	Cuihua Jiang (CHN) 34.768s
2004	Anna Mearses (AUS) 33.952	Yonghua Jiang (CHN) 34.112	Natalia Tsylinskaya (BLR) 34.167

3000 MetresIndividual Pursuit

1992	Petra Rossner (GER) 3:41.753	Kathryn Watt (AUS) 3:43.438	Rebecca Twigg (USA) 3:52.429
1996	Antonella Bellutti (ITA) 3:33.595	Marion Clignet (FRA) 3:38.571	Judith Arnt (GER) 3:38.744
2000	Leontien Zijlaard (NED) 3:31.570	Marion Clignet (FRA) 3:34.636	Yvonne McGregor (GBR) 3:35.492
2004	Sarah Ulmar (NZL) 3:24.537	Katie MacTier (AUS) 3:27:650	Leontien Zijlaard-van Moosel (NED) 3:27.037

1896-1988 Event not held

Individual Road Race

1984	Connie Carpenter-Phinney (USA) 2h 11:14.0	Rebecca Twigg (USA) 2h 11:14.0	Sandra Schumacher (FRG) 2h 11:14.0
1988	Monique Knol (NED) 2h 00.52	Jutta Niehaus (FRG) close	Laima Zilporitee (URS) close
1992	Kathryn Watt (AUS) 2h 04:02	Jeannie Longo-Ciprelli (FRA) 2h 05:02	Monique Knol (NED) 2h 05:03
1996	Jeannie Longo-Ciprelli (FRA) 2h 36:13	Imelda Chiappa (USA) 2h 36.38	Clara Hughes (CAN) 2h 36.44
2000	Leontien Zijlaard (NED) 3:06:31	Hanka Kupfernagel (GER) 3:06:31	Diana Ziliute (LTU) 3:06:31
2004	Sara Carrigan (AUS) 3:24:24	Judith Arndt (GER) 3:24:31	Olga Slusaryeva (RUS) 3:25:03

1896-1980, 1996 Event not held
Event held over 79.2km in 1984; 82km in 1988; 81km in 1992; 104km in1996; 119.7km in 2000; 118.8km in 2004

Road Individual Time Trial

Held over 26km in 1996; 31.2km in 2000

1996	Zulfiya Zabirova (RUS) 36:40	Jeannie Longo-Ciprelli (FRA) 37:00	Clara Hughes (CAN) 37:13
2000	Leontien Zijlaard (NED) 42:00	Mari Holden (USA) 42:37	Jeannie Longo-Ciprelli (FRA) 42:52
2004	Leontien Zijlaard-van Moorsel (NED)	Deidre Demet-Barry (USA) 31:35.62	Karin Theurig (GER) 31:54.89
	31:11.53		

1896-1992 Event not held

Points Race

1996	Nathalie Lancien (FRA) 24pts	Ingrid Haringa (NED) 23	Lucy Tyler-Sharman (UAS) 17
2000	Antonella Bellutti (ITA) 19pts	Leontien Zijlaard (NED) 16	Olga Slusaryeva (RUS) 15
2004	Olga Slusaryeva (RUS) 20pts	Belem Mendez (MEX) 14	Maria Lisa Williams (COL) 12[1]

1896-1992 Event not held

[1]*Maria Luisa Williams (COL) finished third, was initially disqualified, but later reinstated*

Mountain Bike

Introduced in 1996

Men's Cross-Country

1996	Bart Brentjens (NED) 2:17.38	Thomas Frischknecht (SUI) 2:20.14	Miguel Martinez (FRA) 2:20.26
2000	Miguel Martinez (FRA) 2:09:02.50	Filip Meirhoeghe (BEL) 2:10:05.51	Christoph Sauser (SUI) 2:11:21.00
2004	Julien Absalon (FRA) 2:15:02	Jose Hermida (ESP) 2:16:02	Bart Brentjens (NED) 2:17:05

Women's Cross-Country

1996	Paola Pezzo (ITA) 1:50.51	Alison Sydor (CAN) 1:51.58	Susan DiMattei (USA) 1:52.36
2000	Paola Pezzo (ITA) 1:49:24.38	Barbara Baller (SUI) 1:49:51.42	Margarita Fulliana (ESP) 1:49:57.39
2004	Gunn-Rita Dahle (NOR) 1:56:51	Marie-Helene Premont (CAN) 1:57:50	Sabine Spitz (GER) 1:59:21

EQUESTRIAN

Grand Prix (Jumping)

1900	Aimé Haegeman (BEL) *Benton II*	Georges van der Poële (BEL) *Windsor Squire*	Louis de Champsavin (FRA) *Terpsichore*
1912	Jean Cariou (FRA) 186pts *MIgnon*	Rabod von Kröcher (GER) 186 *Dohna*	Emanuel de Blomaert de Sove (BEL) 185 *Clonmore*
1920	Tommaso Lequio (ITA) 2 faults *Trebecco*	Alessandro Valerio (ITA) 3 *Cento*	Gustaf Lewenhaupt (SWE) 4 *Mon Coeur*
1924	Alphonse Gemuseus (SUI) 3 faults *Lucette*	Tommaso Lequio (ITA) 8.75 *Trebecco*	Adam Krolikiewicz (POL) 10 *Picador*
1928	Frantisek Ventura (TCH) no faults *Eliot*	Pierre Bertrand de Balanda (FRA) 2 *Papillon*	Charles Kuhn (SUI) 4 *Pepita*
1932	Takeichi Nishi (JPN) 8pts *Uranus*	Harry Chamberlain (USA) 12 *Show Girl*	Clarence von RosenJr (SWE) 16 *Empire*
1936	Kurt Hasse (GER) 4 faults *Tora*	Henri Rang (ROM) 4 *Delius*	József von Platthy (HUN) 8 *Sellö*
1948	Humbeto Mariles Cortés (MEX) 6.25 faults *Arete*	Rubén Uriza (MEX) 8 *Harvey*	Jean d'Orgeix (FRA) 8 *Sucre de Pomme*
1952	Pierre Jonquères d'Oriola (FRA) no faults *Ali Baba*	Oscar Cristi (CHI) 4 *Bambi*	Fritz Thiedemann (GER) 8 *Meteor*
1956	Hans Günter Winkler (GER) 4 faults *Halla*	Raimondo d'Inzeo (ITA) 8 *Merano*	Piero d'Inzeo (ITA) 11 *Uruguay*
1960	Raimondo d'Inzeo (ITA) 12 faults *Posillipo*	Piero d'Inzeo (ITA) 16 *The Rock*	David Broome (GBR) 23 *Sunslave*
1964	Pierre Jonquères d'Oriola (FRA) 9 faults *Lutteur*	Hermann Schriddle (GER)12.75 *Dozent*	Peter Robeson (GBR) 16 *Firecrest*
1968	William Steinkraus (USA) 4 faults *Snowbound*	Marian Coakes (GBR) 8 *Stroller*	David Broome (GBR) 12 *Mister Softee*
1972	Graziano Mancinelli (ITA) 8 faults *Ambassador*	Ann Moore (GBR) 8 *Psalm*	Neal Shapiro (USA) 8 *Sloopy*
1976	Alwin Schockemöhle (FRG) no faults *Warwick Rex*	Michael Vaillancourt (CAN) 12 *Branch County*	François Mathy (BEL) 12 *Gai Luron*
1980	Jan Kowalcyzk (POL) 8 faults *Artemor*	Nikolai Korolkov (URS) 9.50 *Espadron*	Joaquim Perez Heras (MEX) 12 *Alymony*
1984	Joe Fargis (USA) 4 faults *Touch of Class*	Conrad Homfeld (USA) 4 *Abdullah*	Heidi Robbiani (SUI) 8 *Jessica V*
1988	Pierre Durand (FRA) 1.25 faults *Jappeloup*	Greg Best (USA) 4 *Gem Twist*	Karsten Huck (FRG) 8 *Nepomuk*
1992	Ludger Beerbaum (GER) no faults *Classic Touch*	Piet Raymakers (NED) 0.25 *Ratina Z*	Norman Dello Joio (USA) 4.75 *Irish*
1996	Ulrich Kirchkoff (GER) 1.00 fault *Jus De Pommes*	Willi Melliger (SUI) 4.00 *Calvaro*	Alexandra Ledermann (FRA) 4.00 *Rochet M*
2000	Jeroen Dubbeldam (NED) 4.00 faults *Sjiem*	Albert Voorn (NED) 4 *Lando*	Khaled al Eid (KSA) 4 *Khashim al Aan*

2004   Rodrigo Ressoa (BRA) 8 faults[1]   Chris Kappler (USA) 8   Marco Kutscher (GER) 9
         Baloubet du Rouet   *Royal Kaliber*   *Montender*
1896,1904-1908 Event not held
[1]*Cian O'Connor (IRL) on* Waterford Crystal *placed first with 4 faults but was disqualified*

Grand Prix (Jumping) Team

1912	SWEDEN 25pts	FRANCE 32	GERMANY 40
1920	SWEDEN 14 pts	BELGIUM 16.25	ITALY 18.75
1924	SWEDEN 42.25pts	SWITZERLAND 50	PORTUGAL 53
1928	SPAIN 4 pts	POLAND 8	SWEDEN 10
1932[1]	–	–	–
1936	GERMANY 44.00pts	NETHERLANDS 51.50	PORTUGAL 56.00
1948	MEXICO 34.25 pts	SPAIN 56.50	GREAT BRITAIN 67
1952	GREAT BRITAIN 40.75 pts	CHILE 45.75	UNITED STATES 52.25
1956	GERMANY 40 pts	ITALY 66	GREAT BRITAIN 69
1960	GERMANY 46.50 pts	UNITED STATES 66	ITALY 80.50
1964	GERMANY 68.50 pts	FRANCE 77.75	ITALY 88.50
1968	CANADA 102.75 pts	FRANCE 110.50	FRG 117.25
1972	FRG 32 pts	UNITED STATES 32.25	ITALY 48
1976	FRANCE 40 pts	FRG 44	BELGIUM 63
1980	SOVIET UNION 16 pts	POLAND 32	MEXICO 39.25
1984	UNITED STATES 12 pts	GREAT BRITAIN 36.75	FRG 39.25
1988	FRG 17.25 pts	UNITED STATES 20.50	FRANCE 27.50
1992	NETHERLANDS 12.00pts	AUSTRIA 16.75	FRANCE 24.75
1996	GERMANY 1.75pts	UNITED STATES 12.00	BRAZIL 17.25
2000	GERMANY 15pts	SWITZERLAND 16	BRAZIL 24
2004	UNITED STATES 20pts[2]	SWEDEN 20	GERMANY dna

1896-1908 Event not held
[1]*There was a team competition but no nation had three riders complete the course;* [2]*Germany placed first with 8pts, but one of their horses was disqualified later, and the team relegated to third*

Grand Prix (Dressage)

1912	Carl Bonde (SWE) 15pts	Gustaf-Adolf Boltenstern Sr (SWE) 21	Hans von Blixen-Finecke (SWE) 32
	Emperor	*Neptun*	*Maggie*
1920	Janne Lundblad (SWE) 27.9375pts	Bertil Sandström (SWE) 26.3125	Hans von Rosen (SWE) 25.1250[1]
	Uno	*Sabel*	*Running Sister*
1924	Ernst Linder (SWE) 276.4pts	Bertil Sandström (SWE) 275.8	Xavier Lesage (FRA) 265.8
	Piccolomini	*Sabel*	*Plumard*
1928	Carl von Langen (GER) 237.42pts	Charles Marion (FRA) 231.00	Ragnar Olsson (SWE) 229.78
	Draüfgänger	*Linon*	*Günstling*
1932	Xavier Lesage (FRA) 1031.25pts	Charles Marion (FRA) 916.25	Hiram Tuttle (USA) 901.50
	Taine	*Linon*	*Olympic*
1936	Heinz Pollay (GER) 1760pts	Friedrich Gerhard (GER) 1745.4	Alois Podhajsky (AUT) 1721.5
	Kronos	*Absinth*	*Nero*
1948	Hans Moser (SUI) 492.5pts	André Jousseaume (FRA) 480.0	Gustaf-Adolf Boltenstern Jr (SWE) 477.5
	Hummer	*Harpagon*	*Trumpf*
1952	Henri St Cyr (SWE) 561pts	Lis Hartel (DEN) 541.5	André Jousseauame (FRA) 541.0
	Master Rufus	*Jubilee*	*Harpagon*
1956	Henri St Cyr (SWE) 860pts	Lis Hartel (DEN) 850	Liselott Linsenhoff (GER) 832
	Juli	*Jubilee*	*Adular*
1960	Sergei Filatov (URS) 2144pts	Gustav Fischer (SUI) 2087	Josef Neckermann (GER) 2082
	Absent	*Wald*	*Asbach*
1964	Henri Chammartin (SUI) 1504pts	Harry Boldt (GER) 1503	Sergei Filatov (URS) 1486
	Woermann	*Remus*	*Absent*
1968	Ivan Kizimov (URS) 1572pts	Josef Neckermann (FRG) 1546	Reiner Klimke (FRG) 1527
	Ikhov	*Mariano*	*Dux*
1972	Liselott Linsenhoff (FRG) 1229pts	Yelena Petuchkova (URS) 1185	Josef Neckermann (FRG) 2082
	Piaff	*Pepel*	*Venetia*
1976	Christine Stückelberger (SUI) 1486	Harry Boldt (FRG) 1435	Reiner Klimke (FRG) 1395
	Granat	*Woycek*	*Mehmed*
1980	Elisabeth Theuer (AUT) 1370pts	Yuri Kovshov (URS) 1300	Viktor Ugyumov (URS) 1234
	Mon Cherie	*Igrok*	*Shkval*
1984	Reiner Klimke (FRG) 1504pts	Anne Grethe Jensen (DEN) 1442	Otto Hofer (SUI) 1364
	Ahlerich	*Martzog*	*Limandus*
1988	Nicole Uphoff (FRG) 1521pts	Margit Otto Crepin (FRA) 1462	Christine Stückelberger (SUI) 1417
	Rembrandt	*Corlandus*	*Gauguin De Lully*
1992	Nicole Uphoff (FRG) 1626pts	Isabell Werth (GER) 1551	Klaus Balkenhol (GER) 1515
	Rembrandt	*Gigolo*	*Goldstern*

1996	Isabell Werth (GER) 235.09pts	Anky van Grunsven (NED) 233.02	Sven Rothenberger (NED) 224.94
	Gigolo	*Bonfire*	*Weyden*
2000	Anky van Grunsven (NED) 239.18pts	Isabell Werth (GER) 234.19	Ulla Salzgeber (GER) 225.88
	Bonfire	*Gigolo*	*Rusty*
2004	Anky van Grusven (NED) 79.278pts	Ulla Salzgeber (GER) 78.833	Beatriz Ferrer-Salat (ESP) 76.667
	Salinero	*Rusty*	~~Beauvalais~~

1896-1908 Event not held
[1]Gustaf-Adolf Boltenstern Sr (SWE) on Iron finished third with 26.1875pts but was disqualified

Grand Prix (Dressage Team)

1928	GERMANY 669.72pts	SWEDEN 650.86	NETHERLANDS 642.96
1932	FRANCE 2828.75pts	SWEDEN 2678	UNITED STATES 2576.75
1936	GERMANY 5074pts	FRANCE 4846	SWEDEN 4660.5
1948[1]	FRANCE 1269pts	UNITED STATES 1256	PORTUGAL 1182
1952	SWEDEN 1597.5pts	SWITZERLAND 1759	GERMANY 1501
1956	SWEDEN 2475pts	GERMANY 2346	SWITZERLAND 2346
1964	GERMANY 2558pts	SWITZERLAND 2526	SOVIET UNION 2311
1968	FRG 2699pts	SOVIET UNION 2657	SWITZERLAND 2547
1972	SOVIET UNION 5095pts	FRG 5083	SWEDEN 4849
1976	FRG 5155pts	SWITZERLAND 4684	UNITED STATES 4670
1980	SOVIET UNION 4383pts	BULGARIA 3580	ROMANIA 3346
1984	FRG 4955pts	SWITZERLAND 4673	SWEDEN 4630
1988	FRG 4302pts	SWITZERLAND 4164	CANADA 3969
1992	GERMANY 5224pts	NETHERLANDS 4742	USA 4643
1996	GERMANY 5553pts	NETHERLANDS 5437	UNITED STATES 5309
2000	GERMANY 5632pts	NETHERLANDS 5579	UNITED STATES 5166
2004	GERMANY 74.653pts	SPAIN 72.917	UNITED STATES 71.500

1896-1924, 1960 Event not held.
[1]Sweden were originally declared winners with 1366pts but were subsequently disqualified one year later

Three-Day Event

1912	Axel Nordlander (SWE) 46.59pts	Friedrich von Rochow (GER) 46.42	Jean Cariou (FRA) 46.32
	Lady Artist	*Idealist*	*Cocotte*
1920	Helmer Mörner (SWE) 1775pts	Age Lundström (SWE) 1738.75	Ettore Caffaratti (ITA) 1733.75
	Germania	*Yrsa*	*Traditore*
1924	Adolf van de Voort van Zijp (NED) 1976pts *Silver Piece*	Fröde Kirkebjerg (DEN) 1853.5 *Meteor*	Sloan Doak (USA) 1845.5 *Pathfinder*
1928	Charles Pahud de Mortanges (NED) 1969.82pts *Marcroix*	Gerard de Kruyff (NED) 1967.26 *Va-t-en*	Bruno Neumann (GER) 1944.42 *Ilja*
1932	Charles Pahud de Mortanges (NED) 1813.83pts *Marcroix*	Earl Thomson (USA) 1811 *Jenny Camp*	Clarence von Rosen Jr (SWE) 1809.42 *Sunnyside Maid*
1936	Ludwig Stubbendorff (GER) 37.7pts *Nurmi*	Earl Thomson (USA) 99.9 *Jenny Camp*	Hans Mathiesen Lunding (DEN) 102.2 *Jason*
1948	Bernard Chevallier (FRA) +4pts *Aiglonne*	Frank Henry (USA) -21 *Swing Low*	Robert Selfelt (SWE) -25 *Claque*
1952	Hans von Blixen-Finecke (SWE) 28.33 faults *Jubal*	Guy Lefrant (FRA) 54.50 *Verdun*	Wilhelf Büsing (GER) 55.50 *Hubertus*
1956	Petrus Kasenman (SWE) 66.53 flts *Illuster*	August Lütke-Westhues (GER) 84.87 *Trux van Kamax*	Frank Weldon (GBR) 85.48 *Kilbarry*
1960	Lawrence Morgan (AUS) +7.15pts *Salad Days*	Neale Lavis (AUS) -16.50 *Mirrabooka*	Anton Bühler (SUI) -51.21 *Gay Spark*
1964	Mauro Checcoli (ITA) 64.40pts *Surbean*	Carlos Moratorio (ARG) 56.40 *Chalan*	Fritz Ligges (GER) 49.20 *Donkosak*
1968	Jean-Jaques Guyon (FRA) 38.86pts *Pitou*	Derek Allhusen (GBR) 41.61 *Lochinvar*	Michael Page (USA) 52.31 *Faster*
1972	Richard Meade (GBR) 57.73pts *Laurieston*	Alessa Argenton (ITA) 43.33 *Woodland*	Jan Jonsson (SWE) 39.67 *Sarajevo*
1976	Edmund Coffin (USA) 114.99pts *Bally-Cor*	Michael Plumb (USA) 125.85 *Better & Better*	Karl Schultz (FRG) 129.45 *Madrigal*
1980	Federico Roman (ITA) 108.60pts *Rossinan*	Aleksandr Blinov (URS) 120.80 *Galzun*	Yuriy Salinikov (URS) 151.60 *Pintset*
1984	Mark Todd (NZL) 51.60pts *Charisma*	Karen Stives (USA) 54.20 *Ben Arthur*	Virginia Holgate (GBR) 56.80 *Priceless*
1988	Mark Todd (NZL) 42.60pts *Charisma*	Ian Stark (GBR) 52.80 *Sir Wattie*	Virginia Leng (GBR) 62.00 *Master Craftsman*
1992	Matthew Ryan (AUS) 70pts *Kibah Tic Toc*	Herbert Blocker (GER) 81.30 *Feine Dame*	Blyth Tait (NZL) 87.60 *Messiah*

1996	Blyth Tait (NZL) 56.80pts	Sally Clark (NZL) 60.40	Kerry Millikin (USA) 73.70
	Ready Teddy	*Squirrel Hill*	*Out & About*
2000	David O'Connor (USA) 34.00pts	Andrew Hoy (AUS) 39.80	Mark Todd (NZL) 42.00
	Custom Made	*Swizzle In*	*Eyespy*
2004	Leslie Law (GBR) 44.40pts (1)	Kim Severson (USA) 45.20	Pippa Funnell (GBR) 46.60
	Shear L'Eau	*Winsome Adante*	*Primmore's Pride*

1896-1908 Event not held
[1]*Bettina Hoy (GER) on Ringwood Cockatoo originally placed first with 41.60pts but was then relegated to ninth with 55.60*

Three-Day Event Team

1912	SWEDEN 139.06pts	GERMANY 138.48	UNITED STATES 137.33
1920	SWEDEN 5057pts	ITALY 4375	BELGIUM 4560
1924	NETHERLANDS 5297.5pts	SWEDEN 4743.5	ITALY 4512.5
1928	NETHERLANDS 5865.68pts	NORWAY 5395.68	POLAND 5067.92
1932	UNITED STATES 5038.08pts	NETHERLANDS 4689.08	–[1]
1936	GERMANY 676.75pts	POLAND 991.70	GREAT BRITAIN 9195.90
1948	UNITED STATES 161.50pts	SWEDEN 165.00	MEXICO 305.25
1952	SWEDEN 221.49pts	GERMANY 235.49	UNITED STATES 587.16
1956	GREAT BRITAIN 355.48pts	GERMANY 475.61	CANADA 572.72
1960	AUSTRALIA 128.18pts	SWITZERLAND 386.02	FRANCE 515.71
1964	ITALY 85.80pts	UNITED STATES 65.86	GERMANY 56.73
1968	GREAT BRITAIN 175.93pts	UNITED STATES 245.87	AUSTRALIA 331.26
1972	GREAT BRITAIN 95.53pts	UNITED STATES 10.81	FRG 18.00
1976	UNITED STATES 441.00pts	FRG 584.60	AUSTRALIA 599.54
1980	SOVIET UNION 457.00pts	ITALY 656.20	MEXICO 1172.85
1984	UNITED STATES 186.00pts	GREAT BRITAIN 189.20	FRG 234.00
1988	FRG 225.95pts	GREAT BRITAIN 256.80	NEW ZEALAND 271.20
1992	AUSTRALIA 288.60pts	NEW ZEALAND 290.80	GERMANY 300.30
1996	AUSTRALIA 203.85pts	UNITED STATES 261.10	NEW ZEALAND 268.55
2000	AUSTRALIA 145.80pts	GREAT BRITAIN 161.00	UNITED STATES 175.80
2004	FRANCE 140.40pts	GREAT BRITAIN 143.00	UNITED STATES 145.60

1896-1908 Event not held
[1]*No other teams finished*

DISCONTINUED EVENTS

Equestrian High Jump

1900	Dominique Gardére (FRA) 1.85m *Canéla*	–	André Moreaux (FRA) 1.70m
	Gian Giorgio Trissino (ITA) 1.85m *Oreste*		*Ludlow*

Equestrian Long Jump

1900	Constant van Langhendonck (BEL) 6.10m	Federico Caprilli (ITA) 5.70m	de Bellegarde (FRA) 5.30m
	Extra Dry	*Oreste*	*Tolla*

Figure Riding

Open only to soldiers below the rank of NCO

1920	Bouckaert (BEL) 30,500pts	Field (FRA) 29,500	Finet (BEL) 29.000

Figure Riding, Teams

1920	BELGIUM 87,500pts	FRANCE 81,083	SWEDEN 59,416

FENCING

Men

Foil

Titles are assessed on both wins (2pts) and draws (1pt) so, as in 1928, the winner does not necessarily have the most wins

1896	Emile Gravelotte (FRA) 4 wins	Henri Callott (FRA) 3	Perikles Mavromichalis-Pierrakos (GRE) 2
1900	Emile Cost (FRA) 6 wins	Henri Masson (FRA) 5	Jacques Boulenger (FRA) 4
1904	Ramón Fonst (CUB) 3 wins	Albertson Van Zo Post (USA) 2[1]	Charles Tatham[1] (USA) 1
1906	Georges Dillon-Kavanagh (FRA) dna	Gustav Casmir (GER) dna	Pierre d'Hugues (FRA) dna
1912	Nedo Nadi (ITA) 7 wins	Pietro Speciale (ITA) 5	Richard Verderber (AUT) 4
1920	Nedo Nadi (ITA) 10 wins	Philippe Cattiau (FRA) 9	Roger Ducret (FRA) 9
1924	Roger Ducret (FRA) 6 wins	Philippe Cattiau (FRA) 5	Maurice van Damme (BEL) 4
1928	Lucien Gaudin (FRA) 9 wins	Ermin Casmir (GER) 9	Giulio Gaudini (ITA) 9

1932	Gustavo Marzi (ITA) 9 wins	Joseph Lewis (USA) 6	Giulio Bocchino (ITA) 4
1936	Giulio Guadini (ITA) 7 wins	Edward Gardère (FRA) 6	Giorgio Bocchino (ITA) 4
1948	Jean Buhan (FRA) 7 wins	Christian d'Oriola (FRA) 5	Lajos Maszlay (HUN) 4
1952	Christian d'Oriola (FRA) 8 wins	Edouard Gardère (FRA) 6	Manlio di Rosa (ITA) 5
1956	Christian d'Oriola (FRA) 6 wins	Giancarlo Bergamini (ITA) 5	Antonio Spallino (ITA) 5
1960	Viktor Zhdanovich (URS) 7 wins	Yuriy Sissikin (URS) 4	Albert Axelrod (USA) 3
1964	Egon Franke (POL) 3 wins	Jean-Claude Magnan (FRA) 2	Daniel Revenu (FRA) 1
1968	Ion Drimba (ROM) 4 wins	Jenö Kamuti (HUN) 3	Daniel Revenu (FRA) 3
1972	Witold Woyda (POL) 5 wins	Jenö Kamuti (HUN) 4	Christian Nöel (FRA) 2
1976	Fabio Dal Zotto (ITA) 4 wins	Alexander Romankov (URS) 4	Bernard Talvard (FRA) 3
1980	Vladimir Smirnov (URS) 5 wins	Paskal Jolyot (FRA) 5	Alexander Romankov (URS) 5
1984	Mauro Numa (ITA)	Matthias Behr (FRG)	Stefano Cerioni (ITA)
1988	Stefano Cerioni (ITA)	Udo Wagner (GDR)	Alexander Romankov (URS)
1992	Phillipe Omnes (FRA)	Sergei Goloubiski (EUN)	Elvis Gregory (CUB)
1996	Alessandro Puccini (ITA)	Lionel Plumenail (FRA)	Franck Boidin (FRA)
2000	Young-Ho Kim (KOR)	Ralf Bissdorf (GER)	Dimitri Chevchenko (RUS)
2004	Brice Guyart (FRA)	Salvatore Sanzo (ITA)	Andrea Cassara (ITA)

[1]*Van Zo Post was an American who competed for Cuba in the team events*

Épée

1900	Ramón Fonst (CUB)	Louis Perrée (FRA)	Léon Sée (FRA)
1904	Ramón Fonst (CUB)	Charles Tatham (USA)	Albertson Van Zo Post (USA)[1]
1906	Georges de la Falaise (FRA) dna	Georges Dillon-Kavanagh (FRA) dna	Alexander van Blijenburgh (NED) dna
1908	Gaston Alibert (FRA) 5 wins	Alexandre Lippmann (FRA) 4	Eugène Olivier (FRA) 4
1912	Paul Anspach (BEL) 6 wins	Ivan Osiier (DEN) 5	Philippe Le Hardy de Beaulieu (BEL) 4
1920	Armand Massard (FRA) 9 wins	Alexandre Lippmann (FRA) 7	Gustave Buchard (FRA) 6
1924	Charles Delporte (BEL) 8 wins	Roger Ducret (FRA) 7	Nils Hellsten (SWE) 7
1928	Lucien Gaudin (FRA) 8 wins	Georges Buchard (FRA) 7	George Calman (USA) 6
1932	Giancarlo Cornaggia-Medici (ITA) 8	Georges Buchard (FRA) 7	Carlo Agostini (ITA) 7
1936	Franco Riccardi (ITA) 5 wins	Saverio Ragno (ITA) 6	Giancarlo Cornaggia-Medici (ITA) 6
1948	Luigi Cantone (ITA) 7 wins	Oswald Zappelli (SUI) 5	Edoardo Mangiarotti (ITA) 5
1952	Edoardo Mangiarotti (ITA) 7 wins	Dario Mangiarotti (ITA) 6	Oswald Zappelli (SUI) 6
1956	Carlo Pavesi (ITA) 5 wins	Giuseppe Delfino (ITA) 5	Edoardo Mangiarotti (ITA) 5
1960	Giuseppe Delfino (ITA) 5 wins	Allan Jay (GBR) 5	Bruno Khabarov (URS) 4
1964	Grigori Kriss (URS) 2 wins	William Hoskyns (GBR) 2	Guram Kostava (URS) 1
1968	Gyözö Kulcsár (HUN) 4 wins	Grigori Kriss (URS) 4	Gianluigi Saccaro (ITA) 4
1972	Csaba Fenyvesi (HUN) 4 wins	Jacques la Degaillerie (FRA) 3	Gyözö Kulcsár (HUN) 3
1976	Alexander Pusch (FRG) 3 wins	Jürgen Hehn (FRG) 3	Gyözö Kulcsár (HUN) 3
1980	Johan Harmenberg (SWE) 4 wins	Ernö Kolczonay (HUN) 3	Philippe Riboud (FRA) 3
1984	Philippe Boisse (FRA)	Björne Väggö (SWE)	Philippe Riboud (FRA)
1988	Arnd Schitt (FRG)	Philippe Riboud (FRA)	Andrei Chouvalov (URS)
1992	Eric Srecki (FRA)	Pavel Kolobkov (EUN)	Jean-Michel Henry (FRA)
1996	Alexander Beketov (RUS)	Ivan Trevejo Perez (CUB)	Geza Imre (HUN)
2000	Pavel Kolobkov (RUS)	Hugues Obry (FRA)	Sang-Ki Lee (KOR)
2004	Marcel Fischer (SUI)	Lei Wang (CHN)	Pavel Kolobkov (RUS)

1896 Event not held
[1]*See footnote to foil*

Sabre

1896	Jean Georgiadis (GRE) 4 wins	Telemachos Karakalos (GRE) 3	Holger Nielsen (DEN) 2
1900	Georges de la Falaise (FRA) dna	Léon Thiébault (FRA) dna	Siegfried Flesch (AUT) dna
1904	Manuel Diaz (CUB) 4 wins	William Grebe (USA) 3	Albertson Van Zo Post (USA) (1)
1906	Jean Georgiadis (GRE) dna	Gustav Casmir (GER) dna	Federico Cesarano (ITA) dna
1908	Jeno Fuchs (HUN) 6 wins	Béla Zulavsky (HUN) 6	Vilem Goppold von Lobsdorf (BOH) 4
1912	Jeno Fuchs (HUN) 6 wins	Béla Békéssy (HUN) 5	Ervin Mészaros (HUN) 5
1920	Nedo Nadi (ITA) 11 wins	Aldo Nadi (ITA) 9	Adrianus EW de Jong (NED) 7
1924	Sándor Posta (HUN) 5 wins	Roger Ducret (FRA) 5	János Garai (HUN) 5
1928	Odön Tersztyansky (HUN) 9 wins	Attila Petschauer (HUN) 9	Bino Bini (ITA) 8
1932	György Piller (HUN) 8 wins	Giulio Gaudini (ITA) 7	Endre Kabos (HUN) 5
1936	Endre Kabos (HUN) 7 wins	Gustavo Marzi (ITA) 6	Aladár Gerevich (HUN) 6
1948	Aladár Gerevich (HUN) 7 wins	Vincenzo Pinton (ITA) 5	Pál Kovács (HUN) 5
1952	Pál Kovács (HUN) 8 wins	Aladár Gerevich (HUN) 7	Tibor Berczelly (HUN) 5
1956	Rudolf Kárpáti (HUN) 6 wins	Jerzy Pawlowski (POL) 5	Lev Kuznyetsov (URS) 4
1960	Rudolf Kárpáti (HUN) 5 wins	Zoltán Horvath (HUN) 4	Wladimiro Calarese (ITA) 4
1964	Tibor Pézsa (HUN) 2 wins	Claude Arabo (FRA) 2	Umar Mavlikhanov (URS) 1
1968	Jerzy Pawlowski (POL) 4 wins	Mark Rakita (URS) 4	Tribor Pézsa (HUN) 3
1972	Viktor Sidiak (URS) 4 wins	Peter Maroth (HUN) 3	Vladimir Nazilimov (URS) 3

1976	Viktor Krovopouskov (URS) 5 wins	Vladimir Nazlimov (URS) 4	Viktor Sidiak (URS) 3
1980	Viktor Krovopouskov (URS) 5 wins	Mikhail Burtsev (URS) 4	Imre Gedovari (HUN) 3
1984	Jean François Lamour (FRA)	Marco Marin (ITA)	Peter Westbrook (USA)
1988	Jean François Lamour (FRA)	Janusz Olech (POL)	Giovanni Scalzo (ITA)
1992	Bence Szabo (HUN)	Marco Marin (ITA)	Jean François Lamour (FRA)
1996	Sergei Podnyakov (RUS)	Stanislav Sharikov (RUS)	Damien Touya (FRA)
2000	Mihai Covaliu (ROM)	Mathieu Gourdain (FRA)	Wiradech Kothny (GER)
2004	Aldo Montano (ITA)	Zsolt Nemcsik (HUN)	Vladislav Tretiak (UKR)

[1]See footnote to foil

Team

Foil

1904	CUBA/USA[1]	UNITED STATES	_[2]
1920	ITALY	FRANCE	UNITED STATES
1924	FRANCE	BELGIUM	HUNGARY
1928	ITALY	FRANCE	ARGENTINA
1932	FRANCE	ITALY	UNITED STATES
1936	ITALY	FRANCE	GERMANY
1948	FRANCE	ITALY	BELGIUM
1952	FRANCE	ITALY	HUNGARY
1956	ITALY	FRANCE	GERMANY
1960	SOVIET UNION	ITALY	GERMANY
1964	SOVIET UNION	POLAND	FRANCE
1968	FRANCE	SOVIET UNION	POLAND
1972	POLAND	SOVIET UNION	FRANCE
1976	FRG	ITALY	FRANCE
1980	FRANCE	SOVIET UNION	POLAND
1984	ITALY	FRG	FRANCE
1988	SOVIET UNION	FRG	HUNGARY
1992	GERMANY	CUBA	POLAND
1996	RUSSIA	POLAND	CUBA
2000	FRANCE	CHINA	ITALY
2004	ITALY	CHINA	RUSSIA

1896-1900, 1906-1912 Event not held
[1]See footnote to foil; [2]No other teams entered

Sabre

1906	GERMANY	GREECE	NETHERLANDS
1908	HUNGARY	ITALY	BOHEMIA
1912	HUNGARY	AUSTRIA	NETHERLANDS
1920	ITALY	FRANCE	NETHERLANDS
1924	ITALY	HUNGARY	NETHERLANDS
1928	HUNGARY	ITALY	POLAND
1932	HUNGARY	ITALY	POLAND
1936	HUNGARY	ITALY	GERMANY
1948	HUNGARY	ITALY	UNITED STATES
1952	HUNGARY	ITALY	FRANCE
1956	HUNGARY	POLAND	SOVIET UNION
1960	HUNGARY	POLAND	ITALY
1964	SOVIET UNION	ITALY	POLAND
1968	SOVIET UNION	ITALY	HUNGARY
1972	ITALY	SOVIET UNION	HUNGARY
1976	SOVIET UNION	ITALY	ROMANIA
1980	SOVIET UNION	ITALY	HUNGARY
1984	ITALY	FRANCE	ROMANIA
1988	HUNGARY	SOVIET UNION	ITALY
1992	UNIFIED TEAM	HUNGARY	FRANCE
1996	RUSSIA	HUNGARY	ITALY
2000	RUSSIA	FRANCE	GERMANY
2004	FRANCE	ITALY	RUSSIA

1896-1904 Event not held

Épée

1906	FRANCE	GREAT BRITAIN	BELGIUM
1908	FRANCE	GREAT BRITAIN	BELGIUM
1912	BELGIUM	GREAT BRITAIN	NETHERLANDS
1920	ITALY	BELGIUM	FRANCE
1924	FRANCE	BELGIUM	ITALY
1928	ITALY	FRANCE	PORTUGAL
1932	FRANCE	ITALY	UNITED STATES
1936	ITALY	SWEDEN	FRANCE
1948	FRANCE	ITALY	SWEDEN
1952	ITALY	SWEDEN	SWITZERLAND
1956	ITALY	HUNGARY	FRANCE
1960	ITALY	GREAT BRITAIN	SOVIET UNION
1964	HUNGARY	ITALY	FRANCE
1968	HUNGARY	SOVIET UNION	POLAND
1972	HUNGARY	SWITZERLAND	SOVIET UNION
1976	SWEDEN	FRG	SWITZERLAND
1980	FRANCE	POLAND	SOVIET UNION
1984	FRG	FRANCE	ITALY
1988	FRANCE	FRG	SOVIET UNION
1992	GERMANY	HUNGARY	UNIFIED TEAM
1996	ITALY	RUSSIA	FRANCE
2000	ITALY	FRANCE	CUBA
2004	FRANCE	HUNGARY	GERMANY

1896-1904 Event not held

Women

Foil

1924	Ellen Osiier (DEN) 5 wins	Gladys Davis (GBR) 4	Grete Heckscher (DEN) 3
1928	Helène Mayer (GER) 7 wins	Muriel Freeman (GBR) 6	Olga Oelkers (GER) 4
1932	Ellen Preis (AUT) 9 wins	Heather Guinness (GBR) 8	Erna Bogen (HUN) 7
1936	Ilona Elek (HUN) 6 wins	Helène Mayer (GER) 5	Ellen Preis (AUT) 5
1948	Ilona Elek (HUN) 6 wins	Karen Lachmann (DEN) 5	Ellen Müller-Preis (AUT) 5
1952	Irene Camber (ITA) 5 wins	Ilona Elek (HUN) 5	Karen Lachmann (DEN) 4
1956	Gillian Sheen (GBR) 6 wins	Olga Orban (ROM) 6	Renée Garilhe (FRA) 5
1960	Heidi Schmid (GER) 6 wins	Valentina Rastvorova (URS) 5	Maria Vicol (ROM) 4
1964	Ildikó Ujlaki-Rejtö (HUN) 2 wins	Helga Mees (GER) 2	Antonella Ragno (ITA) 2
1968	Elena Noivkova (URS) 4 wins	Pilar Roldan (MEX) 3	Ildikó Ujlaki-Rejtö (HUN) 3
1972	Antonella Ragno-Lonzi (ITA) 4 wins	Ildikó Bóbis (HUN) 3	Galina Gorokhova (URS)
1976	Ildikó Schwarczenberger (HUN) 4 wins	Maria Collino (ITA) 4	Elena Novikova-Belova (URS) 3
1980	Pascale Trinquet (FRA) 4 wins	Magda Maros (HUN) 3	Barbara Wysoczanska (POL) 3
1984	Jujie Luan (CHN)	Cornelia Hanisch (FRG)	Dorina Vaccaroni (ITA)
1988	Anja Fichtel (FRG)	Sabine Bau (FRG)	Zita Funkenhauser (FRG)
1992	Giovanna Trillini (ITA)	Wang Huifeng (CHN)	Tatyana Sadovskaya (EUN)
1996	Laura Badea (ROM)	Valentin Vezzali (ITA)	Giovanna Trillini (ITA)
2000	Valentina Vezzali (ITA)	Rita König (GER)	Giovanna Trillini (ITA)
2004	Valentina Vezzali (ITA)	Giovanna Trillini (ITA)	Sylwia Gruchala (POL)

1896-1920 Event not held

Épée

1996	Laura Flessel (FRA)	Valerie Bartlois (FRA)	Györgyi Horvathné-Szalay (HUN)
2000	Timea Nagy (HUN)	Gianna Hablützel-Bürki (SUI)	Laura Flessel-Colovic (FRA)
2004	Timea Nagy (HUN)	Laura Flessel-Colovic (FRA)	Maureen Nisima (FRA)

1896-1992 Event not held

Sabre

2004	Mariel Zagunis (USA)	Xue Tan (CHN)	Sanda Jacobson (USA)

1896-2000 Event not held

Team

Foil

1960	SOVIET UNION	HUNGARY	ITALY
1964	HUNGARY	SOVIET UNION	GERMANY
1968	SOVIET UNION	HUNGARY	ROMANIA

1972	SOVIET UNION	HUNGARY	ROMANIA
1976	SOVIET UNION	FRANCE	HUNGARY
1980	FRANCE	SOVIET UNION	HUNGARY
1984	FRG	ROMANIA	FRANCE
1988	FRG	ITALY	HUNGARY
1992	ITALY	GERMANY	ROMANIA
1996	ITALY	ROMANIA	GERMANY
2000	ITALY	POLAND	GERMANY

1896-1956, 2004 Event not held

Épée

1996	FRANCE	ITALY	RUSSIA
2000	RUSSIA	SWITZERLAND	CHINA
2004	RUSSIA	GERMANY	FRANCE

1896-1992 Event not held

DISCONTINUED EVENTS

Foil for Fencing Masters

| 1896 | Léon Pyrgos (GRE) | Jean Perronnet (FRA) | – |
| 1900 | Lucien Mérignac (FRA) | Alphonse Kirchhoffer (FRA) | Jean-Baptiste Mimiague (FRA) |

Épée for Fencing Masters

| 1900 | Albert Ayat (FRA) | Emile Bougnol (FRA) | Henri Laurent (FRA) |
| 1906 | Cyrille Verbrugge (BEL) | Carlo Gandini (ITA) | Ioannis Raissis (GRE) |

Épée for Amateurs and Fencing Masters

| 1900 | Albert Ayat (FRA) | Ramón Fonst (CUB) | Léon Sée (FRA) |

Sabre for Fencing Masters

| 1900 | Antonio Conte (ITA) | Italo Santelli (ITA)[1] | Milan Neralic (AUT) |
| 1906 | Cyrille Verbrugge (BEL) | Ioannis Raissis (GRE) | – |

[1]*Santelli actually lived in Hungary, and so there has been some confusion as to his nationality*

Three Cornered Sabre

| 1906 | Gustav Casmir (GER) | George van Rossem (NED) | Péter Tóth (HUN) |

Single Sticks

| 1904 | Albertson Van Zo Post (USA)[1] | William Grebe (USA) | William O'Connor (USA) |

[1]*See footnote to foil*

FOOTBALL

Men

1900	GREAT BRITAIN	FRANCE	BELGIUM
1904	CANADA	UNITED STATES	UNITED STATES
1906	DENMARK	GREECE	GREECE
1908	GREAT BRITAIN	DENMARK	NETHERLANDS
1912	GREAT BRITAIN	DENMARK	NETHERLANDS
1920	BELGIUM	SPAIN	NETHERLANDS
1924	URUGUAY	SWITZERLAND	SWEDEN
1928	URUGUAY	ARGENTINA	ITALY
1936	ITALY	AUSTRIA	NORWAY
1948	SWEDEN	YUGOSLAVIA	DENMARK
1952	HUNGARY	YUGOSLAVIA	SWEDEN
1956	SOVIET UNION	YUGOSLAVIA	BULGARIA
1960	YUGOSLAVIA	DENMARK	HUNGARY
1964	HUNGARY	CZECHOSLOVAKIA	GERMANY
1968	HUNGARY	BULGARIA	JAPAN
1972	POLAND	HUNGARY	GDR[1]
			SOVIET UNION[1]
1976	GDR	POLAND	SOVIET UNION

1980	CZECHOSLOVAKIA	GDR	SOVIET UNION
1984	FRANCE	BRAZIL	YUGOSLAVIA
1988	SOVIET UNION	BRAZIL	FRG
1992	SPAIN	POLAND	GHANA
1996	NIGERIA	ARGENTINA	BRAZIL
2000	CAMEROON	SPAIN	CHILE
2004	ARGENTINA	PARAGUAY	ITALY

1896-1932 Event not held
¹Tie declared after extra time played

Women

1996	UNITED STATES	CHINA	NORWAY
2000	NORWAY	UNITED STATES	GERMANY
2004	UNITED STATES	BRAZIL	GERMANY

1896-1992 Event not held

GYMNASTICS

Men

Team

1904	USA/AUSTRIA 374.43	UNITED STATES 356.37	UNITED STATES 349.69
1906	NORWAY 19.00	DENMARK 18.00	ITALY 16.71
1908	SWEDEN 438	NORWAY 425	FINLAND 405
1912	ITALY 265.75	HUNGARY 227.25	GREAT BRITAIN 184.50
1920	ITALY 359.855	BELGIUM 346.745	FRANCE 340.100
1924	ITALY 839.058	FRANCE 820.528	SWITZERLAND 816.661
1928	SWITZERLAND 1718.652	CZECHOSLOVAKIA 1712.250	YUGOSLAVIA 1648.750
1932	ITALY 541.850	UNITED STATES 522.275	FINLAND 509.995
1936	GERMANY 657.430	SWITZERLAND 654.802	FINLAND 638.468
1948	FINLAND 1358.3	SWITZERLAND 1356.7	HUNGARY 1330.35
1952	SOVIET UNION 575.4	SWITZERLAND 567.5	FINLAND 564.2
1956	SOVIET UNION 568.25	JAPAN 566.40	FINLAND 555.95
1960	JAPAN 575.20	SOVIET UNION 572.70	ITALY 559.05
1964	JAPAN 577.95	SOVIET UNION 575.45	GERMANY 565.10
1968	JAPAN 575.90	SOVIET UNION 571.10	GDR 557.15
1972	JAPAN 571.25	SOVIET UNION 564.05	GDR 559.70
1976	JAPAN 576.85	SOVIET UNION 576.45	GDR 654.65
1980	SOVIET UNION 589.60	GDR 581.15	HUNGARY 575.00
1984	UNITED STATES 591.40	CHINA 590.80	JAPAN 586.70
1988	SOVIET UNION 593.350	GDR 588.450	JAPAN 585.600
1992	UNIFIED TEAM 585.450	CHINA 580.375	JAPAN 578.250
1996	RUSSIA 576.778	CHINA 575.539	UKRAINE 571.541
2000	CHINA 231.919	UKRAINE 230.306	RUSSIA 230.019
2004	JAPAN 173.821	UNITED STATES 172.933	ROMANIA 172.384

1896-1900 Event not held

Individual Combined Exercises

1900	Gustave Sandras (FRA) 302	Noël Bas (FRA) 295	Lucien Démanet (FRA) 293
1904¹	Julius Lenhart (AUT) 69.80	Wilhelm Weber (GER) 69.10	Adolf Spinnler (SUI) 67.99
1906²	Pierre Paysse (FRA) 97	Alberto Braglia (ITA) 95	Georges Charmoille (FRA) 94
1906	Pierre Paysse (FRA) 116	Alberto Paglia (ITA) 115	Georges Charmoille (FRA) 113
1908	Alberto Braglia (ITA) 317.0	S Walter Tysal (GBR) 312.0	Louis Ségura (FRA) 297.0
1912	Alberto Braglia (ITA) 135.0	Louis Ségura (FRA) 132.5	Adolfo Tunesi (ITA) 131.5
1920	Giorgio Zampori (ITA) 88.35	Marco Torres (FRA) 87.62	Jean Gounot (FRA) 87.45
1924	Leon Stukelj (YUG) 110.340	Robert Prazák (TCH) 110.323	Bedrich Supcik (TCH) 106.930
1928	Georges Miez (SUI) 247.500	Herman Hänggi (SUI) 246.625	Leon Stukelj (YUG) 244.875
1932	Romeo Neri (ITA) 140.625	István Pelle (HUN) 134.925	Heikki Savolainen (FIN) 134.575
1936	Alfred Schwarzmann (GER) 113.100	Eugen Mack (SUI) 112.334	Konrad Frey (GER) 111.532
1948	Veikko Huhtanen (FIN) 229.7	Walter Lehmann (SUI) 229.0	Paavo Aaltonen (FIN) 228.8
1952	Viktor Chukarin (URS) 115.70	Grant Shaginyan (URS) 114.95	Josef Stalder (SUI) 114.75
1956	Viktor Chukarin (URS) 114.25	Takashi Ono (JPN) 114.20	Yuri Titov (URS) 113.80
1960	Boris Shakhlin (URS) 115.95	Takashi Ono (JPN) 115.90	Yuri Titov (URS) 115.60
1964	Yukio Endo (JPN) 115.95	Shuji Tsurumi (JPN) 115.40 Viktor Lisitsky (URS) 115.40	–
1968	Sawao Kato (JPN) 115.90	Mikhail Voronin (URS) 115.85	Akinori Nakayama (JPN) 115.65

1972	Sawao Kato (JPN) 114.650	Eizo Kenmotsu (JPN) 114.575	Akinori Takayama (JPN) 114.325
1976	Nikolai Andrianov (URS) 116.650	Sawao Kato (JPN) 115.650	Mitsuo Tsukahara (JPN) 115.375
1980	Alexander Dityatin (URS) 118.050	Nikolai Andrianov (URS) 118.225	Stoyan Deltchev (BUL) 118.000
1984	Koji Gushiken (JPN) 118.700	Peter Vidmar (USA) 118.675	Li Ning (CHN) 118.575
1988	Vladimir Artemov (URS) 119.125	Valeriy Lyukhine (URS) 119.025	Dmitry Bilozertchev (URS) 118.975
1992	Vitali Scherbo (EUN) 59.025	Grigori Mistyutin (EUN) 58.925	Valeri Belenki (EUN) 58.625
1996	Li Xiaoshuang (CHN) 58.423	Alexei Nemov (RUS) 58.374	Vitali Scherbo (BLR) 58.197
2000	Alexei Nemov (RUS) 58.474	Wei Yang (CHN) 58.361	Alexander Beresch (UKR) 58.212
2004	Paul Hamm (USA) 57.823	Dae Eun Kim (KOR) 57.811	Tae Young Yang (KOR) 57.774

1896 Event not held

[1]*Lenhart was a member of the Philadelphia Club, USA, which won the team event;* [2]*Two competitions in 1906, one of five events and one of six*

Floor Exercises

1932	István Pelle (HUN) 9.60	Georges Miez (SUI) 9.47	Mario Lertora (ITA) 9.23
1936	Georges Miez (SUI) 18.666	Josef Walter (SUI) 18.500	Konrad Frey (GER) 18.466
			Eugen Mack (SUI) 18.466
1948	Ferenc Pataki (HUN) 38.7	János Mogyorosi-Klencs (HUN) 38.4	Zdenek Ruzicka (TCH) 38.1
1952	William Thoresson (SWE) 19.25	Tadao Uesako (JPN) 19.15	–
		Jerzy Jokiel (POL) 19.15	
1956	Valentin Muratov (URS) 19.20	Nobuyuki Aihara (JPN) 19.10	–
		Viktor Chukharin (URS) 19.10	
1960	Nobuyuki Aihara (JPN) 19.450	Yuri Titov (JPN) 19.325	Franco Menichelli (ITA) 19.275
1964	Franco Menichelli (ITA) 19.45	Viktor Lisitsky (URS) 19.35	–
		Yukio Endo (JPN) 19.35	
1968	Sawao Kato (JPN) 19.475	Akinori Nakayama (JPN) 19.400	Takeshi Kato (JPN) 19.275
1972	Nikolai Andrianov (URS) 19.175	Akinori Nakayama (JPN) 19.125	Shigeru Kasamatsu (JPN) 19.025
1976	Nikolai Andrianov (URS) 19.450	Vladimir Marchenko (URS) 19.425	Peter Kormann (USA) 19.300
1980	Roland Brückner (GDR) 19.750	Nikolay Andrianov (URS) 19.725	Aleksandr Dityatin (URS) 19.700
1984	Li Ning (CHN) 19.925	Yun Lou (CHN) 19.775	Koji Sotomura (JPN) 19.700
			Philippe Vatuone (FRA) 19.700
1988	Sergei Kharikov (URS) 19.925	Vladimir Artemov (URS) 19.900	Lou Yun (CHN) 19.850
			Yukio Iketani (JPN) 19.850
1992	Li Xiaoshuang (CHN) 9.925	Grigori Misyutin (EUN) 9.787	–
	Yukio Iketani (JPN) 9.787		
1996	Ioannis Melissanidis (GRE) 9.950	Li Xiaoshuang (CHN) 9.837	Alexei Nemov (RUS) 9.800
2000	Igor Wirovs (LAT) 9.812	Alexei Nemov (RUS) 9.800	Jordan Jovtchev (BUL) 9.787
2004	Kyle Shewfelt (CAN) 9.787	Marian Dragulescu (ROM) 9.787	Jordan Jovtchev (BUL) 9.775

1896-1928 Event not held

Parallel Bars

1896	Alfred Flatow (GER) dna	Jules Zutter (SUI)	Hermann Weingärtner (GER)
1904	George Eyser (USA) 44	Anton Heida (USA) 43	John Duha (USA) 40
1924	August Güttinger (SUI) 21.63	Robert Prazák (TCH) 21.61	Giorgio Zampori (ITA) 21.45
1928	Ladislav Vácha (TCH) 18.83	Josip Primozic (YUG) 18.50	Hermann Hänaggi (SUI) 18.08
1932	Romeo Neri (ITA) 18.97	István Pelle (HUN) 18.60	Heikki Savolainen (FIN) 18.27
1936	Konrad Frey (GER) 19.067	Michael Reusch (SUI) 109.034	Alfred Schwarzmann (GER) 18.967
1948	Michael Reusch (SUI) 39.5	Veikkö Huhtanen (FIN) 39.3	Christian Kipfer (SUI) 39.1
			Josef Stalder (SUI) 39.1
1952	Hans Eugster (SUI) 19.65	Viktor Chukharin (URS) 19.60	Josef Stalder (SUI) 19.50
1956	Viktor Chukharin (URS) 19.20	Masami Kubota (JPN) 19.15	Takashi Ono (JPN) 19.10
			Masao Takemoto (JPN) 19.10
1960	Boris Shakhlin (URS) 19.400	Giovanni Carminucci (ITA) 19.375	Takashi Ono (JPN) 19.350
1964	Yukio Endo (JPN) 19.675	Shuji Tsurumi (JPN) 19.450	Franco Menichelli (ITA) 19.350
1968	Akinori Nakayama (JPN) 19.475	Mikhail Voronin (URS) 19.425	Vladimir Klimenko (URS) 19.225
1972	Sawao Kato (JPN) 19.475	Shigeru Kasamatsu (JPN) 19.375	Eizo Kenmotsu (JPN) 19.25
1976	Sawao Kato (JPN) 19.675	Nikolai Andrianov (URS) 19.500	Mitsuo Tsukahara (JPN) 19.475
1980	Alexander Tkachev (URS) 19.775	Alexander Dityatin (URS) 19.750	Roland Brückner (GDR) 19.650
1984	Bart Conner (USA) 19.950	Nobuyuki Kajitani (JPN) 19.925	Mitchell Gaylord (USA) 19.850
1988	Vladimir Artemov (URS) 19.925	Valeriy Lyukhine (URS) 19.900	Sven Tippelt (GDR) 19.750
1992	Vitali Scherbo (EUN) 9.900	Li Jing (CHN) 9.812	Guo Linyao (CHN) 9.800
			Igor Korobchinkski (EUN) 9.800
			Masayuki Matsunaga (JPN) 9.800
1996	Rustam Sharipov (UKR) 9.837	Jair Lynch (USA) 9.825	Vitali Scherbo (BLR) 9.800
2000	Xiaopeng Li (CHN) 9.825	Joo-Hyung Lee (KOR) 9.812	Alexei Nemov (RUS) 9.800
2004	Valeri Goncharov (UKR) 9.787	Hiroyuki Tomita (JPN) 9.775	Xiaopeng Li (CHN) 9.762

1900, 1906-1920 Event not held

Pommel Horse

1896	Jules Zutter (SUI) dna	Hermann Weingärtner (GER)	Gyula Kakas (HUN)
1904	Anotn Heida (USA) 42	George Eyser (USA) 33	William Merz (USA) 29
1924	Josef Wilhelm (SUI) 21.23	Jean Gutweiniger (SUI) 21.13	Antoine Rebetez (SUI) 20.73
1928	Hermann Hänggi (SUI) 19.75	Georges Miez (SUI) 19.25	Heikki Savolainen (FIN) 18.83
1932	István Pelle (HUN) 19.07	Omero Bonoli (ITA) 18.87	Frank Haubold (USA) 18.57
1936	Konrad Frey (GER) 19.333	Eugen Mack (SUI) 19.167	Albert Bachmann (SUI) 19.067
1948	Paavo Aaltonen (FIN) 38.7	–	
	Veikkö Huhtanen (FIN) 38.7		
	Heikki Savolainen (FIN) 38.7		
1952	Viktor Chukarin (URS) 19.50	Yevgeni Korolkov (URS) 19.40	–
	Grant Shaginyan (URS) 19.40		
1956	Boris Shakhlin (URS) 19.25	Takashi Ono (JPN) 19.20	Viktor Chukarin (URS) 19.10
1960	Eugen Ekman (FIN) 19.375	–	Shuji Tsurumi (JPN) 19.150
	Boris Shakhlin (URS) 19.375		
1964	Miroslav Cerar (YUG) 19.525	Shuji Tsurumi (JPN) 19.325	Yuri Tsapenko (URS) 19.200
1968	Miroslav Cerar (YUG) 19.325	Olli Laiho (FIN) 19.225	Mikhail Voronin (URS) 19.200
1972	Viktor Klimenko (URS) 19.125	Sawao Kato (JPN) 19.00	Eizo Kenmotsu (JPN) 18.950
1976	Zoltán Magyar (HUN) 19.700	Eizo Kenmotsu (JPN) 19.575	Nikolai Andrianov (URS) 19.525
1980	Zoltán Magyar (HUN) 19.925	Alexander Dityatin (URS) 19.800	Michael Nikolay (GDR) 19.775
1984	Li Ning (CHN) 19.950	–	Timothy Daggert (USA) 19.825
	Peter Vidmar (USA) 19.950		
1988	Lubomir Gueraskov (BUL) 19.950		
	Zsolt Borkai (HUN) 19.950		
	Dmitri Bilozertchev (URS) 19.950		
1992	Vitali Scherbo (EUN) 9.925	–	Andreas Wecker (GER) 9.887
	Pae Gil-su (PRK) 9.925		
1996	Lin Donghua (SUI) 9.875	Marius Urzica (ROM) 9.825	Alexei Nemov (RUS) 9.787
2000	Marius Urzica (ROM) 9.862	Eric Poujade (FRA) 9.825	Alexei Nemov (RUS) 9.800
2004	Haibin Teng (CHN) 9.837	Marius Daniel Urzica (ROM) 9.825	Takehiro Kashima (JPN) 9.787

1900, 1906-1920 Event not held

Rings

1896	Ioannis Mitropoulos (GRE) dna	Hermann Weingärtner (GER)	Petros Persakis (GRE)
1904	Herman Glass (USA) 45	William Merz (USA) 35	Emil Voight (USA) 32
1924	Franco Martino (ITA) 21.553	Robert Prazák (TCH) 21.483	Ladislav Vácha (TCH) 21.430
1928	Leon Skutelj (YUG) 19.25	Ladislav Vácha (TCH) 19.17	Emanuel Löffler (TCH) 18.83
1932	George Gulack (USA) 18.97	William Denton (USA) 18.60	Giovanni Lattuada (ITA) 18.50
1936	Alois Hudec (TCH) 19.433	Leon Skutelj (YUG) 18.867	Matthias Volz (GER) 18.667
1948	Karl Frei (SUI) 39.60	Michael Reusch (SUI) 39.10	Zdenek Ruzicka (TCH) 38.30
1952	Grant Shaginyan (URS) 19.75	Viktor Chakarin (URS) 19.55	Hans Eugster (SUI) 19.40
			Dimitri Leonkin (URS) 19.40
1956	Albert Azaryan (URS) 19.35	Valentin Muratov (URS) 19.15	Masao Takemoto (JPN) 19.10
			Masami Kubota (JPN) 19.10
1960	Albert Azaryan (URS) 19.475	Boris Shakhlin (URS) 19.500	Velik Kapsazov (BUL) 19.425
			Takashi Ono (JPN) 19.425
1964	Takuji Hayata (JPN) 19.475	Franco Menichelli (ITA) 19.425	Boris Shakhlin (URS) 19.400
1968	Akinori Nakayama (JPN) 19.450	Mikhail Voronin (URS) 19.325	Sawao Kato (JPN) 19.225
1972	Akinori Nakayama (JPN) 19.350	Mikhail Voronin (URS) 19.325	Mitsuo Tsukahara (JPN) 19.225
1976	Nikolai Andrianov (URS) 19.875	Alexander Ditiyatin (URS) 19.550	Danut Grecu (ROM) 19.500
1980	Alexander Ditiyatin (URS) 19.875	Alexander Tkachev (URS) 19.725	Jiri Tabak (TCH) 19.600
1984	Koji Gushiken (JPN) 19.850	–	Mitchell Gaylord (USA) 19.825
	Li Ning (CHN) 19.850		
1988	Holger Behrendt (GDR) 19.925	–	Sven Tippelt (GDR) 19.875
	Dmitri Bilozerchev (URS) 19.925		
1992	Vitali Scherbo (EUN) 9.937	Li Jing (CHN) 9.875	Li Xiaoshuang (CHN) 9.862
			Andreas Wecker (GER) 9.862
1996	Yuri Chechi (ITA) 9.887	Szilveszter Csollany (HUN) 9.812	–
		Dan Burnica (ROM) 9.812	
2000	Szilveszter Csollany (HUN) 9.850	Dimothenis Tampakos (GRE) 9.762	Jordan Jovtchev (BUL) 9.737
2004	Dimosthenis Tampakos (GRE) 9.862	Jordan Jovtchev (BUL) 9.850	Yuri Chechi (ITA) 9.812

1900, 1906-1920 Event not held

Horizontal Bar

1896	Hermann Weingärtner (GER) dna	Alfred Flatow (GER)	unknown
1904	Anton Heida (USA) 40	–	George Eyser (USA) 39
	Edward Henning (USA) 40		

1924	Leon Stukelj (YUG) 19.730	Jean Gutweniger (SUI) 19.236	André Higelin (FRA) 19.163
1928	Georges Miez (SUI) 19.17	Romeo Neri (ITA) 19.00	Eugen Mack (SUI) 18.92
1932	Dallas Bixler (USA) 18.33	Heikkl Savolainen (FIN) 18.07	Einari Teräsvirta (FIN) 18.07[1]
1936	Aleksanteri Sarvaala (FIN) 19.367	Konrad Frey (GER) 19.267	Alfred Schwarzmann (GER) 19.233
1948	Josef Stalder (SUI) 39.7	Walter Lehmann (SUI) 39.4	Veikkö Huhtanen (FIN) 39.2
1952	Jack Günthard (SUI) 19.55	Josef Stalder (SUI) 19.50	–
		Alfred Schwarzmann (GER) 19.50	
1956	Takashi Ono (JPN) 19.60	Yuri Titov (URS) 19.40	Masao Takemoto (JPN) 19.30
1960	Takashi Ono (JPN) 19.60	Masao Takemoto (JPN) 19.525	Boris Shakhlin (URS) 19.475
1964	Boris Shakhlin (URS) 19.625	Yuri Titov (URS) 19.55	Miroslav Cerar (YUG) 19.50
1968	Mikhail Voronin (URS) 19.550	–	Eizo Kenmotsu (JPN) 19.375
	Akinori Nakayama (JPN) 19.550		
1972	Mitsuo Tsukahara (JPN) 19.725	Sawao Kato (JPN) 19.525	Shigeru Kasamatsu (JPN) 19.450
1976	Mitsuo Tsukahara (JPN) 19.675	Eizo Kenmotsu (JPN) 19.500	Eberhard Gienger (FRG) 19.475
			Henry Boërio (FRA) 19.475
1980	Stoyan Deltchev (BUL) 19.825	Alexander Dityatin (URS) 19.750	Nikolai Andrianov (URS) 19.675
1984	Shinje Morisue (JPN) 20.00	Tong Fei (CHN) 19.955	Koji Gushiken (JPN) 19.950
1988	Vladimir Artemov (URS) 10.900	–	Holger Behrendt (GDR) 19.800
	Valeri Lyukhine (URS) 19.900	Marius Germann (ROM) 19.800	
1992	Trent Dimas (USA) 9.875	Andreas Wecker (GER) 9.837	–
		Grigori Misyutin (EUN) 9.837	
1996	Alexei Nemov (RUS) 9.787	Yeo Hong-Chul (KOR) 9.756	Vitali Scherbo (BLR) 9.724
2000	Alexei Nemov (RUS) 9.787	Benjamin Varonian (FRA) 9.787	Joo-Hyung Lee (KOR) 9.775
2004	Igor Cassina (ITA) 9.812	Paul Hamm (USA) 9.812	Isao Yoneda (JPN) 9.78

1000, 1900-1920 Event not held
[1]Teräsvirta conceded second place to Savolainen

Horse Vault

1896	Carl Schuhmann (GER) dna	Jules Zutter (SUI)	–
1904	Anton Heida (USA) 36	–	William Merz (USA) 31
	George Eyser (USA) 36		
1924	Frank Kriz (USA) 9.98	Jan Koutny (TCH) 9.97	Bohumil Morkovsky (TCH) 9.93
1928	Eugen Mack (SUI) 9.58	Emanuel Löffler (TCH) 9.50	Stane Derganc (YUG) 9.46
1932	Savino Guglielmetti (ITA) 18.03	Alfred Jochim (USA) 17.77	Edward Carmichael (USA) 17.53
1936	Alfred Schwarzmann (GER) 19.200	Eugen Mack (SUI) 18.967	Matthias Volz (GER) 18.467
1948	Paavo Aaltonen (FIN) 39.10	Olavi Rove (FIN) 39.00	János Mogyorosi-Klencs (HUN) 38.50
			Ferenc Pataki (HUN) 38.50
			Leos Sotornik (TCH) 38.50
1952	Viktor Chukarin (URS) 19.20	Masao Takemoto (JPN) 19.15	Tadao Uesako (JPN) 19.10
			Takashi Ono (JPN) 19.10
1956	Helmuth Bantz (GER) 18.85	–	Yuri Titov (URS) 18.75
	Valentin Muratov (URS) 18.85		
1960	Takashi Ono (JPN) 19.350	–	Vladimir Portnoi (URS) 19.225
	Boris Shakhlin (URS) 19.350		
1964	Haruhiro Yamashita (JPN) 19.600	Viktor Lisitsky (URS) 19.325	Hannu Rantakari (FIN) 19.300
1968	Mikhail Voronin (URS) 19.000	Yukio Endo (JPN) 18.950	Sergei Diomidov (URS) 18.925
1972	Klaus Koste (GDR) 18.850	Viktor Klimenko (URS) 18.825	Nikolai Andrianov (URS) 18.800
1976	Nikolai Andrianov (URS) 19.450	Mitsuo Tsukahara (JPN) 19.375	Hiroshi Kajiyama (JPN) 19.275
1980	Nikolai Andrianov (URS) 19.825	Alexander Dityatin (URS) 19.800	Roland Brückner (GDR) 19.775
1984	Lou Yun (CHN) 19.950	Li Ning (CHN) 19.825	–
		Koji Gushiken (JPN) 19.825	
		Mitchell Gaylord (USA) 19.825	
		Shinje Morisue (JPN) 19.825	
1988	Lou Yun (CHN) 19.875	Sylvio Kroll (GDR) 19.862	Park Jong-Hoon (KOR) 19.775
1992	Vitali Scherbo (EUN) 9.856	Grigori Misyutin (EUN) 9.781	Yoo Ok-Youl (KOR) 9.762
1996	Andreas Wecker (GER) 9.850	Krasimir Dounev (BUL) 9.825	Vitali Shcherbo (BLR) 9.800
			Fan Bin (CHN) 9.800
			Alexei Nemov (RUS) 9.800
2000	Gervasio Deferr (ESP) 9.712	Alexei Bondarenko (RUS) 9.587	Lezek Blanik (POL) 9.475
2004	Gervasio Deferr (ESP) 9.737	Evgeni Sapronenko (LAT) 9.706	Marian Dragulescu (ROM) 9.612

1900, 1906-1920 Event not held

Women

Team

1928	NETHERLANDS 316.75	ITALY 289.00	GREAT BRITAIN 258.25
1936	GERMANY 506.50	CZECHOSLOVAKIA 503.60	HUNGARY 499.00

1948	CZECHOSLOVAKIA 445.45	HUNGARY 440.55	UNITED STATES 422.63
1952	SOVIET UNION 527.03	HUNGARY 520.96	CZECHOSLOVAKIA 503.32
1956	SOVIET UNION 444.80	HUNGARY 443.50	ROMANIA 438.20
1960	SOVIET UNION 382.320	CZECHOSLOVAKIA 373.323	ROMANIA 372.053
1964	SOVIET UNION 380.890	CZECHOSLOVAKIA 379.989	JAPAN 377.889
1968	SOVIET UNION 382.85	CZECHOSLOVAKIA 382.20	GDR 379.10
1972	SOVIET UNION 380.50	GDR 376.55	HUNGARY 368.25
1976	SOVIET UNION 390.35	ROMANIA 387.15	GDR 385.10
1980	SOVIET UNION 394.90	ROMANIA 393.50	GDR 392.55
1984	ROMANIA 392.20	UNITED STATES 391.20	CHINA 388.60
1988	SOVIET UNION 395.475	ROMANIA 394.125	GDR 390.875
1992	UNIFIED TEAM 395.666	ROMANIA 395.079	UNITED STATES 394.704
1996	UNITED STATES 389.225	RUSSIA 388.40	ROMANIA 388.246
2000	ROMANIA 154.608	RUSSIA 154.403	CHINA 154.008
2004	ROMANIA 114.283	UNITED STATES 113.584	RUSSIA 113.235

1896-1924, 1932 Event not held

Individual Combined Exercises

1952	Maria Gorokhovskaya (URS) 76.78	Nina Bocharova (URS) 75.94	Margit Korondi (HUN) 75.82
1956	Larissa Latynina (URS) 74.933	Agnes Keleti (HUN) 74.633	Sofia Muratova (URS) 74.466
1960	Larissa Latynina (URS) 77.031	Sofia Muratova (URS) 76.696	Polina Astakhova (URS) 76.164
1964	Vera Cáslavská (TCH) 77.564	Larissa Laytnina (URS) 76.998	Polina Astakhova (URS) 76.965
1968	Vera Cáslavská (TCH) 78.25	Zinaida Voronina (URS) 76.85	Natalya Muchinskaya (URS) 76.75
1972	Ludmila Tourischeva (URS) 77.025	Karin Janz (GDR) 76.875	Tamara Lazakovitch (URS) 76.850
1976	Nadia Comaneci (ROM) 79.275	Nelli Kim (URS) 78.675	Ludmila Tourischeva (URS) 78.625
1980	Yelena Davydova (URS) 79.150	Maxi Gnauck (GDR) 79.075	–
		Nadia Comaneci (ROM) 79.075	
1984	Mary Lou Retton (USA) 79.175	Ecaterina Szabo (ROM) 79.125	Simona Pauca (ROM) 78.675
1988	Yelena Chouchounova (URS) 79.662	Daniela Silivas (ROM) 79.637	Svetlana Bogunskaya (URS) 79.40
1992	Tatyana Gutsu (EUN) 39.737	Shannon Miller (USA) 39.725	Lavinia Milosovici (ROM) 39.687
1996	Lilia Podkopayeva (UKR) 39.255	Gina Gogean (ROM) 39.075	Lavinia Milosovici (ROM) 39.067
			Simona Amanar (ROM) 39.067
2000	Simona Amanar (ROM) 38.642	Maria Olaru (ROM) 38.581	Xuan Liu (CHN) 38.418
2004	Carly Patterson (USA) 38.387	Svetlana Khorkina (RUS) 38.211	Nan Zhang (CHN) 38.049

1896-1948 Event not held

Asymmetric Bars

1952	Margit Korondi (HUN) 19.40	Maria Gorokhovskaya (URS) 19.26	Agnes Keleti (HUN) 19.16
1956	Agnes Keleti (HUN) 18.966	Larissa Latynina (URS) 18.833	Sofia Muratova (URS) 18.800
1960	Polina Astakhova (URS) 19.616	Larissa Latynina (URS) 19.416	Tamara Lyukhina (URS) 19.399
1964	Polina Astakhova (URS) 19.332	Katalin Makray (HUN) 19.216	Larissa Latynina (URS) 19.199
1968	Vera Cáslavská (TCH) 19.650	Karin Janz (GDR) 19.500	Zinaida Voronina (URS) 19.425
1972	Karin Janz (GDR) 19.675	Olga Korbut (URS) 19.450	–
		Erika Zuchold (GDR) 19.450	
1976	Nadia Comaneci (ROM) 20.00	Teodora Ungureanu (ROM) 19.800	Marta Egervari (HUN) 19.775
1980	Maxi Gnauck (GDR) 19.875	Emila Eberle (ROM) 19.850	Steffi Kräker (GDR) 19.775
			Melita Rühn (ROM) 19.775
			Maria Filatova (URS) 19.775
1984	Ma Yanhong (CHN) 19.950	–	Mary Lou Retton (USA) 19.800
	Julianne McNamara (USA) 19.950		
1988	Daniela Silivas (ROM) 20.00	Dagmar Kersten (GDR) 19.987	Yelena Chouchounova (URS) 19.962
1992	Lu Li (CHN) 10.000	Tatyana Gutsu (EUN) 9.975	Shannon Miller (USA) 9.962
1996	Svetlana Khorkina (RUS) 9.850	Wengji Bi (CHN) 9.837	–
		Amy Chow (USA) 9.837	
2000	Svetlana Khorkina (RUS) 9.862	Jie Ling (CHN) 9.837	Yun Yang (CHN) 9.787
2004	Emilie Lepennec (FRA) 9.687	Terin Humphrey (USA) .662	Courtney Kipets (USA) 9.637

1896-1948 Event not held

Balance Beam

1952	Nina Bocharova (URS) 19.22	Maria Gorokhovskaya (URS) 19.13	Margit Korondi (HUN) 19.02
1956	Agnes Keleti (HUN) 18.80	Eva Bosáková (TCH) 18.63	–
		Tamara Manina (URS) 18.63	
1960	Eva Bosáková (TCH) 19.283	Larissa Latynina (URS) 19.233	Sofia Muratova (URS) 19.232
1964	Vera Cáslavská (TCH) 19.449	Tamara Manina (URS) 19.399	Larissa Latynina (URS) 19.382
1968	Natalya Kuchinskaya (URS) 19.650	Vera Cáslavská (TCH) 19.575	Larissa Petrik (URS) 19.250
1972	Olga Korbut (URS) 19.575	Tamara Lazokovitch (URS) 19.375	Karin Janz (GDR) 18.975

1976	Nadia Comaneci (ROM) 19.950	Olga Korbut (URS) 19.725	Teodora Ungureanu (ROM) 19.700
1980	Nadia Comaneci (ROM) 19.800	Yelena Davydova (URS) 19.750	Natalya Shaposhnikova (URS) 19.725
1984	Simona Pauca (ROM) 19.800	–	Kathy Johnson (USA) 19.650
	Ecaterina Szabo (ROM) 19.800		
1988	Daniela Silivas (ROM) 19.924	Yelena Chouchounova (URS) 19.875	Gabriela Potorac (ROM) 19.837
			Phoebe Mills (USA) 19.837
1992	Tayana Lyssenko (EUN) 9.975	Lu Li (CHN) 9.912	–
		Shannon Miller (USA) 9.912	
1996	Shannon Miller (USA) 9.862	Lilia Podkopayeva (UKR) 9.825	Gina Gogean (ROM) 9.787
2000	Xuan Liu (CHN) 9.825	Yekaterina Lobaznyuk (RUS) 9.787	Yelena Prodounova (RUS) 9.775
2004	Catalina Ponor (ROM) 9.787	Carly Patterson (USA) 9.775	Alexandra Eremia (ROM) 9.700
1896-1948 Event not held			

Floor Exercises

1952	Agnes Keleti (HUN) 19.36	Maria Gorokhoskaya (URS) 19.20	Margit Korondi (HUN) 19.00
1956	Larissa Altynina (URS) 18.733	–	Elena Leustean (ROM) 18.70
	Agnes Keleti (HUN) 18.733		
1960	Larissa Latynina (URS) 19.583	Polina Astakhova (URS) 19.532	Tamara Lyukhina (URS) 19.449
1964	Larissa Latynina (URS) 19.599	Polina Astakhova (URS) 19.500	Anikó Jánosi (HUN) 19.300
1968	Larissa Petrik (URS) 19.675	–	Natalya Kuchinskaya (URS) 19.650
	Vera Cáslavská (TCH) 19.675		
1972	Olga Korbut (URS) 19.575	Ludmila Tourischeva (URS) 19.550	Tamara Lazakovitch (URS) 19.450
1976	Nelli Kim (URS) 19.850	Ludmila Tourischeva (URS) 19.825	Nadia Comaneci (ROM) 19.750
1980	Nelli Kim (URS) 19.875	–	Natalya Shaposhnikova (URS) 19.825
	Nadia Comaneci (ROM) 19.875		Maxi Gnauck (GDR) 19.825
1984	Ecaterina Szabo (ROM) 19.975	Julianne McNamara (USA) 19.950	Mary Lou Retton (USA) 19.775
1988	Daniela Silivas (ROM) 19.937	Svetlana Bogunskaya (URS) 19.887	Diana Doudeva (BUL) 19.850
1992	Lavinia Milosovici (ROM) 10.000	Henrietta Onodi (HUN) 9.950	Tatyana Gutsu (EUN) 9.912
			Christina Bontas (ROM) 9.912
			Shannon Miller (USA) 9.912
1996	Lilia Podkopayeva (UKR) 9.887	Simona Amanar (ROM) 9.850	Dominique Dawes (USA) 9.837
2000	Yelena Zamolodchikova (RUS) 9.850	Svetlana Khorkina (RUS) 9.812	Simona Amanar (ROM) 9.712
2004	Catalina Ponor (ROM) 9.750	Nicoleta Sofronie (ROM) 9.562	Patricia Moreno (ESP) 9.487
1896-1948 Event not held			

Horse Vault

1952	Yelena Kalinchuk (URS) 19.20	Maria Gorokhoskaya (URS) 19.19	Galina Minaitscheva (URS) 19.16
1956	Larissa Latynina (URS) 18.833	Tamara Manina (URS) 18.800	Ann-Sofi Colling (SWE) 18.733
			Olga Tass (HUN) 18.733
1960	Margarita Nikolayeva (URS) 19.316	Sofia Muratova (URS) 19.049	Larissa Latynina (URS) 19.016
1964	Vera Cáslavská (TCH) 19.483	Larissa Latynina (URS) 19.283	–
		Birgit Radochla (GER) 19.283	
1968	Vera Cáslavská (TCH) 19.775	Erika Zuchold (GDR) 19.625	Zinaida Voronina (URS) 19.500
1972	Karin Janz (GDR) 19.525	Erika Zuchold (GDR) 19.275	Ludmila Tourischeva (URS) 19.250
1976	Nelli Kim (URS) 19.800	Ludmila Tourischeva (URS) 19.650	–
		Carola Dombeck (GDR) 19.650	
1980	Natalya Shaposhnikova (URS) 19.725	Steffi Kräker (GDR) 19.675	Melita Rühn (ROM) 19.650
1984	Ecaterina Szabo (ROM) 19.875	Mary Lou Retton (USA) 19.850	Lavinia Agache (ROM) 19.750
1988	Svetlana Bogunskaya (URS) 19.905	Gabriela Potorac (ROM) 19.830	Daniela Silivas (ROM) 19.818
1992	Lavinia Milosovici (ROM) 9.925		Tatyana Lyssenko (EUN) 9.912
	Henrietta Onodi (HUN) 9.925		
1996	Simona Amanar (ROM) 9.825	Mo Huilan (CHN) 9.768	Gina Gogean (ROM) 9.750
2000	Yelena Zamolodchikova (RUS) 9.731	Andreea Raducan (ROM) 9.693	Yekaterina Lobaznyuk (RUS) 9.674
2004	Monica Rosu (ROM) 9.656	Annia Hatch (USA) 9.481	Anna Pavlova (RUS) 9.475
1896-1948 Event not held			

Modern Rhythmic

1984	Lori Fung (CAN) 57.950	Doina Staiculescu (ROM) 57.900	Regina Weber (FRG) 57.700
1988	Marina Lobatch (URS) 60.00	Adriana Dounavska (BUL) 59.950	Alexandra Timochenko (URS) 59.875
1992	Aleksandra Timoschenko (EUN) 59.037	Carolina Garcia (ESP) 58.100	Oksana Skaldina (EUN) 57.912
1996	Yekaterina Serebryanskaya (UKR) 39.683	Yanina Batyrchina (RUS) 39.382	Yelena Vitrichenko (UKR) 39.331
2000	Yulia Barsukova (RUS) 39.632	Yulia Raskina (BLR) 39.548	Alina Kabayeva (RUS) 39.466
2004	Alina Kabayeva (RUS) 108.400	Irina Tchachina (RUS) 107.325	Anna Bessonova (UKR) 106.700
1896-1980 Event not held			

Rhythmic Team

1996	SPAIN 38.933	BULGARIA 38.866	RUSSIA 38.365
2000	RUSSIA 39.500	BELARUS 39.500	GREECE 39.283
2004	RUSSIA 51.100	ITALY 49.450	BULGARIA 48.600

1896-1992 Event not held

DISCONTINUED EVENTS

Men

Parallel Bars (Teams)

1896	GERMANY	GREECE	GREECE

Horizontal Bars (Teams)

1896	GERMANY[1]	–	–

[1]Walkover

Rope Climbing

1896	Nicolaos Andriakopoulos (GRE) 23.4sec	Thomas Xenakis (GRE)	–[1]
1904	George Eyser (USA) 7.0	Charles Krause (USA) 7.8	Emil Voigt (USA) 9.8
1906	Georgios Aliprantis (GRE) 11.4	Béla Erödy (HUN) 13.8	Konstantinos Kozantis (GRE) 13.8
1924	Bedrich Supchik (TCH) 7.2	Albert Séguin (FRA) 7.4	August Güttinger (SUI) 7.8
			Ladislav Vácha (TCH) 7.8
1932	Raymond Bass (USA) 6.7sec	William Galbraith (USA) 6.8	Thomas Connelly (USA) 7.0

[1]Fritz Hofmann (GER) did not finish

Club Swinging

1904	Edward Hennig (USA) 13pts	Emil Voigt (USA) 9	Ralph Wilson (USA) 5
1932	George Roth (USA) 8.97pts	Philip Erenberg (USA) 8.90	William Kuhlmeier (USA) 8.63

Tumbling

1932	Rowland Wolfe (USA) 18.90pts	Edward Gross (USA) 18.67	Willliam Herrmann (USA) 19.37

Nine Event Competition

1094	Adolf Spinnler (SUI) 43.49pts	Julius Lenhart (AUT) 43.00	Wilhelm Weber (GER) 41.60

Triathlon

Comprised 100 yards, long jump and shot putt

1904	Max Emmerich (USA) 35.70pts	John Grieb (USA) 34.00	William Merz (USA) 33.90

Four Event Competition

1904	Anton Heida (USA) 161pts	George Eyser (USA) 152	William Merz (USA) 135

Sidehorse Vault

1924	Albert Séguin (FRA) 10.00pts	Jean Gounot (FRA) 9.93	–
		François Gangloff (FRA) 9.93	

Swedish System (Teams)

1912	SWEDEN 937.46pts	DENMARK 898.84	NORWAY 857.21
1920	SWEDEN 1364pts	DENMARK 1325	BELGIUM 1094

Free System (Teams)

1912	NORWAY 114.25pts	FINLAND 109.25	DENMARK 106.25
1920[1]	DENMARK	NORWAY	–

[1]Only two teams competed

Women

Portable Apparatus (Teams)

1952	SWEDEN 74.20pts	SOVIET UNION 73.00	HUNGARY 71.60
1956	HUNGARY 75.20pts	SWEDEN 74.20	POLAND 74.00
			SOVIET UNION 74.00

HANDBALL

Men

1936[1]	GERMANY	AUSTRIA	SWITZERLAND
1972	YUGOSLAVIA	CZECHOSLOVAKIA	ROMANIA
1976	SOVIET UNION	ROMANIA	POLAND
1980	GDR	SOVIET UNION	ROMANIA
1984	YUGOSLAVIA	FRG	ROMANIA
1988	SOVIET UNION	KOREA	YUGOSLAVIA
1992	UNIFIED TEAM	SWEDEN	FRANCE
1996	CROATIA	SWEDEN	SPAIN
2000	RUSSIA	SWEDEN	SPAIN
2004	CROATIA	GERMANY	RUSSIA

1896-1932, 1948-1968 event not held
[1]Field handball played outdoors

Women

1976	SOVIET UNION	GDR	HUNGARY
1980	SOVIET UNION	YUGOSLAVIA	GDR
1984	YUGOSLAVIA	KOREA	CHINA
1988	KOREA	NORWAY	SOVIET UNION
1992	KOREA	NORWAY	UNIFIED TEAM
1996	DENMARK	KOREA	HUNGARY
2000	DENMARK	HUNGARY	NORWAY
2004	DENMARK	KOREA	UKRAINE

1896-1972 Event not held

HOCKEY

Men

1908[1]	ENGLAND	IRELAND	SCOTLAND[2] WALES[2]
1920	ENGLAND[3]	DENMARK	BELGIUM
1928	INDIA	NETHERLANDS	GERMANY
1932	INDIA	JAPAN	UNITED STATES
1936	INDIA	GERMANY	NETHERLANDS
1948	INDIA	GREAT BRITAIN	NETHERLANDS
1952	INDIA	NETHERLANDS	GREAT BRITAIN
1956	INDIA	PAKISTAN	GERMANY
1960	PAKISTAN	INDIA	SPAIN
1964	INDIA	PAKISTAN	AUSTRALIA
1968	PAKISTAN	AUSTRALIA	INDIA
1972	FRG	PAKISTAN	INDIA
1976	NEW ZEALAND	AUSTRALIA	PAKISTAN
1980	INDIA	SPAIN	SOVIET UNION
1984	PAKISTAN	FRG	GREAT BRITAIN
1988	GREAT BRITAIN	FRG	NETHERLANDS
1992	GERMANY	AUSTRALIA	PAKISTAN
1996	NETHERLANDS	SPAIN	AUSTRALIA
2000	NETHERLANDS	KOREA	AUSTRALIA
2004	AUSTRALIA	NETHERLANDS	GERMANY

1896-1906, 1912, 1924 Event not held
[1]Great Britain had four teams entered; [2]Tie for third place; [3]Great Britain represented by England team

Women

1980	ZIMBABWE	CZECHOSLOVAKIA	SOVIET UNION
1984	NETHERLANDS	FRG	UNITED STATES
1988	AUSTRALIA	KOREA	NETHERLANDS
1992	SPAIN	GERMANY	GREAT BRITAIN
1996	AUSTRALIA	KOREA	NETHERLANDS
2000	AUSTRALIA	ARGENTINA	NETHERLANDS
2004	GERMANY	NETHERLANDS	ARGENTINA

1896-1976 Event not held

JUDO

Men

Introduced in 1964
Heavyweight

(Over 80kg – 1964; over 93kg – 1972-76; over 95kg – 1980-96; over 100kg – 2000-04)

1964	Isao Inokuma (JPN)	A Douglas Rogers (CAN)	Parnaoz Chikviladze (URS)
			Anzor Kiknadze (URS)
1972	Willem Ruska (NED)	Klaus Glahn (FRG)	Givi Onashvili (URS)
			Motoki Nishimura (JPN)
1976	Sergei Novrikov (URS)	Gunther Neureuther (FRG)	Sumio Endo (JPN)
			Allen Coage (USA)
1980	Angelo Parisi (FRA)	Dimitar Zaprianov (BUL)	Vladimir Kocman (CZE)
			Radomir Kovacevic (YUG)
1984	Hitoshi Saito (JPN)	Angelo Parisi (FRA)	Cho Yong-Chul (KOR)
			Mark Berger (CAN)
1988	Hitoshi Saito (JPN)	Henry Stöhr (GDR)	Cho Yong-Chul (KOR)
			Grigori Veritchev (URS)
1992	David Khakhaliashvili (EUN)	Naoya Ogawa (JPN)	David Douillet (FRA)
			Imre Csösz (HUN)
1996	David Douillet (FRA)	Ernesto Perez (ESP)	Harry van Barneveld (BEL)
			Frank Moeller (GER)
2000	David Douillet (FRA)	Shinichi Shinohara (JPN)	Indrek Pertelson (EST)
			Tamerlan Timenov (RUS)
2004	Keiji Suzuki (JPN)	Tamerlan Timinov (RUS)	Dennis van der Geest (NED)
			Indrek Pertelson (EST)

1968 Event not held

Light Heavyweight

(Up to 93kg -1972-76; up to 95kg – 1980-96; up to 100kg – 2000-04)

1972	Shoto Chochoshvili (URS)	David Starbrook (GBR)	Chiaki Ishii (BRA)
			Paul Barth (FRG)
1976	Kazuhiro Ninomiya (JPN)	Ramaz Harshiladze (URS)	David Starbrook (GBR)
			Jürg Röthlisberger (SUI)
1980	Robert Van de Walle (BEL)	Tengiz Khubuluri (URS)	Dietmar Lorenz (GDR)
			Henk Numan (NED)
1984	Ha Hyoung-Zoo (KOR)	Douglas Vieira (BRA)	Bjarni Fridriksson (ISL)
			Gunther Neureuther (FRG)
1988	Aurelio Miguel (BRA)	Marc Meiling (FRG)	Robert Van de Walle (BEL)
			Dennis Stewart (GBR)
1992	Antal Kovacs (HUN)	Ray Stevens (GBR)	Dmitri Sergeyev (EUN)
			Theo Meijer (NED)
1996	Pawel Nastula (POL)	Kim Min-Soo (KOR)	Stephane Traineau (FRA)
			Miguel Fernandez (BRA)
2000	Kosei Inoue (JPN)	Nicolas Gill (CAN)	Stephane Traineau (FRA)
			Yuri Stepkin (RUS)
2004	Igor Makarov (BLR)	Sung-Ho Jang (KOR)	Michael Jurack (GER)
			Ariel Zeevi (ISR)

1964-68 Event not held

Middleweight

(Up to 80kg – 1964-76; up to 86kg – 1980-96; up to 90kg – 2000-04)

1964	Isao Okano (JPN)	Wolfgang Hofmann (GER)	James Bergman (USA)
			Eui Tae Kim (KOR)
1972	Shinobu Sekine (JPN)	Oh Seung-Lip (KOR)	Brian Jacks (GBR)
			Jean-Paul Coche (FRA)
1976	Isamu Sonoda (JPN)	Valeri Dvoinikov (URS)	Slavko Obadov (YUG)
			Park Youngchul (KOR)
1980	Jürg Röthlisberger (SUI)	Issac Azcuy Oliva (CUB)	Detlef Ultsich (GDR)
			Alexander Yatskevitch (URS)
1984	Peter Seisenbacher (AUT)	Robert Berland (USA)	Seiki Nose (JPN)
			Walter Carmona (BRA)
1988	PeterSeisenbacher (AUT)	Vladimir Chestakov (URS)	Ben Spijkers (NED)
			Akinobu Osako (JPN)

1992	Waldemar Legien (POL)	Pascal Tayot (FRA)	Hirotaki Okada (JPN)
			Nicolas Gill (CAN)
1996	Jeon Ki-Young (KOR)	Armen Bagdasarov (UZB)	Marko Spittka (GER)
			Mark Huizinga (NED)
2000	Mark Huizinga (NED)	Carlos Honorato (BRA)	Frederick Demontfaucon (FRA)
			Ruslan Mashurenko (UKR)
2004	Zurab Zviadauri (GEO)	Hiroshi Izumi (JPN)	Mark Huizinga (NED)
			Khasanbi Tayov (RUS)

1968 Event not held

Light Middleweight

(Up to 70kg – 1972-76; up to 78kg 1980-96; up to 81kg – 2000-04)

1972	Toyojazu Nomura (JPN)	Anton Zajkowski (POL)	Dietmar Hötger (GDR)
			Anatoli Novikov (URS)
1976	Vladimir Nevzorov (URS)	Koji Kuramoto (JPN)	Partrick Vial (FRA)
			Marian Talaj (POL)
1980	Shota Khabeleri (URS)	Juan Ferrer La Hera (CUB)	Harald Heinke (GDR)
			Bernard Tchoullouyan (FRA)
1984	Frank Wieneke (FRG)	Neil Adams (GBR)	Michel Nowak (FRA)
			Mircea Fratica (ROM)
1988	Waldemar Legien (POL)	Frank Wieneke (FRG)	Torsten Brechot (GDR)
			Bachir Varayev (URS)
1992	Hidehiko Yoshida (JPN)	Jason Morris (USA)	Kim Byung-Joo (KOR)
			Betrand Damaisin (FRA)
1996	Djamel Bouras (FRA)	Toshihiko Koga (JPN)	Soso Liparteliani (GEO)
			In-Chul Cho (KOR)
2000	Makoto Takimoto (JPN)	In-Chul Cho (KOR)	Nuno Delgado (POR)
			Alexei Badolin (EST)
2004	Ilias Iliadis (GRE)	Roman Gontyuk (UKR)	Dmitri Nossov (RUS)
			Flavio Canto (BRA)

1964-68 Event not held

Lightweight

(Up to 63kg – 1964-76; up to 71kg – 1980-96; up to 73kg – 2000-04)

1964	Takehide Nakatani (JPN)	Eric Hänni (SUI)	Oleg Stepanov (URS)
			Aron Bogulubov (URS)
1972	TakaoKawaguchi (JPN)	–[1]	Kim Yong Ik (PRK)
			Jean Jacques Mounier (FRA)
1976	Hector Rodriguez (CUB)	Chang Eun-kyung (KOR)	Felice Mariani (ITA)
			Jozsef Tuncsik (HUN)
1980	Ezio Gamba (ITA)	Neil Adams (GBR)	Karl-Heinz Lehmann (GDR)
			Ravdan Davaadalai (MGL)
1984	Ahn Byeong-Keun (KOR)	Ezio Gamba (ITA)	Luis Onmura (BRA)
			Kerrith Brown (GBR)
1988	Marc Alexandre (FRA)	Sven Loll (GDR)	Michael Swain (USA)
			Guergui Tenadze (URS)
1992	Toshihiko Koga (JPN)	Bertalan Hajtós (HUN)	Chung Hoon (KOR)
			Shay Smadga (ISR)
1996	Kenzo Nakamura (JPN)	Kwak Dae-Sung (KOR)	James Pedro (USA)
			Christophe Gagliano (FRA)
2000	Giuseppe Maddaloni (ITA)	Tiago Camilo (BRA)	Vsevolods Zelanijs (LAT0
			Anatoli Laryukov (BLR)
2004	Won-Hee Lee (KOR)	Vitali Makarov (RUS)	Leandro Guilheiro (BRA)
			James Pedro (USA)

1968 Event not held
[1]*Bakhaavaa Buidaa (MGL) disqualified after positive drug test*

Up to 66kg

(Up to 65kg – 1980-96)

1980	Nikolai Solodukhin (URS)	Tsendying Damdin (MGL)	Ilian Nedkov (BUL)
			Janusz Pawlowski (POL)
1984	Yoshiyuki Matsuoka (JPN)	Hwang Jung-Oh (KOR)	Josef Reiter (AUT)
			Marc Alexandre (FRA)
1988	Lee Kyeung-Keun (KOR)	Janusz Pawlowski (POL)	Bruno Carabeta (FRA)
			Yosuke Yamamoto (JPN)

1992	Rogerio Sampaio (BRA)	Jozsef Csák (HUN)	Udo Quellmalz (GER)
			Israel Hernandez (CUB)
1996	Udo Quellmalz (GER)	Yukimasa Nakamura (JPN)	Israel Plana Hernandez (CUB)
			Henrique Guimares (BRA)
2000	Huseyin Ozkan (TUR)	Larbi Benboudaoud (FRA)	Girolamo Giovinazzo (ITA)
			Georgi Vazagashvili (GEO)
2004	Masato Uchishiba (JPN)	Jozef Krnac (SVK)	Georgi Georgiev (BUL)
			Yordanis Arencibia (CUB)

1964-76 Event no held

Up to 60kg

1980	Thierry Rey (FRA)	Rafael Carbonell (CUB)	Tibor Kinces (HUN)
			Aramby Emizh (URS)
1984	Shinji Hosokawa (JPN)	Kim Jae-Yup (KOR)	Edward Liddie (USA)
			Neil Eckersley (GBR)
1988	Kim Jae-Yup (KOR)	Kevin Asano (USA)	Shinji Hosokawa (JPN)
			Amiran Totikachvili (URS)
1992	Nazim Gousseinov (EUN)	Yoon Hyun (KOR)	Tadamori Koshino (JPN)
			Richard Trautmann (GER)
1996	Tadahiro Nomura (JPN)	Girolamo Giovanazzo (ITA)	Doripalam Narmandakh (MGL)
			Richard Trautmann (GER)
2000	Tadahiro Nomura (JPN)	Bu-Kyung Jung (KOR)	Ajdin Smagulov (KGZ)
			Manolo Poulot (CUB)
2004	Tadahiro Nomura (JPN)	Nestor Khergian (GEO)	Min-Ho Cho (KOR)
			Khashbaatar Tsagaanbaatar (MON)

1964-76 Event not held

DISCONTINUED EVENT

Open Category No Weight Limit

1964	Antonius Geesink (NED)	Akio Kaminaga (JPN)	Theodore Boronovskis (AUS)
			Klaus Glahn (GER)
1972	Willem Ruska (NED)	Vitali Kuznetsov (URS)	Jean-Claude Brondani (FRA)
			Angelo Parisi (GBR)
1976	Haruki Uemura (JPN)	Keith Remfry (GBR)	Shota Chochoshvili (URS)
			Jeaki Cho (KOR)
1980	Dietmar Lorenz (GDR)	Angelo Parisi (FRA)	András Ozsvar (HUN)
			Arthur Mapp (GBR)
1984	Yasuhiro Yamashita (JPN)	Mohamed Rashwan (EGY)	Mihai Cioc (ROM)
			Arthur Schnabel (FRG)

1968 Event not held

Women

Up to 48kg

1992	Cecile Nowak (FRA)	Ryoko Tamura (JPN)	Hulya Senyurt (TUR)
			Amarilis Savon (CUB)
1996	Kye Sun (PRK)	Ryoko Tamura (JPN)	Amarilis Savon (CUB)
			Yolanda Soler (ESP)
2000	Ryoko Tamura (JPN)	Lyubov Bruletova (RUS)	Ann Simons (BEL)
			Anna-Maria Gradante (GER)
2004	Ryoko Tamura-Tani (JPN)	Frederique Jussinet (FRA)	Julia Matijass (GER)
			Feng Gao (CHN)

1964-1988 Event not held

Up to 52kg

1992	Almudena Munoz (ESP)	Noriko Mizuguchi (JPN)	Li Zhongyun (CHN)
			Sharon Rendle (GBR)
1996	Marie-Claire Restoux (FRA)	Hyun Sook-Hee (KOR)	Legna Verdecia (CUB)
			Noriko Sugawara (JPN)
2000	Legna Verdecia (CUB)	Noriko Narazaki (JPN)	Sun-Hui Kye (PRK)
			Yuxiang Liu (CHN)
2004	Dongmei Xian (CHN)	Yuki Yokosawa (JPN)	Ilse Heylen (BEL)
			Amarylis Savon (CUB)

1964-88 Event not held

Up to 57kg

(Up to 56kg – 1992-96)

1992	Miriam Blasco (ESP)	Nicola Fairbrother (GBR)	Chiyori Tateno (JPN)
			Driulis Gonzalez (CUB)
1996	Driulis Gonzalez (CUB)	Jung Sae-Yong (KOR)	Isabel Fernandez (ESP)
			Liu Chuang (CHN)
2000	Isabel Fernandez (ESP)	Driulis Gonzalez (CUB)	Maria Pekli (AUS)
			Kie Kusakabe (JPN)
2004	Yvonne Bönisch (GER)	Sun-Hui Kye (PRK)	Deborah Gravenstin (NED)
			Yurisleidy Lupetey (CUB)

1964-88 Event not held

Up to 63kg

(Up to 61kg – 1992-96)

1992	Catherine Fleury (FRA)	Yael Arad (ISR)	Zhang Di (CHN)
			Yelena Petrova (EUN)
1996	Yuko Emoto (JPN)	Gella Van De Caveye (BEL)	Jenny Gal (NED)
			Jung Sung-Sook (KOR)
2000	Severine Vandenhende (FRA)	Shufang Li (CHN)	Gella Vandacaveye (BEL)
			Sung Sook Jung (KOR)
2004	Ayumi Tanimoto (JPN)	Claudia Heill (AUT)	Driulys Gonzalez (CUB)
			Urska Zolnir (SLO)

1964-88 Event not held

Up to 70kg

(Up to 66kg – 1992-96)

1992	Odalis Reve (CUB)	Emanuela Pierantozzi (ITA)	Kate Howey (GBR)
			Heidi Rakels (BEL)
1996	Min-Sun Cho (KOR)	Aneta Szczepanska (POL)	Claudia Zwiers (NED)
			Xianbo Wang (CHN)
2000	Sibelis Veranes (CUB)	Kate Howey (GBR)	Min-Sun Cho (KOR)
			Ylenia Scapin (ITA)
2004	Masae Ueno (JPN)	Edith Bosch (NED)	Dongya Qin (CHN)
			Annett Böhm (GER)

1964-88 Event not held

Up to 78kg

(Up to 72kg – 1992-96)

1992	Kim Mi-jung (KOR)	Yoko Tanabe (JPN)	Laetitia Meignan (FRA)
			Irene de Kok (NED)
1996	Ulla Werbrouck (HUN)	Yoko Tanabe (JPN)	Ylenia Scapin (ITA)
			Diadenis Luna (CUB)
2000	Lin Tang (CHN)	Celine Lebrun (FRA)	Emanuela Pierantozzi (ITA)
			Simona Richter (ROM)
2004	Noriko Anno (JPN)	Xia Liu (CHN)	Lucia Morico (ITA)
			Yurisel Laborde (CUB)

1964-88 Event not held

Over 78kg (Over 72kg – 1992-96)

1992	Zhuang Xiaoyan (CHN)	Estela Rodriguez (CUB)	Yoko Sakuae (JPN)
			Natalia Lupino (FRA)
1996	Sun Fu-Ming (CHN)	Estela Rodriguez (CUB)	Johanna Hagn (GER)
			Christine Cicot (FRA)
2000	Yuan Hua (CHN)	Daima Beltran (CUB)	Seon-Young Kim (KOR)
			Mayumi Yamashita (JPN)
2004	Maki Tsukada (JPN)	Dayma Beltran (CUB)	Fuming Sun (CHN)
			Tea Donguzashvili (RUS)

1964-88 Event not held

MODERN PENTATHLON

Men

Individual

1912	Gösta Lilliehöök (SWE) 27	Gösta Asbrink (SWE) 28	Georg de Laval (SWE) 30
1920	Gustaf Dyrssen (SWE) 18	Erik de Laval (SWE) 23	Gösta Rüno (SWE) 27
1924	Bo Lindman (SWE) 18	Gustaf Dyrssen (SWE) 39.5	Bertil Uggla (SWE) 45

1928	Sven Thofelt (SWE) 47	Bo Lindman (SWE) 50	Helmuth Kahl (GER) 52
1932	Johan Gabriel Oxenstierna (SWE) 32	Bo Lindman (SWE) 35.5	Richard Mayo (USA) 38.5
1936	Gotthard Handrick (SWE) 31.5	Charles Leonard (USA) 39.5	Silvano Abba (ITA) 45.5
1948	Willie Grut (SWE) 16	George Moore (USA) 47	Gösta Gärdin (SWE) 49
1952	Lars Hall (SWE) 32	Gábor Benedek (HUN) 39	István Szondi (HUN) 41
1956	Lars Hall (SWE) 4843	Olavi Nannonen (FIN) 4774.5	Välnö Korhonen (FIN) 4750
1960	Ferenc Németh (HUN) 5024	Imre Nagy (HUN) 4988	Robert Beck (USA) 4981
1964	Ferenc Török (HUN) 5116	Igor Novikov (URS) 5067	Albert Mokeyev (URS) 5039
1968	Björn Ferm (SWE) 4964	András Balczó (HUN) 4953	Pavel Lednev (URS) 4795
1972	András Balczó (HUN) 5412	Boris Onischenko (URS) 5335	Pavel Lednev (URS) 5328
1976	Janusz Pyciak-Peciak (POL) 5520	Pavel Lednev (URS) 5485	Jan Bartu (TCH) 5466
1980	Anatoli Starostin (URS) 5568	Tamás Szombathelyi (HUN) 5502	Pavel Lednev (URS) 5282
1984	Daniel Massala (ITA) 5469	Svante Rasmuson (SWE) 5456	Carlo Massullo (ITA) 5406
1988	János Martinek (HUN) 5404	Carlo Massullo (ITA) 5379	Vakhtang Yagorachvili (URS) 5367
1992	Arkadiusz Skrzypaszek (POL) 5559	Attila Mizsér (HUN) 5446	Edouard Zenovka (EUN) 5361
1996	Alexander Parygin (KZK) 5551	Eduard Zenovka (RUS) 5530	János Martinek (HUN) 5501
2000	Dimitri Svatkowski (RUS) 5376	Gabor Balogh (HUN) 5353	Pavel Dovgal (BLR) 5338
2004	Andrei Moiseyev (RUS) 5480	Andrejus Zadneprovski (LTU) 5428	Libor Capalini (CZE) 5392

1896-1908 Event not held

Team

1952	HUNGARY 116	SWEDEN 182	FINLAND 213
1956	SOVIET UNION 13 690.5	UNITED STATES 13 482	FINLAND 13 185.5
1960	HUNGARY 14 863	SOVIET UNION 14 309	UNITED STATES 14 192
1964	SOVIET UNION 14 961	UNITED STATES 14 189	HUNGARY 14 173
1968	HUNGARY 14 325	SOVIET UNION 14 248	FRANCE 13 289[1]
1972	SOVIET UNION 15 968	HUNGARY 15 348	FINLAND 14 812
1976	GREAT BRITAIN 15 559	CZECHOSLOVAKIA 15 451	HUNGARY 15 395
1980	SOVIET UNION 16 126	HUNGARY 15 912	SWEDEN 15 845
1984	ITALY 16 060	UNITED STATES 15 568	FRANCE 15 565
1988	HUNGARY 15 886	ITALY 15 571	GREAT BRITAIN 15 276
1992	POLAND 16 018	UNIFIED TEAM 15 924	ITALY 15 760

1896-1948,1996-2004 Event not held
[1]*Sweden finished third but were disqualified when a test indicated that a team member had an excessive level of alcohol*

Women

Introduced in 2000

2000	Stephanie Cook (GBR) 5318	Emily de Riel (USA) 5310	Kate Allenby (GBR) 5273
2004	Zsuzsanna Vörös (HUN) 5448	Jelena Rublevska (LAT) 5380	Georgina Harland (GBR) 5344

ROWING

Men

Single Sculls

1900	Henri Barrelet (FRA) 7:35.6	André Gaudin (FRA) 7:41.6	St George Ashe (GBR) 8:15.6
1904	Frank Greer (USA) 10:08.5	James Juvenal (USA) 2 lengths	Constance Titus (USA) 1 length
1906	Gaston Delaplane (FRA) 5:53.4	Joseph Larran (FRA) 6:07.2	–[1]
1908	Harry Blackstaffe (GBR) 9:26.0	Alexander McCulloch (GBR)1 lgth	Bernhard von Gaza (GER) dna
			Károly Levitsky (HUN) dna
1912	William Kinnear (GBR) 7:47.6	Potydore Veirman (BEL) 1 lgth	Everard Butter (CAN) dna
			Mikhail Kusik (RUS) dna
1920	John Kelly (USA) 7:35.0	Jack Beresford (GBR) 7:36.0	Clarence Hadfield d'Arcy (NZL) 7:48.0
1924	Jack Beresford (GBR) 7:49.2	William Garrett-Gilmore (USA) 7:54.0	Josef Schneider (SUI) 8:01.1
1928	Henry Pearce (AUS) 7:11.0	Kenneth Myers (USA) 7:20.8	David Collett (GBR) 7:19.8
1932	Henry Pearce (AUS) 7:44.4	William Miller (USA) 7:45.2	Guillermo Douglas (URU) 8:13.6
1936	Gustav Schäfer (GER) 8:21.5	Josef Hasenöhri (AUT) 8:25.8	Daniel Barrow (USA) 8:28.0
1948	Mervyn Wood (AUS) 7:24.4	Eduardo Risso (URU) 7:38.2	Romolo Catasta (ITA) 7:51.4
1952	Yuri Tyukalov (URS) 8:12.8	Mervyn Wood (AUS) 8:14.5	Teodor Kocerka (POL) 8:19.4
1956	Vyacheslav Ivanov (URS) 8:02.5	Stuart Mackenzie (AUS) 8:07.0	John Kelly (USA) 8:11.8
1960	Vyacheslav Ivanov (URS) 7:13.96	Achim Hill (GER) 7:20.21	Teodor Kocerka (POL) 7:21.26
1964	Vyacheslav Ivanov (URS) 8:22.51	Achim Hill (GER) 8:26.34	Gottfried Kottmann (SUI) 8:29.68
1968	Henri Jan Wienese (NED) 7:47.80	Jochen Meissner (FRG) 7:52.00	Alberto Demiddi (ARG) 7:57.19
1972	Yuri Malishev (URS) 7:10.12	Alberto Demiddi (ARG) 7:11.53	Wolfgang Güldenpfennig (GDR) 7:14.45
1976	Pertti Karpinnen (FIN) 7:29.03	Peter Kolbe (FRG) 7:31.67	Joachim Dreifke (GDR) 7:38.03
1980	Pertti Karpinnen (FIN) 7:09.61	Vasili Yakusha (URS) 7:11.66	Peter Kersten (GDR) 7:14.88
1984	Pertti Karpinnen (FIN) 7:00.24	Peter Kolbe (FRG) 7:02.19	Robert Mills (CAN) 7:10.38

1988	Thomas Lange (GDR) 6:49.86	Peter Kolbe (FRG) 6:54.77	Eric Verdonk (NZL) 6:58.86
1992	Thomas Lange (GER) 6:51.40	Vaclav Chalupa (CZE) 6:52.93	Kajetan Broniewski (POL) 6:56.82
1996	Xeno Mueller (SUI) 6:44.85	Derek Porter (CAN) 6:47.45	Thomas Lange (GER) 6:47.72
2000	Rob Waddell (NZL) 6:48.90	Xeno Müller (SUI) 6:50.55	Marcus Hacker (GER) 6:50.83
2004	Olaf Tufte (NOR) 6:49.30	Jüri Jaanson (EST) 6:51.52	Ivo Yanakiev (BUL) 6:52.80

1896 Event not held
[1]Only two competitors

Double Sculls

1904	UNITED STATES 10:03.2	UNITED STATES dna	UNITED STATES dna
1920	UNITED STATES 7:09.0	ITALY 7:19.0	FRANCE 7:21.0
1924	UNITED STATES 7:45.0	FRANCE 7:54.8	SWITZERLAND dna
1928	UNITED STATES 6:41.4	CANADA 6:51.0	AUSTRIA 6:48.8
1932	UNITED STATES 7:17.4	GERMANY 7:22.8	CANADA 7:27.6
1936	GREAT BRITAIN 7:20.8	GERMANY 7:26.2	POLAND 7:36.2
1948	GREAT BRITAIN 6:51.3	DENMARK 6:55.3	URUGUAY 7:12.4
1952	ARGENTINA 7:32.2	SOVIET UNION 7:38.3	URUGUAY 7:43.7
1956	SOVIET UNION 7:10.66	UNITED STATES 7:13.16	AUSTRALIA 7:37.4
1960	CZECHOSLOVAKIA 6:47.50	SOVIET UNION 6:50.49	SWITZERLAND 6:50.59
1964	SOVIET UNION 7:10.66	UNITED STATES 7:13.16	CZECHOSLOVAKIA 7:14.23
1968	SOVIET UNION 6:51.82	NETHERLANDS 6:52.80	UNITED STATES 6:54.21
1972	SOVIET UNION 7:01.77	NORWAY 7:02.58	GDR 7:05.55
1976	NORWAY 7:13.20	GREAT BRITAIN 7:15.20	GDR 7:17.45
1980	GDR 6:24.33	YUGOSLAVIA 6:26.34	CZECHOSLOVAKIA 6:29.07
1984	UNITED STATES 6:36.87	BELGIUM 6:38.19	YUGOSLAVIA 6:39.59
1988	NETHERLANDS 6:21.13	SWITZERLAND 6:22.59	SOVIET UNION 6:22.87
1992	AUSTRALIA 6:17.32	AUSTRIA 6:18.42	NETHERLANDS 6:22.82
1996	ITALY 6:16.98	NORWAY 6:18.42	FRANCE 6:19.85
2000	SLOVENIA 6:16.63	NORWAY 6:17.98	ITALY 6:20.49
2004	FRANCE 6:29.00	SLOVENIA 6:31.72	ITALY 6:32.03

1896-1900, 1906-1912 Event not held

Coxless Quadruple Sculls

1976	GDR 6:18.65	SOVIET UNION 6:19.89	CZECHOSLOVAKIA 6:21.77
1980	GDR 5:49.81	SOVIET UNION 5:51.47	BULGARIA 5:52.38
1984	FRG 5:57.55	AUSTRALIA 5:57.98	CANADA 5:59.07
1988	ITALY 5:53.37	NORWAY 5:55.08	GDR 5:56.13
1992	GERMANY 5:45.17	NORWAY 5:47.09	ITALY 5:47.33
1996	GERMANY 5:56.93	UNITED STATES 5:59.10	AUSTRALIA 6:01.65
2000	ITALY 5:45.56	NETHERLANDS 5:47.91	GERMANY 5:48.64
2004	RUSSIA 5:56.85	CZECH REPUBLIC 5:57.43	UKRAINE 5:58.87

1896-1972 Event not held

Coxless Pairs

1904	UNITED STATES 10:57.0	UNITED STATES dna	UNITED STATES dna
1908	GREAT BRITAIN 9:43.0	GREAT BRITAIN 2.5 lengths	CANADA
			GERMANY
1924	NETHERLANDS 8:19.4	FRANCE 8:21.6	[1]
1928	GERMANY 7:06.4	GREAT BRITAIN 7:08.08	UNITED STATES 7:20.4
1932	GREAT BRITAIN 8:00.0	NEW ZEALAND 8:02.4	POLAND 8:08.2
1936	GERMANY 8:16.1	DENMARK 8:19.2	ARGENTINA 8:23.0
1948	GREAT BRITAIN 7:21.11	SWITZERLAND 7:23.9	ITALY 7:31.5
1952	UNITED STATES 8:20.7	BELGIUM 8:23.5	SWITZERLAND 8:32.7
1956	UNITED STATES 7:55.4	SOVIET UNION 8:03.9	AUSTRIA 8:11.8
1960	SOVIET UNION 7:02.01	AUSTRIA 7:03.69	FINLAND 7:03.80
1964	CANADA 7:32.94	NETHERLANDS 7:33.40	GERMANY 7:38.63
1968	GDR 7:26.56	UNITED STATES 7:26.71	DENMARK 7:31.84
1972	GDR 6:53.16	SWITZERLAND 6:57.06	NETHERLANDS 6:58.70
1976	GDR 7:23.31	UNITED STATES 7:26.73	FRG 7:30.03
1980	GDR 6:48.01	SOVIET UNION 6:50.50	GREAT BRITAIN 6:51.47
1984	ROMANIA 6:45.39	SPAIN 6:48.47	NORWAY 6:51.81
1988	GREAT BRITAIN 6:36.84	ROMANIA 6:38.06	YUGOSLAVIA 6:41.01
1992	GREAT BRITAIN 6:27.72	GERMANY 6:32.68	SLOVENIA 6:33.43
1996	GREAT BRITAIN 6:20.09	AUSTRALIA 6:21.02	FRANCE 6:22.15
2000	FRANCE 6:32.97	UNITED STATES 6:33.80	AUSTRALIA 6:34.26
2004	AUSTRALIA 6:30.76	CROATIA 6:32.64	SOUTH AFRICA 6:33.40

1896-1906, 1912-1920 Event not held
[1]Only two pairs

Coxed Pairs

1900 NETHERLANDS 7:34.2	FRANCE I 7:34.4	FRANCE II 7:57.2
1906[1] ITALY I 4:23.0	ITALY II 4:30.0	FRANCE dna
1906[2] ITALY 7:32.4	BELGIUM 8:03.0[3]	FRANCE 8:08.6
1920 ITALY 7:56.0	FRANCE 7:57.0	SWITZERLAND dna
1924 SWITZERLAND 8:39.0	ITALY 8:39.1	UNITED STATES 3m
1928 SWITZERLAND 7:42.6	FRANCE 7:48.4	BELGIUM 7:59.4
1932 UNITED STATES 8:25.8	POLAND 8:31.2	FRANCE 8:41.2
1936 GERMANY 8:36.9	ITALY 8:49.7	FRANCE 8:54.0
1948 DENMARK 8:00.5	ITALY 8:12.2	HUNGARY 8:25.2
1952 FRANCE 8:28.6	GERMANY 8:32.1	DENMARK 8:34.9
1956 UNITED STATES 8:26.1	GERMANY 8:29.2	SOVIET UNION 8:31.0
1960 GERMANY 7:29.14	SOVIET UNION 7:30.17	UNITED STATES 7:34.58
1964 UNITED STATES 8:21.23	FRANCE 8:23.15	NETHERLANDS 8:23.42
1968 ITALY 8:04.81	NETHERLANDS 8:06.80	DENMARK 8:08.07
1972 GDR 7:17.25	CZECHOSLOVAKIA 7:19.57	ROMANIA 7:21.36
1976 GDR 7:58.99	SOVIET UNION 8:01.82	CZECHOSLOVAKIA 8:03.28
1980 GDR 7:02.54	SOVIET UNION 7:03.35	YUGOSLAVIA 7:04.92
1984 ITALY 7:05.99	ROMANIA 7:11.21	UNITED STATES 7:12.81
1988 ITALY 6:58.79	GDR 7.00.63	GREAT BRITAIN 7:01.95
1992 GREAT BRITAIN 6:49.83	ITALY 6:50.98	ROMANIA 6:51.58

1896,1904, 1908-1912,1996-2004 Event not held
[1]*Over 1000m,* [2]*Over 1600m,* [3]*Greek cox*

Fours

1904 UNITED STATES 9:05.8	UNITED STATES dna	UNITED STATES dna
1908 GREAT BRITAIN 8:34.0	GREAT BRITAIN 1.5 lengths	NETHERLANDS
		CANADA
1924 GREAT BRITAIN 7:08.6	CANADA 7:18.0	SWITZERLAND 2 lengths
1928 GREAT BRITAIN 6:36.0	UNITED STATES 6:37.0	ITALY 6:31.6
1932 GREAT BRITAIN 6:58.2	GERMANY 7:03.0	ITALY 7:04.0
1936 GERMANY 7:01.8	GREAT BRITAIN 7:06.5	SWITZERLAND 7:10.6
1948 ITALY 6:39.0	DENMARK 6:43.5	UNITED STATES 6:47.7
1952 YUGOSLAVIA 7:16.0	FRANCE 7:18.4	FINLAND 7:23.3
1956 CANADA 7:08.8	UNITED STATES 7:18.4	FRANCE 7:20.9
1960 UNITED STATES 6:26.26	ITALY 6:28.78	SOVIET UNION 6:29.62
1964 DENMARK 6:59.30	GREAT BRITAIN 7:00.47	UNITED STATES 7:01.37
1968 GDR 6:39.18	HUNGARY 6:41.64	ITALY 6:44.01
1972 GDR 6:24.27	NEW ZEALAND 6:25.64	FRG 6:28.41
1976 GDR 6:37.42	NORWAY 6:41.22	SOVIET UNION 6:42.52
1980 GDR 6:08.17	SOVIET UNION 6:11.81	GREAT BRITAIN 6:16.58
1984 NEW ZEALAND 6:03.48	UNITED STATES 6:06.10	DENMARK 6:07.72
1988 GDR 6:03.11	UNITED STATES 6:05.53	FRG 6:06.22
1992 AUSTRALIA 5:55.04	USA 5:56.68	SLOVENIA 5:58.24
1996 AUSTRALIA 6:06.37	FRANCE 6:07.03	GREAT BRITAIN 6:07.28
2000 GREAT BRITAIN 5:56.24	ITALY 5:56.62	AUSTRALIA 5:57.61
2004 GREAT BRITAIN 6:06.98	CANADA 6:07.06	ITALY 6:10.41

1896-1900, 1906, 1912-1920 Event not held

Coxed Fours

1900[1] GERMANY 5:59.0	NETHERLANDS 6:33.0	GERMANY 6:35.0
1900[2] FRANCE 7:11.0	FRANCE 7:18.0	GERMANY 7:18.2
1906 ITALY 8:13.0	FRANCE dna	FRANCE dna
1912 GERMANY 6:59.4	GREAT BRITAIN 2 lengths	NORWAY dna
		DENMARK dna
1920 SWITZERLAND 6:54.0	UNITED STATES 6:58.0	NORWAY 7:02.0
1924 SWITZERLAND 7:18.4	FRANCE 7:21.6	UNITED STATES 1 length
1928 ITALY 6:47.8	SWITZERLAND 7:03.4	POLAND 7:12.8
1932 GERMANY 7:19.0	ITALY 7:19.2	POLAND 7:26.8
1936 GERMANY 7:16.2	SWITZERLAND 7:24.3	FRANCE 7:33.3
1948 UNITED STATES 6:50.3	SWITZERLAND 6:53.3	DENMARK 6:58.6
1952 CZECHOSLOVAKIA 7:33.4	SWITZERLAND 7:36.5	UNITED STATES 7:37.0
1956 ITALY 7:19.4	SWEDEN 7:22.4	FINLAND 7:30.9
1960 GERMANY 6:39.12	FRANCE 6:41.62	ITALY 6:43.72
1964 GERMANY 7:00.44	ITALY 7:02.84	NETHERLANDS 7:06.46
1968 NEW ZEALAND 6:45.62	GDR 6:48.20	SWITZERLAND 6:49.04

1972 FRG 6:31.85	GDR 6:33.30	CZECHOSLOVAKIA 6:35.64
1976 SOVIET UNION 6:40.22	GDR 6:42.70	FRG 6:46.96
1980 GDR 6:14.51	SOVIET UNION 6:19.05	POLAND 6:22.52
1984 GREAT BRITAIN 6:18.64	UNITED STATES 6:20.28	NEW ZEALAND 6:23.68
1988 GDR 6:10.74	ROMANIA 6:13.58	NEW ZEALAND 6:15.78
1992 ROMANIA 5:59.37	GERMANY 6:00.34	POLAND 6:03.27

1896, 1904, 1908,1996-2004 Event not held
[1]Two separate finals were held in 1900

Eights

1900 UNITED STATES 6:09.8	BELGIUM 6:13.8	NETHERLANDS 6:23.0
1904 UNITED STATES 7:50.0	CANADA dna	–[1]
1908 GREAT BRITAIN I 7:52.0	BELGIUM 2 lengths	GREAT BRITAIN
		CANADA
1912 GREAT BRITAIN I 6:15.0	GREAT BRITAIN II 6:19.0	GERMANY dna
1920 UNITED STATES 6:02.6	GREAT BRITAIN 6:05.0	NORWAY 6:36.0
1924 UNITED STATES 6:33.4	CANADA 6:49.0	ITALY 0.75 length
1928 UNITED STATES 6:03.2	GREAT BRITAIN 6:05.6	CANADA 6:03.8
1932 UNITED STATES 6:37.6	ITALY 6:37.8	CANADA 6:40.4
1936 UNITED STATES 6:25.4	ITALY 6:26.0	GERMANY 6:26.4
1948 UNITED STATES 5:56.7	GREAT BRITAIN 6:06.9	NORWAY 6:10.3
1952 UNITED STATES 6:25.9	SOVIET UNION 6:31.2	AUSTRALIA 6:33.1
1956 UNITED STATES 6:35.2	CANADA 6:37.1	AUSTRALIA 6:39.2
1960 GERMANY 5:57.18	CANADA 6:01.52	CZECHOSLOVAKIA 6:04.84
1964 UNITED STATES 6:18.23	GERMANY 6:23.9	CZECHOSLOVAKIA 6:25.11
1968 FRG 6:07.00	AUSTRALIA 6:07.98	SOVIET UNION 6:09.11
1972 NEW ZEALAND 6:08.94	UNITED STATES 6:11.61	GDR 6:11.67
1976 GDR 5:58.29	GREAT BRITAIN 6:00.82	NEW ZEALAND 6:03.51
1980 GDR 5:49.05	GREAT BRITAIN 5:51.92	SOVIET UNION 5:52.66
1984 CANADA 5:41.32	UNITED STATES 5:41.74	AUSTRALIA 5:42.40
1988 FRG 5:46.05	SOVIET UNION 5:48.01	UNITED STATES 5:48.26
1992 CANADA 5:29.53	ROMANIA 5:29.67	GERMANY 5:31.00
1996 NETHERLANDS 5:42.74	GERMANY 5:44.58	RUSSIA 5:45.77
2000 GREAT BRITAIN 5:33.08	AUSTRALIA 5:33.88	CROATIA 5:34.85
2004 UNITED STATES 5:42.48	NETHERLANDS 5:43.75	AUSTRALIA 5:45.38

1896, 1906 Event not held
[1]Only two teams

Lightweight Double Sculls

1996 SWITZERLAND 6:23.27	NETHERLANDS 6:26.48	AUSTRALIA 6:26.69
2000 POLAND 6:21.75	ITALY 6:23.47	FRANCE 6:24.85
2004 POLAND 6:2.93	FRANCE 6:21.46	GREECE 6:23.23

1896-1992 Event not held

Lightweight Fours

1996 DENMARK 6:09.58	CANADA 6:10.13	UNITED STATES 6:12.29
2000 FRANCE 6:01.68	AUSTRALIA 6:02.09	SOUTH AFRICA 6:03.51
2004 DENMARK 6:01.39	AUSTRALIA 6:02.79	ITALY 6:03.74

1896-1992 Event not held

DISCONTINUED EVENTS

Naval Rowing Boats (200m)

1906 ITALY 10:45.0	GREECE dna	GREECE dna

Coxed 16-Man Naval Rowing Boats (3000m)

1906 GREECE 16:35.0	GREECE 17:09.5	ITALY dna

Coxed Fours (Inriggers)

1912 DENMARK 7:47.0	SWEDEN 7:56.2	NORWAY dna

Women

Women's rowing was introduced in 1976 over a course of 1000 metres. From 1988 it was over 2000m

Singles Sculls

1976	Christine Scheiblich (GDR) 4:05.56	Joan Lind (USA) 4:06.21	Elena Antonova (URS) 4:10.24
1980	Sandra Toma (ROM) 3:40.69	Antonina Makhina (URS) 3:41.65	Martina Schröter (GDR) 3:43.54
1984	Valeria Racila (ROM) 3:40.68	Charlotte Geer (USA) 3:43.89	Ann Haesebrouck (BEL) 3:45.72
1988	Jutta Behrednt (GDR) 7:47.19	Anne Marden (USA) 7:50.28	Magdalene Gueorguivea (BUL) 7:53.65
1992	Elisabeta Lipa (ROM) 7:25.54	Annelies Bredael (BEL) 7:26.64	Silken Laumann (CAN) 7:28.85
1996	Ekaterina Khodotovich (BLR) 7:32.21	Silken Laumann (CAN) 7:35.15	Trine Hansen (DEN) 7:37.20
2000	Ekaterina Khodotovich-Karsten (BLR) 7:28.14	Rumyana Neykova (BUL) 7:28.15	Katrin Rutschow-Stomporowski (GER) 7:28.99
2004	Katrin Rutschow-Stomporowski (GER) 7:18.12	Ekaterina Karsten (BLR) 7:22.04	Rumyana Neykova (BUL) 7:23.10

Double Sculls

1976	BULGARIA 3:44.36	GDR 3:47.86	SOVIET UNION 3:49.93
1980	SOVIET UNION 3:16.27	GDR 3:17.63	ROMANIA 3:18.91
1984	ROMANIA 3:26.75	NETHERLANDS 3:29.13	CANADA 3:29.82
1988	GDR 7:00.48	ROMANIA 7:04.36	BULGARIA 7:06.03
1992	GERMANY 6:49.00	ROMANIA 6:51.47	CHINA 6:55.16
1996	CANADA 6:56.84	CHINA 6:58.35	NETHERLANDS 6:58.72
2000	GERMANY 6:55.44	NETHERLANDS 7:00.36	LITHUANIA 7:01.71
2004	NEW ZEALAND 7:01.79	GERMANY 7:02.78	GREAT BRITAIN 7:07.58

Coxed Quadruple Sculls

1976	GDR 3:29.99	SOVIET UNION 3:32.49	ROMANIA 3:32.76
1980	GDR 3:15.32	SOVIET UNION 3:15.73	BULGARIA 3:16.10
1984	ROMANIA 3:14.11	UNITED STATES 3:15.57	DENMARK 3:16.02
1988[1]	GDR 6:21.06	SOVIET UNION 6:23.47	ROMANIA 6:23.81
1992	GERMANY 6:20.18	ROMANIA 6:24.34	UNIFIED TEAM 6:25.07
1996	GERMANY 6:27.44	UKRAINE 6:30.36	CANADA 6:30.38
2000	GERMANY 6:19.62	GREAT BRITAIN 6:21.64	RUSSIA 6:21.65
2004	GERMANY 6:29.29	GREAT BRITAIN 6:31.26	AUSTRALIA 6:34.73[2]

[1]*Not coxed*
[2]*Ukraine finished third in 6:34.31 but disqualified*

Coxless Pairs

1976	BULGARIA 4:01.22	GDR 4:01.64	FRG 4:02.35
1980	GDR 3:30.49	POLAND 3:30.95	BULGARIA 3:32.39
1984	ROMANIA 3:32.60	CANADA 3:36.06	FRG 3:40.50
1988	ROMANIA 7:28.13	BULGARIA 7:31.95	NEW ZEALAND 7:35.68
1992	CANADA 7:06.22	GERMANY 7:07.96	USA 7:08.11
1996	AUSTRALIA 7:01.39	UNITED STATES 7:01.78	FRANCE 7:03.82
2000	ROMANIA 7:11.00	AUSTRALIA 7:12.56	UNITED STATES 7:13.00
2004	ROMANIA 7:06.55	GREAT BRITAIN 7:08.66	BELARUS 7:09.86

Coxed Fours

1976	GDR 3:45.08	BULGARIA 3:38.24	SOVIET UNION 3:49.38
1980	GDR 3:19.27	BULGARIA 3:20.75	SOVIET UNION 3:20.92
1984	ROMANIA 3:19.30	CANADA 3:21.55	AUSTRALIA 3:23.29
1988	GDR 6:56.00	CHINA 6:58.78	ROMANIA 7:01.13

1992-1996-2004 Event not held

Coxless Fours

1992	CANADA 6:30.85	USA 6:31.86	GERMANY 6:32.34

1976-88,1996-2004 Event not held

Eights

1976	GDR 3:33.32	SOVIET UNION 3:36.17	UNITED STATES 3:38.68
1980	GDR 3:03.32	SOVIET UNION 3:04.29	ROMANIA 3:05.63
1984	UNITED STATES 2:59.80	ROMANIA 3:00.87	NETHERLANDS 3:02.92
1988	GDR 6:15.17	ROMANIA 6:17.44	CHINA 6:21.83
1992	CANADA 6:02.62	ROMANIA 6:06.26	GERMANY 6:07.80

1996	ROMANIA 6:19.73	CANADA 6:24.05	BELARUS 6:24.44
2000	ROMANIA 6:06.44	NETHERLANDS 6:09.39	CANADA 6:11.58
2004	ROMANIA 6:17.70	UNITED STATES 6:19.56	NETHERLANDS 6:19.85

Lightweight-Double Sculls

1996	ROMANIA 7:12.78	UNITED STATES 7:14.65	AUSTRALIA 7:16.56
2000	ROMANIA 7:02.64	GERMANY 7:02.95	UNITED STATES 7:06.37
2004	ROMANIA 6:56.05	GERMANY 6:57.33	NETHERLANDS 6:58.54

1976-1992 Event not held

SAILING

Men

Olympic Monotype

1920[1]	NETHERLANDS (Franciscus Hin) (Johannes Hin)	NETHERLANDS (Arnoud van der Biesen) (Petrus Beukers)	–
1924[2]	Léon Huybrechts (BEL)	Henrik Robert (NOR)	Hans Dittmar (FIN)
1928[3]	Sven Thorell (SWE)	Henrik Robert (NOR)	Bertil Broman (FIN)
1932[4]	Jacques Lebrun (FRA)	Adriaan Maas (NED)	Santiago Cansino (ESP)
1936[5]	Daniel Kagchelland (NED)	Werner Krogmann (GER)	Peter Scott (GBR)
1948[6]	Paul Elvström (DEN)	Ralph Evans (USA)	Jacobus de Jong (NED)
1952[7]	Paul Elvström (DEN)	Charles Currey (GBR)	Rickard Sarby (SWE)
1956	Paul Elvström (DEN)	André Nelis (BEL)	John Marvin (USA)
1960	Paul Elvström (DEN)	Aleksandr Chuchelov (URS)	André Nelis (BEL)
1964	Willi Kuhweide (GER)	Peter Barrett (USA)	Henning Wind (DEN)
1968	Valentin Mankin (URS)	Hubert Raudaschl (AUT)	Fabio Albarelli (ITA)
1972	Serge Maury (FRA)	Ilias Hatzipavlis (GRE)	Viktor Potapov (URS)
1976	Jochen Schumann (GDR)	Andrei Balashov (URS)	John Bertrand (AUS)
1980	Esko Rechardt (FIN)	Wolfgang Mayrhofer (AUT)	Andrei Balashov (URS)
1984	Russell Coutts (NZL)	John Bertrand (AUS)	Terry Neilson (CAN)
1988	José Luis Doreste (ESP)	Peter Holmberg (ISV)	John Cutler (NZL)
1992	José Maria van der Ploeg (ESP)	Brian Ledbetter (USA)	Craig Monk (NZL)
1996	Mateusz Kuznierewicz (POL)	Sebastian Godefroid (BEL)	Roy Heiner (NED)
2000	Iain Percy (GBR)	Luca Devoti (ITA)	Fredrik Lööf (SWE)
2004	Ben Ainslie (GBR)	Rafael Trujillo (ESP)	Mateusz Kusznierewicz (POL)

1896-1912 Event not held
[1]12-foot dinghy (note two-handled), no bronze medal; [2]Meulan class, 12-foot dinghy; [3]International 12-foot class; [4]Snowbird class; [5]International Olympia class; [6]Firefly class; [7]1952-2004 Finn class

Sailboard Class

1984[1]	Steve Van Den Berg (NED)	Randall Steele (USA)	Bruce Kendall (NZL)
1988[2]	Bruce Kendall (NZL)	Jan Boersma (AHO)	Michael Gebhardt (USA)
1992[2]	Franck David (FRA)	Michael Gebhardt (USA)	Lars Kleppich (AUS)
1996	Nikolas Kaklamanakis (GRE)	Carlos Espinola (ARG)	Gal Fridman (ISR)
2000	Christoph Sieber (AUT)	Carlos Espinola (ARG)	Aaron McIntosh (NZL)
2004	Gal Fridman (ISR)	Nikolaos Kaklamanakis (GRE)	Nick Dempsey (GBR)

1896-1980 Event not held
[1]Windglider; [2]Lechner; [3]1996-2004 Mistral

International Soling

1972	UNITED STATES	SWEDEN	CANADA
1976	DENMARK	UNITED STATES	GDR
1980	DENMARK	SOVIET UNION	GREECE
1984	UNITED STATES	BRAZIL	CANADA
1988	GDR	UNITED STATES	DENMARK
1992	DENMARK	UNITED STATES	GREAT BRITAIN
1996	GERMANY	RUSSIA	UNITED STATES
2000	DENMARK	GERMANY	NORWAY

1896-1968, 2004 Event not held

International 470

1976	FRG	SPAIN	AUSTRALIA
1980	BRAZIL	GDR	FINLAND

1984	SPAIN	UNITED STATES	FRANCE
1988	FRANCE	SOVIET UNION	UNITED STATES
1992	SPAIN	UNITED STATES	ESTONIA
1996	UKRAINE	GREAT BRITAIN	PORTUGAL
2000	AUSTRALIA	UNITED STATES	ARGENTINA
2004	UNITED STATES	GREAT BRITAIN	JAPAN

1896-1972 Event not held

International Tornado

1976	GREAT BRITAIN	UNITED STATES	FRG
1980	BRAZIL	DENMARK	SWEDEN
1984	NEW ZEALAND	UNITED STATES	AUSTRALIA
1988	FRANCE	NEW ZEALAND	BRAZIL
1992	FRANCE	UNITED STATES	AUSTRALIA
1996	SPAIN	AUSTRALIA	BRAZIL
2000	AUSTRIA	AUSTRALIA	GERMANY
2004	AUSTRIA	UNITED STATES	ARGENTINA

1896-1972 Event not held

International Star

1932	UNITED STATES	GREAT BRITAIN	SWEDEN
1936	GERMANY	SWEDEN	NETHERLANDS
1948	UNITED STATES	CUBA	NETHERLANDS
1952	ITALY	UNITED STATES	PORTUGAL
1956	UNITED STATES	ITALY	BAHAMAS
1960	SOVIET UNION	PORTUGAL	UNITED STATES
1964	BAHAMAS	UNITED STATES	SWEDEN
1968	UNITED STATES	NORWAY	ITALY
1972	AUSTRALIA	SWEDEN	FRG
1980	SOVIET UNION	AUSTRIA	ITALY
1984	UNITED STATES	FRG	ITALY
1988	GREAT BRITAIN	UNITED STATES	BRAZIL
1992	UNITED STATES	NEW ZEALAND	CANADA
1996	BRAZIL	SWEDEN	AUSTRALIA
2000	UNITED STATES	GREAT BRITAIN	BRAZIL
2004	BRAZIL	CANADA	FRANCE

1896-1928, 1976 Event not held

49-er

2000	FINLAND	GREAT BRITAIN	UNITED STATES
2004	SPAIN	UKRAINE	GREAT BRITAIN

1896-1996 Event not held

Flying Dutchman

1956[1]	NEW ZEALAND	AUSTRALIA	GREAT BRITAIN
1960	NORWAY	DENMARK	GERMANY
1964	NEW ZEALAND	GREAT BRITAIN	UNITED STATES
1968	GREAT BRITAIN	FRG	BRAZIL
1972	GREAT BRITAIN	FRANCE	FRG
1976	FRG	GREAT BRITAIN	BRAZIL
1980	SPAIN	IRELAND	HUNGARY
1984	UNITED STATES	CANADA	GREAT BRITAIN
1988	DENMARK	NORWAY	CANADA
1992	SPAIN	UNITED STATES	DENMARK

1896-1952,1996-2004 Event not held
[1]*Sharpie class*

Laser

1996	Robert Scheidt (BRA)	Ben Ainslie (GBR)	Per Moberg (NOR)
2000	Ben Ainslie (GBR)	Robert Scheidt (BRA)	Michael Blackburn (AUS)
2004	Robert Scheidt (BRA)	Andreas Geritzer (AUT)	Vasilij Zbogar (SLO)

1896-1992 Event not held

Women

Sailboard Class

1992[1]	Barbara Kendall (NZL)	Zhang Xiaodong (CHN)	Dorien de Vries (NED)

1996² Lai-Shan Lee (HKG)	Barbara Kendall (NZL)	Alessandra Sensini (ITA)
2000 Alessandra Sensini (ITA)	Amelie Lux (GFR)	Barbara Kendall (NZL)
2004 Faustine Merret (FRA)	Jian Yin (CHN)	Alessandra Sensini (ITA)

1896-1988 Event not held
¹Lechner; ²1996-2004 Mistral

International 470

1988 UNITED STATES	SWEDEN	SOVIET UNION
1992 SPAIN	NEW ZEALAND	UNITED STATES
1996 SPAIN	JAPAN	UKRAINE
2000 AUSTRALIA	UNITED STATES	UKRAINE
2004 GREECE	SPAIN	SWEDEN

1896-1984 Event not held

Europe Class

1992 Linda Andersen (NOR)	Natalia Dufresne (ESP)	Julia Trotman (USA)
1996 Kristine Roug (DEN)	Margriet Matthijsse (NED)	Courtney Becker-Dey (USA)
2000 Shirley Robertson (GBR)	Margriet Matthijsse (NED)	Serena Amoto (ARG)
2004 Siren Sundby (NOR)	Lenka Smidova (CZE)	Signe Livbjerg (DEN)

1896-1988 Event not held

Yngling

2004 GREAT BRITAIN	UKRAINE	DENMARK

1896-2000 Event not held

DISCONTINUED EVENTS

Swallow

1948 GREAT BRITAIN	PORTUGAL	UNITED STATES

International Tompoot

1972 SOVIET UNION	GREAT BRITAIN	UNITED STATES
1976 SWEDEN	SOVIET UNION	UNITED STATES

Dragon

1948 NORWAY	SWEDEN	DENMARK
1952 NORWAY	SWEDEN	GERMANY
1956 SWEDEN	DENMARK	GREAT BRITAIN
1960 GREECE	ARGENTINA	ITALY
1964 DENMARK	GERMANY	UNITED STATES
1968 UNITED STATES	DENMARK	GDR
1972 AUSTRALIA	GDR	UNITED STATES

30 Square Metres

1920 SWEDEN	–	–

40 Square Metres

1920 SWEDEN	–	–

5.5 Metres

1952 UNITED STATES	NORWAY	SWEDEN
1956 SWEDEN	GREAT BRITAIN	AUSTRALIA
1960 UNITED STATES	DENMARK	SWITZERLAND
1964 AUSTRALIA	SWEDEN	UNITED STATES
1968 SWEDEN	SWITZERLAND	GREAT BRITAIN

6 Metres

1908 GREAT BRITAIN	BELGIUM	FRANCE
1912 FRANCE	DENMARK	SWEDEN
1920 NORWAY	BELGIUM	–
1924 NORWAY	DENMARK	NETHERLANDS
1928 NORWAY	DENMARK	ESTONIA
1932 SWEDEN	UNITED STATES	CANADA

1936	GREAT BRITAIN	NORWAY	SWEDEN
1948	UNITED STATES	ARGENTINA	SWEDEN
1952	UNITED STATES	NORWAY	FINLAND

6 Metres (1907 Rating)

| 1920 | BELGIUM | NORWAY | NORWAY |

6.5 Metres

| 1920 | NETHERLANDS | FRANCE | - |

7 Metres

1908	GREAT BRITAIN	-	-
1920	GREAT BRITAIN	-	-
1912 Event not held			

8 Metres

1908	GREAT BRITAIN	SWEDEN	GREAT BRITAIN
1912	NORWAY	SWEDEN	FINLAND
1920	NORWAY	NORWAY	BELGIUM
1924	NORWAY	GREAT BRITAIN	FRANCE
1928	FRANCE	NETHERLANDS	SWEDEN
1932	UNITED STATES	CANADA	–
1936	ITALY	NORWAY	GERMANY

8 Metres

(1907 Rating)

| 1920 | NORWAY | NORWAY | – |

10 Metres

| 1912 | SWEDEN | FINLAND | RUSSIA |

10 Metres

(1907 Rating)

| 1920 | NORWAY | – | – |

10 Metres

(1919 Rating)

| 1920 | NORWAY | – | – |

12 Metres

| 1908 | GREAT BRITAIN | GREAT BRITAIN | – |
| 1912 | NORWAY | SWEDEN | FINLAND |

12 Metres

(1907 Rating)

| 1920 | NORWAY | – | – |

12 Metres

(1919 Rating)

| 1920 | NORWAY | – | – |

0.5 Ton Class

| 1900 | FRANCE | FRANCE | FRANCE |

0.5-1 Ton Class

| 1900 | FRANCE | GREAT BRITAIN | FRANCE |

1-2 Ton Class

| 1900 | SWITZERLAND | FRANCE | FRANCE |

2-3 Ton Class

| 1900 | GREAT BRITAIN | FRANCE | FRANCE |

3-10 Ton Class

1900 FRANCE	NETHERLANDS	FRANCE GREAT BRITAIN

10-20 Ton Class

1900 FRANCE	FRANCE	GREAT BRITAIN

Open Class

1900 GREAT BRITAIN	GERMANY	FRANCE

Over 20 Ton Class

1900 GREAT BRITAIN	GREAT BRITAIN	UNITED STATES

SHOOTING

Men

Free Pistol (50 Metres)

1896	Sumner Paine (USA) 442	Holger Nielsen (DEN) 280	Nikolaos Morakis (GRE) dna
1900	Karl Röderer (SUI) 503	Achille Paroche (FRA) 466	Konrad Stäheli (SUI) 453
1906	Georgios Orphanidis (GRE) 221	Jean Fouconnier (FRA) 219	Aristides Rangavis (GRE) £10
1912	Alfred Lane (USA) 499	Peter Dolfen (USA) 474	Charles Stewart (GBR) 470
1920	Karl Fredorick (USA) 496	Afranio da Costa (BRA) 480	Alfred Lane (USA) 481
1936	Torsten Ullmann (SWE) 559	Erich Krempel (GER) 544	Charles des Jammonières (FRA) 540
1948	Edwin Vazquez Cam (PER) 545	Rudolf Schnyder (SUI) 539	Torsten Ullmann (SWE) 539
1952	Huelet Benner (USA) 553	Angel León de Gozalo (ESP) 550	Ambrus Balogh (HUN) 549
1956	Pentti Linnosvuo (FIN) 556	Makhmud Oumarov ((URS) 556	Offutt Pinion (USA) 551
1960	Alexei Gushkin (URS) 560	Makhmud Oumarov (URS) 552	Yoshihisa Yoshikawa (JPN) 552
1964	Väinö Markkanen (FIN) 560	Franklin Green (USA) 557	Yoshihisa Yoshikawa (JPN) 554
1968	Grigori Kossykh (URS) 562	Heinz Mertel (FRG) 562	Harald Vollmar (GDR) 560
1972	Ragnar Skanakar (SWE) 567	Dan Iuga (ROM) 562	Rudolf Dollinger (AUT) 560
1976	Uwe Potteck (GDR) 573	Harald Vollmar (GDR) 567	Rudolf Dollinger (AUT) 560
1980	Alexander Melentyev (URS) 581	Harald Vollmar (GDR) 568	Lubcho Diakov (BUL) 565
1984	Xu Haifeng (CHN) 566	Ragnar Skanaker (SWE) 565	Wang Yifu (CHN) 564
1988	Sorin Babii (ROM) (566+94) 660	Ragnar Skanaker (SWE) (564+93) 657	Igor Bassinki (URS) (570+87) 657
1992	Konstantin Loukachik (EUN) 658	Wang Yifu (CHN) 657	Ragnar Skanaker (SWE) 657
1996	Boris Kokoryev (RUS) 666.4	Igor Basinski (BLR) 662.1	Roberto Di Donna (ITA) 661.8
2000	Tanyu Kiryakov (BUL) 666.0	Igor Basinski (BLR) 663.3	Martin Tenk (CZE) 662.5
2004	Mikhail Nestruyev (RUS) 663.3	Jong-Oh Jin (PRK) 661.5	Jong-Su Kim (KOR) 657.7

1904-1908,1924-1932 Event not held

Rapid-Fire Pistol

1896	Jean Phrangoudis (GRE) 344	Georgios Orphanidis (GRE)	Holger Nielsen (DEN) dna
1900	Maurice Larrouy (FRA) 58	Léon Moreaux (FRA) 57	Eugene Balme (FRA) 57
1906	Maurice Lecoq (FRA) 250	Léon Moreaux (FRA) 149	Aristides Rangavis (GRE) 245
1908	Paul van Asbroeck (BEL) 490	Réginald Storms (BEL) 487	James Gorman (USA) 485
1912	Alfred Lane (USA) 287	Paul Palén (SWE) 286	Johan von Holst (SWE) 283
1920	Guilherme Paraense (BRA) 274	Raymond Bracken (USA) 272	Fritz Zulauf (SUI) 269
1924	Paul Bailey (USA) 18	Vilhelm Carlberg (SWE) 18	Lennart Hannelius (FIN) 18
1932	Renzo Morigi (ITA) 36	Heinz Hax (GER) 36	Domenico Matteucci (ITA) 36
1936	Cornelius van Oyen (GER) 36	Heinz Hax (GER) 35	Torsten Ullmann (SWE) 34
1948	Károly Takács (HUN) 580	Carlos Diaz Sáenz Valiente (ARG) 571	Sven Lundqvist (SWE) 569
1952	Károly Takács (HUN) 579	Szilárd Kun (HUN) 578	Gheorghe Lichiardopol (ROM) 578
1956	Stefan Petrescu (ROM) 587	Evgeni Shcherkasov (URS) 585	Gheorghe Lichiardopol (ROM) 581
1960	William McMillan (USA) 587	Pentti Linnosvuo (FIN) 587	Aleksandr Zabelin (URS) 587
1964	Penttii Linnosvuo (FIN) 592	Ion Tripsa (ROM) 591	Lubomir Nacovsky (TCH) 590
1968	Jozef Zapedzki (POL) 593	Marcel Rosca (ROM) 591	Renart Suleimanov (URS) 591
1972	Jozef Zapedzki (POL) 593	Ladislav Faita (TCH) 594	Victor Torshin (URS) 593
1976	Norbert Klaar (GDR) 597	Jürgen Wiefel (GDR) 596	Roberto Ferraris (ITA) 595
1980	Corneliu Ion (ROM) 596	Jürgen Wiefel (GDR) 596	Gerhard Petrisch (AUT) 596
1984	Takeo Kamachi (JPN) 595	Corneliu Ion (ROM) 593	Rauno Bies (FIN) 591
1988	Afanasi Kouzmine (URS) (598+100) 698	Ralf Schumann (GDR) (597+99) 696	Zoltán Kovács (HUN) (594+99) 693
1992	Ralf Schumann (GER) 885	Afanasijs Kuzmins (LAT) 882	Vladimir Vokhmyanin (EUN) 882
1996	Ralf Schumann (GER) 698.0	Emil Milev (BUL) 692.1	Vladimir Vokhmyanin (KAZ) 691.5

2000 Sergei Aliferenko (RUS) 687.6	Michel Ansermet (SUI) 686.1	Iulian Raicea (ROM) 684.6
2004 Ralf Schumann (GER) 694.9	Sergei Poliakov (RUS) 692.7	Sergei Aliferenko (RUS) 692.3

1904-1928 Event not held

Small-Bore Rifle – (Prone)[1]

1908 Arthur Carnell (GBR) 387	Harry Humby (GBR) 386	George Barnes (GBR) 385
1912 Frederick Hird (USA) 194	William Milne (GBR) 193	Harry Burt (GBR) 192
1920 Lawrence Nuesslein (USA) 391	Arthur Rothrock (USA) 386	Dennis Fenton (USA) 385
1924 Pierre Coquelin de Lisle (FRA) 398	Marcus Dinwiddie (USA) 396	Josias Hartmann (SUI) 394
1932 Bertil Rönnmark (SWE) 294	Gustavo Huet (MEX) 294	Zoltán Hradetsky-Soos (HUN) 293
1936 Willy Rögeberg (NOR) 300	Ralph Berzsenyi (HUN) 296	Wladyslaw Karás (POL) 296
1948 Arthur Cook (USA) 599	Walter Tomsen (USA) 599	Jonas Jonsson (SWE) 597
1952 Josif Sarbu (ROM) 400	Boris Andreyev (URS) 400	Arthur Jackson (USA) 399
1956 Gerald Ouellette (CAN) 600[2]	Vasiliy Borrisov (IURS) 599	Gilmour Boa (CAN) 598
1960 Peter Kohnke (GER) 590	James Hill (USA) 589	Enrico Pelliccione (VEN) 587
1964 László Hammerl (HUN) 597	Lonas Wigger (USA) 597	Tommy Pool (USA) 596
1968 Jan Kurka (TCH) 598	László Hammerl (HUN) 598	Ian Ballinger (NZL) 597
1972 Li Ho Jun (PRK) 599	Victor Auer (USA) 598	Nicolae Rotaru (ROM) 595
1976 Karlheinz Smieszek (FRG) 599	Ulrich Lind (FRG) 597	Gennadiy Luschikov (URS) 595
1980 Karoly Varga (HUN) 599	Hellfried Helifort (GDR) 599	Petar Zapianov (BUL) 598
1984 Edward Etzel (USA) 599	Michel Bury (FRA) 596	Michael Sullivan (GBR) 596
1988 Mlroslav Varga (TCH) (600+103.9) 703.9	Cha Young-Chul (KOR) (598+104.8) 702.8	Attila Zahonyi (HUN) (597+104.9) 701.9
1992 Lee Eun-Chul (KOR) 702.5	Harald Stenvaag (NOR) 701.4	Stefan Pletikosic (IOP) 701.1
1996 Christian Klees (GER) 704.8	Sergei Belyayev (KAZ) 703.3	Jozef Gobci (SLO) 701.9
2000 Jonas Edman (SWE) 701.3	Torben Grimmel (DEN) 700.4	Sergei Martynov (BLR) 700.3
2004 Matthew Emmons (USA) 703.3	Christian Lusch (GER) 702.2	Sergei Martynov (BLR) 701.6

1896-1906, 1928 Event not held

[1]*In 1908 and 1912 any position allowed; in 1920 it was a standing position;* [2]*Range found to be marginally short – record not allowed*

Small-Bore Rifle – Three Positions (Prone, Kneeling, Standing)

1952 Erling Kongshaug (NOR) 1164	Viho Ylönen (FIN) 1164	Boris Andreyev (URS) 1163
1956 Anatoliy Bogdanov (URS) 1172	Otakar Horinek (TCH) 1172	Nils Sundberg (SWE) 1167
1960 Viktor Shamburkin (URS) 1149	Marat Niyasov (URS) 1145	Klaus Zähringer (GER) 1139
1964 Lones Wigger (USA) 1164	Velitchko Khristov (BUL) 1152	László Hammerl (HUN) 1151
1968 Bernd Klingner (FRG) 1157	John Writer (USA) 1156	Vitali Parkhimovich (URS) 1154
1972 John Writer (USA) 1166	Lanny Bassham (USA) 1157	Werner Lippoldt (GDR) 1153
1976 Lanny Bassham (USA) 1162	Margaret Murdock (USA) 1162	Werner Seibold (FRG) 1160
1980 Viktor Vlasov (URS) 1173	Bernd Hartstein (GDR) 1166	Sven Johansson (SWE) 1185
1984 Malcolm Cooper (GBR) 1173	Daniel Kipkow (SUI) 1163	Alister Allan (GBR) 1162
1988 Malcolm Cooper (GBR) (1180+99.3) 1279	Alister Allan (GBR) (1181+94.6) 1275.6	Kirill Ivanov (URS) (1173+102) 1275.0
1992 Gratchia Petikiane (EUN) 1267.4	Robert Foth (USA) 1266.6	Ryohei Koba (JPN) 1265.9
1996 Jean-Pierre Amat (FRA) 1273.9	Sergei Belyayev (KAZ) 1272.3	Wolfram Waibel (AUT) 1269.6
2000 Rajmond Debevec (SLO) 1275.1	Juha Hirvi (FIN) 1270.5	Harald Stenvaag (NOR) 1268.6
2004 Zhanbo Jia (CHN) 1264.5	Michael Anti (USA) 1263.1	Christian Planer (AUS) 1262.8

1896-1948 Event not held

Running Game Target

1900 Louis Debray (FRA) 20	Pierre Nivet (FRA) 20	Comte de Lambert (FRA) 19
1972 Lakov Zhelezniak (URS) 569	Hanspeter Bellingrodt (COL) 565	John Kynoch (GBR) 562
1976 Alexander Gazov (URS) 579	Alexander Kedyarov (URS) 576	Jerzy Gresziewicz (POL) 571
1980 Igor Sokolov (URS) 589	Thomas Pfeffer (GDR) 589	Alexander Gasov (URS) 587
1984 Li Yuwei (CHN) 587	Helmut Bellingrodt (COL) 584	Shiping Huang (CHN) 581
1988 Tor Heiestad (NOR) (591+98) 689	Hunag Shiping (CHN) (589+98) 686	Gennadi Avramenko (URS) (591+95) 685

1896,1904-1968,1992-2004 Event not held

10m Running Target

1992 Michael Jakosits (GER) 673	Anatoli Asrabayev (EUN) 672	Lubos Racansky (TCH) 670
1996 Ling Yang (CHN) 685.8	Xiao Jun (CHN) 679.8	Miroslav Janus (CZE) 678.4
2000 Ling Yang (CHN) 681.1	Oleg Moldovan (MOL) 681.0	Zhiyuan Niu (CHN) 677.4
2004 Manfred Kurzer (GER) 682.4	Aleksandr Blinov (RUS) 678.0	Dmitri Lykin (RUS) 677.1

1896-1988 Event not held

Olympic Trap Shooting

1900	Roger de Barbarin (FRA) 17	René Guyot (FRA) 17	Justinien de Clary (FRA) 17
1906[1]	Gerald Merlin (GBR) 24	Ioannis Peridis (GRE) 23	Sidney Merlin (GBR) 21
1908[2]	Sidney Merlin (GBR) 15	Anastasios Metaxas (GRE) 13	Gerald Merlin (GBR) 12
1908	Walter Ewing (CAN) 72	George Beattie (CAN) 60	Alexander Maunder (GBR) 57
			Anastasios Metaxas (GRE) 57
1912	James Graham (USA) 96	Alfred Goeldel-Bronikowen (GER) 94	Harry Blau (RUS) 91
1920	Marke Arie (USA) 95	Frank Troeh (USA) 93	Frank Wright (USA) 87
1924	Gyula Halasy (HUN) 98	Konrad Huber (FIN) 98	Frank Hughes (USA) 97
1952	George Généreux (CAN) 192	Knut Holmqvist (SWE) 191	Hans Lijedahl (SWE) 191
1956	Galliano Rossini (ITA) 195	Adam Smelczynski (POL) 190	Alessandro Ciceri (ITA) 188
1960	Ion Dumitrescu (ROM) 192	Galliano Rossini (ITA) 191	Sergei Kalinin (URS) 190
1964	Ennio Mattarelli (ITA) 198	Pavel Senichev (URS) 194	William Morris (USA) 194
1968	Robert Braithwaite (GBR) 198	Thomas Garrigus (USA) 196	Kurt Czekalla (GDR) 196
1972	Angelo Scalzone (ITA) 199	Michel Carrega (FRA) 198	Silvano Basnagi (ITA) 195
1976	Don Haldeman (USA) 190	Armando Marques (POR) 189	Ubaldesco Baldi (ITA) 189
1980	Luciano Giovanetti (ITA) 198	Rustam Yambulatov (URS) 196	Jörg Damme (GDR) 196
1984	Luciano Giovanetti (ITA) 192	Francisco Boza (PER) 192	Daniel Carlisle (USA) 192
1988	Dmitri Monakov (URS) (197+25) 222	Miloslav Bednarik (TCH) (197+25) 222	Frans Peeters (BEL) (195+24) 219
1992	Petr Hrdilicka (CZE) 219	Kazumi Watanabe (JPN) 219	Marco Venturini (ITA) 218
1996	Michael Diamond (AUS) 149	Josh Lakatos (USA) 147.0	Lance Bade (USA) 147.0
2000	Michael Diamond (AUS) 147	Ian Peel (GBR) 142	Giovanni Pellielo (ITA) 140
2004	Aleksei Alipov (RUS) 149	Giovanni Pellielo (ITA) 146	Adam Vella (AUS) 145

1896,1904,1928-1948 Event not held
[1]Single shot; [2]Double shot

Double Trap

1996	Russell Mark (AUS) 189.0	Albano Pera (ITA) 183.0	Zhang Bang (CHN) 183.0
2000	Richard Faulds (GBR) 187	Russell Mark (AUS) 187	Fehaid Al Deehani (KUW) 186
2004	Sheikh Ahmed Al-Maktoum (UAE) 189	Rajyardrahan Rathore (IND) 179	Zheng Wang (CHN) 178

1896-1992 Event not held

Skeet

1968	Yevgeni Petrov (URS) 198	Romano Garagnani (ITA) 198	Konrad Wirnhier (FRG) 198
1972	Konrad Wirnhier (FRG) 195	Yevgeni Petrov (URS) 195	Michael Buchheim (GDR) 195
1976	Josef Panacek (TCH) 198	Eric Swinkels (NED) 198	Wieslaw Gawlikowski (POL) 196
1980	Hans Kjeld Rasmussen (DEN) 196	Lars-Goran Carlsson (SWE) 196	Roberto Garcia (CUB) 196
1984	Matthew Dryke (USA) 198	Ole Rasmussen (DEN) 196	Luca Scribiani Rossi (ITA) 196
1988	Axel Wegner (GDR) (198+24) 222	Alfonso de Iruarrizaga (CHI) (198+23) 221	Jorge Guardiola (ESP) (196+24) 220
1992	Zhang Shan (CHN) 233[1]	Juan Jorge Giha (PER) 222	Bruno Rosetti (ITA) 222
1996	Ennio Falco (ITA) 149.0	Miroslav Rzeprkowski (POL) 148.0	Andrea Benelli (ITA) 147.0
2000	Mykola Milchev (UKR) 150	Petr Malek (CZE) 148	James Graves (USA) 147
2004	Andrea Benell (ITA) 149	Marko Kemppainen (FIN) 149	Juan Miguel Rodriguez (CUB 147

1896-1964 Event not held
[1]First woman to win an Olympic mixed shooting event

Air Pistol

1988	Taniou Kiriakov (BUL) (585+102.9) 687.9	Erich Buljung (USA) (590+97.9) 687.9	Xu Haifeng (CHN) (584+100.5) 684.5
1992	Yifu Wang (CHN) 684.8	Sergei Pyzhano (EUN) 684.1	Sorin Babii (ROM) 684.1
1996	Roberto di Donna (ITA) 684.2	Yifu Wang (CHN) 684.1	Tanyu Kiryakov (BUL) 683.8
2000	Franck Dumoulin (FRA) 688.9	Yifu Wang (CHN) 686.9	Igor Basinski (BLR) 682.7
2004	Yifu Wang (CHN) 690.0	Mikhail Nestruyev (RUS) 689.8	Vladimir Isakov (RUS) 684.3

1896-1984 Event not held

Air Rifle

1984	Philippe Herberle (FRA) 589	Andreas Kronthaler (AUT) 587	Barry Dagger (GBR) 587
1988	Goran Maksimovic (YUG) (594+101.6) 685.6	Nicolas Berhtelot (FRA) (593+101.2) 694.2	Johann Riederer (FRG) (592+102) 694.0
1992	Yuri Fedkine (EUN) 695.3	Franck Badiou (FRA) 691.9	Johann Riederer (GER) 691.7
1996	Artem Khadzhibekov (RUS) 695.7	Wolfram Waibel (AUT) 695.2	Jean-Pierre Amat (FRA) 693.1
2000	Yalin Cai (CHN) 696.4	Artem Khadyibekov (RUS) 695.1	Yevgeni Aleynikov (RUS) 693.8
2004	Qinan Zhu (CHN) 702.7	Jie Li (CHN) 701.3	Jozef Gönci (SVK) 697.4

1896-1980 Event not held

DISCONTINUED EVENTS

Free Rifle (Three Positions)

1896	Georgios Orphanidis (GRE) 1583	Jean Phrangoudis (GRE) 1312	Viggo Jensen (DEN) 1305
1906	Gudbrand Skatteboe (NOR) 977	Konrad Stäheli (SUI) 943	Jean Reich (SUI) 933
1908	Albert Helgerud (NOR) 909	Harry Simon (USA) 887	Ole Saether (NOR) 883
1912	Paul Colas (FRA) 987	Lars Madsen (DEN) 981	Niels Larsen (DEN) 962
1920	Morris Fisher (USA) 996	Niels Larsen (DEN) 989	Östen Östensen (NOR) 980
1924	Morris Fisher (USA) 95	Carl Osburn (USA) 95	Niels Larsen (DEN) 93
1948	Emil Grunig (SUI) 1120	Pauli Janhonen (FIN) 1114	Willy Rögeberg (NOR) 1112
1952	Anatoliy Bogdanov (URS) 1123	Robert Bürchler (SUI) 1120	Lev Vainschtein (URS) 1109
1956	Vasili Borissov (URS) 1138	Allan Erdman (URS) 1137	Vilho Ylönen (FIN) 1128
1960	Hubert Hammerer (AUT) 1129	Hans Spillmann (SUI) 1127	Vasili Borissov (URS) 1127
1964	Gary Anderson (USA) 1153	Shota Kveliashvili (URS) 1151	Martin Gunnarsson (USA) 1136
1968	Gary Anderson (USA) 1157	Vladimir Kornev (URS) 1151	Kurt Müller (SUI) 1148
1972	Lones Wigger (USA) 1155	Boris Melnik (URS) 1155	Lajos Papp (HUN) 1149

1900-1904, 1928-1936 Event not held

Free Rifle

1896[1]	Pantelis Karasevdas (GRE) 2320	Paulas Pavlidis (GRE) 1978	Nicolaos Tricoupes (GRE) 1718
1906[2]	Marcel de Stadelhofen (SUI) 243	Konrad Stäheli (SUI) 238	Léon Moreaux (FRA) 234
1906[3]	Gudbrand Skatteboe (NOR) 339	Louis Richardet (SUI) 332	Konrad Stäheli (SUI) 328
1906[4]	Konrad Stäheli (SUI) 340	Louis Richardet (SUI) 338	Jean Reich (SUI) 320
1906[5]	Gudbrand Skatteboe (NOR) 324	Julius Braathe (NOR) 310	Albert Helgerud (NOR) 305
1908[6]	Jerry Millner (GBR) 98	Kellogg Casey (USA) 93	Maurice Blood (GBR) 92

1900-1904 Event not held

[1]Over 200m; [2]Any position; [3]Prone (300m); [4]Kneeling (300m); [5]Standing (300m) [6]over 1000 yards

Free Rifle (Team)

1906	SWITZERLAND 4596	NORWAY 4534	FRANCE 4511
1908	NORWAY 5055	SWEDEN 4711	FRANCE 4652
1912	SWEDEN 5655	NORWAY 5605	DENMARK 5529
1920	UNITED STATES 4876	NORWAY 4741	SWITZERLAND 4698
1924	UNITED STATES 676	FRANCE 646	HAITI 646

1896-1904 Event not held

Military Rifle

1900[1]	Emil Kellenberger (SUI) 930	Anders Nielsen (DEN) 921	Ole Östmo (NOR) 917
1900[2]	Lars Madsen (DEN) 305	Ole Östmo (NOR) 299	Charles du Verger (BEL) 298
1900[3]	Konrad Stäheli (SUI) 324	Emil Kellenberger (SUI) 314	–
		Anders Nielsen (DEN) 314	
1900[4]	Achille Paroche (FRA) 332	Anders Nielsen (DEN) 330	Ole Östmo (NOR) 329
1906[5]	Léon Moreaux (FRA) 187	Louis Richardet (SUI) 187	Jean Reich (SUI) 183
1906[6]	Louis Richardet (SUI) 238	Jean Reich (SUI) 234	Raoul de Boigne (FRA) 232
1912[1]	Sándor Prokopp (HUN) 97	Carl Osburn (USA) 96	Embret Skogen (NOR) 95
1912[7]	Paul Colas (FRA) 94	Carl Osburn (USA) 94	Joseph Jackson (USA) 93
1920[4]	Otto Olsen (NOR) 60	Léon Johnson (FRA) 59	Fritz Kuchen (SUI) 59
1920[2]	Carl Osburn (USA) 56	Lars Madsen (DEN) 55	Lawrence Nuesslein (USA) 54
1920[8]	Hugo Johansson (SWE) 58	Mauritz Eriksson (SWE) 56	Lloyd Spooner (USA) 56

1904,1908 Event not held

Military Rifle (Team)

1900	SWITZERLAND 4399	NORWAY 4290	FRANCE 4278
1908	UNITED STATES 2531	GREAT BRITAIN 2497	CANADA 2439
1912	UNITED STATES 1687	GREAT BRITAIN 1602	SWEDEN 1570
1920[2]	DENMARK 266	UNITED STATES 255	SWEDEN 255
1920[4]	UNITED STATES 289	FRANCE 283	FINLAND 281
1920[8]	UNITED STATES 287	SOUTH AFRICA 287	SWEDEN 287
1920[9]	UNITED STATES 573	NORWAY 565	SWITZERLAND 563

1896,1904 Event not held

[1]Three positions (300m); [2]Standing (300m); [3]kneeling (300m); [4]Prone (300m); [5]Standing or kneeling (200m); [6]Standing or kneeling (300m); [7]Any Position (600m); [8]Prone; [9]Prone (300m and 600m)

Small Bore Rifle

1908[1]	John Fleming (GBR) 24	MK Matthews (GBR) 24	WB Marsden (GBR) 24

1908[2] William Styles (GBR) 45   HI Hawkins (GBR) 45   Edward Amoore (GBR) 45
1912[2] Wilhelm Carlberg (SWE) 242   Johan von Holst (SWE) 233   Gustaf Ericsson (SWE) 231
1896-1904 Event not held
[1]Moving target; [2]Disappearing target

Small Bore Rifle (Team)

1908	GREAT BRITAIN 771	SWEDEN 737	FRANCE 710
1912[1]	SWEDEN 925	GREAT BRITAIN 917	UNITED STATES 881
1912[2]	GREAT BRITAIN 762	SWEDEN 748	UNITED STATES 744
1920	UNITED STATES 1899	SWEDEN 1873	NORWAY 1866

1896-1904 Event not held
[1]Over 25m; [2]Over 50m

Live Pigeon Shooting

1900	Léon de Lunden (BEL) 21	Maurice Faure (FRA) 20	Donald MacIntosh (AUS) 18
			Crittenden Robinson (USA) 18

Clay Pigeons (Team)

1908	GREAT BRITAIN 407	CANADA 405	GREAT BRITAIN 372
1912	UNITED STATES 532	GREAT BRITAIN 511	GERMANY 510
1920	UNITED STATES 547	BELGIUM 503	SWEDEN 500
1924	UNITED STATES 363	CANADA 360	FINLAND 360

Running Deer Shooting

1908[1]	Oscar Swahn (SWE) 25	Ted Ranken (GBR) 24	Alexander Rogers (GBR) 24
1908[2]	Walter Winans (USA) 46	Ted Ranken (GBR) 46	Oscar Swahn (SWE) 38
1912[1]	Alfred Swahn (SWE) 41	Ake Lundeberg (SWE) 41	Nestori Toivonen (FIN) 41
1912[2]	Ake Lundeberg (SWE) 79	Edvard Benedicks (SWE) 74	Oscar Swahn (SWE) 72
1920[1]	Otto Olsen (NOR) 43	Alfred Swahn (SWE) 41	Harald Natwig (NOR) 41
1920[2]	Ole Lilloe-Olsen (NOR) 82	Fredrik Landelius (SWE) 77	Einar Liberg (NOR) 71
1924[1]	John Boles (USA) 40	Cyril Mackworth-Praed (GBR) 39	Otto Olsen (NOR) 39
1924[2]	Ole Lilloe-Olsen (NOR) 76	Cyril Mackworth-Praed (GBR) 72	Alfred Swahn (SWE) 72

[1]Single shot; [2]Double shot

Running Deer Shooting (Team)

1908	SWEDEN 86	GREAT BRITAIN 85	-
1912	SWEDEN 151	UNITED STATES 132	FINLAND 123
1920[1]	NORWAY 178	FINLAND 159	UNITED STATES 158
1920[2]	NORWAY 343	SWEDEN 336	FINLAND 284
1924[1]	NORWAY 160	SWEDEN 154	UNITED STATES 158
1924[2]	GREAT BRITAIN 263	NORWAY 262	SWEDEN 250

[1]Single shot; [2]Double shot

Running Deer Shooting (Single & Double Shot)

1952	John Larsen (NOR) 413	Per Olof Sköldberg (SWE) 409	Tauno Mäki (FIN) 407
1956	Vitali Romanenko (URS) 441	Per Olof Sköldberg (SWE) 432	Vladimir Sevrugin (URS) 429

Military Revolver

1896	John Paine (USA) 442	Sumner Paine (USA) 380	Nikolaos Morakis (GRE) 205
1906	Louis Richardet (SUI) 253	Alexandros Theophilakis (GRE) 250	Georgios Skotadis (GRE) 240
1906[1]	Jean Fouconnier (FRA) 219	Raoul de Boigne (FRA) 219	Hermann Martin (FRA) 215

1900-1904 Event not held
[1]Model 1873

Duelling Pistol

1906[1]	Léon Moreaux (FRA) 242	Cesare Liverziani (ITA) 233	Maurice Lecoq (FRA) 231
1906[2]	Konstantinos Skarlatos (GRE) 133	Johann von Holst (SWE) 115	Wilhelm Carlberg (SWE) 115

1896-1904 Event not held
[1]Over 20m; [2]Over 25m

Team Event

1900	SWITZERLAND 2271	FRANCE 2203	NETHERLANDS 1876
1908	UNITED STATES 1914	BELGIUM 1863	GREAT BRITAIN 1817
1912[1]	UNITED STATES 1916	SWEDEN 1849	GREAT BRITAIN 1804
1912[2]	SWEDEN 1145	RUSSIA dna	GREAT BRITAIN dna

1920[1] UNITED STATES 2372	SWEDEN 2289	BRAZIL 2264
1920[2] UNITED STATES 1310	GREECE 1285	SWITZERLAND 1270

1904-1906 Event not held
[1]*Over 50m;* [2]*Over 30m*

Women

Introduced in 1984
Sport Pistol

1984 Linda Thom (CAN) 585	Ruby Fox (USA) 585	Patricia Dench (AUS) 583
1988 Nino Saloukvadze (URS) (591+99) 690	Tomoko Hasegawa (JPN) (587+99) 686	Jasna Sekaric (YUG) (591+95) 686
1992 Marina Logvinenko (EUN) 684	Li Duihong (CHN) 680	Dorzhsuren Munkhbayar (MGL) 679
1996 Lui Duihong (CHN) 687.9	Diana Yorgova (BUL) 684.8	Marina Logvinenko (RUS) 684.2
2000 Maria Grozdeva (BUL) 690.3	Luna Tao (CHN) 689.8	Lolita Yevlevskaya (BLR) 686.0
2004 Maria Grozdeva (BUL) 688.2	Lenka Hykova (CZE) 687.8	Irada Ashumova (AZE) 687.3

Small-Bore Rifle -Three Positions

1984 Wu Xiaoxuan (CHN) 581	Ulrike Holmer (FRG) 578	Wanda Jewell (USA) 578
1988 Silvia Sperber (FRG) (590+95.6) 685.6	Vessela Letcheva (BUL) (583+100.2) 683.2	Valentina Tcherkasova (URS) (586+95.4) 681.4
1992 Launi Melli (USA) 684.3	Nonka Matova (BUL) 682.7	Malgorzata Ksiazkiewicz (POL) 681.5
1996 Alexandra Ivosev (YUG) 686.1	Irina Gerasimenok (POL) 680.1	Renata Mauer (POL) 679.8
2000 Renata Mauer-Rozanska (POL) 684.6	Tatyana Goldobina (RUS) 680.9	Maria Feklistova (RUS) 679.9
2004 Lyubov Galkina (RUS) 688.4	Valentina Turisini (ITA) 685.9	Chengyi Wang (CHN) 685.4

Air Pistol

1988 Jasna Sekaric (YUG) (389+100.5) 489.5	Nino Saloukvadze (URS) (390+97.9) 487.9	Marina Dobrantcheva (URS) (385+100.2) 485.2
1992 Marina Logvinenko (EUN) 486.4	Jasna Sekaric (IOP) 486.4	Maria Grusdeva (BUL) 481.6
1996 Olga Klochneva (RUS) 490.1	Marina Logvinenko (RUS) 488.5	Maria Grusdeva (BUL) 488.5
2000 Luna Tao (CHN) 488.2	Jasna Sekaric (YUG) 486.5	Annemarie Forder (AUS) 484.0
2004 Olena Kostevych (UKR) 483.3	Jasna Sekaric (SCG) 483.3	Maria Grozdeva (BUL) 482.3

1984 Event not held

Air Rifle

1984 Pat Spurgin (USA) 393	Edith Gufler (ITA) 391	Wu Xianxuan (CHN) 389
1988 Irina Chilova (URS) (395+103.5) 498.5	Silvia Sperber (FRG) (393+104.5) 497.5	Anna Maloukhina (URS) (394+101.8) 495.8
1992 Yeo Kab-soon (KOR) 498.2	Vesela Letcheva (BUL) 495.3	Aranka Binder (IOP) 495.1
1996 Renata Mauer (POL) 497.6	Petra Horneber (GER) 497.4	Alexandra Ivosev (YUG) 497.2
2000 Nancy Johnson (USA) 497.7	Cho-Hyun Kang (KOR) 497.5	Jing Gao (CHN) 497.2
2004 Du Li (CHN) 502.0	Lyubov Galkina ((RUS) 501.5	Katerina Kurkova (CZE) 501.1

Trap

2000 Daina Gudzineviciute (LTU) 93	Delphine Racinet (FRA) 92	E Gao (CHN) 90
2004 Suzanne Balogh (AUS) 88	Maria Quintana (ESP) 84	Bo-Na Lee (KOR) 83

1984-1996 Event not held

Double Trap

1996 Kim Rhode (USA) 141	Susanne Keirmayer (GER) 139	Deserie Huddleston (AUS) 139
2000 Pia Hansen (SWE) 148	Deborah Gelisio (ITA) 144	Kim Rhode (USA) 139
2004 Kim Rhode (USA) 146	Bo-Na Lee (KOR) 145	E Gao (CHN) 142

1984-1992 Event not held

Skeet

2000 Zemfira Meftakhetdinova (AZE) 98	Svetlana Demina (RUS) 95	Diana Igaly (HUN) 93
2004 Diana Igaly (HUN) 97	Ning Wei (CHN) 93	Zemfira Meftakhetdinova (AZE) 93

1984-1996 Event not held

SOFTBALL

Women

Introduced in 1996

1996 UNITED STATES	CHINA	AUSTRALIA
2000 UNITED STATES	JAPAN	AUSTRALIA
2004 UNITED STATES	AUSTRALIA	JAPAN

SWIMMING

Men

50 Metres Freestyle

1904[1]	Zóltán Halmay (HUN) 28.0	Scott Leary (USA) 28.6	Charles Daniels (USA) dna.
1988	Matti Biondi (USA) 22.14	Thomas Jager (USA) 22.36	Gennadi Prigoda (URS) 22.71
1992	Alexander Popov (EUN) 21.91	Matt Biondi (USA) 22.09	Tom Jager (USA) 22.30
1996	Alexander Popov (RUS) 22.13	Gary Hall Jr (USA) 22.26	Fernando Scherer (BRA) 22.20
2000	Anthony Ervin (USA) 21.98	-	Pieter van den Hoogenband (NED) 22.03
	Gary Hall Jr (USA) 21.98		
2004	Gary Hall Jr (USA) 21.93	Duje Draganja (CRO) 21.94	Roland Schoeman RSA)22.02

1896-1900,1906-1984 Event not held
[1]50 yards – Race re-swum after judges disagreed on result of first race

100 Metres Freestyle

1896[1]	Alfréd Hajós (HUN) 1:22.2	Efstathios Chorophas (GRE) 1:23.0	Otto Herschmann (AUT) dna
1904[2]	Zóltán Halmay (HUN) 1:02.8	Charles Daniels (USA) dna	Scott Leary (USA) dna
1906	Charles Daniels (USA) 1:13.4	Zóltán Halmay (HUN) 1:14.2	Cecil Healy (AUS) dna
1908	Charles Daniels (USA) 1:05.6	Zóltán Halmay (HUN) 1:06.2	Harald Julin (SWE) 1:08.0
1912	Duke Kahanamoku (USA) 1:03.4	Cecil Healy (AUS) 1:04.6	Kenneth Huszagh (USA) 1:05.6
1920	Duke Kahanamoku (USA) 1:01.4	Pua Kealoha (USA) 1:02.2	William Harris (USA) 1:03.0
1924	Johnny Weissmuller (USA) 59.0	Duke Kahanamoku (USA) 1:01.4	Sam Kahanamoku (USA) 1:01.8
1928	Johnny Weissmuller (USA) 58.6	István Bárány (HUN) 59.8	Katsuo Takaishi (JPN) 1:00.0
1932	Yasuji Miyazaki (JPN) 58.2	Tatsugo Kawaishi (JPN) 58.6	Albert Schwartz (USA) 58.8
1936	Ferenc Csik (HUN) 57.6	Masanori Yusa (JPN) 57.9	Shigeo Arai (JPN) 58.0
1948	Walter Ris (USA) 57.3	Alan Ford (USA) 57.8	Géza Kádas (HUN) 58.1
1952	Clarke Scholes (USA) 57.4	Hiroshi Suzuki (JPN) 57.4	Göran Larsson (SWE) 58.2
1956	Jon Hendricks (AUS) 55.4	John Devitt (AUS) 55.8	Gary Chapman (AUS) 56.7
1960[3]	John Devitt (AUS) 55.2 (55.16)	Lance Larson (USA) 55.2 (55.10)	Manuel dos Santos (BRA) 55.4
1964	Don Schollander (USA) 53.4	Bobbie McGregor (GBR) 53.5	Hans-Joachim Klein (GER) 54.0
1968	Mike Wenden (AUS) 52.2	Ken Walsh (USA) 52.8	Mark Spitz (USA) 53.0
1972	Mark Spitz (USA) 51.22	Jerry Heidenreich (USA) 51.65	Vladimir Bure (URS) 51.77
1976	Jim Montgomery (USA) 49.99	Jack Babashoff (USA) 50.81	Peter Nocke (FRG) 51.31
1980	Jörg Woithe (GDR) 50.40	Per Holmertz (SWE) 50.91	Per Johansson (SWE) 51.29
1984	Ambrose Gaines (USA) 49.80	Mark Stockwell (AUS) 50.24	Per Johansson (SWE) 50.31
1988	Matt Biondi (USA) 48.63	Chris Jacobs (USA) 49.08	Stephan Caron (FRA) 49.62
1992	Alexander Popov (EUN) 49.02	Gustavo Borges (BRA) 49.43	Stephan Caron (FRA) 49.50
1996	Alexander Popov (RUS) 48.74	Gary Hall Jr (USA) 48.81	Gustavo Borges (BRA) 49.02
2000	Pieter van den Hoogenband (NED) 48.30	Alexander Popov (RUS) 48.69	Gary Hall Jr (USA) 48.73
2004	Pieter van den Hoogenband (NED) 48.17	Roland Schoeman (RSA) 48.23	Ian Thorpe (AUS) 48.56

1900 Event not held
[1]Some confusion exists about second and third finishers; [2]100 yards; [3]Larson's original manual timing of 55.1 was revised by the judges (Automatic timings shown were unofficial)

200 Metres Freestyle

1900	Frederick Lane (AUS) 2:25.2	Zóltán Halmay (HUN) 2:31.4	Karl Ruberi (AUT) 2:32.0
1904[1]	Charles Daniels (USA) 2:44.2	Francis Gailey (USA) 2:46.0	Emil Rausch (GER) 2:56.0
1968	Mike Wenden (AUS) 1:55.2	Don Schollander (USA) 1:55.8	John Nelson (USA) 1:58.1
1972	Mark Spitz (USA) 1:52.78	Steven Genter (USA) 1:53.73	Werner Lampe (FRG) 1:53.99
1976	Bruce Furniss (USA) 1:50.29	John Naber (USA) 1:50.50	Jim Montgomery (USA) 1:50.58
1980	Sergei Kopliakov (URS) 1:49.81	Andrei Krylov (URS) 1:50.76	Graeme Brewer (AUS) 1:51.60
1984	Michael Gross (FRG) 1:47.44	Michael Heath (USA) 1:49.10	Thomas Fahrner (FRG) 1:49.69
1988	Duncan Armstrong (AUS) 1:747.25	Anders Holmertz (SWE) 1:47.89	Matt Biondi (USA) 1:47.99
1992	Yevgeni Sadovyi (EUN) 1:46.70	Anders Holmertz (SWE) 1:46.86	Antti Kasvio (FIN) 1:47.63
1996	Danyon Loader (NZL) 1:47.63	Gustavo Borges (BRA) 1:48.08	Daniel Kowalski (AUS) 1:48.25
2000	Pieter van den Hoogenband (NED) 1:45.35	Ian Thorpe (AUS) 1:45.83	Massimiliano Rosolino (ITA) 1:46.65
2004	Ian Thorpe (AUS) 1:44.71	Pieter van den Hoogenband (NED) 1:45.23	Michael Phelps (USA) 1:45.32

1896, 1906-1964 Event not held
[1]220 yards

400 Metres Freestyle

1896[1]	Paul Neuman (AUT) 8:12.6	Antonios Pepanos (GRE) 30m	Efstathios Choraphas (GRE) dna

1904²	Charles Daniels (USA) 6:16.2	Francis Gailey (USA) 6:22.0	Otto Wahle (AUT) 6:39.0
1906	Otto Scheff (AUT) 6:23.8	Henry Taylor (GBR) 6:24.4	John Jarvis (GBR) 6:27.2
1908	Henry Taylor (GBR) 5:36.8	Frank Beaurepaire (AUS) 5:44.2	Otto Scheff (AUT) 5:46.0
1912	George Hodgson (CAN) 5:24.4	John Hatfield (GBR) 5:25.8	Harold Hardwick (AUS) 5:31.2
1920	Norman Ross (USA) 5:26.8	Ludy Langer (USA) 5:29.2	George Vernot (CAN) 5:29.8
1924	Johnny Weismuller (USA) 5:04.2	Arne Borg (SWE) 5:05.6	Andrew Charlton (AUS) 5:06.6
1928	Alberto Zorilla (ARG) 5:01.6	Andrew Charlton (AUS) 5:03.6	Arne Borg (SWE) 5:04.6
1932	Buster Crabbe (USA) 4:48.4	Jean Taris (FRA) 4:48.5	Tautomu Oyokota (JPN) 4:52.3
1936	Jack Medica (USA) 4:44.5	Shumpei Uto (JPN) 4:45.6	Shozo Makino (JPN) 4:48.1
1948	William Smith (USA) 4:41.0	James McLane (USA) 4:43.4	John Marshall (AUS) 4:47.7
1952	Jean Boiteux (FRA) 4:30.7	Ford Konno (USA) 4:31.3	Per-Olof Ostrand (SWE) 4:35.2
1956	Murray Rose (AUS) 4:27.3	Tsuyoshi Yamanaka (JPN) 4:30.4	George Breen (USA) 4:32.5
1960	Murray Rose (AUS) 4:18.3	Tsuyoshi Yamanaka (JPN) 4:21.4	John Konrads (AUS) 4:21.8
1964	Don Schollander (USA) 4:12.2	Frank Wiegand (GER) 4:14.9	Allan Wood (AUS) 4:15.1
1968	Mike Burton (USA) 4:09.0	Ralph Hutton (CAN) 4:11.7	Allan Mosconi (FRA) 4:13.3
1972	Brad Cooper (AUS) 4:00.27	Steven Genter (USA) 4:01.94	Tom McBeen (USA) 4:02.64
1976	Brian Goodell (USA) 3:51.93	Tim Shaw (USA) 3:52.54	Vladimir Raskatov (URS) 3:55.76
1980	Vladimir Salnikov (URS) 3:51.31	Andrei Krylov (URS) 3:53.24	Ivar Stukolkin (URS) 3:55.76
1984	George DiCarlo (USA) 3:51.23	John Mykkkanen (USA) 3:51.49	Justin Lemberg (AUS) 3:51.79
1988	Uwe Dassler (GDR) 3:46.95	Duncan Armstrong (AUS) 3:47.15	Artur Wojdat (POL) 3:47.34
1992	Yevgeni Sadovyi (EUN) 3:45.00	Kieren Perkins (AUS) 3:45.16	Anders Holmertz (SWE) 3:46.77
1996	Danyon Loader (NZL) 3:47.97	Paul Palmer (GBR) 3:49.00	Daniel Kowalski (AUS) 3:48.39
2000	Ian Thorpe (AUS) 3:40.59	Massimiliano Rosolino (ITA) 3:43.40	Klete Keller (USA) 3:47.00
2004	Ian Thorpe (AUS) 3:43.10	Grant Hackett (AUS) 3:43.36	Klete Keller (USA) 3:44.11

1900 Event not held
¹500m; ²440 yards

1500 Metres Freestyle

1896¹	Alfréd Hajós (HUN) 18:22.2	Jean Andreou (GRE) 21:03.4	Efstathios Choraphas (GRE) dna
1900²	John Jarvis (GBR) 13:40.2	Otto Wahle (AUT) 14:53.6	Zóltán Halmay (HUN) 15:16.4
1904³	Emil Rausch (GER) 27:18.2	Géza Kiss (HUN) 28:28.2	Francis Gailey (USA) 28:54.0
1906³	Henry Taylor (GBR) 28:28.0	John Jarvis (GBR) 30:31.0	Otto Scheff (AUT) 30.59.0
1908	Henry Taylor (GBR) 22:48.4	Sydney Battersby (GBR) 22:51.2	Frank Beaurepaire (AUS) 22:56.2
1912	George Hodgson (CAN) 22:00.0	John Hatfield (GBR) 22:39.0	Harold Hardwick (AUS) 23:15.4
1920	Norman Ross (USA) 22:23.2	George Vernot (CAN) 22:36.4	Frank Beaurepaire (AUS) 23:04.0
1924	Andrew Charlton (AUS) 20:06.6	Arne Borg (SWE) 20:41.4	Frank Beaurepaire (AUS) 21:48.4
1928	Arne Borg (SWE) 19:51.8	Andrew Charlton (AUS) 20:02.6	Buster Crabbe (USA) 20:28.8
1932	Kusuo Kitamura (JPN) 19:12.4	Shozo Makino (JPN) 19:14.1	James Christy (USA) 19:39.5
1936	Noboru Terada (JPN) 19:13.7	Jack Medica (USA) 19:34.0	Shumpei Uto (JPN) 19:34.5
1948	James McLane (USA) 19:18.5	John Marshall (AUS) 19:31.3	György Mitro (HUN) 19:43.2
1952	Ford Konno (USA) 18:30.0	Shiro Hasizune (JPN) 18:41.4	Tetsuo Okamoto (JPN) 18:51.3
1956	Murray Rose (AUS) 17:58.9	Tsuyoshi Yamanaka (JPN) 18:00.3	George Breen (USA) 18:08.2
1960	John Konrads (AUS) 17:19.6	Murray Rose (AUS) 17:21.7	George Breen (USA) 17:30.6
1964	Bob Windle (AUS) 17:01.7	John Nelson (USA) 17:03.0	Allan Wood (AUS) 17:07.7
1968	Mike Burton (USA) 16:38.9	John Kinsella (USA) 16:57.3	Greg Brough (AUS) 17:04.7
1972	Mike Burton (USA) 15:52.58	Graham Windeatt (AUS) 15:58.48	Doug Northway (USA) 16:09.25
1976	Brian Goodell (USA) 15:02.40	Bobby Hackett (USA) 15:03.91	Steve Holland (AUS) 15:04.66
1980	Vladimir Salnikov (URS) 14:58.27	Alexander Chaev (URS) 15:14.30	Max Metzker (AUS) 15:14.49
1984	Michael O'Brien (USA) 15:05.20	George DiCarlo (USA) 15:10.59	Stefan Pfeiffer (FRG) 15:12.11
1988	Vladimir Salnikov (URS) 15:00.40	Stevan Pfeiffer (FRG) 15:02.69	Uwe Dassler (GDR) 15:06.15
1992	Kieren Perkins (AUS) 14:43.48	Glen Housman (AUS) 14:55.29	Jörg Hoffmann (GER) 15:02.29
1996	Kieren Perkins (AUS) 14:56.40	Daniel Kowalski (AUS) 15:02.43	Graeme Smith (GBR) 15:02.48
2000	Grant Hackett (AUS) 14:48.33	Kieren Perkins (AUS) 14:53.59	Chris Thompson (USA) 14:56.81
2004	Grant Hackett (AUS) 14:43.40	Larsen Jensen (USA) 14:45.29	David Davies (GBR) 14:45.95

¹1200m; ²1000m; ³1 mile

100 Metres Breaststroke

1968	Don McKenzie (USA) 1:07.7	Vladimir Kossinky (URS) 1:08.0	Nikolai Pankin (URS) 1:08.0
1972	Nobutaka Taguchi (JPN) 1:04.94	Tom Bruce (USA) 1:05.43	John Hencken (USA) 1:05.61
1976	John Hencken (USA) 1:03.11	David Wilkie (GBR) 1:03.43	Arvidas Iuozaytis (URS) 1:04.23
1980	Duncan Goodhew (GBR) 1:03.34	Arsen Miskarov (URS) 1:03.92	Peter Evans (AUS) 1:03.96
1984	Steve Lundquist (USA) 1:01.65	Victor Davis (CAN) 1:01.99	Peter Evans (AUS) 1:02.97
1988	Adrian Moorhouse (GBR) 1:02.04	Karoly Guttler (HUN) 1:02.05	Dmitri Volkov (URS) 1:02.20
1992	Nelson Dreibel (USA) 1:01.50	Norbert Rósza (HUN) 1:01.68	Phil Rogers (AUS) 1:01.76
1996	Frederik Deburghgraeve (BEL) 1:00.65	Jeremy Linn (USA) 1:00.77	Mark Warnecke (GER) 1:01.33
2000	Domenico Fioravanti (ITA) 1:00.46	Ed Moses (USA) 1:00.73	Roman Sloudnov (RUS) 1:00.91

2004   Kosuke Kitajima (JPN) 1:00.08   Brendan Hansen (USA) 1:00.25   Hugues Duboscq (FRA) 1:00.88
1896-1964 Event not held

200 Metres Breaststroke

1908	Frederick Holman (GBR) 3:09.2	William Robinson (GBR) 3:12.8	Pontus Hansson (SWE) 3:14.6
1912	Walter Bathe (GER) 3:01.8	Wilhelm Lützow (GER) 3:05.2	Kurt Malisch (GER) 3:08.0
1920	Häken Malmroth (SWE) 3:04.4	Thor Henning (SWE) 3:09.2	Arvo Aaltonen (FIN) 3:12.2
1924	Robert Shelton (USA) 2:56.5	Joseph de Combe (BEL) 2:59.2	William Kirschbaum (USA) 3:01.0
1928	Yoshiyuki Tsuruta (JPN) 2:48.8	Erich Rademacher (GER) 2:50.6	Teofilo Ylidefonzo (PHI) 2:56.4
1932	Yoshiyuki Tsuruta (JPN) 2:46.4	Reizo Koike (JPN) 2:46.4	Teofilo Ylidefonzo (PHI) 2:47.1
1936	Tetsuo Hamuro (JPN) 2:42.5	Erwin Sietas (GER) 2:42.9	Reizo Koike (JPN) 2:44.2
1948	Joseph Verdeur[1] (USA) 2:39.3	Keith Carter (USA) 2:40.2	Robert Sohl (USA) 2:43.9
1952	John Davies[1] (AUS) 2:34.4	Bowen Stassforth (USA) 2:34.7	Herbert Klein (GER) 2:35.9
1956	Masaru Furukawa[2] (JPN) 2:34.7	Masahiro Yoshimura (JPN) 2:36.7	Charis Yunitschev (URS) 2:36.8
1960	William Mulliken (USA) 2:37.4	Yoshihiko Osaki (JPN) 2:38.0	Weiger Mensonides (NED) 2:39.7
1964	Ian O'Brien (AUS) 2:27.8	Georgi Prokopenko (URS) 2:28.2	Chester Jastremski (USA) 2:29.6
1968	Felipe Munoz (MEX) 2:28.7	Vladimir Kossinsky (URS) 2:29.2	Brian Job (USA) 2:29.9
1972	John Hencken (USA) 2:21.55	David Wilkie (GBR) 2:23.67	Nobutaka Taguchi (JPN) 2:23.88
1976	David Wilkie (USA) 2:15.11	John Hencken (USA) 2:17.26	Rick Colella (USA) 2:19.20
1980	Robertas Shulpa (URS) 2:15.85	Alban Vermes (HUN) 2:16.93	Arsen Miskarov (URS) 2:17.28
1984	Victor Davis (CAN) 2:13.34	Glenn Beringen (AUS) 2:15.79	Etienne Dagon (SUI) 2:17.41
1988	József Szabó (HUN) 2:13.52	Nick Gillingham (GBR) 2:14.12	Sergio Lopez (ESP) 2:15.21
1992	Mike Barrowman (USA) 2:10.16	Norbert Rózsa (HUN) 2:11.23	Nick Gillingham (GBR) 2:11.29
1996	Norbert Rózsa (HUN) 2:12.57	Károly Guttler (HUN) 2:13.03	Andrei Korneyev (RUS) 2:13.17
2000	Domenico Fioravanti (ITA) 2:10.87	Toronce Parkin (RSA) 2:12.50	Davide Rummolo (ITA) 2:12.73
2004	Kosuke Kitajima (JPN) 2:09.44	Daniel Gyurta (HUN) 2:10.80	Brendan Hansen (USA) 2:10.87

1896-1906 Event not held
[1]*Used the then permissible butterfly stroke;* [2]*Used the then permissible underwater technique*

100 Metres Backstroke

1904[1]	Walter Brack (GER) 1:16.8	Georg Hoffmann (GER) 1:18.0	Georg Zacharias (GER) 1:19.6
1908	Arno Bieberstein (GER) 1:24.6	Ludvig Dam (DEN) 1:26.6	Herbert Haresnape (GBR) 1:27.0
1912	Harry Hebner (USA) 1:21.2	Otto Fahr (GER) 1:22.4	Paul Kellner (GER) 1:24.0
1920	Warren Kealoha (USA) 1:15.2	Ray Kegeris (USA) 1:16.2	Gérard Blitz (BEL) 1:19.0
1924	Warren Kealoha (USA) 1:13.2	Paul Wyatt (USA) 1:15.4	Károly Bartha (HUN) 1:17.8
1928	George Kojac (USA) 1:08.2	Walter Laufer (USA) 1:10.0	Paul Wyatt (USA) 1:12.0
1932	Masaji Kiyokawa (JPN) 1:08.6	Toshio Irie (JPN) 1:09.8	Kentaro Kawatsu (JPN) 1:10.0
1936	Adolf Kiefer (USA) 1:05.9	Albert Van de Weghe (USA) 1:07.7	Masaji Kiyokawa (JPN) 1:08.4
1948	Allen Stack (USA) 1:06.4	Robert Cowell (USA) 1:06.5	Georges Vallerey (FRA) 1:07.8
1952	Yoshinobu Oyakawa (JPN) 1:05.4	Gilbert Bozon (FRA) 1:06.2	Jack Taylor (USA) 1:06.4
1956	David Thiele (AUS) 1:02.2	John Monckton (AUS) 1:03.2	Frank McKinney (USA) 1:04.5
1960	David Thiele (AUS) 1:01.9	Frank McKinney (USA) 1:02.1	Robert Bennett (USA) 1:02.3
1968	Roland Matthes (GDR) 58.7	Charles Hickox (USA) 1:00.2	Ronnie Mills (USA) 1:00.5
1972	Roland Matthes (GDR) 56.58	Mike Stamm (USA) 57.70	John Murphy (USA) 58.35
1976	John Naber (USA) 55.49	Peter Rocca (USA) 56.34	Roland Matthes (GDR) 57.22
1980	Bengt Baron (SWE) 56.53	Viktor Kuznetsov (URS) 56.99	Vladimir Dolgov (URS) 57.63
1984	Richard Carey (USA) 55.79	David Wilson (USA) 56.35	Mike West (CAN) 56.49
1988	Daichi Suzuki (JPN) 55.05	David Berkoff (USA) 55.18	Igor Polianski (URS) 55.20
1992	Mark Tewksbury (CAN) 53.98	Jeff Rouse (USA) 54.04	David Berkoff (USA) 54.78
1996	Jeff Rouse (USA) 54.10	Rodolfo Cabrera (CUB) 54.98	Neisser Bent (CUB) 55.02
2000	Lenny Krayzelburg (USA) 53.72	Matt Welsh (AUS) 54.07	Stev Theloke (GER) 54.82
2004	Aaron Peirsol (USA) 54.06	Markus Rogan (AUT) 54.35	Tomomi Morita (JPN) 54.36

1896-1900, 1906,1964 Event not held
[1]*100 yards*

200 Metres Backstroke

1900	Ernst Hoppenberg (GER) 2:47.0	Karl Ruberl (AUT) 2:56.0	Johannes Drost (NED) 3:01.0
1964	Jed Graef (USA) 2:10.3	Gary Dilley (USA) 2:10.5	Robert Bennett (USA) 2:13.1
1968	Roland Matthes (GDR) 2:09.6	Mitchell Ivey (USA) 2:10.6	Jack Horsley (USA) 2:10.9
1972	Roland Matthes (GDR) 2:02.82	Mike Stamm (USA) 2:04.09	Mitchell Ivey (USA) 2:04.33
1976	John Naber (USA) 1:59.19	Peter Rocca (USA) 2:00.55	Don Harrigan (USA) 2:01.35
1980	Sándor Wladár (HUN) 2:01.93	Zóltán Verraszto (HUN) 2:02.40	Mark Kerry (AUS) 2:03.14
1984	Richard Carey (USA) 2:00.23	Frederic Delcourt (FRA) 2:01.75	Cameron Henning (CAN) 2:02.37
1988	Igor Polianski (URS) 1:59.37	Frank Baltrausch (GDR) 1:59.50	Paul Kingsman (NZL) 2:00.48
1992	Martin Lopez-Zubero (ESP) 1:58.47	Vladimir Selkov (EUN) 1:58.87	Stefano Battistelli (ITA) 1:59.40
1996	Brad Bridgewater (USA) 1:58.54	Tripp Schwenk (USA) 1:58.99	Emanuele Meris (ITA) 1:59.18

2000 Lenny Krayzelburg (USA) 1:56.76	Aaron Piersol (USA) 1:57.35	Matt Welsh (AUS) 1:57.59
2004 Aaron Peirsol (USA) 1:54.95	Markus Rogan (AUT) 1:57.35	Razvan Florea (ROM) 1:57.56

1896,1904-1960 Event not held

100 Metres Butterfly

1968 Doug Russell (USA) 55.9	Mark Spitz (USA) 56.4	Ross Wales (USA) 57.2
1972 Mark Spitz (USA) 54.27	Bruce Robertson (CAN) 55.56	Jerry Heidenreich (USA) 55.74
1976 Matt Vogel (USA) 54.35	Joe Bottom (USA) 54.50	Gary Hall (USA) 54.65
1980 Pär Arvidsson (SWE) 54.92	Roger Pyttel (GDR) 54.94	David Lopez (ESP) 55.13
1984 Michael Gross (FRG) 53.08	Pablo Morales (USA) 53.23	Glenn Buchanan (AUS) 53.85
1988 Anthony Nesty (SUR) 53.00	Matt Biondi (USA) 53.01	Andy Jameson (GBR) 53.30
1992 Pablo Morales (USA) 53.32	Rafal Szukala (POL) 53.35	Anthony Nesty (SUR) 53.41
1996 Denis Pankratov (RUS) 52.27	Scott Miller (AUS) 52.53	Vladislav Kulikov (RUS) 52.13
2000 Lars Frölander (SWE) 52.00	Michael Klim (AUS) 52.18	Geoff Huegill (AUS) 52.22
2004 Michael Phelps (USA) 51.25	Ian Crocker (USA) 51.29	Andriy Serdinov (UKR) 51.36

1896-1964 Event not held

200 Metres Butterfly

1956 William Yorzyk (USA) 2:19.3	Takashi Ishimoto (JPN) 2:23.8	György Tumpek (HUN) 2:23.9
1960 Mike Troy (USA) 2:12.8	Neville Hayes (AUS) 2:14.6	David Gillanders (USA) 2:15.3
1964 Kevin Berry (AUS) 2:06.6	Carl Robie (USA) 2:07.5	Fred Schmidt (USA) 2:09.3
1968 Carl Robie (USA) 2:08.7	Martyn Woodroffe (GBR) 2:09.0	John Ferris (USA) 2:09.3
1972 Mark Spitz (USA) 2:00.70	Gary Hall (USA) 2:02.86	Robin Backhaus (USA) 2:03.23
1976 Mike Bruner (USA) 1:59.23	Steven Gregg (USA) 1:59.54	William Forrester (USA) 1:59.96
1980 Sergey Fesenko (URS) 1:59.76	Phil Hubble (GBR) 2:01.20	Roger Pyttel (GDR) 2:01.39
1984 Jon Sieben (AUS) 1:57.04	Michael Gross (FRG) 1:57.40	Rafael Castro (VEN) 1:57.51
1988 Michael Gross (FRG) 1:56.94	Benny Nielsen (DEN) 1:58.24	Anthony Mosse (NZL) 1:58.28
1992 Mel Stewart (USA) 1:56.26	Danyon Loader (NZL) 1:57.93	Franck Esposito (FRA) 1:58.51
1996 Denis Pankratov (RUS) 1:56.51	Tom Malchow (USA) 1:57.44	Scott Miller (AUS) 1:57.48
2000 Tom Malchow (USA) 1:55.35	Denys Sylantyev (UKR) 1:55.76	Justin Norris (AUS) 1:56.17
2004 Michael Phelps (USA) 1:54.04	Takashi Yamamoto (JPN) 1:54.56	Stephen Parry (GBR) 1:55.52

1896-1952 Event not held

200 Metres Individual Medley

1968 Charles Hickox (USA) 2:12.0	Greg Buckingham (USA) 2:13.0	John Ferris (USA) 2:13.3
1972 Gunnar Larsson (SWE) 2:07.17	Tim McKee (USA) 2:08.37	Steve Furniss (USA) 2:08.45
1984 Alex Baumann (CAN) 2:01.42	Pablos Morales (USA) 2:03.05	Neil Cochran (GBR) 2:04.38
1988 Tamás Darnyi (HUN) 2:00.17	Patrick Kühl (GDR) 2:01.61	Vadim Yarochtchouk (URS) 2:02.40
1992 Tamás Darnyi (HUN) 2:00.76	Gregory Burgess (USA) 2:00.97	Attila Czene (HUN) 2:01.00
1996 Attila Czene (HUN) 1:59.91	Jani Sievinen (FIN) 2:00.13	Curtis Myden (CAN) 2:01.13
2000 Massimiliano Rosolino (ITA) 1:58.98	Tom Dolan (USA) 1:59.77	Tom Wilkens (USA) 2:00.87
2004 Michael Phelps (USA) 1:57.14	Ryan Lochtel (USA) 1:58.78	George Bovell (TRI) 1:58.80

1896-1964,1976-1980 Event not held

400 Metres Individual Medley

1964 Richard Roth (USA) 4:45.4	Roy Saari (USA) 4:47.1	Gerhard Hetz (GER) 4:51.0
1968 Charles Hickox (USA) 4:48.4	Gary Hall (USA) 4:48.7	Michael Holthaus (GER) 4:51.4
1972 Gunnar Larsson (SWE) 4:31.98	Tim McKee (USA) 4:31.98	András Hargitay (HUN) 4:32.70
1976 Rod Strachan (USA) 4:23.68	Tim McKee (USA) 4:24.62	Andrei Smirnov (URS) 4:26.90
1980 Alexander Sidorenko (URS) 4:22.89	Sergei Fesenko (URS) 4:23.43	Zóltán Verraszto (HUN) 4:24.24
1984 Alex Baumann (CAN) 4:17.41	Ricardo Prado (BRA) 4:18.45	Robert Woodhouse (AUS) 4:20.50
1988 Tamás Darnyi (HUN) 4:14.75	David Wharton (USA) 4:17.36	Stefano Battistelli (ITA) 4:18.01
1992 Tamás Darnyi (HUN) 4:14.23	Erik Namesnik (USA) 4:15.57	Luca Sacchi (ITA) 4:16.34
1996 Tom Dolan (USA) 4:14.90	Eric Namesnik (USA) 4:15.25	Curtis Myden (CAN) 4:16.28
2000 Tom Dolan (USA) 4:11.76	Erik Vendt (USA) 4:14.23	Curtis Myden (CAN) 4:15.33
2004 Michael Phelps (USA) 4:08.26	Erik Vendt (USA) 4:11.81	Laszlo Cseh (HUN) 4:12.15

1896-1960 Event not held

4x100 Metres Freestyle Relay

1964 UNITED STATES 3:33.2	GERMANY 3:37.2	AUSTRALIA 3:39.1
1968 UNITED STATES 3:01.7	SOVIET UNION 3:34.2	AUSTRALIA 3:34.7
1972 UNITED STATES 3:26.42	SOVIET UNION 3:29.72	GDR 3:32.42
1984 UNITED STATES 3:19.03	AUSTRALIA 3:19.68	SWEDEN 3:22.69
1988 UNITED STATES 3:16.53	SOVIET UNION 3:18.33	GDR 3:19.82

1992	UNITED STATES 3:16.74	UNIFIED TEAM 3:17.56	GERMANY 3:17.90
1996	UNITED STATES 3:15.41	RUSSIA 3:17.06	GERMANY 3:17.20
2000	AUSTRALIA 3:13.67	UNITED STATES 3:13.86	BRAZIL 3:17.40
2004	SOUTH AFRICA 3:13.17	NETHERLANDS 3:14.36	UNITED STATES 3:14.62

1896-1960, 1976-1980 Event not held

4x200 Metres Freestyle Relay

1906[1]	HUNGARY 16:52.4	GERMANY 17:16.2	GREAT BRITAIN nta
1908	GREAT BRITAIN 10:55.6	HUNGARY 10:59.0	UNITED STATES 11:02.8
1912	AUSTRALASIA[2] 10:11.6	UNITED STATES 10.20.2	GREAT BRITAIN 10:28.2
1920	UNITED STATES 10:04.4	AUSTRALIA 10:25.4	GREAT BRITAIN 10:37.2
1924	UNITED STATES 9:53.4	AUSTRALIA 10:02.2	SWEDEN 10:06.8
1928	UNITED STATES 9:36.2	JAPAN 9:41.4	CANADA 9:47.8
1932	JAPAN 8:58.4	UNITED STATES 9:10.5	HUNGARY 9:31.4
1936	JAPAN 8:51.5	UNITED STATES 9:03.0	HUNGARY 9:12.3
1948	UNITED STATES 8:46.0	HUNGARY 8:48.4	FRANCE 9:08.0
1952	UNITED STATES 8:31.1	JAPAN 8:33.5	FRANCE 8:45.9
1956	AUSTRALIA 8:23.6	UNITED STATES 8:31.5	SOVIET UNION 8:34.7
1960	UNITED STATES 8:10.2	JAPAN 8:13.2	AUSTRALIA 8:13.8
1964	UNITED STATES 7:52.1	GERMANY 7:59.3	JAPAN 8:03.8
1968	UNITED STATES 7:35.78	AUSTRALIA 7:53.7	SOVIET UNION 8:01.6
1972	UNITED STATES 7:35.78	FRG 7:41.69	SOVIET UNION 7:45.70
1976	UNITED STATES 7:23.22	SOVIET UNION 7:27.97	GREAT BRITAIN 7:32.11
1980	SOVIET UNION 7:20.50	GDR 7:28.60	BRAZIL 7:29.30
1984	UNITED STATES 7:15.69	FRG 7:16.73	GREAT BRITAIN 7:24.78
1988	UNITED STATES 7:12.51	GDR 7:13.68	FRG 7:14.35
1992	UNIFIED TEAM 7:11.95	SWEDEN 7:15.31	UNITED STATES 7:16.23
1996	UNITED STATES 7:14.84	SWEDEN 7:17.56	GERMANY 7:17.71
2000	AUSTRALIA 7:07.05	UNITED STATES 7:12.64	NETHERLANDS 7:12.70
2004	UNITED STATES 7:07.33	AUSTRALIA 7:07.46	ITALY 7:11.83

1896-1904 Event not held
[1]4x250m; [2]Composed of three Australians and a New Zealander

4x100 Metres Medley Relay

1960	UNITED STATES 4:05.4	AUSTRALIA 4:12.0	JAPAN 4:12.2
1964	UNITED STATES 3:38.5	GERMANY 4:01.6	AUSTRALIA 4:02.3
1968	UNITED STATES 3:54.9	GDR 3:57.5	SOVIET UNION 4:00.7
1972	UNITED STATES 3:48.16	GDR 3:52.12	CANADA 3:52.26
1976	UNITED STATES 3:42.22	CANADA 3:43.23	FRG 3:47.29
1980	AUSTRALIA 3:45.70	SOVIET UNION 3:45.92	GREAT BRITAIN 3:47.71
1984	UNITED STATES 3:39.30	CANADA 3:43.23	AUSTRALIA 3:43.25
1988	UNITED STATES 3:36.93	CANADA 3:39.28	SOVIET UNION 3:39.96
1992	UNITED STATES 3:36.93	UNIFIED TEAM 3:38.56	CANADA 3:39.96
1996	UNITED STATES 3:34.84	RUSSIA 3:37.55	AUSTRALIA 3:39.56
2000	UNITED STATES 3:33.73	AUSTRALIA 3:35.27	GERMANY 3:35.88
2004	UNITED STATES 3:30.68	GERMANY 3:33.62	JAPAN 3:35.22

1896-1956 Event not held

DISCONTINUED SWIMMING EVENTS

100 Metres Freestyle (Sailors)

| 1896 | Ioannis Maloknis (GRE) 2:20.4 | Spiridon Khasapis (GRE) nta | Dimitrios Drivas (GRE) nta |

200 Metres Obstacle Event

| 1900 | Frederick Lane (AUS) 2:38.4 | Otto Wahle (AUT) 2:40.0 | Peter Kemp (GBR) 2:47.4 |

400 Metres Breaststroke

1904	Georg Zacharias (GER) 7:23.6	Walter Brack (GER) 20m	Jamison Hardy (USA) dna
1912	Walter Bathe (GER) 6:29.6	Thor Henning (SWE) 6:35.6	Percy Courtman (GBR) 6:36.4
1920	Hakan Malmroth (SWE) 6:31.8	Thor Henning (SWE) 6:45.2	Arvo Aaltonen (FIN) 6:48.0

880 Yards Freestyle

| 1904 | Emil Rausch (GER) 13:11.4 | Francis Gailey (USA) 13:23.4 | Géza Kiss (HUN) nta |

4000 Metres Freestyle

1900	John Jarvis (GBR) 58:24.0	Zoltán Halmay (HUN) 1:08:55.4	Louis Martin (FRA) 1:13.08.4

Underwater Swimming

1900	Charles de Vendeville (FRA) 188.4	André Six (FRA) 185.4	Peder Lykkeberg (DEN) 147.0

Plunge for Distance

1904	Paul Dickey (USA) 19.05m	Edgar Adams (USA) 17.53m	Leo Goodwin (USA) 17.37m

200 Metres Team Swimming

1900	GERMANY 32pts	FRANCE 51	FRANCE 61

4x50 Yards Relay

1904	United States (New York AC) 2:04.6	United States (Chicago AC) nta	United States (Missouri AC) nta

Plain High Diving

1912	Erik Adlerz (SWE) 40.0	Hjalmar Johansson (SWE) 39.3	John Jansson (SWE) 39.1
1920	Arvid Wallmann (SWE) 183.5	Nils Skoglund (SWE) 183.0	John Jansson (SWE) 175.0
1924	Richmond Eve (AUS) 160.0	John Jansson (SWE) 157.0	Harold Clarke (GBR) 158.0

Women

50 Metres Freestyle

1988	Kristin Otto (GDR) 25.49	Yang Wenyi (CHN) 25.64	Katrin Meissner (GDR) 25.71
			Jill Sterkel (USA) 25.71
1992	Yang Wenyi (CHN) 24.79	Zhuang Yong (CHN) 25.08	Angel Martino (USA) 25.23
1996	Amy van Dyken (USA) 24.87	Le Jingyi (CHN) 24.90	Sandra Volker (GER) 25.14
2000	Inge de Bruijn (NED) 24.32	Therese Alshammar (SWE) 24.51	Dara Torres (USA) 24.63
2004	Inge de Bruijn (NED) 24.58	Malia Matella (FRA) 24.89	Lisbeth Lenton (AUS) 24.91

1896-1984 Event not held

100 Metres Freestyle

1912	Fanny Durack (AUS) 1:22.2	Wilhelmina Wylie (AUS) 1:25.4	Jennie Fletcher (GBR) 1:27.0
1920	Etheda Bleibtrey (USA) 1:13.6	Irene Guest (USA) 1:17.0	Frances Schroth (USA) 1:17.2
1924	Ethel Lackie (USA) 1:12.4	Mariechen Wehselau (USA) 1:12.8	Gertrude Ederle (USA) 1:14.2
1928	Albina Osipowich (USA) 1:11.0	Eleanor Garatti (USA) 1:11.4	Joyce Cooper (GBR) 1:13.6
1932	Helene Madison (USA) 1:06.8	Willemijntje den Ouden (NED) 1:07.8	Eleanor Garatti-Saville (USA) 1:08.2
1936	Henrika Mastenbroek (NED) 1:05.9	Jeanette Campbell (ARG) 1:06.4	Gisela Arendt (GER) 1:06.6
1948	Greta Andersen (DEN) 1:06.3	Ann Curtis (USA) 1:06.5	Marie-Louise Vaessen (NED) 1:07.6
1952	Katalin Szöke (HUN) 1:06.8	Johanna Termeulen (NED) 1:07.0	Judit Temes (HUN) 1:07.1
1956	Dawn Fraser (AUS) 1:02.0	Lorraine Crapp (AUS) 1:02.3	Faith Leech (AUS) 1:05.1
1960	Dawn Fraser (AUS) 1:01.2	Chris von Saltza (USA) 1:02.8	Natalie Steward (GBR) 1:03.1
1964	Dawn Fraser (AUS) 59.5	Sharon Stouder (USA) 59.9	Kathleen Ellis (USA) 1:00.8
1968	Jan Henne (USA) 1:00.0	Susan Pedersen (USA) 1:00.3	Linda Gustavson (USA) 1:00.3
1972	Sandra Neilson (USA) 58.59	Shirley Babashoff (USA) 59.02	Shane Gould (AUS) 59.06
1976	Kornelia Ender (GDR) 55.65	Petra Priemer (GDR) 56.49	Enith Brigitha (NED) 56.65
1980	Barbara Krause (GDR) 54.79	Caren Metschuck (GDR) 55.16	Ines Diers (GDR) 55.65
1984	Carrie Steinsiefer (USA) 55.92	–	Annemarie Verstappen (NED) 56.08
	Nancy Hogshead (USA) 55.92		
1988	Kristin Otto (GDR) 54.93	Zhuang Yong (CHN) 55.47	Catherine Plewinski (FRA) 55.49
1992	Zhuang Yong (CHN) 54.64	Jenny Thompson (USA) 54.84	Franziska van Almsick (GER) 54.94
1996	Le Jingyi (CHN) 54.50	Sandra Volker (GER) 54.88	Angel Martino (USA) 54.93
2000	Inge de Bruijn (NED) 53.83	Therese Alshammar (SWE) 54.33	Jenny Thompson 54.43
			Dara Torres (USA) 54.43
2004	Jodie Henry (AUS) 53.84	Inge de Bruijn (NED) 54.16	Natalie Coughlin (USA) 54.40

1896-1908 Event not held

200 Metres Freestyle

1968	Debbie Meyer (USA) 2;10.5	Jan Henne (USA) 2:11.0	Jane Barkman (USA) 2:11.2
1972	Shane Gould (AUS) 2:03.56	Shirley Babashoff (USA) 2:04.33	Keena Rothhammer (USA) 2:04.92
1976	Kornelia Ender (GDR) 1:59.26	Shirley Babashoff (USA) 2:01.22	Enith Brigitha (NED) 2:01.40
1980	Barbara Krause (GDR) 1:58.33	Ines Diers (GDR) 1:59.64	Carmela Schmidt (GDR) 2:01.44

1984	Mary Wayte (USA) 1:59.23	Cynthia Woodhead (USA) 1:59.50	Annemarie Verstappen (NED) 1:59.69
1988	Heike Friedrich (GDR) 1;57.65	Silvia Poll (CRC) 1:58.67	Manuela Stellmach (GDR) 1:59.01
1992	Nicole Haislett (USA) 1:57.90	Franziska van Almsick (GER) 1:58.00	Kirsten Kielglass (GER) 1:59.67
1996	Claudia Poll (CRC) 1:58.16	Franziska van Almsick (GER)1:58.57	Dagmar Hase (GER) 1:59.56
2000	Susie O'Neill (AUS) 1:58.24	Martina Moravcova (SVK) 1:58.32	Claudia Poll (CRC) 1:58.81
2004	Camelia Potec (ROM) 1:58.03	Federica Pellegrini (ITA) 1:58.22	Solenne Figues (FRA) 1:58.45

1896-1964 Event not held

400 Metres Freestyle

1920[1]	Etheda Bloibtrey (USA) 4.34.0	Margaret Woodbridge (USA) 4:42.8	Frances Schroth (USA) 4:52.0
1924	Martha Norelius (USA) 6:02.2	Helen Wainwright (USA) 6:03.8	Gertrude Ederle (USA) 6:04.8
1928	Martha Norelius (USA) 5:42.8	Marie Braun (NED) 5:57.8	Jospehine McKim (USA) 6:00.2
1932	Helene Madison (USA) 5:28.5	Lenore Kight (USA) 5:28.6	Jennie Maakal (RSA) 5:47.3
1936	Henrika Mastenbroek (NED) 5:26.4	Ragnhild Hveger (DEN) 5:27.5	Lenore Kight-Wingard (USA) 5:29.0
1948	Ann Curtis (USA) 5:17.8	Karen Harup (DEN) 5:21.2	Cathy Gibson (GBR) 5:22.5
1952	Valeria Gyenge (HUN) 5:12.1	Eva Novak (HUN) 5:13.7	Evelyn Kawamoto (USA) 5:14.6
1956	Lorraine Crapp (USA) 4:54.6	Dawn Fraser (AUS) 5:02.5	Sylvia Ruuska (USA) 5:07.1
1960	Chris von Salza (USA) 4:50.6	Jane Cederquist (SWE) 4;53.9	Catharina Lagerberg (NED) 4:56.9
1964	Virginia Duenkel (USA) 4:43.3	Marilyn Ramenofsky (USA) 4:44.6	Terri Stickles (USA) 4:47.2
1968	Debbie Meyer (USA) 4;31.8	Linda Gustavson (USA) 4:35.5	Karen Moras (AUS) 4:37.0
1972	Shane Gould (AUS) 4:19.04	Novella Calligaris (ITA) 4:22.44	Gudrun Wegner (GDR) 4:23.11
1976	Petra Thuemer (GDR) 4:09.89	Shirley Babashoff (USA) 4:10.46	Shannon Smith (CAN) 4:14.60
1980	Ines Diers (GDR) 4:08.76	Petra Schneider (GDR) 4.09.16	Carmela Schmidt (GDR) 4:10.86
1984	Tiffany Cohen (USA) 4:07.10	Sarah Hardcastle (GBR) 4:10.27	June Croft (GBR) 4:11.49
1988	Janet Evans (USA) 4:03.85	Heike Friedrich (GDR) 4;05.94	Anke Möhring (GDR) 4:06.62
1992	Dagmar Hase (GER) 4:07.18	Janet Evans (USA) 4:07.37	Hayley Lewis (AUS) 4:11.22
1996	Michelle Smith (IRL) 4:07.25	Dagmar Hase (GER) 4:08.30	Kirsten Vlieghuis (NED) 4:08.70
2000	Brooke Bennett (USA) 4:05.80	Diana Munz (USA) 4:07.07	Claudia Poll (CRC) 4:07.83
2004	Laure Manaudou (FRA) 4;05.34	Otylia Jedrzejczak (POL) 4:05.84	Kaitlin Sandeno (USA) 4:06.19

1896-1912 Event not held
[1]300m

800 Metres Freestyle

1968	Debbie Meyer (USA) 9:24.0	Pamela Kruse (USA) 9:35.7	Maria Ramirez (MEX) 9:38.5
1972	Keena Rothhammer (USA) 8:53.68	Shane Gould (AUS) 8:56.39	Novella Calligaris (ITA) 8:57.46
1976	Petra Thuemer (GDR) 8:37.14	Shirley Babashoff (USA) 8:37.59	Wendy Weinberg (USA) 8:42.60
1980	Michelle Ford (AUS) 8:28.9	Ines Diers (GDR) 8:32.55	Heike Dähne (GDR) 8:33.48
1984	Tiffany Cohen (USA) 8:24.95	Michele Richardson (USA) 8:30.73	Sarah Hardcastle (GBR) 8:32.60
1988	Janet Evans (USA) 8:20.20	Astrid Strauss (GDR) 8:22.09	Julie McDonald (AUS) 8:22.93
1992	Janet Evans (USA) 8:25.52	Hayley Lewis (AUS) 8:30.34	Jana Henke (GER) 8:30.99
1996	Brooke Bennett (USA) 8:27.89	Dagmar Hase (GER) 8:29.91	Kirsten Vlieghuis (NED) 8:30.84
2000	Brooke Bennett (USA) 8:19.67	Jana Klochkova (UKR) 8:22.66	Kaitlin Sandeno (USA) 8:24.29
2004	Ai Shibata (JPN) 8:24.54	Laure Manaudou (FRA) 8:24.96	Diana Munz (USA) 8:26.61

1896-1964 Event not held

100 Metres Breaststroke

1968	Djurdjica Bjedov (YUG) 1:15.8	Galina Prozumenschchikova[1] (URS) 1:15.9	Sharon Wichman (USA) 1:16.1
1972	Catherine Carr (USA) 1:13.58	Galina Stepanova (URS) 1:14.99	Beverley Whitfield (AUS) 1:15.73
1976	Hannelore Anke (GDR) 1:11.16	Lubov Rusanova (URS) 1:13.04	Marina Kosheveya (URS) 1:13.30
1980	Ute Geweniger (GDR) 1:10.22	Elvira Vasilkova (URS) 1:10.41	Susanne Nielsson (DEN) 1:11.16
1984	Petra Van Staveren (NED) 1:09.88	Anne Ottenbrite (CAN) 1:10.69	Catherine Poirot (FRA) 1:10.70
1988	Tania Dangalakova (BUL) 1:07.95	Antoaneta Frankeva (BUL) 1:08.74	Silke Hörner (GDR) 1:08.83
1992	Yelena Rudkovskaya (EUN) 1:08.00	Anita Nall (USA) 1:08.17	Samantha Riley (AUS) 1:09.25
1996	Penny Heyns (RSA) 1:07.73	Amanda Beard (USA) 1:08.09	Samantha Riley (AUS) 1:09.18
2000	Megan Quann (USA) 1:07.05	Leisel Jones (AUS) 1:07.49	Penny Heyns (RSA) 1:07.55
2004	Xuejuan Luo (CHN) 1:06.64	Brooke Hanson (AUS) 1:07.15	Leisel Jones (AUS) 1:07.16

1896-1964 Event not held
[1]Later Stepanova

200 Metres Breaststroke

1924	Lucy Morton (GBR) 3:33.2	Agnes Geraghty (USA) 3:34.0	Gladys Carson (GBR) 3:35.4
1928	Hilde Schrader (GER) 3:12.6	Mietje Baron (NED) 3:15.2	Lotte Mühe (GER) 3:17.6
1932	Claire Dennis (AUS) 3:06.3	Hideko Maehata (JPN) 3:06.4	Else Jacobsen (DEN) 3:07.1
1936	Hideko Maehata (JPN) 3:03.6	Martha Genenger (GER) 3:04.2	Inge Sörensen (DEN) 3:07.8

1948	Petronella van Vliet (NED) 2:57.2	Nancy Lyons (AUS) 2:57.7	Eva Novák (HUN) 3:00.2
1952	Eva Székely[1] (HUN) 2:51.7	Eva Novák (HUN) 2:54.4	Helen Gordon (GBR) 2:57.6
1956	Ursula Happe[2] (GER) 2:53.1	Eva Székely (HUN) 2:54.8	Eva-Maria ten Elsen (GER) 2:55.1
1960	Anita Lonsbrough (GBR) 2:49.5	Wiltrud Urselmann (GER) 2:50.0	Barbara Göbel (GER) 2:53.6
1964	Galina Prozumenshchikova (URS) 2:46.4	Claudia Kolb (USA) 2:47.6	Svetlana Babanina (URS) 2:48.6
1968	Sharon Wichman (USA) 2:44.4	Djurdjica Bjedov (YUG) 2:46.4	Galina Prozumenshchikova (URS) 2:47.0
1972	Beverley Whitfield (AUS) 2:41.7	Dana Schoenfield (USA) 2:42.05	Galina Stepanova (URS) 2:42.36
1976	Marina Kosheveya (URS) 2:33.35	Marina Yurchenia (URS) 2:36.08	Lubov Rusanova (URS) 2:36.22
1980	Lina Kachushite (URS) 2:29.54	Svetlana Varganova (URS) 2:29.61	Yulia Bogdanova (URS) 2:32.39
1984	Anne Ottenbrite (CAN) 2:30.38	Susan Rapp (USA) 2:31.15	Ingrid Lempereur (BEL) 2:31.40
1988	Silke Hörner (GDR) 2:26.71	Huang Xiaomin (CHN) 2:27.49	Antoaneta Frankeva (BUL) 2:28.34
1992	Kyoko Iwasaki (JPN) 2:26.65	Li Lin (CHN) 2:26.85	Anita Nall (USA) 2:26.88
1996	Penny Heyns (RSA) 2:25.41	Amanda Beard (USA) 2:25.75	Agnes Kovacs (HUN) 2:26.57
2000	Agnes Kovacs (HUN) 2:24.35	Kristy Kowal (USA) 2:24.56	Amanda Beard (USA) 2:25.35
2004	Amanda Beard (USA) 2:23.37	Leisel Jones (AUS) 2:23.60	Anne Poleska (POL) 2:25.82

1896-1920 Event not held
[1]*Used then permitted butterfly stroke;* [2]*Used then permitted underwater technique*

100 Metres Backstroke

1924	Sybil Bauer (USA) 1:23.2	Phyllis Harding (GBR) 1:27.4	Aileen Riggin (USA) 1:28.2
1928	Marie Braun (NED) 1:22.0	Ellen King (GBR) 1:22.2	Joyce Cooper (GBR) 1:22.8
1932	Eleanor Holm (USA) 1:19.4	Philomena Mealing (AUS) 1:21.3	Valerie Davies (GBR) 1:22.5
1936	Dina Senff (NED) 1:18.9	Hendrika Mastenbroek (NED) 1:19.2	Alice Bridges (USA) 1:19.4
1948	Karen Harup (DEN) 1:14.4	Suzanne Zimmermann (USA) 1:16.0	Judy Davies (AUS) 1:16.7
1952	Joan Harrison (RSA) 1:14.3	Geertje Wielema (NED) 1:14.5	Jean Stewart (NZL) 1:15.8
1956	Judy Grinham (GBR) 1:12.9	Carin Cone (USA) 1:12.9	Margaret Edwards (GBR) 1:13.1
1960	Lynn Burke (USA) 1:09.3	Natalie Steward (GBR) 1:10.8	Satoko Tanaka (JPN) 1:11.4
1964	Cathy Ferguson (USA) 1:07.7	Cristine Caron (FRA) 1:07.9	Virginia Duenkel (USA) 1:08.0
1968	Kaye Hall (USA) 1:06.2	Elaine Tanner (CAN) 1:06.7	Jane Swaggerty (USA) 1:08.1
1972	Melissa Belote (USA) 1:05.78	Andrea Gyarmati (HUN) 1:06.26	Susie Atwood (USA) 1:06.34
1976	Ulrike Richter (GDR) 1:01.83	Birgit Treiber (GDR) 1:03.41	Nancy Garapick (CAN) 1:03.71
1980	Rica Reinisch (GDR) 1:00.86	Ina Kleber (GDR) 1:02.07	Petra Reidel (GDR) 1:02.64
1984	Theresa Andrews (USA) 1:02.55	Betsy Mitchell (USA) 1:02.63	Jolanda De Rover (NED) 1:02.91
1988	Kristin Otto (GDR) 1:00.89	Krisztina Egerszegi (HUN) 1:01.56	Cornelia Sirch (GDR) 1:01.57
1992	Krysztina Egerszegi (HUN) 1:00.68	Tunde Szabo (HUN) 1:01.14	Lea Loveless (USA) 1:01.43
1996	Beth Botsford (USA) 1:01.19	Whitney Hedgepeth (USA) 1:01.47	Marianne Kriel (RSA) 1:02.12
2000	Diana Mocanu (ROM) 1:00.21	Mai Nakamura (JPN) 1:00.55	Nina Schiwanevskaya (ESP) 1:00.89
2004	Natalie Coughlin (USA) 1:00.37	Kirsty Coventry (ZIM) 1:00.50	Laure Manaudou (FRA) 1:00.88

1896-1920 Event not held

200 Metres Backstroke

1968	Lillian Watson (USA) 2:24.8	Elaine Tanner (CAN) 2:27.4	Kaye Hall (USA) 2:28.9
1972	Melissa Belote (USA) 2:19.19	Susie Atwood (USA) 2:20.38	Donna Marie Gurr (CAN) 2:23.22
1976	Ulrike Richter (GDR) 2:13.43	Birgit Treiber (GDR) 2:14.97	Nancy Garapick (CAN) 2:15.60
1980	Rica Reinisch (GDR) 2:11.77	Cornelia Polit (GDR) 2:13.75	Birgit Treiber (GDR) 2:14.14
1984	Jolanda De Rover (NED) 2:12.38	Amy White (USA) 2:13.04	Aneta Patrascoiu (ROM) 2:13.29
1988	Krysztina Egerszegi (HUN) 2;09.29	Kathrin Zimmermann (GDR) 2:10.61	Cornelia Sirch (GDR) 2:11.45
1992	Krysztina Egerszegi (HUN) 2:07.06	Dagmar Hase (GER) 2:09.46	Nicole Stevenson (AUS) 2:10.20
1996	Krysztina Egerszegi (HUN) 2:07.83	Whitney Hedgepeth (USA) 2:11.98	Cathleen Rund (GER) 2:12.06
2000	Diana Mocanu (ROM) 2:08.16	Roxana Maracineanu (FRA) 2:10.25	Miki Nakao (JPN) 2:11.05
2004	Kirsty Coventry (ZIM) 2:09.19	Stanislava Komarova (US) 2:09.72	Reiko Nakamura (JPN) 2:09.88
			Antje Buschschulte (GER) 2:09.88

1896-1964 Event not held

100 Metres Butterfly

1956	Shelley Mann (USA) 1:11.0	Nancy Ramey (USA) 1:11.9	Mary Sears (USA) 1:14.4
1960	Carolyn Schuler (USA) 1:09.5	Marianne Heemskerk (NED) 1:10.4	Janice Andrew (AUS) 1:12.2
1964	Sharon Stouder (USA) 1:04.7	Ada Kok (NED) 1:05.6	Kathleen Ellis (USA) 1:06.0
1968	Lynette McClements (AUS) 1:05.5	Ellie Daniel (USA) 1:05.8	Susan Shields (USA) 1:06.2
1972	Mayumi Aoki (JPN) 1;03.34	Roswitha Beier (GDR) 1:03.61	Andrea Gyarmati (HUN) 1:03.73
1976	Kornelia Ender (GDR) 1:00.13	Andrea Pollack (GDR) 1:00.98	Wendy Bognoli (USA) 1:01.17
1980	Caren Metschuck (GDR) 1:00.42	Andrea Pollack (GDR) 1:00.90	Christiane Knacke (GDR) 1:01.44
1984	Mary Meagher (USA) 59.26	Jenna Johnson (USA) 1.00.19	Karin Seick (FRG) 1:00.36
1988	Kristin Otto (GDR) 59.00	Birte Weigang (GDR) 59.45	Qian Hong (CHN) 59.52
1992	Qian Hong (CHN) 58.62	Chrissy Ahmann-Leighton (USA) 58.74	Catherine Plewinski (FRA) 59.01
1996	Amy van Dyken (USA) 59.13	Liu Limin (CHN) 59.14	Angel Martino (USA) 59.23

| 2000 | Inge de Bruijn (NED) 56.61 | Martina Moravcova (SVK) 57.97 | Dara Torres (USA) 58.20 |
| 2004 | Petria Thomas (AUS) 57.72 | Otylia Jedrzejczak (POL) 57.84 | Inge de Bruijn (NED) 57.99 |

1896-1952 Event not held

200 Metres Butterfly

1968	Ada Kok (NED) 2:24.7	Helga Lindner (GDR) 2:24.8	Ellie Daniel (USA) 2:25.9
1972	Karen Moe (USA) 2:15.57	Lynn Colella (USA) 2:16.34	Ellie Daniel (USA) 2:26.74
1976	Andrea Pollack (GDR) 2:11.41	Ulrike Tauber (GDR) 2:12.45	Rosemarie Gabriel (GDR) 2:12.86
1980	Ines Geissler (GDR) 2:10.44	Sybille Schönrock (GDR) 2:10.45	Michelle Ford (AUS) 2:11.66
1984	Mary Meagher (USA) 2:06.90	Karen Phillips (AUS) 2:10.56	Ina Beyermann (FRG) 2:11.91
1988	Kathleen Nord (GDR) 2:09.51	Birte Weigang (GDR) 2:09.91	Mary Meagher (USA) 2:10.80
1992	Summer Sanders (USA) 2:08.67	Wang Xiaohong (CHN) 2:09.01	Susie O'Neill (AUS) 2:09.03
1996	Susie O'Neill (AUS) 2:07.76	Petria Thomas (AUS) 2:09.82	Michelle Smith (IRL) 2:09.91
2000	Misty Hyman (USA) 2:05.88	Susie O'Neill (AUS) 2:06.58	Petria Thomas (AUS) 2:07.12
2004	Otylia Jedrzejczak (POL) 2:06.05	Petria Thomas (AUS) 2:06.36	Yuko Nakanishi (JPN) 2:08.04

1896-1964 Event not held

200 Metres Individual Medley

1968	Claudia Kolb (USA) 2:24.7	Susan Pedersen (USA) 2:28.8	Jan Henne (USA) 2:31.4
1972	Shane Gould (AUS) 2:23.07	Kornelia Ender (GDR) 2:23.59	Lynn Vidali (USA) 2:24.06
1984	Tracy Caulkins (USA) 2:12.64	Nancy Hogshead (USA) 2:15.17	Michele Pearson (AUS) 2:15.92
1988	Daniela Hunger (GDR) 2:12.59	Yelena Dendoberova (URS) 2:13.31	Noemi Ildiko Lung (ROM) 2:14.85
1992	Li Lin (CHN) 2:11.65	Summer Sanders (USA) 2:11.91	Daniela Hunger (GDR) 2:13.62
1996	Michelle Smith (IRL) 2:13.93	Marianne Limpert (CAN) 2:14.35	Lin Li (CHN) 2:14.74
2000	Jana Klochkova (UKR) 2:10.68	Beatrice Caslaru (ROM) 2:12.57	Cristina Teuscher (USA) 2:13.32
2004	Jana Klochkova (UKR) 2:11.14	Amanda Beard (USA) 2:11.70	Kirsty Coventry (ZIM) 2:12.72

1896-1964, 1976-1980 Event not held

400 Metres Individual Medley

1964	Donna De Varona (USA) 5:18.7	Sharon Finneran (USA) 5:24.1	Martha Randall (USA) 5:24.1
1968	Claudia Kolb (USA) 5:08.5	Lynn Vidali (USA) 5:22.2	Sabine Steinbach (GDR) 5:25.3
1972	Gail Neall (AUS) 5:02.97	Loolie Cliff (CAN) 5:03.57	Novella Calligaris (ITA) 5:03.99
1976	Ulrike Tauber (GDR) 4:42.77	Cheryl Gibson (CAN) 4:48.10	Becky Smith (CAN) 4:50.48
1980	Petra Schneider (GDR) 4:36.29	Sharron Davies (GBR) 4:46.83	Agnieszka Czopek (POL) 4:48.17
1984	Tracy Caulkins (USA) 4:39.24	Suzanne Landells (AUS) 4:48.30	Petra Zindler (FRG) 4:48.57
1988	Janet Evans (USA) 4:37.76	Noemi Ildiko Lung (ROM) 4:39.46	Daniela Hunger (GDR) 4:39.76
1992	Krysztina Egerszegi (HUN) 4:36.54	Li Lin (CHN) 4:36.73	Summer Sanders (USA) 4:37.58
1996	Michelle Smith (IRL) 4:39.18	Allison Wagner (USA) 4:42.03	Krysztina Egerszegi (HUN) 4:42.53
2000	Jana Klochkova (UKR) 4:33.59	Yasuko Tajima (JPN) 4:35.96	Beatrice caslaru (ROM) 4:37.18
2004	Jana Klochkova (UKR) 4:34.83	Kaitlin Sandeno (USA) 4:34.95	Georgina Bardach (ARG) 4:37.51

1896-1960 Event not held

4x100 Metres Freestyle Relay

1912	GREAT BRITAIN 5:52.8	GERMANY 6:04.6	AUSTRIA 6:17.0
1920	UNITED STATES 5:11.6	GREAT BRITAIN 5:40.8	SWEDEN 5:43.6
1924	UNITED STATES 4:58.8	GREAT BRITAIN 5:17.0	SWEDEN 5:35.6
1928	UNITED STATES 4:47.6	GREAT BRITAIN 5:02.8	SOUTH AFRICA 5:13.4
1932	UNITED STATES 4:38.0	NETHERLANDS 4:47.5	GREAT BRITAIN 4:52.4
1936	NETHERLANDS 4:36.0	GERMANY 4:36.8	UNITED STATES 4:40.2
1948	UNITED STATES 4:29.2	DENMARK 4:29.6	NETHERLANDS 4:31.6
1952	HUNGARY 4:24.4	NETHERLANDS 4:29.0	UNITED STATES 4:30.1
1956	AUSTRALIA 4:17.1	UNITED STATES 4:19.2	SOUTH AFRICA 4:25.7
1960	UNITED STATES 4:08.9	AUSTRALIA 4:11.3	GERMANY 4:19.7
1964	UNITED STATES 4:03.8	AUSTRALIA 4:06.9	NETHERLANDS 4:12.0
1968	UNITED STATES 4:02.5	GDR 4:05.7	CANADA 4:07.2
1972	UNITED STATES 3:55.19	GDR 3:55.55	FRG 3:57.93
1976	UNITED STATES 3:44.82	GDR 3:45.50	CANADA 3:48.81
1980	GDR 3:42.71	SWEDEN 3:48.93	NETHERLANDS 3:49.51
1984	UNITED STATES 3:43.43	NETHERLANDS 3:44.40	FRG 3:45.56
1988	GDR 3:40.63	NETHERLANDS 3:43.39	UNITED STATES 3:44.25
1992	UNITED STATES 3:39.46	CHINA 3:40.12	GERMANY 3:41.60
1996	UNITED STATES 3:39.29	CHINA 3:40.48	GERMANY 3:41.48
2000	UNITED STATES 3:36.61	NETHERLANDS 3:39.83	SWEDEN 3:40.30
2004	AUSTRALIA 3:35.94	UNITED STATES 3:36.39	NETHERLANDS 3:37.59

1896-1908 Event not held

4 X 200 Metres Freestyle Relay

1996	UNITED STATES 7:59.87	GERMANY 8:01.55	AUSTRALIA 8:05.47
2000	UNITED STATES 7:57.80	AUSTRALIA 7:58.52	GERMANY 7:58.64
2004	UNITED STATES 7:53.42	CHINA 7:55.97	GERMANY 7:57.35

1896-1992 Event not held

4 X 100 Metres Medley Relay

1960	UNITED STATES 4:41.1	AUSTRALIA 4:45.9	GERMANY 4:47.6
1964	UNITED STATES 4:33.9	NETHERLANDS 4:37.0	SOVIET UNION 4:39.2
1968	UNITED STATES 4:28.3	AUSTRALIA 4:30.0	FRG 4:36.4
1972	UNITED STATES 4:20.75	GDR 4:24.91	FRG 4:26.46
1976	GDR 4:06.95	UNITED STATES 4:14.55	CANADA 4:15.22
1980	GDR 4:06.67	GREAT BRITAIN 4:12.24	SOVIET UNION 4:13.61
1984	UNITED STATES 4:08.34	FRG 4:11.97	CANADA 4:12.98
1988	GDR 4:03.74	UNITED STATES 4:07.90	CANADA 4:10.49
1992	UNITED STATES 4:02.54	GERMANY 4:05.19	UNIFIED TEAM 4:06.44
1996	UNITED STATES 4:02.88	AUSTRALIA 4:05.08	CHINA 4:07.34
2000	UNITED STATES 3:58.30	AUSTRALIA 4:01.59	JAPAN 4:04.16
2004	AUSTRALIA 3:57.32	UNITED STATES 3:59.12	GERMANY 4:00.72

1896-1956 Event not held

DIVING

Men

Springboard

1908	Albert Turner (GER) 85.5	Kurt Behrens (GER) 85.3	George Giadzik (USA) 80.8
			Gottlob Walz (GER) 80.8
1912	Paul Günther (GER) 79.23	Hans Luber (GER) 76.78	Kurt Behrens (GER) 73.73
1920	Louis Kuehn (USA) 675.4	Clarence Pinkston (USA) 655.3	Louis Balbach (USA) 649.5
1924	Albert White (USA) 696.4	Pete Desjardins (USA) 693.2	Clarence Pinkston (USA) 653
1928	Pete Desjardins (USA) 185.04	Michael Galitzen (USA) 174.06	Farid Simaika (EGY) 172.46
1932	Michael Galitzen (USA) 161.38	Harold Smith (USA) 158.54	Richard Degener (USA) 151.82
1936	Richard Degener (USA) 163.57	Marshall Wayne (USA) 159.56	Al Greene (USA) 146.29
1948	Bruce Harlan (USA) 163.64	Mlller Anderson (USA) 157.29	Samuel Lee (USA) 145.52
1952	David Browning (USA) 205.29	Miller Anderson (USA) 199.84	Robert Clotworthy (USA) 184.92
1956	Robert Clotworthy (USA) 159.56	Donald Harper (USA) 156.23	Joaquin Capilla Pérez (MEX) 162.30
1960	Gary Tobian (USA) 170.00	Samuel Hall (USA) 167.08	Juan Botella (MEX) 162.30
1964	Kenneth Sitzberger (USA) 159.90	Francis Gorman (USA) 157.63	Larry Andreasen (USA) 143.77
1968	Bernard Wrightson (USA) 170.15	Klaus Dibiasi (ITA) 159.74	James Henry (USA) 158.09
1972	Vladimir Vasin (URS) 594.09	F Giorgio Cagnotto (ITA) 591.63	Craig Lincoln (USA) 577.29
1976	Philip Boggs (USA) 619.05	F Giorgio Cagnotto (ITA) 570.48	Alexander Kosenkov (URS) 567.24
1980	Alexander Portnov (URS) 905.025	Carlos Giron (MEX) 892.140	F Giorgio Cagnotto (ITA) 871.500
1984	Greg Louganis (USA) 754.41	Tan Liangde (CHN) 662.31	Ronald Merriott (USA) 661.32
1988	Greg Louganis (USA) 730.80	Tan Liangde (CHN) 704.88	Li Deliang (CHN) 665.28
1992	Mark Lenzi (USA) 676.530	Tan Liangde (CHN) 645.570	Dmitri Sautin (EUN) 627.780
1996	Ni Xiong (CHN) 701.46	Yu Zhoucheng (CHN) 690.93	Mark Lenzi (USA) 686.49
2000	Ni Xiong (CHN) 708.72	Fernando Platas (MEX) 708.42	Dimitri Sautin (RUS) 703.20
2004	Bo Peng (CHN) 787.38	Alexandre Despatie (CAN) 755.97	Dmitri Sautin (RUS) 753.27

1896-1906 Event not held

Springboard Synchronised

Introduced in 2000

2000	CHINA 365,58	RUSSIA 329.97	AUSTRALIA 322.86
2004	GREECE 353.34	GERMANY 350.01	AUSTRALIA 349.59

Platform

1904[1]	George Shelton (USA) 12.66	Georg Hoffmann (GER) 11.66	Frank Kehoe (USA) 11.33
			Alfred Braunschweiger (GER) 11.33
1906	Gottlob Walz (GER) 156.00	Georg Hoffmann (GER) 150.20	Otto Satzinger (AUT) 147.40
1908	Hajalmar Johansson (SWE) 83.75	Karl Malmström (SWE) 78.73	Arvid Spangberg (SWE) 74.00
1912	Erik Adlerz (SWE) 73.94	Albert Zürner (GER) 72.60	Gustaf Blomgren (SWE) 69.56
1920	Clarence Pinkston (USA) 100.67	Erik Adlerz (SWE) 99.08	Haig Prieste (USA) 93.73
1924	Albert White (USA) 97.46	David Fall (USA) 97.30	Clarence Pinkston (USA) 94.60

1928	Pete Desjardins (USA) 98.74	Farid Simiaka (EGY) 99.58	Michael Galitzen (USA) 92.34
1932	Harold Smith (USA) 124.80	Michael Galitzen (USA) 124.28	Frank Kurtz (USA) 121.98
1936	Marshall Wayne (USA) 113.58	Elbert Root (USA) 110.60	Hermann Stork (GER) 110.31
1948	Samuel Lee (USA) 130.05	Bruce Harlan (USA) 122.30	Joaquin Capilla Pérez (MEX) 113.52
1952	Samuel Lee (USA) 156.28	Joaquin Capilla Pérez (MEX) 145.21	Günther Haase (GER) 141.31
1956	Joaquin Capilla Pérez (MEX) 152.44	Gary Tobian (USA) 152.41	Richard Connor (USA) 149.79
1960	Robert Webster (USA) 165.56	Gary Tobian (USA) 165.25	Brian Phelps (GBR) 157.13
1964	Robert Webster (USA) 148.58	Klaus Dibiasi (ITA) 147.54	Thomas Gompf (USA) 153.93
1968	Klaus Dibiasi (ITA) 164.18	Alvaro Gaxiola (MEX) 154.49	Edwin Young (USA) 153.93
1972	Klaus Dibiasi (ITA) 504.12	Richard Rydze (USA) 480.75	F Giorgio Cagnotto (ITA) 475.83
1976	Klaus Dibiasi (ITA) 600.51	Greg Louganis (USA) 576.99	Vladimir Aleynik (URS) 548.61
1980	Falk Hoffmann (GDR) 835.650	Vladimir Aleynik (URS) 819.705	David Ambartsumyan (URS) 817.440
1984	Greg Louganis (USA) 710.91	Bruce Kimball (USA) 643.50	Li Kongzheng (CHN) 638.28
1988	Greg Louganis (USA) 638.61	Ni Xiong (CHN) 637.47	Jesus Mena (MEX) 594.39
1992	Sun Shunwei (CHN) 677.310	Scott Donie (USA) 633.630	Ni Xiong (CHN) 600.150
1996	Dmitri Sautin (RUS) 692.34	Jan Hempel (GER) 663.27	Hailiang Xiao (CHN) 658.20
2000	Liang Tian (CHN) 724.53	Jia Hu (CHN) 713.55	Dimitri Sautin (RUS) 679.26
2004	Jia Hu (CHN) 748.08	Mathew Helm (AUS) 730.56	Liang ian (CHN) 729.66

1896-1900 Event not held
[1]*Combined springboard and platform event*

Platform Synchronised

Introduced in 2000

2000	RUSSIA 365.04	CHINA 358.74	GERMANY 338.88
2004	CHINA 383.88	GREAT BRITAIN 371.52	AUSTRALIA 366.84

Women

Springboard

1920	Aileen Riggin (USA) 539.9	Helen Wainwright (USA) 534.8	Thelma Payne (USA) 534.1
1924	Elizabeth Becker (USA) 474.5	Aileen Riggin (USA) 460.4	Caroline Fletcher (USA) 434.4
1928	Helen Meany (USA) 78.62	Dorothy Poynton (USA) 75.62	Georgia Coleman (USA) 73.78
1932	Georgia Coleman (USA) 87.52	Katherine Rawls (USA) 82.56	Jane Fauntz (USA) 82.12
1936	Majorie Gestring (USA) 89.27	Katherine Rawls (USA) 88.35	Dorothy Poynton-Hill (USA) 82.36
1948	Victoria Draves (USA) 108.74	Zoe Ann Olsen (USA) 108.23	Patricia Elsener (USA) 101.30
1952	Patricia McCormick (USA) 147.30	Madeleine Moreau (FRA) 139.34	Zoe Ann Jensen (USA) 127.57
1956	Patricia McCormick (USA) 142.36	Jeanne Stunyo (USA) 125.89	Irene MacDonald (CAN) 121.40
1960	Ingrid Krämer (GER) 155.81	Paula Myers-Pope (USA) 141.24	Elizabeth Ferris (GBR) 139.09
1964	Ingrid Krämer-Engel (GER) 145.00	Jeanne Collier (USA) 138.36	Mary Willard (USA) 138.18
1968	Sue Gossick (USA) 150.77	Tamara Pogozheva (URS) 145.30	Keala O'Sullivan (USA) 145.23
1972	Micki King (USA) 450.03	Ulrika Knape (SWE) 434.19	Marina Janicke (GDR) 430.92
1976	Jennifer Chandler (USA) 506.19	Christa Kohler (GDR) 469.41	Cynthia McIngvale (USA) 466.83
1980	Irina Kalinina (URS) 725.910	Martina Proeber (GDR) 698.895	Karin Guthke (GDR) 685.245
1984	Sylvie Bernier (CAN) 530.70	Kelly McCormick (USA) 527.46	Christina Seufert (USA) 517.62
1988	Gao Min (CHN) 580.23	Li Qing (CHN) 534.33	Kelly Anne McCormick (USA) 533.19
1992	Gao Min (CHN) 572.400	Irina Laschko (EUN) 514.140	Brita Baldus (GER) 503.070
1996	Fu Mingxia (CHN) 547.68	Irina Laschko (RUS) 512.19	Annie Pelletier (CAN) 509.64
2000	Fu Mingxia (CHN) 609.42	Jingjing Guo (CHN) 597.81	Dörte Lindner (GER) 574.35
2004	Jingjing Guo (CHN) 633.15	Minzia Wu (CHN) 612.00	Yulia Pakhalina (RUS) 610.62

1896-1912 Event not held

Springboard Synchronised

Introduced in 2000

2000	CHINA 345.12	CANADA 312.03	AUSTRALIA 301.50
2004	CHINA 352.14	RUSSIA 340.92	CANADA 327.78

Platform

1912	Greta Johnson (SWE) 39.9	Lisa Regnell (SWE) 36.0	Isabelle White (GBR) 34.0
1920	Stefani Fryland-Clausen (DEN) 34.6	Eileen Armstrong (GBR) 33.3	Eva Ollivier (SWE) 33.3
1924	Caroline Smith (USA) 10.5	Elizabeth Becker (USA) 11.0	Hjördis Töpel (SWE) 15.5
1928	Elizabeth Pinkston (USA) 31.6	Georgia Coleman (USA) 30.6	Lala Sjöqvist (SWE) 29.2
1932	Dorothy Poynton (USA) 40.26	Georgia Coleman (USA) 35.56	Marion Roper (USA) 35.22
1936	Dorothy Poynton-Hill (USA) 33.93	Velma Dunn (USA) 33.63	Käthe Köhler (GER) 33.43
1948	Victoria Draves (USA) 68.87	Patricia Elsener (USA) 66.28	Birte Christoffersen (DEN) 66.04

1952 Patricia McCormick (USA) 79.37	Paula Myers (USA) 71.63	Juno Irwin (USA) 70.49
1956 Patricia McCormick (USA) 84.85	Juno Irwin (USA) 81.64	Paula Myers (USA) 81.58
1960 Ingrid Krämer (GER) 91.28	Paula Myers-Pope (USA) 88.94	Ninel Krutova (URS) 86.99
1964 Lesley Bush (USA) 99.80	Ingrid Krämer-Engel (GER) 98.45	Galina Alekseyeva (URS) 97.60
1968 Milena Duchkova (TCH) 109.59	Natalia Lobanova (URS) 105.14	Ann Peterson (USA) 101.11
1972 Ulrika Knape (SWE) 390.00	Milena Duchkova (TCH) 370.92	Marina Janicke (GDR) 360.54
1976 Elena Vaytsekhovskaya (URS) 406.59	Ulrika Knape (SWE) 402.60	Deborah Wilson (USA) 401.07
1980 Martina Jäschke (GDR) 596.250	Servard Emirzyan (URS) 576.465	Liana Tsotadze (URS) 575.925
1984 Zhou Jihong (CHN) 435.51	Michele Mitchell (USA) 431.19	Wendy Wyland (USA) 422.07
1988 Xu Yanmei (CHN) 445.20	Michele Mitchell (USA) 436.95	Wendy Williams (USA) 400.44
1992 Fu Mingxia (CHN) 461.430	Yelena Mirochina (EUN) 411.630	Mary Ellen Clark (USA) 401.910
1996 Fu Mingxia (CHN) 521.58	Annika Walter (GER) 429.22	Mary Ellen Clark (USA) 472.95
2000 Laura Wilkinson (USA)	Li Na (CHN) 542.01	Anne Montminy (CAN) 540.15
2004 Chantelle Newbery (AUS) 590.31	Lishi Lao (CHN) 576.30	Loudy Tourky (AUS) 561.66

1896-1908 Event not held

Platform Synchronised

Introduced in 2000

2000 RUSSIA 332.64	CHINA 321.60	UKRAINE 290.34
2004 CHINA 336.90	RUSSIA 330.84	AUSTRALIA 309.30

SYNCHRONISED SWIMMING

Solo

1984 Tracie Ruiz (USA) 198.467	Carolyn Waldo (CAN) 195.300	Miwako Motoyoshi (JPN) 187.050
1988 Carolyn Waldo (CAN) 200.150	Tracie Ruiz-Conforto (USA) 197.633	Miwako Motoyoshi (JPN) 191.850
1992 Kristen Babb-Sprague (USA) 191.848	–	Fumiko Okuno (JPN) 187.056
Sylvia Frechette (CAN) 191.717[1]		

1896-1980, 1996-2004 Event not held

[1]*There was a controversial judging mix up, and belatedly Frechette was promoted to joint gold medallist*

Duet

1984 UNITED STATES 195.584	CANADA 194.234	JAPAN 187.992
1988 CANADA 197.717	UNITED STATES 197.284	JAPAN 190.159
1992 UNITED STATES 192.175	CANADA 189.394	JAPAN 186.868
1996 UNITED STATES 99.720	CANADA 98.367	JAPAN 97.753
2000 RUSSIA 99.580	JAPAN 98.650	FRANCE 97.437
2004 RUSSIA 99.334	JAPAN 98.417	UNITED STATES 96.918

1896-1980 Event not held

Team

1996 UNITED STATES 99.720	CANADA 98.367	JAPAN 97.753
2000 RUSSIA 99.146	JAPAN 98.860	CANADA 97.357
2004 RUSSIA 99.501	JAPAN 98.501	UNITED STATES 97.418

1896-1992 Event not held

WATER POLO

Men

1900[1] GREAT BRITAIN	BELGIUM	FRANCE
1908 GREAT BRITAIN	BELGIUM	SWEDEN
1912 GREAT BRITAIN	SWEDEN	BELGIUM
1920 GREAT BRITAIN	BELGIUM	SWEDEN
1924 FRANCE	BELGIUM	UNITED STATES
1928 GERMANY	HUNGARY	FRANCE
1932 HUNGARY	GERMANY	UNITED STATES
1936 HUNGARY	GERMANY	BELGIUM
1948 ITALY	HUNGARY	NETHERLANDS
1952 HUNGARY	YUGOSLAVIA	ITALY
1956 HUNGARY	YUGOSLAVIA	SOVIET UNION
1960 ITALY	SOVIET UNION	HUNGARY
1964 HUNGARY	YUGOSLAVIA	SOVIET UNION
1968 YUGOSLAVIA	SOVIET UNION	HUNGARY
1972 SOVIET UNION	HUNGARY	UNITED STATES

1976	HUNGARY	ITALY	NETHERLANDS
1980	SOVIET UNION	YUGOSLAVIA	HUNGARY
1984	YUGOSLAVIA	UNITED STATES	FRG
1988	YUGOSLAVIA	UNITED STATES	SOVIET UNION
1992	ITALY	SPAIN	UNIFIED TEAM
1996	SPAIN	CROATIA	ITALY
2000	HUNGARY	RUSIA	YUGOSLAVIA
2004	HUNGARY	SERBIA/MONTENEGRO	RUSSIA

1896, 1904-06 Event not held
[1]Entries were from clubs, not international teams

Women

Introduced in 2000

2000	AUSTRALIA	UNITED STATES	RUSSIA
2004	ITALY	GREECE	UNITED STATES

TABLE TENNIS

Introduced in 1988

Men

Singles

1988	Yoo Nam-Kyu (KOR)	Kim Ki-Taik (KOR)	Erik Lindh (SWE)
1992	Jan-Ove Waldner (SWE)	Jean-Philippe Gatien (FRA)	Ma Wenge (CHN)
			Kim Taek-Soo (KOR)
1996	Liu Guoliang (CHN)	Wang Tao (CHN)	Jörg Rosskoff (GER)
2000	Linghui Kong (CHN)	Jan-Ove Waldner (SWE)	Guoliang Liu (CHN)
2004	Seung-Min Ryu (KOR)	Hao Wang (CHN)	Liqin Wang (CHN)

Doubles

1988	CHINA	YUGOSLAVIA	KOREA
1992	CHINA	GERMANY	KOREA
			KOREA
1996	CHINA	CHINA	KOREA
2000	CHINA	CHINA	FRANCE
2004	CHINA	HONG KONG	DENMARK

Women

1988	Chen Jing (CHN)	Li Huifen (CHN)	Jiao Zhimin (CHN)
1992	Deng Yaping (CHN)	Qiao Hong (CHN)	Hyung Jung-Hwa (KOR)
			Li Bun-Hui (PRK)
1996	Deng Yaping (CHN)	Jing Chen (TPE)	Qiao Hong (CHN)
2000	Nan Wang (CHN)	Ju Li (CHN)	Jing Chen (TPE)
2004	Yining Zhang (CHN)	Hyang-Mi Kim (PRK)	Kyung-Ah Kim (KOR)

Doubles

1988	KOREA	CHINA	YUGOSLAVIA
1992	CHINA	CHINA	KOREA
			PRK
1996	CHINA	CHINA	KOREA
2000	CHINA	CHINA	KOREA
2004	CHINA	KOREA	CHINA

TAEKWONDO

Introduced in 2000

Men

Up to 58kg

2000	Michail Mouroutsos (GRE)	Gabriel Esparza (ESP)	Chih-Hsiung Huang (TPE)
2004	Mu Yen Chu (TPE)	Oscar Salazar Blanco (MEX)	Tamer Bayoumi (EGY)

Up to 68kg

2000	Steven Lopez (USA)	Joon-Sik Sin (KOR)	Hadi Saeibonehkohal (IRI)
2004	Hadi Saei Bonehkohal (IRI)	Chih-Hsiung Huang (TPE)	Myeong-Seob Song (KOR)

Up to 80kg

2000	Angel Fuentes (CUB)	Faissal Ebnoutalib (GER)	Victor Garibay (MEX)
2004	Steven Lopez (USA)	Bahri Tanrikulu (TUR)	Yossef Karami (IRI)

Over 80kg

2000	Kyong-Hun Kim (KOR)	Daniel Trenton (AUS)	Pascal Gentil (FRA)
2004	Dae Sung Moon (KOR)	Alexandros Nikolaidis (GRE)	Pascal Gentil (FRA)

Women

Up to 49kg

2000	Lauren Burns (AUS)	Urdia Rodriguez (CUB)	Shu-Ju Chi (TPE)
2004	Shih Hsin Chen (TPE)	Yanelis Labrada Diaz (CUB)	Yaowapa Boorapolchai (THA)

Up to 57kg

2000	Jae-Eun Jung (KOR)	Hieu Ngan Tran (VIE)	Hamide Bikcin (TUR)
2004	Ji Won Jang (KOR)	Nia Abdallah (USA)	Iridia Salazar Blanco (MEX)

Up to 67kg

2000	Sun-Hee Lee (KOR)	Trude Gunderesen (NOR)	Yoriko Okamoto (JPN)
2004	Wei Luo (CHN)	Elisavet Mystakidou (GRE)	Kyung Sun Hwang (KOR)

Over 67kg

2000	Zhong Chen (CHN)	Natalya Ivanova (RUS)	Dominique Bosshart (CAN)
2004	Zhong Chen (CHN)	Myriam Bavarel (FRA)	Adriana Carmona (VEN)

TENNIS

Men

Singles

1896[1]	John Boland (GBR)	Dionysios Kasdaglis (GRE)	Momcilló Tapavica (HUN)
			Konstantinos Paspatis (GRE)
1900[1]	Hugh Doherty (GBR)	Harold Mahoney (GBR)	Reginald Doherty (GBR)
			Arthur Norris (GBR)
1904[1]	Beals Wright (USA)	Robert LeRoy (USA)	Edgar Leonard (USA)
			Alphonzo Bell (USA)
1906	Max Décugis (FRA)	Maurice Germot (FRA)	Zdenek Zemla (BOH)
1908	Josiah Ritchie (GBR)	Otto Froitzheim (GER)	Wilberforce Eves (GBR)
1908[2]	Wentworth Gore (GBR)	George Caridia (GBR)	Josiah Ritchie (GBR)
1912	Charles Winslow (RSA)	Harold Kitson (RSA)	Oscar Kreuzer (GER)
1912[2]	André Gobert (FRA)	Charles Dixon (GBR)	Anthony Wilding (NZL)
1920	Louis Raymond (RSA)	Ichiya Kumagae (JPN)	Charles Winslow (GBR)
1924	Vincent Reynolds (USA)	Henri Cochet (FRA)	Umberto De Morpurgo (ITA)
1988[1]	Miloslav Mecir (TCH)	Tim Mayotte (USA)	Stefan Edberg (SWE)
			Brad Gilbert (USA)
1992[1]	Marc Rosset (SUI)	Jordi Arrese (ESP)	Goran Ivanisevic (CRO)
			Andrei Cherkasov (EUN)
1996	Andre Agassi (USA)	Sergi Bruguera (ESP)	Leander Paes (IND)
2000	Yevgeni Kafelnikov (RUS)	Thomas Haas (GER)	Arnaud di Pasquale (FRA)
2004	Nicolas Massu (CHI)	Mardy Fish (USA)	Fernando Gonzalez (CHI)

1928-1984 Event not held
[1]Two bronze medals; [2]Indoor tournaments

Doubles

1896	GBR/GERMANY	GREECE	GREAT BRITAIN/AUSTRALIA
1900[1]	GREAT BRITAIN	USA/FRANCE	FRANCE
			GREAT BRITAIN
1904[1]	UNITED STATES	UNITED STATES	UNITED STATES
			UNITED STATES
1906	FRANCE	GREECE	BOHEMIA
1908	GREAT BRITAIN	GREAT BRITAIN	GREAT BRITAIN
1908[2]	GREAT BRITAIN	GREAT BRITAIN	SWEDEN
1912	SOUTH AFRICA	AUSTRIA	FRANCE

1912² FRANCE	SWEDEN	GREAT BRITAIN
1920 GREAT BRITAIN	JAPAN	FRANCE
1924 UNITED STATES	FRANCE	FRANCE
1988¹ UNITED STATES	SPAIN	CZECHOSLOVAKIA
		SWEDEN
1992¹ GERMANY	SOUTH AFRICA	CROATIA
		ARGENTINA
1996 AUSTRALIA	GREAT BRITAIN	GERMANY
2000 CANADA	AUSTRALIA	SPAIN
2004 CHILE	GERMANY	CROATIA

1928-1984 Event not held
¹Two bronze medals; ²Indoor tournaments

Women

Singles

1900¹ Charlotte Cooper (GBR)	Hélène Prévost (FRA)	Marion Jones (USA)
		Hedwiga Rosenbaumova (BOH)
1906 Esmee Simiriotou (GRE)	Sophia Marinou (GRE)	Euphrosine Paspati (GRE)
1908 Dorothea Chambers (GBR)	Dorothy Boothby (GBR)	Joan Winch (GBR)
1908² Gwen Eastlake-Smith (GBR)	Angela Greene (GBR)	Märtha Adlerstrahle (SWE)
1912 Marguerite Broquedis (FRA)	Dora Köring (GER)	Molla Bjurstedt (NOR)
1912² Ethel Hannam (GBR)	Thora Castenschoid (DEN)	Mabel Parton (GBR)
1920 Suzanne Lenglen (FRA)	Dorothy Holman (GBR)	Kitty McKane (GBR)
1924 Helen Wills (USA)	Julie Vlasto (FRA)	Kitty McKane (GBR)
1988¹ Steffi Graf (FRG)	Gabriela Sabatini (ARG)	Zina Garrison (USA)
		Manuela Maleyeva (BUL)
1992¹ Jennifer Capriati (USA)	Steffi Graf (GER)	Mary-Jo Fernandez (USA)
		Arantxa Sanchez-Vicario (ESP)
1996 Lindsay Davenport (USA)	Arantxa Sanchez-Vicario (ESP)	Jana Novotna (CZE)
2000 Venus Williams (USA)	Yelena Dementyeva (RUS)	Monica Seles (USA)
2004 Justine Henin-Hardenne (BEL)	Amelie Mauresmo (FRA)	Alicia Molik (AUS)

1928-1984 Event not held
¹Two bronze medals; ²Indoor tournaments

Doubles

1920 GREAT BRITAIN	GREAT BRITAIN	FRANCE
1924 UNITED STATES	GREAT BRITAIN	GREAT BRITAIN
1988¹ UNITED STATES	CZECHOSLOVAKIA	AUSTRALIA
		FRG
1992¹ UNITED STATES	SPAIN	AUSTRALIA
		UNIFIED TEAM
1996 UNITED STATES	CZECH REPUBLIC	SPAIN
2000 UNITED STATES	NETHERLANDS	BELGIUM
2004 CHINA	SPAIN	ARGENTINA

1928-1984 Event not held
¹Two bronze medals

Mixed Doubles

1900¹ GREAT BRITAIN	FRANCE/GBR	BOHEMIA/GBR
		UNITED STATES/GBR
1906 FRANCE	GREECE	GREECE
1912 GERMANY	SWEDEN	FRANCE
1912² GREAT BRITAIN	GREAT BRITAIN	SWEDEN
1920 FRANCE	GREAT BRITAIN	CZECHOSLOVAKIA
1924 UNITED STATES	UNITED STATES	NETHERLANDS

1928-2004 Event not held
¹Two bronze medals; ²Indoor tournaments

TRAMPOLINING

Introduced in 2000
(Part of the Gymnastics programme)

Men

2000 Alexander Moskalenko (RUS) 41.70	Ji Wallace (AUS) 39.30	Mathieu Turgeon (CAN) 39.10
2004 Yuri Nikitin (UKR) 41.50	Alexander Moskalenko (RUS) 41.20	Henrik Stehlik (GER) 40.80

Women

2000	Irina Karavayeva (RUS) 38.90	Oxana Tsyhuleva (UKR) 37.70	Karen Cockburn (CAN) 37.40
2004	Anna Dogonadze (GER) 39.60	Karen Cockburn (CAN) 39.20	Shanshan Huang (CHN) 39.00

TRIATHLON

Introduced in 2000
(Consists of a 1500m swim, 40km cycle and 10km run)

Men

2000	Simon Whitfield (CAN) 1:48:24	Stephan Vuckovic (GER) 1:48:37	Jan Rehula (CZE) 1:48:46
2004	Hamish Carter (NZL) 1:51:07.73	Bevan Docherty (NZL) 1:51:15.60	Sven Riederer (SUI) 1:51:33.26

Women

2000	Brigitte McMahon (SUI) 2:00:40	Michellie Jones (AUS) 2:00:42	Magali Messmer (SUI) 2:01:08
2004	Kate Allen (AUT) 2:04:43.45	Loretta Harrop (AUS) 2:04:50.17	Susan Williams (USA) 2:05:08.92

VOLLEYBALL

Men

1964	SOVIET UNION	CZECHOSLOVAKIA	JAPAN
1968	SOVIET UNION	JAPAN	CZECHOSLOVAKIA
1972	JAPAN	GDR	SOVIET UNION
1976	POLAND	SOVIET UNION	CUBA
1980	SOVIET UNION	BULGARIA	ROMANIA
1984	UNITED STATES	BRAZIL	ITALY
1988	UNITED STATES	SOVIET UNION	ARGENTINA
1992	BRAZIL	NETHERLANDS	USA
1996	NETHERLANDS	ITALY	YUGOSLAVIA
2000	YUGOSLAVIA	RUSSIA	ITALY
2004	BRAZIL	ITALY	RUSSIA

1896-1960 Event not held

Women

1964	JAPAN	SOVIET UNION	POLAND
1968	SOVIET UNION	JAPAN	POLAND
1972	SOVIET UNION	JAPAN	NORTH KOREA
1976	JAPAN	SOVIET UNION	SOUTH KOREA
1980	SOVIET UNION	GDR	BULGARIA
1984	CHINA	UNITED STATES	JAPAN
1988	SOVIET UNION	PERU	CHINA
1992	CUBA	UNIFIED TEAM	USA
1996	CUBA	CHINA	BRAZIL
2000	CUBA	RUSSIA	BRAZIL
2004	CHINA	RUSSIA	CUBA

1896-1960 Event not held

WEIGHTLIFTING

Men

Flyweight

Up to 52kg 1972-92; up to 54kg 1996

1972	Zygmunt Smalcerz (POL) 337.5kg	Lajos Szücs (HUN) 330	Sándor Holczreitzer (HUN) 327.5
1976	Alexander Voronin (URS) 242.5kg	György Köszegi (HUN) 237.5	Mohammad Nassiri (IRI) 235
1980	Kanybek Osmonoliev (URS) 245kg	Bong Chol Ho (PRK) 245	Gyond Si Han (PRK) 245
1984	Zeng Guoqiang (CHN) 235kg	Zhou Peishujn (CHN) 235	Kazushito Manabe (JPN) 232.5
1988	Sevdalin Marinov (BUL) 270kg	Chun Byung-Kwan (KOR) 260	He Zhuogiang (CHN) 257.5
1992	Ivan Ivanov (BUL) 265kg	Lin Qisheng (CHN) 262.5	Traian Ciharean (ROM) 252.5
1996	Halil Mutlu (TUR) 287.5kg	Zhang Xiangsen (CHN) 280.0	Sevdalin Minchev (BUL) 277.5

1896-1968, 2000-04 Event not held

Bantamweight

Up to 56kg 1948-92; up to 59kg 1996; up to 56kg 2000

1948	Joseph de Pietro (USA) 307.5kg	Julian Creus (GBR) 297.5	Richard Tom (GBR) 295
1952	Ivan Udolov (URS) 315kg	Mahmoud Namdjou (IRI) 307.5	Ali Mirzai (IRI) 300
1956	Charles Vinci (USA) 342.5kg	Vladimir Stogov (URS) 337.5	Mahmoud Namdjou (IRI) 332.5
1960	Charles Vinci (USA) 345kg	Yoshinobu Miyake (JPN) 337.5	Esmail Khan (IRI) 330
1964	Alexei Vakhonin (URS) 357.5kg	Imre Földi (HUN) 355	Shiro Ichinoseki (JPN) 347.5
1968	Mohammed Nassiri (IRI) 367.5kg	Imre Földi (HUN) 367.5	Henryk Trebicki (POL) 357.5
1972	Imre Földi (HUN) 377.5kg	Mohammed Nassiri (IRI) 370	Gennadi Chetin (URS) 367.5
1976	Norair Nurikyan (BUL) 262.5kg	Grzegorz Cziura (POL) 252.5	Kenkichi Ando (JPN) 250
1980	Daniel Nunez (CUB) 275kg	Yurik Sarkasian (URS) 270	Tadeusz Demboncyzk (POL) 265
1984	Wu Shude (CHN) 267.5kg	Lai Runming (CHN) 265	Masahiro Kotaka (JPN) 252.5
1988	Oksen Mirzoyan (URS) 292.5kg[1]	He Yingqiang (CHN) 287.5	Liu Shoubin (CHN) 267.5
1992	Chun Byung-kwan (KOR) 287.5kg	Liu Shoubin (CHN) 277.5	Luo Jianming (CHN) 277.5
1996	Tang Ningsheng (CHN) 307.5kg	Leonidas Sabanis (GRE) 305	Nikolay Pechalov (BUL) 302.5
2000	Halil Mutlu (TUR) 305kg	Wu Wenxiong (CHN) 287.5[2]	Zhang Xiangxiang (CHN) 287.5
2004	Halil Mutlu (TUR) 295kg	Meijin Wu (CHN) 287.5	Sedat Artuc (TUR) 280

1896-1936 Event not held

[1] *Mitko Grablev (BUL) finished in first place with 297.5kg but was subsequently disqualified,* [2] *Ivan Ivanov (BUL) finished in second place with 292.5kg but was disqualified*

Featherweight

Up to 60kg 1920-92; up to 64kg 1996; up to 62kg 2000

1920	Frans de Haes (BEL) 220kg	Alfred Schmidt (EST) 212.5	Eugene Ryther (SUI) 210
1924[1]	Pierino Gabetti (ITA) 402.5kg	Andreas Stadler (AUT) 385	Arthur Reinmann (SUI) 382.5
1928	Franz Andrysek (AUT) 287.5kg	Pierino Gabetti (ITA) 282.5	Hans Wölpert (GER) 282.5
1932	Raymond Suvigny (FRA) 287.5kg	Hans Wölpert (GER) 282.5	Anthony Terlazzo (USA) 280
1936	Anthony Terlazzo (USA) 312.5kg	Saleh Mohammed Soliman (EGY) 305	Ibrahim Shams (EGY) 300
1948	Mahmoud Fayad (EGY) 332.5kg	Rodney Wilkes (TRI) 317.5	Jaffar Salmassi (IRI) 312.5
1952	Rafael Chimishkyan (URS) 337.5kg	Nikolai Saksonov (URS) 332.5	Rodney Wilkes (TRI) 332.5
1956	Isaac Berger (USA) 352.5kg	Yevgeni Minayev (URS) 342.5	Marian Zielinski (POL) 335
1960	Yevgeni Minayev (URS) 372.5kg	Isaac Berger (USA) 362.5	Sebastiano Mannironi (ITA) 352.5
1964	Yoshinobu Miyake (JPN) 397.5kg	Isaac Berger (USA) 382.5	Mieczyslaw Nowak (POL) 377.5
1968	Yoshinobu Miyake (JPN) 392.5kg	Dito Shanidze (URS) 387.5	Yoshiyuki Miyake (JPN) 385
1972	Norair Nurikyan (BUL) 402.5kg	Dito Shanidze (URS) 400	Janos Benedek (HUN) 390
1976	Nikolai Kolesnikov (URS) 285kg	Georgi Todorov (BUL) 280	Kuzumasa Hirai (JPN) 275
1980	Viktor Mazin (URS) 290kg	Stefan Dimitrov (BUL) 287.5	Marek Seweryn (POL) 282.5
1984	Chen Weiqiang (CHN) 282.5kg	Gelu Radu (ROM) 280	Tsai Wen-Yee (TPE) 272.5
1988	Naim Suleymanoglu (TUR) 342.5kg	Stefan Topourov (BUL) 312.5	Ye Huanming (CHN) 287.5
1992	Naim Suleymanoglu (TUR) 320kg	Nikolai Pechalov (BUL) 305	He Yingqiang (CHN) 295
1996	Naim Suleymanoglu (TUR) 357.5kg	Valerios Leonidis (GRE) 332.5	Jiangang Xiao (CHN) 322.5
2000	Nikolay Pechalov (CRO) 325kg	Leonidis Sabanis (GRE) 317.5	Gennadi Oleschuk (BLR) 317.5
2004	Zhiyong Shi (CHN) 325kg	Maosheng Le (CHN) 312.5	Israel José Rubio (VEN) 280[2]

1896-1912 Event not held

[1] *Aggregate of five lifts.* [2] *Leonidas Sampas (GRE) finished third with 312.5kg but disqualified.*

Lightweight

Up to 67.5kg 1920-92; up to 70kg 1996; up to 69kg 2000

1920	Alfred Neuland (EST) 257.5kg	Louis Williquet (BEL) 240	Florimond Rooms (BEL) 230
1924[1]	Edmond Décottignies (FRA) 440kg	Anton Zwerina (AUT) 427.5	Bohumil Durdis (TCH) 425
1928[2]	Kurt Helbig (GER) 322.5kg Hans Haas (AUT) 322.5	–	Fernand Arnout (FRA) 302.5
1932	René Duverger (FRA) 325kg	Hans Haas (AUT) 307.5	Gastone Pierini (ITA) 302.5
1936[2]	Anwar Mohammed Mesbah (EGY) 342.5kg Robert Fein (AUT) 342.5	–	Karl Jensen (GER) 327.5
1948	Ibrahim Shams (EGY) 360kg	Attia Hamouda (EGY) 360	James Halliday (GBR) 340
1952	Tommy Kono (USA) 362.5kg	Yevgeni Lopatin (URS) 350	Verne Barberis (AUS) 350
1956	Igor Rybak (URS) 380kg	Ravil Khabutdinov (URS) 372.5	Chang-Hee Kim (KOR) 370
1960	Viktor Bushuyev (URS) 397.5kg	Howe-Liang Tan (SIN) 380	Abdul Wahid Aziz (IRQ) 380
1964	Waldemar Baszanowksi (POL) 432.5kg	Vladimir Kaplunov (URS) 432.5	Marian Zielinski (POL) 420
1968	Waldemar Baszanowksi (POL) 437.5kg	Parviz Jalayer (IRI) 422.5	Marian Zielinski (POL) 420
1972	Mukharbi Kirzhinov (URS) 460kg	Mladen Koutchev (BUL) 450	Zbigniev Kaczmarek (POL) 437.5
1976[3]	Pyotr Korol (URS) 305kg	Daniel Senet (FRA) 300	Kazimierz Czarnecki (POL) 295
1980	Yanko Rusev (BUL) 342.5kg	Joachim Kunz (GDR) 335	Mintcho Pachov (BUL) 325
1984	Yao Jingyuan (CHN) 320kg	Andrei Socaci (ROM) 312.5	Journi Gronman (FIN) 312.5

1988	Joachim Kunz (GDR) 340kg	Israil Militossian (URS) 337.5	Li Jinhe (CHN) 325
1992	Israil Militossian (EUN) 337.5kg	Yoto Yotov (BUL) 327.5	Andreas Behm (GER) 320
1996	Zhan Xugang (CHN) 357.5kg	Kim Myong-Nam (PRK) 345.0	Attila Feri (HUN) 340.0
2000	Galabin Bojevski (BUL) 357.5kg	Georgi Markov (BUL) 352.5	Sergei Lavrenov (BLR) 340
2004	Guozheng Zhang (CHN) 347.5kg	Bae-Young Lee (KOR) 342.5	Nikolay Pechalov (CRO) 365

1896-1912 Event not held
[1]Aggregate of five lifts; [2]Tie breaker rule relating to bodyweight not yet introduced. [3]Zbigniew Kaczmarek (POL) finished in first place with 307.5kg but was subsequently disqualified

Middleweight

Up to 75kg 1920-92; up to 76kg 1996; up to 77kg 2000

1920	Henri Gance (FRA) 245kg	Pietro Bianchi[1] (ITA) 237.5	Albert Pettersson (SWE) 237.5
1924[2]	Carlo Galimberti (ITA) 492.5kg	Alfred Neuland (EST) 455	Jaan Kikas (EST) 450
1928	Roger Francois (FRA) 335kg	Carlo Galimberti (ITA) 332.5	August Scheffer (NED) 327.5
1932	Rudolf Ismayr (GER) 345kg	Carlo Galimberti (ITA) 340	Karl Hipfinger (AUT) 337.5
1936	Khadr El Thouni (EGY) 387.5kg	Rudolf Ismayr (GER) 352.5	Adolf Wagner (GER) 352.5
1948	Frank Spellman (USA) 390kg	Peter George (USA) 412.5	Sung-Jip Kim (KOR) 380
1952	Peter George (USA) 400kg	Gérard Gratton (CAN) 390	Sung-Jip Kim (KOR) 382.5
1956	Fyodor Bogdanovski (URS) 420kg	Peter George (USA) 412.5	Ermanno Pignatti (ITA) 382.5
1960	Aleksandr Kurinov (URS) 437.5kg	Tommy Kono (USA) 427.5	Gyözö Veres (HUN) 405
1964	Hans Zdrazila (TCH) 445kg	Viktor Kurentsov (URS) 440	Masashi Ouchi (JPN) 437.5
1968	Viktor Kurentsov (URS) 475kg	Masashi Ouchi (JPN) 455	Károly Bakos (HUN) 440
1972	Yordan Bikov (BUL) 485kg	Mohamed Trabulsi (LIB) 472.5	Anselmo Silvino (ITA) 470
1976	Yordan Bikov (BUL) 335kg	Vartan Militosyan (URS) 330	Peter Wenzel (GDR) 327.5
1980	Asen Zlatev (BUL) 360kg	Aleksandr Pervy (URS) 357.5	Nedeltcho Kolev (BUL) 345
1984	Karl-Heinz Radschinsky (FRG) 340kg	Jaques Demers (CAN) 335	Dragomir Cioroslan (ROM) 332.5
1988	Borislav Guidikov (BUL) 375kg	Ingo Steinhöfel (GDR) 360	Alexander Varbanov (BUL) 357.5
1992	Fedor Kassapu (EUN) 357.5kg	Pablo Lara (CUB) 357.5	Kim Myong-nam (PRK) 352.5
1996	Pablo Lara (CUB) 367.5kg	Yoto Yotov (BUL) 360.0	Jon Chol-Ho (PRK) 357.5
2000	Zhan Xugang (CHN) 367.5kg	Viktor Mitrou (GRE) 367.5	Arsen Melikyan (ARM) 365
2004	Taner Sagir (TUR) 375kg	Sergei Filimunov (KAZ) 372.5	Oleg Perepetchenov (RUS) 365

1896-1912 Event not held
[1]Bianchi and Pettersson drew lots for the silver medal; [2]Aggregate of five lifts

Light Heavyweight

Up to 82.5kg 1920-92; up to 83kg 1996; up to 85kg 2000)

1920	Ernest Cadine (FRA) 290kg	Fritz Hünenberger (SUI) 275	Erik Pettersson (SWE) 272.5
1924[1]	Charles Rigoulot (FRA) 502.5kg	Fritz Hünenberger (SUI) 490	Leopold Friedrich (AUT) 490
1928	Said Nosseir (EGY) 355kg	Louis Hostin (FRA) 352.5	Johannes Verheijen (NED) 337.5
1932	Louis Hostin (FRA) 372.5kg	Svend Olsen (DEN) 360	Henry Duey (USA) 330
1936	Louis Hostin (FRA) 372.5kg	Eugen Deutsch (GER) 365	Ibrahim Wasif (EGY) 360
1948	Stanley Stanczyk (USA) 417.5kg	Harold Sakata (USA) 380	Gösta Magnussen (SWE) 375
1952	Trofim Lomakin (URS) 417.5kg	Stanley Stanczyk (USA) 415	Arkadi Vorobyev (URS) 407.5
1956	Tommy Kono (USA) 447.5kg	Vassili Stepanov (URS) 427.5	James George (USA) 417.5
1960	Ireneusz Palinski (POL) 442.5kg	James George (USA) 430	Jan Bochenek (POL) 420
1964	Rudolf Plukfelder (URS) 475kg	Géza Tóth (HUN) 467.5	Gyözö Veres (HUN) 467.5
1968	Boris Selitsky (URS) 485kg	Vladimir Belyayev (URS) 485	Norbert Ozimek (POL) 472.5
1972	Leif Jenssen (NOR) 507.5kg	Norbert Ozimek (POL) 497.5	György Horváth (HUN) 495
1976[2]	Valeriy Shary (URS) 365kg	Trendachil Stoichev (BUL) 360	Peter Baczako (HUN) 345
1980	Yurik Vardanyan (URS) 400kg	Blagoi Blagoyev (BUL) 372.5	Dusan Poliacik (TCH) 367.5
1984	Petre Becheru (ROM) 355kg	Robert Kabbas (AUS) 342.5	Ryoji Isaoka (JPN) 340
1988	Israil Arsamokov (URS) 377.5kg	István Messzi (HUN) 370	Lee Hyung-Kun (KOR) 367.5
1992	Pyrros Dimas (GRE) 370kg	Krzysztof Siemion (POL) 370	–[3]
1996	Pyrros Dimas (GRE) 392.5kg	Marc Huster (GER) 382.5	Andrzej Cofalik (POL) 372.5
2000	Pyrros Dimas (GRE) 390kg	Marc Huster (GER) 390	George Asanidze (GEO) 390
2004	Georgi Asanidze ((GEO) 382.5kg	Andrei Rybakov (BLR) 380	Pyrros Dimas (GRE) 377.5

1896-1912 Event not held
[1]Aggregate of five lifts; [2]Blagoi Blagoyev (BUL) finished in second place with 362.5kg but was subsequently disqualified; [3]Ibrghim Samadov (EUN) placed third but was disqualified, no bronze medal awarded

Middle Heavyweight

Up to 90kg 1952-92; up to 91kg 1996; up to 94kg 2000

1952	Norbert Schemansky (USA) 445kg	Grigori Nowak (URS) 410	Lennox Kilgour (TRI) 402.5
1956	Arkadi Vorobyev (URS) 462.5kg	David Sheppard (USA) 442.5	Jean Debuf (FRA) 425
1960	Arkadi Vorobyev (URS) 472.5kg	Trofim Lomakin (URS) 457.5	Louis Martin (GBR) 445
1964	Vladimir Golovanov (URS) 487.5kg	Louis Martin (GBR) 475	Ireneusz Palinski (POL) 467.5

1968	Kaarlo Kanganiemi (FIN) 517.5kg	Jan Talts (URS) 507.5	Marek Golab (POL) 495
1972	Andon Nikolov (BUL) 525kg	Atanas Chopov (BUL) 517.5	Hans Bettembourg (SWE) 512.5
1976	David Rigert (URS) 382.5kg	Lee James (USA) 362.5	Atanas Chopov (BUL) 360
1980	Péter Baczakó (HUN) 377.5kg	Rumen Alexandrov (BUL) 375	Frank Mantek (GDR) 375
1984	Nicu Vlad (ROM) 392.5kg	Dumitru Petre (ROM) 360	David Mercer (GBR) 352.5
1988	Anatoli Khrapati (URS) 412.5kg	Nail Moukhamediarov (URS) 400	Slawomir Zawada (POL) 400
1992	Kakhi Kakhiashvili (EUN) 412.5kg	Sergei Syrtsov (EUN) 412.5	Serguisz Wolczaniecki (POL) 392.5
1996	Alexei Petrov (RUS) 402.5kg	Leonidas Kokas (GRE) 390.0	Oliver Caruso (GER) 390.0
2000	Akakios Kakiasvilis (GRE) 405kg[1]	Szymon Kolecki (POL) 405	Alexei Petrov (RUS) 402.5
2004	Milen Dobrerv (BUL) 407.5kg	Khadjimourad Akayev (RUS) 405	Eduard Tjukin (RUS) 397.5

1890-1948 Event not held
[1]Same person as 1992 winner

Heavyweight

1920-48 class over 82.5kg; 1952-68 class over 90kg; 1972-92 class up to 110kg; 1996 up to 108kg; up to 105kg 2000

1896[1]	Launceston Eliot (GBR) 71kg	Viggo Jensen (DEN) 57.2	Alexandros Nikolopoulos (GRE) 57.2
1896[2]	Viggo Jensen (DEN) 111.5kg	Launceston Eliot (GBR) 111.5	Sotirios Versis (GRE) 90
1904[3]	Oscar Osthoff (USA) 48pts	Frederick Winters (USA) 45	Frank Kungler (USA) 10
1904[2]	Perikles Kaklousis (GRE) 111.5kg	Oscar Osthoff (USA) 84.36	Frank Kungler (USA) 79.83
1906[1]	Josef Steinbach (AUT) 76.55kg	Tullio Camilotti (ITA) 73.75	Heinrich Schneidereit (GER) 70.75
1906[2]	Dimitrios Tofalos (GRE) 142.5kg	Josef Steinbach (AUT) 136.5	Alexandre Maspoli (FRA) 129.5
			Heinrich Rondl (GER) 129.5
			Heinrich Schneidereit (GER) 129.5
1920	Filippo Bottino (ITA) 270kg	Joseph Alzin (LUX) 225	Louis Bernot (FRA) 250
1924[4]	Giuseppe Tonani (ITA) 517.5kg	Franz Aigner (AUT) 515	Harald Tammer (EST) 497.5
1928	Josef Strassberger (GER) 372.5kg	Arnold Luhaäär (EST) 360	Jaroslav Skobla (TCH) 375.5
1932	Jaroslav Skobla (TCH) 380kg	Václav Psenicka (TCH) 377.5	Josef Strassberger (GER) 377.5
1936	Josef Manger (GER) 410kg	Václav Psenicka (TCH) 402.5	Arnold Luhaäär (EST) 400
1948	John Davis (USA) 452.2kg	Norbert Schemansky (USA) 425	Abraham Charité (NED) 412.5
1952	John Davis (USA) 460kg	James Bradford (USA) 437.5	Humberto Selvetti (ARG) 432.5
1956	Paul Anderson (USA) 500kg	Humberto Selvetti (ARG) 500	Alberto Pigaiani (ITA) 452.5
1960	Yuriy Vlasov (URS) 537.5kg	James Bradford (USA) 512.5	Norbert Schemansky (USA) 500
1964	Leonid Zhabotinsky (URS) 572.5kg	Yuri Vlasov (URS) 570	Norbort Schemansky (USA) 537.5
1968	Leonid Zhabotinsky (URS) 572.5kg	Serge Reding (BEL) 555	Joseph Dube (USA) 555
1972	Jan Talts (URS) 580kg	Alexandre Kraitchev (BUL) 562.5	Stefan Grützner (GDR) 555
1976[5]	Yuri Zaitsev (URS) 385kg	Krastio Semerdiev (BUL) 385	Tadousz Rutkowski (POL) 377.5
1980	Leonid Taranenko (URS) 422.5kg	Valentin Christov (BUL) 385	György Szalai (HUN) 390
1984	Norberto Oberburger (ITA) 390kg	Stefan Tasnadi (ROM) 380	Guy Carlton (USA) 377.5
1988	Yuriy Zakharevich (URS) 455kg	József Jacsó (HUN) 427.5	Ronny Weller (GDR) 425
1992	Ronny Weller (GER) 432.5kg	Artur Akoyev (EUN) 430	Stefan Botev (BUL) 417.5
1996	Timur Taimazov (UKR) 430.0kg	Sergei Syrtsov (RUS) 420.0	Nicu Vlad (ROM) 420.0
2000	Hossain Tavakoli (IRI) 425kg	Alan Tsagayev (BUL) 422.5	Said Saif Asaad (QAT) 420
2004	Dmitri Berestov (RUS) 425kg	Igor Razoronov (UKR) 420[6]	Gleb Pisarevski (RUS) 415

1900,1908-1912 Event not held
[1]One-hand lift; [2]Two-hand lift; [3]Dumbbell Lift; [4]Aggregate of five lifts; [5]Valentin Christov (BUL) finished first with 400kg but disqualified; [6]Ferenc Gyurkovics (HUN) finished second with 420kg but disqualified.

Super-Heavyweight

Over 110kg 1972-92; over 108kg 1996; over 105kg 2000

1972	Vasili Alexeyev (URS) 640kg	Rudolf Mang (FRG) 610	Gerd Bonk (GDR) 572.5
1976	Vasili Alexeyev (URS) 440kg	Gerd Bonk (GDR) 405	Helmut Losch (GDR) 387.5
1980	Sultan Rakhmanov (URS) 440kg	Jürgen Heuser (GDR) 410	Tadeusz Rutkowski (POL) 407.5
1984	Dinko Lukin (AUS) 412.5kg	Mario Martinez (USA) 410	Manfred Nerlinger (FRG) 397.5
1988	Alexander Kurlovich (URS) 462.5kg	Manfred Nerlinger (FRG) 430	Martin Zawieja (FRG) 415
1992	Alexander Kurlovich (EUN) 450kg	Leonid Taranenko (EUN) 425	Manfred Nerlinger (GER) 412.5
1996	Andrei Chemerkin (RUS) 457.5kg	Ronny Weller (GER) 455.0	Stefan Botev (AUS) 455.0
2000	Hossein Reza Zadeh (IRI) 472.5kg	Ronny Weller (GER) 467.5	Andrei Chemerkin (RUS) 462.5[1]
2004	Hossein Reza Zadeh (IRI) 472.5kg	Viktors Scerbatihs (LAT) 455	Velichko Cholakov (BUL) 447.5

1896-1968 Event not held
[1]Ashot Danielyan (ARM) finished in third place with 465kg but was disqualified

DISCONTINUED EVENT

Up to 100kg

1980-92; up to 99kg 1996

1980	Ota Zaremba (TCH) 395kg	Igor Nikitin (URS) 392.5	Alberto Blanco (CUB) 385
1984	Rolf Milser (FRG) 385kg	Vasile Gropa (ROM) 382.5	Pekka Niemi (FIN) 367.5
1988	Pavel Kuznetsov (URS) 425kg	Nicu Vlad (ROM)[1] 402.5	Peter Immesberger (FRG) 367.5
1992	Viktor Tregubov (EUN) 410kg	Timur Taimazov (EUN) 402.5	Waldemar Malak (POL) 400
1996	Akakios Kakiasvilis (GRE)[2] 420.0kg	Anatoli Khrapati (KAZ) 410.0	Denis Gotfrid (UKR) 402.5

1896-1976 Event not held

[1]*Andor Szanyi (HUN) finished second with 407.5kg but was subsequently disqualified;* [2]*Won 1992 middle-heavyweight class representing Unified Team*

Women

(Introduced in 2000)

Up to 48kg

2000	Tara Nott (USA)[1] 185kg	Raema Lisa Rumbewas (INA) 185	Sri Indriyani (INA) 182.5
2004	Nurcan Taylan (TUR) 210kg	Zhuo Li (CHN) 205	Aree Wiratthaworn (THA) 200

[1]*Izabela Dragneva (BUL) finished in first place with 190kg but was disqualified*

Up to 53kg

2000	Xia Yang (CHN) 225kg	Feng-Ying Li (TPE) 212.5	Winarni Binti Slamet (INA) 202.5
2004	Udomporn Polsak (THA) 222.5kg	Raema Lisa Rumbewas (INA) 210	Mabel Mosquera (COL) 197.5

Up to 58kg

2000	Soraya Jiminez Mendivil (MEX) 222.5kg	Song Hui Ri (PRK) 220	Khassaraporn Suta (INA) 210
2004	Yanqing Chen (CHN) 237.5kg	Song Hui Ri (PRK) 232.5	Wandee Kameaim (THA) 230

Up to 63kg

2000	Xiamin Chen (CHN) 242.5kg	Valentina Popova (RUS) 235	Ioanna Chatziioannou (GRE) 222.5
2004	Natalya Skakun (UKR) 242.5kg	Hanna Batsyushka (BLR) 242.5	Tatsiana Stukalava (BLR) 222.5

Up to 69kg

2000	Weining Li (CHN) 242.5kg	Erzsabet Markus (HUN) 242.5	Karnam Malleswari (IND) 240
2004	Chunhong Liu (CHN) 275kg	Eszter Krutzler (HUN) 262.5	Zarema Kasayeva (RUS) 262.5

Up to 75kg

2000	Maria Urrutia (CUB) 245kg	Ruth Ogbeifo (NGR) 245	Yi-Hang Kuo (TPE) 245
2004	Pawina Thongsuk (THA) 272.5kg	Natalia Zabolotnaya (RUS) 272.5	Valentina Popova (RUS) 265

Over 75kg

2000	Ding Meiyuan (CHN) 300kg	Agata Wrobel (POL) 295	Cheryl Haworth (USA) 270
2004	Gonghong Tang (CHN) 305kg	Mi Ran Jang (KOR) 302.5	Ageta Wrobel (POL) 290

WRESTLING

Bodyweight classes have changed over time.

Men
Free-Style

Bantamweight

1904 up to 125lb (56.70kg); 1908 119lb (54kg); up to 56kg 1924-1936; up to 57kg 1948-1996; up to 58kg 2000; up to 55kg 2004

1904	Isidor Niflot (USA)	August Wester (USA)	Z B Strebler (USA)[1]
1908	George Mehnert (USA)	William Press (GBR)	Aubert Coté (CAN)
1924	Kustaa Pihlajamaki (FIN)	Kaarlo Mäkinen (FIN)	Bryant Hines (USA)
1928	Kaarlo Mäkinen (FIN)	Edmond Spapen (BEL)	James Trifunov (CAN)
1932	Robert Pearce (USA)	Odön Zombori (HUN)	Aatos Jaskari (FIN)
1936	Odön Zombori (HUN)	Ross Flood (USA)	Johannes Herbert (GER)
1948	Nasuk Akar (TUR)	Gerald Leeman (USA)	Charles Kouyov (FRA)
1952	Shohachi Ishii (JPN)	Rashid Mamedbekov (URS)	Kha-Shaba Jadav (IND)
1956	Mustafa Dagistanli (TUR)	Mohamad Yaghoubi (IRI)	Mikhail Chakhov (URS)
1960	Terrence McCann (USA)	Nejdet Zalev (BUL)	Tadeusz Trojanowski (POL)
1964	Yojiro Uetake (JPN)	Hüseyin Akbas (TUR)	Aidyn Ibragimov (URS)
1968	Yojiro Uetake (JPN)	Donald Behm (USA)	Abutaleb Gorgori (IRI)
1072	Hideaki Yanagida (JPN)	Richard Sanders (USA)	László Klinga (HUN)
1976	Vladimir Yumin (URS)	Hans-Dieter Brüchert (GDR)	Masao Arai (JPN)
1980	Sergei Beloglazov (URS)	Li Ho Pyong (PRK)	Dugarsuren Ouinbold (MGL)
1984	Hideyaki Tomiyama (JPN)	Barry Davis (USA)	Kim Eui-Kon (KOR)
1988	Sergei Beloglazov (URS)	Askari Mohammadian (IRI)	No Kyung-Sun (KOR)
1992	Alejandro Puerto Diaz (CUB)	Sergei Smal (EUN)	Kim Yong-sik (PRK)
1996	Kendall Cross (USA)	Giga Sissaouri (CAN)	Ri Yong-Sam (PRK)
2000	Alirezas Dabir (IRI)	Yevgeni Buslovich (UKR)	Terry Brands (USA)
2004	Mavlet Batirov (RUS)	Stephen Abas (USA)	Chikara Tanabe (JPN)

1896-1900, 1906, 1912-1920 Event not held
[1]First name often misreported as Zenon

Featherweight

1904 up to 135lb (61.24kg); 1908 up to 133lb (60.30kg); up to 60kg 1920; up to 61kg 1924-1936; up to 63kg 1948-1968; up to 62kg 1972-1996; up to 63kg 2000; up to 60kg 2004

1904	Benjamin Bradshaw (USA)	Theodore McLear (USA)	Charles Clapper (USA)
1908	George Dole (USA)	James Slim (GBR)	William McKie (GBR)
1920	Charles Ackerly (USA)	Samuel Gerson (USA)	PW Bernard (GBR)
1924	Robin Reed (USA)	Chester Newton (USA)	Katsutoshi Naito (JPN)
1928	Allie Morrison (USA)	Kustaa Pihlajamäki (FIN)	Hans Minder (SUI)
1932	Hermanni Pihlajamäki (FIN)	Edgar Nemir (USA)	Einar Karlsson (SWE)
1936	Kustaa Pihlajamaki (FIN)	Francis Millard (USA)	Gösta Jönsson (SWE)
1948	Gazanfer Bilge (TUR)	Ivar Sjölin (SWE)	Adolf Müller (SUI)
1952	Bayram Sit (TUR)	Nasser Givétchi (IRI)	Josiah Henson (USA)
1956	Shozo Sasahara (JPN)	Joseph Mewis (BEL)	Erkki Penttilä (FIN)
1960	Mustafa Dagistanli (TUR)	Stantcho Ivanov (BUL)	Vladimir Rubashbili (URS)
1964	Osamu Watanabe (JPN)	Stantcho Ivanov (BUL)	Nodar Khokhashvili (URS)
1968	Masaaki Kaneko (JPN)	Enyu Todorov (BUL)	Shamseddin Seyed-Abbassi (IRI)
1972	Zagalav Abdulbekov (URS)	Vehbi Akdag (TUR)	Ivan Krastev (BUL)
1976	Yang Jung-Mo (KOR)	Zeveg Oidov (MGL)	Gene Davis (USA)
1980	Magomedgasan Abushev (URS)	Mikho Doukov (BUL)	Georges Hadjioannidis (GRE)
1984	Randy Lewis (USA)	Kosei Akaishi (JPN)	Lee Jeung-Keun (KOR)
1988	John Smith (USA)	Stepan Sarkissian (URS)	Simeon Chterev (BUL)
1992	John Smith (USA)	Askari Mohammadian (IRI)	Lazaro Reinoso (CUB)
1996	Thomas Brands (USA)	Jae-Sung Jang (KOR)	Elbrus Tedeyev (UKR)
2000	Murad Oumakhanov (RUS)	Serafim Barzakov (BUL)	Jae-Sung Jang (KOR)
2004	Yandro Miguel Quintana (CUB)	Masoud Jokar (IRI)	Kenji Inoue (JPN)

1896-1900, 1906, 1912 Event not held

Lightweight

1904 up to 145lb (65.77kg); 1908 up to 146³/₄lb (66.60kg); up to 67.5kg 1920; up to 66kg 1924-1936; up to 67kg 1948-1960; up to 70kg 1964-1968; up to 68kg 1972-1996; up to 69kg 2000; up to 66kg 204)

1904	Otton Roehm (USA)	Rudolph Tesing (USA)	Albert Zirkel (USA)
1908	George de Relwyskow (GBR)	William Wood (GBR)	Albert Gingell (GBR)

1920	Kalle Anttila (FIN)	Gottfried Svensson (SWE)	Peter Wright (GBR)
1924	Russell Vis (USA)	Volmart Wickström (FIN)	Arvo Haavisto (FIN)
1928	Osvald Käpp (EST)	Charles Pacome (FRA)	Eino Leino (FIN)
1932	Charles Pacome (FRA)	Károly Kápáti (HUN)	Gustaf Klarén (SWE)
1936	Károly Kápáti (HUN)	Wolfgang Ehrl (GER)	Hermanni Pihlajamäki (FIN)
1948	Celál Atik (TUR)	Gösta Frandfors (SWE)	Hermanni Pihlajamäki (FIN)
1952	Olle Anderberg (SWE)	Thomas Evans (USA)	Djahanbakte Tovfighe (IRI)
1956	Emamali Habibi (IRI)	Shigeru Kasahara (JPN)	Alimberg Bestayev (URS)
1960	Shelby Wilson (USA)	Viktor Sinyavskiy (URS)	Enyu Dimov (BUL)
1964	Enyu Valtschev (BUL)[1]	Klaus-Jürgen Rost (GER)	Iwao Horiuchi (JPN)
1968	Abdollah Movahed Ardabili (IRI)	Enyu Valtschev (BUL)[1]	Sereeter Danzandarjaa (MGL)
1972	Dan Gable (USA)	Kikuo Wada (JPN)	Ruslan Ashuraliev (URS)
1976	Pavel Pinigin (URS)	Lloyd Keaser (USA)	Yasaburo Sagawara (JPN)
1980	Saipulla Absaidov (URS)	Ivan Yankov (BUL)	Saban Sejdi (YUG)
1984	You In-Tak (KOR)	Andrew Rein (USA)	Jukka Rauhala (FIN)
1988	Arsen Fadzayev (URS)	Park Jang-Soon (KOR)	Nate Carr (USA)
1992	Arsen Fadzayev (EUN)	Valentin Getzov (BUL)	Kosei Akaishi (JPN)
1996	Vadim Bogiyev (RUS)	Townsend Saunders (USA)	Zaza Zazirov (UKR)
2000	Daniel Igali (CAN)	Arsen Gitinov (RUS)	Lincoln McIlravy (USA)
2004	Elbrus Tadeyev (UKR)	Jamill Kelly (USA)	Makhach Murtazaliev (RUS)

1896-1900, 1906, 1912 Event not held
[1]Valtschev competed as Dimov in 1960

Welterweight

1904 up to 158lb (71.67kg); up to 72kg 1924-1936; up to 73kg 1948-1960; up to 74kg 1972-1996; up to 76kg 2000; up to 74kg 2004

1904	Charles Erikson (USA)	William Beckmann (USA)	Jerry Winholtz (USA)
1924	Hermann Gehri (SUI)	Eino Leino (FIN)	Otto Müller (SUI)
1928	Arvo Haavisto (FIN)	Lloyd Appleton (USA)	Maurice Letchford (CAN)
1932	Jack van Bebber (USA)	Daniel MacDonald (CAN)	Eino Leino (FIN)
1936	Frank Lewis (USA)	Ture Andersson (SWE)	Joseph Schleimer (CAN)
1948	Yasar Dogu (TUR)	Richard Garrard (AUS)	Leland Merrill (USA)
1952	William Smith (USA)	Per Berlin (SWE)	Abdullah Modjtabavi (IRI)
1956	Mitsuo Ikeda (JPN)	Ibrahim Zengin (TUR)	Vakhtang Balavadze (URS)
1960	Douglas Blubaugh (USA)	Ismail Ogan (TUR)	Mohammed Bashir (PAK)
1964	Ismail Ogan (TUR)	Guliko Sagaradze (URS)	Mohamad-Ali Sanatkaran (IRI)
1968	Mahmut Atalay (TUR)	Daniel Robin (FRA)	Dagvasuren Purev (MGL)
1972	Wayne Wells (USA)	Jan Karlsson (SWE)	Adolf Seger (FRG)
1976	Jiichiro Date (JPN)	Mansour Barzegar (IRI)	Stanley Dziedzic (USA)
1980	Valentin Raitchev (URS)	Jamtsying Davaajav (MGL)	Dan Karabin (TCH)
1984	David Schultz (USA)	Martin Knosp (FRG)	Saban Sejdi (YUG)
1988	Kenneth Monday (USA)	Adlan Varayev (URS)	Rakhmad Sofiadi (BUL)
1992	Park Jang-soon (KOR)	Kenneth Monday (USA)	Amir Khadem (IRI)
1996	Buvaisar Saityev (RUS)	Park Jang-soon (KOR)	Taykuo Ota (JPN)
2000	Brandon Slay (USA)[1]	Eui-Jae Moon (KOR)	Adam Bereket (TUR)
2004	Buvaisar Saityev (RUS)	Gennadi Laliyev (KAZ)	Ivan Fundora (CUB)

1896-1906, 1912 Event not held
[1]Alexander Leipold (GER) finished in first place but was disqulaified

Middleweight

1908 up to 161lb (73kg); 1920 up to 165.1/4lb (75kg); up to 79kg 1924-1960; up to 87kg 1964-1968; up to 82kg 1972-1996; up to 85kg 2000; up to 84kg 2004

1908	Stanley Bacon (GBR)	George de Relwyskow (GBR)	Frederick Beck (GBR)
1920	Eino Reino (FIN)	Väinö Penttala (FIN)	Charles Johnson (USA)
1924	Fritz Hagmann (SUI)	Pierre Ollivier (BEL)	Vilho Pekkala (FIN)
1928	Ernst Kyburz (SUI)	Donald Stockton (CAN)	Samuel Rabin (GBR)
1932	Ivar Johansson (SWE)	Kyösti Luukko (FIN)	József Tunyogi (HUN)
1936	Emile Poilvé (FRA)	Richard Voliva (USA)	Ahmet Kirecci (TUR)
1948	Glen Brand (USA)	Adil Candemir (TUR)	Erik Lindén (SWE)
1952	David Tsimakuridze (URS)	Gholam Reza Takhti (IRI)	György Gurics (HUN)
1956	Nikola Stantchev (BUL)	Daniel Hodge (USA)	Georgi Skhirtladze (URS)
1960	Hasan Güngör (TUR)	Georgi Skhirtladze (URS)	Hans Antonsson (SWE)
1964	Prodan Gardshev (BUL)	Hasan Güngör (TUR)	Daniel Brand (USA)
1968	Boris Mikhailovich Gurevich (URS)	Munkbat Jigjid (MGL)	Prodan Gradshev (BUL)
1972	Leven Tediashvili (URS)	John Peterson (USA)	Vasile Jorga (ROM)
1976	John Peterson (USA)	Viktor Novoshilev (URS)	Adolf Seger (FRG)
1980	Ismail Abilov (BUL)	Magomedhan Aratsilov (URS)	István Kovács (HUN)

1984	Mark Schultz (USA)	Hideyuki Nagashima (JPN)	Chris Rinke (CAN)
1988	Han Myung-woo (KOR)	Necmi Gencalp (TUR)	Josef Lohyna (TCH)
1992	Kevin Jackson (USA)	Elmadi Zhabraylov (EUN)	Razul Khadem Azghadi (IRI)
1996	Khadshimurad Magomedov (RUS)	Yang Hyun-Mo (KOR)	Amir Khadem Azghadi (IRI)
2000	Adam Saityev (RUS)	Yoel Romero (CUB)	Mogamed Ibragimov (MKD)
2004	Cael Sanderson (USA)	Eui-Jae Moon (KOR)	Sazhid Sazhidov (RUS)

1896-1906, 1912 Event not held

Heavyweight

1904 over 158lb (71.6kg); over 73kg 1908; over 82.5kg 1920; over 87kg 1924-1960; over 97kg 1964-1968; up to 100kg 1972-1996; up to 97kg 2000; up to 96kg 2004

1904	Bernhuff Hansen (USA)	Frank Kungler (USA)	Fred Warmbold (USA)
1908	George O'Kelly (GBR)	Jacob Gundersen (NOR)	Edmond Barrett (GBR)
1920	Robert Roth (SUI)	Nathan Pendleton (USA)	Ernst Nilsson (SWE)[1]
			Frederick Meyer (USA)[1]
1924	Harry Steele (USA)	Henry Wernli (SUI)	Andrew McDonald (GBR)
1928	Johan Richthoff (SWE)	Aukusti Sihovlla (FIN)	Edmond Dame (FRA)
1932	Johan Richthoff (SWE)	Joh Riley (USA)	Nikolaus Hirschl (AUT)
1936	Kristjan Palusalu (EST)	Josef Klapuch (TCH)	Hjalmar Nyström (FIN)
1948	Gyula Bóbis (HUN)	Bertil Antonsson (SWE)	Joseph Armstrong (AUS)
1952	Arsen Mekokishvili (URS)	Bertil Antonsson (SWE)	Kenneth Richmond (GBR)
1956	Hamit Kaplan (TUR)	Hussein Mekhmedov (BUL)	Taisto Kangasniemi (FIN)
1960	Wilfried Dietrich (GER)	Hamit Kaplan (TUR)	Savkus Dzarassov (URS)
1964	Alexander Ivanitsky (URS)	Liutvi Djiber (BUL)	Hamit Kaplan (TUR)
1968	Alexander Medved (URS)	Osman Duraliev (BUL)	Wilfried Dietrich (FRG)
1972	Ivan Yaragin (URS)	Khorloo Baianmunkh (MGL)	József Csatári (HUN)
1976	Ivan Yaragin (URS)	Russell Helickson (USA)	Dimo Kostov (BUL)
1980	Ilya Mate (URS)	Slavtcho Tchervenkov (BUL)	Julius Strnisko (TCH)
1984	Lou Banach (USA)	Joseph Atiyeh (SYR)	Vasile Pascasu (ROM)
1988	Vasile Pascasu (ROM)	Leri Khabelov (URS)	William Scherr (USA)
1992	Leri Khabelov (EUN)	Heiko Balz (GER)	Ali Kayali (TUR)
1996	Kurt Angle (USA)	Abbas Jadidi (IRI)	Arwat Sabejew (GER)
2000	Saghid Murtasaliyev (RUS)	Islam Bairamukov (KAZ)	Yeidar Kurtanadze (GEO)
2004	Khadjimourat Gatsalov (RUS)	Magomed Ibragimov (UZB)	Alireza Heidari (IRI)

1896-1900, 1906, 1912 Event not held
[1]*Tie for third place*

Super-Heavyweight

Over 100kg 1972-1984; up to 130kg 1988-2000; up to 120kg 2004

1972	Alexander Medved (URS)	Osman Duraliev (BUL)	Chris Taylor (USA)
1976	Soslan Andiev (URS)	Jozsef Balla (HUN)	Ladislau Simon (ROM)
1980	Soslan Andiev (URS)	Jozsef Balla (HUN)	Adam Sandurski (POL)
1984	Bruce Baumgartner (USA)	Bob Molle (CAN)	Ayhan Taskin (TUR)
1988	David Gobedjichvili (URS)	Bruce Baumgartner (USA)	Andreas Schröder (GDR)
1992	Bruce Baumgartner (USA)	Jeff Thue (CAN)	David Gobedjhichvili (EUN)
1996	Mahmut Demir (TUR)	Alexei Medvedev (BUL)	Bruce Baumgartner (USA)
2000	David Mussulbes (RUS)	Artur Taymazov (UZB)	Alexis Rodriguez (CUB)
2004	Artur Taymazov (UZB)	Alireza Rezaei (IRI)	Aydin Polatci (TUR)

1896-1968 Event not held

Greco-Roman

Bantamweight

Up to 58kg 1924-1928; up to 56kg 1932-1936; up to 57kg 1948-1996; up to 58kg 2000; up to 55kg 2004

1924	Eduard Pütsep (EST)	Anselm Ahlfors (FIN)	Väinö Ikonen (FIN)
1928	Kurt Leucht (GER)	Jindrich Maudr (TCH)	Giovanni Gozzi (ITA)
1932	Jakob Brendel (GER)	Marcello Nizzola (ITA)	Louis François (FRA)
1936	Márton Lörincz (HUN)	Egon Svensson (SWE)	Jakob Brendel (GER)
1948	Kurt Pettersén (SWE)	Aly Mahmoud Hassan (EGY)	Habil Kaya (TUR)
1952	Imre Hódos (HUN)	Zakaria Chihab (LIB)	Artem Teryan (URS)
1956	Konstantin Vyrupayev (URS)	Evdin Vesterby (SWE)	Francisco Horvat (ROM)
1960	Oleg Karavayev (URS)	Ion Cernea (ROM)	Petrov Dinko (BUL)
1964	Masamitsu Ichiguchi (JPN)	Vladen Trostiansky (URS)	Ion Cernea (ROM)
1968	János Varga (HUN)	Ion Baciu (ROM)	Ivan Kochergin (URS)
1972	Rustem Kazakov (URS)	Hans-Jürgen Veil (FRG)	Risto Björlin (FIN)
1976	Pertti Ukkola (FIN)	Iván Frgic (YUG)	Farhat Mustafin (URS)
1980	Shamil Serikov (URS)	Jozef Lipien (POL)	Benni Ljungbeck (SWE)
1984	Pasquale Passarelli (FRG)	Masaki Eto (JPN)	Haralambos Holidis (GRE)

1988	Andras Sike (HUN)	Stoyan Balov (BUL)	Haralambos Holidis (GRE)
1992	An Han-Bong (KOR)	Rifat Yildiz (GER)	Sheng Zetian (CHN)
1996	Yovei Melnichenko (KAZ)	Denis Hall (USA)	Sheng Zetian (CHN)
2000	Armen Nazarian (BUL)	In-Sub Kim (KOR)	Sheng Zetian (CHN)
2004	Istvan Majoros (HUN)	Geydar Mamedalyev (RUS)	Artiom Kiouregkian (GRE)

1896-1920 Event not held

Featherweight

Up to 60kg 1912-1920; up to 62kg 1924-1928, 1948-1960, 1972-1996; up to 61kg 1932-1936; up to 63kg 1964-1968, 2000; p to 60kg 2004

1912	Kaarlo Koskelo (FIN)	Georg Gerstacker (GER)	Otto Lasanen (FIN)
1920	Oskari Friman (FIN)	Hekki Kähkönen (FIN)	Fridtjof Svensson (SWE)
1924	Kalle Antila (FIN)	Aleksanteri Toivola (FIN)	Erik Malmberg (SWE)
1928	Voldemar Väli (EST)	Erik Malmberg (SWE)	Giacomo Quaglia (ITA)
1932	Giovanni Gozzi (ITA)	Wolfgang Ehrl (GER)	Lauri Koskela (FIN)
1936	Yasar Erkan (TUR)	Aarne Reini (FIN)	Einar Karlsson (SWE)
1948	Mehmet Oktav (TUR)	Olle Anderberg (SWE)	Ferenc Tóth (HUN
1952	Yakov Punkin (URS)	Imre Polyák (HUN)	Abdel Rashed (EGY)
1956	Rauno Mäkinen (FIN)	Imre Polyák (HUN)	Roman Dzneladze (URS)
1960	Muzahir Sille (TUR)	Imre Polyák (HUN)	Konstantin Vyrupayev (URS)
1964	Imre Polyák (HUN)	Roman Rurua (URS)	Branko Marttinovic (YUG)
1968	Roman Rurua (URS)	Hideo Fujimoto (JPN)	Simeon Popescu (ROM)
1972	Gheorghi Markov (BUL)	Heniz-Helmut Wehling (GDR)	Kazimierz Lipien (POL)
1976	Kazimierz Lipien (POL)	Nelson Davidian (URS)	László Réczi (HUN)
1980	Stilianos Migiakis (GRE)	István Tóth (HUN)	Boris Kramorenko (URS)
1984	Kim Weon-Kee (KOR)	Kent-Olle Johansson (SWE)	Hugo Dietsche (SUI)
1988	Kamandar Madjidov (URS)	Jivko Vanguelov (BUL)	An Dae-Hyun (KOR)
1992	Akif Pirim (TUR)	Sergei Martynov (EUN)	Juan Luis Maren Delis (CUB)
1996	Wlodzimierz Zawadzki (POL)	Juan Luis Maren Delis (CUB)	Akif Pirim (TUR)
2000	Varteres Samourgachev (RUS)	Juan Luis Maren Delis (CUB)	Akkaki Chachua (GEO)
2004	Ji-Hyun Jung (KOR)	Roberto Monzon (CUB)	Armen Nazarian (BUL)

1896-1920 Event not held

Lightweight

Up to 75kg 1906; up to 47lb (66.6kg) 1908; up to 67.5kg 1912-1928; up to 66kg 1932-1936; up to 67kg 1948-1960; up to 70kg 1964-1968; up to 68kg 1972-1996; up to 69kg 2000; up to 66kg 2004

1906	Rudolf Watzl (AUT)	Karl Karlsen (DEN)	Ferenc Holuban (HUN)
1908	Enrico Porro (ITA)	Nikolav Orlov (URS)	Avid Lindén-Linko (FIN)
1912	Eemil Wäre (FIN)	Gustaf Malmström (SWE)	Edvin Matiasson (SWE)
1920	Eemil Wäre (FIN)	Taavi Tamminen (FIN)	Fritjof Andersen (NOR)
1924	Oskari Friman (FIN)	Lajos Keresztes (HUN)	Kalle Westerlund (FIN)
1928	Lajos Keresztes (HUN)	Eduard Sperling (GER)	Eduard Westerlund (FIN)
1932	Erik Malmberg (SWE)	Abraham Kurland (DEN)	Eduard Sperling (GER)
1936	Lauri Koskela (FIN)	Josef Herda (TCH)	Voldemar Väli (EST)
1948	Gustaf Freij (SWE)	Aage Eriksen (NOR)	Károly Ferencz (HUN)
1952	Shazam Safim (URS)	Gustaf Freij (SWE)	Mikulás Athanasov (TCH)
1956	Kyösti Lentonen (FIN)	Riza Dogan (TUR)	Gyula Tóth (HUN)
1960	Avtandil Koridza (URS)	Branislav Martinovic (YUG)	Gustaf Freij (SWE)
1964	Kazim Avvaz (TUR)	Valeriu Bularca (ROM)	David Gvantseladze (URS)
1968	Munji Mumemura (JPN)	Stevan Horvat (YUG)	Petros Galaktopoulos (GRE)
1972	Shamii Khisamutdinov (URS)	Stoyan Apostolov (BUL)	Gian Matteo Ranzi (ITA)
1976	Suren Nalbandyan (URS)	Stefan Rusu (ROM)	Heinz-Helmut Wehling (GDR)
1980	Stefan Rusu (ROM)	Andrzej Supron (POL)	Lars-Erik Skiold (SWE)
1984	Vlado Lisjak (YUG)	Tapio Sipila (FIN)	James Martinez (USA)
1988	Levon Djoulfalakian (URS)	Kim Sung-Moon (KOR)	Tapio Sipila (FIN)
1992	Attila Repka (HUN)	Islam Dougutchyev (EUN)	Rodney Smith (USA)
1996	Ryzsard Wolny (POL)	Ghani Yalouz (FRA)	Alexander Tretyakov (RUS)
2000	Filberto Azcuy (CUB)	Katsuhiko Nagata (JPN)	Alexei Glouchkov (RUS)
2004	Farid Mansurov (AZE)	Seref Eroglu (TUR)	Mkhitar Manukyan (KAZ)

1896-1904 Event not held

Welterweight

Up to 72kg 1932-1936; up to 73kg 1948-1960; up to 78kg 1964-1968; up to 74kg 1972-1996; up to 76kg 2000; up to 74kg 2004

1932	Ivar Johansson (SWE)	Väinö Kajander (FIN)	Ercole Gallegatti (ITA)
1936	Rudolf Svedberg (SWE)	Fritz Schäfer (GER)	Eino Virtanen (FIN)
1948	Gösta Andersson (SWE)	Miklós Szilvási (HUN)	Henrik Hansen (DEN)

1952	Miklós Szilvási (HUN)	Gösta Andersson (SWE)	Khalil Taha (LIB)
1956	Mithat Bayrak (TUR)	Vladimir Maneyov (URS)	Per Berlin (SWE)
1960	Mithat Bayrak (TUR)	Günther Maritschnigg (GER)	René Schiermeyer (FRA)
1964	Anatoli Kolesov (URS)	Cyril Todorov (BUL)	Bertil Nyström (SWE)
1968	Rudolf Vesper (GDR)	Daniel Robin (FRA)	Károly Bajkó (HUN)
1972	Vitezslav Macha (TCH)	Petros Galaktopoulos (GRE)	Jan Karlsson (SWE)
1976	Anatoli Kykov (URS)	Vitezslav Macha (TCH)	Karlhienz Helbing (FRG)
1980	Ferenc Kocsis (HUN)	Anatoli Bykov (URS)	Mikko Huhtala (FIN)
1984	Jonko Salomaki (FIN)	Roger Tallroth (SWE)	Stefan Rusu (ROM)
1988	Kim Young-Nam (KOR)	Daoulet Tourlykhanov (URS)	Jozof Tracz (POL)
1992	Mnatsakan Iskandaryan (EUN)	Jozef Tracz (POL)	Torbjörn Kornbakk (SWE)
1996	Fliberto Azcuy (CUB)	Marko Asell (FIN)	Jozef Tracz (POL)
2000	Murat Kardanov (RUS)	Matt Lindland (USA)	Marko Yli-Hannukselä (FIN)
2004	Alexander Dokturishvili (UZB)	Marko Yli-Hannukselä (FIN)	Varteres Samourgachev (RUS)

1896-1928 Event not held

Middleweight

Up to 85kg 1906; up to 161lb (73kg) 1908; up to 75kg 1912-1928; up to 79kg 1932-1960; up to 87kg 1964-1968; up to 82kg 1972-1996; up to 85kg 2000; up to 84kg 2004

1906	Verner Weckman (FIN)	Rudolf Lindmayer (AUT)	Robert Bebrens (USA)
1908	Frithiof Märtensson (SWE)	Mauritz Andersson (SWE)	Anders Andersen (DEN)
1912	Claes Johansson (SWE)	Martin Klein (URS)	Alfred Asikainen (FIN)
1920	Carl Westergren (OWD)	Artur Lindfors (FIN)	Matti Perttilä (FIN)
1924	Eduard Westerlund (SWE)	Artur Lindfors (FIN)	Roman Steinberg (EST)
1928	Väinö Kokkinen (FIN)	László Papp (HUN)	Albert Kusnetz (EST)
1932	Väinö Kokkinen (FIN)	Jean Földeák (GER)	Axel Cadier (SWE)
1936	Ivar Johansson (SWE)	Ludwig Schweikert (GER)	József Palotás (HUN)
1948	Axel Grönberg (SWE)	Muhlis Tayfur (TUR)	Ercole Gallegatti (ITA)
1952	Axel Grönborg (SWE)	Kalervo Rauhala (FIN)	Nikolai Belov (URS)
1956	Givi Kartiziya (URS)	Dimiter Dobrev (BUL)	Rune Jansson (SWE)
1960	Dimiter Dobrev (BUL)	Lothar Metz (GER)	Ion Taranu (ROM)
1964	Branislav Simic (YUG)	Jiri Kormanik (TCH)	Lothar Metz (GER)
1968	Lothar Metz (GDR)	Valentin Olenik (URS)	Branislav Simic (YUG)
1972	Csaba Hegedus (HUN)	Anatoli Nazarenko (URS)	Milan Nenadic (YUG)
1976	Momir Petkovic (YUG)	Vladimir Cheboksarov (URS)	Ivan Kolev (BUL)
1980	Gennadi Korban (URS)	Jan Polgowicz (POL)	Pavel Pavlov (BUL)
1984	Ion Draica (ROM)	Dimitrios Thanapoulos (GRE)	Soren Claeson (SWE)
1988	Mikhail Mamiachvili (URS)	Tibor Komaromi (HUN)	Kim Sang-Kyu (KOR)
1992	Peter Farkas (HUN)	Piotr Stepien (POL)	Daoulet Tourlykhanov (EUN)
1996	Hamza Yerlikaya (TUR)	Thomas Zander (GER)	Valeri Tsilent (BLR)
2000	Hamza Yerlikaya (TUR)	Sandor Bardosi (HUN)	Muchran Vakhtangadze (GEO)
2004	Aleksei Michine (RUS)	Ara Abrahamian (SWE)	Vyacheslav Makarenko (BLR)

1896-1904 Event not held

Heavyweight

Open 1896; over 85kg 1906; over 93kg 1908; over 82.5kg 1912-1928; over 81kg 1932-1960; over 91kg 1964 to 1968; up to 100kg 1972-1996; p to 97kg 2000; up to 96kg 2004

1896	Carl Schuhmann (GER)	Georgios Tsitas (GRE)	Stephanos Christopoulos (GRE)
1906	Sören Jensen (DEN)	Henri Baur (AUT)	Marcel Dubois (BEL)
1908	Richard Weisz (HUN)	Alexander Petrov (RUS)	Sören Jensen (DEN)
1912	Yrjö Saarela (FIN)	Johan Olin (FIN)	Sören Jensen (DEN)
1920	Adolf Lindfors (FIN)	Poul Hansen (DEN)	Martti Nieminen (FIN)
1924	Henri Deglane (FRA)	Edil Rosenqvist (FIN)	Raymund Badó (HUN)
1928	Rudolf Svensson (SWE)	Hjalmar Nyström (FIN)	Georg Gehring (GER)
1932	Carl Westergren (SWE)	Josef Urban (TCH)	Nikolaus Hirschl (AUT)
1936	Kristjan Palusalu (EST)	John Nyman (SWE)	Kurt Hornfischer (GER)
1948	Ahmet Kireççi (TUR)	Tor Nilsson (SWE)	Guido Fantoni (ITA)
1952	Johannes Kotkas (URS)	Josef Ruzicka (TCH)	Tauno Kovanen (FIN)
1956	Anatoliy Parfenov (URS)	Wilfried Dietrich (GER)	Adelmo Bulgarelli (ITA)
1960	Ivan Bogdan (URS)	Wilfried Dietrich (GER)	Bohumil Kubat (TCH)
1964	István Kozma (HUN)	Anatoliy Roschin (URS)	Wilfried Dietrich (GER)
1968	István Kozma (HUN)	Anatoliy Roschin (URS)	Petr Kment (TCH)
1972	Nicolae Martinescu (ROM)	Nikolai Yakovenko (URS)	Ferenc Kiss (HUN)
1976	Nikolai Bolboshin (URS)	Kamen Goranov (BUL)	Andrzej Skrzylewski (POL)
1980	Gheorghi Raikov (BUL)	Roman Bierla (POL)	Vasile Andrei (ROM)
1984	Vasile Andrei (ROM)	Greg Gibson (USA)	Jozef Tertelje (YUG)
1988	Andrzej Wronski (POL)	Gerhard Himmel (FRG)	Dennis Koslowski (USA)

1992	Hector Milian (CUB)	Dennis Koslowski (USA)	Sergei Demyashkevich (EUN)
1996	Andreas Wronski (POL)	Sergei Lishvan (BLR)	Mikael Ljungberg (SWE)
2000	Mikael Ljungberg (SWE)	David Saldadze (UKR)	Garrett Lowney (USA)
2004	Karim Ibrahim (EGY)	Ramaz Nozadze (GEO)	Mehmet Ozal (TUR)

1900-1904 Event not held

Super-Heavyweight

Over 100kg 1972-1984 ; up to 130kg 1988-2000; up to 120kg 2004

1972	Anatoli Roschin (URS)	Alexandre Tomov (BUL)	Victor Dolipschi (ROM)
1976	Alexander Kolchinsky (URS)	Alexandre Tomov (BUL)	Roman Codreanu (ROM)
1980	Alexander Kolchinsky (URS)	Alexandre Tomov (BUL)	Hassan Bchara (LIB)
1984	Jeffrey Blatnick (USA)	Refik Memisevic (YUG)	Victor Dolipschi (ROM)
1988	Alexander Karelin (URS)	Ranguel Guerovski (BUL)	Tomas Johansson (SWE)
1992	Alexander Karelin (EUN)	Tomas Johansson (SWE)	Ioan Grigoras (ROM)
1996	Alexander Karelin (RUS))	Matt Ghaffari (USA)	Sergei Moureiko (MDA)
2000	Rulon Gardner (USA)	Alexander Karelin (RUS)	Dimitri Debelka (BLR)
2004	Khasan Baroyev (RUS)	Georgi Tsurtsumia (KAZ)	Rulon Gardner (USA)

1896-1968 Event not held

DISCONTINUED EVENTS

Free-Style

Light Flyweight

Weight up to 48kg

1904	Robert Curry (USA)	John Heim (USA)	Gustav Thiefenthaler (USA)
1972	Roman Dmitriev (URS)	Ognian Nikolov (BUL)	Ebrahim Javadpour (IRI)
1976	Khassan Issaev (BUL)	Roman Dmitriev (URS)	Akira Kudo (JPN)
1980	Claudio Pollio (ITA)	Jang Se Hong (PRK)	Sergei Kornilayev (URS)
1984	Robert Weaver (USA)	Takashi Irie (JPN)	Son Gab-Do (KOR)
1988	Takashi Kobaysahi (JPN)	Ivan Tozorov (BUL)	Sergei Karemtchakov (URS)
1992	Kim Il (PRK)	Kim Jong-shin (KOR)	Vougar Oroudzhov (EUN)
1996	Kim Il (PRK)	Armen Mkrchyan (ARM)	Alexis Vila (CUB)

1896-1900, 1906-1968; 2000-04 Event not held

Flyweight

1904 up to 115lb (52.16kg); up to 52kg 1958-1996; up to 54kg 2000; up to 55kg 2004

1904	George Mehnert (USA)	Gustave Bauer (USA)	William Nelson (USA)
1948	Lennart Viitala (FIN)	Halit Balamir (TUR)	Thure Johansson (SWE)
1952	Hasan Gemici (TUR)	Yushu Kitano (JPN)	Mahmoud Mollaghessemi (IRI)
1956	Mirian Tslkalamanidze (URS)	Mohamad-Ali Khojastenpour (IRI)	Hüseyin Akbas (TUR)
1960	Ahmet Bilek (TUR)	Masayuki Matsubara (JPN)	Mohamad Saifpour Saidabadi (IRI)
1964	Yoshikatsu Yoshida (JPN)	Chang-sun Chang (KOR)	Said Aliaakbar Haydari (IRI)
1968	Shigeo Nakata (JPN)	Richard Sanders (USA)	Surenjav Sukhbaatar (MGL)
1972	Kiyomi Kato (JPN)	Arsen Alakhverdyev (URS)	Hyong Kim Gwong (PRK)
1976	Yuji Takada (JPN)	Alexander Ivanov (URS)	Jeon Hae-Sup (KOR)
1980	Anatoli Beloglazov (URS)	Wladyslaw Stecyk (POL)	Nermedin Selimov (BUL)
1984	Saban Trstena (YUG)	Kim Jong-Kyu (KOR)	Yuji Takada (JPN)
1988	Mitsuru Sato (JPN)	Saban Trstena (YUG)	Vladimir Togouzov (URS)
1992	Li Hak-Son (PRK)	Larry Lee Jones (USA)	Valentin Jordanov (BUL)
1996	Valentin Jordanov (BUL)	Namik Abdullayev (AZE)	Maulen Mamirov (KAZ)
2000	Namik Abdullayev (AZE)	Samuel Henson (USA)	Amiran Kartanov (GRE)

1896-1900, 1906-1936; 2004 Event not held

Light-Heavyweight

1920 up to 82.5kg; up to 87kg 1924-1960; up to 97kg 1964-1968; up to 90kg 1972-1996

1920	Anders Larsson (SWE)	Charles Courant (SUI)	Walter Maurer (USA)
1924	Joh Spellman (USA)	Rudolf Svensson (SWE)	Charles Courant (FRA)
1928	Thure Sjöstedt (SWE)	Anton Bögli (SUI)	Henri Lefebre (FRA)
1932	Peter Mehringer (USA)	Thure Sjöstedt (SWE)	Eddie Scarf (AUS)
1936	Knut Fridell (SWE)	August Neo (EST)	Erich Siebert (GER)
1948	Henry Wittenberg (USA)	Fritz Stöckli (SUI)	Bengt Fahlkvist (SWE)
1952	Wiking Palm (SWE)	Henry Wittenberg (USA)	Adil Atan (TUR)
1956	Gholam Reza Tahkti (IRI)	Boris Kulayev (URS)	Peter Blair (USA)
1960	Ismet Atli (TUR)	Gholam Reza Tahkti (IRI)'	Anatoli Albul (URS)
1964	Alexander Medved (URS)	Ahmet Ayik (TUR)	Said Mustafafov (BUL)
1968	Ahmet Ayik (TUR)	Shota Lomidze (URS)	József Csatári (HUN)
1972	Ben Peterson (USA)	Gennadi Strakhov (URS)	Károly Bajkó (HUN)

1976	Levan Tediashvili (URS)	Ben Peterson (USA)	Stelica Morcov (ROM)
1980	Sanasar Oganesyan (URS)	Uwe Neupert (GDR)	Aleksandr Cichon (POL)
1984	Ed Banach (USA)	Akira Ota (JPN)	Noel Loban (GBR)
1988	Makharbek Khadartsev (URS)	Akira Ota (JPN)	Kim Tae-Woo (KOR)
1992	Makharbek Khadartsev (EUN)	Kenan Simsek (TUR)	Christopher Campbell (USA)
1996	Rasul Khadem Azghadi (IRI)	Makharbek Khadartsev (RUS)	Eldar Kurtanidze (GEO)

1896-1912; 2000-04 Event not held

Greco-Roman

Light Flyweight

Up to 48kg

1972	Gheorghe Berceanu (ROM)	Rahim Ahabadi (IRI)	Stefan Anghelov (BUL)
1976	Alexei Shumanov (URS)	Gheorghe Berceanu (ROM)	Stefan Anghelov (BUL)
1980	Zaksylik Ushkempirov (URS)	Constantin Alexandru (ROM)	Ferenc Seres (HUN)
1984	Vincenzo Maenza (ITA)	Markus Scherer (FRG)	Ikuzo Saito (JPN)
1988	Vincenzo Maenza (ITA)	Andrzej Glab (POL)	Bratan Tzenov (BUL)
1992	Oleg Kutcherenko (EUN)	Vincenzo Maenza (ITA)	Wiber Sanchez (CUB)
1996	Sim Kwon-Ho (KOR)	Alexander Pavlov (BLR)	Zafar Gulyov (RUS)

1896-1968 Event not held

Flyweight

Up to 52kg 1948-1996; up to 54kg 2000

1948	Pietro Lombardi (ITA)	Kenan Olcay (TUR)	Reino Kangasmäki (FIN)
1952	Boris Maksimovich Gurevich (URS)	Ignazio Fabra (ITA)	Leo Honkala (FIN)
1956	Nikolai Solovyov (URS)	Ignazio Fabra (ITA)	Durum Ali Egribas (TUR)
1960	Dumitru Pirvulescu (ROM)	Osman Sayed (UAR)	Mohamad Paziraye (IRI)
1964	Tsutomu Hanahara (JPN)	Angel Kerezov (BUL)	Dumitru Pirvulescu (ROM)
1968	Petar Kirov (BUL)	Vladimir Bakulin (URS)	Miroslav Zeman (TCH)
1972	Petar Kirov (BUL)	Koichiro Hirayama (JPN)	Giuseppe Bognanni (ITA)
1976	Vitali Konstantinov (URS)	Nicu Ginga (ROM)	Koichiro Kirayama (JPN)
1980	Vakhtang Blagidze (URS)	Lajos Racz (HUN)	Mladen Mladenov (BUL)
1984	Atsuji Miyahama (JPN)	Daniel Aceves (MEX)	Bang Dae-Du (KOR)
1988	Jon Ronningen (NOR)	Atsuji Miyahama (JPN)	Lee Jae-Suk (KOR)
1992	Jon Ronningen (NOR)	Alfred Ter-Mkrttchian (EUN)	Min Kyung-Kap (KOR)
1996	Arman Nazaryan (ARM)	Brandon Paulson (USA)	Andrei Kalashnikov (UKR)
2000	Kwon-Ho Sim (KOR)	Lazaro Rivas (CUB)	Yong-Gyun Kang (PRK)

1896-1936 Event not held

Light-Heavyweight

Up to 205lb (93kg) 1908; up to 82.5kg 1912-1928; up to 87kg 1932-1960; up to 97kg 1964-1968, 2000; up to 90kg 1972-1996

1908	Verner Weckman (FIN)	Yrjö Saarala (FIN)	Carl Jensen (DEN)
1912	–[1]	Anders Ahlgren (SWE)	Béla Varga (HUN)
		Ivor Böhling (FIN)	
1920	Claes Johansson (SWE)	Edil Rosenqvist (SWE)	Johannes Eriksen (DEN)
1924	Carl Westergren (SWE)	Rudolf Svensson (SWE)	Onni Pellinen (FIN)
1928	Ibrahim Moustafa (EGY)	Adolf Rieger (GER)	Onni Pellinen (FIN)
1932	Rudolf Svensson (SWE)	Onni Pellinen (FIN)	Mario Gruppioni (ITA)
1936	Axel Cadier (SWE)	Edwins Bietags (LAT)	August Néo (EST)
1948	Karl-Erik Nilsson (SWE)	Kaelpo Gröndahl (FIN)	Ibrahim Orabi (EGY)
1952	Kaelpo Gröndahl (FIN)	Shalva Shikhladze (URS)	Karl-Erik Nilsson (SWE)
1956	Valentin Nikolayev (URS)	Petko Sirakov (BUL)	Karl-Erik Nilsson (SWE)
1960	Tevfik Kis (TUR)	Krali Bimbalov (BUL)	Givi Kartoziya (URS)
1964	Boyan Radev (BUL)	Per Svensson (SWE)	Heinz Kiehl (GER)
1968	Boyan Radev (BUL)	Nikolai Yakovenko (URS)	Nicolae Martinescu (ROM)
1972	Valeri Rezantsev (URS)	Josip Corak (YUG)	Czeslaw Kwiecinski (POL)
1976	Valeri Rezantsev (URS)	Stoyan Ivanov (BUL)	Czesalw Kwiecinski (POL)
1980	Norbert Nottny (HUN)	Igor Kanygin (URS)	Petre Disu (ROM)
1984	Steven Fraser (USA)	Ilie Matei (ROM)	Frank Andersson (SWE)
1988	Atanas Komchev (BUL)	Harri Koskela (FIN)	Vladimir Popov (URS)
1992	Maik Bullmann (GER)	Hakki Basar (TUR)	Gogui Kogouachvili (EUN)
1996	Vyachetslav Oleynik (UKR)	Jacek Fafinski (POL)	Maik Bullmann (GER)

1896-1906 Event not held
[1]Ahlgren and Böhling declared equal second after 9 hours of wrestling.

All-around

1906	Sören Jensen (DEN)	Verner Weckmann (FIN)	Rudolf Watzl (AUT)

Women

Introduced in 2004
48kg
2004	Irina Merlini (UKR)	Chiharu Icho (JPN)	Patricia Miranda (USA)

55kg
2004	Saori Yoshida (JPN)	Tonya Verbeek (CAN)	Anna Gomis (FRA)

63kg
2004	Kaori Icho (JPN)	Sara McMann (USA)	Lise Legrand (FRA)

72kg
2004	Xu Wang (CHN)	Gouzel Manyourova (RUS)	Kyoko Hamaguchi (JPN)

DISCONTINUED SPORTS

CRICKET
1900	GREAT BRITAIN	FRANCE	–

CROQUET
Simple à la Boule
1900	Aumoitte (FRA)	Johin (FRA)	Waydelich (FRA)

Simple à deux boules
1900	Waydelich (FRA)	Vignerot (FRA)	Sautereau (FRA)

Doubles
1900	FRANCE	-	–

GOLF
Men
Singles
1900	Charles Sands (USA)	Walter Rutherford (GBR)	David Robertson (GBR)
1904	George Lyon (CAN)	Chandler Egan (USA)	Burt McKinnie (USA)

Team
1904	United States	United States	–

Women
Singles
1900	Margaret Abbott (USA)	Pauline Whittier (USA)	Daria Pratt (USA)

JEU DE PAUME
1908	Jay Gould (USA)	Eustace Mills (GBR)	Neville Lytton (GBR)

LACROSSE
1904	CANADA	UNITED STATES	CANADA
1908	CANADA	GREAT BRITAIN	–

MOTORBOATING
Open Class
1908	FRANCE	-	-

60 Foot Class

| 1908 | GREAT BRITAIN | – | – |

8 Metre Class

| 1908 | GREAT BRITAIN | – | – |

POLO

1900	GREAT BRITAIN	GREAT BRITAIN	FRANCE
1908	GREAT BRITAIN	GREAT BRITAIN	GREAT BRITAIN
1920	GREAT BRITAIN	SPAIN	UNITED STATES
1924	ARGENTINA	UNITED STATES	GREAT BRITAIN
1936	ARGENTINA	GREAT BRITAIN	MEXICO

ROQUE

| 1904 | Charles Jacobus (USA) | Smith Streeter (USA) | Charles Brown (USA) |

RACKETS

Singles

| 1908 | Evan Noel (GBR) | Henry Leaf (GBR) | John Jacob Astor (GBR) |

Doubles

| 1908 | GREAT BRITAIN | GREAT BRITAIN | GREAT BRITAIN |

RUGBY UNION

1900	FRANCE	GERMANY	GREAT BRITAIN
1908	AUSTRALIA	GREAT BRITAIN	–
1920	UNITED STATES	FRANCE	–
1924	UNITED STATES	FRANCE	ROMANIA

TUG OF WAR

1900	SWEDEN/DENMARK[1]	FRANCE	–
1904	UNITED STATES	UNITED STATES	UNITED STATES
1906	GERMANY	GREECE	SWEDEN
1908	GREAT BRITAIN	GREAT BRITAIN	GREAT BRITAIN
1912	SWEDEN	GREAT BRITAIN	–
1920	GREAT BRITAIN	NETHERLANDS	BELGIUM

1896 Event not held
[1]*Combined team*

WINTER GAMES

ALPINE SKIING

Men

	Gold	Silver	Bronze

Downhill

1948	Henri Oreiller (FRA) 2:55.0	Franz Gabl (AUT) 2:59.1	Karl Molitor (SUI) 3:00.3
			Rolf Olinger (SUI) 3:00.3
1952	Zeno Colò (ITA) 2:30.8	Othmar Schneider (AUT) 2:32.0	Christian Pravda (AUT) 2:32.4
1956	Anton Sailer (AUT) 2:52.2	Raymond Fellay (SUI) 2:55.7	Andreas Molterer (AUT) 2:56.2
1960	Jean Vuarnet (FRA) 2:06.0	Hans-Peter Lanig (GER) 2:06.5	Guy Périllat (FRA) 2:06.9
1964	Egon Zimmerman (AUT) 2:18.16	Léo Lacroix (FRA) 2:18.90	Wolfgang Bartels (GER) 2:19.48
1968	Jean-Claude Killy (FRA) 1:59.85	Guy Périllat (FRA) 1:59.93	Jean-Daniel Dätwyler (SUI) 2:00.32
1972	Bernhard Russi (SUI) 1:51.43	Roland Collombin (SUI) 1:52.07	Heinrich Messner (AUT) 1:52.40
1976	Franz Klammer (AUT) 1:45.73	Bernhard Russi (SUI) 1:46.06	Herbert Plank (ITA) 1:46.59
1980	Leonhard Stock (AUT) 1:45.50	Peter Wirnsberger (AUT) 1:46.12	Steve Podborski (CAN) 1:46.62
1984	Bill Johnson (USA) 1:45.59	Peter Müller (SUI) 1:45.86	Anton Steiner (AUT) 1:45.95
1988	Pirmin Zurbriggen (AUT) 1:59.63	Peter Müller (SUI) 2:00.14	Franck Piccard (FRA) 2:01.24
1992	Patrick Ortlieb (AUT) 1:50.37	Franck Piccard (FRA) 1:50.42	Günther Mader (AUT) 1:50.47
1994	Tommy Moe (USA) 1:45.75	Kjetil André Aamodt (NOR) 1:45.79	Edward Podivinsky (CAN) 1:45.87
1998	Jean Luc Cretier (FRA) 1:50.11	Lasse Kjus (NOR) 1:50.51	Hannes Trink (AUT) 1:50.63
2002	Fritz Strobl (AUT) 1:39.13	Lasse Kjus (NOR) 1:39.35	Stephan Eberharter (AUT) 1:39.41
2006	Antoine Deneriaz (FRA) 1:48.80	Michael Walchhofer (AUT) 1:49.52	Bruno Kernen (SUI) 1:49.82

1924-1936 Event not held

Slalom

1948	Edi Reinalter (SUI) 2:10.3	James Couttret (FRA) 2:10.8	Henri Oreiller (FRA) 2:12.8
1952	Othmar Schneider (AUT) 2:00.0	Stein Eriksen (NOR) 2:01.2	Guttorm Berge (NOR) 2:01.7
1956	Anton Sailer (AUT) 3:14.7	Chiharu Igaya (JPN) 3:18.7	Stig Sollander (SWE) 3:20.2
1960	Ernst Hinterseer (AUT) 2:08.9	Matthias Leitner (AUT) 2:10.3	Charles Bozon (FRA) 2:10.4
1964	Josef Stiegler (AUT) 2:21.13	William Kidd (USA) 2:21.27	James Hengu (USA) 2:21.52
1968	Jean-Claude Killy (FRA) 1:39.73	Herbert Huber (AUT) 1:39.82	Alfred Matt (AUT) 1:40.09
1972	Francisco Fernández Ochoa (ESP) 1:49.27	Gustavo Thöni (ITA) 1:50.28	Rolando Thöni (ITA) 1:50.30
1976	Piero Gros (ITA) 2:03.29	Gustavo Thöni (ITA) 2:03.73	Willy Frommelt (LIE) 2:04.28
1980	Ingemar Stenmark (SWE) 1:44.26	Phil Mahre (USA) 1:44.76	Jacques Lüthy (SUI) 1:45.06
1984	Phil Mahre (USA) 1:39.21	Steve Mahre (USA) 1:39.62	Didier Bouvet (FRA) 1:40.20
1988	Alberto Tomba (ITA) 1:39.47	Frank Wörndl (FRG) 1:39.53	Paul Frommelt (LIE) 1:39.84
1992	Finn Christian Jagge (NOR) 1:44.39	Alberto Tomba (ITA) 1:44.67	Michael Tritscher (AUT) 1:44.85
1994	Thomas Stangassinger (AUT) 2:02.02	Alberto Tomba (ITA) 2:02.17	Jure Kosir (SLO) 2:02.5
1998	Hans Petter Buraas (NOR) 1:49.31	Ole Christian Furuseth (NOR) 1:50.64	Thomas Sykora (AUT) 1:50.68
2002	Jean-Pierre Vidal (FRA) 1:41.06	Sebastien Amiez (FRA) 1:41.82	Benjamin Raich (AUT) 1:42.41[1]
2006	Benjamin Raich (AUT) 1:43.14	Reinfried Herbst (AUT) 1:43.97	Rainer Schönfelder (AUT) 1:44.15

1924-1936 Event not held
[1]Alain Baxter (GBR) finished in third place but was disqualified

Giant Slalom

1952	Stein Eriksen (NOR) 2:25.0	Christian Pravda (AUT) 2:26.9	Toni Spiss (AUT) 2:28.8
1956	Anton Sailer (AUT) 3:00.1	Andreas Molterer (AUT) 3:06.3	Walter Schuster (AUT) 3:07.2
1960	Roger Staub (SUI) 1:48.3	Josef Stiegler (AUT) 1:48.7	Ernst Hinterseer (AUT) 1:49.1
1964	François Bonlieu (FRA) 1:46.71	Karl Schranz (AUT) 1:47.09	Josef Steigler (AUT) 1:48.05
1968	Jean-Claude Killy (FRA) 3:29.28	Willy Favre (SUI) 3:31.50	Heinrich Messner (AUT) 3:31.83
1972	Gustavo Thöni (ITA) 3:09.62	Edmund Bruggmann (SUI) 3:10.75	Werner Mattle (SUI) 3:10.99
1976	Heini Hemmi (SUI) 3:26.97	Ernst Good (SUI) 3:27.17	Ingemar Stenmark (SWE) 3:27.41
1980	Ingemar Stenmark (SWE) 2:40.74	Andreas Wenzel (LIE) 2:41.49	Hans Enn (AUT) 2:42.51
1984	Max Julen (SUI) 2:41.18	Jure Franko (YUG) 2:41.41	Andreas Wenzel (LIE)
1988	Alberto Tomba (ITA) 2:06.37	Hubert Strolz (AUT) 2:07.41	Pirmin Zurbriggen (SUI) 2:08.39
1992	Alberto Tomba (ITA) 2:06.98	Marc Girardelli (LUX) 2:07.30	Kjetil André Aamodt (NOR) 2:07.82
1994	Markus Wasmeier (GER) 2:52.46	Urs Kälin (SUI) 2:52.48	Christian Mayer (AUT) 2:52.58
1998	Hermann Maier (AUT) 2:38.51	Stephan Eberharter (AUT) 2:39.26	Michael von Grünigen (SUI) 2:39.69
2002	Stephan Eberharter (AUT) 2:23.28	Bode Miller (USA) 2:24.16	Lasse Kjus (NOR) 2:24.32
2006	Benjamin Raich (AUT) 2:35.00	Joel Chenal (FRA) 2:35.07	Hermann Maier (AUT) 2:35.16

1924-1948 Event not held

Super Giant Slalom

1988	Franck Piccard (FRA) 1:39.66	Helmut Mayer (AUT) 1:40.96	Lars-Börje Eriksson (SWE) 1:41.08
1992	Kjetil André Aamodt (NOR) 1:13.04	Marc Girardelli (LUX) 1:13.77	Jan Einar Thorsen (NOR) 1:13.83
1994	Markus Wasmeier (GER) 1:32.53	Tommy Moe (USA) 1:32.61	Kjetil André Aamodt (NOR) 1:32.93
1998	Hermann Maier (AUT) 1:34.82	Hans Knauss (AUT) 1:35.43	–
		Didier Cuche (SUI) 1:35.43	
2002	Kjetil André Aamodt (NOR) 1:21.58	Stephan Eberharter (AUT) 1:21.68	Andreas Schifferer (AUT) 1:21. 83
2006	Kjetil André Aamodt (NOR) 1:30.65	Hermann Maier (AUT)	Ambrosi Hoffmann (SUI) 1:30.98

1924-1984 Event not held

Alpine Combination (Downhill and Slalom)

1936	Franz Pfnür (GER) 99.25pts	Gustav Lantschner (GER) 96.26	Emile Allais (FRA) 94.69
1948	Henri Orellier (FRA) 3.27pts	Karl Molitor (SUI) 6.44	James Couttet (FRA) 6.95
1988	Hubert Strolz (AUT) 36.55pts	Bernhard Gstrein (AUT) 43.45	Paul Accola (SUI) 48.24
1992	Josef Polig (ITA) 14.58pts	Gianfranco Martin (ITA) 14.90	Steve Locher (SUI) 18.16
1994	Lasse Kjus (NOR) 3:17.53	Kjetil André Aamodt (NOR) 3:18.55	Harald Strand Nielsen (NOR) 3:19.14
1998	Mario Reiter (AUT) 3:08.06	Lasse Kjus (NOR) 3:08.65	Christian Mayer (AUT) 3:10.11
2002	Kjetil André Aamodt (NOR) 3:17.56	Bode Miller (USA) 3:17.84	Benjamin Raich (AUT) 3:18.26
2006	Ted Ligety (USA) 3:09.35	Ivica Kostelic (CRO) 3:09.88	Rainer Schönfelder ((AUT) 3:10.67

1924-1932,1952-1984 Event not held

Women

Downhill

1948	Hedy Schlunegger (SUI) 2:28.3	Trude Beiser (AUT) 2:29.1	Resi Hammerer (AUT) 2:30.2
1952	Trude Jochum-Beiser (AUT) 1:47.1	Annemarie Buchner (GER) 1:48.0	Giuliana Mimuzzo (ITA) 1:49.0
1956	Madeleine Berthod (SUI) 1:40.7	Frieda Dänzer (SUI) 1:45.4	Lucile Wheeler (CAN) 1:45.9
1960	Heidi Beibl (GER) 1:37.6	Penelope Pitou (USA) 1:38.6	Traudl Hecher (AUT) 1:38.9
1964	Christl Haas (AUT) 1:55.39	Edith Zimmerman (AUT) 1:56.42	Traudl Hecher (AUT) 1:56.66
1968	Olga Pall (AUT) 1:40.87	Isabelle Mir (FRA) 1:41.33	Christl Haas (AUT) 1:41.41
1972	Marie-Thérèse Nadig (SUI) 1:36.68	Annemarie Pröll (AUT) 1:37.00	Susan Corrock (USA) 1:37.68
1976	Rosi Mittermaier (FRG) 1:46.16	Brigitte Totschnig (AUT) 1:46.68	Cindy Nelson (USA) 1:47.50
1980	Annemarie Moser-Pröll (AUT) 1:37.52	Hanni Wenzel (LIE) 1:38.22	Marie-Thérèse Nadig (SUI) 1:38.36
1984	Michela Figini (SUI) 1:13.36	Maria Walliser (SUI) 1:13.41	Olga Charvátová (TCH) 1:13.53
1988	Marina Kiehl (FRG) 1:25.86	Brigitte Oertli (SUI) 1:26.61	Karen Percy (CAN) 1:26.62
1992	Kerin Lee-Gartner (CAN) 1:52.55	Hilary Lindh (USA) 1:52.61	Veronika Wallinger (AUT) 1:52.64
1994	Katja Seizinger (GER) 1:35.93	Picabo Street (USA) 1:36.59	Isolde Kostner (ITA) 1:36.85
1998	Katja Seizinger (GER) 1:28.89	Pernilla Wiberg (SWE) 1:29.18	Florence Masnada (FRA) 1:29.37
2002	Carole Montillet (FRA) 1:39.56	Isolde Kostner (ITA) 1:40.01	Renata Götschl (AUT) 1:40.39
2006	Michaela Dorfmeister (AUT) 1:56.49	Martina Schild (SUI) 1:56.86	Anja Paerson (SWE) 1:57.13

1924-1936 Event not held

Slalom

1948	Gretchen Fraser (USA) 1:57.2	Antoinette Meyer (SUI) 1:57.7	Erika Mahringer (AUT) 1:58.0
1952	Andrea Mead-Lawrence (USA) 2:10.6	Ossi Reichert (GER) 2:11.4	Annemarie Buchner (GER) 2:13.3
1956	Renée Colliard (SUI) 1:52.3	Regina Schöpf (AUT) 1:55.4	Yevgeniya Sidorova (URS) 1:56.7
1960	Anne Heggtveit (CAN) 1:49.6	Betsy Snite (USA) 1:52.9	Barbi Henneberger (GER) 1:56.6
1964	Christine Goitschel (FRA) 1:29.86	Marielle Goitschel (FRA) 1:30.77	Jean Saubert (USA) 1:31.36
1968	Marielle Goitschel (FRA) 1:25.86	Nancy Greene (CAN) 1:26.15	Annie Famose (FRA) 1:27.89
1972	Barbara Cochran (USA) 1:31.24	Danièlle Debernard (FRA) 1:31.26	Florence Steurer (FRA) 1:32.69
1976	Rosi Mittermaier (FRG) 1:30.54	Claudia Giordani (ITA) 1:30.87	Hanni Wenzel (LIE) 1:32.20
1980	Hanni Wenzel (LIE) 1;25.09	Christa Kinshofer (FRG) 1:26.50	Erika Hess (SUI) 1:27.89
1984	Paoletta Magoni (ITA) 1:36.47	Perrine Pelen (FRA) 1:37.38	Ursula Konsett (LIE) 1:37.50
1988	Vreni Schneider (SUI) 1:36.69	Mateja Svet (YUG) 1:38.37	Christa Kinshofer-Güthlein (FRG) 1:38.40
1992	Petra Kronberger (AUT) 1:32.68	Annelise Coberger (NZL) 1:33.10	Blanca Fernández-Ochoa (ESP) 1:33.35
1994	Vreni Schneider (SUI) 1:56.01	Elfi Eder (AUT) 1:56.36	Katja Koren (SLO) 1:56.61
1998	Hilde Gerg (GER) 1:32.40	Deboarah Compagnoni (ITA) 1:32.46	Zali Steggall (AUS) 1:32.67
2002	Janica Kostelic (CRO) 1:46.10	Laure Pequegnot (FRA) 1:46.17	Anja Paerson (SWE) 1:47.09
2006	Anja Paerson (SWE) 1:29.04	Nicole Hosp (AUT) 1:29.33	Marlies Schild (AUT) 1:29.79

1924-1936 Event not held

Giant Slalom

1952	Andrea Mead-Lawrence (USA) 2:06.8	Dagmar Rom (AUT) 2:09.0	Annemarie Buchner (GER) 2:10.0
1956	Ossi Reichert (GER) 1:56.5	Josefine Frandl (AUT) 1:57.8	Dorothea Hochleitner (AUT) 1:58.2
1960	Yvonne Rüegg (SUI) 1:39.9	Penelope Pitou (USA) 1:40.0	Giuliana Chenal-Minuzzo (ITA) 1:40.2

1964	Marielle Goitschel (FRA) 1:52.24	Christine Goitschel (FRA) 1:53.11	–
		Jean Saubert (USA) 1:53.11	
1968	Nancy Greene (CAN) 1:51.97	Annie Famose (FRA) 1:54.61	Fernande Bochatay (SUI) 1:54.74
1972	Marie-Thérèse Nadig (SUI) 1:29.90	Annemarie Pröll (AUT) 1:30.75	Wiltrud Drexel (AUT) 1:32.35
1976	Kathy Kreiner (CAN) 1:29.13	Rosi Mittermaier (FRG) 1:29.25	Danièlle Debernard (FRA) 1:29.95
1980	Hanni Wenzel (LIE) 2:41.66	Irene Epple (FRG) 2:42.12	Perrine Pelen (FRA) 2:42.41
1984	Debbie Armstrong (USA) 2:20.98	Christin Cooper (USA) 2:21.38	Perrine Pelen (FRA) 2:21.40
1988	Vreni Schneider (SUI) 2:06.49	Christa Kinshofer-Güthlein (FRG) 2:07.42	Maria Walliser (SUI) 2:07.72
1992	Pernilla Wiberg (SWE) 2:12.74	Diann Roffe (USA) 2:13.71	–
		Anita Wachter (AUT) 2:13.71	
1994	Deborah Compagnoni (ITA) 2:30.47	Martina Ertl (GER) 2:32.19	Vreni Schneider (SUI) 2:32.97
1998	Deborah Compagnoni (ITA) 2:50.59	Alexandra Meissnitzer (AUT) 2:52.39	Katja Seizinger (GER) 2:52.61
2002	Janica Kostelic (CRO) 2:30.01	Anja Paerson (SWE) 2:31.33	Sonja Nef (SUI) 2:31.67
2006	Julia Mancuso (USA) 2:09.19	Tanja Poutiainen (FIN) 2:09.86	Anna Ottosson (SWE) 2:10.33

1924-1948 Event not held

Super Giant Slalom

1988	Sigrid Wolf (AUT) 1:19.03	Michela Figini (SUI) 1:20.03	Karen Percy (CAN) 1:20.29
1992	Deborah Compagnoni (ITA) 1:21.22	Carole Merle (FRA) 1:22.63	Katja Seizinger (GER) 1:23.19
1994	Diann Roffe (USA) 1:22.15	Svetlana Gladischeva (RUS) 1:22.44	Isolde Kostner (ITA) 1:22.45
1998	Picabo Street (USA) 1:18.02	Michaela Dorfmeister (AUT) 1:18.03	Alexandra Meissnitzer (AUT) 1:18.09
2002	Daniela Ceccarelli (ITA) 1:13.59	Janica Kostelic (CRO) 1:13.64	Karen Putzer (ITA) 1:13.86
2006	Michaela Dorfmeister (AUT) 1:32.47	Janica Kostelic (CRO) 1:32.74	Alexandra Meissnitzer (AUT) 1:33.06

1924-1984 Event not held

Alpine Combination (Downhill and Slalom)

1936	Christel Cranz (GER) 97.06pts	Käthe Grasegger (GER) 95.26	Laila Schou Nilsen (NOR) 93.48
1948	Trude Beiser (AUT) 6.58pts	Gretchen Fraser (USA) 6.95	Erika Mahringer (AUT) 7.04
1988	Anita Wachter (AUT) 29.25pts	Brigitte Oertli (SUI) 29.48	Maria Walliser (SUI) 51.28
1992	Petra Kronberger (AUT) 2.55pts	Anita Wachter (AUT) 19.39	Florence Masnada (FRA) 21.38
1994	Pernilla Wiberg (SWE) 3:05.16	Vreni Schneider (SUI) 3:05.29	Alenka Dovzan (SLO) 3:06.64
1998	Katja Seizinger (GER) 2:40.74	Martina Ertl (GER) 2:40.92	Hilde Gerg (GER) 2:41.50
2002	Janica Kostelic (CRO) 2:43.28	Renata Götschl (AUT) 2:44.77	Martina Ertl (GER) 2:45.16
2006	Janica Kostelic (CRO) 2:51.08	Marlies Schild (AUT) 2:51.58	Anja Paerson (SWE) 2:51.63

1924-1932,1952-1984 Event not held

BIATHLON RESULTS

Men

10,000 Metres

1980	Frank Ulrich (GDR) 32:10.69	Vladimir Alikin (URS) 32:53.10	Anatoliy Alyabiev (URS) 33:09.16
1984	Eirik Kvalfoss (NOR) 30:53.8	Peter Angerer (FRG) 31:02.4	Matthias Jacob (GDR) 31:10.5
1988	Frank-Peter Roetsch (GDR) 25:08.1	Valeri Medvedtsev (URS) 25:23.7	Sergei Tchepikov (URS) 25:29.4
1992	Mark Kirchner (GER) 26:02.3	Ricco Gross (GER) 26:18.0	Harri Eloranta (FIN) 26:26.6
1994	Sergei Chepikov (RUS) 28:07.0	Ricco Gross (GER) 28:13.0	Sergei Tarasov (RUS) 28:27.4
1998	Ole Einar Bjørndalen (NOR) 27:16.2	Frode Andersson (NOR) 28:17.8	Ville Räikkönen (FIN) 28:21.7
2002	Ole Einar Bjørndalen (NOR) 24:51.3	Sven Fischer (GER) 25:20.2	Wolfgang Perner (AUT) 25:44.4
2006	Sven Fischer (GER) 26:11.6	Halvard Hanevold (NOR) 26:19.8	Frode Andresen (NOR) 26:31.3

1924-1976 Event not held

12,500 Metres Pursuit

2006	Vincent Defrasne (FRA) 35:20.2	Ole Einar Bjørndalen (NOR) 35:22.9	Sven Fischer (GER) 35:35.8

1924-2002 Event not held

Combined Pursuit

Comprises the 10km race noted above plus a 12.5km race

2002	Ole Einar Bjørndalen (NOR) 57:25.9	Raphael Poirée (FRA) 58:8.9	Ricco Gross (GER) 58:21.9

1924-1998, 2006 Event not held

15,000 Metres Mass Start

2006	Michael Greis (GER) 47:20.0	Tomasz Sikora (POL) 47:26.3	Ole Einer Bjørndalen (NOR) 47:32.3

1924-2002 Event not held

20,000 Metres

1960 Klas Lestander (SWE) 1:33:21.6	Antii Tyrväinen (FIN) 1:33:57.7	Aleksandr Privalov (URS) 1:34:54.2
1964 Vladimir Melyanin (URS) 1:20:26.8	Alexander Privalov (URS) 1:23:42.5	Olav Jordet (NOR) 1:24:38.8
1968 Magnar Solberg (NOR) 1:13:45.9	Alexander Tikhonov (URS) 1:14:40.4	Vladimir Gundartsev (URS) 1:18:27.4
1972 Magnar Solberg (NOR) 1:15:55.5	Hans-Jörg Knauthe (GDR) 1:16:07.6	Lars Arvidsson (SWE) 1:16:27.03
1976 Nikolai Kruglov (URS) 1:14:12.26	Heikki Ikola (FIN) 1:15:54.10	Alexander Elizarov (URS) 1:16:05.57
1980 Anatoli Alyabiev (URS) 1:08:16.31	Frank Ullrich (GDR) 1:13:21.4	Eberhard Rösch (GDR) 1:11:11.73
1984 Peter Angerer (FRG) 1:11:52.7	Frank-Peter Roetsch (GDR) 1:13:21.4	Eirik Kvalfoss (NOR) 1:14:02.4
1988 Frank-Peter Roetsch (GDR) 56:33.3	Valeri Medvedtsev (URS) 56:54.6	Johann Pasler (ITA) 57:10.1
1992 Yevgeni Redkine (EUN) 57:34.4	Mark Kirchner (GER) 57:40.8	Mikael Löfgren (SWE) 57:59.4
1994 Sergei Tarasov (RUS) 57:25.3	Frank Luck (GER) 57:28.7	Sven Fischer (GER) 57:41.9
1998 Halvard Hanevold (NOR) 56:16.4	Pier Carrara (ITA) 56:21.9	Alexei Aidarov (BLR) 56:46.5
2002 Ole Einar Bjørndalen (NOR) 51:03.3	Frank Luck (GER) 51:39.4	Viktor Maigourov (RUS) 51:40.6
2006 Michael Greis (GER) 54:23.0	Ole Einer Bjørndalen (NOR) 54:39.0	Halvard Hanevold (NOR) 55:31.9

1924-1956 Event not held

Relay

4x7500 Metres

1968 SOVIET UNION 2:13:02.4	NORWAY 2:14:50.2	SWEDEN 2:17:26.3
1972 SOVIET UNION 1:51:44.92	FINLAND 1:54:37.22	GDR 1:54:57.67
1976 SOVIET UNION 1:57:55.64	FINLAND 2:01:45.58	GDR 2:04:08.61
1980 SOVIET UNION 1:34:03.27	GDR 1:34:50.99	FRG 1:37:30.26
1984 SOVIET UNION 1:38:51.7	NORWAY 1:39:03.9	FRG 1:39:05.1
1988 SOVIET UNION 1:22:30.0	FRG 1:23:37.4	ITALY 1:23:51.5
1992 GERMANY 1:24:43.5	UNIFIED TEAM 1:25:06.3	SWEDEN 1:25:38.2
1994 GERMANY 1:30:22.1	RUSSIA 1:31:23.6	FRANCE 1:32:31.3
1998 GERMANY 1:21:36.2	NORWAY 1:21:56.3	RUSSIA 1:22:19.3
2002 NORWAY 1:23:42.3	GERMANY 1:24:27.6	FRANCE 1:24:36.6
2006 GERMANY 1:21:51.5	RUSSIA 1:22:12.4	FRANCE 1:22:35.1

1924-1964 Event not held

Women

(Introduced in 1992)
7500 Metres

1992 Anfissa Reztsova (EUN) 24:29.2	Antje Misersky (GER) 24:45.1	Yelena Belova (EUN) 24:50.8
1994 Myriam Bédard (CAN) 26:08.8	Svetlana Paramygina (BLR) 26:09.9	Valentina Tserbe (UKR) 26:10.0
1998 Galina Kukleva (RUS) 23:08.0	Uschi Disl (GER) 23:08.7	Katrin Apel (GER) 23:32.4
2002 Kati Wilhelm (GER) 20:41.4	Uschi Disl (GER) 20:57.0	Magdalena Forsberg (SWE) 21:20.4
2006 Florence Baverel-Robert (FRA) 22:31.4	Anna Olofsson (SWE) 22:33.8	Lilia Efremova (UKR) 22:38.0

10,000 Metres Pursuit

2006 Kati Wilhelm (GER) 36:43.6	Martina Glagow (GER) 37:57.2	Albina Akhatova (RUS) 38:05.0

1992-2002 Event not held

12,500 Metres Mass Start

2006 Anna Olofsson (SWE) 40:36.5	Kati Wilhelm (GER) 40:55.3	Uschi Disl (GER) 41:18.4

1992-2002 Event not held

Combined Pursuit

Comprises the 7.5km race noted above plus a 10km race

2002 Olga Pyleva (RUS) 52:51.9	Kati Wilhelm (GER) 52:57.2	Irina Nikoultina (BUL) 53:00.0

1992-1998, 2006 Event not held

15,000 Metres

1992 Antje Misersky (GER) 51:47.2	Svetlana Paramygina (EUN) 51:58.5	Myriam Bédard (CAN) 52:15.0
1994 Myriam Bédard (CAN) 52:06.6	Anne Briand (FRA) 52:53.3	Ursula Disl (GER) 53:15.3
1994 Ekaterina Dafovska (BUL) 54:52.0	Yelena Petrova (UKR) 55:09.8	Ursula Disl (GER) 55:17.9
2002 Andrea Henkel (GER) 47:29.1	Liv Grete Poirée (NOR) 47:37.0	Magdalena Forsberg (SWE) 48:08.3
2006 Svetlana Ishmouratova (RUS) 49:24.1	Martina Glagow (GER) 50:34.9[1]	Albina Akhatova (RUS) 50:55.0

[1] *Olga Pyleva (RUS) disqualified after placing second in 50:09.6*

Relay

4x7500 Metres

1992[1]	FRANCE 1:15:55.6	GERMANY 1:16:18.4	UNIFIED TEAM 1:16:54.6
1994	RUSSIA 1:47:19.5	GERMANY 1:51:16.5	FRANCE 1:52:28.1
1998	GERMANY 1:40:13.6	RUSSIA 1:40:25.2	NORWAY 1:40:37.3
2002	GERMANY 1:27:55.0	NORWAY 1:28:25.6	RUSSIA 1:29:19.7
2006[2]	RUSSIA 1:16:12.5	GERMANY 1:17:03.2	FRANCE 1:18:38.7

[1]Only three per team; [2]4 x 6000 Metres

BOBSLEDDING

Men

2-Man Bob

1932	UNITED STATES I 8:14.14	SWITZERLAND II 8:16.28	UNITED STATES II 8:29.15
1936	UNITED STATES I 5:29.29	SWITZERLAND II 5:30.64	UNITED STATES II 5:33.96
1948	SWITZERLAND II 5:29.2	SWITZERLAND I 5:30.4	UNITED STATES II 5:35.3
1952	GERMANY I 5:24.54	UNITED STATES I 5:26.89	SWITZERLAND I 5:27.71
1956	ITALY I 5:39.14	ITALY II 5:31.45	SWITZERLAND I 5:37.46
1964	GREAT BRITAIN I 4:21.90	ITALY II 4:22.02	ITALY I 4:22.63
1968	ITALY I 4:41.54[1]	FRG I 4:41.54	ROMANIA 4:44.46
1972	FRG II 4:47.07	FRG I 4:58.84	SWITZERLAND I 4:59.33
1976	GDR II 3:44.42	FRG I 3:44.99	SWITZERLAND I 3:45.70
1980	SWITZERLAND II 4:09.36	GDR II 4:10.93	GDR I 4:11.08
1984	GDR II 3:28.56	GDR I 3:26.04	SOVIET UNION II 3:26.16
1988	SOVIET UNION I 3:53.48	GDR I 3:54.19	GDR II 3:54.64
1992	SWITZERLAND I 4:03.26	GERMANY I 4:03.55	GERMANY II 4:03.63
1994	SWITZERLAND I 3:30.81	SWITZERLAND II 3:30.86	ITALY I 3:31.01
1998	ITALY I 3:37.24	–	GERMANY I 3:37.89
	CANADA I 3:27.24		
2002	GERMANY I 3:10.11	SWITZERLAND I 3:10.20	SWITZERLAND II 3:10.62
2006	GERMANY I 3:43.38	CANADA 3:43.59	SWITZERLAND 3:43.73

1924-1928,1960 Event not held
[1]Italy had fastest single run

4-Man Bob[1]

1924	SWITZERLAND I 5:45.54	GREAT BRITAIN II 5:48.83	BELGIUM I 6:02.29
1928[2]	UNITED STATES II 3:20.5	UNITED STATES I 3:21.0	GERMANY II 3:21.9
1932	UNITED STATES I 7:53.68	UNITED STATES II 7:55.70	GERMANY I 8:00.04
1936	SWITZERLAND II 5:19.85	SWITZERLAND I 5:22.73	GREAT BRITAIN I 5:23.41
1948	UNITED STATES II 5:20.1	BELGIUM 5:21.3	UNITED STATES I 5:21.5
1952	GERMANY 5:07.84	UNITED STATES I 5:10.48	SWITZERLAND I 5:11.70
1956	SWITZERLAND I 5:10.44	ITALY II 5:12.10	UNITED STATES I 5:12.39
1964	CANADA 4:14.46	AUSTRIA 4:15.48	ITALY II 4:15.60
1968[2]	ITALY I 2:17.39	AUSTRIA I 2:17.48	SWITZERLAND I 2:18.04
1972	SWITZERLAND 4:43.07	ITALY I 4:43.83	FRG I 4:43.92
1976	GDR I 3:40.43	SWITZERLAND II 3:40.89	FRG I 3:41.37
1980	GDR I 3:59.92	SWITZERLAND I 4:00.87	GDR II 4:00.97
1984	GDR I 3:20.22	GDR II 3:20.78	SWITZERLAND I 3:21.39
1988	SWITZERLAND I 3:47.51	GDR I 3:47.58	SOVIET UNION II 3:48.26
1992	AUSTRIA I 3:53.90	GERMANY I 3:53.92	SWITZERLAND I 3:54.13
1994	GERMANY II 3:27.78	SWITZERLAND I 3:27.84	GERMANY I 3:28.01
1998[3]	GERMANY II 2:39.41	SWITZERLAND I 2:40.01	GREAT BRITAIN I 2:40.06
			FRANCE 2:40.06
2002	GERMANY I 3:07.51	UNITED STATES I 3:07.81	UNITED STATES II 3:07.86
2006	GERMANY I 3:40.42	RUSSIA 3:40.55	SWITZERLAND 3:40.83

1960 Event not held
[1]5-man teams allowed until 1932; [2]two runs only; [3]three runs only

Women

Introduced in 2002

2-Woman Bob

2002[1]	UNITED STATES II 1:37.76	GERMANY I 1:38.06	GERMANY II 1:38.29
2006	GERMANY 3:49.98	UNITED STATES 3:50.69	ITALY 3:51.01

[1]Two runs only

CURLING

Men

1924	GREAT BRITAIN	SWEDEN	FRANCE
1998	SWITZERLAND	CANADA	NORWAY
2002	NORWAY	CANADA	SWITZERLAND
2006	CANADA	FINLAND	UNITED STATES

1928-1994 Event not held

Women

1998	CANADA	DENMARK	SWEDEN
2002	GREAT BRITAIN	SWITZERLAND	CANADA
2006	SWEDEN	SWITZERLAND	CANADA

1924-1994 Event not held

FIGURE SKATING

Men

Year	Gold	Silver	Bronze
1908[1]	Nikolai Panin (RUS) 219pts	Arthur Cumming (GBR) 164	George Hall-Say (GBR) 104
1908	Ulrich Salchow (SWE) 1886.5pts	Richard Johansson (SWE) 1826.0	Per Thorén (SWE) 1787.0
1920	Gillis Grafström (SWE) 2838.5pts	Andreas Krogh (NOR) 2634	Martin Stixrud (NOR) 2561.5
1924	Gillis Grafström (SWE) 2575.25pts	Willy Böckl (AUT) 2518.75	Georges Gautschi (SUI) 2233.5
1928	Gillis Grafström (SWE) 2698.25pts	Willy Böckl (AUT) 2682.50	Robert von Zeebroeck (BEL) 2578.75
1932	Karl Schäfer (AUT) 2602.0pts	Gillis Grafström (SWE) 2514.5	Montgomery Wilson (CAN) 2448.3
1936	Karl Schäfer (AUT) 2959.0pts	Ernst Baier (GER) 2805.3	Felix Kaspar (AUT) 2801.0
1948	Richard Button (USA) 1720pts	Hans Gerschwiler (SUI) 1630.1	Edi Rada (AUT) 1603.2
1952	Richard Button (USA) 1730.3pts	Helmut Seibt (AUT) 1621.3	James Grogan (USA) 1627.4
1956	Hayes Alan Jenkins (USA)1497.95pts	Ronald Robertson (USA) 1492.1	David Jenkins (USA) 1465.41
1960	David Jenkins (USA) 1440.2pts	Karol Divin (TCH) 141.3	Donald Jackson (CAN) 1401.0
1964	Manfred Schnelldorfer (GER) 1916.9pts	Alain Calmar (FRA) 1876.5	Scott Allen (USA) 1873.6
1968	Wolfgang Schwarz (AUT) 1894.1pts	Tim Woods (USA) 1891.6	Patrick Péra (FRA) 1864.5
1972	Ondrej Nepela (TCH) 2739.1pts	Sergey Tchetveroukhin (URS) 2672.4	Patrick Péra (FRA) 2653.1
1976	John Curry (GBR) 192.74pts	Vladimir Kovalyev (URS) 187.64	Toller Cranston (CAN) 187.38
1980	Robin Cousins (GBR) 189.48pts[2]	Jan Hoffmann (GDR) 189.72 (2)	Charles Tickner (USA) 187.06
1984	Scott Hamilton (USA) 3.4pl	Brian Orser (CAN) 5.6	Jozef Sabovtchik (TCH) 7.4
1988	Brian Boitano (USA) 3.0pl	Brian Orser (CAN) 4.2	Viktor Petrenko (URS) 7.8
1992	Viktor Petrenko (EUN) 1.5pl	Paul Wylie (USA) 3.5	Petr Barna (TCH) 4.0
1994	Alexei Urmanov (RUS) 1.5pl	Elvis Stojko (CAN) 3.0	Philippe Candeloro (FRA) 6.5
1998	Ilya Kulik (RUS) 1.5pl	Elvis Stojko (CAN) 4.0	Philippe Candeloro (FRA) 4.5
2002	Alexei Yagudin (RUS) 1.5pl	Yevgeni Pluschenko (RUS) 4.0	Timothy Goebel (USA) 4.5
2006	Yevgeni Pluschenko (RUS) 258.33pts	Stephane Lambiel (SUI) 231.31	Jeffrey Buttle (CAN) 227.59

1912 Event not held
[1]Special figures competition; [2]Majority of judges favoured Cousins.

Women

Year	Gold	Silver	Bronze
1908	Madge Syers (GBR) 1262.5pts	Elsa Rendschmidt (GER) 1055.0	Dorothy Greenhough-Smith (GBR) 960.0
1920	Magda Mauroy-Julin (SWE) 913.5pts	Svea Norén (SWE) 887.75	Theresa Weld (USA) 898.0
1924	Herma Planck-Szabó (AUT) 2094.25pts	Beatrix Loughran (USA) 1959.0	Ethel Muckelt (GBR) 1750.0
1928	Sonja Henie (NOR) 2452.25pts	Fritzi Berger (AUT) 2248.50	Beatrix Loughran (USA) 2254.50
1932	Sonja Henie (NOR) 2302.5pts	Fritzi Berger (AUT) 2167.1	Maribel Vinson (USA) 2158.5
1936	Sonja Henie (NOR) 2971.4pts	Cecilia Colledge (GBR) 2926.8	Vivi-Anne Hultén (SWE) 2763.2
1948	Barbara-Ann Scott (CAN) 1467.7pts	Eva Pawlik (AUT) 1418.3	Jeanette Altwegg (GBR) 1405.5
1952	Jeanette Altwegg (GBR) 1455.8pts	Tenley Albright (USA) 1432.2	Jacqueline du Bief (FRA) 1422.0
1956	Tenley Albright (USA) 1866.30pts	Carol Heiss (USA) 1848.24	Ingrid Wendl (AUT) 1753.91
1960	Carol Heiss (USA) 1490.1pts	Sjoukje Dijkstra (NED) 1424.8	Barbara Roles (USA) 1414.8
1964	Sjoukje Dijkstra (NED) 20.18.5pts	Regine Heitzer (AUT) 1945.5	Petra Burka (CAN) 1940.0
1968	Peggy Fleming (USA) 1970.5pts	Gabrielle Seyfert (GDR) 1882.3	Hana Maskova (TCH) 1828.8
1972	Beatrix Schuba (AUT) 2751.5pts	Karen Magnussen (CAN) 2763.2	Janet Lynn (USA) 2663.1
1976	Dorothy Hamill (USA) 193.80pts	Dianne De Leeuw (NED) 190.24	Christine Errath (GDR) 188.16
1980	Anett Pötzsch (GDR) 189.00pts	Linda Fratianne (USA) 188.30	Dagmar Lurz (FRG) 183.04
1984	Katarina Witt (GDR) 3.2pl	Rosalyn Sumners (USA) 4.6	Kira Ivanova (URS) 9.2
1988	Katarina Witt (GDR) 4.2pl	Elizabeth Manley (CAN) 4.6	Debra Thomas (USA) 6.0
1992	Kristi Yamaguchi (USA) 1.5pl	Midori Ito (JPN) 4.0	Nancy Kerrigan (USA) 4.0
1994	Oksana Baiul (UKR) 2.0pl	Nancy Kerrigan (USA) 2.5	Lu Chen (CHN) 5.0

1998	Tara Lipinski (USA) 2.0pl	Michelle Kwan (USA) 2.5	Lu Chen (CHN) 5.0
2002	Sarah Hughes (USA) 3.0pl	Irina Slutskaya (RUS) 3.0	Michelle Kwan (USA) 3.5
2006	Shisuka Arakawa (JPN) 191.34pts	Sasha Cohen (USA) 183.36	Irina Slutskaya (RUS) 181.44

1912 Event not held

Pairs

1908	GERMANY 56.0pts	GREAT BRITAIN 51.5	GREAT BRITAIN 48.0
1920	FINLAND 80.75pts	NORWAY 72.75	GREAT BRITAIN 66.25
1924	AUSTRIA 74.50pts	FINLAND 71.75	FRANCE 69.25
1928	FRANCE 100.50pts	AUSTRIA 99.25	AUSTRIA 93.25
1932	FRANCE 76.7pts	UNITED STATES 77.5	HUNGARY 76.4
1936	GERMANY 103.0pts	AUSTRIA 102.7	HUNGARY 97.6
1948	BELGIUM 123.5pts	HUNGARY 122.2	CANADA 121.0
1952	GERMANY 102.6pts	UNITED STATES 100.6	HUNGARY 97.4
1956	AUSTRIA 101.8pts	CANADA 101.9	HUNGARY 99.3
1960	CANADA 80.4pts	GERMANY 76.8	UNITED STATES 76.2
1964[1]	CANADA 98.5pts	SOVIET UNION 104.4	GERMANY 103.6
1968	SOVIET UNION 315.2pts	SOVIET UNION 312.3	FRG 304.4
1972	SOVIET UNION 420.4pts	SOVIET UNION 419.4	GDR 411.8
1976	SOVIET UNION 140.54pts	GDR 136.35	GDR 134.57
1980	SOVIET UNION 147.26pts	SOVIET UNION 143.80	GDR 140.52
1984	SOVIET UNION 1.4pl	UNITED STATES 2.8	SOVIET UNION 3.8
1988	SOVIET UNION 1.4pl	SOVIET UNION 2.8	UNITED STATES 4.2
1992	UNIFIED TEAM 1.5pl	UNIFIED TEAM 3.0	CANADA 4.5
1994	RUSSIA 1.5pl	RUSSIA 3.0	CANADA 4.5
1998	RUSSIA 2.0pl	RUSSIA 3.5	GERMANY 6.0
2002[2]	RUSSIA	–	CHINA 4.5
	CANADA		
2006	RUSSIA 204.46pts	CHINA 189.73	CHINA 186.91

1912 Event not held

[1]Marika Kilius & Hansjürgen Bäumler (GER) were second, then disqualified, and then reinstated; [2]Canada promoted to equal first place after protests about unfair judging which had placed them second

Ice Dance

1976	SOVIET UNION 209.92pts	SOVIET UNION 204.88	UNITED STATES 202.64
1980	SOVIET UNION 205.48pts	HUNGARY 204.52	SOVIET UNION 201.86
1984	GREAT BRITAIN 2.0pl	SOVIET UNION 4.0pl	SOVIET UNION 7.0pl
1988	SOVIET UNION 2.0pl	SOVIET UNION 4.0pl	CANADA 6.0pl
1992	UNIFIED TEAM 2.0pl	FRANCE 4.4	UNIFIED TEAM 5.6
1994	RUSSIA 3.4pl	RUSSIA 3.8	GREAT BRITAIN 4.8
1998	RUSSIA 2.0pl	RUSSIA 4.0	FRANCE 7.0
2002	FRANCE 2.0pl	RUSSIA 4.0	ITALY 6.0
2006	RUSSIA 200.64 pts	UNITED STATES 196.06	UKRAINE 195.85

1908-1972 Event not held

FREESTYLE SKIING

Men

Moguls

1992	Edgar Grospiron (FRA) 25.81pts	Olivier Allamand (FRA) 24.87	Nelson Carmichael (USA) 24.82
1994	Jean-Luc Brassard (CAN) 27.74pts	Sergei Shoupletsov (RUS) 26.90	Edgar Grospiron (FRA) 26.64
1998	Jonny Moseley (USA) 26.93pts	Janne Lahtela (FIN) 26.01	Sami Mustonen (FIN) 25.76
2002	Janne Lahtela (FIN) 27.97pts	Travis Mayer (USA) 27.59	Richard Gay (FRA) 26.91
2006	Dale Begg-Smith (AUS) 26.77pts	Mikko Ronkainen (FIN) 26.62	Toby Dawson (USA) 26.30

1924-1988 Event not held

Aerials

1994	Andreas Schönbächler (SUI) 234.67pts	Phillippe Laroche (CAN) 228.23	Lloyd Langlois (CAN) 222.44
1998	Eric Bergoust (USA) 255.64pts	Sebastien Foucras (FRA) 248.79	Dmitri Daschinsky (BLR) 240.79
2002	Aleš Valenta (CZE) 257.02pts	Joe Pack (USA) 251.64	Alexei Grischin (BLR) 252.19
2006	Xiaopeng Han (CHN) 250.77pts	Dmitri Dashinsky (BLR) 248.68	Vladimr Lebedyeva (RUS) 246.76

1924-1992 Event not held

Women

Moguls

1992	Donna Weinbrecht (USA) 23.69pts	Yelizaveta Kozhevnikova (EUN) 23.50	Stine Lise Hattestad (NOR) 23.04
1994	Stine Lise Hattestad (NOR) 25.97pts	Elizabeth McIntyre (USA) 25.89	Yelizaveta Kozhevnikova (EUN) 25.81
1998	Tae Satoya (JPN) 25.06	Tatyana Mittermayer (GER) 24.62	Kari Traa (NOR) 24.09
2002	Kari Traa (NOR) 25.94pts	Shannon Bahrke (USA) 25.06	Tae Satoya (JPN) 24.85
2006	Jennifer Heil (CAN) 26.50pts	Kari Traa (NOR) 25.65	Sandra Laoura (FRA) 25.37

1924-1988 Event not held

Aerials

1994	Lina Cheryasova (UZB) 166.84pts	Marie Lindgren (SWE) 165.88	Hilde Synnøve Lid (NOR) 164.13
1998	Nikki Stone (USA) 193.00pts	Xu Nannan (CHN) 186.97	Colette Brand (SUI) 171.83
2002	Alisa Camplin (AUS) 193.47pts	Veronica Brenner (CAN) 190.02	Deidra Dionne (CAN) 189.26
2006	Evelyne Leu (SUI) 202.55pts	Nina Li (CHN) 197.39	Alisa Camplin (AUS) 191.39

1924-1992 Event not held

ICE HOCKEY

Men

1920	CANADA	UNITED STATES	CZECHOSLOVAKIA
1924	CANADA	UNITED STATES	GREAT BRITAIN
1928	CANADA	SWEDEN	SWITZERLAND
1932	CANADA	UNITED STATES	GERMANY
1936	GREAT BRITAIN	CANADA	UNITED STATES
1948	CANADA	CZECHOSLOVAKIA	SWITZERLAND
1952	CANADA	UNITED STATES	SWEDEN
1956	SOVIET UNION	UNITED STATES	CANADA
1960	UNITED STATES	CANADA	SOVIET UNION
1964	SOVIET UNION	SWEDEN	CZECHOSLOVAKIA
1968	SOVIET UNION	CZECHOSLOVAKIA	CANADA
1972	SOVIET UNION	UNITED STATES	CZECHOSLOVAKIA
1976	SOVIET UNION	CZECHOSLOVAKIA	FRG[1]
1980	UNITED STATES	SOVIET UNION	SWEDEN
1984	SOVIET UNION	CZECHOSLOVAKIA	SWEDEN
1988	SOVIET UNION	FINLAND	SWEDEN
1992	UNIFIED TEAM	CANADA	CZECHOSLOVAKIA
1994	SWEDEN	CANADA	FINLAND
1998	CZECH REPUBLIC	RUSSIA	FINLAND
2002	CANADA	UNITED STATES	RUSSIA
2006	SWEDEN	FINLAND	CZECH REPUBLIC

[1]*Three-way tie for bronze with the USA and Finland decided on goal average.*

Women

1998	UNITED STATES	CANADA	FINLAND
2002	CANADA	UNITED STATES	SWEDEN
2006	CANADA	SWEDEN	UNITED STATES

1924-1994 Events not held

LUGEING

Men

Singles

1964	Thomas Köhler (GER) 3:26.77	Klaus Bonsack (GER) 3:27.04	Hans Plenk (GER) 3:30.15
1968	Manfred Schmid (AUT) 2:52.48	Thomas Köhler (GDR) 2:52.66	Klaus Bonsack (GDR) 2:55.33
1972	Wolfgang Scheidel (GDR) 3:27.58	Harald Ehrig (GDR) 3:28.39	Wolfram Fiedler (GDR) 3:28.73
1976	Detlef Günther (GDR) 3:27.688	Josef Fendt (FRG) 3:28.196	Hans Rinn (GDR) 3:28.574
1980	Bernhard Glass (GDR) 2:54.796	Paul Hildgartner (ITA) 2:55.372	Anton Winkler (FRG) 2:56.545
1984	Paul Hildgartner (ITA) 3:04.258	Sergey Danilin (URS) 3:04.962	Valeriy Dudin (URS) 3:05.012
1988	Jens Müller (GDR) 3:05.548	Georg Hackl (FRG) 3:05.916	Yuriy Khartchenko (URS) 3:06.274
1992	Georg Hackl (GER) 3:02.363	Markus Prock (AUT) 3:02.669	Markus Schmidt (AUT) 3:02.942
1994	Georg Hackl (GER) 3:21.571	Markus Prock (AUT) 3:21.584	Armin Zöggeler (ITA) 3:21.833
1998	Georg Hackl (GER) 3:18.436	Armin Zöggeler (ITA) 3:18.939	Jens Müller (GER) 3:19.093
2002	Armin Zöggeler (ITA) 2:57.91	Georg Hackl (GER) 2:58.270	Markus Prock (AUT) 2:58.283
2006	Armin Zöggeler (ITA) 3:26.088	Albert Demtschenko (RUS) 3:26.198	Martins Rubenis (LAT) 3:26.445

1924-1960 Event not held

2-Man

1964	AUSTRIA 1:41.62	AUSTRIA 1:41.91	ITALY 1:42.87
1968	GDR 1:35.85	AUSTRIA 1:36.34	FRG 1:37.29
1972	ITALY 1:28.35	–	GDR 1:29.16
	GDR 1:28.35		
1976	GDR 1:25.604	FRG 1:25.889	AUSTRIA 1:25.919
1980	GDR 1:19.331	ITALY 1:19.606	AUSTRIA 1:19.795
1984	FRG 1:23.620	SOVIET UNION 1:23.660	GDR 1:23.887
1988	GDR 1:31.940	GDR 1:32.039	FRG 1:32.274
1992	GERMANY 1:32.053	GERMANY 1:32.239	ITALY 1:32.298
1994	ITALY 1:36.720	ITALY II 1:36.769	GERMANY 1:36.945
1998	GERMANY 1:41.105	UNITED STATES I 1:41.127	UNITED STATES II 1:41.217
2002	GERMANY 1:26.082	UNITED STATES 1:26.216	UNITED STATES 1:26.220
2006	AUSTRIA 1:34.497	GERMANY 1:34.807	ITALY 1:34.930

1924-1960 Event not held

Women

Singles

1964	Ortrun Enderlein (GER) 3:24.67	Ilse Geisler (GER) 3:27.42	Helene Thurner (AUT) 3:29.06
1968	Erica Lechner (ITA) 2:28.66	Christa Schmuck (FRG) 2:29.37	Angelika Dünhaupt (FRG) 2:29.56
1972	Anna-Maria Müller (GDR) 2:59.18	Ute Rührold (GDR) 2:59.49	Margit Schumann (GDR) 2:59.54
1976	Margit Schumann (GDR) 2:50.621	Ute Rührold (GDR) 2:50.846	Elisabeth Demleitner (FRG) 2:51.056
1980	Vera Sosulya (URS) 2:36.537	Melitta Sollmann (GDR) 2:37.657	Ingrida Amantova (URS) 2:37.817
1984	Steffi Martin (GDR) 2:46.570	Bettine Schmidt (GDR) 2:46.873	Ute Weiss (GDR) 2:47.248
1988	Steffi Martin-Walter (GDR) 3:03.973	Ute Weiss-Oberhoffner (GDR) 3 :04.105	Cerstin Schmidt (GDR) 3:04.181
1992	Doris Neuner (AUT) 3:06.696	Angelika Neuner (AUT) 3:06.769	Susi Erdmann (GER) 3:07.115
1994	Gerda Weissensteiner (ITA) 3:15.517	Susi Erdman (GER) 3:16.276	Andrea Tagwerker (AUT) 3:16.652
1998	Silke Kraushaar (GER) 3:23.779	Barbara Niedernhuber (GER) 3:23.781	Angelika Neuner (AUT) 3:24.253
2002	Sylke Otto (GER) 2:52.464	Barbara Niedernhuber (GER) 2:52:785	Silke Kraushaar (GER) 2:52.865
2006	Sylke Otto (GER) 3:07.979	Silke Kraushaar (GER) 3:08.115	Tatjana Hüfner (GER) 3:08.460

1924-1960 Event not held

SKELETON SLED

Men

1928[1]	Jennison Heaton (USA) 3:01.8	John Heaton (USA) 3:02.8	Earl of Northesk (GBR) 3:05.1
1948[2]	Nino Bibbia (ITA) 5:23.2	John Heaton (USA) 5:24.6	John Crammond (GBR) 5:25.1
2002	Jim Shea (USA) 1:41.96	Martin Rettl (AUT) 1:42.01	Gregor Stähli (SUI) 1:42.15
2006	Duff Gibson (CAN) 1:55.88	Jeffery Pain (CAN) 1:56.14	Gregor Stähli (SUI) 1:56.80

1924, 1932-1936, 1952-1998 Event not held
[1]Aggregate of three runs; [2]Aggregate of six runs

Women

2002	Tristan Gale (USA) 1:45.11	Lea Ann Parsley (USA) 1:45.21	Alex Coomber (GBR) 1:45.37
2006	Maya Pedersen (SUI) 1:59.83	Shelley Rudman (GBR) 2:01.06	Melissa Hollingsworth-Richards (CAN) 2:01.41

1924-1998 Event not held

MILITARY PATROL

1924	SWITZERLAND	FINLAND	FRANCE

1928-2006 Event not held

NORDIC SKIING

Men

Sprint (freestyle)

2002[1]	Tor Arne Hetland (NOR) 2:56.9	Peter Schlickenrieder (GER) 2:57.0	Cristian Zorzi (ITA) 2:57.2
2006[2]	Björn Lind (SWE) 2:26.5	Roddy Darragon (FRA) 2:27.1	Thobias Fredrksson (SWE) 2:27.8

1924-1998 Event not held
[1]1480m; [2]1325m

Team Sprint

2006	SWEDEN 17:02.9	NORWAY 17:03.5	RUSSIA 17:05.2

1924-2002 Event not held

15,000 Metres

1924[1]	Thorleif Haug (NOR) 1:14:31.0	Johan Gröttumsbraaten (NOR) 1:15.51.0	Tipani Niku (FIN) 1:16:26.0
1928[2]	Johan Gröttumsbraaten (NOR) 1.37.01.0	Ole Hegge (NOR) 1:39:01.0	Reidar Ödegaard (NOR) 1:40:11.0
1932[3]	Sven Utterström (SWE) 1:23:07.0	Axel Wikström (SWE) 1:25:07.0	Veli Saarinen (FIN) 1:25:24.0
1936[1]	Erik-August Larsson (SWE) 1:14:38.0	Oddbjörn Hagen (NOR) 1:15:33.0	Pekka Niemi (FIN) 1:16:59.0
1948[1]	Martin Lundström (SWE) 1:13:50.0	Nils Östensson (SWE) 1:14:22.0	Gunnar Eriksson (SWE) 1:16:06.6
1952[1]	Hallgeir Brenden (NOR) 1:1:34.0	Tapio Mäkelä (FIN) 1:2:09.0	Paavo Lonkila (FIN) 1:2:20.0
1956	Hallgeir Brenden (NOR) 49:39.0	Sixten Jernberg (SWE) 50:14.0	Pavel Koltschin (URS) 50:17.0
1960	Haakon Brusveen (NOR) 51:55.5	Sixten Jernberg (SWE) 51:58.6	Veikko Hakulinen (FIN) 52:03.0
1964	Eero Mäntyranta (FIN) 50:54.1	Harald Grönningen (NOR) 51:34.8	Sixten Jernberg (SWE) 51:42.2
1968	Harald Grönningen (NOR) 47:54.2	Eero Mäntyranta (FIN) 47:56.1	Gunnar Larsson (SWE) 48:33.7
1972	Sven-Ake Lundback (SWE) 45:28.24	Fedor Simsachov (URS) 46:00.84	Ivar Formo (NOR) 44:19.25
1976	Nikolai Bayukov (URS) 43:58.47	Yevgeni Belyayev (URS) 44:01.10	Arto Koivisto (FIN) 44:19.25
1980	Thomas Wassberg (SWE) 41:25.63	Juha Mieto (FIN) 41:57.64	Ove Aunli (NOR) 452:28.62
1984	Gunde Svan (SWE) 41:25.6	Aki Karvonen (FIN) 41:34.9	Harri Kirvesniemi (FIN) 41:45.6
1988	Michael Deviatyarov (URS) 41:18.9	Pal Mikkelsplass (NOR) 41:33.4	Vladimir Smirnov (URS) 41:40.5
2002	Andrus Veerpalu (EST) 37:07.4	Frode Estil (NOR) 37:43.4	Jaak Mae (EST) 37:50.8
2006	Andrus Veerpalu (EST) 38:01.3	Lukas Bauer (CZE) 38:15.8	Tobias Angerer (GER) 38:20.5

1992-1994 Event not held
[1]Distance 18km; [2]Distance 19.7km; [3]Distance 18.2km

Combined Pursuit[1]

1992	Bjørn Dahlie (NOR) 1:05:37.9	Vegard Ulvang (NOR) 1:06:31.3	Giorgio Vanzetta (ITA) 1:06:31.2
1994	Bjørn Dahlie (NOR) 1:00:08.8	Vladimir Smirnov (KZK) 1:00:38.0	Silvio Fauner (ITA) 1:01:48.6
1998	Thomas Alsgaard (NOR) 1:07:01.7	Bjørn Dahlie (NOR) 1:07:02.8	Vladimir Smirnov (URS) 1:07:31.5
2002[2]	Frode Estil (NOR) 49:48.9	–	Per Olofsson (SWE) 49:52.9
	Thomas Alsgaard (NOR) 49:48.9		
2006	Evgeni Dementiev (RUS) 1:17:0.8	Frode Estil (NOR) 1:17:01.4	Pietro Piller Cottrer (ITA) 1:17:01.7

1924-1988 Event not held
[1]From 1992-1998 15km (freestyle) times were added to the 10km (classical) race. In 2002 the second race was a 10km (freestyle) one. In 2006 both races were over 15km; [2]Johann Mühlegg (ESP) finished first in 49:20.4 but disqualified

30,000 Metres (freestyle)

1956	Veikko Hakulinen (FIN) 1:44:06.0	Sixten Jernberg (SWE) 1:44:30.0	Pavel Koltschin (URS) 1:45:45.0
1960	Sixten Jernberg (SWE) 1:56:03.9	Rolf Rämgard (SWE) 1:51:16.9	Nikolai Anikin (URS) 1:52:28.2
1964	Eero Mäntyranta (FIN) 1:30:50.7	Harald Grönningen (NOR) 1:32:02.3	Igor Voronchikin (URS) 1:32:15.8
1968	Franco Nones (ITA) 1:35:29.2	Odd Martinsen (NOR) 1:36:28.9	Eero Mäntyranta (FIN) 1:36:55.3
1972	Vyacheslav Vedenine (URS) 1:36:31.2	Paal Tyldum (NOR) 1:37:25.3	Johannes Harviken (NOR) 1:37:32.4
1976	Sergei Savelyev (URS) 1:30:29.38	William Koch (USA) 1:30:57.84	Ivan Garanin (URS) 1:31:09.29
1980	Nikolai Simyatov (URS) 1:27:02.80	Vassili Rochev (URS) 1:27:34.22	Ivan Lebanov (BUL) 1:28:03.87
1984	Nikolai Simyatov (URS) 1:28:56.3	Alexander Zavyalov (URS) 1:24:35.1	Gunde Svan (SWE) 1:29:35.7
1988	Alexei Prokurorov (URS) 1:24:26.3	Vladimir Smirnov (URS) 1:24:35.1	Vegard Ulvang (NOR) 1:25:11.6
1992	Vegard Ulvang (NOR) 1:22:27.8	Bjørn Dahlie (NOR) 1:23:14.0	Terje Langli (NOR) 1:23:42.5
1994	Thomas Alsgaard (NOR) 1:12:26.4	Bjørn Dahlie (NOR) 1:13:13.6	Mika Myllylä (FIN) 1:14:14.0
1998	Mika Myllylä (FIN) 1:33:55.8	Erling Jeune (NOR) 1:35:27.1	Silvio Fauner (ITA) 1:36:08.5
2002[1]	Christian Hoffmann (AUT) 1:11:31.0	Mikhail Botvinov (AUT) 1:11:32.3	Kristen Skjeldal (NOR) 1:11:42.7

1924-1952, 2006 Event not held
[1]Johann Mühlegg (ESP) finished first in 1:09:28.9 but disqualified

50,000 Metres (classical)

1924	Thorleif Haug (NOR) 3:44:32.0	Thoralf Strömstad (NOR) 3:46:23.0	Johan Gröttumsbraaten (NOR) 3:47:46.0
1928	Per Erik Hedlund (SWE) 4:52:03.0	Gustaf Jonsson (SWE) 5:05:30.0	Volger Andersson (SWE) 5h 05:46.0
1932	Veli Saarinen (FIN) 4:28:00.0	Väinö Likkanen (FIN) 4:28:20.0	Arne Rustadstuen (NOR) 4:31:53.0
1936	Elis Wiklung (SWE) 3:30:11.1	Axel Wikström (SWE) 3:33:20.0	Nils-Joel Englund (SWE) 3:34:10.0
1948	Nils Karlsson (SWE) 3:47:48.0	Harald Eriksson (SWE) 3:52:20.0	Benjamin Vanninen (FIN) 3:38:28.0
1952	Veikko Hakulinen (FIN) 3:33:33.0	Eero Kolehmainen (FIN) 3:38:11.0	Magnar Estenstad (NOR) 3:57:28.0
1956	Sixten Jernberg (SWE) 2:50:27.0	Veikko Hakulinen (FIN) 2:51:45.0	Fedor Terentyev (URS) 2h 53:32.0
1960	Kalevi Hämäläinen (FIN) 2:59:06.3	Veikko Hakulinen (FIN) 2:59:26.7	Rolf Rämgard (SWE) 3:02:46.7

1964	Sixten Jernberg (SWE) 2:43:52.6	Assar Rönnlund (SWE) 2:44:58.2	Arto Tiainen (FIN) 2:45:30.4
1968	Olle Ellefsäter (NOR) 2:28:45.8	Vyacheslav Vedenine (URS) 2:29:02.5	Josef Haas (SUI) 2:29:14.8
1972	Paal Tyldrum (NOR) 2:43:14.75	Magne Myrmo (NOR) 2:43:29.45	Vyacheslav Vedenine (URS) 2:44:00.19
1976	Ivar Formo (NOR) 2:37:30.50	Gert-Dietmar Klause (GDR) 2:38:13.21	Benny Södergren (SWE) 2:39:39.21
1980	Nikolai Simyatov (URS) 2:27:24.60	Juha Mieto (FIN) 2:30:20.52	Alexander Savyalov (URS) 2;30:51.52
1984	Thomas Wassberg (SWE) 2:15:55.8	Gunde Svan (SWE) 2:16:00.7	Aki Karvonen (FIN) 2:17:04.7
1988	Gunde Svan (SWE) 2:04:30.9	Maurilio De Zolt (ITA) 2:05:36.4	Andreas Grünenfelder (SUI) 2:06:01.9
1992	Bjørn Dahlie (NOR) 2:03:41.5	Maurilio De Zolt (ITA) 2:04:39.1	Giorgio Vanzetta (ITA) 2:06:42.1
1994	Vladimir Smirnov (KZK) 2:07:20.0	Myka Myllylä (FIN) 2:08:41.9	Sture Sivertsen (NOR) 2:08:49.0
1998	Bjørn Dahlie (NOR) 2:05:08.2	Niklas Jonsson (SWE) 2:05:16.3	Christian Hoffmann (AUT) 2:06:01.8
2002[1]	Mikhail Ivanov (RUS) 2:06:20.8	Andrus Veerpalu (EST) 2:06:44.5	Odd-Bjørnhjelmeset (NOR) 2:08:41.5
2006	Georgio Di Centa (ITA) 2:06:11.8	Evgeni Dementiev (RUS) 2:06:12.6	Mikhail Botvinov (AUT) 2:06:12.7

[1]Johann Mühlegg (ESP) finished first in 2h 06:05.9 but was disqualified

4x10,000 Metres Relay

1936	FINLAND 2:41:33.0	NORWAY 2:41:39.0	SWEDEN 2:43:03.0
1948	SWEDEN 2:32:08.0	FINLAND 2:41:06.0	NORWAY 2:44:33.0
1952	FINLAND 2:20:16.0	NORWAY 2:23:13.0	SWEDEN 2:24:13.0
1956	SOVIET UNION 2:15:30.0	FINLAND 2:16:31.0	SWEDEN 2:17:42.0
1960	FINLAND 2:18:45.6	NORWAY 2:18:46.4	SOVIET UNION 2:21:21.6
1964	SWEDEN 2:18:34.6	FINLAND 2:18:42.4	SOVIET UNION 2:18:46.9
1968	NORWAY 2:08:33.5	SWEDEN 2:10:13.2	FINLAND 2:10:56.7
1972	SOVIET UNION 2:04:47.94	NORWAY 2:04:57.6	SWITZERLAND 2:07:00.06
1976	FINLAND 2:07:59.72	NORWAY 2:09:58.36	SOVIET UNION 2:10:51.46
1980	SOVIET UNION 1:57:03.6	NORWAY 1:58:45.77	FINLAND 2:00:00.18
1984	SWEDEN 1:55:06.3	SOVIET UNION 1:55:16.5	FINLAND 1:56:31.4
1988	SWEDEN 1:43:58.6	SOVIET UNION 1:44:11.3	CZECHOSLOVAKIA 1:45:22.7
1992	NORWAY 1:39:26.0	ITALY 1:40:52.7	FINLAND 1:41:22.9
1994	ITALY 1:41:15.0	NORWAY 1:41:15.4	FINLAND 1:42:15.6
1998	NORWAY 1:40:55.7	ITALY 1:40:55.9	FINLAND 1:42:15.5
2002	NORWAY 1:32:45.5	ITALY 1:32:45.8	GERMANY 1:33:34.5
2006	ITALY 1:43:45.7	GERMANY 1:44:01.4	SWEDEN 1:44:01.7

1924-1932 Event not held

Women

Sprint (freestyle)

2002[1]	Yulia Tchepalova (RUS) 3:10.6	Evi Sachenbacher (GER) 3:12.2	Anita Moen (NOR) 3:12.7
2006[2]	Chandra Crawford (CAN) 2:12.3	Claudia Künzel (GER) 2:13.0	Alena Sidko (RUS) 2:13.2

1924-1998 Event not held
[1]1480m; [2]1145m

Team Sprint

2006	SWEDEN 16:36.9	CANADA 16:37.5	FINLAND 16:3.2

1924-2002 Event not held

10,000 Metres (classical)

1952	Lydia Wideman (FIN) 41:40.0	Mirja Hietamies (FIN) 42:39.0	Siiri Rantanen (FIN) 42:50.0
1956	Lyubov Kozyryeva (URS) 38:11.0	Radya Yeroschina (URS) 38:16.0	Sonja Edström (SWE) 38:23.0
1960	Maria Gusakova (URS) 39:46.6	Lyubov Baranova-Kozyryeva (URS) 40:04.2	Radya Yeroschina (URS) 40:06.0
1964	Klaudia Boyarskikh (URS) 40:24.3	Yevdokia Mekshilo (URS) 40:26.6	Maria Gusakova (URS) 40:46.6
1968	Toini Gustafsson (SWE) 36:46.5	Berit Mördre (NOR) 37:54.6	Inger Aufles (NOR) 37:59.9
1972	Galina Kulakova (URS) 34:17.8	Alevtina Olunina (URS) 34:54.1	Marjatta Kajosmaa (FIN) 34:56.5
1976	Raisa Smetanina (URS) 30:13.41	Helena Takalo (FIN) 30:14.28	Galina Kulakova (URS) 30:38.61
1980	Barbara Petzold (GDR) 30:31.54	Hilkka Riihivuori (FIN) 30:35.05	Helena Takalo (FIN) 30:45.25
1984	Marja-Liisa Hämäläinen (FIN) 31:44.2	Raisa Smetanina (URS) 32:02.9	Brit Petersen (NOR) 32:12.7
1988	Vida Ventsene (URS) 30:08.3	Raisa Smetanina (URS) 30:17.0	Marjo Matikainen (FIN) 30:20.5
2002[1]	Bente Skari (NOR) 28:05.6	Yulia Tchepalova (RUS) 28:09.9	Stefania Belmondo (ITA) 28:45.8
2006	Kristina Smigun (EST) 27:51.4	Marit Bjørgen (NOR) 28:12.7	Hiilde Pedersen (NOR) 28:14.0

1924-1948,1992-1998 Event not held
[1]Olga Danilova (RUS) finished second in 28:08.1 but was disqualified

Combined Pursuit[1]

1992	Lyubov Yegorova (EUN) 40:07.7	Stefania Belmondo (ITA) 40:31.8	Yelena Välbe (EUN) 40:51.7
1994	Lyubov Yegorova (RUS) 41:38.1	Manuela di Centa (ITA) 41:46.4	Stefania Belmondo (ITA) 42:21.1

1998 Larissa Lazutina (RUS) 46:06.9	Olga Danilova (RUS) 46:13.4	Katerina Neumannova (CZE) 46:14.2
2002[2] Beckie Scott (CAN) 25:09.9	Katerina Neumannova (CZE) 25:10.0	Viola Bauer (GER) 25:11.5
2006 Kristina Smigun (EST) 42:48.7	Katerina Neumannova (CZE) 42:50.6	Evgenia Medvedyeva-Abruzova (RUS) 43:03.2

1924-1988 Event not held
[1]*From 1992-1998 10km (freestyle) times were added to 5km (classical) race times. In 2002 second race was 5km (freestyle) In 2006 both races were over 7.5km;* [2]*Olga Danilova (RUS) and Larissa Lazutina (RUS) finished in first and second places in 24:52.1 and 24:59.0 respectively, but were disqualified*

15,000 Metres (freestyle)

1992 Lyubov Yegorova (EUN) 42:20.8	Marjut Lukharinen (FIN) 43:29.9	Yelena Välbe (EUN) 43:42.3
1994 Manuela di Centa (ITA) 39:44.5	Lyubov Yegorova (RUS) 41:03.0	Nina Gavrilyuk (RUS) 41:10.4
1998 Olga Danilova (RUS) 46:55.4	Larissa Lazutina (RUS) 47:01.0	Anita Moen-Guidon (NOR) 47:52.6
2002[1] Stefania Belmondo (ITA) 39:54.4	Katerina Neumannova (CZE) 40:01.3	Yulia Tchepalova (RUS) 40:02.1

1924-1988, 2006 Event not held
[1]*Larissa Lazutina (RUS) finished second in 39:56.2 but was disqualified*

30,000 Metres (classical)

1992 Stefania Belmondo (ITA) 1:22:30.1	Lyubov Yegorova (EUN) 1:22:52.0	Yelena Välbe (EUN) 1:24:13.9
1994 Manuela di Centa (ITA) 1:25:41.6	Marit Wold (NOR) 1:25:57.8	Marja-Liisa Hämäläinen (FIN) 1:26:13.6
1998 Yulia Tchepalova (RUS) 1:22:01.5	Stefania Belmondo (ITA) 1:22:11.7	Larissa Lazutina (RUS) 1:20:15.7
2002[1] Gabriella Paruzzi (ITA) 1:30:57.1	Stefania Belmondo (ITA) 1:31:01.6	Bente Skari (NOR) 1:31:36.3
2006 Katerina Neumannova (CZE) 1:22:25.4	Yulia Tchepalova (RUS) 1:22:26.8	Justyna Kowalcyzk (POL) 1:22:27.5

1924-1988 Event not held
[1]*Larissa Lazutina (RUS) finished first in 1:29:09.0 but was disqualified*

4x5000 Metres Relay[1]

1956 FINLAND 1:09:01.0	SOVIET UNION 1:09:28.0	SWEDEN 1:09:48.0
1960 SWEDEN 1:04:21.4	SOVIET UNION 1:05:02.6	FINLAND 1:06:27.5
1964 SOVIET UNION 59:20.2	SWEDEN 1:01:27.0	FINLAND 1:02:45.1
1968 NORWAY 57:30.0	SWEDEN 57:51.0	SOVIET UNION 58:13.6
1972 SOVIET UNION 48:46.15	FINLAND 49:19.37	NORWAY 49:51.49
1976 SOVIET UNION 1:07:49.75	FINLAND 1:08:36.57	GDR 1:09:57.95
1980 GDR 1:02:11.10	SOVIET UNION 1:03:18.30	NORWAY 1:04:13.50
1984 NORWAY 1:06:49.7	CZECHOSLOVAKIA 1:01:33.0	FINLAND 1:07:36.7
1988 SOVIET UNION 59:51.1	NORWAY 1:01:33.0	FINLAND 1:01:53.8
1992 UNIFIED TEAM 59:34.8	NORWAY 59:56.4	ITALY 1:00:25.9
1994 RUSSIA 57:12.5	NORWAY 57:42.6	ITALY 58:42.6
1998 RUSSIA 55:33.5	NORWAY 55:38.0	ITALY 56:53.3
2002 GERMANY 49:30.6	NORWAY 49:31.9	SWITZERLAND 50:03.6
2006 RUSSIA 54:47.7	GERMANY 54:57.7	ITALY 54:58.7

1924-1952 Event not held
[1]*Over three stages prior to 1976*

DISCONTINUED

Men

10,000 Metres (classical)

1992 Vegard Ulvang (NOR) 27:36.0	Marco Alberello (ITA) 27:55.2	Christer Majbäck (SWE) 27:56.4
1994 Bjørn Dahlie (NOR) 24:20.1	Vladimir Smirnov (KZK) 24:38.3	Marco Alberello (ITA) 24:42.3
1998 Bjørn Dahlie (NOR) 27:24.5	Markus Gander (AUT) 27:32.5	Mika Myllylä (FIN) 27:40.1

1924-1988 Event not held

Women

5,000 Metres (classical)

1964 Klaudia Boyarskikh (URS) 17:50.5	Mirja Lehtonen (FIN) 17:52.9	Alevtina Koltschina (URS) 18:08.4
1968 Toini Gustafsson (SWE) 16:45.2	Galina Kulakova (URS) 16:48.4	Alevtina Koltschina (URS) 16:51.6
1972 Galina Kulakova (URS) 17:00.50	Marjatta Kajosmaa (FIN) 17:05.50	Helena Sikolova (TCH) 17:07.32
1976 Helena Takalo (FIN) 15:48.69	Raisa Smetanina (URS) 15:49.73	Nina Baldycheva (URS) 16:12.82[1]
1980 Raisa Smetanina (URS) 15:06.92	Hikka Riihivuori (FIN) 15:11.96	Kvetoslava Jeriová (TCH) 15:23.44
1984 Marja-Liisa Hämäläinen (FIN) 17:04.0	Berit Aunli (NOR) 17:41.1	Kvetoslava Jeriová (TCH) 17:18.3
1988 Marjo Matikainen (FIN) 15:04.0	Tamara Tikhonova (URS) 15:05.3	Vida Ventsene (URS) 15:11.1

1992	Marjut Lukkarinen (FIN) 14:13.8	Lyubov Yegorova (EUN) 14:14.7	Yelena Valbe (EUN) 14:22.7
1994	Lyubov Yegorova (RUS) 14:08.8	Manuela di Centa (ITA) 14:28.3	Marja-Liisa Kirvesniemi (FIN) 14:36.0
1998	Larissa Lazutina (RUS) 17:37.9	Katerina Neumannova (CZE) 17:42.7	Bente Martinsen (NOR) 17:49.4

1924-1960 Event not held
[1]Galina Kulakova (RUS) finished third but disqualified

20,000 Metres (freestyle)

1984	Marja-Liisa Hämäläinen (FIN) 1:01:45.0	Raisa Smetanina (URS) 1:02:26.7	Anne Jahren (NOR) 1:03:13.06
1988	Tamara Tikhonova (URS) 55:53.6	Anfissa Reztsov (URS) 56:12.8	Raisa Smetanina (URS) 57:22.1

1924-1980 Event not held

NORDIC COMBINED

Sprint

2002	Samppa Lajunen (FIN)	Ronny Ackermann (GER)	Felix Gottwald (AUT)
2006	Felix Gottwald (AUT)	Magnus Moan (NOR)	Georg Hettich (GER)

1924-1998 Event not held

Individual[1]

1924[2]	Thorleif Haug (NOR)	Thoralf Strömstad (NOR)	Johan Gröttumsbraaten (NOR)
1928[2]	Johan Gröttumsbraaten (NOR)	Hans Vinjarengen (NOR)	John Snersrud (NOR)
1932	Johan Gröttumsbraaten (NOR) 446.0	Ole Stenen (NOR) 436.05	Hans Vinjarengen (NOR) 434.60
1936	Oddbjörn Hagen (NOR) 430.30	Olaf Hoffsbakken (NOR) 419.80	Sverre Brodahl (NOR) 408.10
1948	Heikki Hasu (FIN) 448.80	Martti Huhtala (FIN) 433.65	Sven Israelsson (SWE) 433.40
1952	Simon Slattvik (NOR) 431.621	Heikki Hasu (FIN) 447.50	Sverre Stenersen (NOR) 436.355
1956	Sverre Stenersen (NOR) 455.0	Bengt Eriksson (SWE) 437.4	Franciszek Gron-Gasienica (POL) 436.8
1960	Georg Thoma (GER) 457.952	Tormod Knutsen (NOR) 453.000	Nikolai Gusakow (URS) 452.000
1964	Tormod Knutsen (NOR) 469.28	Nikolai Kiselyev (URS) 453.04	Georg Thoma (GER) 452.88
1968	Frantz Keller (FRG) 449.04	Alois Kälin (SUI) 447.94	Andreas Kunz (GDR) 444.10
1972	Ulrich Wehling (GDR) 413.34	Rauno Miettinen (FIN) 405.55	Karl-Heinz Luck (GDR) 398.80
1976	Ulrich Wehling (GDR) 423.39	Urban Hettich (FRG) 418.90	Konrad Winkler (GDR) 417.47
1980	Ulrich Wehling (GDR) 432.20	Jouko Karjalainen (FIN) 429.50	Konrad Winkler (GDR) 425.32
1984	Tom Sandberg (NOR) 422.595	Jouko Karjalainen (FIN) 416.900	Jukka Ylipulli (FIN) 410.825
1988	Hippolyt Kempf (SUI)	Klaus Sulzenbacher (AUT)	Allar Levandi (URS)
1992	Fabrice Guy (FRA)	Sylvain Guillaume (FRA)	Klaus Sulzenbacher (AUT)
1994	Fred Børre Lunberg (NOR)	Takanori Kono (JPN)	Bjarte Engen Vik (NOR)
1998	Bjarte Engen Vik (NOR)	Samppa Lajunen (FIN)	Valeri Stolyarov (RUS)
2002	Samppa Lajunen (FIN)	Jaakko Tallus (FIN)	Felix Gottwald (AUT)
2006	Georg Hettich (GER)	Felix Gottwald (AUT)	Magnus Moan (NOR)

[1]1924-1952 Distance 18km, since then 15km; [2]1924-1928 scoring different from 1932 onwards

Team

1988	FRG	SWITZERLAND	AUSTRIA
1992	JAPAN	NORWAY	AUSTRIA
1994	JAPAN	NORWAY	SWITZERLAND
1998	NORWAY	FINLAND	FRANCE
2002	FINLAND	GERMANY	AUSTRIA
2006	AUSTRIA	GERMANY	FINLAND

1924-1984 Event not held

SKI-JUMPING

Normal Hill

1924-1988 70m; From 1992 90m

1924[1]	Jacob Tullin Thams (NOR) 18 960	Narve Bonna (NOR) 18 689	Anders Haugen (USA) 17 916
1928	Alf Andersen (NOR) 19 208	Sigmund Ruud (NOR) 18 542	Rudolf Burkert (TCH) 17 937
1932	Birger Ruud (NOR) 228.1	Hans Beck (NOR) 227.0	Kaare Wahlberg (NOR) 219.5
1936	Birger Ruud (NOR) 232.0	Sven Eriksson (SWE) 230.5	Reidar Andersen (NOR) 228.9
1948	Petter Hugsted (NOR) 228.1	Birger Ruud (NOR) 226.6	Thorleif Schjeldrup (NOR) 225.1
1952	Arnfinn Bergmann (NOR) 226.0	Torbjørn Falkanger (NOR) 221.5	Karl Holmström (SWE) 219.5
1956	Antti Hyvärinen (FIN) 229.9	Aulis Kallakorpi (FIN) 225.0	Harry Glass (GER) 224.5
1960	Helmut Recknagel (GER) 227.2	Niilio Halonen (FIN) 222.6	Otto Leodolter (AUT) 219.4
1964	Veikko Kankkonen (FIN) 229.9	Toralf Engan (NOR) 226.3	Torgeir Brandtzäg (NOR) 222.9
1968	Jiri Taska (TCH) 216.5	Reinhold Bachler (AUT) 214.2	Baldur Preiml (AUT) 212.6

1972	Yukio Kasaya (JPN) 244.2	Akitsuga Konno (JPN) 234.8	Seiji Aochi (JPN) 229.5
1976	Hans-Georg Aschenbach (GDR) 252.0	Jochen Danneberg (GDR) 246.2	Karl Schnabl (AUT) 242.0
1980	Toni Innauer (AUT) 266.3	Manfred Dekker (GDR) 249.2 Hirokazu Yagi (JPN) 249.2	–
1984	Jens Weissflog (GDR) 215.2	Matti Nykänen (FIN) 214.0	Jari Puikkonen (FIN) 212.8
1988	Matti Nykänen (FIN) 229.1	Pavel Ploc (TCH) 212.1	Jiri Malec (TCH) 211.8
1992	Ernst Vettori (AUT) 222.8	Martin Höllwarth (AUT) 218.1	Toni Nieminen (FIN) 217.0
1994	Espen Bredesen (NOR) 282.0	Lasse Ottesen (NOR) 268.0	Dieter Thoma (GER) 260.5
1998	Jani Soininen (FIN) 234.5	Kazuyoshi Funaki (JPN) 233.5	Andreas Wiidhoelz (AUT) 232.5
2002	Simon Ammann (SUI) 269.0	Sven Hannawald (GER) 267.5	Adam Malysz (POL) 263.0
2006	Lars Bystøl (NOR) 266.5	Matti Hautamäki (FIN) 265.5	Roar Ljøkelsøy (NOR) 264.5

[1]Originally Thorleif Haug (NOR) was placed third due to incorrect calculations at the time. Error corrected in 1974.

Large Hill

1964-1988 90m; from 1992 120m

1964	Toralf Engan (NOR) 230.7	Veikko Kankkonen (FIN) 228.9	Torgeir Brandtzaeg (NOR) 227.2
1968	Vladimir Belousov (URS) 231.3	Jiri Raska (TCH) 229.4	Lars Grini (NOR) 214.3
1972	Wojciech Fortuna (POL) 219.9	Walter Steiner (SUI) 219.8	Rainer Schmidt (GDR) 219.3
1976	Karl Schnabl (AUT) 234.8	Toni Innauer (AUT) 232.9	Henry Glass (GDR) 221.7
1980	Jouko Törmäinen (FIN) 271.0	Hubert Neuper (AUT) 262.4	Jari Puikkonen (FIN) 248.5
1984	Matti Nykänen (FIN) 232.2	Jens Weissflog (GDR) 213.7	Pavel Ploc (TCH) 202.9
1988	Matti Nykänen (FIN) 224.0	Erik Johnson (NOR) 207.9	Matjaz Debelak (YUG) 207.7
1992	Toni Nieminen (FIN) 239.6	Martin Höllwarth (AUT) 227.3	Heinz Kuttin (AUT) 214.8
1994	Jens Weissflog (GER) 274.5	Espen Bredesen (NOR) 266.5	Andreas Goldberger (AUT) 255.0
1998	Kazuyoshi Funaki (JPN) 272.3	Jani Soininen (FIN) 260.8	Mashiko Harada (JPN) 258.3
2002	Simon Ammann (SUI) 281.4	Adam Malysz (POL) 267.9	Matti Hautamäki (FIN) 256.0
2006	Thomas Morgernstern (AUT) 276.9	Andreas Koffler (AUT) 276.8	Lars Bystøl (NOR) 250.7

1924-1960 Event not held

Large Hill – Team

1988	FINLAND 634.4	YUGOSLAVIA 625.5	NORWAY 596.1
1992	FINLAND 644.4	AUSTRIA 642.9	CZECHOSLOVAKIA 620.1
1994	GERMANY 970.1	JAPAN 956.9	AUSTRIA 918.9
1998	JAPAN 933.0	GERMANY 897.4	AUSTRIA 881.5
2002	GERMANY 974.1	FINLAND 974.0	SLOVENIA 946.3
2006	AUSTRIA 984.0	FINLAND 976.6	NORWAY 950.1

1924-1984 Event not held

SNOWBOARDING

Introduced in 1998

Men

Halfpipe

1998	Gian Simmen (SUI) 85.2	Daniel Franck (NOR) 82.4	Ross Powers (USA) 82.1
2002	Ross Powers (USA) 46.1	Danny Kass (USA) 42.5	Jarret Thomas (USA) 42.1
2006	Shaun White (USA) 46.8	Danny Kass (USA) 44.0	Markku Koski (FIN) 41.5

Giant Slalom[1]

1998	Ross Rebagliati (CAN) 2:03.96	Thomas Prugger (ITA) 2:03.98	Ueli Kestenholz (SUI) 2:04.08
2002	Philip Schoch (SUI)	Richard Richardsson (SWE)	Chris Klug (USA)
2006	Philip Schoch (SUI)	Simon Schoch (SUI)	Siegfried Grabner (AUT)

[1]From 2002 two competitors race in parallel

Cross

2006	Seth Westcott (USA)	Radoslav Zidek (SVK)	Paul-Henri Delerue (FRA)

Women

Halfpipe

1998	Nicola Thost (GER) 74.6	Stine Brun Kjeldaas (NOR) 74.2	Shannon Dunn (USA) 72.8
2002	Kelly Clark (USA) 47.9	Dorianne Vidal (FRA) 43.0	Fabienne Reuteler (SUI) 39.7
2006	Hannah Teter (USA) 46.4	Gretchen Bleiler (USA) 43.4	Kjersti Buaas (NOR) 42.0

Giant Slalom[1]

1998	Karine Ruby (FRA) 2:17.34	Heidi Renoth (GER) 2:19.17	Brigitte Koeck (AUT) 2:19.42
2002[1]	Isabelle Blanc (FRA)	Karine Ruby (FRA)	Lidia Trettel (ITA)
2006	Daniela Meuli (SUI)	Amelie Kober (GER)	Rosey Fletcher (USA)

[1]From 2002 two competitors race in parallel

Cross

2006	Tanja Freiden (SUI)	Lindsay Jacobellis (USA)	Dominique Maltais (CAN)

SPEED SKATING

Men

500 Metres

1924	Charles Jewtraw (USA) 44.0	Oskar Olsen (NOR) 44.2	Roald Larsen (NOR) 44.8
			Clas Thunberg (FIN) 44.8
1928	Clas Thunberg (FIN) 43.4	–	John Farrrell (USA) 43.6
	Bernt Evensen (NOR) 43.4		Roald Larsen (NOR) 43.6
			Jaako Friman (FIN) 43.6
1932	John Shea (USA) 43.4	Bernt Evensen (NOR) 5m	Alexander Hurd (CAN) 8m
1936	Ivar Ballandgrud (NOR) 43.4	Georg Krog (NOR) 43.5	Leo Friesinger (USA) 44.0
1948	Finn Helgesen (NOR) 43.1	Kenneth Bartholomew (USA) 43.2	–
		Thomas Byberg (NOR) 43.2	
		Robert Fitzgerald (USA) 43.2	
1952	Kenneth Henry (USA) 43.2	Donald McDermott (USA) 43.9	Arne Johansen (NOR) 44.0
			Gordon Audley (CAN) 44.0
1956	Yevgeni Grishin (URS) 40.2	Rafael Gratsch (URS) 40.8	Alv Gjestvang (NOR) 41.0
1960	Yevgeni Grishin (URS) 40.2	William Disney (USA) 40.3	Rafael Gratsch (URS) 40.4
1964	Richard McDermott (USA) 40.1	Yevgeni Grishin (URS) 40.6	–
		Vladimir Orlov (URS) 40.6	
		Alv Gjestvang (NOR) 40.6	
1968	Erhard Keller (FRG) 40.3	Richard McDermott (USA) 40.5	–
		Magne Thomassen (NOR) 40.5	
1972	Erhard Keller (FRG) 39.44	Hasse Börjes (SWE) 39.69	Valeri Muratov (URS) 39.80
1976	Yevgeni Kulikov (URS) 39.17	Valeri Muratov (URS) 39.25	Daniel Immerfall (USA) 39.54
1980	Eric Heiden (USA) 38.03	Yevgeni Kulikov (URS) 38.37	Lieuwe de Boer (NED) 38.48
1984	Sergei Fokitchev (URS) 38.19	Yoshihiro Kitazawa (JPN) 38.30	Gaétan Boucher (CAN) 38.39
1988	Uwe-Jens Mey (GDR) 36.45	Jan Ykema (NED) 36.76	Akira Kuriowa (JPN) 36.77
1992	Uwe-Jens Mey (GER) 37.14	Toshiyuki Kuriowa (JPN) 37.18	Junichi Inoue (JPN) 37.26
1994	Alexander Golubyev (RUS) 36.33	Sergei Klevchenya (RUS) 36.39	Manabu Horii (JPN) 36.53
1998[1]	Hiroyasu Shimizu (JPN) 1:11.35	Jeremy Wotherspoon (CAN) 1:11.84	Kevin Overland (CAN) 1:11.86
2002	Casey FitzRandolph (USA) 1:09.23	Hiroyasu Shimizu (JPN) 1:09.26	Kip Carpenter (USA) 1:09.47
2006	Joey Cheek (USA) 1:09.76	Dmirti Dorofeyev (RUS) 1:10.41	Kang Seok Lee (KOR) 1:10.43

[1]In 1998 the event changed to an aggregate of the times from two races

1000 Metres

1976	Peter Mueller (USA) 1:19.32	Jörn Didriksen (NOR) 1:20.45	Valeri Muratov (URS) 1:20.57
1980	Eric Heiden (USA) 1:15.18	Gaétan Boucher (CAN) 1:16.68	Frode Rönning (NOR) 1:16.91
	Vladimir Lobanov (URS) 1:16.91		
1984	Gaétan Boucher (CAN) 1:15.80	Sergei Khlebnikov (URS) 1:16.63	Kai Arne Engelstad (NOR) 1:16.75
1988	Nikolai Gulyayev (URS) 1:13.03	Uwe-Jens Mey (GDR) 1:13.11	Igor Gelezovsky (URS) 1:13.19
1992	Olaf Zinke (GER) 1:14.85	Kim Moon-Yan (KOR) 1:14.86	Yukinori Miyabe (JPN) 1:14.92
1994	Dan Jansen (USA) 1:12.43	Igor Zhelezovsky (BLR) 1:12.72	Sergei Klevchenya (RUS) 1:12.85
1998	Ids Postma (NED) 1:10.64	Jan Bos (NED) 1:10.71	Hiroyasu Shimizu (JPN) 1:11.00
2002	Gerard van Velde (NED) 1:07.18	Jan Bos (NED) 1:07.53	Joey Cheek (USA) 1:07.61
2006	Shani Davis (USA) 1:08.89	Joey Cheek (USA) 1:09.16	Erben Wennemars (NED) 1:09.32

1924-1972 Event not held

1500 Metres

1924	Clas Thunberg (FIN) 2:20.8	Roald Larsen (NOR) 2:20.0	Sigurd Moen (NOR) 2:25.6
1928	Clas Thunberg (FIN) 2:21.1	Bernt Evensen (NOR) 2:21.9	Ivar Ballangrud (NOR) 2:22.6
1932	John Shea (USA) 2:57.5	Alexander Hurd (CAN) 5m	William Logan (CAN) 6m
1936	Charles Mathiesen (NOR) 2:19.2	Ivar Ballangrud (NOR) 2:20.2	Birger Wasenius (FIN) 2:20.9
1948	Sverre Farstad (NOR) 2:17.6	Ake Seyffarth (SWE) 2:18.1	Odd Lundberg (NOR) 2:18.9

1952	Hjalmar Andersen (NOR) 2:20.4	Willem van der Voort (NED) 2:20.6	Roald Aas (NOR) 2:21.6
1956	Yevgeni Grischin (URS) 2:08.6	–	Tiovo Salonen (FIN) 2:09.4
	Yuri Mikhailov (URS) 2:08.6		
1960	Roald Aas (NOR) 2:10.4	–	Boris Stenin (URS) 2:11.5
	Yevgeni Grishin (URS) 2:10.4		
1964	Ants Antson (URS) 2:10.3	Cornelis Verkerk (NED) 2:10.6	Villy Haugen (NOR) 2:11.25
1968	Cornelis Verkerk (NED) 2:03.4	Ard Schenk (NED) 2:05.0	–
		Ivar Eriksen (NOR) 2:05.0	
1972	Ard Schenk (NED) 2:02.96	Roar Grönvold (NOR) 2:04.26	Göran Claeson (SWE) 2:05.89
1976	Jan Egil Storholt (NOR) 1:59.38	Yuri Kondakov (URS) 1:59.97	Hans Van Holden (NED) 2:00.87
1980	Eric Heiden (USA) 1:55.44	Kai Stenshjemmet (NOR) 1:56.81	Terje Andersen (NOR) 1:56.92
1984	Gaétan Boucher (CAN) 1:58.36	Sergei Khlebnikov (URS) 1:58.83	Oleg Bogyev (URS) 1:58.89
1988	André Hoffmann (GDR) 1:52.06	Eric Flaim (USA) 1:52.12	Michael Hadschieff (AUT) 1:52.31
1992	Johann-Olav Koss (NOR) 1:54.81	Ådne Søndrål (NOR) 1:54.85	Leo Visser (NED) 1:54.90
1994	Johann-Olav Koss (NOR) 1:51.29	Rintje Ritsma (NED) 1:51.99	Flako Zandstra (NED) 1:52.38
1998	Ådne Søndrål (NOR) 1:47.87	Ids Postma (NED) 1:48.13	Rintje Ritsma (NED) 1:48.52
2002	Derek Parra (USA) 1:43.95	Jochen Uytdehaage (NED) 1:44.57	Ådne Søndrål (NOR) 1:45.26
2006	Enrico Fabris (ITA) 1:45.97	Shani Davis (USA) 1:46.13	Chad Hedrick (USA) 1:46.22

5000 Metres

1924	Clas Thunberg (FIN) 8:39.0	Julius Skutnabb (FIN) 8:48.4	Roald Larsen (NOR) 2:00.87
1928	Ivar Ballangrud (NOR) 8:50.5	Julius Skutnabb (FIN) 8:59.1	Bernt Evensen (NOR) 9:01.1
1932	Irving Jaffee (USA) 9:40.8	Edward Murphy (USA) 2m	William Logan (CAN) 4m
1936	Ivar Ballangrud (NOR) 8:19.6	Birger Wasenius (FIN) 8:23.3	Antero Ojala (FIN) 8:30.1
1940	Reidar Liaklev (NOR) 8:29.4	Odd Lundberg (NOR) 8:32.7	Göthe Hedlund (SWE) 8:34.8
1952	Hjalmar Andersen (NOR) 8:10.6	Kees Broekman (NED) 8:21.6	Sverre Haugli (NOR) 8:22.4
1956	Boris Schilkov (URS) 7:48.7	Sigvard Ericsson (SWE) 7:56.7	Oleg Gontscharenko (URS) 7:57.5
1960	Viktor Kositschkin (URS) 7:51.3	Knut Johannesen (NOR) 8:00.8	Jan Pesman (NED) 8:05.1
1964	Knut Johannesen (NOR) 7:38.4	Per Moe (NOR) 7:38.6	Anton Maier (NOR) 7:42.0
1968	Anton Maier (NOR) 7:22.4	Cornelis Verkerk (NED) 7:23.2	Petrus Nottet (NED) 7:25.5
1972	Ard Schenk (NED) 7:23.6	Roar Grönvold (NOR) 7:28.18	Sten Stensen (NOR) 7:33.39
1976	Sten Stensen (NOR) 7:24.48	Piet Kleine (NED) 7:26.47	Hans Van Helden (NED) 7:26.54
1980	Eric Heiden (USA) 7:02.29	Kai Stenshjammet (NOR) 7:03.28	Tom Oxholm (NOR) 7:05.59
1984	Tomas Gustafson (SWE) 7:12.28	Igor Malkov (URS) 7:12.30	René Schöfisch (GDR) 7:17.49
1988	Tomas Gustafson (SWE) 6:44.63	Leendert Visser (NED) 6:44.98	Gerard Kemkers (NED) 6:45.92
1992	Geir Karlstad (NOR) 6:59.97	Falko Zandstra (NED) 7:02.28	Leo Visser (NED) 7:04.96
1994	Johann-Olav Koss (NOR) 6:34.96	Kjell Storelid (NOR) 6:42.68	Rintje Ritsma (NED) 6:43.94
1998	Gianni Romme (NED) 6:22.20	Rintje Ritsma (NED) 6:28.24	Bart Veldkamp (BEL) 6:28.31
2002	Jochen Uytdehaage (NED) 6:14.66	Derek Parra (USA) 6:17.98	Jens Boden (GER) 6:21.73
2006	Chad Hedrick (USA) 6:14.68	Sven Kramer (NED) 6:16.40	Enrico Fabris (ITA) 6:18.25

10,000 Metres

1924	Julius Skutnabb (FIN) 18:04.8	Clas Thunberg (FIN) 18:97.8	Roald Larsen (NOR) 18:12.2
1932	Irving Jaffee (USA) 19:13.6	Ivar Ballangrud (NOR) 5m	Frank Stack (CAN) 6m
1936	Ivar Ballangrud (NOR) 17:24.3	Birger Wasenius (FIN) 17:28.2	Max Stiepl (AUT) 17:30.0
1948	Ake Seyffarth (SWE) 17:26.3	Lauri Parkkinen (FIN) 17:36.0	Pentti Lammio (FIN) 17:42.7
1952	Hjalmar Andersen (NOR) 16:45.8	Kees Broekman (NED) 17:10.6	Carl-Erik Asplund (SWE) 17:16.6
1956	Sigvard Ericsson (SWE) 16:35.9	Knut Johannesen (NOR) 16:36.9	Oleg Gontscharenko (URS) 16:42.3
1960	Knut Johannesen (NOR) 15:46.6	Viktor Kositschkin (URS) 15:49.2	Kjell Bäckman (SWE) 16:14.2
1964	Jonny Nilsson (SWE) 15:50.1	Anton Maier (NOR) 16:06.0	Knut Johannesen (NOR) 16:06.3
1968	Johnny Höglin (SWE) 15:23.6	Anton Maier (NOR) 15:23.9	Orjan Sandler (SWE) 15:31.8
1972	Ard Schenk (NED) 15:01.35	Cornelis Verkerk (NED) 15:04.70	Sten Stensen (NOR) 15:07.08
1976	Piet Kleine (NED) 14:50.59	Sten Stensen (NOR) 14:53.30	Hans Van Helden (NED) 15:02.02
1980	Eric Heiden (USA) 14:28.13	Piet Kleine (NED) 14:36.03	Tom Oxholm (NOR) 14:36.60
1984	Igor Malkov (URS) 14:39.90	Tomas Gustafson (SWE) 14:39.95	René Schöfisch (GDR) 14:46.91
1988	Tomas Gustafson (SWE) 13:48.20	Michael Hadschieff (AUT) 13:56.11	Leendert Visser (NED) 14:00.55
1992	Bart Veldkamp (NED) 14:12.12	Johann-Olav Koss (NOR) 14:14.58	Geir Karlstad (NOR) 14:18.13
1994	Johann-Olav Koss (NOR) 13:30.55	Kjell Storelid (NOR) 13:49.25	Bart Veldkamp (NED) 13:56.73
1998	Gianni Romme (NED) 13:15.33	Bob de Jong (NED) 13:25.76	Rintje Ritsma (NED) 13:28.19
2002	Jochen Uytdehaage (NED) 12:58.92	Gianni Romme (NED) 13:10.03	Lasse Saetre (NOR) 13:16.92
2006	Bob de Jongh (NED) 13:01.57	Chad Hedrick (USA) 13:05.40	Carl Verheijen (NED) 13:08.80

1928 Event abandoned

Team Pursuit

2006	ITALY 3:44.46	CANADA 3:47.28	NETHERLANDS 3:44.53[1]

1924-2002 Event not held
[1]*Winners of B final*

DISCONTINUED EVENT

All-Round Championship

Aggregate of placings in 500m, 1500m, 5km and 10km

1924	Clas Thunberg (FIN) 5.5pts	Roald Larsen (NOR) 9.5	Julius Skutnabb (FIN) 11

Women

500 Metres

1960	Helga Haase (GER) 45.9	Natalya Donchenko (URS) 46.0	Jeanne Ashworth (USA) 46.1
1964	Lydia Skoblikova (URS) 45.0	Irina Yegorova (URS) 45.4	Tatyana Sidorova (URS) 45.5
1968	Ludmila Titova (URS) 46.1	Mary Meyers (USA) 46.3	–
		Dianne Holum (USA) 46.3	
		Jennifer Fish (USA) 46.3	
1972	Anne Henning (USA) 43.33	Vera Krasnova (URS) 44.01	Ludmila Titova (URS) 44.45
1976	Sheila Young (USA) 42.76	Catherine Priestner (CAN) 43.12	Tatyana Averina (URS) 43.17
1980	Karin Enke (GDR) 41.78	Leah Poulos-Mueller (USA) 42.26	Natalya Petruseva (URS) 42.42
1984	Christa Rothenburger (GDR) 41.02	Karin Enke (GDR) 41.28	Natalya Chive (URS) 41.50
1988	Bonnie Blair (USA) 39.10	Christa Rothenburger (GDR) 39.12	Karin Enke-Kania (GDR) 39.24
1992	Bonnie Blair (USA) 40.33	Ye Qiaobo (CHN) 40.51	Christa Rothenburger-Luding (GER) 40.57
1994	Bonnie Blair (USA) 39.25	Susan Auch (CAN) 39.61	Franziska Schenk (GER) 39.70
1998[1]	Catriona LeMay Doan (CAN) 1:16.60	Susan Auch (CAN) 1:16.93	Tomomi Okazaki (JPN) 1:17.10
2002	Catriona LeMay Doan (CAN) 1:14.75	Monique Garbrecht-Enfieldt (GER) 1:14.94	Sabine Völker (GER) 1:15.19
2006	Svetlana Zhurova (RUS) 1:16.57	Manli Wang (CHN) 1:16.78	Hui Ren (CHN) 1:16.87

[1]*In 1998 the event changed to an aggregate of the times from two races*

1000 Metres

1960	Klara Guseva (URS) 1:34.1	Helga Haase (GER) 1:34.3	Tamara Rylova (URS) 1:34.8
1964	Lydia Skoblikova (URS) 1:33.2	Irina Yegorova (URS) 1:34.3	Kaija Mustonen (FIN) 1:34.8
1968	Carolina Geijssen (NED) 1:32.6	Ludmila Titova (URS) 1:32.9	Dianne Holum (USA) 1:33.4
1972	Monika Pflug (FRG) 1:31.40	Atje Keulen-Deelstra (NED) 1:31.61	Anne Henning (USA) 1:31.62
1976	Tatyana Averina (URS) 1:28.43	Leah Poulos (USA) 1:28.57	Sheila Young (USA) 1:29.14
1980	Natalya Petruseva (URS) 1:24.10	Leah Poulos-Mueller (USA) 1:25.41	Sylvia Albrecht (GDR) 1:26.46
1984	Karin Enke (GDR) 1:21.61	Andrea Schöne (GDR) 1:22.83	Natalya Petruseva (URS) 1:23.21
1988	Christa Rothenburger (GDR) 1:17.65	Karin Enke-Kania (GDR) 1:17.70	Bonnie Blair (USA) 1:18.31
1992	Bonnie Blair (USA) 1:21.90	Ye Qiaobo (CHN) 1:21.92	Monique Garbrecht (GER) 1:22.10
1994	Bonnie Blair (USA) 1:18.74	Anke Baier (GER) 1:20.12	Ye Qiaobo (CHN) 1:20.22
1998	Marianne Timmer (NED) 1:16.51	Christine Witty (USA) 1:16.79	Catriona LeMay Doan (CAN) 1:17.37
2002	Christine Witty (USA) 1:13.83	Sabine Völker (GER) 1:13.96	Jennifer Rodriguez (USA) 1:14.24
2006	Marianne Timmer (NED) 1:16.05	Cindy Klassen (CAN) 1:16.09	Anni Freisinger (GER) 1:16.11

1500 Metres

1960	Lydia Skoblikova (URS) 2:25.2	Elvira Seroczynska (POL) 2:25.7	Helena Pilejeyk (POL) 2:27.1
1964	Lydia Skoblikova (URS) 2:22.6	Kaija Mustonen (FIN) 2:25.5	Berta Kolokoltseva (URS) 2:27.1
1968	Kaija Mustonen (FIN) 2:22.4	Carolina Geijssen (NED) 2:22.7	Christina Kaiser (NED) 2:24.5
1972	Dianne Holum (USA) 2:20.85	Christina Baas-Kaiser (NED) 2:21.05	Atje Keulen-Deelstra (NED) 2:22.05
1976	Galina Stepanskaya (URS) 2:16.58	Sheila Young (USA) 2:17.06	Tatyana Averina (URS) 2:17.96
1980	Annie Borckink (NED) 2:10.95	Ria Visser (NED) 2:12.35	Sabine Becker (GDR) 2:12.38
1984	Karin Enke (GDR) 2:03.42	Andrea Schöne (GDR) 2:05.29	Natalya Petruseva (URS) 2:05.78
1988	Yvonne Van Gennip (NED) 2:00.68	Karin Enke-Kania (GDR) 2:00.82	Andrea Schöne-Ehrig (GDR) 2:01.49
1992	Jacqueline Börner (GER) 2:05.87	Gunda Niemann (GER) 2:05.92	Seiko Hashimoto (JPN) 2:06.88
1994	Emese Hunyady (AUT) 2:02.19	Svetlana Fedotkin (RUS) 2:02.69	Gunda Niemann (GER) 2:03.41
1998	Marianne Timmer (NED) 1:57.58	Gunda Niemann-Stirnemann (GER) 1:58.86	Christine Witty (USA) 1:58.97
2002	Anni Friesinger (GER) 1:54.02	Sabine Völker (GER) 1:54.97	Jennifer Rodriguez (USA) 1:55.32
2006	Cindy Klassen (CAN) 1:55.27	Kristina Groves (CAN) 1:56.74	Ireen Wust (NED) 1:56.90

3000 Metres

1960	Lydia Skobilova (URS) 5:14.3	Valentina Stenina (URS) 5:16.9	Eevi Huttunen (FIN) 5:21.0
1964	Lydia Skobilova (URS) 5:14.9	Valentina Stenina (URS) 5:18.5	–
		Pil-Hwa Han (PRK) 5:18.5	
1968	Johanna Schut (NED) 4:56.2	Kaija Mustonen (FIN) 5:01.0	Christina Kaiser (NED) 5:01.3

1972	Christina Baas-Kaiser (NED) 4:52.14	Dianne Holum (USA) 4:58.67	Atje Keulen-Deelstra (NED) 4:59.91
1976	Tayana Averina (URS) 4:45.19	Andrea Mitscherlich (GDR) 4:45.23	Lisbeth Korsmo (NOR) 4:45.24
1980	Bjørg Eva Jensen (NOR) 4:32.13	Sabine Becker (GDR) 4:32.79	Beth Heiden (USA) 4:33.77
1984	Andrea Mitscherlich-Schöne (GDR) 4:24.79	Karin Enke (GDR) 4:26.33	Gabi Schönbrunn (GDR) 4:33.13
1988	Yvonne Van Gennip (NED) 4:11.94	Andrea Schöne-Ehrig (GDR) 4:12.09	Gabi Schönbrunn-Zange (GDR) 4:16.92
1992	Gunda Niemann (GER) 4:19.90	Heike Warnicke (GER) 4:22.88	Emese Hunyadi (AUT) 4:24.64
1994	Svetlana Bazhanova (RUS) 4:17.43	Emese Hunyadi (AUT) 4:18.14	Claudia Pechstein (GER) 4:18.34
1998	Gunda Niemann-Stirnemann (GER) 4:07.29	Claudia Pechstein (GER) 4:08.47	Anni Friesinger (GER) 4:09.44
2002	Claudia Pechstein (GER) 3:57.70	Renate Groenewold (NED) 3:58.94	Cindy Klassen (CAN) 3:58.97
2006	Ireen Wust (NED) 4:02.43	Renate Groenewold (NED) 4:03.48	Cindy Klassen (CAN) 4:04.37

5000 Metres

1988	Yvonne Van Gennip (NED) 7:14.13	Andrea Schöne-Ehrig (GDR) 7:17.2	Gabi Schönbrunn-Zange (GDR) 7:21.61
1992	Gunda Niemann (GER) 7:31.57	Heike Warnicke (GER) 7:37.59	Claudia Pechstein (GER) 7:39.80
1994	Claudia Pechstein (GER) 7:14.37	Gunda Neimann (GER) 7:14.88	Hiromi Yamamoto (JPN) 7:19.68
1998	Claudia Pechstein (GER) 6:59.61	Gunda Niemann-Stirnemann (GER) 6:59.65	Lyudmila Prokasheva (KZK) 7:11.14
2002	Claudia Pechstein (GER) 6:46.91	Gretha Smit (NED) 6:49.22	Clara Hughes (CAN) 6:53.53
2006	Clara Hughes (CAN) 6:59.07	Claudia Pechstein (GER) 7:00.08	Cindy Klassen (CAN) 7:00.57

1960-1984 Event not held

Team Pursuit

2006	GERMANY 3:01.25	CANADA 3:02.91	RUSSIA nta

1960-2002 Event not held

SHORT-TRACK SPEED SKATING

Men

500 Metres

1994	Chae Ji-Hoon (KOR) 43.45	Mirko Vuillermin (ITA) 43.47	Nicky Gooch (GBR) 43.68
1998	Takafuni Nishitani (JPN) 42.862	An Yulong (CHN) 43.022	Hitoshi Uematsu (JPN) 43.713
2002	Marc Gagnon (CAN) 41.802	Jonathan Guilmette (CAN) 41.994	Rusty Smith (USA) 42.027
2006	Apolo Anton Ohno (USA) 41.935	Francois-Louis Tremblay (CAN) 42.002	Hyun-Soo Ahn (KOR) 42.089

1924-1992 Event not held

1000 Metres

1992	Kim Ki-Hoon (KOR) 1:30.76	Frederic Blackburn (CAN) 1:31.11	Lee Joon-Ho (KOR) 1:31.16
1994	Kim Ki-Hoon (KOR) 1:34.57	Chae Ji-Hoon (KOR) 1:34.92	Marc Gagnon (CAN) 1:33.03[1]
1998	Kim Dong-Sung (KOR) 1:32.375	Jiajun Li (CHN) 1:32.428	Eric Bedard (CAN) 1:32.661
2002	Steven Bradbury (AUS) 1:29.109	Apolo Anton Ohno (USA) 1:30.160	Mathieu Turcotte (CAN) 1:30.563
2006	Hyun-Soo Ahn (KOR) 1:26.739	Ho-Suk Lee (KOR) 1:26.764	Apolo Anton Ohno (USA) 1:26.927

1924-1988 Event not held
[1] *As no other finisher in A final, the winner of the B Final was placed third*

1500 Metres

2002[1]	Apolo Anton Ohno (USA) 2:18.541	Jiajun Li (CHN) 2:18.731	Marc Gagnon (CAN) 2:18.806
2006	Hyun-Soo Ahn (KOR) 2:25.341	Ho-Suk Lee (KOR) 2:25.600	Jiajun Li (CHN) 2:26.005

1924-1998 Event not held
[1] *Dong-Sung Kim (KOR) finished first but was disqualified*

5000 Metres Relay

1992	SOUTH KOREA 7:14.02	CANADA 7:14.06	JAPAN 7:18.18
1994	ITALY 7:11.74	UNITED STATES 7:13.37	AUSTRALIA 7:13.68
1998	CANADA 7:32.075	KOREA 7:06.776	CHINA 7:11.559
2002	CANADA 6:51.579	ITALY 6:56.327	CHINA 6:59.633
2006	KOREA 6:43.376	CANADA 6:43.707	UNITED STATES 6:47.990

1924-1988 Event not held

Women

500 Metres

1992	Cathy Turner (USA) 47.04	Li Yan (CHN) 47.08	Hwang Ok-Sil (PRK) 47.23
1994	Cathy Turner (USA) 45.98	Zhang Yanmei (CHN) 46.44	Amy Peterson (USA) 46.76
1998	Annie Perreault (CAN) 46.568	Yang Yang S (CHN) 46.627	Chun Lee Kyung (KOR) 46.335[1]
2002	Yang Yang A (CHN) 44.187	Evgeniya Radanova (BUL) 44.252	Wang Chunlu (CHN) 44.272
2006	Meng Wang (CHN) 44.345	Evgeniya Radanova (BUL) 44.374	Anouk LeBlanc-Boucher (CAN) 44.759

1924-1988 Event not held

[1]Isabelle Charest (CAN) was third but disqualified – winner of B final placed third

1000 Metres

1994	Chun Lee-Kyung (KOR) 1:36.87	Nathalie Lambert (CAN) 1:36.97	Kim So-Hee (KOR) 1:37.09
1998	Chun Lee-Kyung (KOR) 1:42.776	Yang Yang S (CHN) 1:43.343	Won Hye-Kyung (KOR) 1:43.361
2002	Yang Yang A (CHN) 1:36.391	Gi-Hyun Ko (KOR) 1:36.427	Yang Yang S (CHN) 1:37.008
2006	Sun-Yu Jin (KOR) 1:32.859	Meng Wang (CHN) 1:33.079	Yang Yang A (CHN) 1:33.937

1924-1992 Event not held

1500 Metres

2002	Gi-Hyun Ko (KOR) 2:31.581	Eun-Kyung Choi (KOR) 2:31.610	Evgeniya Radanova (BUL) 2:31.723
2006	Sun-Yu Jin (KOR) 2:23.494	Eun-Kyung Choi (KOR) 2:24.069	Meng Wang (CHN) 2:24.469

1924-1998 Event not held

3000 Metres Relay

1992	CANADA 4:36.62	UNITED STATES 4:37.85	UNIFIED TEAM 4:42.69
1994	KOREA 4:26.64	CANADA 4:32.04	UNITED STATES 4:39.34
1998	KOREA 4:16.260	CHINA 4:16.383	CANADA 4:21.205
2002	KOREA 4:12.793	CHINA 4:13.236	CANADA 4:15.738
2006	KOREA 4:17.040	CANADA 4:17.336	ITALY 4:20.030

1924-1988 Event not held

Index